DICTIONARY OF
FILM MAKERS

Dictionary of

FILM

MAKERS

by Georges Sadoul

TRANSLATED, EDITED, AND UPDATED BY

Peter Morris

UNIVERSITY OF CALIFORNIA PRESS
BERKELEY AND LOS ANGELES

University of California Press
Berkeley and Los Angeles
© 1972 by The Regents of the University of California
Translated with the permission of Editions du Seuil,
Paris. Originally published as *Dictionnaire des
Cinéastes, 1965.*
Designed by W. H. Snyder
Library of Congress Catalog Card Number: 78-136028
ISBN: 0-520-01864-8 (cloth)
0-520-02151-7 (paper)

Preface

BY GEORGES SADOUL

For this Dictionary we used the definition of "Film Maker" given by Louis Delluc in 1922, to include "Organizers, directors, artists, industrialists who have contributed something to the artistic industry of the cinema."

The present volume contains a thousand entries devoted to directors, scriptwriters, cinematographers, art directors, composers, producers, inventors — but not actors and actresses. At least 10,000 entries would be necessary — not for an international *Who's Who* which would require at least 100,000 names, but just in order to include all those who have contributed to the rapid worldwide development of the art of the cinema since 1895. This Dictionary does not pretend to be "exhaustive." In order to be accessible to everyone, both in format and in price, it could not attempt to emulate the monumental Italian *Filmlexicon degli Autori* whose seven volumes contain well over 50,000 entries, including actors.

The necessity of making a selection has led us to choose, sometimes arbitrarily, one film maker over another of equal importance; but we have attempted to include here the representatives of 60 countries without limiting ourselves to the best-known film industries. Twenty-five years devoted to film history, numerous study travels in four continents, devoted collaborators and excellent French and foreign reference works have not prevented errors and gaps in a volume which contains about 20,000 dates and film titles. Certain omissions (rightly or wrongly) are deliberate. Others not. If one attempted to bring to the public only a perfect work one would never be able to print the manuscript. Publication is the best means of provoking corrections and additional information. We appeal to readers to send us these so that one day a revised and corrected edition can be published. Our predecessors proceeded no differently.

Here is the method we have followed. The date of a film is in principle that of the first public screening, not of its conception, beginning or end of production, or private screening. In this we have followed the historians of literature who use the date of the first edition, of a book's release to the public, as the identifying one.

Each of our entries (apart from those of a few lines) is comprised of a critical appraisal, followed by a filmography. All have been abridged and many do not list all the films of a prolific film maker.

The director's filmographies are the key to this Dictionary. For other film makers we cite only film titles with their directors, whose entries should be referred to for additional information. This part has been retained to facilitate consultation but it does not signify that we have pretended to settle the old question about the "author" of a film. In certain cases, the principal "author" might be less the credited director than a star (such as Douglas Fairbanks), a producer (such as Zanuck), a scriptwriter (such as Zavattini), or even a writer whose literary work has been adapted (such as Victor Hugo). A film is almost always a collective creation and each collaborator, from the least technician to the most famous star, in small part or large, is one of the authors. Moreover, certain major comedians can be considered as the principal authors of films which they themselves did not always "direct." Thus, we have included brief entries for Buster Keaton, Max Linder, Harold Lloyd, and others.

In the entries for important directors we have quite often quoted from interviews, statements, or critical articles. Sometimes we have had to paraphrase these while respecting the spirit. In the filmographies we have given (whenever possible) original-language titles and the French titles which are not often a literal translation but the title chosen, for good or ill, by the distributor. A thousand important films have been given only by title, followed by an asterisk, indicating that this work is described in more detail in our complementary *Dictionary of Films*.

In order to be able to publish a volume for wide distribution it was necessary to accept limitations on the number of entries and therefore to eliminate some categories of film makers. We have not included technicians though we know that they are of major importance (editors, sound engineers, and camera operators). We have cited few producers and no exhibitors, distributors, or exporters.

It is our hope that this present volume, such as it is, will be of assistance to cinephiles — that elite of spectators who now count themselves in millions around the world.

Introduction

TO THE ENGLISH EDITION
BY PETER MORRIS

I am pleased to have had the opportunity of bringing Georges Sadoul's valuable *Dictionary of Film Makers* to English-speaking readers. In preparing this edition I have taken advantage of his invitation to revise and correct factual information in the original. In particular many of the filmographies have been expanded and additional biographical information has been included in many of the entries.

More recent development of certain film makers' work has led me to revise completely several of the entries. I have also added many new entries, notably for directors who established their reputations in the sixties (e.g., Bertolucci, Forman, Skolimowski) but also for certain cameramen, writers, and composers whose work seemed to me to merit inclusion. In each case entries authored by me are indicated by an asterisk. In some cases I have added additional information or a critical appraisal of the film maker's recent work; these are indicated in the text by square brackets [ ]. In all, the Dictionary has been expanded by some 15%.

The original format has been retained with minor revisions. The film maker's name is followed by an indication (in parentheses) of his original name or other names under which he worked (*also* = also known as). The arrangement is entirely alphabetical by letter. "Mc" and "Mac" are interfiled as "Mac" as is now common practice though, of course, the correct spelling has been retained. Certain names have been cross-referenced for convenience and to avoid confusion over surname prefixes (e.g., Philippe de Broca is entered under "Broca" but cross-referenced from "de Broca," and similarly with Erich von Stroheim, and others).

The filmographies for many entries have been expanded and in every case up-dated; for some directors the filmographies have been completed. Filmographies which are not complete have been indicated by the use of "notably" preceding the filmography, to indicate that a selection has been made. Original-language film titles have been used in directors' filmographies wherever possible but not for other film makers where a cross reference to the director is possible. For reasons of space, titles in common languages (French, German, Italian) have not been translated when the English release title is merely a translation of the original; it has usually been given when it substantially differs. For other languages (Russian, Swedish, Japanese, etc.) an English title is given even though this may only be a literal translation and not a release title.

Film dates, given in parentheses after the title and without the "19," do not include the country of origin except where this is not the same as that in which the film maker normally worked. For film makers who worked on a group of films in one country and later in another country, the films' country of origin is given only at the beginning and end of each series of films (e.g., Lubitsch). In any case, the films' nationality is often indicated by the language of the titles.

As Sadoul points out, publication is a means of provoking emendations and I join with him in welcoming corrections or additional information for inclusion in a later edition.

Inevitably not everyone will agree with Sadoul's assessment of certain film makers, nor with mine. But the particular merit of the original over other dictionaries is its critical and historical appraisals rather than its being only an assemblage of facts. It is this quality which I hope I have retained in this edition. I am indebted to the Canadian Film Institute's Film Study Center and the British Film Institute's Information Department, without access to which the preparation of this volume would have been impossible.

Abbreviations

ALSO	Also known as	ED	Editor
ANIM	Animator	MUS	Composer
ART DIR	Art Director/Production Designer	PHOTOG	Director of Photography
		PROD	Producer/Executive Producer
ASSIST	Assistant		
CHOREOG	Choreographer/Dance Director	PSEUD	Pseudonym
		Q.V.	See
DIR	Director	SCEN	Scenarist/Script-writer

Film makers are listed under their professional names. Actual or alternate names follow in parentheses.

An asterisk following a title indicates a film described in the companion *Dictionary of Films*. An asterisk preceding an entry indicates that the entry was added or significantly expanded by the translator.

COUNTRY ABBREVIATIONS USED IN FILMOGRAPHIES

Aust	Austria	Gr	Greece
Austral	Australia	Hung	Hungary
Belg	Belgium	It	Italy
Brit	Britain	Mex	Mexico
Bulg	Bulgaria	Neth	Netherlands
Czech	Czechoslovakia	Nor	Norway
Den	Denmark	Pol	Poland
Fin	Finland	Rum	Rumania/Romania
Fr	France	Sp	Spain
Ger	Germany	Swed	Sweden
GDR	German Democratic Republic/East Germany	Switz	Switzerland
		Yugos	Yugoslovia
GFR	German Federal Republic/West Germany		

AAES, Erik (also, in France, Eric Aèss) ART DIR Denmark. (Nordby April 27, 1899–) One of the best art directors of international stature, as exemplified by his work with Dreyer (*q.v.*) on *Ordet** and *Vredens dag** with Marcel L'Herbier (*q.v.*) on *Feu Mathias Pascal**, with Cavalcanti (*q.v.*) on *Yvette, En rade**, and *Le Capitaine Fracasse,* and with Renoir (*q.v.*) on *La Petite marchande d'allumettes**. Since 1929, he has largely confined his activities to the Danish cinema, with the exception of Cavalcanti's *Herr Puntila und sein Knecht Matti** (55), and André de Toth's *Hidden Fear* (57).

ABBAS, Khwaja Ahmad DIR/SCEN/PROD India. (Panipat June 7, 1914–) A powerful force in the Indian cinema, both as film maker and journalist. Began his film career as scriptwriter and later directed his own films. Creator of two key Indian films: *Dharti Ke Lal/Children of the Earth** (46), rural poverty and dispossessed peasantry in Bengal; *Shehar aur Sapna/The City and the Dream* (63), produced on a shoestring budget and filmed in the slums and on the roads. [Also notably,
SCEN: *Naya Sansar, Awara*, Shri 420.*
DIR: *Munna** (54), much influenced by neorealism and the first Hindi film produced without songs and dances, *Pardesi/The Traveller* (57) (co-production with USSR, V. M. Pronin co-dir), *The Celestial Palace* (66).]

ABULADZE, Tenghis DIR USSR. (Koutaissi, Georgia Jan 31, 1924–) Young Georgian director who has directed a number of documentaries and made his first feature as co-director with Chkheidze (*q.v.*) on *Lurdzha Magdany/Magdana's Donkey** (55), awarded a prize at Cannes, a compassionate and expressive film in the realist tradition. Also, *Somebody Else's Children* (59) (co-dir: Djaparidze), *Me, Grandmother, Iliko, and Illarion* (63), *The Prayer* (68).

ABU SAIF, Salah DIR Egypt. (April 12, 1915–) With the younger Youssef Shahine (*q.v.*), he is the best director of the modern Egyptian cinema. An expression of popular life and a feeling for human truths characterize his best films: *The Monster, A Woman's Youth,* and *The Beginning and the End.* He began his career in films as an editor and became a director after the war.
DIR: *Daiman Fi Kalbi/Always in My Heart* (47), *El Muntakem/The Avenger* (47), *Mughammarat Antar wa Abla/ The Adventures of Antar and Abla* (48), *Shariah el Bahlawane/Street of the Puppet Show* (49), *El Sakr/The Falcon* (50), *Laka Yom Ya Zalem/Your Day Will Come* (51), *El Hub Bahdala/Love is a Scanda`* (51), *El Osta Hassen/Foreman Hassan* (52), *Raya and Sekina* (53), *El Wahsh/The Monster** (54), *Chabab Emraa/A Woman's Youth* (56), *El Fatawa/The Tough* (56), *El Wessada el Khalia/The Empty Pillow* (57), *La Anam/No Tomorrow* (57), *Mugarem Fi Ijaza/Thief on Holiday* (58), *El Tarik el Masdud/The Barred Road* (58), *Ana Hurra/I'm Free* (59), *Bint Sabatashar/A Girl of Seventeen* (59), *Bayn el Samaa wa el Ard/Between Heaven and Earth* (59), *Lawet el Hub/ Agony of Love* (59), *Bedaya wa Nehayat/The Beginning and the End* (60), *La Tutfi el Shems/The Sun Will Never Set* (61), *Ressalah min emraa Maghoola/Letter from an Unknown Woman* (62), *Cairo 30* (66), *El Zawga el Sania/ The Second Wife* (67), *El Cadia 68/ Case 68* (68), *Awdit el Roh/The Return of the Spirit* (69).

ACHARD, Marcel SCEN/DIR France. (Sainte-Foy-lès-Lyon July 5, 1900–) Member of French Academy. With an appealing sense of fantasy, he revived the *comédie boulevardière* after 1925 and created a new tradition for it.
SCEN (notably): *Jean de la lune* (31) (dir: Jean Choux), *Mayerling* (36) (dir: Anatole Litvak), *Alibi* (37) (dir: Pierre Chenal), *Gribouille* (37) (dir: Marc Allégret), *Orage* (38) (dir: Marc Allégret), *Félicie Nanteuil* (42) (dir: Marc Allégret), *Madame de** (53) (dir: Ophüls), *La Femme et le Pantin* (59) (dir: Julien Duvivier).
DIR (notably): *Jean de la lune* (49) (remake), *La Valse de Paris* (50).

ACHAREKAR M. R. ART DIR India. (Bombay Nov 14, 1905–) One of the best Indian designers. He has collaborated with Mehboob Khan (*q.v.*) on *Aan** and with Raj Kapoor (*q.v.*) on *Shri 420/Mister 420, Awara**, and *Jagte Raho**.

***ADAM, Ken** ART DIR Britain. (Berlin 1921–)Moved to Britain from Germany before the war and has been in films since 1947. Most noted for his stylish designs for the James Bond series: *Dr. No** (62), *Goldfinger** (64), *Thunderball** (65), *You Only Live Twice** (67). Other notable films include *Queen of Spades* (48), *Around the World in Eighty Days* (56) (European scenes), *Night of the Demon** (58), *The Ipcress File* (65), *Funeral in Berlin* (66), *Chitty Chitty Bang Bang* (68).

***ADLER, Buddy (Maurice Adler)** PROD USA. (USA June 22 1906–July 12 1960) One of the most notable Hollywood producers. With Columbia from 1947–54. Joined 20th-Century Fox in 1954 and became head of the studio in 1956. Died while preparing *Cleopatra**. Main films: *Salome* (53), *From Here to Eternity** (53), *Love is a Many Splendored Thing* (55), *Bus Stop** (56), *Anastasia* (56), *Heaven Knows, Mr. Allison* (57), *South Pacific* (58), *Inn of the Sixth Happiness* (58).

ADRIAN (Gilbert Adrian) COSTUMES USA. (Naugatuk, USA 1903–1959) One of the best Hollywood costume designers and set decorators in the early sound period. With MGM for many years, his precise, luxurious, sophisticated approach found its best outlet in the period films of Greta Garbo and George Cukor. Best work: for Edmund Goulding *Love* (27), for Lubitsch *The Merry Widow** (34), for Mamoulian *Queen Christina* (33), for Clarence Brown *Anna Karenina* (35), *Conquest* (38), for George Cukor *David Copperfield* (35), *Camille* (36), for Robert Z. Leonard *The Great Ziegfield* (36).

AÈSS, Eric see AAES, ERIK

AGOSTINI, Philippe PHOTOG/DIR France. (Paris August 11, 1910–) As director of photography for Bresson (*q.v.*), Daquin (*q.v.*), Carné (*q.v.*), Grémillon (*q.v.*), and Ophüls (*q.v.*), he contributed much to the typical French visual style of the Forties and early Fifties. In 1958 began to direct his own films. Assist Photog on *Quai des brumes**.
PHOTOG (notably): for Duvivier *Carnet de Bal** (37), for Benoit-Lévy *Itto* (34), for Autant Lara *Lettres d'amour* (42), *Douce** (43), for Bresson *Les Anges du péché** (43), *Les Dames du bois de Boulogne** (45), for Carné *Les Portes de la nuit** (46), for Ophüls *Le Plaisir** (51), for Jules Dassin *Du rififi chez les hommes** (55).
DIR: *Le Naïf aux quarante enfants* (58), *Le Dialogue des Carmélites* (59), *Rencontres* (62), *La Soupe aux poulets* (63).

AGRADOOT *pseud* collective DIR/SCEN/PROD Nishith Bannerjee Agragami (1924–) PHOTOG Bibhuti Lata (1915–) Among the best Bengali directors, humanistic and concerned with both emotion and contemporary life. Most notable films include *Santralpa* (49), *Sagarika* (50), *Sree Jagannath* (50), and *Sahajatri* (51), *Babla* (51), *Kar Papay* (52), *Andi* (52), *Agni Pariksha* (54), *Anupama* (55), *Sabar Oparay* (55), *Shilpi* (57).

AKAT, Lütfü DIR Turkey. (Istanbul 1916–) The most prolific and well-known Turkish director with two or three features a year since 1952.
DIR (notably): *Unutlan sir* (47), *Damga* (47), *Vurun kahpeye* (48), *Ingiliz Kemal Lawrens'e karsi* (49), *Kaatil* (53), *Beyaz mendil* (55), *Ak altin* (57).

ALDO, G. R. (Aldo Graziati) PHOTOG Italy/France. (Scorze Jan 1, 1902–Albara di Painiga Nov 14, 1953) The greatest

2

postwar Italian cinematographer, noted for his excellent sense of black and white and his talent for composition. After being a studio photographer in France, he became famous for his photography for Visconti (*q.v.*) on *La Terra trema**. He collaborated also with Orson Welles (*q.v.*) on *Othello** and with De Sica (*q.v.*) on *Miracle in Milan** and *Umberto D**. He died in an automobile accident during the production of *Senso**.

ALDRICH, Robert B. DIR USA. (Cranston, Rhode Island August 9, 1918–) [Joined RKO in 1943 as production clerk, then became second assistant director. From 1946 to 1948 was assistant director, unit production manager, writer at Enterprises Studios. Continued as associate producer and assistant until 1952 when he directed 17 of the NBC TV series *The Doctor* and four of the *China Smith* series. During his years as assistant (see below) he worked with Renoir (*q.v.*), Losey (*q.v.*), Wellman (*q.v.*), and Chaplin (*q.v.*). He directed his first feature in 1953 and received major recognition with *Apache* in 1954.] His style is powerful, persuasive, and a little hysterical. He often dealt with social themes in his early films, notably in *Apache, Attack, The Big Knife* and that marvelous reversal of the conventional thriller, *Kiss Me Deadly*. He has said of himself: "I portray heroic characters. I am opposed to the idea of fatalism. Everyone must take his own actions even if he is broken. Voluntary sacrifice is the acme of moral integrity. Suicide is a gesture of revolt: it is necessary to pay the price of strife . . . I loath showing despicable characters who are merely black; this is a question less of finding excuses than explanations . . . I have a weakness for flowery language but during rehearsals I become aware of what could be excessive and I make it more humane . . . Love with a capital L has never been depicted in my films. It is the basis of life, of mankind, but the attachment which a man can have to a way of life or a cause is perhaps more durable than the attachment to a woman."
[ASSIST: for Renoir *The Southerner** (45), for Leslie Fenton *Pardon My Past* (45), for Wellman *The Story of G.I. Joe* (46), for Lewis Milestone *The Strange Love of Martha Vickers* (46), *Arch of Triumph* (48), *The Red Pony* (49), for Albert Lewin *The Private Affairs of Bel Ami* (47), for Robert Rossen *Body and Soul* (47), for Abraham Polonsky *Force of Evil* (48), for Richard Fleischer *So This is New York* (48), for Richard Wallace *A Kiss for Corliss* (49), for Ted Tetzlaff *The White Tower* (50), for Irving Reis *Of Men and Music* (50), *New Mexico* (50), for Joseph Losey *M** (51), *The Prowler* (51), for Charles Lamont *Abbott and Costello Meet Captain Kidd* (52), for Charles Chaplin *Limelight** (52). Also associate producer on *The First Time* (51), *Ten Tall Men* (51), *When I Grow Up* (51).]
DIR: *The Big Leaguer* (53), *World for Ransom* (54), *Apache** (54), *Vera Cruz* (54), *Kiss Me Deadly** (55), *The Big Knife** (55), *Autumn Leaves* (56), *Attack** (56), *The Garment Center/ The Garment Jungle* (57) (Aldrich replaced as director by Vincent Sherman (who received credit) when production almost completed), *Ten Seconds to Hell* (58), *The Angry Hills* (59), *The Last Sunset* (61), *Sodoma e Gomorra/Sodom and Gomorrah* (It62), *Whatever Happened to Baby Jane?* (62), *Four for Texas* (63), *Hush . . . Hush, Sweet Charlotte* (64), *The Flight of the Phoenix* (66), *The Dirty Dozen* (67), *The Legend of Lylah Clare* (68), *The Killing of Sister George* (68), *Whatever Happened to Aunt Alice?* (68), *Too Late the Hero* (69), *The Grissom Gang* (70). Has produced many of his later films and was co-scriptwriter on *Ten Seconds to Hell*.

*ALEA, Tomas Guttierrez DIR Cuba. (1928–) Trained at the Centro Sperimentale di Cinema in Rome. Organizer of the cinema section of the cultural division of the rebel army and later a founder member of ICAIC (Instituto Cubano del Arte e Industria Cinematograficos). Made several documentaries, *Esta Tierra Nuestra* (59), *Asamblea General* (59), *Muerte al Invasor* (61) (with Santiago Alvarez); directed the first post-Revolution feature, *Historias de la Revolucion* (60), three episodes of the Revolution presented in a semidocumentary style. In 1968 his *Memories of Underdevelopment* was the first Cuban feature to make an international critical impact. DIR: *Historias de la Revolucion* (60), *Las Doce Sillas* (62), *Cumbite* (64) (a visually powerful peasant drama set in

3

Haiti), *Muerte de un Burocrata* (66), *Memorias del Desarrollo* (68). Projected, *La Tierra Prometida* (71), about the Inquisition.

ALEKAN, Henri PHOTOG France. (Paris Feb 10, 1909–) Trained by Schüfftan (*q.v.*) this cinematographer was a great postwar revelation, as much at home with the documentary approach of *La Bataille du rail* as with the stylized *La Belle et la bête*. In more recent years he has specialized in color. Assistant, with Agostini (*q.v.*) and Page (*q.v.*), to Schüfftan (*q.v.*) on *Quai des brumes**.
PHOTOG (notably): for Clément, *La Bataille du rail** (45), *Les Maudits** (47); for Carné, *La Marie du port* (50), *Juliette ou la Clef des songes* (51); for Cocteau, *La Belle et la bête** (46); for Duvivier, *Anna Karenina* (Brit48); for Yves Allégret, *Une si jolie petite plage** (48); for Gance, (co-photog) *Austerlitz* (60); for Delanoy, *La Princesse de Clèves;* for Gatti, *The Other Cristobal* (Cuba63). Also *Topkapi* (64), *Triple Cross* (66), *Mayerling* (68), *Figures in a Landscape* (70).

ALEXANDROV, Grigori V. (Grigori Mormonenko) DIR USSR. (Yekaterinburg Feb 23, 1903–) Originally Eisenstein's (*q.v.*) right-hand man and collaborator, he made his own name famous with *Jazz Comedy* (34). Drawing on American burlesque, serials, musicals, and even animated cartoons, but with an original, very Russian style of its own, it was a worldwide success. He followed this up with the less successful *Circus* and *Volga-Volga* and, after the war, *Spring,* featuring his wife Lyuba Orlova. He returned to contemporary problems with *Meeting on the Elbe* in 1949 and in 1952, directed a biographical film on the composer, Glinka. His entertaining earthy approach and verve have earned him a place among film makers of international caliber.
CO-DIR/CO-SCEN (with Eisenstein): *October**, *The General Line**, *Que Viva Mexico**.
DIR: *Romance sentimentale* (Fr31), *Women's Crusade/Woman's Weal, Woman's Woe* (Switz31), *Internationale* (33) (both these are experimental documentaries), *Vesyolye Rebyata/Jazz Comedy** (34), *Cirk/Circus** (36), *Report of Comrade Stalin on Proposed Constitution of the USSR to the Eighth Extraordinary Congress of the Soviets* (37), *1 Maja/May 1st* (38) (both documentaries), *Volga-Volga* (38), *Svetlyi Put/ Bright Path/Tanya* (40), *Film Report on the War No. 4* (41), *Odna Semja/ One Family* (43), *Kapiskie Liudi/Those From the Caspian* (44), *Vesna/Spring** (47), *Vstrecha na Elbe/Meeting on the Elbe* (49)(photog: Tisse, mus: Shostakovich), *Kompozitor Glinka/Glinka* (52) (photog: Tisse), *Chelovieku cheloviek/From Man to Man* (58) (documentary), *Russki Suvenir/Russian Souvenirs* (60), *Lenin v Shveitzarii/Lenin in Switzerland* (66), *October,* revised version of original (67).

ALEXEIEFF, Alexandre ANIM France. (Kazan, Russia August 5, 1901–) The complete work of this great French animator lasts barely two hours on the screen but represents more than thirty years of continuing experiments with plastic techniques. Originally a talented engraver and illustrator, he developed after 1930 the pin-screen method of illuminating thousands of pins, set at various levels in a screen, to produce depth and design. In *Une nuit sur le mont Chauve* (33) set to Mussorgsky's music he used this method to create the effect of animated engravings, full of strange beauty and fantastic details. His prewar short commercials are supreme examples of the form — plastic poems of shapes, light, movement, and color. During the war in Canada he returned to the pin-screen with his collaborator Claire Parker and made the beautiful *En Passant* set to French-Canadian folk music. Back in France after the war, he had again to concentrate on commercials before making for Orson Welles the remarkable pin-screen prologue for *The Trial* and the short film *Le Nez* based on the Gogol story. If only for his invention of the revolutionary pin-screen technique with its limitless possibilities, he would merit a place in film history. But he is also as great an artist as his peers in the "eighth art": Emile Reynaud, Emile Cohl, Norman McLaren, Karel Zeman, Jiri Trnka (all *q.v.*).
ANIM: *Une nuit sur le mont Chauve** (33), *La Belle au bois dormant* (35) (puppets); Commercials: *Lingner Werke* (35), *L'Orchestre automatique* (35), *Parade des chapeaux* (36), *Le Trône de France* (36), *Franck Aroma* (37–39), *Crème Simon, Les Vêtements Sigrand,*

4

Huilor, L'Eau d'Evian, Les Fonderies Martin, Les Oranges de Jaffa, Les Cigarettes Bastos, Les Gaines Roussel, Ceupa (37–39), *En Passant* (Can43), *Fumées* (51), *Masques* (52), *Nocturnes* (54), *Pure Beauté* (54), *Rimes* (54), *Le Buisson ardent* (55), *Sève de la terre* (55), *Bain d'X* (56), *Osram* (56), *Quatre temps* (57), *Cent pour Cent* (57), *Constance* (58), *Anonyme* (58); titles for *Cocinor* (57), titles and prologue for *The Trial** (62); *Le Nez* (63).

ALGAR, James DIR/SCEN USA. (Modesto, USA 1914–) Best known as specialist in Walt Disney's true-life adventure series, which used trick montages of animal life: *Beaver Valley* (50), *The Living Desert** (53), *The Vanishing Prairie* (54), *Secrets of Life* (57), *White Wilderness* (57). Also produced *The Incredible Journey* (63), *The Gnome-Mobile* (67).

ALLEGRET, Marc DIR France. (Bâle, Switzerland Dec 22, 1900–) Began with a documentary when he traveled with André Gide to the Congo, then during the Thirties directed a number of polished films, notably *Mam'zelle Nitouche* (with Raimu), *Le Lac-aux-dames, Sous les yeux d'Occident* (based on Joseph Conrad's novel), *Orage* (with Jean-Louis Barrault, Michèle Morgan, Charles Boyer), and *Entrée des artistes.* His work since the war has been less interesting but usually effective. A great discoverer of talent, he gave their first real chances to, among others, Simone Simon, Jean-Pierre Aumont (both in *Les beaux jours*), Michèle Morgan (in *Gribouille*), Danièle Delorme, Gérard Philipe (both in *Les Petites du quai aux fleurs*), and Brigitte Bardot (in *Futures vedettes*). Brother of Yves Allégret.
DIR: *Voyage au Congo* (27) (documentary), *Papoul* (29), *La Meilleure bobonne* (30), *J'ai quelque chose à vous dire* (30), *Mam'zelle Nitouche* (31), *La Petite chocolatière* (31), *Les Amants de minuit* (31), *Le Blanc et le Noir* (31) (co-dir: Florey), *Attaque nocturne* (31), *Fanny* (32), *Le Lac-aux-dames* (34), *L'Hôtel du libre échange* (34), *Les Beaux jours* (35), *Sous les yeux d'Occident* (36), *Les Amants terribles* (36), *Aventure à Paris* (36), *Sans famille* (36), *La Dame de Malacca* (37), *Gribouille* (37), *Razumoff* (37), *Orage* (38), *Entrée des artistes* (38), *La Corsaire* (39),

Parade en sept nuits (41), *Felicie Nanteuil* (42), *La Belle aventure* (42), *L'Arlésienne* (42), *Les Petites du quai aux fleurs* (43), *Lunegarde* (44), *Pétrus* (46), *Blanche Fury* (Brit47), *Marie Chapdelaine* (50), *The Naked Heart* (Brit50), *La Demoiselle et son revenant* (51), *Blackmailed* (Brit51), *Avec André Gide* (51) (documentary), *L'Occultisme et la Magie* (52) (documentary), *Jean Coton* (53) (documentary), *Julietta* (53), *L'Amante di Paride* (It54), *Femmina* (It54), *Futures vedettes* (55), *L'Amant de Lady Chatterley* (55), *En effeuillant la marguerite* (56), *L'Amour est en jeu* (57), *Sois belle et tais-toi* (58), *Un drôle de dimanche* (58), *Les Affreux* (59), *Les Démons de Minuit* (61) (co-dir: Charles Gérard), *Les Parisiennes* (62) (one episode), *L'Abominable Homme des douanes* (63), *Lumière* (66) (documentary), *Expo 1900* (66) (documentary), *Le Bal du comte d'Orgel* (69).

ALLEGRET, Yves DIR France. (Paris Oct 13, 1907–) Brother of Marc Allégret. Although he directed several prewar films and worked as an assistant to Jean Renoir (*q.v.*), he only succeeded in establishing himself after the war when he became recognized as a specialist in the *film noir* with *Une si jolie petite plage, Dédée d'Anvers,* and *Manèges.* His abilities and humanism were later revealed in *Les Miracles n'ont lieu qu'une fois, Les Orgueilleux,* and *La Meilleure Part.*
DIR: *Ténériffe* (32) (short), *Prix et Profit* (32), *Le Gagnant* (35), *Vous n'avez rien à déclarer?* (36) (co-dir: Léo Joannon), *Jeune fille de France* (38), *Les Deux timides* (42) (under name Y. Champlain), *La Boîte aux rêves* (44), *Les Démons d l'Aube* (46), *Dédée d'Anvers* (47), *Une si jolie petite plage** (48), *Manèges* (50), *Les Miracles n'ont lieu qu'une fois* (51), *Les Sept péchés capitaux* (51) (one episode), *Nez-de-cuir* (52), *La Jeune folle* (52), *Les Orgueilleux* (53), *Mam'zelle Nitouche* (53), *Oasis* (54), *La Meilleure Part* (56), *Méfiez-vous fillettes* (57), *La Fille de Hambourg* (58), *Quand la femme s'en mêle* (58), *L'Ambitieuse* (59), *Le Chien de pique* (61), *Germinal* (Hung63), *Johnny Banco* (66), *L'Invasion* (70).

ALOV, Alexander DIR USSR. (Kharkov 1923–) One of the best of the younger generation of Soviet film makers who

5

always works in collaboration with Vladimir Naumov. Trained at the All-Union State Institute of Cinematography (VGIK) in Moscow under Savchenko (*q.v.*), began as assistant to Savchenko on *Taras Schevchenko* and completed it when Savchenko died during production. Concentrates on fast-paced, dramatic action films largely dealing with the Russian Civil War and the Second World War.

DIR (all with Naumov): *Trevozhnaya molodost/Turbulent Youth* (55), *Pavel Korchagin** (57), *Veter/The Wind* (59), *Mir vkhodyashchemu/Peace to the Newcomer* (61), *Moneta/The Coin* (63) (for TV), *Skvenei anekdot/An Ugly Story* (65).

AMADORI, Luis Cesar DIR Argentina. (Pescara, Italy May 28, 1902–) Prolific Argentinian director, at the height of his renown during the Peron regime.

DIR (notably): *Puerto Nuevo* (36), *Napoleon* (41), *Carmen* (43), *Madame Sans Gêne* (45), *Mosquita muerta* (46), *Albeniz* (47), *Una mujer sin cabeza* (48), *Don Juan Tenorio* (49), *Pescado* (Mex51), *La Pasion desnuda* (52), *La Bella Fioraia* (It/Sp58).

*AMBROSIO, Arturo PROD/DIR Italy. (Turin 1869–Rome 1960) A pioneer of the Italian cinema who produced in Turin many of the first Italian costume spectaculars: *The Last Days of Pompeii* (1908), *The Slave of Carthage* (1910), *Dante e Beatrice* (1912) and the 1924 version of *Quo Vadis**. He also produced the famous Robinet comedies with Marcel Fabré. Also directed among others *Theodora* (21) from the play by Victorien Sardou and *Cenere* (16) with Eleonara Duse and Febo Mari.

*AMIDEI, Sergio SCEN Italy. (Trieste Oct 30, 1904–) Made his name with his script for *Rome, Open City* which he wrote in secret with Rossellini (*q.v.*) and became one of the best neorealist scriptwriters. Has worked for (always in collaboration with other writers) De Sica (*q.v.*), Zampa (*q.v.*), Lizzani (*q.v.*). SCEN (notably): for Rossellini, *Rome, Open City**, *Paisa**, *Il Generale della Rovere, Viva l'Italia, Stromboli, Angst/ La Peura, Era notte a Roma, La Machina ammazzacattivi;* for Castellani, *Sotto il sole di Roma;* for De Sica *Sciuscia**; for Luigi Zampa, *Anni difficili;*

for Carlo Lizzani, *Cronache di poveri amanti**, *Il Processo di Verona.*

ANDERSON, Lindsay DIR Britain. (Bangalore, India April 17, 1923–) Critic, writer, theater director and film maker, and the principal driving force behind the *free cinema* movement of the mid-Fifties. [His articles in *Sight and Sound* (notably, *Stand Up! Stand Up!*) demanded a new sense of commitment in the cinema. A manifesto by the founders of *free cinema* stressed their common "belief in freedom, in the importance of the individual and in the significance of the everyday"] and Anderson himself expressed this in his poetic impression of Covent Garden *Every Day Except Christmas* and in his first feature *This Sporting Life*, still one of the best from the "kitchen sink" period of British films. [*If . . .* , too, is a speculation on the nature of individualism. His time between films is devoted to the theater, where he is equally renowned as a director at the National Theater. Co-founder in 1947 of the film magazine *Sequence* and frequently a critic for *Sight and Sound, New Statesman, The Times,* etc.]

DIR (shorts): *Meet the Pioneers* (48), *Idlers that Work* (50), *Three Installations* (52), *Wakefield Express* (53), *O Dreamland* (54), *Trunk Conveyor* (54), *Green and Pleasant Land* (54), *Henry* (54), *The Children Upstairs* (54), *Thursday's Children* (54) (co-dir: Guy Brenton), *£20 a Ton* (55), *Foot and Mouth* (55), *Every Day Except Christmas* (57), five episodes of the *Robin Hood* TV Series: *Secret Mission, The Imposters, Isabella, The Haunted Hill, Ambush* (56–57), *March to Aldermaston* (59) (co-scriptwriter with several others), *Raz, Dwa, Trzy/The Singing Lesson* (Pol67), *The White Bus* (67) (originally intended as a episode in a feature). Also supervised editing of *Together* (55) (dir: Lorenza Mazetti) and was production manager of James Broughton's *The Pleasure Garden* (53). Also directed several TV commercials. Walter Lasally (*q.v.*) photographed many of the documentaries.

DIR (features): *This Sporting Life** (63), *If . . .** (68).

*ANGER, Kenneth DIR USA. (Santa Monica, California 1932–) With Maya Deren (*q.v.*) the most important name

6

in the development of the New American Cinema. Fascinated by magic, myth, and ritual, he began film-making at an early age and made his first significant contribution with *Fireworks* (47), a brilliant portrait of homosexuality. After several evocative works in Europe he created the obsessive *Scorpio Rising* (63), a societal poem.

DIR: *Who Has Been Rocking My Dream Boat?* (41), *Tinsel Tree* (42), *Prisoner of Mars* (42), *The Nest* (43), *Escape Episode* (44), *Drastic Demise* (45), *Escape Episode* (46) (re-edited sound version), *Fireworks* (47), *Puce Moment* (49), *La Lune des lapins* (Fr50), *Eaux d'Artifice* (It53), *Inauguration of the Pleasure Dome/Lord Shiva's Dream* (54), *Thelema Abbey* (It55), *Scorpio Rising** (63), *Kustom Kar Kommando* (64), *Invocation of My Demon Brother* (Brit69).

ANKERSTJERNE, Johan PHOTOG Denmark. (Randers Jan 17, 1886–) The best cameraman during the early (1911–20) period of the Danish cinema. Photographed many of August Blom's (*q.v.*) films from 1911–16 and worked with Benjamin Christensen (*q.v.*), for whom he created the unforgettable images of *Häxan**.

ANNENKOV, Georges COSTUMES France. (Petropavlovsk, Russia 1901–) Arrived in France with Chagall and Pougny after having directed in the Soviet Union the mass pantomime *The Capture of the Winter Palace*. He developed into a skillful and polished designer whose approach suited Max Ophüls during his last French period: *La Ronde**, *Le Plaisir**, *Lola Montès**.

ANOUILH, Jean SCEN France. (Bordeaux June 23, 1910–) Leading French dramatist of the Second World War and postwar period (whose work ranges from romantic fatalism in his *Pièces noires* to savage tragicomedy in the *Pièces grincantes* and to gentle delicacy in his *Pièces roses*) has also written several film scripts since 1936.

SCEN (notably): *Les Dégourdis de la Onzième* (36) (dir: Christian-Jaque), *Monsieur Vincent* (47) (dir: Maurice Cloche), *Anna Karenina* (Brit47) (dir: Julien Duvivier), *Pattes blanches* (48) (dir: Jean Grémillon), *Caroline chérie* (50) (dir: R. Pottier), *Le Chevalier de la nuit* (53), *La Ronde** (64) (dir: Roger Vadim).

DIR: *Le Voyageur sans bagage* (43) (based on his own play), *Deux sous le violette* (52).
Several of his plays have been filmed, notably, *Waltz of the Toreadors* (62) (dir: John Guillermin) and *Becket* (64) (dir: Peter Grenville).

ANSCHUTZ, Ottomar INVENTOR Germany. (Lissa, Poland May 16, 1846–Berlin 30, 1907) One of the inventors of the film camera. In the period after 1882 he took successive photos of men and animals in movement, which he later set in motion in his Elektrotachyscope, patented in 1887, perfected in 1890.

***ANSTEY, Edgar** DIR Britain. (Watford 1907–) One of the founders, with John Grierson (*q.v.*), of the British documentary school of the Thirties, to which he contributed many notable films, including *Granton Trawler* (34), *Housing Problems* (35) (co-dir: Arthur Elton), *Enough to Eat* (36). He was head of production at the Shell Film Unit during the war. In 1949, he established the film unit of the British Transport Commission (now British Transport Films) and there has produced many notable documentaries, including *Terminus, Snow*, and others.

ANTHEIL, George MUS USA. (Trenton, USA June 8, 1900–1961) An avant-garde musician who was a pupil of Stravinsky in Paris. Made his debut in the cinema with a *bruitiste* sound track for Léger's *Ballet mécanique**. In Hollywood after 1940, he created only conventional scores, especially for the films of Cecil B. DeMille (*q.v.*) and Stanley Kramer (*q.v.*).

ANTOINE, André DIR France. (Limoges Jan 31, 1858–Le Pouliguen Oct 19, 1943) This influential theater director and manager came to film too late (at 60 years old) in his career to exercise the same kind of influence on the still adolescent cinema. However many films he directed he was usually restricted to adaptations of well-known authors and had his *L'Alouette et la Mésange* (from his own script, using nonprofessional actors) refused distribution. The striking vision of Paris at war he created in *Le Coupable* and the lyricism of *La Terre* would lead one to think that his *Les Frères Corses, Les Travailleurs de la mer* (from Victor Hugo), and *Mademoiselle de La Seiglière* might be significant films, but they have unfortunately disappeared. The best French film makers of the Twenties did not understand how much the founder of the Théâtre Libre and one of the proponents of the "new naturalism" anticipated the future of the cinema and particularly Italian neorealism. But before his final retirement from the film studios, he wrote: "People have been mistaken, from the beginnings of the cinema, in adopting theatrical methods for an art which is nothing like it . . . The kingdom of tomorrow will belong to plastic artists more than literary ones . . . On the stage, the view is fixed. In the cinema, it is perpetually in motion . . . The most valuable improvement that could be made would be to avoid using studios, *even, and especially for interiors* . . . Then we would be able to note the difference possible between the cinema, which is living, outdoor *creation,* and the theater, whose principle, on the other hand, is the imitation of nature." Retired as director of the Odéon in 1916. From 1930–1940 he was film critic for *Journal*. His son, André-Paul Antoine, has written scripts for Duvivier, Christian-Jaque, Pierre Chenal, Raymond Bernard (all *q.v.*), and others.

DIR: *Les Frères Corses* (16), *Le Coupable** (17), *Les Travailleurs de la mer* (18), *Israel* (18), *Mademoiselle de La Seiglière* (20), *La Terre** (21), *L'Alouette et la Mésange* (22), *L'Arlésienne* (22) (based on the play by Alphonse Daudet).

ANTONIONI, Michelangelo DIR Italy. (Ferrara Sept 29, 1912–) One of the most important film makers of the second half of this century. Passionately involved with his themes, his best work is characterized by an avoidance of traditional narrative structure in favor of character studies in depth and analyses of the anguish and unease of the modern world. Born among the middle-class and knowing these people best, his films have been almost entirely set in the bourgeois milieu, with the notable exception of *Il Grido,* the hopeless odyssey of a worker in the northern plains of Italy. Always, the environment of his characters plays a major role in the themes of his films. He developed an early interest in the cinema and theater, contributed in the late Thirties to *Cinema,* and continued writing as a film critic until 1949. His first film experience was as a scriptwriter during the gestation period of neorealism and his first films were documentaries. In films like *Gente del Po, N.U.,* and *L'Amorosa Menzogna* hints of his vision of the world and even his obsessions are already present. His first features are largely exploratory, but he established himself with *Le Amiche* in 1955 from a story by Cesare Pavese. In relation to this he said: "My profession is making films, but this is also the profession of living, of relating to my fellow-men, having experiences." *L'Avventura,* his first major international success, made him famous and he followed this with *L'Eclisse* and *La Notte,* the second and third parts of a trilogy focusing on women in modern society. He has described, at various times, his themes and approach: "My opinions, my mistakes, that which is most personal in my experiences will convey my message if I am sincere. To be sincere implies making something that is somewhat autobiographical. The experience that mainly contributed to make me a director is the bourgeois background from which I came . . . In the first place and above all I like women. Perhaps this is because I understand them better. I was raised among women and in their environment. I have been criticized for observing everything from a distance. This is not at all deliberate, only my method of telling the story. This 'distancing' is perhaps also modesty. I manage to imagine a moving scene but I cannot direct it. Perhaps this is because I am moved before others. Perhaps it is also because I am from the north, from Ferrara, a town where the people hide their emotions entirely . . . I am very concerned during shooting to follow the character until I sense the necessity of slackening my grip. The acting becomes good through the images, which is a plastic fact. Gray tones and threatening skies are often characteristic of my films . . . In trying to explain to the actor what he must do, one risks making his acting mechanical or turning him into a second director. . . . I attach great importance to the sound-track, to natural sounds and noises more than to music. . . . Our drama is incommunicability which isolates us one from the other. Its permanence misleads us and prevents us from resolving our problems. I am not a moralist. I neither have, nor pretend to have, a solution. But perhaps the critics are right and not the artist. You and not I. Because who ever knows what he himself is saying?"

ASSIST: Carné's *Les Visiteurs du soir* (42), Fulchignoni's *I Due Foscari* (42). CO-SCEN: Fulchignoni's *I Due Foscari* (42), Rossellini's *Un Pilota ritorna* (42), de Santis' *Caccia Tragica* (47), Fellini's *Lo Sceicco Bianco* (52) and all his own films.

DIR (shorts): *Gente del Po* (43–47), *N.U./Nettezza Urbana* (48), *L'Amorosa Menzogna* (48–49), *Superstizione* (49), *Sette Canne, un Vestito* (50), *La Villa dei Mostri* (50), *la Funivia del Faloria* (50).

DIR (features): *Cronaca di un Amore* (50), *I Vinti* (52), *La Signora Senza Camelie* (53), *L'Amore in Citta** (53) (one episode), *Le Amiche** (55), *Il Grido** (57), *L'Avventura** (60), *La Notte** (60), *L'Eclisse** (62), *Deserto Rosso** (64), *I Tre Volti* (65) (one episode, not released, negative destroyed by producer), *Blow-Up** (Brit66), *Zabriskie Point* (USA69).

Has also worked as a theater director, was 2nd Unit Dir for Lattuada's *La Tempesta* (58) and completed *Nel Segno di Roma* after the director, Guido Brignone, died in the final stages of production.

ARAKELIAN, Hagop MAKE-UP France. (Ekaterinodar, Russia Oct 9, 1894–) Trained by the great Shakhatuni, he become renowned as the best French make-up artist after his film in the Thirties. He created Jean Marais' monstrous face in Cocteau's *La Belle et la bête** and in some respects created Brigitte Bardot since he was responsible for her make-up on her first successes, including Vadim's *Et Dieu créa la femme**. Also founded the IDHEC make-up department in 1946.

ARCADY, Jean (A. Brachalinoff) ANIM France. (Sofia, Bulgaria Jan 12, 1912–) Exceptional animator and special effects technician who has contributed much to French cartoons and films on art: [*Kapok, l'esquimau* (43), *Astre et désastre* (45), *Leonardo da Vinci* (52), *Légendes cruelles* (52), *Prélude pour voix, orchestre et caméra* (60), *Savoir choisir* (61), *L'Ondomane* (61), *Mar-*

quet (62). He has also worked as technical and music collaborator on over 40 films.]

***ARNOLD, Jack** DIR/PROD USA. (New Haven, USA Oct 14, 1912–) Began his career as a Broadway actor, joined Universal in 1952 and made his name with a series of science-fiction films, during the Fifties. He has also produced and directed thrillers, westerns, and comedies and now concentrates on production, especially in TV (*It's About Time, Gilligan's Island*).

DIR (notably): *It Came From Outer Space* (53), *The Glass Webb* (53), *The Creature from the Black Lagoon* (54), *Revenge of the Creature* (55), *The Man From Bitter Ridge* (55), *Tarantula* (55), *The Vampire* (57), *The Incredible Shrinking Man* (57), *No Name on the Bullet* (59), *The Mouse that Roared* (Brit59), *A Global Affair* (63), *Hello, Down There* (68).

ARNSTAM, Leo DIR USSR. (Dniepropetrovsk 1905–) A trained musician whose first film work was in 1931 as director of sound for *Alone**. In 1932 he co-wrote *Counterplan*;* in 1936 he directed his first film, *Podrugi/Girl Friends**; and in 1944 the equally notable *Zoya*. Also (notably): *Glinka* (46), *Romeo and Juliet* (55) from the Prokofiev ballet.

ARRATO, Ubaldo PHOTOG Italy. (Ovada March 23, 1897–Rome Dec 1947). Italian cameraman, trained 1918–1930, worked with Max Ophüls on *La Signora di Tutti* (34) and Rossellini, notably on *Rome, Open City**.

ARZNER, Dorothy DIR/ED USA. (San Francisco Jan 3, 1900–) Editor during the Twenties on, e.g., *Blood and Sand* (22) and *The Covered Wagon** (23) and became Hollywood's only woman director of the Thirties, notably on *Nana/Lady of the Boulevards** (34), *Craig's Wife* (35), *The Bride Wore Red* (37), *Dance, Girl, Dance* (40), *First Comes Courage* (43). Films in the Twenties include *Fashions for Women* (27), *Ten Modern Commandments* (27), and *Get Your Man* (27).

ASQUITH, Anthony DIR Britain. (London Nov 9, 1902–Feb 1968) With Alfred Hitchcock (*q.v.*) the strongest force in the British cinema of the Thirties and one of the most important British directors. Passionately devoted to the cinema, tasteful and intelligent, he has varied between quasi-documentary portraits of English life and theatrical adaptations, but his style has always been part of his attempt to avoid the Korda (*q.v.*) "international" approach and find an authentic English character. The son of Lord Asquith, he went to Hollywood in 1926 to study film-making and in 1928 in Britain was assistant to Sinclair Hall on *Boadicea*. His first feature, *Shooting Stars* (28), a burlesque, used revolutionary effects. He continued his experiments in audio-visual counterpoint and the portrayal of English life with *A Cottage on Dartmoor* (29); in *Tell England* (30) he depicted the Gallipoli expedition during the First World War. He became internationally famous as a master of stage adaptations with *Pygmalion* (38) from Shaw's play. He made what is certainly his masterpiece, *The Way to the Stars*, at the end of the war. Thereafter, the evolution of the cinema somewhat stranded him in the two genres that appealed to him, but he continued to make civilized, entertaining films until his death.

DIR: *Shooting Stars* (28) (co-dir: A. V. Bramble), *Underground* (29), *The Runaway Princess* (29), *A Cottage on Dartmoor* (29), *Tell England* (30) (co-dir: Geoffrey Barkas), *Dance, Pretty Lady* (32), *The Lucky Number* (33), *Forever England* (35), *Moscow Nights* (36), *Pygmalion** (38) (co-dir: Leslie Howard), *French Without Tears* (39), *Freedom Radio* (40), *Quiet Wedding* (41), *Cottage to Let* (41), *Uncensored* (42), *We Dive at Dawn* (43), *The Demi-Paradise* (43), *Welcome to Britain* (43) (co-dir: B. Meredith), *Fanny by Gaslight* (44), *The Way to the Stars** (45), *While the Sun Shines* (47), *The Winslow Boy* (48), *The Woman in Question/ Five Angles on Murder* (50), *The Browning Version* (51), *The Importance of Being Earnest* (52), *The Net* (53), *The Final Test* (53), *Carrington, V.C./ Court Martial* (54), *The Young Lovers* (54), *Orders to Kill* (58), *Libel* (59), *The Doctor's Dilemma* (59), *The Millionairess* (60), *Guns of Darkness* (62), *Two Living, One Dead* (62), *An Evening with the Royal Ballet* (63) (co-dir), *The V.I.P.'s* (63), *The Yellow Rolls Royce* (64). Also production supervision on English version of *Unfinished Symphony* (34); script for *Marry Me* (32) and *Letting in the Sunshine* (33); and director of shorts, *Guide Dogs for the Blind* (39), *Channel Incident* (40), *Rush Hour* (40), *Two Fathers* (44), *On Such a Night* (56).

ASTRUC, Alexandre DIR France. (Paris July 13, 1923–) A stylist with a deep insight into the elaboration of visual imagery as a means of elucidating human relationships. He established a considerable reputation as a film critic and journalist for *Combat* and *L'Ecran Française* and renewed interest in the German silent cinema and the work of Murnau. Evolved the idea of "caméra-stylo" in 1948: "By it I mean the cinema will gradually break free from the tyranny of the visual, from the image for its own sake, from the immediate and concrete demands of the narrative, to become a means of writing as supple and subtle as written language . . . With the development of 16mm and television, the day is not far off when everyone will possess a projector, will go to the local shop and rent films written on any subject, of any form . . . The fundamental problem of the cinema is how to express thought. The creation of this language has preoccupied all the theoreticians and writers in the history of cinema, from Eisenstein down to the scriptwriters and adaptors of the sound cinema."

He worked on two 16mm shorts as assistant to Marc Allégret (*q.v.*) and Marcel Achard (*q.v.*) and collaborated on two scripts before making his first professional film, *Le Rideau cramoisi*, in 1952. This and his first feature, *Les Mauvaises rencontres*, 1955, are in some ways precursors of the *nouvelle vague*. Apart from his early films, most of his films are from imposed subjects and adapted from existing works. Few have had any real commercial success. It is ironic that the man who so passionately attacked the filming of famous novels and plays should himself have had to use the "caméra-stylo" in just this way. ASSIST: Marc Allégret's *Blanche Fury* (Brit47), Marcel Achard's *Jean de la lune* (49).

CO-SCEN: *La P . . . respecteuse* (52) (dir: Pagliero), *Luther* (unfilmed).

DIR (shorts): *Aller et Retour* (48) in 16 mm, *Ulysse ou les Mauvaises ren-*

contres (49) in 16 mm, *Le Rideau cramoisi** (52), *Les Puits et le Pendule* (63) for TV, *Evariste Galois* (64).
DIR (features): *Les Mauvaises rencontres** (55), *Une Vie** (58), *La Proie pour l'ombre** (60), *L'Education sentimentale 61* (61) (freely based on Flaubert), *La Longue marche* (66), *Flammes sur l'Adriatique* (68).

AUBERT, Louis PROD France. (Mayenne 1879–Les Sables d'Olonne May 17, 1944) A pioneer of the French film industry who as exhibitor, distributor, and producer always followed his own motto: "The cinema is very simple — two columns, one for receipts, the other for expenses."

AUDIARD, Michel SCEN France. (Paris May 15, 1920–) Brilliant French dialogue writer in the *boulevardier* manner who since 1950 has followed in the footsteps of Henri Jeanson (*q.v.*). He has worked with Jean Delannoy (*q.v.*), Denys de la Patellière (*q.v.*), André Hunebelle, etc.

AUDRY, Jacqueline DIR France. (Orange Sept 25, 1908–) One of the few French female directors, noted for her tasteful and delicate Colette adaptations. Almost all her features have been scripted by her husband, Pierre Laroche (*q.v.*).
DIR (notably): *Les Chevaux du Vercors* (43) (documentary), *Les Malheurs de Sophie* (45), *Sombre dimanche* (48), *Gigi* (48), *Minne l'ingénue libertine* (50), *Olivia* (51), *Huis clos* (54) (from Sartre), *Mitsou* (56) (from Colette), *La Garçonne* (57), *L'Ecole de cocottes* (57), *Le Sécret du chevalier d'Eon* (60), *Cadavres en vacances* (61), *Les Petits Matins* (61), *Soledad* (66), *Le Lis de mer* (70).

AUGUST, Joseph PHOTOG USA (1890–1947) Trained with Thomas Ince (*q.v.*) and W. S. Hart. From 1925 to 1945 he was the usual cameraman for John Ford, for whom he created the memorable images of *The Informer** (35). [Also, notably, *Man's Castle** (33), *Twentieth Century** (34), *The Plough and the Stars* (37), *Gunga Din* (39), *The Hunchback of Notre Dame* (40), *All That Money Can Buy* (41), *They Were Expendable* (45).]

AURENCHE, Jean SCEN France (Pierrelatte Sept 11, 1904–) Usually collaborates with Pierre Bost (*q.v.*), with whom he has written many of the best postwar French films, notably those of Claude Autant-Lara (*q.v.*), which are mostly adaptations of novels.
SCEN (notably): for Carné *Hotel du Nord* (38); for Autant-Lara, *Lettres d'amour* (42), *Le Mariage de Chiffon* (42), *Journal d'une femme en blanc* (65); with Pierre Bost, *Douce** (43), *Sylvie et la fantôme* (45), *Le Diable au corps** (47), *Occupe-toi d'Amélie** (49), *L'Auberge rouge** (51), *Le Blé en herbe/Ripening Seed* (54), *Le Rouge et le noir* (54), *Marguerite de la nuit* (55), *En cas de malheur** (58), *Le Jouer* (58), *Non Uccidere** (61), for Christian-Jaque, *Les Dégourdis de la onzième* (36) (co-scen: Jean Anouilh), *Madame Sans-Gêne* (62); for Jean Delannoy, *La Symphonie pastorale* (46), *Dieu a besoin des hommes* (50); for René Clément, *Au-delà des grilles* (48), *Jeux interdits** (52).

AURIC, Georges MUS France/Britain. (Lodève Feb 15, 1899–) The most famous French composer, representative of the best romantic tradition in symphonic film music. A member of the Groupe des Six and the author of several orchestral compositions and ballet scores. Contributed much to films by Cocteau, Clair, Vadim, Ophüls, Cavalcanti, and to several British films. Later became director of the Paris Opéra. Notable films: *Le Sang d'un poète** (30) (dir: Cocteau), *A nous la liberté** (31) (dir: Clair), *Lac aux dames* (34) (dir: Marc Allégret), *Orage* (38) (dir: M. Allégret), *Entrée des artistes* (38) (dir: M. Allégret), *L'Alibi* (37) (dir: Pierre Chénal), *L'Éternel retour** (43) (dir: Delannoy), *Dead of Night** (45) (dir: Cavalcanti), *Caesar and Cleopatra** (45) (dir: Gabriel Pascal), *La Belle et la bête** (46) (dir: Cocteau), *It Always Rains on Sunday** (47) (dir: Robert Hamer), *Hue and Cry** (47) (dir: Charles Crichton), *Les Parents terribles** (48) (dir: Cocteau), *Orphée* (51) (dir: Cocteau), *Lavender Hill Mob** (51) (dir: Charles Crichton), *Moulin Rouge** (52) (dir: Huston), *Roman Holiday** (53) (dir: Wyler), *Le Salaire de la peur** (53) (dir: Clouzot), *Du rififi chez les hommes** (55) (dir: Dassin), *Lola Montès** (55) (dir: Ophüls), *Le Mys-*

tère Picasso* (56) (dir: Clouzot), *Les Bijoutiers du clair de lune* (58) (dir: Vadim), *Celui qui doit mourir** (57) (dir: Dassin), *Bonjour Tristesse* (57) (dir: Preminger), *La Chambre ardente* (62) (dir: Duvivier), *The Innocents* (61) (dir: Jack Clayton), *Thomas l'Imposteur* (65) (dir: Franju).

AUTANT-LARA, Claude DIR France. (Luzarches Aug 5, 1903–) Became active in the cinema from the age of sixteen, designed sets and costumes for Marcel L'Herbier (*q.v.*) and later for Jean Renoir (*q.v.*) and Jacque Catelain; was also assistant to René Clair (*q.v.*). He directed an avant-garde short, *Fait divers*, in 1923, then a documentary, *Vittel* (26), and *Construire un feu* (27–28), an early wide-screen experiment from a Jack London story. From 1930 to 1932 he directed French versions of American films in Hollywood and, after his return to France, directed a number of shorts. His pre-1942 features were commissioned and did not at all appeal to him but he had to accept them in order to make a living until *Le Diable au corps* (47) brought him international fame. It is perhaps not surprising that he has said: "The director must consider himself surrounded by enemies. What I mean by this is that, in a business where the taste of one man must prevail, he is surrounded by people who want to do nothing but impose their own tastes." The war gave him the chance to emerge from the shadows, and after the charming, outdated *Le Mariage de Chiffon* and *Lettres d'amour* in 1942, his satire of the bourgeoisie in *Douce/Love Story* (43) seemed especially astringent during the Pétainist period. Waspish satirical views of conventional morality characterize his films in the first postwar decade. An attack on the recent war through a portrait of an earlier one is the key to *Le Diable au corps,* still his best film. He dissected the ridiculous characters of "la Belle époque" in *Occupe-toi d'Amélie,* brought violent Voltairean satire to *L'Auberge rouge,* and depicted the bitter occupation years in *La Traversée de Paris.* His films, however, are not all equally successful. He has tended to concentrate on staging well-written adaptations of classic novels and plays. This may perhaps be because the cover of a well-known work allows him to say more without interference

from the censor (whom he has perpetually attacked). In order to make *Non Uccidere,* a film close to his heart for ten years, he had to accept many commercial films.

ART DIR: for L'Herbier, *Le Carnaval des vérités* (19), *L'Homme du large* (20), *Villa Destin* (21), *Don Juan et Faust* (22), *L'Inhumaine** (23), *Le Diable au coeur* (27); for Jean Renoir, *Nana** (26); for Jacque Catelain, *Le Marchard de plaisir* (23).

ASSIST: to René Clair on *Paris qui dort** (23), *Le Voyage imaginaire* (25).

DIR (shorts): *Fait divers* (23), *Vittel* (26), *Construire en feu* (27–28), *Le Gendarme est sans pitié, Un client sérieux, Monsieur le duc, La Peur des coups, Invite Monsieur à dîner* (all 32–33).

DIR (features): *Ciboulette* (33), *My Partner Master Davis/The Mysterious Mr. Davis* (Brit36), *L'Affair du Courrier de Lyon* (37), *Le Ruisseau* (38), *Fric-frac* (39), *Le Mariage de Chiffon* (42), *Lettres d'amour* (42), *Douce** (43), *Sylvie et le fantôme* (45), *Le Diable au corps** 47), *Occupe-toi d'Amélie** (49), *L'Auberge rouge** (51), *Les Sept péchés capitaux* (52) (one episode), *Le Bon Dieu sans confession* (53), *Le Blé en herbe/Ripening Seed* (54) (from Colette), *Le Rouge et le noir* (54) (from Stendhal), *Marguerite de la nuit* (55), *La Traversée de Paris* (56), *En cas de malheur** (58), *Le Jouer* (58), *Les Regates de San Francisco* (59), *La Jument verte* (59), *Le Bois des amants* (60), *Non Uccidere** (61), *Vive Henri IV, Vive l'amour* (61), *Le Comte de Monte Cristo* (61), *Le Meurtrier* (63), *Le Magot de Joséfa* (63), *Journal d'une femme en blanc/ Woman in White* (65), *Une femme en blanc se révolte* (66), *Le Plus vieux métier du monde* (67) (one episode), *Le Franciscain de Bourges* (67), *Les Patates* (69). Most post-43 films SCEN Aurenche, Bost ART DIR Max Douy.

AVERY, Tex ANIM USA. (Dallas, Texas 1918–) Began in cartoons with Charles Mitz and with Walter Lantz. Before 1940 he collaborated with Chuck Jones (*q.v.*) at Warner Brothers, where they invented Bugs Bunny. He was largely responsible for ferociously savage cartoons and for the characters "Chilly Willy," "Lucky Ducky," and "Droopy."

Although he never abandoned the typical Disney animals and graphic design, he revolutionized cartoons with his ruthless, violent, anarchic sense of comic fantasy, often quasi-surrealistic. His films are typically based on a rhythmic chase and fight to the death. [Among his best films are *Kingsize Canary* (47) and *The Cat That Hated People* (49). Others include: *Dumb-Hounded* (43), *The Shooting of Dan McGoo* (45), *Half-Pint Pigmy* (47), *Bad Luck Blackie* (49), *Car of Tomorrow* (52), *Deputy Droopy* (54), *Polar Pests* (58).]

BABURAO PAINTER DIR/PROD India. (Kolhapur 1892–) Pioneer of the Indian cinema. Designer for D. G. Phalke (*q.v.*) from 1913–19. Founded the Maharashtra Film Company in Kolhapur in 1921 and gave V. Shantaram (*q.v.*) his first chance to direct. Main films from 1921–26 include *Sarahandri, Sinhegarh, Sati Padmini, Sarkari Praser.* Also, *Swajara Doran* (30), *Vishwamitra* (52).

BAC, André PHOTOG France. (Paris Dec 14, 1905–) Excellent French cameraman who has worked with Grémillon, *Le Six juin à l'aube** (45); with Daquin, *Le Point du jour** (49); with Autant-Lara *Occupe-toi d'Amélie** (49), *L'Auberge rouge** (51); with Yves Robert, *La Famille Fenouillard* (60), *La Guerre des boutons* (62), *Bébert et l'Omnibus* (63).

BACHELET, Jean PHOTOG France. (Azans Oct 8, 1894–) Began his career in Russia before 1914 and is especially notable for his consistently remarkable work with Jean Renoir during his best period, from *Nana** to *La Règle du jeu**.

BACON, Lloyd DIR USA. (San Jose Jan 16, 1889–Burbank Nov 15, 1955) Began his career as an actor in Chaplin shorts and was trained by Mack Sennett. He became one of the most prolific Hollywood directors, largely under contract to Warners; most of his work is competent but routine. He directed among others *42nd Street*, Footlight Parade* (33), *Gold Diggers of 1937* (36), and *Call Me Mister* (51), whose qualities derive largely from Busby Berkeley's (*q.v.*) choreography.

BADRAKHAN, Ahmed DIR Egypt. (Sept 18, 1909–) One of the pioneers of the Egyptian cinema who since 1932 specialized in melodramas and films with songs. Since the revolution he has made several patriotic films including: *Allah Maana/God is on Our Side* (54), *Mustafa Kamel* (53).

BAKY, Josef von DIR Germany/German Federal Republic. (Hungary March 23, 1902–1966) Prolific German film maker, formerly assistant to Geza von Bolvary (*q.v.*); directed first film in 1936. Notable for *Intermezzo* (36), *Annelie* (41), *Münchausens Abenteuer** (43), *Der Träumende Mund/Dreaming Lips* (52).

BALCON, (Sir) Michael PROD Britain. (Birmingham May 19, 1896–) Perhaps the most powerful single force in the British film industry. Beginning as a distributor in 1919, he formed Gainsborough and in 1931 became director of production at Gaumont British. He gave Hitchcock his first chance to direct (*The Pleasure Garden*) and produced his best British films. In 1938 he became head of production at Ealing Studios, where he produced the famous Ealing comedies and dramas and trained the postwar generation of British directors: Charles Frend, Robert Hamer, Charles Crichton, Mackendrick, Harry Watt, Henry Cornelius (all *q.v.*), etc. In 1959, he founded Bryanston Films; he took over British Lion in 1964 and has been connected with Woodfall.

BALDI, Gian Vittorio DIR Italy. (Bologna Oct 30, 1930–) Documentary film maker who has tried to portray men living their lives, "to discover and reproduce the beauty that is found in every natural gesture and in spontaneous dialogue." Originally a critic.
DIR: *Il Pianto delle Zitelle* (59), *Vigilia di mezza estate* (59), *Via dei Cessati Spiriti* (59), *La Casa delle Vedove* (60),

Luciano (60), *Il Bar di Gigi* (61), *L'Italiane e l'Amore* (61) (one episode), *Il Corrida di Sposa* (62), Luciano (62) (same material as 60), *Le Adolescenti* (65) (one episode), *Riltratto di Pina* (66), *Fuoco* (70).

*BALLARD, Lucien PHOTOG USA. (1908–) One of the most professional and accomplished of American cinematographers, his work has ranged from Sternberg's *Morocco* (1930), through Kubrick's *The Killing* (56), to the recent color films, *Will Penny*, *The Wild Bunch*, and *True Grit*. He has worked for both Boetticher (*q.v.*) and Peckinpah (*q.v.*).
PHOTOG (notably): *Morocco* (30), *The Devil is a Woman**(35), *Crime and Punishment* (36), *The King Steps Out* (36), *Fixed Bayonets* (51), *The Magnificent Matador* (55), *The Killing* (56), *Band of Angels* (57), *Anna Lucasta* (58), *Buchanan Rides Alone* (58), *Ride the High Country** (61), *Will Penny* (67), *The Wild Bunch** (68), *True Grit* (69), *The Ballad of Cable Hogue* (70), *The Master of the Islands* (70).

BAN, Frigyes DIR Hungary. (Kosicich, Hungary 1902–) Veteran director of some forty films from 1939 to date, among which is *The Soil under Your Feet* (48), the first major postwar production of the newly nationalized Hungarian film industry and one of the best of its early productions.
[DIR (notably): *Talpalatanyi föld/The Soil under Your Feet* (48), *Semmelweis* (52), *Rakoczi Ladnagya/Rakoczi's Lieutenant* (53), *Szegeny gazdagok/ Fatia Negra* (59), *Büdosviz/Healing Water* (64).]

BANOS, Ricardo de DIR Spain. (Barcelona Aug 27, 1882–Aug 8, 1939) Pioneer director of the Spanish cinema.
DIR (notably): *Secrets of the Confession* (06), *Don Juan Tenorio* (10), *The Lovers of Teruel* (12), *The White Gypsy* (19), *Don Juan Tenorio* (21), *El Relicario* (33).

BANTON, Travis COSTUMES USA. (Texas Aug 18, 1894–) Hollywood designer of plush costumes whose work typifies the Hollywood period films of 1925–45. Worked for Frank Borzage (*q.v.*), Lubitsch (*q.v.*), Ophüls (*q.v.*) (on *Letter From an Unknown Woman*), and, notably, for Sternberg on the Dietrich films:

Morocco* (30), *Dishonored* (31), *Shanghai Express** (32), *The Scarlet Empress* (34), *The Devil is a Woman** (35).

BARATIER, Jacques DIR France. (Montpellier March 8, 1918–) Originally a drama critic, then worked in radio and made several shorts, *Désordres* (49), *Paris la nuit*(55), before making his first feature, the poetic *Goha* in Tunisia in 1957. Idealistic and devoted to experiment.
DIR: *Goha** (57), *La Poupée* (62), *Dragées au poivre* (63), *L'Or du duc* (65), *Le Désordre à vingt ans* (67), *La Décharge* (70).

BARDEM, Juan Antonio DIR Spain. (Madrid June 2, 1922–) With his friend Berlanga (*q.v.*) he gave the Spanish cinema a new lease on life and an international standing. Stylistically vigorous and sincere, he has expressed the realities of his country better than anyone (except Buñuel) in *Comicos*, *La Venganza* and particularly in *Death of a Cyclist* and *Calle Mayor*. The son of actors Rafael Bardem and Mathilde M. Sampiero, he was educated in agriculture, then in 1947 received a diploma from the Madrid film school. He made his name as a scriptwriter on Berlanga's *Welcome, Mr. Marshall!* in 1952. In 1955, the young film maker took stock of the Spanish cinema: "After 60 years the Spanish cinema is politically ineffective, socially false, intellectually infirm, aesthetically empty, industrially rickety. We now want to fight for a national cinema with love, sincerity, and honor." Later he added: "Undoubtedly a film maker cannot himself hope to change the world. Nonetheless, he must make a contribution. He must devote all his efforts towards a positive, useful cinema that will reveal the reality of things so that they will change. The Spanish spirit is realistic in literature as it is in painting. I consider the cinema deeply rooted in reality. It is the witness of its time. It is necessary to say as much as possible, as quietly as possible. Briefly, to shun the baroque and return to classicism." "An artist cannot transplant his roots; I can speak only of that which I know well: Spain."
SCEN: for Berlanga, *Bienvenido, Mr. Marshall!** (52), *Novio a la vista* (53); and for all his own films.
DIR: *Paseo sobre una guerra antigua* (48)

15

(16mm short, co-dir: Berlanga), *Barajas, Aeropuerto Internacional* (50) (short), *Esa pareja feliz* (51) (co-dir: Berlanga), *Comicos* (53), *Felices Pascuas* (54), *Muerte de un ciclista** (55), *Calle Mayor** (56), *La Venganza* (57), *Sonatas* (59), *A las Cinco de la Tarde* (60), *Los Innocentes* (62), *Nunca Pasa Nada* (63), *Los Pianos Mecanicos* (64), *El Ultimo Dia de la Guerra/The Last Day of the War* (69).

BARKER, Reginald DIR USA. (Scotland 1886–Hollywood Sept 25, 1937) The best director of Thomas Ince (*q.v.*) productions and one of those who made the western an art form. Directed many of the William S. Hart classics from 1914 to 1917, including *Hell's Hinges* (16) and *Between Men* (15), but did not direct *The Aryan**, though often credited with it. Also (notably): *The Wrath of the Gods* (14), *The Coward* (15), *The Iron Strain* (16), both with Charles Ray, *Shadows* (19), *The Hell Cat* (18), *The Storm* (22).

BARKER, William George PHOTOG/DIR/PROD Britain (1867–1951) Pioneer of the British cinema, excellent cameraman of everyday scenes from 1897 to 1912, when he became a director of features. He later turned exclusively to production. Photographed F. R. Benson's *Richard III* (11). [Directed, notably, *Sixty Years a Queen* (13) (a dramatized exposition of Queen Victoria's reign), *East Lynne* (13). Produced *The German Spy Peril* (14), *The Road to Ruin* (14), *Jane Shore* (15), *Rogues of London* (15), and many others.]

BARNET, Boris V. DIR USSR. (Moscow June 16, 1902–Riga Jan 1965) The best Soviet director of comedies, gentle and lyrical in his approach, full of warmth in his perceptive observation of behavior. Originally a boxer, he trained in films under Kuleshov. After his excellent silent films, like *The House on Trubnaya Square* (28) and *Girl with the Hat-Box* (27), he created his masterpiece, *Okraina* in 1933. In 1959 in a conversation with me he said: "I am not a theoretical man, but I take the material for my films from life. For good or ill, I have always tried to show a modern period, men truly set in Soviet times. But it is not easy and one might in this regard think of a Japanese painter. Until he is 40 he paints still lifes. Between 40 and 60, birds. After 60, herons and ducks. He must wait until he is a hundred before finding the dignity to take up the subject of man. But is one ever sure of having sufficient time? Personally I like the droll aspects of a drama and the tragic elements of comedy. It is a question of proportions, not always easy to find." Acted in Kuleshov's *The Strange Adventure of Mr. West in the Land of the Bolsheviks** (24), Otsep's *Der Lebende Leichnam/A Living Corpse* (USSR/Germany 29), his own *Miss Mend*.

DIR (notably): *Miss Mend* (26) (co-dir: Otsep), *Devushka s korobkoi/Girl with the Hat-Box* (27), *Doma na Trubnoi/The House on Trubnaya Square** (28) *Moskva v Octyabr'/Moscow in October* (29), *Ledolom/Thaw* (31), *Okraina/Outskirts** (33), *U samovo sinevo morya/By the Bluest of Seas* (36), *Noch v Sentyabr'/A Night in September* (39), *Manhood* (41) and *A Priceless Head* (42) (both part of series *Fighting Film Albums*), *Podvig razvedchika/The Scout's Exploit* (47), *Liana* (55), *The Poet* (57), *Anoushka* (61).

BARON, Auguste INVENTOR France. (Paris 1853–Paris June 1, 1938) Remarkable, but unlucky inventor both of the sound cinema (1896–1899) and of multiscreen: Cinématorama (1896), Multirama (1912).

BARONCELLI, Jacques de DIR France. Bouillargues June 25, 1881–Paris Jan 12 1951) One of the first Frenchmen to take the cinema seriously as an art form. Descended from an aristocrat family, he was a journalist until he was overwhelmed by the cinema after seeing *The Cheat**. Notable especially as a good adapter (*Le Père Goriot, Ramuntcho*) he had also a sense of the open air and the sea (*Pêcheurs d'Islande*). Directed more than 80 films from 1915 to 1947, including: *La Maison de l'espoir* (15) (first film), *Le Roi de la mer* (17), *Ramuntcho* (19), *Le Père Goriot* (21), *Nêne* (23), *Pêcheurs d'Islande* (24) (from Pierre Loti), *La Femme et le Pantin* (29) (from Pierre Louys), *Crainquebille** (33) (from Anatole France), *Michel Strogoff* (37) (from Jules Verne), *La Duchess de Langeais* (42) (from Balzac), *Rocambole* (48) (from Ponson Du Terrail).

BARRETO, Vitor de Lima DIR Brazil (1905–) Met justifiable international fame with *O Cangaceiro,* about bandits of honor in the Robin Hood style.
DIR (notably): *Painel* (50) (short), *Santuario* (51) (short), *O Cangaceiro** (53), *A Primeira Missa* (61).

BARROS, José Leitao de DIR Portugal. (Lisbon 1896–) His best films, like *Nazare* (28), *Maria do Mar* (29), and *Alla Ariba* (42), are notable for their beautiful images and their use of exteriors and, occasionally, nonprofessional actors. However, he has had to accept many mediocre commissioned films: *The Dead Queen* (45), *Camoëns* (46), etc.

BARSACQ, Léon ART DIR France. (Crimea Oct 18, 1906–Dec 1969) One of the French art directors who knew how best to create an "atmosphere," as exemplified in his work for Renoir, *La Marseillaise*;* for Carné, *Les Enfants du paradis*;* for Leenhardt, *Les Dernières Vacances;* for Clément, *Le Chateau de verre;* and for many of Clair's later films, *Le Silence est d'or*, La Beauté du diable*, Les Belles de nuit*, Les Grandes Manoeuvres*, Porte des Lilas*.* His work in the Sixties was of considerably less interest.

BARTOSCH, Berthold ANIM France. (Bohemia Dec 29, 1893–) Primarily an architect, born in Austro-Hungary, and famous in the cinema for one film: *L'Idée* (34), a symbolic interpretation of humanity's response to idealism, based on woodcuts by Frans Masereel with music by Arthur Honegger (*q.v.*). Earlier Bartosch had worked with Lotte Reiniger (*q.v.*). *L'Idée* is revolutionary in its use of multiplane animation (before Disney).

*BARUA, Pramathesh Chandra DIR/SCEN India. (Gauripur, Assam 1900–Calcutta Nov 29, 1951) Son of the Rajah of Gauripur and widely traveled abroad, where he had observed film production, he made several attempts to break into films (notably in 1931 by producing Debaki Bose's *Aparadhi*) and eventually joined New Theatres in Calcutta. His first success, which he directed, adapted, and acted in, with *Devdas*. Thereafter he became a powerful influence on the development of Bengali cinema and trained

Bimal Roy (*q.v.*), Debaki Bose (*q.v.*), and Nitin Bose (*q.v.*). Wrote many of his own scripts and acted in several of his own films.
DIR (notably): *Devdas** (35), *Maya/Illusion* (36), *Mukti/Liberation* (37), *Adhikar/Authority* (38), *Zindigi* (39), *Prija Banhabi* (40). His work declined rapidly in the Forties.

BARZMAN, Ben SCEN USA/Britain. (Toronto, Canada Oct 12, 1910–) One of the best of the Hollywood scriptwriters who suffered from the Hollywood witch-hunts, he continued to work in Europe after leaving Hollywood at the same time as Losey. Contributed to American films under various pseudonyms until 1963, when he again used his own name. [SCEN (notably): for George Marshall, *True to Life* (42); for Losey, *The Boy with Green Hair* (USA48), *Stranger on the Prowl* (It51), *Time Without Pity* (Brit56), *Blind Date** (Brit59); for Edward Dmytryk, *Give Us This Day* (Brit 49); for Dassin, *He Who Must Die** (Fr57); for Lawrence Harvey, *The Ceremony* (Brit63); for Anthony Mann, *The Fall of the Roman Empire* (USA63), *The Heroes of Telemark* (65); for John Guillermin, *The Blue Max* (Brit66).]

BASS, Saul ANIM USA (Neden 1920–) Title designer whose work, especially for Preminger, often surpasses in art and poetry the films for which they are ostensibly the prologue.
Titles for: *Around the World in 80 Days, West Side Story*, Spartacus, Vertigo*, Psycho*, The Big Country, North by Northwest*, It's a Mad, Mad, Mad, Mad World, Carmen Jones*, Exodus*, The Man with the Golden Arm*, Bonjour Tristesse, Anatomy of a Murder, Saint Joan*, Bunny Lake is Missing,* and many others.
DIR: *The Searching Eye* (64), *From Here to There* (64), *Why Man Creates* (68) (all shorts).

BATCHELOR, Joy *see* HALAS, JOHN

BAUER, Yevgeni DIR USSR. (188?–Crimea summer, 1917) The first artist in Tsarist Russia to devote himself to the cinema in a period when there were mainly docile directors churning out mediocre films for the big Pathé and Drankov companies. Originally a painter, he became an art director and director for these companies before joining Khanzhonkov, who gave his talents almost free rein. In three and a half years he directed nearly 60 films. Completely enamored of beautifully dressed, decadent heroes and heroines in splendid sets, he specialized in sophisticated dramas, many of them featuring Ivan Mozhukhin.

DIR (notably): *The Secret of Professor Insarov's Portrait* (13), *Volnaya ptitsa/ Freed Bird* (13) *Ditya bolshova goroda/ Child of the Big City* (14), *Slezi/Tears* (14), *Zhizn v smerti/Life in Death* (14), *Pesn torzhestvuyushchei liubvi/Song of Triumphant Love* (15), *Obozhzhenniue krylya/Singed Wings* (15), *Korleva ekrana/Queen of the Screen* (16), *Zhizn za zhizn/A Life for a Life* (16), *Grif starovo bortza/Griffon of an Old Warrior* (16), *Revolutsioner/Revolutionist* (17), *Nabat/The Alarm* (17), *Korol Parizha/The King of Paris* (17).

BECKER, Jacques DIR France. (Paris Sept 15, 1906–Paris Feb 21, 1960) A director of integrity who was Renoir's (*q.v.*) assistant from 1931 to 1939 and who followed the realistic path of his mentor, but with an intensely personal and carefully detailed style of his own. He began by creating a kind of social tableau of France, offering a very careful and realistic portrait of peasant life in *Goupi Mains-Rouges,* of fashionable Paris in *Falbalas,* of a pair of working-class lovers in postwar Paris in *Antoine et Antoinette,* and of the Saint-Germain-des-Près youth in *Rendez-vous de juillet.* His most perfectly created visual work is *Casque d'or,* a portrait of Parisian apaches at the turn of the century and a tribute to the time of Feuillade (*q.v.*). He tried his hand at sophisticated comedies and was forced to accept several commissioned films, but acquitted himself well even with these. Then, just before his death he regained his true creative power with *Le Trou,* a rigorous but totally engrossing film. He has described his art and ideas: "The effectiveness of a film is dependent on the application of a rigorous logic to the development of the story. In a true film everything must be foreseen, the smallest suspect detail destroys the value of the whole." "Causes don't interest me as much as a theme. The story (the anecdote, the tale) is of little importance to me. Only the characters, who become *my* characters, obsess me to the point where I can't stop think-ing about them. They excite me just as people I meet by chance during the day excite me and about whom I am curious to the point of being caught staring at strangers." "People have been wrong in believing, roughly, that I have tried at any price to be 'social.' This impression is caused by the fact that in my films they become quite involved with the characters. That is my somewhat entomological side: whatever happens in France, I am French, I make films about French people, I look at French people, I am interested in French people." Began a feature *L'Or du Cristobal* in 1939 that he was not able to complete. He completed his first feature after his return from captivity in Germany in 1942.

ASSIST: to Jean Renoir on, e.g., *Boudu sauvé des eaux*, Chotard et compagnie, Madam Bovary, Les Bas Fonds*, Une partie de campagne*, La Grande Illusion*, La Marseillaise*.*

DIR: *Le Commissaire est bon enfant* (34) (short, co-dir: Pierre Prévert), *Tête de turc* (35) (5-reel film that Becker refused later to acknowledge as his), *L'Or du Christobal* (39) (taken over by Jean Stelli, Becker refused to acknowledge it as his work), *Dernier atout* (42), *Goupi Mains-Rouges** (43), *Falbalas* (45), *Antoine et Antoinette** (47), *Rendez-vous de juillet** (49), *Edouard et Caroline* (51), *Casque d'or** (52), *Rue de l'Estrapade* (53), *Touchez pas au grisbi** (54), *Ali-Baba et les 40 voleurs* (54), *Les Aventures d'Arsène Lupin* (56), *Montparnasse 19* (57) (originally to have been made by Ophüls but entirely redesigned by Becker), *La Trou** (60).

BEK-NAZAROV, Amo DIR USSR. (Armenia 1892–) The father of the Armenian cinema, which he established after having been an actor in Moscow and having been director of many films in Georgia.

DIR (notably): *U pozernovo stolba/In the Pillory* (24), *Natella* (26), *Namus/ Honor* (26) (first Armenian film), *Zare* (27), *Khaz-Push* (27), *The House on a Volcano* (28), *Pepo* (35), *Zanguezour* (38), *David-Bek* (44), *Anait* (48), *The New Residence* (55).

*BELLOCCHIO, Marco DIR Italy. (1940–) Young, deeply political film maker who studied at the Centro Sperimentale in Rome and has remarkable economy of expression, comparable in some ways to the approach of the French *nouveau* *roman: I Pugni in Tasca/Fists in the Pocket* (65) and *La Cina è vicina/China is Near* (66). Although less incisive than the earlier film, this latter is a powerful psychological and political portrait. Also episode in *Amore è Rabbia* (It/Fr67–69) (not in English version), *Nel Nome del Padre* (71).

BELLON, Yannick DIR France. (Biarritz April 6, 1924–) Woman documentary film maker with an intense, lively, and intelligent perception. Also an editor.
DIR (notably): *Goémons* (47), *Colette* (50), *Varsovie quand même* (53), *Un matin comme les autres* (54), *Le Second souffle* (59), *Zaa le petit chameau blanc* (60), *Le Bureau des mariages* (62).

BENACERRAF, Margot DIR Venezuela. (Caracas Aug 14, 1926–) After making a documentary, *Reveron*, directed in 1958 the best film ever made in Venezuela, the remarkable *Araya**.

BENEDEK, Laslo DIR/SCEN/PHOTOG/ED USA/Britain/Germany/France. (Budapest March 5, 1907–) Born in Hungary, he became a cameraman and editor in Germany and France in the early Thirties and was scriptwriter in England 1935–37. He moved to the USA in 1937 and worked in various capacities before directing his first film in 1948. Responsible for two notable Hollywood films of the Fifties, *The Wild One* and *Death of a Salesman*, but his work since has been totally without interest.
DIR (notably): *The Kissing Bandit* (48), *Port of New York* (49), *Death of a Salesman** (51), *The Wild One** (54), *Kinder, Mütter, und ein General* (Ger55), *Moment of Danger/Malaga* (Brit60), *Recours en grâce* (Fr60), *Namu, the Killer Whale* (66), *The Daring Game* (68), *The Night Visitor* (70).

BENOIT-LEVY, Jean DIR France. (Paris April 25, 1888–Paris Aug 2, 1959) The apostle of educational films in France (400 shorts 1920–40); worked in USA from 1941–46 and for UNESCO in Paris from 1946. Gave Jean Epstein his start in films and co-directed with Marie Epstein several fiction films, of which the most famous are: *La Maternelle* (33), *Itto* (34), *La Mort du cygne* (37). Also: *Pasteur* (22) (co-dir: Jean Epstein), *Hélène* (36), *Altitude 3200* (37).

BERARD, Christian ART DIR France. (Paris 1902–Paris Feb 13, 1949) The greatest set designer of the French theater from 1935–49, he made major contributions to three films by his friend, Jean Cocteau: *La Belle et la bête**, *L'Aigle à deux têtes*, *Les Parents terribles**.

BERGLUND, Sven INVENTOR Sweden. (Stockholm July 20, 1881–Berlin May 10, 1937) Would appear to have been, with Eugène Lauste (*q.v.*), the first to have recorded sound on film by an optical process (1906–11). After demonstrating the process in Stockholm, 1921, and Berlin, 1922, he established Filmfototon, which was absorbed in 1928 by Tobis. Continued his experiments on stereoscopic film in Berlin after 1933. Committed suicide in 1937, undoubtedly to escape the Gestapo.

BERGMAN, Ingmar DIR/SCEN Sweden. (Uppsala July 4, 1918–) The most famous contemporary Swedish director. Preoccupied with metaphysical musings about human relationships, God, and the Devil, he has followed in the footsteps of his mentors, Sjöström (*q.v*) and Stiller (*q.v.*), with an unparalleled sense of theme, character, poetic lyricism, atmosphere, and an overwhelming pessimism. The son of a pastor to the royal court, he was trained in the Swedish theater, was assistant at the Swedish Opera from 1940–42, worked on scripts at Svensk Filmindustri from 1940–44, and wrote scripts for Sjöberg (*q.v.*) and Molander (*q.v.*). His first films as director reflect the influence of Marcel Carné and French poetic realism. He made his name with two almost metaphysical studies of the problems of male-female relationships, *Prison* (48) and *Thirst* (49), and women play a major role in films such as *Summer Interlude*, *Waiting Women*, *Summer with Monika* and *A Lesson in Love*. He had already established an international reputation when the public at large discovered him through *Smiles of a Summer Night* (55), even though this acidulous satire was generally considered only a charming comedy. He was taken seriously after *The Seventh Seal*, despite its somewhat simplistic philosophy. It doesn't match the profundity of *Wild Strawberries* (perhaps his masterpiece), in which he portrayed a man facing the problems of his past life – a theme he had earlier explored in the tragicomedy *Sawdust and Tinsel.* He became somewhat uncertain in his forties but found a new forcefulness and approach in *Through a Glass Darkly, Winter Light,* and *The Silence,* whose sparse, intense styles he has further developed in his recent films. He has discussed himself and his work at various times (somewhat paraphrased): "Art lost its basic creative drive the moment it was separated from worship . . . In former days the artist remained unknown and his work was to the glory of God . . . I want to be one of the artists in the cathedral on the great plain . . . Regardless of whether I believe or not, whether I am Christian or not, I would play my part in the collective building of the cathedral." "When I was younger, work was an exciting game for me . . . now it has become a bitter fight." "If my original ideas have enough strength to make a film, I decide to materialize it. Then comes something very difficult and complicated: the transformation of rhythms, moods, atmosphere, tensions, sequences, tones and scents into words, into an understandable script . . . I have never had any ambition to be an author. I am a film maker not an author." "The human face is the starting point for our work. The camera must take part only like a totally objective observer. The actor's most beautiful means of expression is his look. Simplicity, concentration, an awareness of details, these must be the constant factors in each scene and each ensemble." "My first commandment is always to be interesting. The public has a right to demand from me sensation, emotion, joy, rejuvenation. Everything is allowed except that which leads to failure; the most dangerous roads are in the end the only practical ones." Bergman has continued to work in the theater as a director and playwright and also for TV.

SCEN: for Sjöberg *Hets/Torment** (44), *Sista Paret ut/Last Pair Out* (51), for Molander *Kvinna utan ansikte/Woman without a Face* (47), *Eva* (48), *Franskild/Divorced* (51), for Alf Kjellin *Lustgarden/Pleasure Garden* (61), and all his own films except *Music in Darkness, Thirst, This Can't Happen Here, The Virgin Spring.*

DIR: *Kris/Crisis* (46), *Det Regnar pa var Kärlek/It Rains on Our Love* (46), *Skepp till Indialand/A Ship Bound for India* (47), *Musik i Mörker/Music in Darkness* (48), *Hamnstadt/Port of Call* (48), *Fängelse/Prison* (48), *Törst/Thirst** (49), *Till Glädje/To Joy* (50), *Sant Händer inte Här/This Can't Happen Here/High Tension* (50), *Sommarlek/Summer Interlude** (51), *Kvinnors Väntan/Waiting Women* (52) *Sommaren med Monika/Summer with Monika** (52), *Gycklarnas Afton/Sawdust and Tinsel/The Naked Night** (53), *En Lektion i Karlek/A Lesson in Love* (54), *Kvinnodröm/Journey into Autumn** (55), *Sommarnattens Leende/Smiles of a Summer Night** (55), *Det Sjunde Inseglet/The Seventh Seal** (56), *Smultronstället/Wild Strawberries** (57), *Nära Livet/So Close to Life/Brink of Life* (58), *Ansiktet/The Face/The Magician* (58), *Jungfrukällen/The Virgin Spring** (60), *Djävulens Öga/The Devil's Eye* (60), *Sasom i en Spegel/Through a Glass Darkly** (61), *Nattsvardsgästerna/Winter Light** (63), *Tystnaden/The Silence** (63), *For atte inte Tala om Alla Dessa Kvinnor/Now about All These Women* (64), *Stimulantia* (65) (one episode, released 67), *Persona* (66), *Vargtimmen/Hour of the Wolf** (68), *Skammen/Shame* (68), *Riten/The Rite/The Ritual* (69) (for TV), *En passion/A Passion* (69), *Faro Document* (70).

BERKELEY, Busby (William Berkeley Enos) DIR/CHOREOG USA. (Los Angeles Nov 29, 1895–) The best American choreographer of the Thirties. His career began on Broadway as choreographer, producer, impresario; moved to Hollywood soon after the introduction of sound to be dance director for the films of Eddie Cantor and others. Joined Warner Brothers in 1933 and developed there the masterful, cinematic style that became his trademark: kaleidoscopic visual stagings of chorus girls, using every conceivable camera device and angle. He is far more the author of such musical masterpieces of the Thirties as *42nd Street* and *Gold Diggers of 1933* than their credited directors. He has recently returned to the Broadway stage.

[CHOREOG: *Whoopee* (30), *Kiki* (31), *Palmy Days* (31), *Flying High* (31), *Night World* (32), *Bird of Paradise* (32) (dir: King Vidor), *The Kid from Spain* (32) (dir: Leo McCarey), *42nd Street** (33), *Gold Diggers of 1933** (33), *Footlight Parade* (33) (dir: Lloyd Bacon), *Roman Scandals* (33), *Wonder Bar* (34) (dir: Lloyd Bacon), *Fashions of 1934*

(34) (dir: William Dieterle), *Twenty Million Sweethearts* (34), *Dames* (34), *Go into Your Dance* (35), *In Caliente* (35) (dir: Lloyd Bacon), *Stars over Broadway* (35) (dir: William Keighley), *Gold Diggers of 1937** (36) (dir: Lloyd Bacon), *Singing Marine* (37) *Varsity Show* (37), *Gold Diggers in Paris** (38), *Ziegfeld Girl* (41) (dir: Robert Z. Leonard), *Lady Be Good* (41) (dir: Norman Z. McLeod), *Born to Sing* (41), *Calling All Girls* (42) (short), *Three Cheers for the Girls* (43) (short), *Girl Crazy* (43) (dir: Norman Taurog), *Two Weeks with Love* (50), *Call Me Mister* (51) (dir: Lloyd Bacon), *Two Tickets to Broadway* (51), *Million Dollar Mermaid* (52) (dir: Mervyn LeRoy), *Small Town Girl* (53), and all his own musicals. DIR: *She Had to Say Yes* (33), *Gold Diggers of 1935** (35), *Bright Lights* (35), *I Live for Love* (35), *Stage Struck* (36), *The Go Getter* (37), *Hollywood Hotel* (37), *Men Are Such Fools* (38), *Garden of the Moon* (38), *Comet Over Broadway* (38), *They Made Me a Criminal* (39), *Broadway Serenade* (39), *Babes in Arms* (39), *Fast and Furious* (39), *Forty Little Mothers* (40), *Strike Up the Band* (40), *Blonde Inspiration* (41), *Babes on Broadway* (41), *For Me and My Gal* (42), *The Gang's All Here* (43), *Cinderella Jones* (46), *Take Me out to the Ball Game/Everybody's Cheering* (49) and as 2nd unit director on *Easy to Love* (53), *Rose Marie* (54), *Jumbo* (62).]

BERLANGA, Luis Garcia DIR Spain. (Valencia June 12, 1921–) With his friend, Bardem (*q.v.*), he gave birth to a new Spanish cinema with *Welcome, Mr. Marshall!* Originally a journalist, like Bardem he was trained at the Madrid film school. He is a masterful satirist and has followed in his best films (notably *Placido*) the great Spanish picaresque tradition. He has said of himself: "I want to show only the goodness of men through the social order and mankind. As a man, I am a liberal, as an individual, a Christian. What pleases me is to make films. I like to live and be left in peace." This latter wish has not always been granted, since his films have often fallen afoul of the censor. Has scripted all his own films. DIR (notably): *Paseo sobre una guerra antigua* (48) (16 mm short, co-dir: Bardem), *El Circo* (49) (16mm short), *Esa pareja feliz* (51) (co-dir: Bardem), *Bienvenido, Mr. Marshall!** (52), *Calabuch* (56), *Los Jueves Milagro* (57), *Placido* (61), *Les Quatres verités* (62) (one episode), *El Verdugo/The Executioner** (63), *Las Pirañas* (67).

BERLIN, Irving (Israel Baline) MUS USA. (Russia May 11, 1888–) The most famous American composer of popular songs and musicals has contributed to numerous Hollywood films. After contributing songs to a number of early sound films, his first major film success came with *Top Hat** (35) and *Follow the Fleet* (36), both directed by Mark Sandrich. [Others, including films based on his stage musicals: *On the Avenue* (36), *Alexander's Ragtime Band* (38), *Carefree* (38), *Second Fiddle* (39), *Louisiana Purchase* (41), *Holiday Inn* (42), *This is the Army* (43), *Blue Skies* (46), *Easter Parade* (48), *Annie Get Your Gun* (50), *Call Me Madame* (52), *There's No Business Like Show Business* (54), *White Christmas* (54), *Sayonara* (57).]

BERNARD, Guy MUS France. (Chauny May 19, 1907–) One of the best French film composers, famous especially for his score for *Guernica*, with counterpoint by Eluard, Picasso, and Alain Resnais. Notable scores include: for Leenhardt, *Naissance du cinéma* (46) and *Les Dernières Vacances** (48); for Marcel Cravenne, *Danse de mort* (46); for Yannick Bellon, *Goémons* (47) and *Varsovie quand même* (53); for Alain Resnais, *Guernica** (50); for Nicole Vedrès *Paris 1900** (47); for Jean Vidal, *Zola* (54).

BERNARD, Raymond DIR France. (Paris Oct 10, 1891–) The son of Tristan Bernard, he began his career by adapting his father's plays. An honest, conscientious, and professional director, his best films have been his version of *Les Misérables* and spectaculars such as *Miracle des loups*. He is also a stage actor. DIR (notably): *Jeanne Doré* (17) (with Sarah Bernhardt), *Le Petit Café* (19) (from his father's play, with Max Linder), *Le Secret de Rosette Lambert* (20), *Le Miracle des loups* (24), *Le Jouer d'échecs* (27), *Tarakanova* (29), *Les Croix de bois** (32), *Les Misérables** (34), *Tartarin de Tarascon* (35), *Marthe Richard* (37), *J'étais une aventurière* (38), *Les Otages* (39), *Un ami viendra* *ce soir* (46), *Maya* (49), *La Dame aux camélias* (53), *Le Septième Commandement* (57).

BERNARD-AUBERT, Claude DIR France. (Durtal May 26, 1930–   ) An extremist, but sincere, he expressed his hatred of the Indochina War (in which he had been involved) in his best film: *Patrouille de choc* (57), the diary of a combatant. Also: *Les Tripes au soleil* (59), *Match contre la mort* (59), *Les Lâches vivent d'espoir* (61), *A fleur de peau* (62), *A l'aube du troisième jour* (63).

BERNARD-DESCHAMPS, Dominique DIR France. (Bordeaux 1892–   ) In the cinema since 1914, but made his best films after 1930: *Le Rosiér de Madame Husson* (32), *M. Coccinelle* (38). Collaborated with Professor Chrétien after 1935 on the development of his Hypergonar lens, the basis of cinemascope.

BERNHARDT, Curtis (also, Kurt Bernhardt) DIR USA/Germany. (Worms, Germany April 15, 1899–   ) Trained in Berlin, he later churned out UFA-style melodramas in Paris, London, and particularly Hollywood. [His *The Last Company* in Germany with Conrad Veidt and Emil Jannings seemed to indicate talent, but his French and British films were mediocre. Moved to France in 1934, Britain in 1935, and Hollywood in 1940. His first Hollywood film of any merit was *Conflict* (45), a Germanic-style thriller with Humphrey Bogart and Sidney Greenstreet. He even managed to nullify the charms of *The Merry Widow,* and his *Miss Sadie Thompson* is a poor remake of *Rain.*] DIR (notably): *Qualen der Nacht* (26), *Schinderhannes* (28), *die Letzte Kompagnie/The Last Company* (30), *Der Mann, der den Mord beging/The Man Who Murdered* (31), *Der Rebell* (32), *Der Tunnel* (33), *L'Or dans la rue* (Fr34), *Beloved Vagabond* (Brit36), *Devotion* (USA43), *Conflict* (45), *A Stolen Life* (46), *Possessed* (48), *The High Wall* (48), *Payment on Demand* (51), *The Blue Veil* (51), *Sirocco* (51), *The Merry Widow** (52), *Miss Sadie Thompson* (54), *Beau Brummel* (54), *Interrupted Melody* (56), *Gaby* (56), *Kisses for My President* (64).

*BERNSTEIN, Elmer MUS USA. (New York 1922–   ) Excellent composer whose work ranges from jazz-like, popular themes to heavily orchestrated epics for many Hollywood films. Notable scores: *Sudden Fear* (52), *The Man with the Golden Arm** (55), *The Ten Commandments* (56), *The Tin Star* (57), *The Sweet Smell of Success** (57), *God's Little Acre* (58), *Desire under the Elms* (58), *Some Came Running** (59), *The Magnificent Seven** (60), *Birdman of Alcatraz* (62), *Walk on the Wild Side* (62), *To Kill a Mockingbird* (62), *The Sons of Katie Elder* (65), *Baby the Rain Must Fall* (65), *Return of the Seven** (66), *Hawaii* (66), *Thoroughly Modern Millie* (67), *A Walk in the Spring Rain* (68), *The Liberation of L. B. Jones* (69).

BERTHOMIEU, André DIR France. (Rouen Feb 16, 1903–Paris April 10, 1960) The most prolific of French directors with over sixty films to his name from 1926 to 1960, including several good ones: *Pas si bête* (29), *Le Morte en fuite* (36), and others.

*BERTOLUCCI, Bernardo DIR Italy (Parma March 16, 1940–   ) Young film maker of serious moral sensibility and political interests who made his name with *Before the Revolution* (64), a thematically dense and visually bold film. Though he has worked on documentaries and for TV, his films are more influenced by the later Visconti (*q.v.*) and Rossellini (*q.v.*) and by Godard (*q.v.*) and Pasolini (*q.v.*) than by conventional Italian neorealist roots. His *Partner* (68) is a portrait of modern intellectual man; *The Conformist* (69) and *The Spider's Strategy* (70) both deal ostensibly with Italy's fascist past but are philosophically complex works with a more visually assured and less grandiose style than his earlier features. Assistant to Pasolini on *Accattone** (61) and has scripted all his own films. DIR: *La Commare Secca/The Grim Reaper* (62), *Prima della Rivoluzione/ Before the Revolution** (64), *La Via del Petrolio* (65) (3-part film for TV), *Il Canale* (67), *Amore è rabbia/Vangelo 70* (67) (one episode), *Partner* (68), *Il Conformista/The Conformist* (69), *Strategia del ragno/The Spider's Strategy* (70) (for TV).

BERTRAND, Paul ART DIR France. (Chalon-sur-Saône April 4, 1915–   ) Trained by Alexandre Trauner (*q.v.*), he was René

22

Clément's (*q.v.*) designer on *Les Maudits** (47), *Jeux interdits** (52), *Gervaise* (56), and *Plein Soleil* (60), to all of which he brought his sense of poetic realism.

*BIBERMAN, Herbert J. DIR USA. (Philadelphia March 4, 1900–June 1971) One of the Hollywood Ten imprisoned for contempt of Congress in 1950–51. Originally an actor and theater director (he directed the first Bolshevik play seen in the USA) he became a scriptwriter in Hollywood (*King of Chinatown, New Orleans, Road to Yesterday*) and directed his first unremarkable films: *One Way Ticket* (35), *Meet Nero Wolfe* (36). His only other Hollywood film was *The Master Race* (44), a bitterly anti-Nazi film, though he also produced a western, *Abilene Town* (46). He made the brilliant *Salt of the Earth** in 1954 and spent much of his time thereafter in political and social agitation against the Hollywood system. He did not make another film until 1968, *Slaves,* an often brilliantly structured analysis of 19th-century slavery in America.

BIELEK, Pal'o DIR Czechoslovakia. (Banska Bistrica Oct 11, 1910–) An outstanding figure in the Slovakian cinema in Bratislava, first as an actor before the war with, e.g., Martin Fric (*q.v.*), then after the war as scriptwriter and the best Slovakian director. All his films have Slovakian themes.
DIR: *Far Freedom* (45) (documentary), *Vlcie diery/Foxholes* (48), *Priehrada/ The Dam* (50), *Lazy sa pohli/The Mountains are Stirring* (52), *V piatok trinasteho/Friday the 13th* (53), *Styridsatstyri/Forty-four* (57), *Kapitan Dabac/ Captain Dabac* (59), *Janosik, I* (62), *Janosik, II* (63), *Majster kat/The Hangman* (65), *Traja/Trio* (69).

BIRRI, Fernando DIR Argentina (Santa-Fé March 13, 1925–) One of the most vigorous young Argentinian directors, interested in social themes, especially in *Tiredie* (60) (short) and *Los Inundados* (62).

BITZER, Billy PHOTOG USA. (Boston April 21, 1874–Hollywood 1944) One of the greatest cameramen of all time. Began in 1899, joined Biograph and worked with D. W. Griffith (*q.v.*), photographing all his major films with an unusual feeling for visual form and for humanity.

BLACHE, Alice *see* GUY-BLACHÉ, ALICE

BLACKBURN, Maurice MUS Canada. (Québec, 1914–) An inventive composer who created scores for McLaren's (*q.v.*) *Blinkety Blank, A Fantasy, Lines Vertical, Lines Horizontal,* using synthetic sounds.

*BLACKTON, James Stuart DIR/PROD USA. (Sheffield, Britain Jan 5, 1875–Hollywood Aug 13, 1941) A neglected American pioneer, equal in artistic importance to D. W. Griffith (*q.v.*). During his years with Vitagraph as director and producer (in the sense of "artistic supervisor") he is credited with the development of frame by frame animation of people and objects (dubbed *mouvement américain* in France after his *Haunted Hotel* in 1907) and with the systematic use since 1908 (and before Griffith) of a kind of medium close-up (still called *plan américain* in France). This is evident in *Scenes of True Life* (1908) which, through this and its new approach to theme and acting style, exercised a universal influence well before 1911, when Griffith's films were first noticed in Europe. He also produced the first American series of classical adaptations, especially of Shakespeare. He became interested in films after interviewing Edison in 1895 as a journalist; in 1896 he established Vitagraph with his friend Albert E. Smith. In 1897 they turned to production and were joined in 1899 by William T. Rock, a partnership that continued until 1925. Their first film (1897) was a story film, *The Burglar on the Roof* (dir: Blackton, photog: Smith): in 1898 they made the propagandistic *Tearing Down the Spanish Flag,* a theme Blackton returned to in 1914–16 with his war propaganda films, *The Glory of the Nation, Womanhood, The Common Cause, Safe for Democracy, Missing, The Battle Cry of Liberty, The Battle Cry of Peace.* He made his first animation film in 1906, *Humorous Phases of Funny Faces,* three years before the famous *Gertie the Dinosaur.* Established the Vitagraph acting troupe in 1907. In 1911 he set up the Vitagraph studio in Hollywood. In 1917 he withdrew from Vitagraph to produce independently for Famous Players. In 1921 he went to Britain to make *The Glorious*

Adventure, a period film in Prizmacolor with Lady Diana Manners and Victor McLaglen. After several more commercially successful films he returned to the USA and Vitagraph, where he remained until the company was sold to the Warner brothers (*q.v.*) in 1925. He retired a millionaire but lost his fortune in the 1929 crash and was reduced in the Thirties to showing his old films in sideshows, delivering a funny commentary and dressed up as a turn-of-the-century film maker. He died following an automobile accident in 1941.

DIR and/or PROD (notably): *The Burglar on the Roof* (1897), *Tearing Down the Spanish Flag* (1898), *A Gentleman of France* (03), *Sherlock Holmes* (05), *Monsieur Beaucaire* (05), *Raffles, the Amateur Craftsman* (06), *And the Villain Still Pursued Her* (06), *The Jail Bird and How He Flew* (06), *Humorous Phases of Funny Faces* (06) (anim), *The San Francisco Earthquake* (06), *A Modern Oliver Twist* (06), *The Haunted Hotel** (07), *Lightning Sketches* (07) (anim), *The Easterner* (07), *Francesca di Rimini* (07), *Liquid Electricity* (07), *The Mill Girl* (07), *Salome* (07), *Get Me a Step Ladder* (08), *Scenes of True Life* (08), *Richard III* (08), *The Merchant of Venice* (08), *Julius Caesar* (08), *Anthony and Cleopatra* (08), *Princess Nicotine or the Smoke Fairy* (09) (anim), *The Magic Fountain Pen** (09) (anim), *Napoleon Bonaparte and Empress Josephine of France/Napoleon Man of Destiny* (09), *A Midsummer Night's Dream** (09), *An Alpine Echo* (09), *The Auto Maniac* (09), *Oliver Twist* (09), *Saul and David* (09), *The Way of the Cross* (09), *Richilieu* (09), *The Romance of an Umbrella* (09), *Les Misérables** (09), *The Life of Moses* (09–10), *Twelfth Night* (10), *Uncle Tom's Cabin* (10), *A Brother's Devotion* (10), *Convict 796* (10), *Chew-Chew Land* (10), *True Life* (10), *Fruits of Vengeance* (10), *The New Stenographer* (11), *A Tale of Two Cities* (11), *The Derelict Reporter* (11), *The Mate of the John M* (11), *The Spirit of the Light* (11), *The Wooing of Winifred* (11), *The Two Portraits* (12), *Lincoln's Gettysburg Address* (12), *Alma's Champion* (12), *The Pink Pajama Girl* (12), *At the Eleventh Hour* (12), *The Diamond Brooch* (12), *The Light of St. Bernard* (12), *Beau Brummel* (13), *Love's Sunset* (13), *The Vengeance of Durand* (13), *Love, Luck, and Gasoline* (14), *A Million Dollar Bid* (14), *Battle Cry of Peace* (15), *Womanhood* (17), *The Glory of a Nation* (17), *Country Life* (17) (series), *The Glorious Adventure* (Brit22), *A Gypsy Cavalier* (Brit23), *The Virgin Queen* (Brit23), *Redeeming Sin* (24), *The Clean Heart* (24), *The Happy Warrior* (25), *Tides of Passion* (25), *The Gilded Highway* (25), *Bride of the Storm* (26), *Hell Bent for Heaven* (26), *The Passionate Quest* (26). Also, produced the John Bunny, Flora Finch comedies; the Weary Willy comedies.

BLASETTI, Alessandro DIR Italy. (Rome July 3, 1900–) Blasetti and Camerini (*q.v.*) are the best directors of the mediocre period in Italian cinema from 1935 to 1945. Film critic 1924–28. Carlo Lizzani wrote of him: "He had, since 1928, the ability to stir the stagnant waters of the Italian cinema. He directed *Sole* then *1860,* which marked the highest peak of the Italian cinema during the Fascist period: *The Old Guard* marks his collusion with the regime. But what was his *La Corona di ferro* if not the dreams of the ordinary man, the protagonist of *Four Steps in the Clouds,* a film that indicated a return to drama based on everyday life?" His postwar films have been mainly comedies or spectaculars. Has also worked in the theater.

DIR: *Sole* (29) (scen: Blasetti, Vergano), *Nerone/Nero* (30), *Resurrectio/Resurrection* (31), *Terra Madre* (31), *Palio* (32), *La Tavola dei Poveri* (32), *I Mille di Garibaldi/1860** (33), *Vecchia Guardia/The Old Guard* (33), *Aldebaran* (35), *La Contessa di Parma/The Countess of Parma* (37), *Ettore Fieramosca* (38), *Un'avventura di Salvator Rosa* (40), *La Corona di ferro* (41), *La Cena delle beffe* (41), *Quattro passi fra le nuvole/Four Steps in the Clouds** (42), *Un Giorno nella Vita/A Day of Life* (46), *Fabiola* (48), *Prima Communione/First Communion* (50), *Altri Tempi/Infidelity* (52), *La Fiammata* (52), *Tempi Nostri* (53), *Peccato che sia una Canaglia* (54), *Europa di Notte/European Nights* (59), *Io Amo, Tu Ami/I Love, You Love* (61), *Io, io, io e . . . gli altri* (65), *Simon Bolivar/La Epopeya de Simon Bolivar* (It/Sp/Venezuela69), *10 Giugno 1940* (70) (TV, one episode).

BLEIMAN, Mikhail SCEN USSR. (Rostov 1904–) Notable Soviet scenarist who collaborated with Ermler (*q.v.*) on *A Great Citizen** (38, 39), and *She Defends Her Country** (43).

BLIOKH, Yakov DIR USSR. (Odessa 1895–Moscow 1957) Documentary film maker who began his career as production manager on *Battleship Potemkin** (25) and who created an unforgettable portrait of a Chinese metropolis with *A Shanghai Document** (28).

BLOM, August DIR Denmark. (Copenhagen Dec 26, 1869–Copenhagen Jan 10, 1947) The principal name, with Holger-Madsen (*q.v.*), associated with the early artistic development of the Danish cinema, a specialist in lavish melodramas and the discoverer of such stars as Asta Nielsen, Olaf Fönss, and Else Froelich. [His *Atlantis* (13), for example, is technically complex for its period, with an interrelated use of locations and a sophisticated morality. An outstanding success, it is considered by many historians to be the most important film made before Griffith's (*q.v.*), features, and it had considerable influence on his work. Notable is Blom's use of parallel action and double exposure. Blom, who was also an actor, directed his first film in 1910.] DIR (notably): *Hamlet* (10), *Livets Storme* (10), *Robinson Crusoe* (10), *Balletdanserinden* (11), *Guvernorens Datter* (12), *Atlantis* (13), *Pressens Magt* (13), *Revolutions Bryllup* (14), *Verdens Undergang* (15), *Maharajaens Yndlingshustru* (18), *Prometheus* (19), *Hendes Naade Dragonem* (25).

BLOMBERG, Erik PHOTOG/DIR Finland. (Helsinki Sept 18, 1913–) Since 1936 he has been the best Finnish cinematographer. He became a director and established an international reputation in 1952 with his first film, *White Reindeer**.

*BOETTICHER, Budd (Oscar Boetticher, Junior) DIR USA. (Chicago July 29, 1916–) With Peckinpah (*q.v.*), whom he perhaps influenced, he is the best modern director of westerns. Having become involved in bull-fighting in Mexico, he was hired as technical adviser for Mamoulian's *Blood and Sand* (41), became an assistant director in 1943–44, and directed his first film in 1944. Of his early films, Boetticher says: "I was really working in the dark . . . (They) only took 8, 10, 12 days and there isn't a bit of directing in

them." After several not very interesting films, except for *The Bullfighter and the Lady, Seminole,* and *The Magnificent Matador,* he made the brilliant *Seven Men from Now* and received his first serious critical attention in André Bazin's famous analysis (see *Dictionary of Films*). Since then he has made a series of remarkable westerns and a classic thriller, *The Rise and Fall of Legs Diamond* (60). His films reflect a classic moral confrontation that has its roots in the early westerns of Thomas Ince (*q.v.*) and William S. Hart. Andrew Sarris describes them as "Constructed partly as allegorical odysseys and partly as floating crap games where every character took turns at bluffing about his hand until the final showdown." Boetticher says of himself: "I have never made a film either for something or anti-something . . . I think (Daves) and (Ford) are the best people for landscape that I know, but I have the impression at times that they let the landscapes take over from the people. I've never done that. I like very simple landscapes in my films — desert or rocks . . . I prefer that because it's the actors who count . . . I don't think I have ever really brought off a successful study of a woman, except Alice Diamond in *Legs Diamond* and the girls in *The Magnificent Matador* and *The Bullfighter and the Lady.* What is important is what the heroine has caused to happen, or what she represents . . . She herself is of no importance." Burt Kennedy (*q.v.*) has written most of his scripts since 1956; Boetticher wrote the script for Don Siegel's *Two Mules for Sister Sara* (70). ASSIST: *Destroyer* (43) (dir: William Seiter), *The More the Merrier* (43) (dir: George Stevens), *The Desperadoes* (43) (dir: Charles Vidor), *Cover Girl* (44) (dir: Charles Vidor). DIR: *One Mysterious Night* (44), *The Missing Juror* (44), *Youth on Trial* (44), *A Guy, a Gal, and a Pal* (45), *Assigned to Danger* (48), *Behind Locked Doors* (48), *Black Midnight* (49), *Wolf Hunters* (49), *Killer Shark* (50), *The Bullfighter and the Lady* (51), *The Sword of D'Artegnan* (51) (TV), *The Cimarron Kid* (51), *Bronco Buster* (52), *Red Ball Express* (52), *Horizons West* (52), *City Beneath the Sea* (53), *Seminole* (53), *The Man from the Alamo* (53), *Wings of the Hawk* (53), *East of Sumatra* (53), *The Magnificent Matador* (55), *The Killer is Loose* (55), *Seven Men from*

*Now** (56), *The Tall T* (57), *Decision at Sundown* (57), *Buchanan Rides Alone* (58), *Ride Lonesome* (59), *Westbound* (59), *Comanche Station* (60), *The Rise and Fall of Legs Diamond* (60), *Olle* (67) (documentary), *A Time for Dying* (69). Also 55–60, several TV programs.

BOISROND, Michel DIR France. (Châteauneuf Oct 9, 1921–) Has directed many of Brigitte Bardot's commercial successes: *Cette sacrée gamine* (56), *Une Parisienne* (57), *Voulez-vous danser avec moi?* (59). [Also: *Le Chemin des écoliers* (59), *Un soir sur le plage* (60), *Comment réussir en amour* (62), *L'Homme qui valait des milliards* (67), *La Leçon particulière* (68), *Aux purs tout est pur* (68). Assistant to Clair on *La Beauté du diable** (49), *Les Belles de nuit** (52), *Les Grandes Manoeuvres** (55).]

BOLOGNINI Mauro DIR Italy. (Pistoia 1923–) Trained as assistant to Zampa, Delannoy, Yves Allégret (all *q.v.*), he developed into a somewhat mannered director with a taste for elegant images but whose films usually have great flair. His best film is *Il Bell'Antonio* (60). His most recent films have been largely "episodes." [DIR (notably): *Gli Innamorati* (55), *Giovani mariti* (57), *La Notte brava* (59), *Il Bell'Antonio* (60), *La Giornata balorda* (60), *La Viaccia* (61), *Senilita* (61), *Agostino* (63), *La Corruzione* (64), *I Tre Volti* (64) (one episode), *La Bambole* (64) (one episode), *Mademoiselle de Maupin* (65), *La Donna e una cosa mervigliosa* (65), *Le Streghe* (66) (one episode), *Le Fate* (66) (one episode), *Le Plus vieux métier du monde* (67) (one episode), *Metello* (71).]

BOLVARY Geza von DIR Germany. (Budapest Dec 28, 1897–) Prolific German director, mediocre specialist in operetta films; over 50 films before, during, and after the Nazi regime.

BONDARCHUK, Sergei DIR USSR. (Ukraine 1920–) Famous postwar Russian actor (*Cavalier of the Golden Star**, *The Grasshopper*, *Othello**, etc.) who became a director in the late Fifties. He suffered much in the Second World War when he was 20 but has taken as his motto a phrase of Gorky's: "Man is made for happiness as the bird is for flight." His experiences are reflected in his first film, *Destiny of a Man* (59), and in his choice of later subjects, though these have led him into directing spectaculars.
DIR: *Sudba Cheloveka/Destiny of a Man** (59), *Voina i Mir/War and Peace** (64–67), *Waterloo* (It/USSR70).

BONNARDOT, Jean-Claude DIR France. (Paris Dec 26, 1923–) Trained as a maker of short films, he directed in Korea *Moranbong* (59), which was banned by the French censors until 1964, despite its humanistic theme and admirable qualities. Later he directed an admirable thriller, *Ballade pour un voyou* (63).

***BOORMAN, John** DIR Britain/USA. (Britain 1933–) Ex-TV director who attracted attention with the thriller, *Point Blank*, a quasi allegory replete with visual pyrotechnics. Later films have not fulfilled his earlier promise and *Leo the Last* is disappointing.
DIR: *Catch Us if You Can/Having a Wild Weekend* (Brit66), *Point Blank* (USA 67), *Hell in the Pacific* (USA68), *Leo the Last* (Brit69).
'**37** ·

BOROWCZYK, Walerian ANIM/DIR Poland/France. (Kwilcz Oct 21, 1923–) Studied painting and worked as a graphic artist until 1955. Made his first animated films with Jan Lenica (*q.v.*). His animated films have a satiric, bitter power, with strange, fantastic surrealistic images and overtones of horrific tragedy. His (un-animated) feature films are similar but the dramatic structure with actors seems less able to sustain his vision. He has worked in France since 1959.
DIR: *Once Upon a Time* (57), *Love Requited* (57), *Dom/House* (58) (all co-dir: Lenica), *School* (58), *Les Astronautes* (59) (co-dir: Chris Marker), *Le Dernier voyage de Gulliver* (60), *Le Concert de M. et Mme. Kabal* (62), *L'Encyclopédie de grand'maman* (63), *Rennaissance* (63), *Les Jeux des anges* (64), *Le Dictionnaire de Joachim* (65), *Rosalie* (66), *Le Théâtre de Monsieur et Madame Kabal* (67) (feature), *Gavotte* (67), *Diptyque* (67), *Goto l'île d'amour* (68) (feature), *Le Phonographe* (69), *Blanche* (70) (feature).

BORZAGE, Frank DIR USA. (Salt Lake City April 23, 1893–Hollywood 1961) A largely unrecognized director but the equal of his contemporaries, John Ford,

Howard Hawks, or King Vidor (all *q.v.*). A product of the commercial cinema, had about 15 artistically productive years 1925–40 before returning to the standard Hollywood product. No director has shown better than he the intimate warmth of human love in a profoundly united couple. His lovers are rarely isolated from their environment but are carefully depicted as part of their times, most commonly crisis-ridden America. In addition to his understanding of human relationships and his poetic tenderness, he had a social awareness and many of his films express a hatred of war. When war ravaged the world for the second time in his life he resigned himself to directing merely competent commercial films. He worked as a coal miner, became an actor for the Lubin Company and Thomas Ince (*q.v.*), and a director of westerns for Universal on, e.g., *The Pitch O'Chance* and several Will Rogers films.

DIR: *Ashes of Desire* (19), *Humoresque* (20), *Song of Love* (23), *Children of Dust* (23), *The Nth Commandment* (23), *Secrets* (24), *The Lady* (25), *Circle* (25), *The Marriage License* (26), *The Greater Glory* (26), *Seventh Heaven** (27), *Street Angel* (28), *They Had to See Paris* (29), *The River** (29), *Liliom* (30), *Bad Girl* (31), *Young America* (31), *A Farewell to Arms* (32), *Secrets* (33), *A Man's Castle** (33), *Flirtation Walk* (34), *No Greater Glory** (34), *Little Man, What Now?** (34), *Living on Velvet* (35), *Desire* (36) (supervised by Lubitsch), *Hearts Divided* (36), *The Big City* (37), *The Green Light* (37), *History is Made at Night* (37), *Mannequin* (38), *The Shining Hour* (38), *Three Comrades* (38), *Disputed Passage* (39), *Strange Cargo* (40), *Flight Command* (40), *Smiling Through* (41), *Stage Door Canteen* (43), *His Butler's Sister* (43), *Till We Meet Again* (44), *The Spanish Main* (45), *I've Always Loved You* (46), *Magnificent Doll* (47), *Moonrise* (48), *China Doll* (58), *The Big Fisherman* (61), *Atlantis, the Lost Kingdom** (It63) (completed by Edgar G. Ulmer).

BOSE, Debaki Kumar DIR/PROD India. (Akalpoush, Bengal Nov 25, 1898–) With P. C. Barua (*q.v.*), one of the founders of the Calcutta school at New Theatres and the best Bengali film maker of the Thirties. A militant nationalist in his youth and a devotee of the Vishnava evangelical movement, he brought to the Indian film an integrated sense of music, song, and action in creating his lyric, devotional dramas such as *The Devotee* (33). His *Seeta* (33) was the first Indian film to be shown at the Venice Festival. Younger directors like Bimal Roy (*q.v.*) and Satyajit Ray (*q.v.*) learned much from Bose and from his artistic expression of his Bengali cultural roots. Began his career writing and acting in *Flames of Flesh* (25).

DIR (notably): *Pansahar* (29), *Aparadhi/ The Culprit* (31) (for P. C. Barua), *Chandidas* (32), *Puran Bhagat/The Devotee* (33), *Seeta* (33), *Vidyapathi* (37), *Inquilbad* (37), *Apnagar* (41), *Kewi/ The Poet* (49). Also, between 1935–47, *Meerabai, Nartaki, Sonera, Sansar, Kusha Laila, Chandra Keshar, Ratna Deep, Sagar Sangame*. In later years he has concentrated on production.

BOSE, Nitin DIR/PHOTOG India. (Calcutta 1901–) Began as a cameraman for Debaki Bose (*q.v.*) on, e.g., *Chandidas* (32), which he later directed in a Hindi version. He became a director for New Theatres and was one of the leading directors of the Calcutta school during the Thirties. According to M. Garga he directed "social films and tragedies in which the rich and the poor are caught up in a merciless battle and in which the good, like the bad and the indifferent, are powerfully characterized." Between 1930–40 he directed films like *Bhagya Chakra/The Wheel of Fate* (35), *The President, The Enemy, Mother Earth and Marriage*. After 1950 he moved to Bombay and became a leading director there. He is a cousin of Satyajit Ray (*q.v.*) and Ray occasionally watched him at work at New Theatres in the Forties.

BOSSAK, Jerzy DIR Poland. (Rostov 1910–) A precise but emotional documentary film maker who has contributed much to the development of the Polish short film and the encouragement of young talent. Originally a journalist and film critic, he joined the progressive Start group in 1930. In 1943, he formed, with Aleksander Ford (*q.v.*), the film section of the Polish Army in the USSR, and with Ford directed *Maidanek* (44) on the death camp and *The Battle of Kolberg* (45) among others. He has directed many short and medium length documentaries, including: *Powodz/Storm over Po-*

27

land/Flood (46), *Pokoj zdobedzie swiat/ Peace Will Win* (51) (co-dir: Joris Ivens), *Wrzesien 1939/September 1939* (61) (compilation feature), *Requiem dia 500,000* (63), *Dokumenty walki* (67). He is head of the Kamera film group and teaches at the Lodz Film School.

BOST, Pierre SCEN France. (Lasalle Sept 5, 1901–) Originally a writer, he became one of the best postwar French script-writers in his collaboration with Jean Aurenche (*q.v.*).

BOSUSTOW, Stephen ANIM USA. (Canada Nov 6, 1911–) Worked for Ub Iwerks (*q.v.*) and Walter Lantz, and for Walt Disney (*q.v.*) until 1941, when he left him during the famous strike. Worked independently and förmed UPA with a staff of six in 1943. Although UPA revolutionized animated film production in the Forties and although he later received Academy Awards for *Mr. Magoo** and *Gerald McBoing Boing,* the credit for this is more due to John Hubley (*q.v.*), Peter Burness (*q.v.*), Robert Cannon (*q.v.*), and others. He gave up directing after *Swab Your Choppers* (47) to concentrate on production and, after the departure of its more creative talents, UPA ended up as much of an assembly line as the later Disney, as witnessed by *Magoo's Arabian Nights.* Notable among his earlier films as director are *Brotherhood of Man* (43) (co-dir: Robert Cannon) and *Hell Bent for Election* (44) (co-dir: Chuck Jones).

*BOULTING, John DIR Britain. (Bray Nov 21, 1913–) **and Roy** (Bray Nov 21, 1913–) Twins as prolific as quads who have made many films in collaboration, alternating as producer/director. They formed Charter Films in 1937, with Roy directing. John directed his first film in 1945. During the war Roy made the notable documentaries *Desert Victory, Burma Victory,* and *Tunisian Victory* (with Frank Capra). John made the excellent *Brighton Rock* (47) from Graham Greene's story and in the Fifties they made a series of satirical comedies, notably, *I'm Alright Jack* and *Lucky Jim.* Recent work has been dull.
DIR (John): *Journey Together* (45), *Brighton Rock* (47), *Seven Days to Noon* (50), *The Magic Box* (51), *Private's Progress* (56), *Lucky Jim* (57),

I'm Alright Jack (59), *Heaven's Above* (63), *Rotten to the Core* (65).
DIR (Roy): *The Landlady* (37) (short), *Consider Your Verdict* (37), *Trunk Crime* (39), *Inquest* (39), *Pastor Hall* (40), *Dawn Guard* (41) (short), *Thunder Rock* (42), *They Serve Abroad* (42) (short), *Desert Victory* (43) (documentary), *Tunisian Victory* (44) (documentary), *Burma Victory* (45) (documentary), *Fame is the Spur* (47), *The Guinea Pig* (48), *High Treason* (51), *Singlehanded* (51), *Sea Gulls over Sorrento* (54), *Josephine and Men* (55), *Run for the Sun* (USA56), *Brothers-in-Law* (57), *Carlton-Browne of the F.O.* (59), *Suspect* (60), *A French Mistress* (60), *The Family Way* (66), *Twisted Nerve* (68), *There's a Girl in My Soup* (70).

BOURGEOIS, Gérard DIR France. (Geneva Aug 18, 1874–Paris Dec 15, 1944) Pioneer French film maker with a theatrical background who made admirable use of depth of field in his best film, *Les Victimes de l'alcool* (11), a version of Zola's *L'Assommoir.*

BOURGOIN, Jean (Yves Bourgoin) PHOTOG France. (Paris March 4, 1913–) An excellent cameraman who gained experience with Renoir on *La Vie est à nous** and *La Marseillaise** and later specialized in color.
PHOTOG (notably): for Tati, *Mon oncle*;* for Baratier, *Goha*;* for Orson Welles, *Confidential Report*;* for Becker, *Goupi mains-rouges*;* for Molinaro, *Une fille pour l'été;* for Y. Allégret, *Les Démons de l'aube, Dédée d'Anvers, Manèges;* for Cayatte, *Les Amants de Vérone, Justice est faite*, Nous sommes tous des assassins*.*

BOURGUIGNON, Serge DIR France/USA. (Maignelay Sept 3, 1928–) Studied at the Institut des Hautes Etudes Cinématographiques (IDHEC). He is passionately devoted to the cinema, delighting in beautiful images and the exotic, but he is sometimes a little mannered. His *Sundays and Cybele* won an Academy Award.
DIR (notably): *Sikkim, terre secrète* (57) (documentary), *Les Quatre Sourires* (60) (documentary), *Les Dimanches de Ville-d'Avray/Sundays and Cybele* (62), *The Reward* (USA65), *A Coeur joie/*

Two Weeks in September (67), *The Picasso Summer* (69).

BOYER, François SCEN France. (Sézanne March 30, 1920–) Began by scripting René Clément's *Les Jeux interdits** from his own novel and ten years later met with equal success in *La Guerre des boutons* (62).

BOYTLER, Arcady DIR Mexico/USSR. (Aug 31, 1895–) Originally an actor in Russia trained by Stanislavski, he directed the Russian comedy series, *Arcady*, in 1916. Later he moved to Mexico, where he directed the excellent *La Mujer del puerto** in 1933 and Cantinflas's screen debut in 1938.

BRACHO, Julio DIR Mexico (190?–) Theatrical background with Copeau and Stanislavski; he became during the Forties one of the best Mexican directors. His best film is *Distinto amanacer*.

***BRAKHAGE, Stan** DIR USA. (Kansas City 1933–) One of the most influential and most prolific film makers of the American underground. Directed his first film at 18 and has worked as a director of commercials in order to have the freedom to make his own films. He is enchanted with the technical possibilities of the camera and all his films exude a sense of delight in the physical world. *Scenes from Under Childhood*, an autobiographical film, is his latest work. His films include: *Interim* (51), *Desistfilm* (53), *Unglassed Windows Cast a Terrible Reflection* (53), *In Between* (54), *The Way to Shadow Garden* (55), *Reflections on Black* (55), *Wonder Ring* (55), *Flesh of Morning* (56), *Nightcats* (57), *Daybreak* (57), *White Eye* (57), *Anticipation of the Night* (57), *Loving* (57), *Colorado Legend* (59), *Prelude* (61), *The Dead* (61), *Thin Line Lyre Triangular* (63), *Window Water Baby Moving* (63), *The Art of Vision* (61–65), *Fire of Waters* (66), *Lovemaking* (68) (episodes), *Scenes from Under Childhood* (2 episodes completed, 1969).

BRAUNBERGER, Pierre PROD France. (Paris July 29, 1905–) Perhaps the single most influential producer in France, courageous and farsighted in his choice of directors from the French *avant-garde* of 1925 to the *nouvelle vague;* has worked with, among many others, Jean Renoir, René Clair, Buñuel, Resnais, Jean Rouch, Reichenbach, Jacques Rivette, Truffaut, Godard (all *q.v.*).

BRDECKA, Jiři ANIM/SCEN Czechoslovakia. (Moravia Dec 24, 1917–) Excellent director of cartoons who has often worked with Trnka (*q.v.*) and has written scripts for many important fiction and animated films.
[SCEN (notably): for Jasny, *That Cat**; for Lipsky, *Lemonade Joe* (64); for Weiss, *Appassionata* (59); for Trnka, *The Emperor's Nightingale**, *Old Czech Legends**, *A Midsummer Night's Dream.* ANIM (notably): *Love and the Dirigible* (47), *A Comic History of Aviation* (58), *Look Out!* (59), *Our Red Riding Hood* (60), *Gallina Vogelbirdae* (63), *A Minstrel's Song* (64), *Why Do You Smile Mona Lisa?* (66).]

BRECHT, Bertolt SCEN Germany. (Augsbourg Feb 10, 1898–Berlin Aug 14, 1956) The influential German poet, dramatist, and theoretician has occasionally collaborated on films, but until Cavalcanti's *Puntila** was unhappy with screen adaptations of his work. His *Dreigroschenoper** (31) was filmed by Pabst and later remade; he co-wrote the script for Slatan Dudow's *Kuhle Wampe** (32), wrote the original story for Fritz Lang's *Hangmen Also Die* (43), and wrote the song for Ivens' *Das Lied der Ströme* (54). His influence on the cinema has been considerable and both Losey (*q.v.*) and John Hubley (*q.v.*) were his disciples.

***BRENON, Herbert** DIR USA/Britain. (Dublin Jan 13, 1880–Los Angeles June 21, 1958) Hollywood pioneer who began as scriptwriter and editor with the Imp Company in 1909. First film in 1912. He directed two spectaculars, *Ivanhoe* (13) and *Across the Atlantic* (13), in Britain and made Annette Kellerman a star with *Neptune's Daughter* (14); made Nazimova famous with *War Brides* (16) and directed other important stars of the period: Theda Bara (in *The Two Orphans**), Pola Negri, and Louise Brooks. He returned to Britain in the mid-Thirties and made a number of mediocre films. His sentimental melodramas made him one of the most famous Hollywood names of the Twenties.

BRESSON, Robert DIR France. (Bromont-la-Mothe, Sept 25, 1907–) The Jansenist of the French cinema, though he has developed a humanistic classical abstraction and is not at all coldly doctrinaire. He became involved in the cinema in 1933 but he considers that his career really began with his first feature, made during the war: *Les Anges du péché*, a drama set in the closed world of a convent. His next film, *Les Dames du bois de Boulogne*, freely based on a Diderot story and updated to a contemporary period, is a searing work, as luminous as the exceptionally vivid gas lighting. It was a commercial failure and Bresson did not make another film for some years until his Bernanos adaptation, *Le Journal d'un curé de campagne*. This marked a turning point in his work, a more rigorous exactness in approach: from this film on he has avoided professional actors, sets, and florid dialogue in order to reach a more direct contact with life (though his style is quite different from neorealism). In order to capture human expression, psychology, and behavior he submits his characters to a rigorously refined and austere visual staging, most often set in a restricted environment, a closed world. His masterpiece, *Un condamné à mort s'est échappé*, is bare and intense, constructed out of gestures and objects, the essence of the courage and atmosphere of the French Resistance. *Pickpocket*, a reworking of the theme of *Crime and Punishment*, deals more directly with the theme of submission and salvation, follows the style of his earlier work, and creates a profoundly forceful sense of reality. In *Procès de Jeanne d'Arc*, his most severe film, he reached the summit of abstraction. [The figure of the donkey Balthasar in *Au hasard, Balthasar* is a study in innocence, a complex and profound symbol. His two most recent films, *Mouchette* (from Bernanos) and *Une Femme douce* (from Dostoevski) are far less severe than his preceding films, the first a study in withdrawal comparable to *Le Journal d'un curé de compagne*, the second an evocation of spiritual sterility. *Une Femme douce* is also Bresson's first color film.] He has said, at various times, of his work: "A film must be the work of one man, and reach the public as such. The cinema must express itself not through images but through the relationships of images, which is not at all the same thing. In the same way, a painter does not express himself through colors but

through a relationship of colors. If an initial, neutral image is suddenly brought together with another, it vibrates, life bursts through. This isn't so much the life of the story or of the characters, it is the life of the film. As soon as the image comes alive one is creating cinema. The cinema is not a spectacle, it is in the first place a style. . . . I try more and more in my films to suppress what is called plot. Plot is a novelist's trick. I want to and, indeed, do make myself as much of a realist as possible, using only raw material taken from real life. But in the end I find I have a realism that is not simply 'reality.' . . . An actor, even (and particularly) a talented actor, gives us too simple an image of a human being, and therefore a false image. . . . In a film what I am looking for is a march towards the unknown. In any case, the basis is nature, man, not the actor." André Bazin wrote: "Like Dreyer, Bresson is naturally drawn towards the most sensual qualities of the face which . . . is only the licensed impression of the being, the visible tracing of the soul. Bresson literally strips away all superfluous elements from his characters.

SCEN: *C'était un musicien* (33) (dir: F. Zelnick, M. Gleize), *Les Jumeaux de Brighton* (36) (dir: Claude Heymann), *Courrier sud* (37) (dir: Pierre Billon), and for all his own films.

DIR: *Les Affaires publiques* (34) (short feature), *Les Anges du péché** (43), *Les Dames du bois de Boulogne** (45), *Le Journal d'un curé de campagne** (50), *Un condamné à mort s'est échappé** (56), *Pickpocket** (59), *Procès de Jeanne d'Arc** (62), *Au hasard, Balthasar* (66), *Mouchette** (66), *Une Femme douce/A Gentle Creature* (69), *Quatre nuits d'un rêveur* (71).

*BROCA, Philippe de DIR France. (Paris 1935–) He originally made shorts in Africa, became assistant to Chabrol (*q.v.*) and Truffaut (*q.v.*), directed his first features in 1960, the extremely successful *Love Game* and *The Joker*. A film maker with a deft sense of sophisticated comedy, and of social and sexual satire.

DIR: *Les Jeux de l'amour* (60), *Le Farceur* (60), *L'Amant de cinq jours** (61), *Cartouche* (61), *Les Sept péchés capitaux* (61) (one episode), *Les Veinards* (62) (one episode), *L'Homme de Rio* (63), *Un monsieur de cam-*

pagnie (64), *Les Tribulations d'un Chinois en Chine* (65), *Le Roi de coeur* (66), *Le Plus vieux métier du monde* (67) (one episode), *La Diable par la queue* (68), *La Poudre d'escampette* (70).

BRONSTON, Samuel PROD USA (Russia 1910?–) Independent Hollywood producer who founded Samuel Bronston Productions based in Madrid (with the backing of Dupont) and made the super spectacles *King of Kings* and *El Cid.* In 1964, *The Fall of the Roman Empire* heralded his own.
[PROD: *The Adventures of Martin Eden* (42), *Jack London* (43), *A Walk in the Sun** (45), *John Paul Jones* (59), *King of Kings* (60), *El Cid** (61), *55 Days at Peking* (63), *Circus World/The Magnificent Showman* (64), *The Fall of the Roman Empire* (64).]

BROOK, Peter DIR Britain (London March 21, 1925–) Famous British stage producer (since 1945) who has made several notable films.
[DIR: *The Beggar's Opera* (53), *Moderato cantabile* (60), *Lord of the Flies* (62), *The Persecution and Assassination of Jean-Paul Morat as Performed by the Inmates of the Asylum of Charenton under the Direction of the Marquis de Sade** (66), *Red, White, and Zero* (67) (one episode), *Tell Me Lies* (68), *King Lear* (Brit/Den70).]

BROOKS, Richard DIR/SCEN USA. (Philadelphia May 18, 1912–) Originally a novelist (Dmytryk's *Crossfire** is based on his novel), theatrical producer, and radio/TV writer, he entered films as a scriptwriter in 1942. He is an interesting film maker when he directs his own scripts, as in *Blackboard Jungle* and *Elmer Gantry,* and, despite its naïveté, *Something of Value.* But he can become totally mediocre when he has to play by the Hollywood rules. All his films since *Something of Value* (57) have been from his own scripts. He has said of his work: "Though I write a script, I don't have real control over my film because the studio can transform the completed film in the editing. I also regret not being able to choose my actors freely, like most American directors." "Your film can be no better than the script. If the story is bad, the actors can be sublime, the music magnificent, the color breath-taking, but your film will, in the end, be a failure." He has produced his own films since 1965.
SCEN: *White Savage* (52) (dir: Arthur Lubin), *Cobra Women* (45) (dir: Robert Siodmak), *My Best Gal* (44) (dir: Anthony Mann), *Brute Force* (47) (dir: Jules Dassin), *To the Victor* (48) (dir: Delmer Daves), *Key Largo* (48) (dir: John Huston), *Any Number Can Play* (49) (dir: Mervyn LeRoy), *Mystery Street* (50) (dir: John Sturges), *Storm Warning* (50) (dir: Stuart Heisler) and for all his own films except *The Last Time I Saw Paris, The Flame and the Flesh, Take the High Ground* and *The Catered Affair.*
DIR: *Crisis* (50), *The Light Touch* (51), *Deadline USA* (52), *Battle Circus* (53), *Take the High Ground* (53), *The Last Time I Saw Paris* (53), *The Flame and the Flesh* (54), *The Blackboard Jungle** (55), *The Last Hunt* (56), *The Catered Affair/Wedding Breakfast* (56), *Something of Value** (57), *The Brothers Karamazov* (58), *Cat on a Hot Tin Roof* (58), *Elmer Gantry** (60), *Sweet Bird of Youth* (62), *Lord Jim* (65), *The Professionals* (60), *In Cold Blood* (67), *The Happy Ending* (69).

BROWN, Clarence DIR USA. (Clinton May 10, 1890–) Formerly assistant to Maurice Tourneur (*q.v.*) – with whom he co-directed the memorable *Last of the Mohicans* (20) – he became one of Hollywoods veterans, sometimes capable of real achievements, as in *The Flesh and the Devil** (27), *The Trail of '98* (28), and *Intruder in the Dust** (49). [Also, notably: *The Eagle* (25), *Anna Karenina* (35), *Ah! Wilderness* (35), *Conquest/Marie Walewska* (37), *Of Human Hearts* (38), *The Human Comedy* (43), *National Velvet* (45), *The Yearling* (47), *Song of Love* (47). His last film was *Plymouth Adventure* (52) but he produced Delmer Daves's *Never Let Me Go* (53) before retiring.]

BROWNING, Tod DIR USA. (Louisville, Kentucky July 12, 1882–Santa Monica Oct 6, 1962) Originally a vaudeville and circus performer, he became an actor for Griffith, then his assistant in 1916 on *Intolerance**, and finally joined Fox as director in 1917. During the Twenties and Thirties he was the master of the American horror film genre and made Lon Chaney and Bela Lugosi famous.

31

He has sometimes been called "the Edgar Allan Poe of the cinema" and, in any case, is a "dark angel" whose phantasmagoric creations were much admired around 1925 by the surrealists. He took a singular delight in grotesque characters and built his best films around them. In 1928 he said: "While I am working on a subject for Lon Chaney, I never consider the plot. This writes itself after I have conceived the characters. *The Unknown* came to me after I thought of a man without arms. For *The Road to Mandalay*, the initial idea is simply that of a man so frightfully ugly that he is ashamed to reveal himself to his own daughter. In this way one can develop any story." Many of his films are from his own scripts. He retired after 1939 and lived in comfort on his savings in Santa Monica.

DIR (notably): *Jim Bludso* (17), *The Brazen Beauty* (18), *The Wicked Darling* (19) (with Chaney), *The Virgin of Stamboul* (20), *Outside the Law* (21) (with Chaney), *Under Two Flags* (22), *Man Under Cover* (22), *The White Tiger* (23), *Drifting* (23), *The Unholy Three** (25) (with Chaney), *The Mystic* (25), *The Blackbird* (26) (with Chaney), *The Road to Mandalay* (26) (with Chaney), *The Unknown* (27) (with Chaney), *London After Midnight* (27) (with Chaney), *London After Midnight* (27) (with Chaney), *The Show* (27) (with Chaney), *West of Zanzibar* (28) (with Chaney), *Big City* (28), *Where East is East* (29) (with Chaney), *The Thirteenth Chair* (29), *Outside the Law* (30), *The Iron Man* (31), *Dracula** (31) (with Lugosi), *Freaks** (32), *Fast Workers* (33), *Mark of the Vampire* (35) (with Lugosi), *The Devil Doll* (36), *Miracles for Sale* (39).

BRUMBERG, Valentina and Zinaida ANIM USSR. (Moscow Aug 2, 1899 and Aug 2, 1900–) Their cartoons use human characters more than animals, as in *The Young Samoyed* (29). Since 1940 their work has been quite conventional.

BRUNIUS, John W. DIR Sweden. (Stockholm Dec 26, 1884–Stockholm Dec 16, 1937) After a theatrical background, he developed into the best Swedish silent director apart from Sjöström (*q.v.*) and Stiller (*q.v.*). His films in the Twenties are largely elaborate period films.

DIR: *Mästerkatten i stövlar/Puss in Boots* (18), *Synnöve Solbakkien* (19), *Ah, i morron kväll/Oh, Tomorrow Night* (19), *Thora van Deken* (20), *Gyurkovisarna* (20), *Kvarnen/The Mill* (21), *En Lyckoriddare/A Fortune Hunter* (21), *En Vild fagel/A Wild Bird* (21), *Harda Viljor/Hard Wills* (22), *Karlekens Ögon/The Eyes of Love* (22), *Johan Ulfstjerna* (23), *En Piga bland Pigor/A Maid among Maids* (24), *Karl XII/Charles XII*, Parts I, II (25), *Fänrik Stals Sägner/Tales of Ensign Steel*, Parts I, II (26), *Gustaf Wasa*, Parts I, II (26), *Vi Tva/The Two of Us* (30), *Doktorns Hemlighet/The Doctor's Secret* (30), *Längtan till Havet/Longing for the Sea* (31), *Havets Melodi/Melody of the Sea* (34), (co-dir), *Falska Greta/False Greta* (34). All the films until 1926 PHOTOG Hugo Edlund.

*BRYAN, John ART DIR/PROD Britain. (London 1911–London 1969) Trained as a theater designer in the Thirties, he eventually developed into one of the cinema's most distinctive designers, notable for his period films: the Shaw adaptations *Pygmalion*, etc., the two Dickens adaptations by David Lean (*q.v.*) *Great Expectations* (which won him an Oscar) and *Oliver Twist*, and more recently *Becket*. Began producing in the early Fifties.

ART DIR (notably): Asquith's *Pygmalion**, *Fanny by Gaslight*, Gabriel Pascal's *Major Barbara*, *Caesar and Cleopatra**, David Lean's *Great Expectations*, *Oliver Twist*, *The Passionate Friends*, *Madeleine*, Albert Lewin's *Pandora and the Flying Dutchman*, Peter Glenville's *Becket*.

PROD (notably): Ronald Neane's *The Card*, *The Horse's Mouth*, Robert Parrish's *The Purple Plain*, Stuart Burge's *There Was a Crooked Man*, de Sica's *After the Fox*, Robert Freeman's *The Touchables*.

BUCHOWETZKI, Dimitri (Dmitri Bukhovetzky) DIR Germany/France/USA. (Russia 1895–USA 1932) Originally a director in Russia he emigrated to Germany and made his name with a series of exotic costume dramas, many with Emil Jannings. [He was invited to Hollywood in 1924 but his seven films there were not successful and he returned to Europe with the arrival of sound.]

DIR (notably): *Die Brüder Karamosoff* (20) (co-dir: Carl Froelich), *Danton* (21), *Sappho* (21), *Die Gräfin von Paris* (22), *Othello** (22), *Peter der Grosse* (22), *das Karusell des Lebens* (23), *The Crown of Lies* (USA26), *Valencia* (USA26), *Weib im Dschungel* (30), *Die Nacht der Entscheidung* (31).

BULAJIC, Velko (Veljko) DIR Yugoslavia. (Montenegro March 23, 1928–) One of the best of the younger Yugoslav directors who trained at the Centro Sperimentale in Rome and who made documentaries before turning to features. His documentary on the Skopje disaster, *Skopje 1963,* won many international awards.
DIR: *Vlak bez voznog redu/Train without a Timetable* (58), *Rat/War* (60), *Uzavreli Graniczna/Boom Town* (61), *Kozara/Hill of Death** (62), *Skopje 1963* (64) (documentary), *Pogled u zjenicu sunca/A Glance at the Pupil of the Sun* (66), *Bitka na Neretvi/Battle on the River Neretva* (69) (with Sergei Bondarchuk).

BUNUEL, Luis DIR Spain/France/Mexico. (Calanda, Aragon Feb 22, 1900–) Infinitely tender under an apparent cruelty, uncompromising, understanding, totally honest and faithful to himself, his art, his ideals and his friends. If Vigo (*q.v.*) can be called the Rimbaud of the cinema he is the Lautréamont. Born in Aragon like Goya (one of his idols), he studied at Madrid University with Garcia Lorca, Dali, Juan Vicens, Rafael Alberti, and others. He left Spain in 1925 to escape the dictatorship of Primo de Rivera and in order to find freedom in France. He worked as assistant to Jean Epstein (*q.v.*), whom he admired, from 1926 to 1928. But then "surrealism revealed to me that man cannot dispense with the moral sense. I believed in the total freedom of man, but I saw in surrealism a discipline to follow and it led me to take a marvelous and poetic, large step forward" (in *Un chien andalou* and *L'Age d'or*). After breaking with surrealism, directing *Land Without Bread,* and working as an executive producer with the Spanish Republicans, he had a very unhappy, abortive period in the USA (from 1938), where he worked for the Museum of Modern Art in New York and directed shorts for the American

army. Then he was invited to Mexico to direct commercial films and found his voice again with *Los Olvidados*. Thereafter he has directed in Mexico, Spain, and France a series of powerful masterpieces, *Subida al Cielo, Él, Nazarin, Viridiana, El Angel Exterminador,* and *Belle de jour.* He has said: "I have always been an atheist, thank God . . . I believe it is necessary to find God in man, it's a very straightforward attitude." "Apart from my first three films, I have only made films that have been commissioned. I have not made them badly but always morally worthy; I have always followed my surrealist precept: 'the prostitution of art is not excused by having to eat.' I am opposed to conventional morality, traditional fantasies, sentimentalism, all the moral trash of society. Bourgeois morality is, for me, amoral because it is based on extremely unjust institutions: religion, nationalism, the family, and other pillars of society." He has discussed his conception of the cinema: "It will be enough for the white eyelid of the screen to reflect the light that is proper to it in order to make the universe jump. But for the time being we can sleep quietly, for the cinematographic light is securely smothered." "The cinema is a marvelous and dangerous weapon if it is in the hands of a free spirit. It is the best instrument for expressing the world of dreams, emotions, instincts. It seems to have been invented to express the life of the subconscious, whose roots lie at the heart of poetry. However, it shouldn't be thought I am for a cinema exclusively dedicated to fantasy and mystery . . . I ask the cinema to be a witness, to take account of the world, which is to say all that is important in reality. Reality has many levels and can have a thousand different meanings for different people. I want to have an integral vision of reality; I want to enter the marvelous universe of the unknown." "As far as I'm concerned, the private drama of one individual could not interest anyone worthy of living in his times. If the spectator shares the joys, sadnesses, agonies of a character on the screen, it could only be because they are a reflection of the joys sadnesses, and agonies of society at large and are therefore his own. Unemployment, lack of security, the fear of war, etc., affect everyone today, therefore the spectator."

33

ASSIST: for Jean Epstein *Mauprat* (26), *La Chute de la Maison Usher** (28).

DIR: *Un chien andalou** (Fr28), *L'Age d'or** (Fr30), *Las Hurdes/Land Without Bread** (Sp32), *Gran Casino* (Mex47), *El Gran Calavera* (Mex49), *Los Olvidados** (Mex50), *Susana* (Mex51), *La Hija del Engano* (Mex51), *Una Mujer sin Amor* (Mex51), *Subida al Cielo** (Mex 51), *El Bruto* (Mex52), *Robinson Crusoe* (Mex52), *Cumbres Borrascosas** (Mex52), *La Illusion viaja en Tranvia* (Mex53), *El Rio y la Muerte* (Mex54), *Ensayo de un Crimen** (Mex55), *Cela s'appelle l'aurore** (Fr/It55), *La Mort en ce Jardin/Evil Eden* (Fr/Mex56), *Nazarin* (Mex58), *La Fièvre mont à El Pao/Republic of Sin* (Fr/Mex59), *The Young One** (Mex60), *Viridiana** (Sp/Mex61), *El Angel Exterminador** (Mex 62), *Le Journal d'une femme de chambre** (Fr64), *Simon del Desierto* (Mex65), *Belle de jour** (Fr67), *La Voie lactée/The Milky Way* (Fr68), *Tristana* (Sp/It/Fr70).

BUREL, Léonce-Henry PHOTOG France. (Indret Nov 23, 1892–) From Gance (*q.v.*) to Bresson (*q.v.*) perhaps the greatest French cameraman, and one of those who has contributed the most to cinematic art.

PHOTOG (notably): for Pouctal, *Alsace* (16); for Abel Gance, *Les Gaz mortels* (17), *Le Droit à la vie* (17), *La Zone de la mort* (17), *Mater Dolorosa** (17), *La Dixième Symphonie** (18), *J'accuse** (19), *La Roue** (22), *Napoléon** (27); for Feyder, *Crainquebille** (22), *Visages d'enfants* (25), *L'Image* (26); for Maurice Tourneur, *L'Équipage* (28); for Mariel L'Herbier, *Nuits de prince* (30); for Jean Renoir, *Boudu sauvé des eaux** (32); for Jean Benoit-Lévy, *La Mort du cygne* (38); for Noël-Noël, *Les Casse-Pieds* (48), *La Vie enchantée* (49); for Bresson, *Le Journal d'un curé de campagne** (50), *Un condamné à mort s'est échappé** (56), *Pickpocket** (59), *Procès de Jeanne d'Arc** (62).

*BURNESS, Peter ANIM USA. (1910–) Originally worked on such cartoons as *Tom and Jerry* and *The Little King,* then joined UPA and became the most prolific director of the *Mr. Magoo** cartoons in the Fifties. Later moved to TV and the Bullwinkle Show.

CABANNE, Christy William DIR USA. (St. Louis 1888–Philadelphia Oct 15, 1950) Important American film pioneer, trained by D. W. Griffith (*q.v.*); directed Lillian Gish in, e.g., *The Rebellion of Kitty Belle* (14), *The Sisters* (14), *Enoch Arden/The Fatal Marriage* (15), directed Douglas Fairbanks's screen debut, *The Lamb** (15), and was co-director on the 1925 *Ben Hur** (notably for the nativity scene). Later, directed many B-pictures.

CACOYANNIS, Michael DIR Greece. (Cyprus 1922–) The first Greek director to give his country's cinema an international reputation and, since the Fifties, one of the best Greek film makers along with Nikos Koundouros (*q.v.*) and George Tzavellas (*q.v.*). He was based in England as a radio and stage producer and actor 1939–50. His early films show an English influence and many of his best films have been photographed by the English cameraman Walter Lassally (*q.v.*). Nevertheless, his *Windfall in Athens, Stella,* and *A Girl in Black* have an authentic national flavor. After several failures, he regained his international stature with *Electra,* a version of the Euripedes tragedy filmed in his own country, and achieved an enormous popular success with *Zorba the Greek.* He writes the scripts for his own films.
DIR: *Kiriakatiko Xypnima/Windfall in Athens* (53), *Stella* (55), *To Koritsi me ta mavra/A Girl in Black** (55), *A Matter of Dignity* (57), *Our Last Spring* (58), *The Wastrel* (60), *Elektra** (61), *Zorba the Greek** (64), *The Day the Fish Came Out.* (67), *The Trojan Women* (71).

CALMETTES, André DIR France. (Paris April 18, 1861–Paris 1942) Also an actor, he co-directed (with Le Bargy), *L'Assassinat du duc de Guise** (08), and *Le Retour d'Ulysse* (08) and was for three years a director with Film d'Art, making *La Tosca* (08) and *La Dame aux Camélias/Camille* (10) with Sarah Bernhardt; *Macbeth** (09) with Mounet-Sully; *Camille Desmoulins* (11) with Madame Lara; *Madame Sans-Gêne* (11) with Madame Réjane.

CAMERINI, Mario DIR Italy. (Rome Feb 6, 1895–) With Blasetti (*q.v.*), the best Italian director of the Thirties, a specialist in somewhat melancholy comedies whose heroes are often ordinary people hoping to meet good fortune. He studied law, was an officer in the *bersaglieri*, was assistant to his cousin Genina (*q.v.*) 1920–23, and became a scriptwriter. He played a role in De Sica's (*q.v*) development. Since 1940 he has concentrated on period films and has made little of interest. Carlo Lizzani wrote of him: "He was the confessor of the middle classes, scrutinizing with an always most prudent art the hearts of the faithful in order to find there any small sins; he never concerned himself with recounting their secret passions nor with making them face the major problems of existence."
DIR (notably): *Jolly, Clown da Circo* (23), *Maciste contre lo Sceicco* (26) (with the original "Maciste," Pagano), *Kiff Tebi* (27), *Rotaie* (29), *Figaro e la Sua Gran Giornata* (31), *Gli Uomini, che Mascazoni* (32), *Il Cappello a tre Punte* (34), *Daro un Milione* (35), *Ma non è Una Cosa Seria* (36) (with De Sica), *Il Signor Max* (37), *Batticuore* (38), *Grandi Magazzini* (39) (with De Sica), *Una Romantica Avventura* (40), *I Promessi Sposi* (40), *Una Storia d'Amore* (42), *T'Amero Sempre* (43), *Two Anonymous Letters* (45), *La Figlia del Capitano* (47), *Molti Sogni per le Strade* (48), *Il Brigante Musolino* (50),

Wife for a Night (51), *Honeymoon Deferred* (52), *Ulisse/Ulysses* (53), *La Bella Mugnaia* (55), *Suor Letizia* (56), *Holiday on Ischia* (58), *Via Margretha* (61), *I Briganti Italiani* (61), *Kali-Yug, Goddess of Vengeance* (63), *Delitto Quasi Perfetto/Imperfect Murder* (66).

CAMUS, Marcel DIR France. (Chappes April 21, 1912–) An assistant for many years (to Decoin, Rouquier, Becker, Astruc), he made a short film, *Renaissance,* in 1950 and in 1956 his first feature, the moving *Mort en Fraude* on the Indochina war. He achieved great international success with the visually striking *Black Orpheus* but his later films have been of far less interest.
DIR: *Mort en Fraude* (56), *Orfeu negro/Black Orpheus** (58), *Os bandeirantes* (60), *L'Oiseau de paradis* (62), *Le Chant du monde* (65), *L'Homme de New York* (67), *Vivre la nuit* (68), *Le Mur de l'Atlantique* (70).

***CANNON, Robert** ANIM USA. (1901–June 5, 1964) A leading animator for UPA during its creative period when it revolutionized the cartoon. Originally with Disney (*q.v.*), he co-directed *Brotherhood of Man* with Bosustow (*q.v.*) and made a notable contribution to UPA with the creation of *Gerald McBoing Boing* (50) and *Christopher Crumpet* (52). His films have very carefully orchestrated, often surrealistic, sound tracks. Among his other films, *Madeline* (52) and *Fudget's Budget* (54) stand out.

CANTAGREL, Marc DIR France. (Paris Dec 1, 1879–Paris Nov 6, 1960) A major figure in the educational and scientific film field, who directed about a hundred shorts.

CAPELLANI, Albert DIR France/USA. (Paris 1870–Paris 1931) One of the earliest pioneers of the cinema as it developed into an art form. Trained in the theater by André Antoine (*q.v.*), he became for Pathé the principal director of SCAGL (Société Cinématographique des Auteurs et Gens de Lettres), adapting in an illustrative style the works of Hugo, Zola, Sue, etc. His masterpiece is *Les Misérables.* Worked also in the USA, was head of the Clara Kimball Young Film Corporation and directed Nazimova in several films.
DIR (notably): *Aladin* (06), *Don Juan*

(07), *Cendrillon* (07), *Les Apprentissages de Boireau* (07), *Le Chat botté* (08), *Jeanne d'Arc** (08), *L'Homme au gants blancs* (08), *L'Assommoir** (09), *Athalie* (10), *L'Évade de Tuileries* (10), *Les Deux Orphelines/The Two Orphans** (10), *Les Misérables** (11), *Les Mystères de Paris* (11), *Le Courrier de Lyon* (11), *Notre-Dame de Paris* (11), *Germinal* (13), *La Glu* (13), *Patrie* (13), *Quatrevingt-treize* (14), *Les Epaves de l'amour* (15), *Le Rêve interdit* (15), *Camille* (USA15), *The Dark Silence* (USA16), *La Vie de Bohème* (16), *Daybreak* (USA17), *Out of the Fog* (USA 19), *The Red Lantern* (USA20), *The Young Diana* (USA22).

CAPRA, Frank DIR USA. (Palermo May 19, 1897–) Famous both as the man who wrote and directed Harry Langdon's best films and for his brilliant series of light comedies in the Thirties, mostly based on scripts by Robert Riskin (*q.v.*). Sicilian born, he emigrated to the USA in 1903 and in 1921 became a gagman for Hal Roach (*q.v.*). He wrote Langdon's first feature and directed his next two, and in 1932 began the series of New Deal comedies that made his name. He wrote of *Mr. Smith Goes to Washington:* "The meaning of a film, it seems to me, is not in its truth or falsity but in the persistence of its ideas and in the way it reaches the public . . . It can be considered less as a reflection of life than as a document of human psychology, a testament of the popular spirit." In order to resolve social injustice, his fables (as invented or adapted by Robert Riskin) often involved "good fairies": gangsters (*Lady for a Day*), millionaires, both generous (*Mr. Deeds*) or converted from their evil ways (*You Can't Take It with You*), and persuasive innocents (*Mr. Smith*). Capra, who himself had many of Mr. Smith's traits, possessed great faith in the myth of the New Deal and reflected his Rooseveltian beliefs in his somewhat utopian films. This is true even of the documentary series *Why We Fight,* which he produced when he was drafted into the army during World War II. When times and the mood changed after the war, this mocking Sicilian never truly recaptured the engaging optimism and good humor of his earlier successes. His qualities and his failings were equally out of fashion in postwar America. Robert Riskin wrote none of his postwar films.

SCEN: for Harry Edwards, *Tramp, Tramp, Tramp** (26); for William Wellman, *Westward the Women* (51); and his own *The Strong Man**, *Say It with Sables, Submarine, Flight, Forbidden, It's a Wonderful Life.*
DIR: *Fultah Fisher's Boarding House* (23) (short), *The Strong Man** (26), *Long Pants** (27), *For the Love of Mike* (27), *That Certain Feeling* (28), *So This Is Love* (28), *The Matinee Idol* (28), *The Way of the Strong* (28), *Say it with Sables* (28), *Submarine* (28), *The Power of the Press* (28), *The Donovan Affair* (29), *The Younger Generation* (29), *Flight* (29), *Ladies of Leisure* (30), *Rain or Shine* (30), *Dirigible* (31), *The Miracle Woman** (31), *Platinum Blonde* (31), *Forbidden* (32), *American Madness* (32), *The Bitter Tea of General Yen* (33), *Lady for a Day** (33), *It Happened One Night** (34), *Broadway Bill* (34), *Mr. Deeds Goes to Town** (36), *Lost Horizon* (37), *You Can't Take It with You** (38), *Mr. Smith Goes to Washington** (39), *Meet John Doe/ John Doe Dynamite* (41), *Arsenic and Old Lace* (41 released 44), *Prelude to War** (42), *The Nazis Strike** (42) (co-dir: Litvak), *Divide and Conquer** (43) (co-dir: Litvak), *The Battle of China** (44) (co-dir: Litvak) (all in *Why We Fight** documentary series), *Tunisian Victory* (44) (co-dir: Boulting) (documentary), *Two Down, One to Go* (45) (documentary) *It's a Wonderful Life* (46), *State of the Union/The World and His Wife* (48), *Riding High* (49) (remake of *Broadway Bill*), *Here Comes the Groom* (51), *A Hole in the Head* (59), *A Pocketful of Miracles** (61) (remake of *Lady For a Day**).
PROD: *Why We Fight** series, and all his own postwar films.

CARBONNAUX, Norbert DIR France. (Neuilly March 28, 1918–) Good French director of comedies who did not fulfill all the hopes of his first films.
DIR (notably): *Les Corsaires du bois de Boulogne* (54), *Courte tête* (56), *Le Temps des oeufs durs* (58), *Candide* (61), *La Gamberge* (62).

*CARDIFF, Jack PHOTOG/DIR Britain. (Yarmouth 1914–) One of the best British cameramen, notable for his color work in Britain and Hollywood. Began as a camera assistant on Robinson's *The Informer** (29) and won an Oscar for his color photography of *Black Narcissus* (47). Began directing with the interesting *Intent to Kill* (58) and later, *Sons and Lovers* (60), but has made little of note since.
PHOTOG (notably): for Paul Czinner, *As You Like It* (36); for Jacques Feyder, *Knight without Armor* (37); for Powell and Pressburger, *A Matter of Life and Death/Stairway to Heaven* (46), *Black Narcissus* (47), *The Red Shoes** (48); for Gabriel Pascal, *Caesar and Cleopatra** (45); for Albert Lewin, *Pandora and the Flying Dutchman* (51); for Hitchcock, *Under Capricorn* (49); for John Huston, *The African Queen** (51); for Mankiewicz, *The Barefoot Contessa** (54); for King Vidor, *War and Peace** (56); for Laurence Olivier, *The Prince and the Showgirl* (57); for Richard Fleischer, *The Vikings* (58).
DIR: *Intent to Kill* (58), *Beyond This Place* (59), *Sons and Lovers* (60), *Scent of Mystery/Holiday in Spain* (60), *The Lion* (62), *My Geisha* (62), *The Long Ships* (64), *Young Cassidy* (64) (replaced John Ford), *The Liquidator* (65), *The Mercenaries/Dark of the Sun* (67), *The Girl on a Motorcycle* (68).

CARLO-RIM (Jean-Marius Richard) SCEN/ DIR France. (Nîmes Dec 19, 1905–) Good French scriptwriter, notably on Tourneur's *Justin de Marseille* (35), Berthomieu's *Le Morte en Fuite* (36), who has also directed several films from his own scripts.
DIR (notably): *Simplet* (42) (co-dir: Fernandel), *L'Armoire volante* (48), *La Maison Bonnadieu* (51), *Virgile* (53), *Escalier de service* (55), *Les Truands* (56), *Contes* (63), (from Maupassant, for TV).

CARNÉ, Marcel DIR France. (Paris Aug 18, 1909–) The master of French poetic realism, exacting, painstaking, and dedicated, whose films since *Jenny* (his first feature, at 27) have exerted an extraordinary international influence. A journalist and film critic in the Twenties, his film making career began as assistant to Feyder (*q.v.*) and Clair (*q.v.*). He made a short in 1929 and a number of very short advertising films in the Thirties with Aurenche (*q.v.*) and Paul Grimault (*q.v.*). As a critic, he asked in 1932: "When will the cinema descend into the streets?" and felt that he couldn't see "without irritation the current cinema shutting itself away, fleeing from life in order to delight in sets and artificiality." He called for a cinema that would be interested, like the novelist Dabit, in particular Parisian districts: "Do you say 'Populism?' One shouldn't be afraid of the word more than the thing itself. Isn't describing the simple life of ordinary people, conveying their working-class atmosphere, better than re-creating the overheated ambience of dance parties?" The style of his films suggests the influence of his *Kammerspiel* mentors: Sternberg, Lupu Pick, Murnau, and Feyder (all *q.v.*), and his pre-1948 films reveal several recurrent themes: unattainable love, the possibility of happiness only in eternity, and villains who are not evil but have fallen into difficulties. His universe like that of Prévert (*q.v.*) is a kind of stage on which good battles with evil. His heroes (often played by Jean Gabin) are honest, courageous men, driven into crime by society — though his professional gangsters are always portrayed as vulgar riffraff. His lovers seek an "elsewhere" where happiness will be possible and eternal, but they are always thwarted by destiny, often symbolized by one of the characters but also by the environment itself. Ultimately, this sense of fatality is an expression of Carné's understanding of the structure of society. The dramatic shape of his theme was not inviolable and became less pessimistic in later years as when the Devil in *Les Visiteurs du soir* finds himself powerless before the still beating hearts of the entwined lovers. At the end of 1940, when his *Quai des brumes* was accused by Vichy moralizers of contributing (along with Gide, Sartre, etc.) to the collapse of France, he replied that it was the job of an artist to be a barometer of his period and that the barometer shouldn't be blamed for the storm it forecasts. In his preceding films with Jacques Prévert, he had metaphorically expressed his pessimism in the face of the rising threat. They both reached their artistic height with *Les Enfants du paradis.* Their next film together, *Les Portes de la nuit,* was an unmerited failure and, apart from the unfinished *La Fleur de l'âge* in 1948, they never worked together again. (Prévert apparently contributed to *La Marie du port* but was not credited.) Nonetheless, some of their earlier themes can be detected in *La Marie du port, L'Air de Paris* and *Les Tricheurs,* though

these had far less public and critical success than Carné's prewar films.
ASSIST PHOTOG: to Georges Périnal on Feyder's *Les Nouveaux Messieurs** (28), to Jules Kruger on Richard Oswald's *Cagliostro* (29).
ASSIST: to René Clair, *Sous les toits de Paris** (29); to Feyder, *Le Grand jeu** (33), *Pension Mimosas** (34), *La Kermesse héroïque** (35).
DIR: *Nogent, Eldorado du dimanche* (29) (short), *Jenny* (36), *Drôle de drame* (37), *Quai des brumes** (38), *Hôtel du Nord* (38), *Le Jour se lève** (39), *Les Visiteurs du soir** (42), *Les Enfants du paradis** (45), *Les Portes de la nuit** (46), *La Marie du port* (50), *Juliette ou la Clef des songes* (51), *Thérèse Raquin** (53), *L'Air de Paris* (54), *Les Pays d'où je viens* (56), *Les Tricheurs* (58), *Du mouron pour les petits oiseaux* (63), *Trois chambres à Manhattan* (65), *Les Jeunes loups* (68), *La Force et le droit* (70), *Les Assassins de l'ordre* (71).
Terrain Vague (1960)

CARRIL, Hugo del DIR Argentina. (Buenos Aires Nov 30, 1912–) Originally a handsome leading actor and singer in the Thirties and Forties, in 1952 he directed the remarkable *Las Aguas bajan Turbias**, which totally broke with the then current conventions of the Argentinian cinema.

CARTIER-BRESSON, Henri DIR France. (Chanteloup, S. et M. 1908–) The most famous modern French photographer also directed *Le Retour* (46), a documentary portrait of returning French prisoners of war and a hauntingly moving human document. He has recently turned to television reportage with less successful results: *California Impressions* (USA 70).

CASERINI, Mario DIR Italy. (Rome 1874– Rome Nov 17, 1920) One of the most famous directors of Italian spectaculars, from 1908 to 1918, who also made a number of comedies and Shakespeare adaptations for Cinès. He directed at least a hundred films including: *Otello** (07), *Garibaldi* (07), *Marco Visconti, Romeo e Giulietta, Giovanna d'Arco/ Joan of Arc** (all 08), *Beatrice Censi, La Gerla di Papa Martin, L'Innominato* (all 09), *Macbeth**, *Amleto/Hamlet**, *Il Cid, Federico Barbarossa, Giovanni delle Bande Nere, Lucrezia Borgia, Messalina* (all 10), *Jane Gray, Antigone.*

Santarellina, L'Ultimo dei Frontignac (at 11), Mater Dolorosa, I Mille, Siegfried (all 12), Florette e Patapon, Il Treno degli Spettri, Ma l'Amor, Mio non Muore (all 13), Nerone e Agrippina (13 or 14), La Gorgona (14), Amor che Uccide (17), Capitan Fracassa (17), Madama Arlecchino (18), Fior d'Amore (20).

CASSAVETES, John DIR USA. (New York 1929–) A well-known stage and film actor, his reputation as one of the best young independent New York film makers was established with *Shadows* (59) and *Too Late Blues* (61), allying a "de-dramatized" story with a deep sensitivity. [His first commercial feature, *A Child is Waiting,* was a disaster (in every sense) and he did not direct again until he returned to his earlier improvisational approach and re-established his reputation with the highly praised *Faces.*]
DIR: *Shadows** (59), *Too Late Blues* (61), *A Child is Waiting* (62), *Faces* (68), *Husbands* (Brit71).

CASTELLANI, Renato DIR Italy. (Finale Ligure Sept 4, 1913–) Originally an assistant to Blasetti (*q.v.*), he wrote Blasetti's *La Corona di Ferro* and Camerini's *Una Romantica Avventura* and in the early Forties established a reputation — with Soldati (*q.v.*) and Lattuada (*q.v.*) — as a decorative film maker. He later joined the neorealist movement and contributed to it a delicate sense of fantasy, notably in the picaresque *Sotto il Sole di Roma* (47) and *Due Soldi di Speranza* (52). He returned to ornamentalism with *Romeo and Juliet* (54) and has since made little of interest.
DIR (notably): *Un Colpo di Pistola* (41), *Zaza* (42), *Sotto il Sole di Roma* (47), *E Primavera* (49), *Due Soldi di Speranza** (52), *Romeo and Juliet* (Brit54), *I Sogni nei Cassetto* (57), *Nella Citta l'Inferno* (59), *Il Brigante* (61), *Mare Matto* (63), *Sotto il Cielo Stellato* (66), *Questi Fantasmi* (67), *Leonardo da Vinci* (71) (TV).

CAUVIN, André DIR Belgium. (Brussels Feb 12, 1907–) Originally a pioneer director of films on art — *Van Eyck* (38), *Hans Memling* (38). During the war became a specialist in documentaries made in the Congo and continued portraying Belgian colonialism until the last voyage of their King in *Bwana Kikoto.*

CAVALCANTI, Alberto DIR/PROD France/Britain/Brazil/etc. (Rio de Janeiro Feb 6, 1897–) Though largely unsung, he is one of the most important film makers in the history of the cinema, making significant and often basic contributions to the French avant-garde 1925–30, to the English documentary and the "Ealing" style 1934–48, and to the renaissance of the Brazilian cinema 1949–52. He was not always able to direct the films as he intended, but those he created in complete freedom are characterized by their sensitivity, their sense of human and social realities, their understanding, their visual refinement, and their reflection of his delight in the cinema. His career began in France in the early Twenties as a set designer for Marcel L'Herbier (*q.v.*) with whom he developed a new style for studio constructions, notably the use of ceilings. He directed his first film in 1926 and in films like *Rien que les heures, En rade, Yvette, La P'tite Lilie,* and *Le Petit Chaperon rouge,* with their descriptions of ordinary life allied to a sense of somewhat melancholy poetic fantasy and the suggestion of an unattainable "elsewhere," he is an obvious forerunner of French poetic realism of the Thirties. After a sterile period he joined John Grierson (*q.v.*) at the British General Post Office (GPO) Film Unit and gave the British documentary movement a new impetus based on his work in France and on new experiments he made in the use of sound (e.g. on *Night Mail**). It was at this time he suggested calling the movement "neorealism." As a producer with the GPO and later with the Crown Film Unit (1939) he made many short documentaries, produced others, and discovered and/or encouraged Len Lye, Pat Jackson, Harry Watt (*q.v.*), Basil Wright (*q.v.*), Chick Fowles, and Humphrey Jennings (*q.v.*). During the war he joined Michael Balcon (*q.v.*) at Ealing Studios and brought the documentary approach and a sense of national and social realities to his fiction films. His own films as director are remarkable, but he also developed many of the postwar English film makers like Charles Frend, Charles Crichton, Basil Dearden, Robert Hamer (all *q.v.*), etc. He was invited to Brazil in 1949 and in São Paolo gathered together the talents he felt necessary to revitalize the Brazilian cinema. He created a movement which, although it soon ran into difficulties with foreign monopolies, had an impact whose ripples have still not subsided. More than this, he directed one film in his country of origin, *O Canto do Mar,* which is of major importance, though totally unknown in Europe. On his return to Europe he directed a Brecht adaptation *Mr. Puntila and His Valet Matti,* which is the only adaptation the exacting Brecht considered faithful to the original. He has since made several other features and directed for British TV.

ART DIR: for L'Herbier, *L'Inhumane** (23), *L'Inondation* (24), *Feu Mathias Pascal** (25); for Catelain, *La Galerie des monstres* (24); for George Pearson, *The Little People* (Brit25).

DIR: *Le Train sans yeux* (26), *Rien que les heures** (26), *Yvette* (27), *En rade** (27) *La P'tite Lilie* (27), *La Jalousie de barbouillé* (27), *Le Capitaine Fracasse* (28), *Vous verrez la semaine prochaine* (29), *Le Petit Chaperon rouge* (29), *A mi-chemin du ciel* (30), *Les Vacances du diable* (30), *Toute sa vie* (30), *Dans une île perdue* (31), *En lisant le journal* (32), *Le Jour du Frotteur* (32), *Revue Montmartroise* (32), *Nous ne ferons jamais le cinema* (32), *Le Truc du Brésilien* (32), *Le Mari garçon* (32), *Coralie et Cie* (33), *Plaisirs deféndus* (33), *Le Tour de chant* (Fr33), *Pett and Pott* (Brit34), *New Rates* (34), *Line to Tcherva Hut* (36), *Coalface* (36), *We Live in Two Worlds* (37), *Who Writes to Switzerland* (37), *Message from Geneve* (37), *Four Barriers* (37), *Men of the Alps* (39), *A Midsummer Day's Work* (39), *Yellow Caesar* (41) (compilation), *Film and Reality* (42) (compilation), *Watertight* (43), *Alice in Switzerland* (42), *Went the Day Well?* (42), *Champagne Charlie* (44), *Dead of Night** (45) (co-dir: Hamer, Crichton, Dearden), *The Life and Adventures of Nicholas Nickleby* (46), *They Made Me a Fugitive* (47), *The First Gentleman* (47), *For Them Tkat Trespass* (Brit48) *Simao o Coalha* (Brazil52), *O Canto do Mar** (54), *Mulher de Verdade* (Brazil 54), *Herr Puntila und sein Knecht Matti** (Aust55), *Die Windrose* (GDR56) (compilation), *La Prima Notte* (It58), *The Monster of Highgate Pond* (Brit60), *Thus Spake Theodor Herzl* (Israel60) (documentary).

PROD (notably): many GPO documentaries, including *Rainbow Dance, Calendar of the Year, North Sea, Speaking from America, Spare Time, The First Days.* Also: *The Foreman Went to France* (Brit42) (dir: Charles Frend), *The Big Blockade* (Brit41) (dir: Charles Frend), *The Halfway House* (Brit43) (dir: Basil Dearden), *Caicaro* (Brazil 50) (dir: Adolfo Celi), *Painel* (50), *Santuario* (51) (both shorts, dir: Lima Barreto), *Terra Sempere Terra* (51), *Volta Redonda* (52) (both dir: John Payne).

ED: for the Marquis de Wavrin's *Au pays scalp* (Fr32).

CAYATTE, André DIR France. (Carcassonne Feb 3, 1909–) Originally a lawyer, journalist, and novelist, he developed into an unexceptional director who made his name with four skillful and sympathetic "judicial" films that have little to offer but their theses: *Justice est faite, Nous sommes tous des assassins, Avant le déluge* and *Le Dossier noir.* Charles Spaak collaborated on the scripts of all four. The best of the series is *Avant le déluge,* with its portrait of the confusion the cold war caused among certain people. André Bazin wrote of the "cybernetics" of Cayatte: "These are not only films with ideals or a thesis, but quite a paradoxical enterprise in which the mechanics of the cinema are used on the spectator. He is suggesting to us a juridical and mechanistic universe populated by automatons; we await the revolt of the robots."

SCEN: for Marc Allégret, *Entrée des artistes;* for Jean Grémillon *Rémorques** and many of his own films.

DIR: *Les Amant de Vérone* (48), *Justice est faite** (50), *Nous sommes tous des assassins** (52), *Avant le déluge** (53), *Le Dossier noir* (55), *Oeil pour oeil* (56), *Le Miroir à deux faces* (58), *Le Passage du Rhin* (60), *Le Glaive et la balance* (62), *La Vie conjugale* (63), *Piège pour Cendrillon* (65), *Les Risques du métier* (67), *Les Chemins de Khatmandou* (69), *Mourir d'aimer* (70).

CAYROL, Jean DIR/SCEN France. (Bordeaux 1911–) Excellent author and poet who has ended using the camera as fluently as the pen. Has written a book on the cinema *Le Droit de Regard.*

SCEN: for Alain Resnais, *Nuit et Brouillard** (56), *Muriel** (63); and for his own films.

DIR: *Les Specialités de la mer* (59) (TV short), *On vous parle* (60), *La Frontière* (61) (short), *Madame se meurt* (61) (short), *De tout pour faire un monde* (62) (short), *Le Coup de grâce* (65), *La Déesse* (66) (short). All except the last, co-dir: Claude Durand.

CECCHI, Emilio PROD/SCEN Italy. (Florence July 14, 1884–Rome 1966) An established Italian essayist and critic who advocated in the Twenties a revival of stylistic formalism and who became artistic director of Cinès on the invitation of the banker L. Toeplitz. At Cinès, from 1932–44, he promoted the careers of Blasetti, Camerini, and Soldati (all *q.v.*) among others.

CECCHI D'AMICO, Suso SCEN Italy. (Rome July 12, 1914–) Excitable, vehement, sometimes a little acidic, she is one of the best Italian script-writers (always in collaboration) who has worked with De Sica (*Bicycle Thieves*, *Miracle in Milan**, *Boccaccio 70*), Zampa (*Vivere in pace*, *l'Onorevole Angelina*), Visconti (*Bellissima*, *Senso**, *Le Notte Bianche**, *Rocco and His Brothers**, *The Leopard**, *Vaghe stelle dell' Orsa*), Antonioni (*I Vinti*, *La Signora senza Camelia*, *L' Amiche**), Castellani (*E Primavera*), Blasetti (*Fabiola*, *Altri Tempi*), Francesco Rosi (*Salvatore Giuliano*, *La Sfida*, *Kean*), Mario Monicelli (*Proibito*, *i Soliti Ignoti*, *Casanova 70*), and Bolognini (*Metello*).

***CHABROL, Claude** DIR France. (Paris June 24, 1930–) Apart from Godard (*q.v.*), he is the most prolific (19 features and three sketches) of the former *nouvelle vague* directors. A dedicated film maker, at his happiest behind a camera, he passed through an artistically sterile period in the Sixties and has recently re-emerged with a series of films from *Les Biches* to *La Rupture* (including his best film to date *Le Boucher*) that can lay justifiable claim to being counted among the best postwar French films. He began as press attaché at 20th Century-Fox in Paris and film critic for *Arts* and *Cahiers du Cinéma;* an inheritance received by his first wife enabled him to make his first films, *Le Beau Serge* (58) and *Les Cousins* (58), both richly detailed explorations of life, one in a village, the other in the city, and the first appearance of his typical pattern of heroes. He followed these with the exquisitely stylized *A double tour* (59) and the poetic, though poorly acted, *Les Bonnes Femmes* (59). The latter, a commercial disaster, heralded a period of other critical and/or commercial failures and Chabrol turned for some years to directing commercial thrillers. With *Les Biches* (68), an exquisite, unhysterical study of obsession and the struggle for dominance, his technical assurance and purity of style became evident. Since then, although he usually makes two films a year, his work has evidenced increasing strength and mastery of the most economical means of expression (e.g., the ending of *La Femme infidèle*) culminating in the brilliant *Le Boucher*, a profoundly compassionate study of emotions and human relationships. He has gathered around him a team of collaborators: SCEN himself and/or Paul Gégauff PHOTOG Jean Rabier ART DIR Guy Littaye MUS Pierre Jansen ED Jacques Gaillard; his actors often include his wife, Stéphane Audran, Michel Bouquet, Michel Duchaussoy, Maurice Ronet, Jean Yanne.
DIR: *Le Beau Serge** (58), *Les Cousins** (58), *A double tour/Web of Passion/ Leda* (59), *Les Bonnes Femmes** (59), *Les Godelureaux* (60), *Les Sept Péchés Capitaux* (61) (one episode), *L'Oeil du malin/The Third Lover* (62), *Ophélia* (62), *Landru/Bluebeard* (62), *Les Plus belles escroqueries du monde* (63) (one episode), *Le Tigre aime la chair fraîche/ The Tiger Likes Fresh Blood* (64), *Marie-Chantal contre le docteur Kha* (65) *Le Tigre se parfume à la dynamite/An Orchid for the Tiger* (65), *La Ligne de demarcation* (66), *Paris vu par . . .* (66) (one episode), *Le Scandale/The Champagne Murders* (66), *La Route de Corinthe* (67), *Les Biches/The Does/The Girl Friends* (68), *La Femme infidele** (68), *Que la bête meure/Killer* (69), *Le Boucher* (69), *La Rupture* (70), *Juste avant la nuit* (70).

***CHANDLER, Raymond** SCEN USA. (Chicago July 23, 1888–La Jolla, California March 26, 1959) American author of crime stories whose work profoundly influenced the postwar Hollywood thriller. He began at Paramount in 1943 and was a scriptwriter or a co-scriptwriter on *Double Indemnity** (44), *And Now Tomorrow* (44), *The Unseen* (45), *The Blue Dahlia* (46), *Strangers on a Train** (51). Several of his novels have been filmed: *Farewell, My Lovely/Murder My Sweet**, *The Big Sleep**, *Brasher Dou-*

bloon (from *The High Window*), *The Lady in the Lake**, *Marlowe* (from *The Little Sister*). His acidic essay, *Writers in Hollywood,* is one of his most famous nonfiction pieces.

CHAPLIN, Charles Spencer DIR USA. (London April 16, 1889–) The greatest genius the cinema has ever produced, justifiably compared to Molière by Delluc and to Shakespeare by Elie Faure. His childhood in London at the end of the Victorian era is like something out of a Dickens novel. His parents were music hall entertainers who fell into poverty and he and his elder brother Syd (1885–1965), were familiar with slums, begging, nights spent in the streets, and children's homes. He made his first stage appearance in 1895 and from the age of six had a busy stage career. In about 1906 he joined the famous pantomime group of Fred Karno and toured extensively with it. In 1910 he went with Karno to the USA; at the end of 1913, having been seen by Mack Sennett, he was persuaded, somewhat reluctantly, to sign a contract with Sennett's Keystone Company. He appeared in 35 films in 1914 for Keystone, all filled with slapstick, wild chases, and custard pies. However, it was in his second film, *Kid Auto Races at Venice,* that he first wore the tramp costume of large shoes, baggy pants, tight coat, and derby hat. In 1915 he signed a contract with Essanay at $1,250 a week and made 14 films. (He directed these and all his later films.) In them the wild slapstick began to take second place to more subtle pantomime and to the development of his character of a little man at odds with the world around him, notably in *The Bank, The Tramp,* and *Work.* At Essanay he first began to work with Rollie Totheroh as cameraman; he continued to use him on all his films up to *Limelight.* His co-actors at Essanay included the delightful Edna Purviance, Leo White, and Lloyd Bacon. In 1916 he signed with Mutual for $10,000 a week and a bonus of $670,000 a year. At Mutual he crossed the abyss that separates talent from genius and created 12 often perfect comedies, as graceful as ballet and full of sustained comedy and psychological characterizations: *The Floorwalker, The Count, The Rink,* and *The Cure.* At the same time, in films like *The Pawnshop, Easy Street, The Immigrant,* and *The Adventurer* he began

to move towards the bold social polemic, and sometimes the tragedy, that marked his later work. His Mutual films, said Delluc, made him as famous as Sarah Bernhardt and Napoleon. He now had total mastery of his means of expression. In a famous early article he described how in the classic ice-cream gag in *The Adventurer,* the first laugh comes from Charlie's embarrassment and the second and bigger laugh when the ice cream falls down the bare back of a dignified woman. This, he felt, showed not only the tendency of the viewer to share in the actor's predicament (sympathetic shivering with cold) but also his delight in seeing the rich and pompous get the worst of things: "If I had dropped the ice cream, for example, on a scrubwoman's neck, instead of getting laughs, sympathy would have been aroused for the woman. Also, because a scrubwoman has no dignity to lose, that point would have been lost." Throughout his career, much of Chaplin's comedy grew out of how his "little man" punctured the pomposity of the upper class. In June 1917 he signed the famous million-dollar contract with First National for eight films of any length. (From 1918 until he left Hollywood all his films were made at his own studios.) His first three shorts, *A Dog's Life, Shoulder Arms,* and *Sunnyside* moved still more firmly in the direction of social criticism and satire. Each film was the result of long and painstaking effort, an ordeal of nervous tension that involved reshooting a scene over and over again until Chaplin was completely satisfied. His first feature, *The Kid,* was a great success and he left the USA for a triumphant tour of Europe. After *The Pilgrim* in 1923, with its nose-thumbing at hypocrisy and convention, he began to suffer mounting attacks from moralists, culminating in a violent campaign (after his divorce from Lita Grey in 1927) that demanded his expulsion from the USA. However, his image of a David battling Goliath, a little man, battered, lovesick, frustrated, but eventually triumphant, endeared him to millions of other "little men" around the world. Although he had formed United Artists in 1919 with D. W. Griffith, Douglas Fairbanks, and Mary Pickford, his First National commitments prevented his making a film for the company until 1923, when he directed (but did not star in) the drama *A Woman of*

Paris. In the preface to this film he wrote: "Humanity is not divided into heroes and villains, but simply men and women. Their passions, for good or ill, have been given them by nature." He made a triumphant return to the screen in *The Gold Rush* (25), but following the hysterical campaign against him in 1927, which brought him close to suicide, a sense of bitterness appeared in *The Circus* (28) which has never since been totally absent from his films. Although talkies had become established, he refused dialogue in favor of music and sound effects in his first sound film, *City Lights*. He spent two years of unrelenting effort on this and created a harrowing film with a profound sense of tragedy. He left the USA for a world tour and on his return made *Modern Times* (36), directly based on the contemporary economic crisis. When fascism and war again threatened the world he prepared the brilliant satire *The Great Dictator* and found himself for the third time the victim of attacks. He married Oona O'Neill in 1943 and, after the war, abandoned his "little man" character in *Monsieur Verdoux*, a derisive, lucid piece of ferocious black comedy. Attacks on him as a Communist during the McCarthy years made it impossible for him to live in the USA; and after the notorious denial of his re-entry permit in 1952 he took up residence with his family in Switzerland. He was unable to attend the premiere of his Shakespearean tragedy *Limelight*, and declared at the time: "I believe in liberty, that is my only political belief; I am for men, that is my nature. I don't believe in technique, in cameras promenading around stars' nostrils; I believe in mime, I believe in style. I have no 'mission.' My aim is to bring pleasure to people." He directed *A King in New York* in Britain in 1957, wrote his autobiography, and in 1962 had his tenth child. He was awarded an honorary doctorate by Oxford University in 1962. He directed *A Countess from Hong Kong* in Britain in 1966 but it received poor reviews and public response.

[In the following filmography, about 15 of the early 1914 Keystone shorts were directed by Henry Lehrmann, Mack Sennett, Mabel Normand, or George Nichols but for convenience they have been included here. Chaplin directed and wrote all his other films, appeared in all but one, and wrote the music for most of his sound films.]

DIR (shorts): *Making a Living, Kid Auto Races at Venice, Mabel's Strange Predicament, Between Showers, A Film Johnnie, Tango Tangles, His Favorite Pastime, Cruel Cruel Love, The Star Boarder, Mabel at the Wheel, Twenty Minutes of Love, Caught in a Cabaret*, Caught in the Rain, A Busy Day, The Fatal Mallet, His Friend the Bandit, The Knockout, Mabel's Busy Day, Mabel's Married Life, Laughing Gas, The Property Man, The Face on the Barroom Floor, Recreation, The Masquerader, His New Profession, The Rounders, The New Janitor, Those Love Pangs, Dough and Dynamite, Gentlemen of Nerve, His Musical Career, His Trysting Place, Tillie's Punctured Romance* (6 reels, dir: Mack Sennett), *Getting Acquainted, His Prehistoric Past* (all 14), *His New Job*, A Night Out, The Champion, In the Park, The Jitney Elopement, The Tramp*, By the Sea, Work*, A Woman*, The Bank*, Shanghaied*, A Night in the Show, Carmen*, Police* (all 15), (*Triple Trouble* (18) is a pastiche of earlier Essanay Chaplins), *The Floorwalker* (16), *The Fireman** (16), *The Vagabond** (16), *One A.M.* (16), *The Count* (16), *The Pawnshop** (16), *Behind the Screen* (16), *The Rink** (16), *East Street** (17), *The Cure* (17), *The Immigrant** (17), *The Adventurer** (17), *A Dog's Life** (18), *The Bond* (18), *Shoulder Arms** (18), *Sunnyside** (19), *A Day's Pleasure* (19), *The Idle Class* (21), *Pay Day** (22), *The Pilgrim** (23).

DIR (features): *The Kid** (21), *A Woman of Paris** (23), *The Gold Rush** (25), *The Circus** (28), *City Lights** (31), *Modern Times** (36), *The Great Dictator** (40), *Monsieur Verdoux** (47), *Limelight** (52), *A King in New York** (Brit57), *A Countess from Hong Kong* (Brit66).

CHARELL, Erik (also Eric Charrell) DIR Germany. (Pressburg 189?–19?) Famous director of stage operettas in the Twenties and Thirties who made his name with only one film, *Der Kongress tanzt** (31), although the producer, Erich Pommer (*q.v.*), seems to have been more responsible for this worldwide success which influenced many subsequent musicals. He made one film in Hollywood: *Caravan* (34).

CHAUTARD, Emile DIR France/USA. (Paris 1881–Hollywood 1934) French pioneer who worked for Eclair from 1909–14 and made his name with *La Poison de l'humanité* (12). He moved to the States in 1914 and was an actor and director during the Twenties.

CHAYEFSKY, Paddy SCEN USA. (New York Jan 29, 1923–) Though more of a teleplay writer than a scenario writer, he had a considerable influence on the American cinema 1955–58 with his adaptations of his own TV plays, quasi-neorealist dramas of ordinary people in everyday situations. He said: "Every thread of human relationships merits a dramatic study. It is far more interesting to know the reasons why a man gets married than why he kills his neighbor." SCEN: for Delbert Mann, *Marty** (55), *Bachelor Party** (57), *Middle of the Night* (58); for Richard Brooks, *The Catered Affair/Wedding Breakfast* (56); for John Cromwell, *The Goddess* (58); for Arthur Hiller, *The Americanization of Emily* (65), *Hospital* (71); for Joshua Logan, *Paint Your Wagon* (68).

CHENAL, Pierre (P. Cohen) DIR France. (Paris 1903–) He made his name in the Thirties with a somewhat studied stylization in several French films, overpraised at the time: *La Rue sans nom* (34), *Crime et châtiment* (35), *Le Dernier tournant/The Postman Always Rings Twice** (39), *L'Alibi* (37) and in Italy with *Il Fu Mattia Pascal/The Late Matthew Pascal** (37). Later followed an international career in Argentina, Chile, the USA (*Native Son*), and back in France with *Clochmerle* (48), but his work has been consistently mediocre.

CHIARINI, Luigi DIR Italy. (June 20, 1900–) Italian film critic and the founder and director, 1935–50, of the Centro Sperimentale (Rome film school). He has also directed several films in the decorative style: *Via delle Cinque Lune* (42), *La Bella Addormentata* (42), *La Locandiera* (43), *L'Ultimo Amore* (46), *Patto col Diavolo* (48).

CHIAURELI, Mikhail DIR USSR. (Tiflis Jan 25, 1894–) Trained as a sculptor, he became a stage actor in 1916 and a film actor in 1921 (Perestiani's and Nikidze's *The Murder of General Gryaznov*), he

directed his first film in 1928. His *Saba* (29) and *Out of the Way!* (31), early in his career, have a direct, almost neorealist style. The latter is a lively burlesque attack on the cult of personality, a cult to which he himself fell prey after 1938 and which he expressed in several of his films on Stalin, notably in the oversimplifications and grandiose imagery of *The Fall of Berlin* (49). DIR: *First Cornet Streshnev* (28) (co-dir: Y. Dzigan), *Saba* (29), *Khabarda!/Out of the Way!* (31), *Posledni maskarad/ The Last Masquerade* (34), *Arsen* (37), *Great Dawn* (38), *Georgi Saakadze*, Part I (42), *Georgi Saakadze*, Part II (43), *Klyatva/The Vow* (46), *Padeniye Berlina/The Fall of Berlin** (49), *Nezabyvayemi 1919 god/The Unforgettable Year of 1919* (52), *Otar's Widow* (58).

CHIRSKOV, Boris SCEN USSR. (Stavropol 1904–) The author of many scripts (*Valeri Chkalov, Zoya, Invasion,* etc.) but notable mainly for his script for Ermler's *Velikii perelom/The Great Turning Point** (46).

CHKEIDZE, Revaz DIR USSR. (Tiflis 1926–) Notable Georgian film maker who studied under Yutkevich (*q.v.*) and Romm (*q.v.*) and whose best film is *Magdana's Donkey,* co-directed with Abuladze (*q.v.*). DIR: *Lurdzha Magdana/Magdana's Donkey** (55), *Nash dvor/Our Courtyard* (56), *Maya iz Tskhneti/Maya from Tshneti* (62), *Otets soldata/A Soldier's Father* (65).

CHOMON, Segundo de PHOTOG France/ Italy. (Teruel Oct 18, 1871–Paris May 2, 1929) A major pioneer in the development of trick effects: 1902, stencil tinting; 1906, frame by frame animation (?). From 1905 to 1911 he made trick films for Pathé (e.g., *Sleeping Beauty* in 1908) and was the first to make artistic and expressive use of the moving camera in Pastrone's *Cabiria** (14).

CHRETIEN, Henri INVENTOR France. (Paris Feb 1, 1879–Washington Feb 6, 1956) Invented and developed the "hypergonar" lens after 1925 (used by Autant-Lara on his 1927–28 *Construire un Feu*), which, when acquired by Spiros Skouras of 20th Century-Fox, became the basis of the anamorphic lens system of Cinema-

44

Scope and eventually established the worldwide preeminence of the wide screen film.

CHRISTENSEN, Benjamin (in USA, Benjamin Christianson) DIR Denmark/USA/Germany. (Viborg Sept 28, 1879–Copenhagen April 13, 1959) originally an opera singer and producer, his film career began in Denmark as writer and actor. He made two atmospheric and visually stylistic thrillers *The Mysterious X* (13) and *Night of Revenge* (15) before making in Sweden the most striking of all film fantasies *Häxan*. [This led to a contract with UFA in Germany, where he acted in Dreyer's *Michaël* and directed three films. He went to Hollywood in 1926 and directed six features — three horror films and three comic horror films (including the remarkable *Seven Footprints to Satan*) — before returning to Denmark in 1930. He made no more films until 1939. Then he made four successful films in four years, though these are largely unknown outside Scandinavia.]
DIR: *Det Hemmelighedsfulde X/The Mysterious X* (Den13), *Haevnens Nat/ The Night of Revenge* (Den15), *Häxan/ Witchcraft Through the Ages** (Swed22), *Unter Juden* (Ger23), *Seine Frau, die Unbekannte* (Ger23), *Die Frau mit den Schlechten Ruf* (Ger25), *The Devil's Circus* (USA26), *Mockery* (USA27), *The Hawk's Nest* (USA28), *The Haunted House* (USA29), *The House of Horror* (USA29), *Seven Footprints to Satan* (USA29), *Skilsmissen Born/Children of Divorce* (Den39), *Barnet/The Child* (Den40), *Gaa med Mig Hjem* (Den41), *Damen med de Sorte Handsker* (Den42).

CHRISTIAN-JAQUE (Christian Maudet) DIR France. (Paris Sept 4, 1904–) Trained at the Beaux Arts and originally an art director and assistant to Duvivier, he has directed some 50 films, of which at least a dozen have been major commercial successes. Undeniably a complete professional, he has a sense of conviction and often of liberality and has created many interesting films: *Las Disparus de Saint-Agil, La Chartreuse de Parme, Si tous les gars du monde* and, above all, *Fanfan la Tulipe*.
DIR (notably). *Francois I*ᵉʳ (36), *Les Pirates du rail* (37), *Les Disparus de Saint-Agil* (38), *L'Assassinat du Père Noël* (41), *La Symphonie fantastique* (42), *Carmen** (42–44), *Sortilèges* (45),
Boule de suif* (45), *Un Revenant* (46), *D'homme à hommes* (48), *La Chartreuse de Parme* (48), *Souvenirs perdus* (50), *Fanfan la Tulipe** (51), *Lucrèce Borgia* (52), *Nana** (55), *Si tous les gars du monde/Race for Life* (56), *Babette s'en va-t-en guerre* (59), *Madame Sans-Gêne* (61), *Les Bonnes causes* (63), *La Tulipe noire* (64), *Le Saint . . .* (66), *La Seconde vérité* (66), *Emma Hamilton* (68).

CHRISTIE, Al PROD/DIR USA. (Ontario, Canada Nov 24, 1886–Hollywood April 14, 1951) Mack Sennett's (*q.v.*) and Hal Roach's (*q.v.*) closest rival as a producer of short comedies in the Twenties. He began as a director of westerns and comedies in 1910 and established his own production company in 1916, which turned out hundreds of short comedies (and occasionally features like *Charley's Aunt* in 1925) featuring comedians like Bobby Vernon, Neal Burns, and Billy Dooley. His comedies were often lively and entertaining with interesting satirical aspects.

CHU, Shih-ling (Tsou Se-ling) DIR Hong Kong. (?–?) A Hong Kong pioneer in the use of the neorealist style who has made at least two interesting films: *The Dividing Wall** (51), and *House Warming** (54).

CHUKRAI, Grigori DIR USSR. (Ukraine 1921–) Simple and honest in approach, he is a key Soviet film maker of the Fifties. Trained by Yutkevich (*q.v.*) and Romm (*q.v.*) and an assistant to Romm in 1953, he developed into the voice of a new Soviet generation, one that had been profoundly affected by the war and the difficult Stalinist years that followed. He himself suffered severely during the war and his experiences are reflected in his films. *The Forty First,* a remake of the earlier film, is an attack on the hero cult; *Ballad of a Soldier* is a sincere and moving portrait of the sufferings of a country at war; *Clear Skies* (less perfect) is a direct criticism of the Stalinist years that resounds like a cry from the heart. He has said of himself: "I am a romantic, a believer in life. Without romance, I could not live. A work of art must move the mind and heart, be strictly directed with a unity of style, and be of service to mankind. War does not obsess me, but I loathe it. It stole from me my best years and my best friends."

DIR: *Nazar Srodolia* (55), *Sorok pervyi/ The Forty-First** (56), *Ballada o soldate/ Ballad of a Soldier** (59), *Chistoie nebo/Clear Skies** (61), *Zhilibyli starik so starukhoi/There Was an Old Man and an Old Woman* (64), *People!* (66), *Stalingrad* (69) (documentary).

CIAMPI, Yves DIR France. (Paris Feb 9, 1921–) A film maker of the Fifties generation (totally ignored in France), he has always demonstrated the greatest integrity, even under the difficult conditions of international co-productions. Began as an amateur film maker and became assistant to Hunebelle. He has filmed also in Japan and Senegal.

DIR (notably): *Les Compagnons de la gloire* (45) (documentary), *Un grand patron* (51), *La Guérisseur* (54), *Les Héros sont fatigués* (55), *Le Vent se lève* (61), *Liberté I* (Senegal62), *La Ciel sur la tête* (65), *A quelques jours près* (68).

CICOGNINI, Alessandro MUS Italy. (Pescara Jan 25, 1906–) One of the most fashionable Italian composers who tends to use traditional, often gay themes. He has collaborated notably with De Sica on *Sciuscia**, *Bicycle Thieves**, *Miracle in Milan**, *Umberto D**, *L'Oro di Napoli, Il Tetto, Yesterday, Today, and Tomorrow;* with Blasetti on *Quatro passi fra le nuvole**, *Prima Communione;* with Comencini on *Pane, Amor e Fantasia;* with Duvivier on *Don Camillo.*

CIULEI, Liviu DIR Romania. (Bucharest July 7, 1923–) Trained as an architect, he had a successful theatrical career as set designer, actor, and director before turning to films, first as actor, then as assistant to Victor Illiu (*q.v.*). His first film was *The Eruption* (59), his second *Valurile Dunariis/The Danube Waves* (63), a lively color film; then the best film of the new Romanian cinema, his third, the striking *Padurea Spinzuratilor/ Forest of the Hanged** (65).

CLAIR, René (René Chomette) DIR France/ Britain/USA. (Paris Nov 11, 1898–) The most French of all film makers and the most famous French film maker after Méliès (*q.v.*) and Linder (*q.v.*). From the first, said Moussinac in 1951, "he proclaimed freedom, that freedom which is common to all of us and which he never stopped defending . . . It seems to me admirable that in all of his films, every Frenchman could recognize a little of himself and every foreigner a little of France." His childhood coincided with the cinema's and, after the war, his career began as a journalist for *L'Intransigéant.* [In 1920 he began playing leads in films by Feuillade (*q.v.*) and Protozanov (*q.v.*), developed an interest in the cinema, and went to Brussels in 1922 to study Jacques de Baroncelli (*q.v.*) at work. He became a film critic and a passionate champion of the cinema, rediscovered the French pioneers, made his first film *Paris qui dort* (23), and flirted briefly with the avant-garde in its search for "pure cinema" (*Entr'acte*).] His mentor in those youthful days was Feuillade and at that time he wrote: "What is basic to the cinema is that which cannot be told. But try to make people (you, me, others) understand that, people warped by some 30 centuries of chattering — poetry, theater, the novel. It is necessary to return them to the primitive state!" After several less successful films, he established his international reputation with *Un Chapeau de paille d'Italie* (27), transforming Labiche's chattering into images. The arrival of sound depressed him and he asked, "Rebirth or death? If chance doesn't thwart the plans of the financiers, you'd better bet on death or at least on a long death-like sleep." But he added: "It will not be impossible for an art appropriate to the sound film to be developed" and himself proved this with *Sous les toits de Paris,* hailed everywhere as the most beautiful film in the world. At the age of barely 30 he reached his artistic peak with *Le Million* (31) and *A nous la liberté* (31). Their success intoxicated Clair less than they made him uneasy; in 1927 he had denounced money as an obstacle to true creation, adding, "the cinema must therefore renounce the relative freedom enjoyed by other arts. Let us resign ourselves to being artisans of ephemeral works. Undoubtedly we will be the sacrificial generation." The unmerited failure of *Le Dernier Milliardaire* (34) led to an exile from France, which the war later prolonged. His British and Hollywood films, even *The Ghost Goes West, The Flame of New Orleans,* and *It Happened Tomorrow,* do not match his greatest French films. In 1946 he re-

46

turned to his native Paris and to a second maturity with more personal films involving true feeling. He warmly evoked the turn of the century and the approach of old age in his tender *homage* to the cinema's pioneers in *Le Silence est d'or* (47). He denounced the technological age and the atomic threat in his "Faust," *La Beauté du diable* (49). He dissected the conventions and behavior of "la Belle Epoque" and revealed their sordid foundations in the elegant tragicomedy *Les Grandes Manoeuvres* (55) and exalted friendship and loyalty in *Porte des Lilas* (57). In the end his universally recognized qualities forced the French Academy to admit to their ranks for the first time a film maker in his own right: "His glory lacked nothing, it was ours that was deficient." He has written several books on the cinema.

DIR: *Paris qui dort** (Fr23), *Entr'acte** (24), *Le Fantôme du Moulin-Rouge* (24) *Le Voyage imaginaire* (25), *La Proie du vent* (26), *Un Chapeau de paille d'Italie** (27), *La Tour* (28) (documentary short), *Les Deux Timides* (28), *Sous les toits de Paris** (30), *Le Million** (31), *A nous la liberté** (31), *Quatorze juillet* (32), *Le Dernier Milliardaire** (34), *The Ghost Goes West** (Brit35), *Break the News* (Brit37), *The Flame of New Orleans* (USA40), *Forever and a Day* (USA42) (one episode), *I Married a Witch** (USA42), *It Happened Tomorrow** (USA43), *And Then There Were None/Ten Little Indians* (USA45), *Le Silence est d'or** (Fr47), *La Beauté du diable** (49), *Les Belles de nuit** (52), *Les Grandes Manoeuvres** (55), *Porte des Lilas** (57), *La Française et l'amour* (60) (one episode), *Tout l'or du monde* (61), *Les Quatre Vérités* (62) (one episode), *Les Fêtes galantes* (65). Also: SCEN for Genina's *Prix de beauté* (29) and for all his own films except *Entr'acte;* PROD Pierre Harts' documentary short, *Un village dans Paris* (Fr39); DIR the uncompleted *Air Pur* in France 1939. In 1920–23, acted in Feuillade's *Parisette, Les Deux Gamines, L'Orpheline;* Protozanov's *Le Sens de la mort, Pour une nuit d'amour;* Loïe Fuller's *Le Lys de la vie.* ASSIST to Baroncelli on *Carillon de minuit* (22), *La Légende de soeur Béatrix* (22).

*CLARKE, Shirley DIR USA. (New York 1925–) Important independent American film maker who, after several ex-perimental shorts (*Dance in the Sun, A Moment in Love, Bridges-go-round*) and documentaries (*Scary Time, Loops, Skyscraper,* with Lewis Jacobs, Willard van Dyke), turned to the quest for realism and established her reputation with her first feature, the Pirandellian *The Connection** (61). Her later *The Cool World* (63) and *Portrait of Jason* (67) were less successful.

CLARKE, T. E. B. SCEN Britain. (Watford June 7, 1907–) Sometimes called the British Zavattini, he wrote several of the most famous Ealing comedies and dramas. Originally a journalist.

SCEN (notably): for Basil Dearden, *Halfway House* (44), *The Blue Lamp* (50); for Cavalcanti, *Champagne Charlie* (44), *Dead of Night** (45); for Charles Crichton *Hue and Cry** (47), *The Lavender Hill Mob** (51), *The Titfield Thunderbolt* (53); for Charles Frend, *Barnacle Bill* (57); for Henry Cornelius, *Passport to Pimlico** (48); for Jack Cardiff, *Sons and Lovers* (60); for Don Chaffey, *The Horse Without a Head* (63).

*CLAYTON, Jack DIR Britain. (1921–) A complete professional who worked his way up through the industry, which he joined when young, assisting on many films since 1945. His first film, the short feature *The Bespoke Overcoat*, won an award at Cannes and his *Room at the Top* brought a new sense of realism to the British cinema and established a pattern of film-making for a decade. He has a sure touch with actors, notably in *The Innocents* (a beautiful visualization of the James story) and in the otherwise gimmicky *The Pumpkin Eater.*

DIR: *The Bespoke Overcoat** (55), *Room at the Top** (58), *The Innocents* (61), *The Pumpkin Eater* (64), *Our Mother's House* (67). Also produced *Three Men in a Boat* (56) (dir: Ken Annakin).

CLEMENT, René DIR France/Italy/Britain. (Bordeaux March 18, 1913–) A precise, intelligent, if sometimes mannered, film maker who, after experience as a cameraman and documentary film maker in the Thirties, developed a realistic approach that he retained for some years. In 1946 he told Jean Quéval: "The cinema is my vocation, even my life. Long before *La Bataille du rail* I was able to draw my first weapons in the fiction film. The anecdote and the triangle drama have had their day. The cinema must respond to the social restlessness of the viewer and must give him hope in wisdom. It is a concept that I believe can be expressed through a social and aesthetic realism." His first feature, *La Bataille du rail,* which merited the success of *Paisà* or *Sciuscià,* was hardly known outside France and his *Les Maudits* was an undeserved failure. After some setbacks he stubbornly returned to his first principles with *Jeux interdits* which although refused by the Cannes Festival was a success at Venice and throughout the world. Perhaps the great success profited him less than his previous failures. After *Knave of Hearts* in Britain and *Gervaise* he began to specialize in large-budget, international co-productions, but he never matched his earlier work. However, he remains one of the best French film makers of the postwar years.

DIR (shorts): *Soigne ton gauche* (37) (with Jacques Tati), *La Grand Chartreuse* (37), *Arabie interdite* (38) (series of three documentaries), *La Bièvre* (39), *Le Tirage* (42), *Ceux du rail* (42), *Toulouse* (43), *La Grande Pastorale* (43), *Chefs de demain* (43), *Mountain* (43).

DIR (features): *La Bataille du rail** (45), *La Père tranquille* (46), *La Belle et la Bête** (46) (co-dir/technical adviser), *Les Maudits** (47), *Le Mure di Malapurga* (It/Fr48), *Le Château de verre* (50), *Jeux interdits** (52), *Knave of Hearts** (Brit54), *Gervaise** (56), *La Diga sul Pacifico/The Sea Wall/This Angry Age* (It58), *Plein Soleil* (It59), *Che Joia Vivere!/Quelle Joie de vivre!* (Fr/It61), *Le Jour et l'heure* (Fr/It 63), *Les Félins/The Cage/Joy House* (63), *Paris brûle-t-il?/Is Paris Burning?* (66), *Ecrit sur le sable* (66), *Passager de la pluie/Rider in the Rain* (Fr/It69).

✓ **CLINE, Edward** DIR USA. (Wisconsin Nov 7, 1892–1961) The best comedy director trained by Mack Sennett (*q.v.*), he collaborated on short films with Buster Keaton from 1920 to 1923 and later directed several W. C. Fields features: *Million Dollar Legs** (32), *My Little Chickadee* (40), *Never Give a Sucker an Even Break** (41), *The Bank Dick* (41).
(44)

CLOCHE, Maurice DIR France. (Commercy June 17, 1907–) A prolific film maker who began by making documentaries in 1933 and who is memorable mainly for his ambitious *Monsieur Vincent* (47), with Pierre Fresnay, photographed by Claude Renoir (*q.v.*). Also, *La Vie est Magnifique* (38), *Cage aux filles* (48), *Né de père inconnu* (50), *Les Filles de la nuit* (57), *Coplan, agent secret* (64), among many others.

CLOEREC, René MUS France. (Paris May 31, 1911–) Autant-Lara's (*q.v.*) favorite composer, notably for *Douce, Diable au corps**, *L'Auberge rouge**, *La Traversee au Paris.* Also in Britain for *Intimate Relations**.

CLOUZOT, Henri-Georges DIR France. (Niort Nov 20, 1907–) The greatest French specialist in thrillers, sometimes incorporating neurotic tensions, and always violence; made his name after the war with the suspenseful effects of his films, his meticulous creation of atmosphere, used of actors, effective style, and a certain taste for visual experiment (notably in *Le Mystère Picasso*). He began his career as a scriptwriter and 1932–33 was assistant to Litvak (*q.v.*) and Dupont (*q.v.*) in Germany. He spent the period 1934–38 in various sanatoria, then returned to scriptwriting and directed his first feature in 1942. His first three films, *L'Assassin habite au 21, Quai des Orfèvres,* and *Le Corbeau* (despite the overemotional accusations of Nazi collaboration which this third film aroused in France) are above all suspense films. He was praised at the time for a certain tendency towards social criticism and affirmed this in *Manon* (49), which was not, however, the equal of the later *Wages of Fear.* At this time he spoke of the importance of preparation, of planning every detail, every movement, before beginning to shoot: "My greatest pleasure is the actual production, the editing . . . Dialogue, which played a major role in my first films, has diminished in importance. *Le Salaire de la peur* is a visual film in which the dialogue is largely in the background. I developed a form of editing built around continuing shocks. I always set light against shadow. I could be accused, because of this, of being simplistic . . . But I pursue a process of simplification in order to accentuate contrasts . . . What do sophisticated, old-fashioned dramas, the recounting of spicy stories matter to us? The social drama, the drama of our times, has arrived. It is those that hold us, those that we hope to fix on the screen." His later projects ran afoul of the censor. But with *Les Diaboliques* and *La Vérité* was he sure he was not returning to a more highly spiced recounting of old-fashioned spicy stories? The earlier pessimism and the taste for the sordid and for neurotic passions has become more marked in his later films.

SCEN: *Un soir de rafle* (31) (dir: Carmine Gallone), *Ma cousine de Varsovie* (38), *Le Révolte* (38) (both dir: Léon Mathet), *Le Duel* (39) (dir: Pierre Fresnay), *Le Monde tremblera* (39) (dir: Richard Pottier), *Le Dernier des six* (41) (dir: Georges Lacombe), *Les Inconnus dans la maison* (41) (dir: Henri Decoin), *Si tous les gars du monde* (56) (dir: Christian-Jaque), and all his own films.

DIR: *La Terreur des Batignolles* (31) (short), *L'Assassin habite au 21* (42), *Le Corbeau** (43), *Quai des Orfèvres** (47), *Manon* (49), *Retour à la vie* (49) (one episode), *Miquette et sa mère* (49), *Le Salaire de la peur** (53), *Les Diaboliques/The Fiends* (55), *Le Mystère Picasso** (56), *Les Espions* (57), *La Vérité** (60), *La Prisonnière/Woman in Chains* (68). Also, an incomplete documentary, *Brésil* (50–51), and an abandoned feature, *L'Enfer* (64).

COCTEAU, Jean DIR/SCEN France. (Maisons-Laffitte July 5, 1889–Milly-la-Forêt Oct 11, 1963) A dominant figure on the French intellectual scene — poet, dramatist, novelist, actor, and painter — who took a great delight in the cinema and worked intermittently with it over 30 years. He saw the cinema as a means of expressing "the frontier incidents between one world and another." The films he directed, from *Le Sang d'un poète* to *Testament d'Orphée,* are a kind of private diary, full of his own ideas, views, and obsessions and his delight in cinematic devices. His fantasy, *La Belle et la Bête,* almost balletic in style, was followed by the claustrophobic dissection of a self-centered family *Les Parents terribles* and the mythological, unforgettable *Orphée.* He has said of himself and of the cinema: "The more I am forced to study the craft of film, the more I perceive its effectiveness is in its intimacy, its confessional and realistic qualites. A film is not a dream that is told but one that we all dream together." "The role of the poet is to act out his thoughts. Suppose then that the film serves us, allows us to show personal things." "Nothing is more truthful than fiction. Nothing more beautiful than the accidental, otherwise it is the train that leaves and arrives at a fixed time." "It is not up to us to obey the public, which does not know what it wants, but to compel the public to follow us." Cocteau's work is unique in the cinema, an always visually fascinating combination of the real and the unreal, personal obsession and ancient myth.

SCEN: *La Comédie de bonheur* (39) (dir: L'Herbier), *Le Baron Fantôme* (43) (dir: Serge de Poligny), *L'Eternel retour** (43) (dir: Jean Delannoy), *Les Dames du bois de Boulogne** (45) (dir: Bresson), *Ruy Blas* (47) (dir: Pierre Billon), *Les Enfants terribles* (50) (dir: Jean-Pierre Melville), *La Princesse de Clèves* (60) (dir: Jean Delannoy), *Thomas l'imposteur* (65) (dir: Georges Franju). Also, commentary for André Zwobada's *Les Noces de sable** (48) and scripts for all his own films.

DIR: *Le Sang d'un poète** (30), *La Belle et la Bête** (46), *L'Aigle a deux têtes* (47), *Les Parents terribles** (48), *Orphée** (49), *Le Testament d'Orphée** (59) and two 16mm shorts, *Coriolan* (50), *Villa Santo-Sospir* (51).

COHL, Emile (Emile Courte) ANIM/DIR France/USA. (Paris Jan 4, 1857–Orly Jan 27, 1938) French pioneer of animation and related genres who was a pupil of André Gill, a famous cartoonist, and was a cartoonist himself until 1907, when he became a director at Gaumont and developed rapidly from trick films to frame-by-frame animation. He was not only an extraordinary technician, the creator and developer of various techniques (animation of line drawings, puppets, objects, combination of cartoons and live action, stop-frame animation, etc.), he was also a great artist, a man of fantastic imagination, fertile inventiveness, and a sure sense of malicious comedy. He was the first to develop a standard character, "Fantoche," (an ordinary but unconquerable man) in his cartoons. He worked in the USA from 1913–15 on the *Snookums* series. All modern animation is descended from Cohl, notably that of Norman McLaren (*q.v.*) after 1940. He was ruined by the war and became destitute. He died in a rest home in 1938 when a candle accidentally set his beard on fire.

DIR: a hundred short films, including: *La Course aux potirons/The Pumpkin Race* (07), *La Vie à rebours* (07), *Fantasmagorie/A Fantasy, Don Quichotte*, Le Cauchemar du Fantoche, Un drame chez les Fantoches, Les Allumettes animées, Le Journal animé, Le Petit soldat qui devient dieu* (all 08), *Les Transfigurations, La Lampe qui file, Les Joyeaux microbes/Magic Cartoons, Les Locataires d'à côté, Génération spontanée, Les Lunettes féeriques* (all 09), *Le Binettoscope, Le Petit Chanteclair, Le Tout Petit Faust, Enfance de l'art, Rien n'est impossible à l'homme* (all 10), *Poudre de vitesse, La Chambre ensorcelée/The Automatic Moving Co., Le Retapeur de cervelle, Aventures d'un bout de papier, Les Melons baladeurs* (all 11), *Les Jouets animés, L'Homme sans tête, Cuisine-Express* (all 12), *Les Aventures de Baron de Crac/Baron Munchausen** (13), *Monsieur Stop* (13), *Aventures de Maltracé* (13), *Snookums* series (USA 13–15), *Les Aventures des Pieds Nickelés* (18).

COLLINS, Alfred DIR Britain. (?–?) British pioneer who in 1903–05 (before Griffith) used a very modern editing syntax with extreme close-ups and a moving camera in tackling social subjects: *The Runaway Match/Marriage by Motor* (03), *Mutiny on a Russian Battleship* (05) (the Potemkin Mutiny). Originally a music hall comedian, he made numerous short comedies and chase films for Gaumont, 1903–10.

COLPI, Henri ED/DIR France. (Switzerland July 12, 1912–) A member of the French *new wave* and a close collaborator of Resnais as editor of several of his films, he directed several shorts in the Fifties and made his feature debut with *Une aussi longue absence* (61) from a Marguerite Duras screenplay. He trained at l'IDHEC, became a film critic, and has written two books on the cinema.

ED (notably): for Resnais, *Nuit et Brouillard*, Hiroshima mon amour*, L'Année dernière à Marienbad*;* for Clouzot, *Le Mystère Picasso*;* for Chaplin, *A King in New York*.*

DIR: *Une aussi longue absence* (61), *Codine* (Rom62), *Pour une étoile sans nom* (66), *Heureux qui comme Ulysse* (69).

COMENCINI, Luigi DIR Italy. (Salo June 8, 1916–) After the neorealist short *Bambini in Città* (46), he was pushed into commercial film-making somewhat in spite of himself with *Pane, Amore e Fantasia* (53), but he has a sense of comic fantasy as witnessed by *Tutti a casa* (60). He has also written scripts. [DIR (notably): *Bambini in Città* (46) (short), *Proibito Rubare* (48), *Persiane Chiuse* (51), *Pane, Amore e Fantasia/Bread, Love, and Dreams* (53), *Pane, Amore e Jalosia/Bread, Love, and Jealousy* (54), *Marita in Città* (58), *Tutti a casa* (60), *Il Compagno Don Camillo* (66), *Il Frigorifero* (71) (co-dir: Mario Monicelli).]

COMMANDON, Jean DIR France. (Jarnac Aug 3, 1877–) A pioneer of the science film who since 1908 has made 100–150 research films in the fields of microscopy, zoology, medicine, botany, etc.

CONNELLY, Marc SCEN USA. (McKeesport Dec 13, 1890–) Well-known dramatist and stage director who contributed to several major Hollywood successes with original scenarios or adaptations of his plays, notably *Beggar on Horseback* (25) (dir: James Cruze) and *Green Pastures** (36), directed by himself and William Keighley. His *Merton of the Movies* was filmed twice: *Merton of the Movies* (24) (dir: James Cruze), *Make Me a Star* (32) (dir: William Beaudine).

CONWAY, Jack DIR USA. (Graceville July 17, 1887–Los Angeles Oct 11, 1952) An honest Hollywood craftsman who was trained by D. W. Griffith (*q.v.*) at Triangle, he directed his first feature film, *The Old Armchair*, in 1912; he also acted for some years. Worked for most of his career with MGM and directed a large number of films, including: *Our Modern Maidens* (28), *The New Moon* (30), *The Unholy Three** (30) (remake), *Arsène Lupin* (32), *Viva Villa** (34), *A Tale of Two Cities* (35), *A Yank at Oxford* (38), *Boom Town* (40), *Crossroads* (42), *The Hucksters* (47).

COOPER, Merian C. DIR/PROD USA. (Jacksonville Oct 24, 1893–) He worked as co-director and producer with Ernest B.

Schoedsack (*q.v.*), with whom he had gone through the First World War, on several well-known early films, from the documentaries, *Grass** (25) and *Chang** (27), to *The Four Feathers* (29) and the marvelous fantasy, *King Kong** (33). [Also produced, notably, *Little Women* (33), *Flying Down to Rio* (33), *She* (35), *The Last Days of Pompeii* (35), *Mighty Joe Young** (49), several John Ford films: *The Lost Patrol** (34), *The Fugitive* (47), *Fort Apache** (48), *She Wore a Yellow Ribbon* (49), *Wagonmaster* (50), *Rio Grande* (50), *The Quiet Man** (52), *The Sun Shines Bright* (53), *The Searchers* (56). Produced *This is Cinerama* (52) and *The Best of Cinerama* (63). Received special Academy Award in 1952 for his "innovations and contributions to the art of the motion picture."]

CORMAN, Roger DIR USA. (Detroit April 5, 1926–) A director who made his name as king of the B-pictures in the Fifties (25 in five years) and as a master of Edgar Allan Poe adaptations in the Sixties. Though his scripts are often uneven and the acting rarely memorable, he has brought to the fantasy, horror, science-fiction, and thriller genres a visual power and a sense of poetic violence. In some respects he can be considered the heir to Tod Browning's (*q.v.*) mantle. He was originally a literary agent and author before he began his film career as a producer in 1954.
[DIR: *Five Guns West* (55), *Apache Woman* (55), *The Day the World Ended* (55), *Swamp Women* (55), *The Oklahoma Woman* (55), *Gunslinger* (56), *It Conquered the World* (56), *Not of this Earth* (56) *The Undead* (56), *The She Gods of Shark Reef* (56), *Naked Paradise* (56), *Attack of the Crab Monsters* (56), *Rock All Night* (56), *Teenage Doll* (57), *Carnival Rock* (57), *Sorority Girl* (57), *The Viking Women and the Sea Serpent* (57), *War of the Satellites* (57), *Machine Gun Kelly* (58), *Teenage Cavemen* (58), *I, Mobster/The Mobster* (58), *A Bucket of Blood* (59), *Crybaby Killer* (59), *The Wasp Woman* (59), *Ski Troop Attack* (60), *The House of Usher/The Fall of the House of Usher** (60), *The Little Shop of Horrors* (60), *The Last Woman on Earth* (60), *Creature from the Haunted Sea* (60), *Atlas* (60), *The Pit and the Pendulum* (61), *The Intruder/The Stranger* (61), *The*

Premature Burial (61), *Tales of Terror* (61), *Tower of London* (62), *The Young Racers* (62), *The Raven* (62), *The Terror* (62), *X — the Man with X-Ray Eyes* (63), *The Haunted Palace* (63), *The Secret Invasion* (63), *The Masque of the Red Death* (64), *The Tomb of Ligeia* (64), *The Wild Angels* (66), *The St. Valentine's Day Massacre* (66), *The Trip* (67), *What's in it for Harry* (68), *Bloody Mama* (70), *Von Richthofen and Brown*, and *Gas, or, It Became Necessary to Destroy the World in Order to Save It* (both 71). Also *The Little Guy* (57), *Reception* (57), both uncompleted.
PROD: *The Monster from the Ocean Floor* (54), *The Fast and the Furious* (54), *Highway Dragnet* (54), and most of his own films.]

CORNELIUS, Henry DIR Britain. (South Africa Aug 18, 1913–London May 3, 1958) Former actor and stage producer in Germany, editor in France and Britain, he made a number of documentary shorts in South Africa (40–45) and co-scripted *It Always Rains on Sunday** for Ealing before making a striking directorial debut with *Passport to Pimlico*. However, apart from *Genevieve*, his other films were disappointing; he declined with the other directors of the British comedy school and died relatively young.
DIR (features): *Passport to Pimlico** (48), *The Galloping Major* (51), *Genevieve* (53), *I Am a Camera* (55), *Next to No Time* (58), *Law and Disorder* (58) (completed by Crichton).

COS, Joachim see ROSAS, ENRIQUE

COTTAFAVI, Vittorio DIR Italy. (Modena Jan 30, 1914–) Prolific Italian director of commercial period spectaculars and melodramas who, curiously, has been compared (for his later work) by some critics to Racine. He studied at the Centro Sperimentale, wrote scripts for Alessandri and Vergano from 1939–48, and has been assistant to Blasetti (*q.v.*) and De Sica (*q.v.*).
DIR: *I Nostri Sogni* (43), *Lo Sconosciuto di San Marino* (48), *La Grande Strada* (48), *La Fiamme die non si Spegne* (49), *Una Donna a Ucciso* (51), *Il Boia di Lilla* (52), *Traviata '53* (53), *In Amore si Pecca in Due* (53), *Una Donna Libera* (54), *Avanzi di Galera* (54), *Nel Gorgo del Paccato* (55), *Fiesta Brava* (Sp56), *The Revolt of the Gladiators* (58), *Le*

Legioni di Cleopatra (59), *Messalina* (59), *La Vendetta di Ercole/The Vengeance of Hercules* (60), *Ercole Alla Conquista di Atlantis/Hercules Conquers Atlantis* (61), *I Cento Cavalieri* (Sp64).

COURANT, Curt (also Curtis, Kurt) PHOTOG Germany/France/Britain/USA. (1895?–) One of the best prewar cinematographers. Began his career in Germany after the First World War and gained experience during the classic German period, mainly on period melodramas and spectaculars. Left Germany in 1933, worked in Britain with Hitchcock (*q.v.*) and achieved his best work during the era of French poetic realism with Carné (*q.v.*) and Renoir (*q.v.*).

PHOTOG (notably): *Hamlet** (Ger20) (dir: Sven Gade), *Peter der Grosse* (Ger 22) (dir: Buchowetzki), *Quo Vadis?** (It/Ger24) (dir: Georg Jacoby, d'Annunzio), *Die Frau im Mond* (Ger29) (dir: Fritz Lang), *Perfect Understanding* (Brit33) (dir: Cyril Gardner), *Ciboulette* (Fr33) (dir: Autant-Lara), *The Man Who Knew Too Much** (Brit34) (dir: Hitchcock), *The Iron Duke* (Brit35) (dir: Victor Saville), *Broken Blossoms** (Brit36) (dir: John Brahm), *Le Puritain* (Fr38) (dir: Jeff Musso), *La Bête humaine** (Fr38) (dir: Renoir), *Louise* (Fr39) (dir: Abel Gance), *Le Jour se lève* (Fr39) (dir: Carné), *De Mayerling à Sarajevo* (Fr40) (dir: Ophüls), *Monsieur Verdoux** (USA47) (dir: Chaplin).

COUSTEAU, Jacques-Yves DIR France. (Saint-André June 11, 1910–) French underwater explorer whose documentaries (notably his two full-length films) have revealed the marvels of underwater life to millions of spectators.

DIR (notably): *Par 18 mètres de fond* (43), *Epaves* (45), *Paysages du silence* (47), *Autour d'un récif* (48), *Dauphins et Cétaces* (49), *Carnets de plongée* (50), *Le Monde du silence** (55) (co-dir: Louis Malle), *Le Monde sans soleil/ World Without Sun* (64), and numerous TV documentaries.

*COUTARD, Raoul PHOTOG/DIR France. (1924–) A press photographer (1951-56), he became associated with several new wave directors, notably Truffaut (*q.v.*) and Godard (*q.v.*). He has a sharp, exhilarating style, full of quick pans and hand-held camera shots. Directed his first feature in 1970: *Hoa*

Binh, a remarkably unsentimental portrait of Vietnamese children caught up in a war without meaning.

PHOTOG (notably): for Truffaut *Tirez sur le pianiste** (60), *Jules et Jim** (61), *L'Amour a vingt ans* (62) (one episode), *La Peau douce* (64), *La Mariée etait en noir/The Bride Wore Black* (67); for Jacques Demy, *Lola** (60); for Jacques Baratier, *La Poupée* (62); for Jean Rouch, *Chronique d'un été* (61); for Philippe de Broca, *Un monsieur de compagnie* (64); for Claude de Givray, *Tire-au-flanc 62** (61); for Raoul Lévy, *Je vous salve Mafia* (65); for Tony Richardson, *The Sailor from Gibraltar* (Brit66); for Costa-Gavras, *L'Aveu* (70); and for most of Godard's (*q.v.*) films.

DIR: *Hoa Binh* (70).

COWARD, Noël SCEN/PROD/DIR Britain. (Teddington Dec 16, 1899–) Actor, producer, playwright, one of the bright lights of the English theater and entertainment world in the Twenties and Thirties who has also contributed over a period of years to the cinema. Many of his plays have been filmed, including *Cavalcade**, *Bittersweet*, *Blithe Spirit*. He has always exuded an urbane, sophisticated wit, at times cynical, at others sentimental.

SCEN: *The Queen Was in the Parlor* (27) (dir: Graham Cutts), *Easy Virtue* (27) (dir: Hitchcock), *The Vortex* (27) (dir: Adrian Brunel), *Bittersweet* (33) (dir: Herbert Wilcox), *The Astonished Heart* (50) (dir: Terence Fisher), *Meet Me Tonight* (52) (dir: Anthony Pelissier), and his own DIR/PROD films.

DIR: *In Which We Serve** (42) (co-dir: David Lean).

PROD: David Lean's *This Happy Breed* (44), *Blithe Spirit* (45), *Brief Encounter** (45), and *In Which We Serve** (42).

CREVENA, Alfredo DIR Mexico (?–) Prolific Mexican film maker who made his name in Europe with the violent and self-indulgent *Revolt of the Hanged* (55).

CRICHTON, Charles DIR Britain. (Wallasey Aug 6, 1910–) One of the most distinctive talents of the Ealing school during the Forties and Fifties, responsible for the extremely successful *Hue and Cry, Lavender Hill Mob*, and *The Titfield Thunderbolt*. He was trained as an editor in the Thirties (*Elephant Boy, Things to Come, The Thief of Bagdad,* etc.) and joined Ealing in 1940, where he came under the influence of Michael Balcon (*q.v.*) and Cavalcanti (*q.v.*) and initially directed documentaries.

DIR: *Young Veterans* (41) (short), *For Those in Peril* (44), *Painted Boats* (45), *Dead of Night** (45) (one episode), *Hue and Cry** (47), *Another Shore* (48), *Against the Wind* (48), *Train of Events* (49) (co-dir: Basil Dearden), *Dance Hall* (50), *The Lavender Hill Mob** (51), *Hunted* (52), *The Titfield Thunderbolt* (53), *The Love Lottery* (53), *The Divided Heart* (54), *The Man in the Sky* (56), *Law and Disorder* (58) (begun by Henry Cornelius), *Floods of Fear* (58), *Battle of the Sexes* (59), *The Boy Who Stole a Million* (60), *The Third Secret* (64), *He Who Rides a Tiger* (65), and many episodes of various TV series.

CROMWELL, John DIR USA. (Toledo Dec 23, 1888–) Veteran Hollywood director, formerly stage actor and producer, who since the early days of sound until 1961 was a conscientious craftsman with an ability with actors and who has occasionally (*Caged, The Goddess*) dealt with somewhat unconventional themes.

DIR (notably): *The Dummy* (29), *Tom Sawyer* (30), *Vice Squad* (31), *The World and the Flesh* (31), *Of Human Bondage* (34), *The Fountain* (34), *Jalna* (35), *Little Lord Fauntleroy* (36), *The Prisoner of Zenda* (37), *Algiers* (38) (remake of *Pépé le Moko**), *Abe Lincoln in Illinois* (40), *The Enchanted Cottage* (45), *Anna and the King of Siam* (46), *Dead Reckoning* (47), *Caged* (50), *The Racket* (51), *Hidden Fear* (57), *The Goddess* (58), *A Matter of Morals* (61).

CROSLAND, Alan DIR USA. (New York Aug 1894–Hollywood July 25, 1936) Mediocre director of some 30 films from 1915 to 1936 who merits a footnote in film history as the director of the first film with synchronized music, *Don Juan* (26), and the first film with dialogue, *The Jazz Singer** (27). Died in a car accident.

CRUZE, James (Jens Cruz Bosen) DIR USA. (Ogden March 27, 1884–Hollywood Aug 4, 1942) Prolific Hollywood director, at his best during the silent period when he made at least two important films, the epic western, *The Covered Wagon,* and the quasi-expressionistic *Beggar on Horseback*. [Originally an actor for David Belasco and Thanhouser (*She, Cymbeline, Dr. Jekyll and Mr. Hyde*), he directed his first feature in 1918. He distrusted talking pictures and was never at ease with them.]

DIR (notably): *Too Many Millions* (18), *The Valley of the Giants* (19), *Terror Island* (20), *Crazy to Marry* (21), *One Glorious Day* (22), *The Dictator* (22), *Hollywood* (23), *Ruggles of Red Gap* (23), *To The Ladies* (23), *The Covered Wagon** (23), *The Garden of Weeds* (24), *The City That Never Sleeps* (24), *The Enemy Sex* (24), *Merton of the Movies* (24), *The Fighting Coward* (24), *Beggar on Horseback* (25), *Welcome Home* (25), *The Goose Hangs High* (25), *Pony Express* (25), *Marriage* (26), *Mannequin* (26), *Waiter from the Ritz* (26), *Old Ironsides* (27), *The City Gone Wild* (27), *On to Reno* (27), *The Great Gabbo* (29), *Man's Man* (29), *If I Had a Million* (32) (one episode), *Washington Merry-Go-Round* (33), *David Harum* (34), *Helldorado* (35), *I Cover the Waterfront* (35), *Sutter's Gold* (36), *The Wrong Road* (37), *The Prison Nurse* (38), *Gangs of New York* (38), *Come On, Leathernecks* (38).

CUKOR, George DIR USA. (New York July 7, 1899–) A former Broadway actor and producer (1921–29) who moved to Hollywood with the coming of sound and specialized in literary adaptations, sophisticated comedies, musical comedies, and period films. Though a director without true artistic genius, his films at their best are tasteful, cultivated, urbane, and intelligently directed. To him we owe the memorable *Dinner at Eight, Little Women, Holiday, Born Yesterday, Heller in Pink Tights, The Philadelphia Story,* and *Keeper of the Flame*. He is a lucid, modest, and sincere man who has spoken of the difficulties of his profession: "I spent five weeks supervising the cutting of *Heller in Pink Tights*. It was worth what it was worth, but at least it had a sense of direction. Unfortunately I had to leave; the film was re-edited in a stupid way and everything was destroyed. Legally I had no rights . . . In Europe, a director is taken more seriously. In Hollywood, when you complete a film, everyone believes he can give you his opinion." He began his film career as dialogue director on Richard Wallace's *River of Romance* (29) and Milestone's *All Quiet on the Western Front** (30). DIR: *Grumpy* (30) (co-dir: Cyril Gardner), *The Virtuous Sin* (30) (co-dir: Louis Gasnier), *The Royal Family of Broadway* (30) (co-dir: Cyril Gardner), *Tarnished Lady* (31), *Girls About Town* (31), *One Hour With You* (32) (taken over by Lubitsch), *What Price Hollywood?* (32), *A Bill of Divorcement* (32), *Rockabye* (32), *Our Betters* (32), *Dinner at Eight** (33), *Little Women* (33), *David Copperfield* (34), *Sylvia Scarlett* (35), *Romeo and Juliet* (36), *Camille* (36), *Holiday** (38), *Zaza* (38), *The Women* (39), *Susan and God/The Gay Mrs. Trexel* (40), *The Philadelphia Story** (40), *A Woman's Face* (41), *Two-Faced Woman* (41), *Her Cardboard Lover* (42), *Keeper of the Flame* (43), *Gaslight** (44) (remake), *Winged Victory* (44), *A Double Life* (47), *Edward My Son* (48), *Adam's Rib* (49), *A Life of Her Own* (50), *Born Yesterday** (50), *The Model and the Marriage Broker* (51), *The Marrying Kind* (52), *Pat and Mike* (52), *The Actress* (53), *It Should Happen to You** (54), *A Star is Born* (54) (remake), *Bhowani Junction* (55), *Les Girls* (57), *Wild is the Wind* (57), *Song Without End* (59) (dir: Charles Vidor, completed by Cukor), *Heller in Pink Tights* (60), *Let's Make Love* (60), *The Chapman Report* (61), *My Fair Lady** (64), *Justine* (69). Also directed documentary, *Resistance and Ohm's Law* (43).

CURTIZ, Michael (in Hungary, Mihaly Kertesz; in Germany, Michael Kertesz) DIR Hungary/Austria/USA. (Budapest Dec 24, 1888–Hollywood, April 10, 1962) An absolute professional whose film career spanned fifty years and over 150 films in a variety of genres — thrillers, horrors, westerns, melodramas, and spectacles. He was acting in films before he was twenty, directed his first film in Hungary in 1912, and was an assistant to Sjöström and Stiller. Ebullient, skillful, and painstaking in his approach to often trivial material (and sometimes antipathetic themes like the proslavery *Sante Fe Trail*) he can include many excellent films and numerous commercial successes among his output: *20,000 Years in Sing-Sing, Black Fury, Angels with Dirty Faces, Mildred Pierce, Casablanca, The Mystery of the Wax Museum, The Charge of the Light Brigade, The Adventures of Robin Hood, Captain Blood.* [A director with Warner Brothers for most of his Hollywood years, he was the industry's most consistent commercially successful director. He once said: "I don't see black and white words in a script when I read it. I see action." His best work is in the Thirties and early Forties.

The following filmography is not necessarily complete in the early years. Curtiz acted in Blom's *Atlantis** in Denmark and apparently directed one film there. It is also said he directed a film in Sweden in 1919 with Garbo (who would then have been 14!).]

[DIR *Ma Es Holnap* (Hung12), *Rabelek* (12), *Az Ejszaka Rabjai* (14), *A Tolonc* (14), *Rank Ban* (14), *A Kolesonkert Csecsemok* (14), *Akit Ketten Szeretnek* (15), *A Karthauzi* (16), *Makkhetes* (16), *A Fekete Szivarvany* (16), *As Ezust Kecske* (16), *A Farkas* (16), *Doktor Ur* (16), *A Magyar Fold Ereje* (16), *Zoard Mester* (17), *A Voros Samson* (17), *Az Utolso Hajnal* (17), *Tavasz a Telben* (17), *A Senka Fia* (17), *A Szentjobi Erdo Titka* (17), *A Kuruzslo* (17), *A Halazcsengo* (17), *A Fold Embre* (17), *Az Ezredes* (17), *Egy Krajcar Tortenete* (17), *A Beke Utja* (17), *Az Arendas Zsido* (17), *Tatarjaras* (17), *Az Ordos* (18), *A Napraforgos Holgy* (18), *Lulu* (18), *Judas* (18), *Kilencvenkilenc* (18), *A Csunya Filu* (18), *Alraune* (18), *A Vig Ozvegy/The Merry Widow* (18), *Varazskeringo* (18), *Lu, a Kokott* (Hung18), *Die Dame mit dem Schwarzen Handschuh* (Aust19), *Der Stern von Damaskus* (19), *Die Gottesgeissel* (20), *Die Dame mit den Sonnenblum* (20), *Wege des Schreckens* (21), *Frau Dorothy's Bekenntnis* (21), *Miss Tutti Frutti* (21), *Herzogin Satanella* (21), *Sodom und Gomorrah* (22/23) (two parts), *Die Lawine* (23), *Der Junge Medardus* (23), *Namenlos* (23), *Ein Spiel ums Leben* (24), *General Babka* (24), *The Uncle from Sumatra* (?) (24), *Harun al Raschid* (24), *Die Slavenkönigin/Moon of Israel* (24), *Das Spielzeug von Paris/Red Heels* (25), *Fiaker Nr.13* (Ger26), *Der Goldene Schmetterling/The Road to Happiness* (Ger26), *The Third Degree* (USA26), *A Million Bid* (27), *The Desired Woman* (27), *Good Time Charley* (27), *Tenderloin* (28), *Noah's Ark* (28), *Hearts in Exile* (29), *Glad Rag Doll* (29), *Madonna of Avenue*

A (29), The Gamblers (29), Mammy (30), Under a Texas Moon (30), The Matrimonial Bed (30), Bright Lights (30), A Soldier's Plaything (30), River's End (30), Damon des Meeres (31) (German version of Lloyd Bacon's Moby Dick), God's Gift to Women (31), The Mad Genius (31), The Woman from Monte Carlo (32), Alias the Doctor (32), The Strange Love of Molly Louvain (32), Doctor X (32), Cabin in the Cotton (32) (co-dir: William Keighley), 20,000 Years in Sing-Sing (33), The Mystery of the Wax Museum (33), The Keyhole (33), Private Detective (33), Goodbye Again (33), The Kennel Murder Case (33), Female (33), Mandalay (34), British Agent (34), Jimmy the Gent (34), The Key/High Peril (34), Black Fury (35), The Case of the Curious Bride (35) Little Big Shot (35), Front Page Woman (35), Captain Blood (35), The Walking Dead (36), The Charge of the Light Brigade (36), Stolen Holiday (36), Mountain Justice (37), Kid Galahad/Battling Bellhop (37), The Perpect Specimen (37), Gold is Where You Find It (38), The Adventures of Robin Hood (38) (co-dir: William Keighley), Four Daughters (38), Four's a Crowd (38), Angels with Dirty Faces* (38), Dodge City (39), Sons of Liberty (39) (short), Daughters Courageous (39), Four Wives (39), The Private Lives of Elizabeth and Essex (39), Virginia City (40), The Sea Hawk (40), The Santa Fe Trail (40), The Sea Wolf (41), Dive Bomber (41), Captains of the Clouds (42), Yankee Doodle Dandy (42), Casablanca* (43), Mission to Moscow (43), This is the Army (43), Passage to Marseilles (44), Janie (44), Roughly Speaking (45), Mildred Pierce (45), Night and Day (46), Life with Father (47), The Unsuspected (47), Romance on the High Seas (48), My Dream is Yours (49), Flamingo Road (49), The Lady Takes a Sailor (49), Young Man with a Horn

(50), Bright Leaf (50), The Breaking Point (50), Jim Thorpe — All American/Man of Bronze (51), Force of Arms (51), I'll See You in My Dreams (52), The Story of Will Rogers (52), The Jazz Singer* (52), Trouble Along the Way (53), The Boy from Oklahoma (54), The Egyptian (54), White Christmas (54), Young at Heart (55) (remake of Four Daughters), We're no Angels (55), The Scarlet Hour (56), The Vagabond King (56) (remake), The Best Things in Life Are Free (56), The Helen Morgan Story (57), The Proud Rebel (58), King Creole (58), The Hangman (59), The Man in the Net (59), The Adventures of Huckleberry Finn (60), A Breath of Scandal (60), Francis of Assisi (61), The Comancheros (61).]

CZINNER, Paul DIR Germany/Britain. (Hungary 1890–) Former Hungarian stage producer who emigrated to Austria, then to Germany in 1919, and to Britain in 1933. His many films with his wife Elizabeth Bergner, largely "boulevard" dramas, have a fine sense of psychological characterization, notably in his best film, Nju. Since 1955 he has tended to concentrate on film reproductions of opera and ballet.
DIR: Homo Immanis (Aust19), Der Unmensch (Aust 19), Inferno (Aust20), Nju (Ger24), Der Geiger von Florenz (Ger26), Liebe (Ger26), Dona Juana (Ger27), Fräulein Else (29), The Woman He Scorned (Brit30), Ariane (31), Der Träumende Mund/Dreaming Lips (Ger32), Catherine the Great (Brit34), Escape Me Never (35), As You Like It (36), Dreaming Lips (37) (remake), Stolen Life (39), Don Giovanni (55), The Bolshoi Ballet (57), The Royal Ballet (59), Der Rosenkavalier (62), Romeo and Juliet (66).
SCEN Eifersucht (Ger26) (dir: Karl Grune), Der Träumende Mund (Ger53), (dir: von Baky), and most of his own films.

DAGUERRE, Mandé INVENTOR France. (Cormeilles Nov 18, 1789–Bry-sur-Marne July 10, 1851) A painter and exhibitor of panoramas and an irrepressible businessman who purchased in 1829 the process invented by Nicéphore Niepce (*q.v.*). In 1837, he marketed the daguerreotype (a single copper-plated print involving a 20 minute pose), the patent to which was purchased by the French government in 1839 and placed in the public domain.

D'AMICO, Suso Cecchi *see* CECCHI D'AMICO, SUSO

*DANIELS, William PHOTOG USA. (Cleveland 1895–June 1970) Notable Hollywood cameraman who gained his experience with Triangle and was with MGM for many years. Photographed many of Greta Garbo's most memorable films, from *Flesh and the Devil** (27) to *Ninotchka** (39). Also, notably, for Stroheim, *Foolish Wives** (21), *Greed** (24), *Merry-Go-Round* (22), *The Merry Widow** (25); for George Cukor, *Dinner at Eight** (33), *Camille* (36); for Jules Dassin, *Brute Force** (47), *Naked City** (48); for Anthony Mann, *Winchester 73* (50). In recent years his work has been less interesting: *Von Ryan's Express* (65), *Valley of the Dolls* (67), *Assault on a Queen* (66), *The Maltese Bippy* (69), *Move* (70). Also produced *Robin and the Seven Hoods* (64), *Assault on a Queen* (66).

DAQUIN, Louis DIR France/Austria/Romania/German Democratic Republic. (Calais May 30, 1908–) A talented film maker who began his career as assistant to Abel Gance (*q.v.*), Pierre Chenal (*q.v.*), Julien Duvivier (*q.v.*), and Jean Grémillon (*q.v.*). His films have a sincerity of approach and certain lyrical qualities that are most evident in his first film, *Nous les gosses* (41). "I distrust formulas," he wrote in 1947. "If 'realism' is an end in itself, it doesn't interest me. If it is the 'means' that will allow me to communicate my hopes, feelings, and beliefs, then hurrah for realism." He portrayed the daily life of ordinary people in *Les Frères Bouquinquant* and created his masterpiece with *Le Point du jour* (48), a film that could have led to the development of a fertile French neorealism. After 1950 and his noble *Maître après Dieu* his beliefs led to his being ostracized by the French film industry and he continued his career abroad, notably with a number of remarkable literary adaptations: Maupassant, *Bel-Ami*, Panait Istrati, *The Thistles of the Baragon*, and Balzac, *Les Arrivistes*.

DIR: *Nous les gosses** (41), *Madame et la mort* (43), *Le Voyageur de la Toussaint* (43), *Premier de cordée* (44), *Patrie* (45), *Les Frères Bouquinquant** (47), *Le Point du jour** (48), *Maître après Dieu* (51), *Bel-Ami* (Aust54), *Ciulinii Baraganului** (Rum57), *Trübe Wasser* (GDR60) (from Balzac), *La Foire aux cancres* (Fr63).

DASSIN, Jules DIR USA/Britain/France/Greece. (Middletown Dec 18, 1912–) One of several American film makers driven out of Hollywood by the McCarthy witchhunt of the late Forties who developed a new career in Europe. From 1936 to 1940 he was a stage actor and producer and a radio scriptwriter. He worked for RKO for a year, joined MGM in 1941 to direct shorts, and made his first feature in 1942. After the notable *Brute Force, Naked City*, and *Thieves' Highway* in Hollywood he built an even more successful career in Europe with *Rififi, He Who Must Die*, and *Never on Sunday*. However, he has also made several failures in recent years. In an interview with Chabrol and Truffaut he discussed his approach to the cinema: "What interests me is truth. The cinema is a mass art, the cheapest form of entertainment. A film must be entertaining. You discover in my films a blend of documentary and poetry. This is my poor search for an expression of truth, restricted by *séries noirs.*" He has collaborated on the scripts of many of his films and acted in a few of them.

DIR (shorts): *Artur Rubinstein* (41), *Pablo Casals* (41), *The Tell-Tale Heart* (41), *Survival* (68) (documentary on the Arab-Israeli conflict).

DIR (features): *Nazi Agent* (42), *The Affairs of Martha* (42), *Reunion in Paris* (42), *Young Ideas* (43), *The Canterville Ghost* (44), *A Letter for Evie* (45), *Two Smart People* (46), *Brute Force** (47), *Naked City** (48), *Thieves' Highway** (49), *Night and the City** (Brit50), *Du Rififi chez les hommes** (Fr55), *Celui qui doit mourir** (Fr/It 57), *La Loi/Where the Hot Wind Blows* (Fr/It58), *Pote Tin Kyriaki/Never on Sunday** (Gr59), *Phaedra* (USA/Gr61), *Topkapi/The Light of Day* (USA/Fr63), *10:30 p.m. Summer* (USA/Sp66), *Uptight* (68), *La Promesse de l'aube/Promise at Dawn* (Fr/USA70).

DAVES, Delmer DIR/SCEN USA. (San Francisco July 24, 1904–) At one time an assistant to James Cruze (*The Covered Wagon**), an actor and assistant scriptwriter, 1927–33, a scriptwriter from 1934, and a director from 1943; his films are extremely variable in quality, though often humanistic. He brought his feeling for dramatic plot to thrillers (*Dark Passage*) and especially to several notable westerns: *Broken Arrow, The Last Wagon, 3:10 to Yuma, Cowboy,* and *The Hanging Tree.*

[SCEN (notably): *The Petrified Forest* (36) (dir:Archie Mayo), *The Go-Getter* (37) (dir: Busby Berkeley), *Love Affair* (39) (dir: Leo McCarey) and most of his own films.

DIR: *Destination Tokyo* (43), *The Very Thought of You* (44), *Hollywood Canteen* (44), *Pride of the Marines* (45), *The Red House* (47), *Dark Passage* (47), *To the Victor* (48), *Task Force* (49), *A Kiss in the Dark* (49), *Broken Arrow* (50), *Bird of Paradise* (51), *Return of the Texan* (52), *The Treasure of the Golden Condor* (53), *Never Let Me Go* (53), *Demetrius and the Gladiators* (53), *Drum Beat* (54), *Jubal* (56), *The Last Wagon* (56), *3:10 to Yuma** (57), *Kings Go Forth* (58), *Cowboy* (58), *The Badlanders* (58), *The Hanging Tree* (59), *A Summer Place* (60), *Parrish* (60), *Susan Slade* (61), *Rome Adventure* (62), *Spencer's Mountain* (63), *Youngblood Hawke* (64), *The Battle of Villa Fiorita* (65).]

*DEARDEN, Basil DIR Britain. (Westcliff Jan 1, 1911–London March 23, 1971) Former actor and stage manager and an assistant on many of the George Formby and Will Hay comedies, he became a scriptwriter with Ealing and developed under Cavalcanti's (*q.v.*) tutelage into a capable director specializing in the handling of contemporary social issues, notably in *The Captive Heart* (46), *Frieda* (47), *The Blue Lamp* (49), *The Pool of London* (50), *Sapphire* (59), *I Believe in You* (51), *Violent Playground* (58), *Victim* (61). Most of his films since 1951 were produced by Michael Relph, who shares producer-director-writer credits on many of them. He died in a car crash in 1971.

DIR: *The Black Sheep of Whitehall* (41) (co-dir: Will Hay), *The Goose Steps Out* (42) (co-dir: Will Hay), *My Learned Friend* (43) (co-dir: Will Hay), *The Bells Go Down* (43), *The Halfway House* (44), *They Came to a City* (44), *Dead of Night** (45) (one episode), *The Captive Heart* (46), *Frieda* (47), *Saraband for Dead Lovers* (48), *Train of Events* (49) (co-dir: Charles Crichton), *The Blue Lamp* (49), *Cage of Gold* (50), *Pool of London* (50), *I Believe in You* (51), *The Gentle Gunman* (52), *The Square Ring* (53), *The Rainbow Jacket* (54), *Out of the Clouds* (54), *The Ship That Died of Shame* (55), *Who Done it?* (56), *The Smallest Show on Earth* (57), *Violent Playground* (58), *Sapphire* (59), *The League of Gentlemen* (60), *Man in the Moon* (60), *The Secret Partner* (61), *Victim* (61), *All Night Long* (62), *Life for Ruth/Walk in the Shadow* (62), *The Mind Benders* (63), *A Place to Go* (63), *Woman of Straw* (64), *Masquerade* (64), *Khartoum* (66), *Only When I Larf* (67), *The Assassination Bureau* (68), *The Man Who Haunted Himself* (70).

D'EAUBONNE, Jean *see* EAUBONNE, JEAN D'

DE BARONCELLI, Jacques *see* BARONCELLI, JACQUES DE

DEBRIE, André INVENTOR France. (Paris Jan 28, 1891–) The most famous French developer and manufacturer of film equipment, responsible for: the Parvo camera (1908); the Matipo printer, the universal stand, and the ultra-high-speed camera (1920–25); three interlocked cameras, with Abel Gance (1926); the Truca equipment (1936); mobile laboratory for instantaneous recording and projection of TV programs on 16mm (1949).

DE BROCA, Philippe see BROCA, PHILIPPE DE

DECAE, Henry PHOTOG France. (Saint-Denis July 31, 1915–) A major contributor to the *nouvelle vague* who began his career as an amateur and a director of short films (1941–44) and who developed later into a specialist, both in location camerawork using high-speed film (*Le Silence de la mer, Le Beau Serge, Les 400 Coups*) and in sensual, languorous photography (*Les Enfants terribles, Les Amants*) — at its best when he shoots in color (*La Ronde, Viva Maria, A double tour*).
PHOTOG (notably): for Melville, *Le Silence de la mer** (47), *Les Enfants terribles* (49), *Bob le Flambeur* (55), *Léon Morin, prêtre** (61), *L'Aîne des Ferchaux* (63), *Le Samourai* (67), *Le Cercle rouge* (70); for Louis Malle, *Ascenseur pour l'échafaud* (57), *Les Amants** (58), *Vie Privée* (61), *Viva Maria* (65), *Le Voleur* (66); for Chabrol, *Le Beau Serge** (58), *Les Cousins** (59), *A double tour* (59), *Les Bonnes femmes** (59); for Truffaut, *Les 400 Coups** (59); for René Clément, *Plein soleil* (59), *Che Joia Vivere* (61), *Le Jour et l'heure* (63), *Les Félins* (63); for Serge Bourgignon *Les Dimanches de Ville-d'Avray* (62); for Jacques Baratier, *Dragées au poivre* (63); [for Vadim, *La Ronde** (64); for Georges Rouquier, *S.O.S. Noronha* (57); for Duvivier, *Diaboliquement vôtre* (67); for Anatole Litvak, *The Night of the Generals* (66); and the Godard, Demy, and Vadim episodes in *Les Septs péchés capitaux* (62); for Henri Verneuil, *The Sicilian Clan* (69); and, less successfully, *The Only Game in Town* (USA70), *Hello-Goodbye* (USA70).]

DECOIN, Henri DIR France. (Paris March 18, 1896–1969) Prolific and conventional director who was originally a journalist, then a scriptwriter and assistant director. DIR (notably): *Abus de confiance* (37), *Premier rendez-vous* (41), *Les Inconus de la maison* (42), *La Fille de diable* (46), *Entre onze heures et minuit* (48), *La Vérité sur Bébé Donge* (52), *Les Amants de Tolède* (53), *Razzia sur chnouf* (55), *Charmants garçons* (57), *La Chatte* (58).

DEGELIN, Emile DIR Belgium. (Diest July 16, 1926–) Good documentary film maker — e.g., *Dock* (55), *Faits divers* (56) — who was less at ease with his first fiction feature, *Si le vent te fait peur* (59).

DE HAAS, Max DIR Netherlands. (Amsterdam Sept 12, 1903–) One of the best Dutch documentary directors who at the start of his career made the ironic and truculent masterpiece, *Ballad of the Top Hat** (36). Also, notably, *LO-LKP* (48), *Men and Microbes* (51), *Maskerage* (52).

DEHNI, Salah DIR Syria. (Deraa Jan 15, 1929–) A former IDHEC (Paris) student who made in Syria in 1958 an interesting documentary on erosion.

DEKEUKELEIRE, Charles DIR Belgium. (Ixelles Feb 27, 1905–) One of the best Belgian documentary film makers, he began in the avant-garde but eventually had to make sponsored films.
DIR (notably): *Combat de boxe* (27), *Impatience* (28), *Flamme blanche* (28), *Histoire de Lourdes* (32), *Terres brulées* (Congo34), *Le Mauvais Oeil* (38), *Au service des prisonniers* (42), *Le Fondateur* (47), *Maisons* (48), *L'Espace d'une vie* (49).

DELANNOY, Jean DIR France. (Noisy-le-Sec Jan 12, 1908–) A prolific director well versed in the traditions of his craft, he has made over 70 films since 1933 and has occasionally achieved real success: *L'Eternel retour, La Symphonie pastorale, Dieu a besoin des hommes*.
DIR (notably): *Paris Deauville* (35), *Pontcarral, colonel d'Empire* (42), *L'Eternel retour** (43), *La Symphonie pastorale* (46), *Les Jeux sont faits* (47), *Dieu a besoin des hommes* (49), *Le Garçon sauvage* (51), *Chiens perdus sans collier* (55), *Notre Dame de Paris* (56), *Maigret tend un piège* (57), *La Princesse de Clèves* (60), *Venus impériale* (62),

Les Amitiés particulières (64), *Le Soleil des voyous* (67), *La Peau de torpedo* (70).

*DE LAURENTIIS, Dino PROD Italy. (1919–) Major Italian producer who ran Ponti-De Laurentiis with Carlo Ponti (*q.v.*) from 1950–57. He has produced several of the major postwar Italian commercial and artistic successes: *Bitter Rice*, Europe 51*, War and Peace*, Gold of Naples, La Strada*, Nights of Cabiria*, The Bible . . . In the Beginning, The Stranger* (Visconti), *Barbarella, Waterloo.*

*DELERUE, Georges MUS France. (Roubaix 1925–) Wide-ranging French composer associated with the *nouvelle vague*, he has a liking for lyrically atmospheric, melancholy themes but at his best can deepen a film's psychological characterizations. He also works for theater, radio, and TV and often conducts.
MUS (notably): for Agnès Varda, *Du côté de la côte, L'Opéra Mouffe;* for Resnais, *Hiroshima, mon amour** (co-mus: Fusco); for Truffaut, *Tirez sur le pianiste*, Jules et Jim*, La Peau douce;* for Godard, *Le Mépris*;* for Broca, *Les Jeux de l'amour, Le Farceur, L'Amant de cinq jours*, Cartouche, Un monsieur de compagnie, Les Tribulations d'un Chinoise en Chine, Le Roi de coeur;* for Kast, *Le Bel âge;* for Colpi, *Une aussi longue absence;* for Melville, *L'Aîné des Ferchaux;* for Alain Robbe-Grillet, *L'Immortelle;* for Malle, *Viva Maria;* for Jean-Louis Richard, *Mata Hari* (64); for Claude Berri, *Le Vieil homme et l'enfant* (66); for Jean Herman, *Le Dimanche de la vie* (68); for Jack Clayton, *The Pumpkin Eater;* for Fred Zinnemann, *A Man for All Seasons;* for Kevin Billington, *Interlude* (68); for Dassin, *La Promesse de l'aube* (70).

DELLUC, Louis DIR/SCEN France. (Cadouin Oct 14, 1890–Paris March 22, 1924) One of the most significant influences on the development of the French cinema — as film maker and critic, proselytizer and founder of film societies. He died too young to reach his full measure as a director but was a remarkable scriptwriter, using, in Dulac's *La Fête espagnole* and his own *Fièvre* and *La Femme de nulle part,* unity of time and place, atmosphere, flashbacks, and psychological characterizations. He was editor of *Le Film,* 1917–19; critic for *Paris-Midi,* 1918–23; founder and editor of *Cinéa,* 1921–23; the author of *Cinéma et Cie,* 1919, *Photogénie* 1920, *La Jungle du cinéma* and *Charlot* 1920, *Drames de cinéma* 1923, and several novels. Around him formed the French impressionist school (sometimes called "the first avant-garde") of Abel Gance (*q.v.*), L'Herbier (*q.v.*), Germaine Dulac (*q.v.*), and Jean Epstein (*q.v.*). Moussinac said "he worked with a relentlessness that he carefully hid." His writings sparkle with meaningful aphorisms: "The masters of the screen are those who speak to the masses." "The mass of the cinema is the entire universe." "The great power of this stumbling art is that it is popular. The cinema is everywhere. Theaters have been built in every country, films have been made throughout the world. It is the best means for people to communicate." "All the time life is creating cinema, it is time the camera created life." "Existing scripts are sad. Have you nothing to say? Take a walk, look around, dream. The streets, subways, street cars, shops are full of a thousand original and powerful comedies to challenge your talent, people of talent." "Art would be pointless if everyone were capable of consciously savoring each passing moment." "Taken from life: this doesn't necessarily mean it is true." "Film, like music, moves and is moving." "The purpose of art is to allow one soul to communicate with another."
SCEN: *La Fête espagnole** (19) (dir: Germaine Dulac), *Le Train sans yeux* (26) (dir: Cavalcanti) and all his own films.
DIR: *Fumée noire* (20) (co-dir: René Coiffart), *L'Americain ou le Chemin d'Ernoa* (20), *Le Tonnere* (20) (short), *Le Silence* (20), *Fièvre** (21), *La Femme de nulle part** (22), *L'Inondation* (24).

DEMARE, Lucas DIR Argentina. (Buenos Aires July 14, 1910–) One of the best Argentinian directors of the Forties; though his films are a little unpolished, they have an authentic national character, typically in *Guerra des Gauchos** (42), *Pampa Barbare* (45), *La Zafra* (58).

DEMILLE, Cecil Blount DIR/PROD USA. (Ashfield Aug 12, 1881–Hollywood Jan 21, 1959) Hollywood personified, a marvelous story teller who made his name with a series of DeMille spectaculars, full of violence, sex, and pseudo religion, but who also excelled in westerns, sophisticated comedies, and sex dramas. More cultured than the other Hollywood founders, he found continuing commercial success over some 60 years by exploiting his formula of sex, tempered by morality and the Bible. He was, in himself, the "Greatest Show on Earth" and epitomized until his death (at almost 80) the world-wide supremacy of the American film industry. His films are a blend of striking visual design and a taste for "sophistication," the most famous of them undoubtedly being his biblical spectaculars: *The Ten Commandments* (23 & 56), *The King of Kings* (27), *The Sign of the Cross* (32), and *Samson and Delilah* (49). His other period films are more uneven and though Delluc admired *Joan the Woman* (17), DeMille often edged toward absurdity in *Cleopatra* (34), *The Crusades* (35), and *The Volga Boatman* (26). In the Twenties he made a notable series of comedies of manners — e.g., *Male and Female, Forbidden Fruit,* and *Fool's Paradise* — that often included sumptuously staged dance numbers. His *The Godless Girl* (29) includes criticism of the penitentiary system. It is also too often forgotten that he was a masterly director of westerns from his early days (*The Squaw Man, The Virginian*) until the latter part of his career (*Unconquered*). His masterpiece in this genre, *Union Pacific,* is an effervescent portrait of the period in which the railways opened up the West.

After experience as a stage producer and playwright (with his brother William) he joined Jesse Lasky as a director in Hollywood in 1913 and later worked for Sam Goldwyn. Louis Delluc wrote of him in 1922: "He makes me think of a manufacturer of luxurious automobiles. When a Rolls, a Cadillac, a Hispano is built, it is likely that they have claim to no other aim but to please that sacred cow, the public, and to give it what it wants. But it is equally likely that this servility and self-effacement strikes a blow at imagination and inspiration . . . Admirably equipped, surrounded by masterly craftsmen, armed with a remarkable, disciplined, and photogenic acting troupe, he searches out the best with a kind of unknowing audacity, a quasi-violent patience, a fecund persistence, in which is laid out a shining, comfortable, beautiful,

and well-oiled future." Everything was not always beautiful in many of the films that he later directed but most of them have a strength that was not to be found in Hollywood after his death.

DIR: *The Squaw Man* (13), *The Virginian* (14), *The Call of the North* (14), *Brewster's Millions* (14), *The Man from Home* (14), *The Rose of the Rancho* (14), *The Girl of the Golden West* (14), *The Warrens of Virginia* (15), *The Unafraid* (15), *The Captive* (15), *Wild Goose Chase* (15), *The Arab* (15), *Chimmie Fadden* (15), *Kindling* (15), *The Cheat** (15), *Carmen** (15), *Temptation* (15), *Maria Rosa* (16), *The Trail of the Lonesome Pine* (16), *The Heart of Nora Flynn* (16), *The Dream Girl* (16), *Joan the Woman** (17), *A Romance of the Redwoods* (17), *The Little American* (17), *The Woman God Forgot* (17), *The Devil Stone* (17), *Old Wives for New* (18), *The Whispering Chorus* (18), *We Can't Have Everything* (18), *Till I Come Back to You* (18), *The Squaw Man* (19) (remake), *Don't Change Your Husband* (19), *For Better, For Worse* (19), *Male and Female* (19), *Why Change Your Wife?* (20), *Something to Think About* (20), *Forbidden Fruit* (21), *The Affairs of Anatol* (21), *Fool's Paradise* (21), *Saturday Night* (22), *Manslaughter* (22), *Adam's Rib* (23), *The Ten Commandments** (23), *Triumph* (24), *The Golden Bed* (25), *The Road to Yesterday* (25), *The Volga Boatmen* (26), *The King of Kings* (27), *Chicago* (28), *The Godless Girl* (29), *Dynamite* (29), *Madame Satan* (30), *The Squaw Man* (31) (remake), *The Sign of the Cross* (32), *This Day and Age* (32), *Four Frightened People* (33), *Cleopatra** (34), *The Crusades* (35), *The Plainsman* (38), *The Buccaneer* (38), *Union Pacific** (39), *Northwest Mounted Police* (40), *Reap the Wild Wind* (42), *The Story of Dr. Wassel* (44), *Unconquered* (47), *Samson and Delilah* (49), *The Greatest Show on Earth* (52), *The Ten Commandments** (56).

PROD: *Silence* (26) (dir: Rupert Julian), *The Buccaneer* (58) (dir: Anthony Quinn), and most of his own films.

*DE MILLE, William Churchill SCEN/DIR/PROD USA. (Washington June 25, 1878– Hollywood March 18, 1955) Elder brother of Cecil B. (but spelled his name de Mille rather than DeMille), active for many years as a playwright, joined Lasky at the same time as his brother as head of the scenario department and as a director. He wrote many scripts for his brother between 1914–20. His work as a director is less well known than that of his brother and most of his films have been lost. He developed a less flamboyant style than Cecil's — perceptive, delicate, and full of psychological nuances. He also produced several of his brother's films, including *Carmen** and *Why Change Your Wife?*, and wrote Hal Roach's *Captain Fury* (39).

DIR (notably): *Miss Lulu Bett* (21), *What Every Woman Knows* (21), *Nice People* (22), *The Marriage Maker* (23), *Only 38* (23), *Craig's Wife* (28), *The Emperor Jones* (33).

*DEMY, Jacques DIR France/USA. (Pont-Château (Loire Atlantique) June 5, 1931–) His films have a fragile, poignant, bittersweet flavor with a characteristic quality of nostalgia, often reminiscent of French poetic realism and of Max Ophüls (*q.v.*). He began his career working with cartoonist Paul Grimault and as assistant to Georges Rouquier, then directed several short films before establishing an international reputation with *Lola* (60), a gentle, gay film and a kind of musical without songs and dances. It was on this film that he established a continuing, fertile collaboration with the designer Bernard Evein (*q.v.*). After *La Baie des anges,* he directed the revolutionary musical, *The Umbrellas of Cherbourg* an audaciously inventive and uninhibited work, splendidly designed in glowing colors. His later films have been less interesting but are noteworthy for his preoccupation with design and decoration and his recurrent themes: "My idea is to make fifty films that will be linked together and that will mutually illuminate each other's meaning through shared characters." He sees the film largely as spectacle and his plots (he writes his own scripts) have a distinctly melodramatic flavor.

ASSIST: to Grimault on commercials (51); to Georges Rouquier, *Lourdes et ses miracles* (54), *Honegger* (55), *SOS Noronha* (57).

DIR (shorts): *Le Sabotier du val de Loire* (55), *Le Bel indifférent* (57), *Musée Grévin* (58) (co-dir: Jean Masson), *La Mer et l'Enfant* (59) (co-dir: Jean Masson), *Ars* (59).

DIR (features): *Lola** (60), *Les Sept péchés capitaux* (62) (one episode), *La Baie des anges* (62), *Les Parapluies de Cherbourg** (64), *Les Demoiselles de Rochefort* (66), *Model Shop* (USA68), *Peau d'âne* (70).

DENOLA, Georges DIR France. (188?–circa 1950) A film pioneer who directed numerous literary adaptations (Balzac, Eugène Sue, Hector Malot, Jules Marey, Octave Feuillet, etc.) for Pathé between 1905–14, including an exceptional *Rocambole* (13–14), in episodes.

*DEREN, Maya DIR USA. (1908–1961) Perhaps the most important figure in the postwar development of the personal, independent film in the USA, she defined her approach in this way: "The great art expressions will come later, as they always have, and they will be dedicated, again, to the *agony* and the *experience* rather than the incident." Her first films, *Meshes of the Afternoon* (43) and *At Land* (44), strikingly individual, injected a new vitality into the independent American cinema. Her later films, less symbolic, but equally personal, are experiments in space and time, explorations of movement, rhythm, and form in which she developed a kind of cine-choreography that eventually reached the commercial screens in, e.g., *West Side Story**. She was an effusive and persuasive proselytizer for a personal cinema, lectured widely, wrote many articles, and is the author of an important book on esthetics, *An Anagram of Ideas on Art, Form, and Film,* 1946.

DIR: *Meshes of the Afternoon** (43) (co-dir: Alexander Hammid), *The Witches Cradle* (43), *At Land** (44), *A Study in Choreography for the Camera* (45), *Ritual in Transfigured Time* (46), *Meditation on Violence* (48), *The Very Eye of Night* (59).

DE ROBERTIS, Francesco DIR Italy. (Foggia Sept 16, 1902–Rome Feb 3, 1959) Former marine officer who directed the semidocumentary *SOS 103* and gave Rossellini the opportunity to direct his first major feature, *La Nave bianca* (41). He organized the Fascist Republic's film industry in Venice (43–45) and later directed several mediocre films.

DE ROCHEMONT, Louis PROD USA. (Boston Jan 13, 1899–) The originator and executive producer of *The March of Time* series (35–43) who later became one of the leading influences on postwar American semidocumentary films as the producer of works by Henry Hathaway (*The House on 92nd Street, Call Northside 777*) and Kazan (*Boomerang**) as well as of *Lost Boundaries* (49) and *Martin Luther* (53). He later became a producer for Cinerama and Cinemiracle. (*See also:* MARK HELLINGER)

DE SANTIS, Giuseppe DIR Italy. (Fondi Feb 11, 1917–) The best film maker of the second neorealist period, with a forceful, baroque style, dedicated and deeply concerned with social and human realities. He studied at the Centro Sperimentale and from 1940–44 was an excellent film critic. He wrote scripts and was Visconti's assistant on *Ossessione* (42) before directing his first feature in 1947. His *Bitter Rice* was a worldwide commercial success but is inferior to his masterpieces, *Caccia Tragica* and *Rome, Ore 11*. As a young critic, he wrote in 1941: "We are fighting for the dawn of an awareness that will lead towards realism. We have learned to scan the unlimited horizons of an imagination that is forever opposed to the miserable conditions of man, his solitude, his difficulties in escaping, and which finds, even in escapism, the imposing strength of reciprocal human communication. Our sympathies are joined always with a cinema that breathes the intimate essence of reality through historical education. Art is the reincarnation of history. The level of civilization cannot be separated from the land that gave birth to it." In this way, during a Fascist regime, he defined the basic tenets of what was to become neorealism and of which he was to become one of the masters. However, his work in the Fifties was less brilliant: he often encountered censorship problems and could not resist accepting new productions – not always with success.
SCENE:Visconti's *Ossessione** (42), Rossellini's *Desiderio** (43), Vergano's *Il Sole Sorge Ancora** (46), and all his own films.
ASSIST: to Visconti, *Ossessione** (42); to Vergano, *Il Sole Sorge Ancora** (46).
DIR: *Caccia Tragica** (47), *Riso Amaro** (49), *Non C'è Pace tra gli Ulivi** (50), *Roma, Ore 11** (51), *Un Marito per Anna Zaccheo/A Husband for Anna* (53), *Giorni d'Amore* (54), *Uomini e*

Lupi/Men and Wolves (56), *Cesta Duga Godinu Dana** (Yugos58), *La Garçonnière* (60), *Italiani brava gente* (USSR/It64).

DE SETA, Vittorio DIR Italy. (Palerma Oct 15, 1923–) Dedicated Sicilian-born director, who made independent documentaries before directing his first feature, the significant *Banditi a Orgosolo*. He writes and photographs all his own films.
DIR (shorts): *Isole de Fucco* (54), *Lu Tempu di li Pisci Spata* (54), *Sulfatara* (55), *Pasqua in Sicilia* (55), *Contadini del Mare* (56), *Parabolo d'Oro* (56), *Pescherecci* (57), *Pastori di Orgosolo* (58), *Un Giorno in Barbagia* (58), *I Dimenticati* (59).
DIR (features): *Banditi a Orgosolo** (61), *Un Uomo a Metà/Almost a Man* (65), *L'Invitata* (70).

DE SICA, Vittorio DIR Italy. (Sora July 7, 1902–) In association with Zavattini (*q.v.*), he played a major role in the development of neorealism 1944–52, creating the often imitated *Bicycle Thieves* and a vast tableau of life in postwar Italy in *Sciuscià, Umberto D, Miracle in Milan,* and, later, in *Il Tetto*. He was well known in Italy in the Thirties as an actor (notably in several of the films of Mario Camerini), directed his first film in 1939, and made several more films before creating his first significant film, *Sciuscià* (46). His style failed to evolve in the Fifties and his work fell into obscurity. He returned to acting, largely in mediocre films, contributed to the vulgarization of neorealism by producing Comencini's *Bread, Love, and Dreams* and resumed directing only in 1960 with *Two Women,* whose commercial success does not outweigh its faults. His films in the Sixties have been slick pastiches, often featuring Sophia Loren; most of them are sex comedies or romantic melodramas. Nonetheless, his earlier work still merits André Bazin's words of 1954: "To explain De Sica, we must go back to the source of his art, namely his tenderness, his love. The quality shared in common by *Miracle in Milan* and *Bicycle Thieves* is the author's inexhaustible love of his characters." "His Neopolitan graciousness becomes, by virtue of the cinema, the greatest love message our period has had the good fortune to hear since Chaplin. I have used the word love. I

should rather have said poetry. Poetry is but the active and creative form of love, its projection into the world."
DIR: *Rose scarlatte* (39) (co-dir: Giuseppe Amato), *Maddaleno zero in condotta* (40), *Teresa Venerdi* (41), *Un Garibaldino al Convento* (42), *I Bambini ci Guardino* (43), *La Porta del Cielo* (44), *Sciuscià* (46), *Ladri di Biciclette/Bicyle Thieves* (49), *Miracolo a Milano* (50), *Umberto D* (52), *Stazione Termini/Indiscretion* (53), *L'Oro di Napoli* (54), *Il Tetto* (55), *La Ciociaria/Two Women* (60), *Il Giudizio Universale* (61), *Boccaccio 70* (61) (one episode), *I Sequestrati di Altona* (It/Fr62), *Il Boom* (63), *Ieri, Oggi, Domani/Yesterday, Today, and Tomorrow* (It/Fr63), *Matrimonio all'Italiana* (It/Fr64), *Un monde nouveau* (Fr65), *Caccia alla Volpe/After the Fox* (65), *La Streghe/The Witches* (It/Fr66) (one episode), *Woman Times Seven* (USA/Fr67), *Gli Amanti/A Place for Lovers* (It/Fr68), *I Girasoli/Sunflower* (It/Fr69), *Le Coppie* (70) (episode), *Il Giardino dei Finz Contini* (71).

DESLAW, Eugène DIR France. (Kiev Dec 8, 1900–) An outstanding Russian-born member of the French avant-garde from 1925, originally interested in abstract films and constructivism, who contributed to the movement's development into documentary.
DIR: *La Marche des machines* (28), *Montparnasse* (29), *La Nuit électrique* (30), *Le Monde en parade* (31), *Négatifs* (32) (co-dir: Jean Darroy), *La Cité universitaire de Paris* (33).

DEVILLE, Michel DIR France. (Boulogne-sur-Mer April 13, 1931–) A specialist in lighthearted, romantic, situation comedies, often elegant but always insubstantial. He was Henri Decoin's (*q.v.*) assistant on 13 films before making his first feature alone in 1960.
DIR: *Une balle dans le canon* (58) (co-dir: C. Gérard), *Ce soir ou jamais* (60), *Adorable menteuse* (61), *A cause, à cause d'une femme* (62), *L'Appartement des filles* (63), *Lucky Jo* (64), *On a volé la Joconde* (66), *Martin Soldat* (66), *Benjamin* (67), *Bye, Bye, Barbara* (68), *L'Ours et la poupée* (69).

DIAMANT-BERGER, Henri PROD/DIR France. (Paris June 9, 1895–) He has directed and/or produced over 100 films since 1920, including *Les Trois Mousquetaires* (21) and *Monsieur Fabre* (51); in 1918 he published *Le Cinéma,* one of the first meaningful monographs on the seventh art.

*DICKINSON, Thorold DIR Britain. (Bristol Nov 16, 1903–) A major talent of the British cinema who has, unfortunately, directed relatively few fiction films. He worked (since 1925) as assistant, editor, scriptwriter, and producer before establishing his reputation as a director with the remarkable *Gaslight* — a film whose negative was destroyed to make way for the American remake. As head of the Army Kinematograph Service film unit during the war he produced 17 short documentaries. After the semi-documentary thriller on the dangers of careless talk during war, *The Next of Kin* (42) — a film that anticipated the Louis de Rochemont (*q.v.*) films in the USA — and *Men of Two Worlds* (46), he created the stylized, brilliantly atmospheric *The Queen of Spades* (49) from the Pushkin story. In Israel in 1955 he made the semidocumentary *Hill 24 Doesn't Answer.* He was head of the United Nations Film Service from 1956–60 and was professor of cinema at the Slade School of Fine Art, University College, London, until 1971. At the UN he wrote and supervised the feature-length documentary, *Power Among Men* (58).
DIR: *The High Command* (37), *Spanish ABC* (38) (documentary), *The Arsenal Stadium Mystery* (39), *Gaslight* (40), *Westward Ho!* (40) (short), *Miss Grant Goes to the Door* (40) (short), *Yesterday is Over Your Shoulder* (40) (short), *The Prime Minister* (41), *The Next of Kin* (42), *Men of Two Worlds* (46), *The Queen of Spades* (49), *Secret People* (52), *Hagiva/Hill 24 Doesn't Answer* (Israel55).

DICKSON, William Kennedy Laurie INVENTOR/DIR USA. (Britain 1860–1937) The inventor of perforated 35mm film around 1890 and more responsible for the development of the Kinetoscope and ensuing cinematographic devices patented by Edison (*q.v.*) than Edison himself, who took little active interest in his work after his initial ideas. He also directed the first Kinetoscope films in 1893–94 and from 1895–1900 those of American Biograph, of which he was one of the founders.

63

DIETERLE, William (Wilhelm) DIR USA/
Germany. (Ludwigshafen July 15, 1893–
) Originally an actor with Max Rein-
hardt (*q.v.*) in Berlin, he was brought
into films by E. A. Dupont (*q.v.*) and directed his first film in 1923, *Der Mensch
am Wege*. After several more films in
Germany, he moved to Hollywood in
1931 and again collaborated with Max
Reinhardt on *A Midsummer Night's
Dream** (35). He established a reputation in the late Thirties with his series
of "biographical" films: *The Story of
Louis Pasteur* (35), *The Life of Emile
Zola** (37), *Juarez* (39), *Dr. Ehrlich's
Magic Bullet* (40). During this period
he also directed several other interesting
films — *Satan Met a Lady** (36), *Blockade* (38), *The Hunchback of Notre
Dame* (40), *All That Money Can Buy*
(40), *Kismet* (44) — before descending
into routine, facile melodramas. He returned to Germany in 1958 and has
directed several films there.

DINESEN, Robert DIR Denmark. (Copenhagen Oct 23, 1874–circa 1940) Good
director during the most creative period
of the Danish cinema, 1910–20. After
making his screen debut alongside Asta
Nielsen, he directed a considerable number of society dramas and thrillers with
his friends Psilander, Olaf Fönss, Lily
Beck, Gunnar Tolnaes, etc. His best film
is *De Fire diaevle/The Four Devils*
(11).

DISNEY, Walt ANIM/PROD USA. (Chicago Dec 5, 1901–Dec 15, 1966) This
most famous of cartoon producers deserves neither the fulsome praise showered on him by critics in the Thirties
nor the universal opprobrium of the
Fifties. He made enormous technical and
esthetic contributions to the development
of animation, 1927–37, and was usually
the first to adapt any technical advance to
the cartoon field: sound, color, stereo-
phony, multiplanar photography, and
later, CinemaScope. [He began his career
as a commercial artist and transferred
to cartoon production in the early Twenties. With the money from his first films
he moved to Hollywood with his collaborator Ub Iwerks (*q.v.*) and made
several films in the *Alice in Cartoonland* series and the *Oswald the Rabbit*
series.] In 1927 he introduced Mortimer
Mouse who, after two films, grew into
the famous *Mickey Mouse** series in

whose animation Ub Iwerks seems to
have played a major role. Later, Disney
introduced a whole menagerie of anthropomorphic characters, including Donald Duck, Pluto, Minnie Mouse, and
Goofy, plus the more free-ranging *Silly
Symphonies** series. His shorts in the
Thirties have a remarkable sense of
rhythm, of visual comedy, of unconventional technical effects and of sound as
an integrated element. They are true
works of the imagination and, although
the product of collective endeavor, carry
the mark of Disney's hand. However,
after the international success of his first
feature, Disney increasingly turned his
attention to administration and supervision of his studio's many side lines: the
copyright reproduction of his characters
on everything from soap to children's
furniture, a TV series, Disneyland, a ski
resort, and Disney World in Florida. His
films, made on an assembly line, ceased
to reflect any real personality and after
the artistic failure of *Fantasia,* Disney
no longer took an interest in creation.
On the later films he is little more than
the credited executive producer and the
films, for all their technical expertise, became largely insipid, cliché-ridden, and
sentimental without true sentiment. In
1948, he produced the first of the gimmicky series of nature documentaries and
in 1953, *The Living Desert*. He began
making live-action fiction features in
1950 with *Treasure Island*, and these
have largely dominated the Disney Studios production since. The familiar Disney style has continued to be evident in
the output of the studios since Walt Disney's death in 1966.
[The following filmography is not complete: a complete Disney filmography
has never been published. It is in three
parts: "animated shorts," "animated features," and "features" (live-action documentaries and fiction films). As indicated
above, Disney played a more important
creative role in the earlier films than the
later but they have been included here
for the sake of convenience. Directors
are not given, but James Algar (*q.v.*)
was responsible for many of the documentaries and Robert Stevenson for many
of the fiction films.]
ANIM (shorts): *Little Red Riding Hood*
(23), *Jack the Giant Killer* (23), *The
Town Musician of Bremen* (23), *The
Three Bears* (23), *Goldilocks* (23), *Alice
in Cartoonland* series (24–25) *Oswald*

the *Rabbit* series (25–26) (26 films), *Plane Crazy* (27), *Galloping Gaucho* (28), *Steamboat Willie* (28), *The Barn Dance* (28), *Skeleton Dance* (29), *Carnival Kid* (29), *Mickey's Follies* (29), *Summer* (30), *Autumn* (30), *The Picnic* (30), *Mother Goose Melodies* (31), *Mickey Steps Out* (31), *The Ugly Duckling* (31), *The Grocery Boy* (32), *The Mad Dog* (32) (Pluto), *Flowers and Trees* (32), *Mickey's Melodrama* (33), *Three Little Pigs* (33), *Mickey's Gala Premier* (33), *Band Concert* (34), *The Grasshopper and the Ants* (34), *Gulliver Mickey* (34), *The Tortoise and the Hare* (34), *Three Orphan Kittens* (35), *Mickey's Man Friday* (35), *Music Land* (35), *Mickey's Circus* (36) (Donald Duck), *Donald and Pluto* (36), *Three Blind Mouseketeers* (36), *Who Killed Cock Robin?* (36), *The Country Cousin* (36), *Don Donald* (37), *The Old Mill* (37), *The Four Seasons* (37), *Clock Cleaners* (37), *Donald and the Magnet** (37), *The Battle Between Classic and Jazz* (37), *Ferdinand the Bull* (38), *Winken, Blinken, and Nod* (38), *Donald's Nephews* (38), *The Autograph Hound* (39), *The Ugly Duckling* (39), *Tugboat Mickey* (39), *Pluto's Dream House* (40), *Lend a Paw* (41), *Der Fuhrer's Face* (42), *Chicken Little* (43), *Tiger Trouble* (44), *Donald's Double Trouble* (46), *Clown of the Jungle* (47), *Toy Tinkers* (49), *Home Made Home* (50), *Father's Day Off* (52), *Melody* (53), *Toot, Whistle, Plunk, and Boom* (53), *Pigs is Pigs* (56), *The Conquest of Space* (54), *Atom the Good Genie* (56), *The Truth About Mother Goose* (57).

ANIM (features): *Snow White and the Seven Dwarfs** (37), *Pinocchio* (39), *Fantasia** (40), *The Reluctant Dragon* (41), *Dumbo* (41), *Bambi** (42), *Saludos Amigos* (42), *The Three Caballeros* (45) (anim and live action), *Make Mine Music* (46), *Song of the South* (46), *Fun and Fancy Free* (47), *Melody Time* (48), *Cinderella* (49), *So Dear To My Heart* (50), *Ichabod and Mr. Toad/Wind in the Willows* (50), *Alice in Wonderland* (51), *Peter Pan* (53), *The Lady and the Tramp* (55), *Sleeping Beauty* (58), *101 Dalmatians* (60), *The Sword in the Stone* (63), *Winnie the Pooh and the Honey Tree* (65), *The Jungle Book* (67), *Winnie the Pooh and the Blustery Day* (68).

LIVE ACTION PROD: *Jungle Cat* (48), *Perri* (48), *Seal Island* (48), *Beaver Valley* (50), *Treasure Island* (50), *Nature's Half Acre* (51), *Water Birds* (51), *The Living Desert** (53), *20,000 Leagues Under the Sea* (53), *The Alaskan Eskimo* (53), *Westward Ho the Wagons* (56), *Davy Crockett* (56), *Old Yeller* (57), *White Wilderness* (58), *The Absent-Minded Professor* (60), *In Search of the Castaways* (61), *Emil and the Detectives** (63), *The Miracle of the White Stallions* (63), *Mary Poppins* (64), *The Monkey's Uncle* (65), *That Darn Cat* (65).

*DI VENANZO, Gianni PHOTOG Italy. (Teramo Dec 18, 1920–Rome Feb 1966) One of the most notable postwar Italian cinematographers who collaborated on many of Antonioni's (*q.v.*) films and was especially skillful in controlling the tone of images. He began his career as assistant to Aldo Tonti (*q.v.*) and Otello Martelli (*q.v.*). His most inspired work was on Fellini's *8½* and Antonioni's *La Notte* and *L'Eclisse*.

PHOTOG (notably): for Antonioni, *Amore in Città** (53), *Le Amiche** (55), *Il Grido** (57), *La Notte** (60), *L'Eclisse** (62); for Carlo Lizzani, *Achtung! Banditi!* (51), *Cronache di Poveri Amanti** (54), *Amore in Città** (53); for Francesco Rosi, *Kean* (56), *La Sfida* (58), *I Magliari* (59), *Salvatore Giuliano** (61), *Le Mani sulla Città** (63), *Il Momenta della Verita* (64); for Mario Monicelli, *I Soliti Ignoti* (58), *Alta Infidelta* (64) (one episode); for Losey, *Eva* (62); for Fellini, *8½** (63), *Giulietta degli Spiriti** (65); for Comencini, *La Ragazza di Babe* (63); for Elio Petri, *La Decima vittima* (65); for Joseph Mankiewicz, *The Honey Pot* (66).

DMYTRYK, Edward DIR USA/Britain. (Grand Forks Sept 4, 1908–) After a long career (1930–39) as editor and later as director of B-pictures (1935–43), he developed into one of the best postwar Hollywood directors, revealing an original approach to thrillers with *Farewell My Lovely* and *Give Us This Day*, and to social films with *Crossfire*. [He was fired by RKO in late 1947 for his alleged Communist sympathies, became one of the renowned "Hollywood Ten" cited for contempt of Congress, and was sentenced to six months in jail. In late 1950, apparently as a result of the Korean War, he changed his mind and agreed to testify before the House Committee on Un-American Activities. On March 10, 1951 he recanted his earlier political beliefs. He returned to Hollywood in 1952 and has since become a prolific director of relatively uninteresting commercial films — though some of them betray a certain uneasiness.

DIR: *The Hawk* (35), *Television Spy* (39), *Emergency Squad* (40), *Golden Gloves* (40), *Mystery Sea Raider* (40), *The First Romance* (40), *The Devil Commands* (41), *Under Age* (41), *Sweetheart of the Campus* (41), *Blond from Singapore* (41), *Confessions of Boston Blackie* (41), *Secrets of the Lone Wolf* (41), *Counter Espionage* (42), *Seven Miles from Alcatraz* (42), *Hitler's Children* (43), *The Falcon Strikes Back* (43), *Behind the Rising Sun* (43), *Captive Wild Woman* (43), *Tender Comrade* (44), *Farewell My Lovely** (44), *Back to Bataan* (45), *Cornered* (46), *Till the End of Time* (46), *Crossfire** (47), *So Well Remembered* (Brit47), *The Hidden Room/Obsession* (Brit48), *Give Us This Day* (Brit49), *Mutiny* (Fr 52), *The Sniper* (USA52), *Eight Iron Men* (52), *The Juggler* (Israel53), *The Caine Mutiny* (54), *Broken Lance* (54), *The End of the Affair* (Brit55), *Soldier of Fortune* (55), *The Left Hand of God* (55), *The Mountain* (56), *Raintree County* (57), *The Young Lions* (58), *Warlock* (59), *The Blue Angel** (59), *The Reluctant Saint* (It61), *A Walk on the Wild Side* (62), *The Carpetbaggers* (63), *Where Love Has Gone* (64), *Mirage* (65), *Alvarez Kelly* (65), *Anzio* (67), *Shalako* (68).]

DOLIN, Boris DIR USSR. (Aug 2, 1903–) A former assistant to Alexander Zguridi (*q.v.*) who developed into his peer as a director of nature films. Notable among his many films are *Zakon velikoi lyubvi/ The Law of the Great Love* (45), about a family of foxes in Siberia, and *Istoria odnogo kolza/The Tale of a Link* (48) on bird migration. [Since 1959 he has been director of the children's film studios in Moscow, where he made *The Surprising Hunt* (60), *Blind Bird* (62), and *More Amazing Than a Fairy Tale* (64).]

*DONEN, Stanley DIR USA/Britain. (Colombia, South Carolina April 13, 1924–) One of the greatest directors of American musicals of the Fifties whose *On the Town, Singin' in the Rain,* and *Funny Face* are masterpieces of the

genre. He began his career as a Broadway chorus dancer in 1940, became choreographic assistant to Gene Kelly in 1941, and in 1942 went to Hollywood with Kelly and the Broadway cast to work on the film version of *Best Foot Forward.* During the next five years he worked as dance director or assistant on 14 films (10 of which were for MGM). In 1949 he and Kelly wrote the script and directed some of the numbers for Busby Berkeley's *Take Me Out to the Ball Game* and the same year he directed his first feature (with Kelly), *On the Town,* a film that broke away entirely from stage-bound dance conventions and returned somewhat to the approach of the early Lubitsch (*q.v.*) and Mamoulian (q.v.) musicals. In 1952, again with Kelly, he created his best film, *Singin' in the Rain,* which contains some gently ironic and nostalgic memories of Busby Berkeley (*q.v.*) musicals. His exuberant and wild *Seven Brides for Seven Brothers* (54) was followed by *It's Always Fair Weather* (55), a superbly choreographed musical about postwar disillusion that was not a complete success. It marked the end of his "realistic" musicals for MGM and the following year he made the glamorous, satirical fantasia, *Funny Face.* Since 1958 (apart from *Damn Yankees*), Donen has concentrated on making fast-moving, modish comedies and comedy-thrillers in a consciously artificial style. Of his recent films, *Two for the Road* (67) stands out as a deeply personal, bittersweet portrait of the difficulties of human relationships.

ASSIST: *Best Foot Forward* (43), *Cover Girl* (44), *Hey Rookie* (44), *Jam Session* (44), *Kansas City Kitty* (44), *Anchors Aweigh* (45), *Holiday in Mexico* (46), *No Leave, No Love* (46), *Living in a Big Way* (47), *This Time for Keeps* (47), *Killer McCoy* (47), *The Big City* (48), *Date with Judy* (48), *The Kissing Bandit* (48), *Take Me Out to the Ball Game* (49) (also script).

DIR: *On the Town** (49) (co-dir: Gene Kelly), *Royal Wedding/Wedding Bells* (50), *Love is Better than Ever/The Light Fantastic* (51), *Singin' in the Rain** (51) (co-dir: Gene Kelly), *Fearless Fagan* (52), *Give a Girl a Break* (53), *Deep in My Heart* (54), *Seven Brides for Seven Brothers* (54), *It's Always Fair Weather* (55) (co-dir: Gene Kelly), *Funny Face** (57), *Kiss Them* for Me (57), The Pajama Game (57) (co-dir: George Abbott), Indiscreet (58), Damn Yankees/What Lola Wants (59) (co-dir: George Abbott), Once More, With Feeling! (59), Surprise Package (Brit60), The Grass is Greener (Brit60), Charade (63), Arabesque (66), Two for the Road (67), Bedazzled (Brit67), Staircase (68). He has produced his own films since 1958.

DONIOL-VALCROZE, Jacques DIR France. (Paris March 15, 1920–) Co-founder with André Bazin of Cahiers du Cinéma in 1952 and an actor and scriptwriter for Pierre Kast (q.v.), he developed later into an intelligent director of satirical comedies (L'Eau à la bouche) and dramas (Le Viol).
DIR: Bonjour, monsieur la Bruyère (56) (short), L'Oeil du maître (57) (short), Les Surmenés (58) (short), L'Eau à la bouche (59), Le Coeur battant (60), La Dénonciation (62), L'Enlèvement d'Antoine Bigut (64) (TV), Jean-Luc Godard (64) (TV), La Bien-aimée (66) (TV), Le Viol (67), La Maison des Bories (69).

DONSKOY, Mark (also Mark Donskoi) DIR USSR. (Odessa March 6 1901–) A good, if not always consistent, director, who achieved well-merited international renown with the Gorki trilogy (38–40) and who had a special gift with literary adaptations (The Rainbow, A Village Schoolteacher, At Great Cost). His Gorki trilogy is especially remarkable for its atmospheric re-creation of life in Tsarist Russia at the turn of the century. Originally a musician and writer, he wrote the script for The Last Stronghold (25), was G. Roshal's assistant on His Excellency in 1927, and directed his first films the same year. He has said a film maker "must be faithful to his artistic calling, to his artistic honesty. The starting point and aim of all artistic creation is the enrichment of mankind; the development of an esthetic of life in order to render it more beautiful in creating beauty for and between men; the discovery of the beauty and goodness hidden in the soul of every man."
DIR: Zhizn/Life (27) (short), V bolshoi gorode/In the Big City (27) (co-dir: M. Averbach), Tsena cheloveka/The Value of Man (28) (co-dir: M. Averbach), Pizhon/The Fop (29), Chuzhoi bereg/Alien Shore/The Other Shore (30), Ogon/Fire (30), Pesn o schaste/Song of Happiness (34), Detstvo Gorkovo/The Childhood of Maxim Gorki* (38) V lyudkyakh/My Apprenticeship/Among People/Out in the World* (39), Moi universiteti/My Universities* (40), Romantiki/Children of the Soviet Arctic (41), Fighting Film Album No. 9: Beacon (41), Kak zakalyalas stal/How the Steel Was Tempered* (42), Mayak/The Lighthouse (42), Raduga/Rainbow* (43), Nepokorenniye/Unconquered (45), Seklskaya uchitelnitsa/A Village Schoolteacher* (46), Alitet ukhodit v gory/Alitet Leaves for the Hills (48), Nashi chempiony / Our Champions / Sporting Fame (50), Mat/Mother* (55), Dorogoi tsenoi/At Great Cost/At a High Price* (57), Foma Gordeyev/Foma Gordeyev (59), Zdravstvyite deti/Hello, Children (62), Serdze materi/Heart of a Mother (66), Vernost materi/A Mother's Devotion (66), Chaliapin (70).

DOS SANTOS, Nelson Pereira see SANTOS, Nelson Pereira dos

DOUY, Max ART DIR France. (Issy-les-Moulineaux June 20, 1914–) One of the best French designers who has assisted or collaborated with Meerson (q.v.), Eugène Lourié, and Trauner (q.v.) and who excels in the creation of distinctive interiors and period films.
[ART DIR (notaby): for Autant-Lara, Le Diable au corps*, L'Auberge rouge*, Occupe-toi d'Amélie*, Le Blé en herbe, Le Rouge et noir, Margeurite de la nuit, La Traversée de Paris, En cas de malheur, Le Jouer, La Jument verte, Le Bois des amants, Non Uccidere*, Vive Henry IV, vive l'amour, Le Comte de Monte Cristo, Le Meurtrier, Le Magot de Joséfa, Le Journal d'un femme en blanc; for Jean Grémillon, Le Ciel est à vous*, Lumière d'été*; for Becker, Dernier a tout, Falbalas; for Bresson, Les Dames du Bois de Boulogne*; for Clouzot, Quai des Orfèvres*, Manon; for Le Chanois, Sans laisser d'adresse*; for Renoir, French Cancan*; for Astruc, Les Mauvaises rencontres*; for Buñuel, Cela s'appelle l'aurore*; for Dassin, Topkapi.]

DOVZHENKO, Alexander DIR USSR. (Ukraine Sept 11, 1894–Moscow Nov 25, 1956) The cinema's greatest epic poet who interwove the eternal themes of love, life, fertility, and death in a series of lyrical hymns dedicated to his native Ukraine. The son of Ukrainian peasants, he had been a teacher and diplomat before taking up painting. But, as he recalled: "In June 1926, after a sleepless night of soul-searching, (I) started for Odessa where I joined a cinema studio. The cinema, I thought, was the one art that was fresh and new . . . I knew little about it — indeed, I very rarely saw films." His first three films were of uneven quality, but his next film was *Zvenigora* (28), at whose legendary screening in Moscow Eisenstein and Pudovkin recognized, "There was a new film person among us." Then came *Arsenal,* which is not far from equaling his masterpiece, *Earth.* His sound films, though always appealing in some respects, are less perfect; many of them ran the gauntlet of political interference. Unforgettable, nonetheless, are the lyrical images of *Ivan,* the impassioned drama of *Aerograd* in the wild Siberian taiga, the earthy power of *Shchors,* and the extraordinary cantata to love and death, youth and old age, which is the heart of *Michurin.* Worn out by life and the various struggles he had had to fight during his career, he died at 62 as he was about to commence shooting *Poem of the Sea.* However, his widow, Yulia Solntseva (1901–), who had worked closely with him, was able to complete this from his original script and created a lyrical epic that is almost throughout worthy of Dovzhenko's genius. She has continued to make films based on scripts and other material he left: *The Flaming Years, The Enchanted Desna, Unforgettable.* He has said of himself and his work: "I am the knight, the partisan of contemporary problems. Our life today can never be spoken of too often. One shouldn't debase oneself contemplating the past or the *folie de grandeur* but turn towards everyday man. Let us understand that a dewdrop can by itself reflect the entire world and the whole of society. And, also that if our country is great it is because the ordinary people are great." "In order to upset, it is necessary to be upset. In order to bring joy and clarity to others it is necessary to have clarity in one's heart and lift it up on high." "Let us not treat the theme of ordinary man as an ordinary theme. A film that is not steeped in human feeling is like a planet without atmosphere. As the Chinese proverb says: a warrior with faults is still a warrior but a gnat without faults is only a gnat." "Let us not be so scared of depicting the delicacy of the human spirit, loving attentions and understanding, kisses. 'Love is wise and perspicacious' says the proverb: it elevates man, embellishes and inspires him, gives him happiness. And if it is contrary it brings a deep spiritual suffering that is found among men wherever they live." "I am not one of those who prepare a detailed script in advance, a shot by shot design. I am a painter by training and the spatial composition of people is not in fact a problem for me that involves this kind of preplanning of my images. I bring in my camera and set it down on the chosen spot. The harmony of particular images is perhaps explained by their close integration with the land."

DIR: *Yagodka Liubvi/The Fruits of Love/The Marriage Trap/Jean Kolbasink The Hairdresser* (26) (short), *Vasya-Reformator/Vasya the Reformer* (26) (co-dir: F. Lopatinsky), *Sumka dipkuriera/The Diplomatic Pouch* (27), *Zvenigora** (28), *Arsenal* *(29), *Zemlya/ Earth** (30), *Ivan** (32), *Aerograd** (35), *Shchors** (39), *Osvobozhdeniye/ Liberation* (40) (co-dir: Solntseva) (documentary), *Bitva za nasha Sovietskaya Ukrainu/The Fight for Our Soviet Ukraine* (43) (co-dir: Solntseva, Y. Avdeyenko under supervision of Dovzhenko) (documentary), *Pobeda na Pravoberezhnoi Ukraine i izgnaniye nemetsikh za predeli ukrainskikh sovietskikh zemel/ Victory in the Ukraine and the Expulsion of the Germans from the Boundaries of the Ukrainian Soviet Land* (45) (co-dir: Solntseva) (compilation documentary), *Michurin/Life in Blossom** (47), *Poema o more/Poem of the Sea** (58) (completed by Solntseva).
SCEN: *Povest'. plamennykh let/The Flaming Years** (61), *Zacharovannaya Desna/ The Enchanted Desna* (65), *Nezabuvaiemoe/Unforgettable* (69) (all dir: Solntseva) and all his own films.

DREVILLE, Jean DIR France. (Vitry-sur Seine Sept 20, 1906–) Excellent craftsman whose prolific output includes several successful films: *Autour de l'argent* (28), *La Cage aux rossignols* (45), *Le Visiteur* (47), *La Bataille de l'eau lourde/Operation Swallow* (47), *Les Casse-Pieds* (48), *Horizons sans fin* (53),

Normandie-Niemen (60), *Lafayette* (61).

DREYER, Carl Theodor DIR Denmark/Sweden/Germany/France. (Copenhagen Feb 3, 1889–March 20, 1968) One of the world's greatest film makers, a man who created in *La Passion de Jeanne d'Arc* one of the "ten most beautiful films in the world" and whose style is characterized by exacting, expressive design and subtle camera movements and by a concentration on the physiognomy and inner psychology of his characters. Originally a journalist, he became a title writer for Nordisk Film in 1912 and from 1912–18 wrote some 25 scripts for August Blom (*q.v.*), Holger-Madsen (*q.v.*), A. W. Sandberg, Karl Mantzius, and others. It was on his initiative that the company began adapting literary works into films. He was also an editor. In the years between *Vampyr* and *Day of Wrath* he was in Britain and North Africa and then returned to journalism in Denmark. The expressive visual quality of his first films quickly developed into an exacting style of realism in which the tiniest detail of the human face or the background became expressive. His increasingly abstract style often reflected a concrete reality; his symbolism is above all a reflection of a spiritual and human condition. The themes of love and death (poetically summarized in *Gertrud*) recur in all his films. He was obsessed by sorcery (*Day of Wrath*, *Vampyr*) and mysticism (*Ordet*); in some respects he was a man from an earlier epoch, but, despite their medieval qualities, his films never seem divorced from contemporary realities. He has said of himself and his work: "There is a close resemblance between a work of art and a human being: both have a soul — which is expressed through style. The creator, through style, fuses the different elements of his work and makes the public see the theme through his eyes." "Only artistic truth has any validity, that is to say, the truth extracted from real life and purged of all secondary aspects. What takes place on the screen is not, and couldn't be, reality. Naturalism is no longer art." "I am not a rebel. I don't believe in revolutions. Too often they carry us many steps backwards. I am more inclined to believe in 'evolutions' with small steps forward . . . Simplification should transform an idea into a symbol. With symbolism one begins to move toward abstraction because symbolism works through suggestion. Abstraction might sound like a bad word to the ears of film makers. But my only desire is that it brings to life the world of the imagination beyond a sterile and tiresome naturalism." "What I seek in my films . . . is a penetration to my actors' deepest thoughts by means of their most subtle expressions. For these are the expressions that reveal the character of the person, his unconscious feelings, the secrets that live in the depths of his soul . . . That is why I always look for actors who are capable of responding to this quest."
DIR (features): *Praesidenten/The President* (Den19), *Blade af Satans Bog/ Leaves from Satan's Book** (Den19), *Prästänken/The Parson's Widow* (Swed 20), *Die Gezeichneten/Love One Another** (Ger22), *Der Var Engang/Once Upon a Time* (Den22), *Michaël* (Ger 24), *Du Skal Aere din Hustru/Master of the House** (Den25), *Glomsdalsbruden/ The Bride of Glomsdale* (Norway25), *La Passion de Jeanne d'Arc** (Fr28), *Vampyr** (Ger/Fr31), *Vredens Dag/Day of Wrath** (Den43), *Tva Människor* (Swed45), *Ordet** (Den55), *Gertrud** (Den64).
DIR (shorts): *Modrehyelpen/Good Mothers* (42), *Water for the Countryside* (45), *Den Danske Landsbykirke/The Danish Village Church* (47), *De Gamle/ The Seventh Age* (47), *De Naede Fargen/They Caught the Ferry* (48), *Thorvaldsen* (49), *The Childhood of Radio* (49), *Storsstroembroen/Storstrom Bridge* (49), *Shakespeare og Kroenberg* (50), *Ronne og Nexos Genoplyging/The Reconstruction of Ronne and Nexos* (54), *Noget om Nordem* (59), all for the Danish film board.

DUARTE, Anselmo DIR Brazil. (Lisbon Oct 17, 1859–) Former Brazilian actor who became a director and won the Palme d'or at Cannes for his *O Pagador de Promessas/The Given Word** (61).

DUDOW, Slatan DIR Germany/German Democratic Republic. (Zaribrod, Bulgaria Jan 30, 1903–Berlin Aug 12, 1963) One of the best German film makers, he studied theater in Berlin (1922), became assistant to Lang (*q.v.*) and Pabst (*q.v.*), and made an experimental short before directing the remarkable socialist docu-

ment *Kühle Wampe* (32) from Brecht's
script. This was banned in Germany
as an insult to Hindenberg and Dudow
himself was exiled from Germany in
1933. He was active as a writer in
Switzerland from 1933 to 1946 and then
returned to the German Democratic
Republic and directed many good films,
including *Stronger than the Night,* a
portrait of the anti-Nazi struggle at
the height of Hitler's power. He scripted
all his postwar films.
DIR: *Seifenblasen/Soap Bubbles* (29),
Kühle Wampe* (32), *Unser täglich Brot/
Our Daily Bread** (49), *Familie Ben-
thin* (50) (co-dir: Kurt Maetzig), *Fra-
uenschicksale* (52), *Stärker als die
Nacht/Stronger than the Night** (54),
Der Hauptman von Köln (56), *Verwir-
rung der Liebe* (59), *Christine* (unfinished, 63).

**DULAC, Germaine (Germaine Saisset-Schnei-
der)** DIR France. (Amiens 1882–Paris
July 1942) One of the first in France
to take the cinema seriously as a major
art form, she was a sensitive, independent, liberal-minded film maker, passionately devoted to experiment and new
ideas. Originally a drama critic and author and a militant women's liberationist,
she dedicated her whole life after 1916
to the cinema. After manifesting her
emotional gifts and visual sense in *Les
Soeurs ennemies* (16) and *Vénus Victrix*
(17), she directed *La Fête espagnole*
(19), based on a script by her friend
Delluc (*q.v.*) and established her name
as one of the strongest forces in the
French impressionist school. After several
more films, including, notably, *La Mort
du soleil,* she created her masterpiece:
La Souriante Madame Beudet (22), a
critique of middle-class married life
(what would today be called "lack of
communication"). Her later features were
so hampered by commercial restrictions
that she joined the "second avant-garde"
with her *La Coquille et le Clergyman*
(based on Antonin Artaud's script) and
her short visual symphonies set to music,
Disque 927 and *Thème et Variations.*
When the introduction of talking films
brought independent production to a
halt, she decided to devote herself to
newsreels and became head of *France-
Actualités* (1930–40). However, she
never gave up her love for the cinema
and for spreading the word; from 1924

on she played a major role in the development of film societies in France.
DIR: *Les Soeurs ennemies* (16), *Géo,
le mystérieux* (17), *Vénus Victrix/ Dans
l'ouragan de la vie* (17), *Ames de fous*
(18), *La Cigarette* (19), *La Fête es-
pagnole** (19), *Malencontre* (20), *La
Belle Dame sans merci* (21), *La Mort
du soleil* (22), *La Souriante Madame
Beudet** (22), *Gosette* (22–23) (six
episodes), *Le Diable dans la ville* (24),
Ame d'artiste (25), *La Folie des vaillants*
(25), *Antoinette Sabrier* (27), *La
Coquille et le Clergyman** (28), *Princess
Mandane* (28), *Disque 927* (29), *Arabesque* (29), *Thème et variations* (30).

DUNAYEVSKY, Isaac MUS USSR. (Ukraine
Jan 30, 1900–Moscow Dec 25, 1955)
Alexandrov's (*q.v.*) close collaborator on
his musical comedies, the composer of
the catchy and popular music and lyrics
of *Jazz Comedy**, *Circus**, *Volga Volga,
Spring**, of the scores for Ivan Pyriev's
(*q.v.*) *Kuban Cossacks* (49), and *The
Rich Bride* (38), and for Pyriev's and
Ivens' *Friendship Triumphs* (GDR/
USSR52).

DUNCAN, F. Martin see MARTIN-DUNCAN, F.

DUNNE, Philip SCEN/DIR USA. (New York
Feb 11, 1908–) For many years an
esteemed Hollywood scriptwriter and for
12 years script supervisor at 20th Century-Fox, he worked with Ford, Mankiewicz, and Preminger (all *q.v.*) and on
every kind of film, from Ford's *How
Green Was My Valley** and Kazan's
Pinky (49) to Allan Dwan's *Suez* (38),
John Cromwell's *Son of Fury* (42),
Henry King's *David and Bathsheba*
(51), and Henry Koster's *The Robe**
(53). In 1955 he decided to become a
director and producer and has since
made several polished, skillful films.
[DIR: *The View from Pompey's Head*
(55), *Prince of Players* (55), *Hilda
Crane* (56), *Three Brave Men* (57),
Ten North Frederick (58), *In Love and
War* (58), *Blue Denim* (60), *Wild in
the Country* (61), *Lisa/The Inspector*
(62), *Blindfold* (66).]

*DUNNING, George ANIM Canada/Brit-
ain. (Toronto 1920–) An imaginative
animator whose career began in 1943
with the National Film Board of Canada,
where he worked on, notably, *J'ai tant
dansé* (in the *Chants Populaires* series)

and *Cadet Rouselle* (46) (with Colin Low) a visualization of a French folk song using cut-out metal shapes and evocative backgrounds. In 1949 he set up his own company, Graphic Associates. In 1956 he moved to England, where he made many sponsored films and TV commercials as well as *The Apple, The Wardrobe,* and *The Flying Man,* the last, a film using blobs of watercolor in a manner derived from Bartosch's (*q.v.*) approach in *L'Idée.* After the three-screen cartoon for Expo '67 in Montreal, *Canada is My Piano,* he returned to Britain to direct the entrancing feature, *Yellow Submarine.* His personal films have strongly irrational, surrealistic themes.

ANIM (notably): *Chants Populaires* (Canada44) (two sequences: No. 2, *J'ai tant dansé,* No. 4, *Auprès de ma blonde*), *Grim Pastures* (44), *Three Blind Mice* (45), *Cadet Rouselle* (46) (co-dir: Colin Low), *The Adventures of Baron Munchausen* (47) (co-dir: Colin Low), *Family Tree* (Canada 47) (co-dir: Evelyn Lambart), *The Story of the Motorcar Engine* (Brit58), *The Wardrobe* (59), *Mr. Know-How* (61), *The Apple* (61), *The Flying Man* (62), *The Ever Changing Motorcar* (62), *Visible Manifestations* (63), *The Adventures of Thud and Blunder* (62–65), *Discovery — Penicillin* (64), *The Beatles* (66) (TV series), *Cool McCool* (66) (TV series), *Canada is My Piano* (Canada67), *Yellow Submarine** (Brit68).

*DUPONT, Ewald André (Andreas) DIR Germany/Britain/USA. (Zeitz, Sachsen Dec 25, 1891–Hollywood Dec 12, 1956) Originally a writer, he became one of Germany's first film critics in 1911. He was brought into films by Erich Pommer (*q.v.*) and made his first films before 1917. He directed some 30 films in Germany, but his most successful period was at the end of the silent era when he directed his best film, *Variety* (25). He moved to Britain in 1927 as a producer-director at Elstree and made several, somewhat ponderous, quasi-expressionistic films before moving to Hollywood in 1933. His work there is of little interest. He was a talent scout and agent 1940–49 and returned to directing in 1950 with, again, mediocre results.

DIR (notably): *Das Alte Gesetz* (Ger23), *Die grüne Manuela* (Ger23), *Baruch* (Ger24), *Der Demütige und die Sangerin*

(Ger25), *Varieté** (Ger25), *Love Me and the World is Mine* (Brit27), *Moulin Rouge** (Brit28), *Piccadilly* (Brit29), *Atlantik* (Ger/Brit29), *Two Worlds* (Brit 30), *Menschen im Käfig/Cape Forlorn/ Love Storm* (Ger30), *Der Läufer von Marathon* (Ger33), *Forgotten Faces* (USA36), *Hell's Kitchen* (39), *The Scarf* (50), *Return to Treasure Island* (54).

DURAND, Jean DIR France. (Paris Dec 15, 1882–Paris 1946) The greatest French director of silent comedies — the maker of some 400 films — whose "cartesianism of the absurd" dominates the *Onésime*, Calino,* and *Zigoto* series (09–14) that feature the Pouitte troupe of acrobats and students he had trained. He was also a specialist in adventure and animal films for his wife, the animal trainer, Berthe Dagmar, and made westerns in the Camargue region in collaboration with Joe Hamman. He made no more films after the arrival of talkies, but before this he had said: "One should be careful of formulas, each script should be treated according to its spirit and each script must have a spirit."

DUVIVIER, Julien DIR France/Britain/USA/ Italy/Germany. (Lille Oct 8, 1896–Oct 31, 1967) The director of some 65 films over 50 years whose best period was in the Thirties. He began as an actor, then became assistant to, among others, Feuillade, André Antoine, and Marcel L'Herbier (all *q.v.*). His first films were mediocre but with the introduction of sound he developed into a good director of actors and demonstrated an ability to create an effective atmosphere. From 1934 to 1938, swept along on the current of French poetic realism, he developed an international reputation with *La Bandera, Pépé le Moko,* and *Carnet de bal* and was considered by some critics to be the equal of Renoir, Clair, Feyder, or Carné (all *q.v.*). After 1940 he returned to his mediocre beginnings but, taken altogether, has directed several craftsmanlike successes with good casts and in collaboration with some excellent writers like Charles Spaak (*q.v.*) and Henri Jeanson (*q.v.*). His two Italian *Don Camillo* films were major international box-office successes.

[DIR: *Haceldama/Le Prix du sang* (19), *Les Roquevillard* (22), *L'Ouragan sur la montagne* (22), *Der Unheimliche Gast/ Le Logis de l'horreur* (Ger22), *Le Reflet* de Claude Mercoeur (23), *Credo ou la tragedie de Lourdes* (23), *Coeurs farouches* (23), *L'Oeuvre immortelle* (Belgium24), *La Machine à refaire la vie* (24) (documentary, co-dir: Henry Lepage), *L'Abbé Constantin* (25), *Poil de carotte* (25), *L'Agonie de Jérusalem* (26), *L'Homme à l'Hispano* (26), *Le Mariage de Mademoiselle Beulemans* (27), *Le Mystère de la Tour Eiffel* (27), *Le Tourbillon de Paris* (28), *La Vie miraculeuse de Thérèse Martin* (29), *La Divine croisière* (29), *Madame Colibri* (29), *Au bonheur des dames* (29), *David Golder* (30), *Les Cinq gentlemen maudits* (31), *Allo, Berlin? Ici Paris* (32), *Poil de carotte* (32) (remake), *La Venus de collège* (32), *La Tête d'un homme* (32), *Le Petit roi* (33), *Le Paquebot, Tenacity* (34), *Marie Chapdelaine* (34), *Golgotha* (35), *La Bandera** (35), *Le Golem/The Legend of Prague** (Czech35), *La Belle Équipe** (36), *Pépé le Moko** (36), *L'Homme du jour* (36), *Carnet de bal/Christine** (37), *The Great Waltz* (USA38), *La Fin du jour* (39), *La Charrettee fantôme* (39), *Un tel père et fils/Heart of a Nation* (40, completed in USA), *Lydia* (Brit40), *Tales of Manhattan* (USA42), *Flesh and Fantasy* (USA43), *The Impostor* (USA 43), *Panique* (46), *Anna Karenina* (Brit47), *Au Royaume des cieux/Woman Hunt* (49), *Black Jack* (50), *Sous le ciel de Paris/Under the Paris Sky* (50), *Il Piccolo mondo di Don Camillo/The Little World of Don Camillo* (It51), *La Fête à Henriette/Henriette* (52), *Il Ritorno di Don Camillo/The Return of Don Camillo* (It53), *L'Affaire Maurizius/On Trial* (53), *Marianne de ma jeunesse* (54), *Voici le temps des assassins/Murder a la carte* (55), *L'Homme à l'imperméable/The Man in the Raincoat* (50), *Pot-Bouille/The House of Lovers* (57), *La Femme et le pantin/A Woman Like Satan* (58), *Marie-Octobre* (58), *Das Kuntstseidene Mädchen/La Grand Vie* (GFR59), *Boulevard* (60), *La Chambre ardente/The Curse and the Coffin* (61), *Le Diable et les dix commandements/The Devil and the Ten Commandments* (62), *Chair de poule/Highway Pick-up* (63), *Diaboliquement votre/Diabolically Yours* (67).

SCEN: *L'Agonie des Aigles* (20) (dir: Bernard Deschamps), *Crépuscule d'épouvante* (21) (dir: Henri Etiévant), *Amours, délices et Rogues* (46) (dir: André Berthomieu), and most of his own films.]

DWAN, Allan DIR/SCEN USA. (Toronto, Canada April 3, 1885–) The most prolific of all American directors, notable for having directed some 400 films and who scripted or produced as many more. His most creative period was 1916–23 when he was working with Douglas Fairbanks. From 1909 to 1915 he made numerous films for Essanay and from 1915–17 worked under Griffith's (*q.v.*) supervision at Triangle. He has since been a competent director of every type of commercial film.

DIR (notably): *The Good Bad Man* (16), *The Half-breed* (16), *Manhattan Madness** (16), *A Modern Musketeer* (18), *Bound in Morocco* (18), *Robin Hood** (22), *The Iron Mask* (29) (all with Douglas Fairbanks), *Human Cargo* (36), *Heidi* (37), *Suez* (38), *The Three Musketeers* (39), *Frontier Marshall** (39), *The Sands of Iwo Jima* (49), *Montana Belle* (52), *Hold Back the Night* (56), *The Most Dangerous Man Alive* (58, released 61).

DZIGAN, Yefim DIR USSR. (Moscow 1898–) Routine Soviet director whose best film was *We from Kronstadt** (36), a success partly owing to his excellent scriptwriter, Vsevolod Vishnevsky (*q.v.*).

EASTMAN, George INVENTOR USA. (Waterville July 12, 1854–Rochester, N.Y. March 14, 1932) A major industrialist, the inventor of roll film, who built the Eastman-Kodak Company into a formidable international monopoly based on the sale of raw film stock. Originally employed in a bank, he established in 1884 a factory for photographic products specializing in roll film, at first on paper, then, in 1888, on celluloid. That same year he introduced the famous Kodak camera, designed to use the new film. From 1889 to 1892 he perfected perforated 35mm celluloid film stock for Edison (*q.v.*), and on these foundations built up a world-wide monopoly of photographic film and equipment that made him a millionaire. 1907–08: Supported the establishment of the powerful Motion Picture Patents Company, the Film Trust. 1908: Industrial struggle with Pathé in which he supported the establishment of a European monopoly. 1909: Pathé and Agfa broke his international film monopoly. 1924: Bought control of Pathé's French and British film stock interests. 1920–30: Introduced 16mm and 8mm film for noncommercial and amateur use (and eventually largely forced the other film gauges, from 9.5mm to 28mm, off the market). 1932: Committed suicide leaving a large part of his immense fortune to the Eastman Foundation. George Eastman House in Rochester, N.Y., now contains a museum of photography and cinematography.

EAUBONNE, Jean d' ART DIR France. (Talence 1903–May 1971) Set designer, art director, trained by Meerson (*q.v.*), with a stylish, baroque approach seen at its best in the postwar French films of Max Ophüls (*q.v.*). Notable work: for Carné, *Jenny;* for Becker, *Rue de l'Estrapade,*

Casque d'Or*, Touchez pas au Grisbi*, Montparnasse 19; for Cocteau, *Le Sang d'un poète*, Orphée*;* for Ophüls, *De Majerling à Sarajevo, La Ronde*, Le Plaisir*, Madame de . . . *, Lola Montès*;* for Feyder, *La Loi du nord.*

*EDESON, Arthur PHOTOG USA. (New York Oct 24, 1891–Feb 1970) One of the greatest of Hollywood cameramen, a master of controlled lighting effects and trick work (notably in several Universal horror films of the Thirties), but equally at home with Douglas Fairbanks' spectaculars and thrillers.
PHOTOG (notably): for John Emerson, *Wild and Woolly* (17); for Fred Niblo, *The Three Musketeers* (21); for Allan Dwan, *Robin Hood** (22); for Raoul Walsh, *The Thief of Bagdad* (24); for Harry Hoyt, *The Lost World* (25); for Henry King, *Stella Dallas** (25); for Roland West, *The Bat* (26); for Lewis Milestone, *All Quiet on the Western Front** (30); for James Whale, *Frankenstein** (31), *The Old Dark House* (32), *The Invisible Man** (33); for Frank Lloyd, *Mutiny on the Bounty* (35); for Howard Hawks, *Sergeant York** (41); for John Huston, *The Maltese Falcon** (41); for Michael Curtiz, *Casablanca** (42); for Jean Negulesco, *The Mask of Dimitrios* (44).

EDISON, Thomas Alva INVENTOR USA. (Milan, USA Feb 11, 1847–West Orange, New Jersey Oct 18, 1931) The most well-known American inventor, developer of the phonograph and the incandescent lamp among numerous other devices, who very quickly understood the possibilities of using moving pictures as a visual complement to his phonograph. He took little interest in the technical and experimental work involved, which was the responsibility of W. K. L.

Dickson (*q.v.*) and Eugène Lauste(*q.v.*), but made a major contribution to the later industrialization of the equipment. He invented the phonograph in 1879; from 1888–94 he developed an interest in "moving" pictures and on Jan. 2, 1891 patented the Kinetoscope. When the Lumière (*q.v.*) Cinématographe was released in 1895, he purchased the patents of Thomas Armat, presented his Vitascope projector on April 23, 1896, and founded his own production company. From 1897–1907 he was involved in legal battles over patent rights with several competitors (the "Patents War"). [In 1907 the Edison Licensees group was formed (including Kalem, Vitagraph, Lubin, Selig, Essanay, Méliès, and Pathé) in which all the members agreed to make royalty payments to Edison. In 1908 the group and other patent holders pooled their resources and established the Motion Picture Patents Company, a powerful monopoly. From 1909 until the trust was broken by court decisions of Oct. 15, 1915 and April 9, 1917, Edison was involved in continuing legal battles with the "Independents." After these cases were lost, Edison lost interest in the cinema and in 1918 closed his studios in the Bronx.]

EFFENDY, Basuki DIR Indonesia. (192?–) A sensitive and humanistic film maker in the developing Indonesian cinema, notable for *Si Menje* (50), *Si Melati* (54).

*EGGELING, Viking ANIM Sweden/Germany. (Lund 1880–Berlin 1925) Swedish painter, one of the co-founders of dada in Zurich, whose schematic, formal abstractions are related to constructivism. In 1919 in Berlin he collaborated with Hans Richter (*q.v.*) in exploring the rhythmical interrelationships of forms and colors in scroll paintings, and in 1921 they both began experimenting with making abstract films. *Diagonal Symphony*, begun in 1921 but not completed until 1924, is an attempt to discover the nature of time in film "analogous to but in no sense dependent upon, the abstract designs of Malevich and Klee." In 1924, he made the somewhat similar *Parallels and Horizontal*.

EISENSTEIN, Sergei Mikhailovich DIR USSR. (Riga Jan 23, 1898–Feb 11, 1948) A titan, a cinematic genius, a Renaissance

man with a deep understanding of the arts, he was at once a creator and a theoretician. [The son of a prosperous ship builder, he was educated in engineering and architecture (14–17), but after two years as an engineer with the Red Army during the Civil War, he decided to become an artist. He had long been interested in the stage and in 1921 took a job as designer at Foregger's experimental theater and later as director at the Proletkult Theater. He was also developing his own theoretical approach to esthetic problems and was deeply interested in the psychological problems of artistic creation.] His stage work was based on what he called "the montage of attractions"; for the Proletkult he directed a free adaptation of Ostrovsky's *Enough Simplicity in Every Wise Man* (which included a short film parody *Gloumov's Diary*), S. Tretiakov's *Listen Moscow!*, and *Gas Masks* — the latter staged in an actual factory. This experience led him to the cinema as a possible better solution for his esthetic problems and in 1924 he directed the ebullient *Strike*. In two months (Sept–Nov, 25), the 27-year-old director filmed *The Battleship Potemkin*. "A feature of this film," he wrote, "was that close-ups, which usually served as explanatory details, became the parts capable of evoking the whole in the perception and feelings of the spectator. This was how the surgeon's pince-nez was utilized: the dangling eyeglasses were made to symbolize their owner . . . I compared this method of treating close-ups with a figure of speech known as synecdoche." This approach he felt allowed him to bring out "the importance of the great events of 1905, of which the *Potemkin* was no more than an individual episode, but one reflecting the greatness of the whole." His theories of "montage of attractions" (not used in *Potemkin*) became "intellectual montage" in *October* (shot without professional actors and studio sets) and "harmonic montage" in *The General Line*. Though these latter films are not the equal of *Potemkin*, Eisenstein was at the peak of his artistic powers when he set out with Alexandrov (*q.v.*) and Tisse (*q.v.*) in August 1929 to travel to Europe and the USA. After working on several abortive projects for Paramount in Hollywood, he signed a contract with Upton Sinclair to film, with Alexandrov and Tisse, the extraordinary epic, *Que Viva Mexico!* in Mexico. The year 1932 marked the beginning of a difficult period for him. Sinclair took the Mexican film (which, when edited, might have surpassed *Potemkin*) out of his hands. He was deeply depressed on his return to the USSR and spent some time in seclusion before returning to Moscow to teach at the Film Institute. [He suffered under official opprobrium that culminated in 1937 in a bitter denunciation by the head of the Soviet cinema of his *Bezhin Meadow* — a project begun in 1935 whose script had been several times rewritten under government orders and whose filming was twice interrupted by Eisenstein's illnesses. Production of the film was halted in March 1937. (In 1966 a 25-minute compilation of stills from fragments of the film was put together using the original script.) After Eisenstein's public excoriation of himself and his errors in this film, he was entrusted with the production of a large-budget epic, *Alexander Nevsky*.] This was his first sound film, an experiment in the orchestration of images and Prokofiev's score, operatic in effect with stylized, expressive acting. His last film, *Ivan the Terrible*, was planned as a trilogy in 1942: the first part was filmed in Alma Ata during the most difficult period of the war; the second completed but banned by Stalin and released only in 1958; the third prepared but never filmed. *Ivan the Terrible* is a monumental operatic tragedy that continued Eisenstein's experiments in the contrapuntal use of image and music and suggested major new possibilities for the cinema's development. He died in 1948 from a heart attack, two weeks after his fiftieth birthday. Two years earlier, ever aware of the cinema's enlarging perspectives, he had offered this prophecy: "No sooner have we mastered the color technique than we have to deal with the problems of volume and space, set us by the stereoscopic cinema that is hardly out of its diapers. Then there is the miracle of television — a living reality staring us in the face, ready to nullify the experience of the silent and sound cinema, which itself has not yet been fully assimilated. There, montage, for instance, was a mere *sequence* (more or less perfect) of the real course of events as seen and creatively reflected through the consciousness and emotions of an artist. Here, it will be the course of events itself, presented the moment they occur. This will be an astonishing meeting of two extremes. The first link in the chain of the developing form of histrionics is the actor, the mime. Conveying to his audiences the ideas and emotions he experiences at that moment, he will hold out his hand to the exponent of the highest form of future histrionics — the TV magician — who quick as a flash will expertly use camera eyes and angles to enthrall the millions-strong TV audiences with his artistic interpretation of an event taking place at that very moment . . . The cinema is fifty years old . . . but how immeasurably little the world of esthetics has achieved in mastering the means and potentialities of the cinema!" DIR: *Stachka/Strike** (24), *Bronenosets Potyomkin/Battleship Potemkin** (25), *Oktyabr'/October/Ten Days that Shook the World** (27), *Staroye i Novoye/Old and New/The General Line** (29), *Que Viva Mexico!** (Mex31/32) (unfinished, footage later released in *Thunder over Mexico* and *Time in the Sun*, etc.), *Bezhin lug/Bezhin Meadow* (35–37) (unfinished, compilation of fragments produced in 1966 by Nahum Kleimann and Sergei Yutkevich, music by Prokofiev), *Alexander Nevsky** (38), *Ivan Grosny/Ivan the Terrible, Part I** (44), *Ivan Grosny/Ivan the Terrible, Part II/ The Boyars' Plot** (46, released 58). Although credited as co-director, Eisenstein had little to do with Alexandrov's *Romance sentimentale* (Fr30).

EISLER, Hanns MUS Germany/USA. (Leipzig July 6, 1898–Berlin Sept 6, 1962) A composer with a deep understanding of the cinema who worked with Brecht, Chaplin, Feyder, Resnais, Ivens, and Lang (all *q.v.*), among others. He studied music in Vienna and was a pupil of Arnold Schoenberg. He left Berlin in 1933, traveled through various countries, and in 1938 moved to the USA, where he scored several Hollywood films. His political beliefs led to his deportation in 1947 and he settled in the German Democratic Republic. MUS (notably): for Victor Trivas, *Niemandsland** (31); for Slatan Dudow, *Kühle Wampe** (32), *Unser täglich Brot** (GDR49); for Joris Ivens, *Pesn o geryakh/Song of Heroes* (USSR32), *Nieuwe Gronden/New Earth** (Neth34), *The 400 Million** (USA38), *Our Russian Front* (USA41) (co-mus: Shostakovich);

for Jacques Feyder, *Le Grand Jeu** (Fr 34); for Joseph Losey, *Pete Roleum and His Cousins* (USA39); for Fritz Lang, *Hangmen Also Die** (USA43); for Clifford Odets, *None But the Lonely Heart* (USA43); for Chaplin, *Monsieur Verdoux** (USA47); for Jean Renoir, *The Woman on the Beach* (USA47); for Louis Daquin, *Bel Ami* (Aust54), *Trübe Wasser* (GDR60); for Pabst, *Herr Puntila und sein Knecht Matti** (Aust55); for Raymond Rouleau, *Les Sorcieres de Salem* (Fr/GDR57); for Erich Engel, *Geschwader Fledermaus* (GDR59); for Alain Resnais, *Nuit et Brouillard** (Fr 55).

SCEN: *Fidelio* (Aust56) (dir: Walter Felsenstein), *Gasparone* (Aust56) (dir: Karl Paryla).

EKK, Nikolai DIR USSR. (Moscow 1898–) A director associated with only one major film: *Putyovkha v zhizn/Road to Life** (31). Originally an actor with Vsevolod Meyerhold, he made documentary films from 1928–30 and later directed the first Soviet color feature *Grunya Kornakova* (36). His other work is mediocre.

EL SHEIKH, Kamel DIR Egypt. (Feb 5, 1918–) The director of some fifty films of uneven quality, but, notably, a film influenced by neorealism, *Hayat ou Maut/Life or Death* (55).

EMERSON, John DIR/SCEN USA. (May 29, 1878–March 9, 1946) Originally a stage actor, director, and dramatist, he joined the cinema and directed and wrote such films as *Geronimo's Last Raid* (12). He joined Triangle (under D. W. Griffith's supervision) and made many of the Douglas Fairbanks's first films, often from scripts by his wife, Anita Loos. He also directed films with Mary Pickford, e.g., *Less Than Dust* (16), Constance Talmadge, and Norma Talmadge, and took on Erich von Stroheim (*q.v.*) as his assistant, giving him his first major acting opportunity. After 1920, he gave up directing and joined his wife in a scriptwriting team, e.g., on *The Love Expert* (20), *Dulcy* (23).

EMMER, Luciano DIR Italy. (Milan Jan 19, 1918–) A major contributor to the field of art documentaries from 1942–54 who brought to life, through editing and evocative music, the works of Giotto, Hieronymus Bosch, Carpaccio, etc. He moved into the fiction field and made a successful debut with the nonchalant and charming *Domenica d'Agosta* (50). He has scripted all his own films.

DIR (documentaries): *Il Covo* (41), *Racconto di Affresco* (41), *Romanzo du un' Epoca* (42), *Destini d'Amore* (42), *Cantico delle Creature* (43), *Il Conte di Luna* (45), *Guerrieri* (46), *Bianchi Pascoli* (47), *Isole nella Laguna* (47), *Sulla Via di Damasco* (48), *Romantici a Venezia* (48), *Il Dramma di Cristo* (48), *La Leggenda di Sant'Orsola* (49), *Piero Della Francesca* (49), *Goya* (50), *Leonardo da Vinci* (52), *Picasso* (54). All except the last two (which are medium-length features), co-dir: Enrico Gras.

DIR (features): *Domenica d'Agosta* (50), *Parigi è sempre Parigi* (51), *Ragazze di Piazza di Spagna* (52), *Camilla* (54), *Il Bigamo* (56), *Il Momento pui Bello* (57), *Paradiso Terrestre/A chacun son paradis* (51) (co-dir: Robert Enrico), *La Ragazza in vetrina* (60).

ENEI, Yevgeni ART DIR USSR. (Hungary 1890–) Designer for many of the best Leningrad film makers, notably, Kozintsev, Trauberg, and Ermler (all *q.v.*), to whose films he contributed many striking sets, including those for *The Cloak**, *Club of the Big Deed**, *Fragment of an Empire**, *The New Babylon**.

*ENFIELD, Cyril Raker (Cy Endfield) DIR USA/Britain. (USA 1914–) Former scenarist and a director of a dozen or so obscure second features for Monogram until *Underworld Story* (50), a thriller with liberal pretensions, and his best film, *The Sound of Fury* (51), an authentic story of a lynching. McCarthyism forced him to leave the USA in 1952 and he spent several years as an obscure writer and director in Britain before making the excellent *Hell Drivers* (57). Though his work is extremely uneven, he has made several tough adventure films and a delightful Jules Verne adaptation, *The Mysterious Island*.

DIR (after 1950): *Underworld Story* (USA50), *The Sound of Fury* (USA51), *Tarzan's Strange Fury* (USA50), *The Limping Man* (Brit53), *The Master Plan* (54), *The Secret* (55), *Impulse* (55), *Child in the House* (56), *Hell Drivers* (57), *Sea Fury* (58), *Jet Storm* (59), *The Mysterious Island* (60), *Hide and Seek* (62), *Zulu* (63), *Sands of the Kala-*

hari (65), *De Sade* (69), *Universal Soldier* (71).

ENGEL, Morris DIR USA. (New York April 8, 1918–) Interesting and sensitive film maker of the independent New York school, originally a photographer, who established an international reputation with *The Little Fugitive** (53) and followed this with *Lovers and Lollipops* (55). His *Weddings and Babies* (58), shot on location, was the first feature to be made with a portable camera with synchronous sound attachment and led to Ricky Leacock's (*q.v.*) work with such equipment.

EPSTEIN, Jean DIR France. (Warsaw March 26, 1897–Paris April 2, 1953) Abel Gance said of him: "He preferred to die a victim rather than live by prostituting his art. I still see his so expressive rhomboidal face whose hair seemed to burn like a black flame from his forehead. I hear his slow, singular voice, chary of words, picking his listeners. Must not this voice still be heard from the depths of the abyss?" His first contacts with the cinema came when he worked on bibliographical research with Auguste Lumière, then briefly with Germaine Dulac, Louis Delluc, and Abel Gance (all *q.v.*) in the early Twenties. The following is a summary of his work and contribution to the cinema based on Henri Langlois' account: "He never left the cinema. His work began in 1922 with *Pasteur* and ended in 1947 with *Le Tempestaire*. His films described as commercial could be signed by him without shame." "*Coeur fidèle* (23) is the triumph of impressionism in motion but also the triumph of the modern spirit. *La Belle Nivernaise* (23) is one of his most pure, most classical, most exquisite works, with its skillful, spare style, its subtle rhythm that cannot be analyzed. After the stresses of *Le Lion des Mogols* (24), his inspiration deserted him and he didn't develop beyond his earlier films." "With *L'Affiche* (24) and *Le Double amour* (25) he began to feel the weight of commercial pressures. *La Chute de la maison Usher* (28) was 'the intensification of acting through the use of slow motion.' Then he turned his back on success and left for Brittany to make what no one in France had made before: *Finis Terrae* (29) and *L'Or des mers* (32), which were made under the particular influence of Soviet films and were attempts to discover a much more realistic sense of wonder." But the sense of wonder born of reality found its most complete expression only in *Mor'Vran* (31). His work during the sound period was totally unappreciated and misunderstood. During the occupation, under the Vichy regime, Epstein was shut off from the studios and the forced inactivity only added to his other persecutions. Their names and Polish origin made him and his sister, Marie Epstein (who collaborated on many of his films), suspect. They were arrested by the Gestapo and only saved from deportation by the Red Cross and several friends. After the war, he worked for the Red Cross, finished his two most famous books, *L'Intelligence d'un machine* (46) and *Le Cinéma du diable* (47), and directed two shorts in Brittany, *Le Tempestaire* (47) and *Les Feux de la mer* (48), the latter for the United Nations.

DIR: *Pasteur* (22) (co-dir: Benoît-Lévy), *Les Vendanges* (22), *L'Auberge rouge** (23), *Coeur fidèle** (23), *La Montagne infidèle* (23), *La Belle Nivernaise** (23), *Le Lion des Mogols* (24), *L'Affiche* (24), *Le Double amour* (25), *Les Aventures de Robert Macaire* (25), *Mauprat* (26), *Au pays de George Sand* (26), *Six et demi-onze** (27), *La Glace à trois faces* (27), *La Chute de la maison Usher** (28), *Finis terrae** (29), *Sa tête* (29), *Le Pas de la mule* (30), *Mor'Vran/La Mer des corbeaux/The Sea of Ravens* (30), *Notre-Dame de Paris* (31), *La Chanson des peupliers* (31), *Le Cor* (31), *L'Or des mers** (32), *Les Berceaux* (32), *La Villanelle des rubans* (32), *Le Vieux Chaland* (32), *L'Homme à l'Hispano* (33), *La Châtelaine du Liban* (33), *Chanson d'Armor* (34), *La Vie d'un grand journal* (34), *Coeur de Gueux* (36), *La Bretagne* (36), *La Bourgogne* (36), *Vive la vie* (37), *La Femme du bout du monde* (37), *Les Bâtisseurs* (38), *Eau vive* (38), *Artères de France* (39), *Le Tempestaire* (47), *Les Feux de la mer* (48).

ERMLER, Friedrich DIR USSR. (Lettonie May 13, 1898–1967) A major film maker, who, after his first films in what would later be called the "neorealistic" manner (*Children of Storm, Katka's Reinette Apples, The Parisian Cobbler*), began directing psychological films with *Fragment of an Empire* and gave to this difficult but cinematic genre two masterpieces: *The Great Citizen* and *The Great*

Turning Point. He has said of himself and his work: "I have been driven by a taste for reality since my first films. This realism could be innate in me, but I nonetheless had to learn it. In the beginning I worked without thinking. I had only the desire to create. However, my films are set out like a reflection of the various Soviet periods. The Civil War is the theme of *The House in the Snow Drifts*, *Katka* describes particular social strata during the New Economic Policy (NEP) period, *The Parisian Cobbler* poses moral problems about young people during the reconstruction, *Counterplan* is the beginning of the Five Year Plans, *Peasants* depicts the struggle of the poor peasants against the kulaks, *The Great Citizen* the fight of the opposition against the Party, *The Great Turning Point*, the last war, the fighting of the partisans of Stalingrad." "The basis of my films generally comes from me, but to develop it, I have always used a scriptwriter. I never adapt a script during filming. I don't have enough talent to improvise. I study it carefully then use it like a conductor uses a music score, knowing what I must draw from the actors and the sets. It is men who matter the most to me and, with actors, their faces." "When I consider what I have made of my life, I would single out *The Great Citizen* and *The Great Turning Point*. They are worth more than all my other films."

DIR: *Deti buri/Children of Storm* (26) (co-dir: Eduard Johanson), *Katkabumazhnyr anyot/Katka's Reinette Apples** (26), *Dom v sugrobakh/The House in the Snow Drifts* (28), *Parizhsky sapozhnik/The Parisian Cobbler* (28), *Oblomok imperii/Fragment of an Empire** (29), *Vstrechnyi/Counterplan** (32) (co-dir: S. Yutkevich), *Krestyaniye/Peasants** (35), *Veliki grazhdanin/A Great Citizen** (Part I, 38; Part II, 39), *Ona zashchishchayet rodinu/She Defends Her Country** (43), *Veliki perelom/The Great Turning Point** (46), *Neokonchennaya povest/An Unfinished Story** (55), *Pervi den/The First Day* (58), *Under the Trial of History* (64), and various films for TV.

ERTUGRUL, Mushin DIR/PROD Turkey. (Istanbul 1888–) The founder of the Turkish cinema, stage dramatist and producer, director of the municipal theater in Istanbul and of the state theater in Ankara. He directed his first film in 1922, the first Turkish color film in 1953 and has made some thirty features in his career and produced many others.

ESCOFFIER, Marcel COSTUMES France. (Monaco Nov 29, 1910–) Notable costume designer, mainly for period films: for Cocteau, *La Belle et la Bête** (with Bérard), *Ruy Blas*, *L'Aigle à deux têtes*, *Orphée**; for Christian-Jaque,*Carmen**, *Fanfan la Tulipe**, *Nana**; for Ophüls, *Lola Montès** (with Georges Annenkov); for Visconti, *Senso** (with Piero Tosi).

ESPINOSA, Julio Garcia DIR Cuba. (193?–) Young Cuban film maker who began under the Batista dictatorship with an interesting social document, *El Megano*, (banned by the censors), and directed the second postrevolution feature, *Cuba Baila* (60).

ETAIX, Pierre DIR France. (Roanne Nov 23, 1928–) Excellent comedian, former circus clown, TV and music-hall actor, and gag writer for Jacques Tati (*q.v.*) on *Mon Oncle**. He acts in and scripts all his own films.
DIR: *La Rupture* (61), *Heureux anniversaire* (61) (both shorts, co-dir: J.-P. Carrière), *Le Soupirant** (62), *Insomnie* (63) (short), *Nous n'irons plus au bois* (63) (short), *Yoyo* (65), *Tant qu'on a la santé* (66), *Le Grand amour* (68), *Pays de Cocagne* (70).

EVEIN, Bernard ART DIR France. (Saint-Nazaire Jan 5, 1929–) Designer who is closely associated with many *nouvelle vague* directors and who has a delicate, poetic sense of reality. He has designed all of Jacques Demy's (*q.v.*) films, which alone marks him as a major talent. Also, notably, for Louis Malle, *Les Amants**, *Zazie dans le Métro**, *Vie privée*, *Le Feu follet**, *Viva Maria!*; for Chabrol, *Les Cousins**, *A double tour*; for Philippe de Broca, *Les Jeux de l'amour*, *L'Amant de cinq jours**; for Agnès Varda, *Cléo de 5 à 7**; for Godard, *Une femme est une femme*; for Alain Cavalier, *L'Insoumis* (64); for Serge Bourguignon, *Les Dimanches de ville d'Avray;* for René Clément, *Le Jour et l'heure*. Also designed costumes for Resnais *L'Année dernière à Marienbad**. Jacques Saulnier has collaborated with him on some of the above.

FABRI, Zoltan DIR Hungary. (1917–)
One of the best Hungarian directors [who
built an international reputation on his
films portraying country life, notably in
Merry-Go-Round. He began his career
as actor, stage manager, and set designer
and often acts as his own art director.]
DIR: *Colony Underground* (51), *Vihar/
The Storm* (52), *Eletjel/Fourteen Lives
in Danger* (54), *Körhinta/Merry-Go-
Round** (55), *Hannibal tanar ur/Profes-
sor Hannibal** (56), *Bolond aprilis/
Summer Clouds* (57), *Edes Anna/Anna*
(58), *Duvad/The Brute* (59), *Ket felido
a pokolban/The Last Goal* (61), *Nap-
pali sötetseg/Darkness in Daytime* (63),
Husz ora/Twenty Hours (64), *Viziva-
rosi nyar/A Hard Summer* (65) (TV),
Utoszezon/Late Season (67), *a Pal utcai
fiuk/The Paul Street Boys* (68), *The
Tot Family* (69).

FANCK, Arnold DIR Germany. (Franken-
thal March 6, 1889–) A pioneer in
the field of "mountain" films who worked
with several talented cameramen (Sepp
Allgeier, Richard Angst, and Hans
Schneeberger) and whose favorite actress was Leni Riefenstahl (*q.v.*). A doctor of geology, he directed his first short
documentaries in 1920 with Dr. Taurn,
eventually moved into fiction films, and
successfully continued his career under
the Nazi regime.
DIR: *Wunder des Schneeschuhs* (20) (co-
dir: Taurn), *Im Kampf mit dem Berg*
(21) (co-dir: Taurn), *Pomperlys Kampf
mit dem Schneeschuh* (22) (co-dir:
Holger Madsen), *Der Berg des Schichsals*
(24), *Der Heilige Berg* (26), *Der Grosse
Sprung* (27), *Die Weisse Hölle vom Piz
Palü/The White Hell of Pitz Palu* (29)
(co-dir: G. W. Pabst), *Stürme über dem
Montblanc* (30), *Der Weisse Rausch*
(31), *S.O.S. Eisberg* (33), *Der Ewige
Traum/König des Mont-blanc* (34), *Die*

Tochter des Samurai (37), *Ein Robinson*
(40).

FAULKNER, William SCEN USA. (1897–July
6, 1962) Famous American novelist,
several of whose works have been filmed
(*Sanctuary* by Tony Richardson, *Intruder in the Dust** by Clarence Brown,
The Sound and the Fury by Martin Ritt,
Tarnished Angels (from *Pylon*) by
Douglas Sirk, *The Reivers* by Mark Ry-
dell) who also worked in Hollywood,
[notably in an intermittent collaboration
with Howard Hawks (*q.v.*): *Today We
Live* (33), *The Road to Glory* (36), *To
Have and Have Not* (45), *The Big
Sleep** (46), *Land of the Pharaohs* (54)
(all co-scenario). Also *Slave Ship* (36)
(dir: Tay Garnett) and numerous contributions to other scripts during the
Thirties and Forties.]

FAUSTMANN, Erik "Hampe" DIR Sweden.
(Stockholm July 3, 1919–1961) Swedish
actor in the Forties and Fifties and a
film maker of the Swedish "middle generation" with a dedicated concern for
portraying social themes.
DIR: *Natt i Hamn/Night in the Harbor*
(43), *Sonja* (43), *Vi Behöver Varann/
We Need Each Other* (44), *Flickan och
Djävulen/The Girl and the Devil* (44),
Brott och Straff/Crime and Punishment
(45), *Harald Handfaste* (46), *När An-
gärna Blommar/When Meadows Bloom*
(46), *Krigsmans Erinran/A Soldier's
Duties* (47), *Lars Harde* (48), *Främ-
mande Hamn/Foreign Harbor* (48),
Smeder pa Luffen/Vagabond Blacksmiths
(49), *Restaurant Intim* (50), *Kvinnan
bakom allt/Woman Behind Everything*
(51 released 56), *Ubat 39/U-Boat 39*
(52), *Hon kom som en Vind/She Came
Like a Wind* (52), *Kvinnohuset/House
of Women* (53), *Gud Fader och Tat-
taren/God and the Gypsy* (54), *Cafe*

79

Lunchrasten (54), *Resa i Natten/Night Journey* (55), *Ingen sa Tokig som Jag/No One Is Crazier Than I Am* (55). Also three short films in 1951.

*FEHER, Friedrich DIR Germany/Britain. (Vienna March 16, 1889–Hollywood 1945) The director of the curious, baroque *Robber Symphony* about whom little is known. He began as an actor and played Alan in *The Cabinet of Dr. Caligari** (for which he claimed artistic responsibility after Weine's death). He made several period and horror films in Germany before leaving there in 1933 because of his Jewish origin, and directed *The Robber Symphony* in Britain. He then moved to the USA, where he acted in minor films. All his films feature his wife, Magda Sonja.
DIR (notably): *Das Blutgeld* (13), *Der Unsichtbare Gast* (19), *Die Rote Hexe* (20), *Tyrannei des Todes* (20), *Die Tänzerin Marion* (20), *Carrière* (21), *Marionetten des Teufels* (23) (2 parts, co-dir: J. Brandt), *Sanin* (25), *Das Graue Haus* (26), *Verbotene Liebe* (26–27), *Mata Hari* (27), *Die Geliebre des Gouverneurs* (27), *Maria Stuart* (27), *Hotelgeheimnisse* (28), *Ihr Junge/Wenn die Geigen klingen* (Ger/Aust/Czech 31), *Le Loup Garou* (32), *Gehetzte Menschen/Steckbrief Z 48/The Robber Symphony** (Brit36).

FEJOS, Paul (Pal) DIR Hungary/USA/Denmark, etc. (Budapest 1898–1963) An oddly changeable film maker whose work has ranged from the mediocre to the brilliant and from experimental to documentary. He began as a set designer, made his directorial debut on commercial films in Hungary, moved to the USA in 1923 to work in bacteriological research, made the experimental low-budget evocation of a suicide, *The Last Moment* (27), and the pre-neorealist masterpiece, *Lonesome* (28), He returned to Europe and made films in France, Austria, Hungary, and Denmark. His films in the Thirties are of lesser interest, despite the undeniable qualities of *Spring Shower*. He became interested in ethnological documentaries and in Thailand in 1939 made a fictionalized portrait of peasant life, *A Handful of Rice,* for a Swedish producer. Earlier he had made several short anthropological documentaries in Madagascar (35–36)

for Nordisk and in the East Indies (37–38) for Svensk Filmindustri before returning to the USA in 1939 to devote himself entirely to anthropological research.
[DIR: *Fekete kapitang/The Black Captain* (Hung20), *Joslat/Prophecy* (Hung20), *Pan* (Hung20), *Lidercnyomas/Nightmare* (Hung20), *Ujraelok/Revived* (Hung21), *Egri csillagok* (Hung23) (unfinished), *The Last Moment* (USA27), *Lonesome** (USA28), *Broadway* (USA 29), *Erik the Great Illusionist/The Last Performance* (USA29), *The Big House** (USA30), (French and German versions only), *Fantômas* (Fr31), *L'Amour à l'Americaine* (Fr31), *Tavaszi Zapor/Spring Shower/Marie** (Hung/Fr32), *Itel a Balaton/The Verdict of Lake Balaton* (Hung32), *Sonnenstrahl* (Aust33), *Fruhlingstimmen* (Aust33), *Flugten fra millionerne* (Den33), *Fange Nr. 1/Prisoner No. 1* (Den35), *Fredlos* (Den35), *Den Gyldne Smil/The Golden Smile* (Den35), *The Bilo* (36), *Dance Contest in Esira* (36) (documentaries for Nordisk, made in Madagascar), *Tambora* (37), *Att Sagla ar Nordvantigt* (38) (documentaries for Svensk Filmindustri, made in the East Indies), *Man och kvinna/A Handful of Rice** (Swed/Thailand39).]

FELLINI, Federico DIR Italy. (Rimini Jan 20, 1920–) Film maker with a powerful personality and an exuberant style, sometimes inconsistent in quality, but who possesses the somewhat rare talent of being able to bring "types" to life. His film career began as a gag writer in 1939 and progressed to scriptwriting. He gained experience during the most creative period of neorealism, working with Rossellini (*q.v.*) on *Rome, Open City,* and *Paisà,* during which period he said he discovered "an Italy unknown to us because for 20 years we had been prisoners of a political regime that had truly blindfolded us." Lattuada (*q.v.*) gave him his first opportunity to direct on *Luci del Varietà* (50). The satire of "heart-throb" heroes, *The White Sheik,* and the autobiographical *I Vitelloni* were both orthodox neorealist films, as was his episode in *Amore in Città.* But *La Strada* (54) marked his break with the movement. "Neorealism had been a major impetus," he said in 1960, "a truly sacred and hallowed guide for everyone. But soon its errors became very serious. If its humble attitude before life was extended also to the camera, then direction was no longer needed. Now as far as I'm concerned, the cinema bears a very close similarity to the circus." *La Strada* is a kind of symbolic circus, with its three heroes — the strong man, the acrobat, and the female clown — its traveling caravan, and its shows. "Astronomical distances separate people," he said then, "they live alongside each other without being aware of their solitude, without ever establishing real relationships among themselves." A kind of mysticism is also evident in his films of which he said: "If by Christian you mean love thy neighbor, then all my films focus on this theme. They show a world without love, people who exploit others, a world in which there is always an ordinary person who wants to give love and lives for love." This idealism does not exclude social criticism. *Il Bidone* is a satire in the *Monsieur Verdoux* manner, depicting the falsity of a social attitude and structure by placing it in another context. Gelsomina in *Nights of Cabiria* is a kind of Don Quixote fighting, lance raised, against the ogres of a corrupt world — a fresco which Fellini painted in *La Dolce Vita*. [His next film, *8½*, marked a new development in Fellini's work, more personal, full of dazzling images, whose blend of comic and poetic fantasy gives an insight into Fellini's preoccupations with memories, life, love, and death. *Juliet of the Spirits*, in many ways his best film, is a profound exploration of the mental world of woman, a fantasy in the most complete sense of the term. *Fellini Satyricon*, for all its imagism, fails to convey his intentions, but his inventive TV document, *The Clowns*, is delightful in its blend of autobiographical elements (the clown with whom Fellini identifies) and its entertaining visual fireworks.]

SCEN (notably): (all in collaboration) for Rossellini, *Roma, Città Aperta**, *Paisà**, *Il Miracolo, Francesco, Giullare di Dio, Europa 51**; for Alberto Lattuada, *Il Delitto di Giovanni Episcopo, Senza Pietà**, *Il Mulino del Po;* for Pietro Germi, *In Nome della Legge**, *Il Cammino della Speranza**, *La Città si Difende, Il Brigante di Tacca del Lupo;* for Mario Bonard, *Avante c'è Porto* (42), *Campo de Fiori* (42); for Riccardo Freda, *Tutta la Città Canta* (43); for

Eduardo Felippo, *Fortunella* (58); and all his own films.

DIR: *Luci del Varietà** (50) (co-dir: Lattuada), *Lo Sceicco Bianco** (52), *I Vitelloni** (53), *Amore in Città** (53) (one episode), *La Strada** (54), *Il Bidone** (55), *Le Notti di Cabiria** (56), *La Dolce Vita** (60), *Boccacio '70* (62) (one episode), *8½** (63), *Giulietta degli Spiriti** (65), *A Tre Passi dal Delirio/Histoires extraordinaires* (67) (one episode), *Fellini Satyricon* (69), *I Clowns* (70) (TV).

FERNANDEZ, Emilio DIR Mexico. (Hondo, Coahuila March 26, 1904–) Mexican film maker (who has also acted in the USA and Mexico) who, during the most creative period in the Mexican cinema in the Forties, established an international reputation with *Maria Candelaria*. He followed this with a series of major national portraits, like the murals of Diego Rivera and Siqueiros, reflecting both the Spanish and Indian traditions and a certain popular taste for melodrama: *Flor Silvestre*, the somewhat cold *Perla* (from a script by Steinbeck), the fiery *Enamorada*, the violent *Rio Escondido* and the stylish and moving *Pueblerina*. But, on the other hand, his work also contains touristic folklore elements and a taste for crudely melodramatic plots that gradually took over from his better qualities. And, when the Mexican film industry drifted into commercialism in the Fifties, he found himself outmoded. All his films from 1943–50 PHOTOG Gabriel Figueroa (*q.v.*), except for *Pepita Jiminez*.

DIR: *La Isla de la Pasion* (41), *Soy puro Mexicano* (42), *Flor Silvestre* (43), *Las Abandonados* (44), *Bugambilia* (44), *Maria Candelaria/Xochimilco** (45), *Pepita Jiminez* (46), *La Perla* (46), *Enamorada* (46), *Rio Escondido** (48), *Maclovia* (48), *Salon Mexico* (49), *Pueblerina* (49), *La Malquerida* (49), *Duelo en la Montañas* (49), *The Torch* (50), *Victimas del Pecado* (50), *Un Dia de Vida* (50), *Islas Marias* (50), *Suave Patria* (51), *La Bien Amada* (51), *Acapulco* (52), *Tu y el Mar* (52), *Cuando levanta la Niebla* (52), *La Red/ The Net* (53), *El Rapto* (53), *La Rosa blanca* (54), *La Rebelion de los Colgados* (54), *Nosotros dos* (Sp54), *La Tierra del Fuego se Apaga* (Argentina 55), *Una Cita de Amor/The Rebel* (56), *El Impostor* (57), *Pueblito, o el*

Amor (61), *A Loyal Soldier of Pancho Villa* (66). Also directed several exteriors for Huston's *The Unforgiven*.

FERRERI, Marco DIR Spain/Italy. (Milan 1928–) Former journalist who was in Spain from 1955–60 and directed there two remarkably ferocious, acerbic satires *El Pisito* and *El Cochecito*. His first Italian feature *Ape Regina*, a satire on Christian marriage, was equally corrosive but his later films have not matched it.

DIR: *El Pisito* (Sp58), *Los Chicos* (Sp 59), *El Cochecito** (Sp59), *Le Italiane è l'Amore* (It61) (one episode), *Ape Regina/The Conjugal Bed* (It63), *La Donna Scimmia* (It64), *Controsesso* (It64) (one episode), *Oggi, Domani, Dopodomani/Paranoia* (It/Fr65) (one episode), *Marcia Nuziale* (It65), *Dillinger è morto* (It68), *Il Seme dell'Uomo* (69), *L'Udienza* (71).

FERREYRA, José A. DIR Argentina. (Buenos Aires 1889–Buenos Aires 1943) Pioneer of the Argentinian cinema who created its artistic foundations. Originally a painter and designer, he was a somewhat bohemian artist with an understanding of popular life, a sure and supple style, and a sense of characters and characterization.

DIR: *Una Noche de Garufa* (15) (short), *El Tango de la Muerte* (17), *Campo Ajuera* (19), *Mientre Buenos Aires duerme* (21), *La Guacha* (21), *La Chica della Calle Florida* (21), *Buenos Aires* (22), *Ciudad de Ensueño* (22), *El Organito de la Tarde* (24), *El Arriero de Yacanto* (24), *Mi Ultimo Canto* (24), *Muchachita de Chiclana* (26), *Perden Viejita* (27), *El Cantar di mi Ciudad* (30), *La Canción del Gaucho* (30), *Muñequitas Portenas** (31), *Calles de Buenos Aires* (34), *Puente Alsina* (35), *Ayudame a Vivir* (36), *Besos Brujos* (37), *Muchachos de la Ciudad* (37), *La Ley que Olvidaron* (38), *Chimbella* (39), *El Hijo del Barrio* (40), *La Mujer y la Selva* (41).

FERRY, Jean SCEN France. (Capens June 16, 1906–) Scriptwriter and dialogue writer, with a background in surrealism, who has written some 50 films, notably those of Clouzot (*q.v.*) and Christian-Jaque (*q.v.*).

FESCOURT, Herni DIR France. (Béziers Nov 23, 1880–Neuilly Aug 9, 1966) Sensi-

tive, cultured, and with a real sense of visual design, he is one of the great French film makers. Originally a musician, journalist, and lawyer, he began directing for Gaumont in 1912 and later directed many tasteful, forceful adaptations of literary works, including an excellent *Les Misérables*. However, his talents were never given the recognition they deserved. He lectured on film at IDHEC after 1942.

DIR: Numerous films for Gaumont 1912–14, including: *La Méthode du professeur Neura, Un mari à l'essai, La Lumière qui tue, La Mort sur Paris, Fille de Prince*. Also (notably): *Mathias Sandorff* (20), *Rouletabille* (22), *Mandrin* (23), *Les Grands* (24), *Les Misérables** (25), *La Maison du Maltais* (27), *L'Occident* (27), *Le Comte de Monte-Cristo* (29), *La Maison de la flèche* (32, in Brit), *Serments* (Swed31), *Pour service de nuit* (Swed31), *L'Occident* (37), *Bar du Sud* (38), *Retour de Flamme* (42).

FEUILLADE, Louis DIR France. (Lunel Feb 19, 1873–Nice Feb 26, 1925) A major pioneer of the French cinema who, in his twenty-year film career, made some 800 films of all types without claiming to be the great artist which, in fact, he was. He was in the cavalry from 1891 to 1895 when he married, became a wine broker and later, a journalist and poet for *La Croix, La Revue mondiale*, etc. He approached Léon Gaumont (*q.v.*) in 1905 with some film scripts, was warmly encouraged by Gaumont's artistic director, Alice Guy (*q.v.*) and in 1906 directed his first films. When Alice Guy left Paris to go to Berlin with her husband she recommended Feuillade as her replacement. His first films were trick films in which he took the camera into the streets to create comedy that often ended in a chase and that included extravagant special effects. Over the next years he worked industriously, directing period films, adventure films, melodramas, "art" films, religious films, and serials. Some 502 films have been identified as his and he certainly made many more. (The filmography below is extremely abridged.) He was also responsible for shaping the careers of Emile Cohl, Jean Durand, Léonce Perre, Musidora, René Cresté, René Navarre, Henri Fescourt, Jacques Feyder, and even René Clair. Abel Gance wrote his first script for Feuillade in 1908. In 1911

Feuillade made his first major contribution with the *La Vie telle qu'elle est* series, which he described as "an attempt, for the first time, to transpose realism into literature, the theater, and the arts." He reached the peak of his artistic development with the superb blend of realism, fantasy, and visual poetry in his episode films: *Fantômas* (13–14), *Les Vampires* (15–16), *Judex* (16), and *Tih Minh* (18). Though largely dismissed at the time by established critics, Breton and Aragon (the future founders of surrealism) were unstinting in their enthusiasm: "It is in *Les Vampires* that the great reality of our century will be found. They are beyond fashion, beyond taste." In 1920 Feuillade wrote: "With rare exceptions I have written all my own scripts. Just as one needs cinematic actors, it is necessary to have writers who specialize in this art. Good adaptations of plays and novels are exceptional. In fact, they are usually desecrations." After the war, when he was worn out with overwork and too little rest, his work lost its earlier imaginative and innovative qualities and he found himself among the "old guard" and was treated like a Philistine. He died in 1925 in Nice, where he had gone to complete his last film, *Le Stigmate*. His work was largely forgotten until after the Second World War, when it was resurrected, largely through screenings at the Cinémathèque Française. Seen there by many young critics (and future *nouvelle vague* directors), Feuillade's work was re-examined and rehabilitated. The one-time "honest artisan" became classed as one of the great masters of the cinema.

DIR (notably): *Le Billet de banque* (06), *C'est papa qui prend la purge* (06), *l'Homme aimanté* (07), *La Légende de la fileuse* (07), *Une dame vraiment bien* (08), *La Récit du colonel* (08), *Le Tic* (08), *Promethée* (08), *Le Collier de la reine* (09), *La Mort de Mozart* (09), *Mater Dolorosa* (09), *La Légende des Phares* (09), *Les Sept péchés capitaux* (10) (7 films in color), *Le Pater* (10), *Bébé* series (10–13) (74 films), *La Vierge d'Argos* (11), *La Vie telle qu'elle est* series (11–13) (17 films), *Dans la brousse* (12), *Le Noël de Francesca* (12), *Le Mort vivant* (12), *L'Anneau fatal* (12), *Le Detective Dervieux* series (12–13) (5 films), *Bout-de-Zan* series (12–16) (53 films), *L'Agonie de Byzance* (13), *Fantômas* series* (13–14) (5

films), *La Vie drôle* series (13–18) (35 films), *Les Fiancés de 1914* (14), *Union sacrée* (15), *Les Vampires* series* (15–16) (10 films), *Le Double jeu* (16), *Le Noël de Poilu* (16), *Judex* (16) (12 episodes), *La Nouvelle Mission de Judex* (17) (12 episodes), *Herr Doktor* (17), *Le Bandeau sur les yeux* (17), *La Fugue de Lily* (17), *L'Homme sans visage* (18), *Les Petites marionnettes* (18), *Vendémiare* (18), *Tih Minh* (18) (12 episodes), *Barrabas* (19) (12 episodes), *L'Engrenage* (19), *Le Nocturne* (19), *L'Énigme* (19), *Les Deux gamines* (20) (12 episodes), *L'Orpheline* (21) (12 episodes), *Parisette* (21) (12 episodes), *Le Fils de Flibustier* (22) (12 episodes), *Belle humeur* series (21–22), *Vindicta* (23) (5 episodes), *L'Orphelin de Paris* (23) (6 episodes), *La Gosseline* (23), *Le Gamin de Paris* (23), *La Fille bien gardée* (24), *Pierrot, Pierrette* (24), *Lucette* (24), *Le Stigmate* (24) (6 episodes). Almost all his films 08–15 PHOTOG Guérin; 16–24, L. Morizet.

FEYDER, Jacques (Jacques Frédérix) DIR France/USA. (Belgium July 21, 1885– Switzerland May 25, 1948) A film maker who remained on the fringes of impressionism in the Twenties and was one of the major creators of poetic realism in the Thirties. The son of a Belgian bourgeois family who intended a military career for him and who insisted he change his name when as a young man he moved to Paris to enter the theater. After numerous small roles (including film ones for Méliès, 1911, and Louis Feuillade, Gaston Ravel, etc.) he got his first chance to direct for Léon Gaumont in 1915 when the war created a shortage of directors. His wife, Françoise Rosay, the star of many of his best films, was seen first in his second film. After some dozen films on which he learned his profession, he established an international reputation in the Twenties with *L'Atlantide*, *Crainquebille* (which Griffith greatly admired), *Visage d'enfants*, *Gribiche*, and especially his Zola adaptation, *Thérèse Raquin*. Following the excellent satire, *Les Nouveaux Messieurs*, he moved to Hollywood as sound films were being introduced and spent a rather unproductive four years there, during which he worked on melodramas, including two Greta Garbo vehicles (*The Kiss*, *Anna Christie*). He returned to France, marking his return with the excellent *Le Grand jeu,* and followed this with *Pension Mimosas,* a characteristic example of poetic realism. The following year he made what is perhaps his most famous film, *La Kermesse héroïque,* a visually rich tribute to the great painters of his native Flanders. His work thereafter fell into decline with *Knight without Armour* (for Korda in London), *Les Gens du voyage,* and *La Loi du nord.* He made the mediocre *Une femme disparaît* in Switzerland during the war and acted as artistic supervisor for two films by other directors before he died. He always felt that the secret of film-making lay in the selection of a story that would appeal to the public, and of a milieu and atmosphere, and in carefully bringing these to life. In 1925 he wrote: "Everything can be translated into screen terms. Everything can be expressed through images. It is possible to make an appealing and moving film as easily from the 10th Chapter of Montesquieu's *L'Esprit des lois* as from a novel by Paul de Kock. But in order to do that one must have a cinematic soul." His predilection for melodrama did not always serve him well on works that were derived from the traditions of Zola and Maupassant (and on which his best collaborators were Marcel Carné (*q.v.*) as assistant and Charles Spaak (*q.v.*) as scriptwriter). Marcel Carné wrote of him: "He dreams of bringing to the screen such-and-such a satirical farce or such-and-such a conflict between workers and management, but he found it necessary always to have recourse to a romantic story. He was minutely careful in his shooting script. Everything was weighed and proportioned with a disconcerting knowledge." He said to Charles Spaak: "To direct is to defend oneself against all those who fuss about around us and to bring back to an intellectual design that which tends to escape." He added that the cinema, which needed life and real people, was often fed on the colorless and the ersatz — a forecast of the sad end of his own career, a career that Abel Gance has rightly said puts him among the cinema's martyrs.

DIR: *M. Pinson, policer* (15), *Têtes des femmes, femmes de tête* (16), *Le Pied qui étrient* (16) (four episodes), *Le Bluff* (16), *Un conseil d'ami* (16), *L'Homme de compagnie* (16), *Tiens, vous êtes à Poitiers* (16), *L'Instinct est maître* (16), *Le Frère de lait* (16), *Le Billard casse* (16), *Abregeons les formalités* (16), *Le Trouvaille de Bûchu* (16), *Le Pardessus de demi-saison* (17), *Les Vieilles femmes de l'hospice* (17), *La Faute d'orthographe* (19), *L'Atlantide** (21), *Crainquebille** (22), *Visages d'enfants* (23–25), *L'Image* (23–25), *Gribiche* (25), *Carmen** (26), *Au pays de roi lepreux* (27), *Thérèse Raquin/Du Sollst Nicht Ehebrechen** (Ger/Fr28), *Les Nouveaux Messieurs** (28), *The Kiss* (USA29), *Anna Christie* (USA29), *The Unholy Night* (USA30) (French version only), *His Glorious Night* (French and German versions only: *Olympia*), *Son of India* (USA31), *Daybreak* (USA31), *Le Grand jeu** (Fr34), *Pension Mimosas** (35), *La Kermesse héroïque** (35), *Knight without Armour* (Brit37), *Fahrendes Volk/Les Gens du voyage* (Ger 38), *La Loi du Nord/La Piste du Nord* (Fr39–42), *Une femme disparaît* (Switz 41); and artistic director for *Maturareise* (Switz43) (dir: S. Steiner), *Macadam* (Fr46) (dir: Marcel Blistène).

SCEN: *Gardiens de Phare** (29) (dir: Jean Grémillon), and all his own films.

FIGUEROA, Gabriel PHOTOG Mexico/USA. (Mexico 1907–) Cameraman steeped in the best Mexican traditions who worked as assistant to Gregg Toland (*q.v.*) in Hollywood, 1935–36. His elaborate, sometimes ornate, visual style, inspired by the frescoes of Diego Rivera and Siqueiros, was a major factor in the best films of Emilio Fernandez (*q.v.*), but he was also able to adopt a sparse style for Buñuel's (*q.v.*) Mexican masterpieces. In recent years he has worked on several Hollywood films.

PHOTOG (notably): for Fernando de Fuentes, *Alla en el Rancho Grande* (36); for Chano Urrueta, *Noche de los Mayas* (39); for Fernandez, *Flor Silvestre* (43), *Maria Candelaria** (45), *Las Abandonadas* (44), *La Perla* (46), *Enamorada* (46), *Rio Escondido** (48), *Maclovia* (48), *La Malquerida* (49), *The Torch* (50), *La Rosa blanca* (55), *La Tierra del Fuego se apago* (55) and others; for Buñuel, *Los Olvidados** (50), *El** (52), *Nazarin** (58), *La Fièvre mont à El Pao* (59), *The Young One** (60), *El Angel Exterminador** (62), *Simon del Desierto* (65); for John Ford, *The Fugitive* (USA47); for John Huston, *Night of the Iguana* (USA64); for Don Siegel *Two Mules for Sister Sarah* (USA70);

for Brian Hutton, *Kelly's Heroes* (USA 70).

*FISCHER, Gunnar PHOTOG Sweden. (Ljungby 1910–) Brilliant cameraman, with a special flair for chiaroscuro effects and evocative outdoor work, who is most famous for his work on 12 of Bergman's (*q.v.*) best films. He joined the industry in 1935 as assistant to Julius Jaenzon (*q.v.*) and photographed his first film in 1939.
PHOTOG (notably): for Erik Faustmann, *Natt i Hamn* (43), *Krigsmans erinran* (47); for Dreyer, *Tva Människor* (45); for Lars-Erik Kjellgren, *Soldat Bom* (48), *Lek pa Regnbagen* (58); for Bergman, *Hamnstadt* (48), *Törst** (49), *Till Glädje* (50), *Sant händer inte Har* (50), *Sommarlek* (51), *Kvinnors Väntan* (52), *Sommaren med Monika** (52), *Sommarnattens Leende** (55), *Det Sjunde Inseglet** (56), *Smultronstället** (57), *Ansiktet* (58), *Djävulens Oga* (60); for Hasse Ekman, *Gabrielle* (54), *Egen ingäng* (56); for Alf Kjellin, *Lustgarden/ Pleasure Garden* (61), *Siska* (62); for Arne Sucksdorff, *Pojken i trädet/Boy in the Trees* (61); for Vilgot Sjöman, *491* (64); for Lars-Magnus Lindgren, *Svarta palmkronor/The Black Palm Trees* (68); for Goran Gentele, *Miss and Mrs. Sweden* (70) and three episodes of *Stimulantia* (65–67).

FISHER, Terence DIR Britain. (London 1904–) An editor in the Thirties who graduated to directing melodramas for the Gainsborough studios and then horror films for Hammer in the Fifties and Sixties. He has made numerous films, from the well-tried stories of *Dracula**, *Frankenstein**, the Phantom of the Opera, Dr. Jekyll, etc., but is far from being a new Tod Browning (*q.vv.*).

*FISCHINGER, Oskar ANIM Germany/USA. (Gelnhausen, Germany 1900–1967) Imaginative pioneer in the field of abstract animated interpretations of musical themes, a disciple of Ruttman (*q.v.*) in the Twenties, who made his first *Film Studies* prior to 1925. He worked on the special effects of a number of films (including Fritz Lang's *Frau im Mond*) and several film commercials. His earlier films have a remarkable unity of sound and image in which geometric forms move in synchronization to the music. In 1933, he made his first color film (in Gasparcolor), *Circles,* and when his *Composition in Blue* won a special prize at Venice in 1935 he was invited to Hollywood by Paramount. There he continued his abstract experiments and designed the Bach sequence in Disney's *Fantasia** (though his contribution was not used in the final film). In 1947, he made the prize-winning *Motion Painting No. 1* using oil painting on glass and invented the Lumigraph "color organ." In the Fifties he made a number of TV commercials and experimented with stereoscopic abstract films. His most notable films include (music source in parentheses): *Study No. 5* (Ger28) (jazz), *Study No. 6* (Ger30) (Guerrero's "Vaya Veronica"), *Study No. 7* (Ger31) (Brahms's "Hungarian Dance No. 5"), *Study No. 8* (Ger31) (Dukas's "The Sorcerer's Apprentice"), *Study No. 9* (Ger31) (Brahms's "Hungarian Dance No. 6"), *Study No. 10* (Ger31) (Verdi's "Aida"), *Study No. 11* (Ger32) (Mozart's minuet "Divertissement"), *Study No. 12* (Ger32) (Rubinstein's "Lichtertanz"), *Coloratura* (Ger32) (trailer for feature film), *Circles* (Ger33) (Grieg, Wagner), *Composition in Blue* (Ger33) (Nicolai's *Merry Wives of Windsor*), *Allegretto* (USA36) (jazz), *An Optical Poem* (USA37), *An American March* (USA39) (Sousa's "Stars and Stripes"), *Motion Painting No. 1* (USA47) (Bach's "Brandenberg Concerto No. 3").

FLAHERTY, Robert DIR USA/Britain. (Iron Mountain, Michigan Feb 16, 1884–New York July 23, 1951) The Jean-Jacques Rousseau of the cinema, and one of its greatest geniuses, who created the "narrative documentary" — a method of filmmaking whose stories, actors, and settings were taken from life itself. His films have a deep human warmth, an understanding of what he called the true spirit of man, and reflect his passionate attention to detail and his interest in everyday behavior and the common feelings of mankind. They demonstrated that every man is capable of "acting out" his own life for the camera. Though he did not use the "camera eye" as a technique for instantaneous documentation and though he used reconstructed scenes, he can justifiably be called the first master of *cinéma-vérité*. He took infinite pains with his work and once said: "Film is the longest distance between two points." After studies at Upper Canada College

in Toronto, he became a mineralogist, developed an interest in the Canadian Arctic, and began exploring there, backed by Sir William Mackenzie, in 1910. In 1917 he took a film camera with him and filmed the expeditions to Baffinland and Belcher Islands, but the negative of this was burned in a fire in Toronto (a print survived but was later lost). In 1920 he decided to return to the North and, backed by a fur company, filmed the daily life of an Eskimo family in *Nanook of the North*. It was a great worldwide success and led to his being offered a completely free hand by Jesse L. Lasky (*q.v.*) of Paramount to make a film anywhere in the world. The result was the admirable portrait of Samoan life, *Moana*, a major critical success, but a film whose modest commercial success did not match Paramount's expectations. For MGM he began production of *White Shadows in the South Seas* with W. S. Van Dyke (*q.v.*), but withdrew when the film was turned into romanticized fiction. With F. W. Murnau (*q.v.*) he began production of the independent *Tabu*, but again withdrew when it appeared they had totally different approaches to the same material. Flaherty left for Europe and was invited by John Grierson to join the British documentary movement. In Britain, with the enthusiastic support of Michael Balcon (*q.v.*) of Gaumont-British, he was able to visit the Aran Islands off the coast of Ireland and create *Man of Aran* with its theme of the struggle of man against the sea. It received more praise than any other Flaherty film since *Nanook* and Alexander Korda (*q.v.*) agreed to back his next film, *Elephant Boy*, in India. But, after filming was completed in India, the studio took over his material, added completely new studio-shot dialogue scenes (directed by Zoltan Korda) and edited the whole to play up the melodrama. In 1939, Pare Lorentz (*q.v.*), head of the US Film Service, invited Flaherty to return to the USA to make a film on the problems of erosion. The result was the epic, *The Land,* a film that was given only limited nontheatrical circulation in the USA and none abroad. Then, backed by Standard Oil, he returned to the dreams of his childhood with the lyrical *Louisiana Story,* his last film. In 1926 he wrote: "The truly great films have yet to be made. They will not be the work of the large studios but of amateurs in the literal sense, of passionate people who will tackle something without commercial aims. And these films will be made with art and truth." Jean Grémillon said of him: "In his so clear eyes he had an intensity and a gentleness which was that of the child he had been, falling asleep in his moccasins, dreaming of Indian country where there was gold. He found that gold: it is what he gave to us. He always searched for the same thing: the mark of man, both in the struggle with nature that he could only master in the enchanted world of childhood and in the sense of wonder at the natural world of *Moana* and *Louisiana Story*. No other film maker spent more time than he in studying and understanding the elements of his theme and in drawing out its profound and basic subject matter."
DIR: *Nanook of tthe North** (20–21), *Moana – a Romance of the Golden Age** (25), *The Pottery Maker* (25) (short), *The Twenty-Four Dollar Island* (26) (short), *Tabu** (31) (co-dir: F. W. Murnau), *Industrial Britain* (Brit32) (completed and ed: John Grierson), *Man of Aran** (Brit34), *Elephant Boy* (Brit37) (co-dir: Zoltan Korda), *The Land** (42), *Louisiana Story** (48). Flaherty also worked on *White Shadows in the South Seas** (28), but little of the final film is attributable to him. [Also, PHOTOG: *Guernica* (49) (ed: David Flaherty), PROD American version of *The Titan: Story of Michelangelo* (Switz 40) (dir: Curt Oertel), *What's Happened to Sugar?* (50), *The Gift of Green* (50) (both, dir: David Flaherty).]

*FLEISCHER, David PROD USA. (New York June 14, 1894–   ) Younger brother of animator Max Fleischer, director on several of his brother's films, and administrative head of the Fleischer Studios in Florida in its heyday. He also claims to have patented in 1929 a technique for drawing sound directly onto film.

*FLEISCHER, Max ANIM/PROD USA. (Austria July 17, 1889–   ) A major American cartoonist who was the only serious rival to Disney in the Thirties. Though Austrian-born, he came to the USA as an infant. He worked first as a newspaper cartoonist and during the First World War made instructional cartoons for the Army. After the war he created his first character, Koko the Clown in the *Out of the Inkwell** series, which mixed animation and live action. One of his other early characters was *Betty Boop,* the first and only cartoon vamp, who was modeled on the singer Helen Kane and had continuing problems with the censor over her sexiness. He made the first *Popeye the Sailor* film in 1933 based on a comic-strip character created by the cartoonist Segar, the plots of which followed a common pattern in which Popeye would become invincible after eating spinach. (Fleischer is said to have had a financial agreement with spinach canning interests.) He also made a series of animated songs with the famous bouncing ball. In 1936 the first medium-length film from the Fleischer Studios (headed by his younger brother) appeared: *Popeye the Sailor Meets Sinbad the Sailor.* Apparently encouraged by the success of Disney's (*q.v.*) *Snow White and the Seven Dwarfts*,* Fleischer made the full-length *Guilliver's Travels** in 1939. It was not a success and his next feature *Mr. Bug Goes to Town/ Hoppity Goes to Town* (41) was a flop. Unable to keep up with developments in animation, he stopped independent work and became production chief of Paramount's cartoon division, from which Popeye cartoons continued to flow in an uninspired stream for some years.

FLEISCHER, Richard DIR USA. (New York Dec 8, 1916–) The son of Max Fleischer (*q.v.*), he studied medicine and dramatic art, joined RKO in 1940 as production assistant, and directed a number of documentaries from 1942 to 1946. (*This is America* series, *Flickers Flashback* series, etc.). His work, though of varied quality, has been largely underestimated, perhaps because he had to work under the thumb of such highly individualistic producers as Stanley Kramer, Walt Disney, and Darryl F. Zanuck (all *q.v.*). His virtuosity and skill are evident in *The Vikings* and even in *20,000 Leagues Under the Sea,* despite their large budgets; but the large budget of the tiresome and solemn *Barabbas* overwhelmed him. The erotic and stylish *Girl in the Red Velvet Swing,* the courageous, violent, and antimilitaristic *Between Heaven and Hell,* and the interesting *Violent Saturday* and *Bandido* are ample compensations for the mediocre intellectual pretentiousness of *Compulsion* or *Crack in the Mirror.* [His *Fantastic Voyage* owes more credit to its designer than to Fleischer but the box-office success of *Dr. Dolittle* inspired producers' confidence in him and he has since made several original films: *The Boston Strangler* and *10 Rillington Place,* both carefully drawn re-creations of actual crimes with excellent performances, stand out against the somewhat bloated *Che!* and *Tora! Tora! Tora!*]
DIR: *Child of Divorce* (46), *Banjo* (47), *So This is New York* (48), *Make Mine Laughs* (48), *Trapped* (49), *The Happy Time* (49), *Follow Me Quietly* (49), *The Clay Pigeon* (50), *The Armored-Car Robbery* (50), *The Narrow Margin* (52), *Arena* (53), *20,000 Leagues Under the Sea* (54), *Violent Saturday* (55), *The Girl in the Red Velvet Swing* (55), *Bandido* (56), *Between Heaven and Hell* (56), *The Vikings* (58), *These Thousand Hills* (59), *Compulsion* (59), *Crack in the Mirror* (60), *The Big Gamble* (61), *Barabbas* (62), *The Fantastic Voyage* (66), *Dr. Dolittle* (67), *The Boston Strangler* (68), *Che!* (69), *Tora! Tora! Tora!* (USA/Jap70), *10 Rillington Place* (Brit70), *Buff* (71), *The Last Run* (71).

FLEMING, Victor DIR USA. (Pasadena Feb 23, 1883–Phoenix Jan 6, 1949) A conscientious technician who began his career as a cameraman, won his spurs with Douglas Fairbanks, developed into a director of melodramas and spectaculars — *Red Dust* (32), *Treasure Island* (24), *The Wizard of Oz* (38), *Dr. Jekyll and Mr. Hyde* (41), *Joan of Arc** (48) — and won his marshal's baton with *Gone With the Wind*,* the credit for which is mainly due to its producer David Selznick (*q.v.*).

FLOREY, Robert DIR USA. (Paris Sept 14, 1900–) French-born film maker who has worked largely in Hollywood since 1921. He was originally a journalist in Paris and worked as Feuillade's assistant in 1920. In 1921 he moved to Hollywood, worked for some years as press agent for Linder and Fairbanks and as assistant to Louis Gasnier, Sternberg, Vidor, and Henry King (all *q.v.*), and then made two experimental short films with Slavko Vorkapich (*q.v.*) in 1928–29. He directed the first Marx Brothers film, *Cocoanuts* (29), collaborated with Chaplin, and has made some 70 films, mostly second features. He was a great enthusiast for the American cinema, writing three books on it in the Twenties and two later. Since 1950 he has directed about 100 films for TV. He also collaborated on the script of the original *Frankenstein**.

DIR (notably): *The Life and Death of 9413, a Hollywood Extra* (28) (short), *The Loves of Zero* (29) (short), *Johann the Coffin Maker* (29) (short), *Cocoanuts* (29) (co-dir: J. Santley), *La Route est belle* (Brit30) (musical in French!), *Le Blanc et le noir* (Fr31) (co-dir: M. Allégret), *The Murders in the Rue Morgue* (32), *Ex-Lady* (33), *The Woman in Red* (34), *Smarty* (34), *Hollywood Boulevard* (36), *Hotel Imperial* (38), *The Face Behind the Mask* (40), *Desert Song* (42), *Lady Gangster* (42), *God is My Co-Pilot* (44), *The Beast With Five Fingers* (46), *Monsieur Verdoux** (47) (as associate dir), *Tarzan and the Mermaids* (47), *Rogues' Regiment* (48), *Outpost in Morocco* (48), *Johnny One-Eye* (49), *Vicious Years* (50), *The Gangster We Made* (50).

FORD, Aleksander DIR Poland. (Lodz Nov 24, 1908–) The most significant force in the artistic development of the Polish cinema, who stubbornly, and despite official opposition, directed several films of international class in the prewar years (*Lenin of the Street, Awakening*) and has made many notably postwar films. He studied art in the Twenties, began directing in 1928, made his first feature in 1930, and was an active member of the Start group after 1932. During the war he worked in the USSR with Bossak (*q.v.*) and organized the Polish Army Film Unit, the basis of the postwar Polish nationalized cinema. He has made several outstanding and highly praised films: *Border Street, The Youth of Chopin, Five Boys from Barska Street,* and *Knights of the Teutonic Order.* As artistic director of the Studio film group after 1955 he played a major role in the encouragement of young directors and the development of the new Polish cinema.

DIR: *Nad Ranem* (29) (short), *Tetno Polskiego Manchesteru/Lodz, the Polish Manchester* (29) (short), *The Mascot* (30), *Legion ulicy/The Legion of the Street* (32), *Przebudzenie/Awakening* (34), *Sabra* (Palestine34), *Forward, Co-operation* (35) (documentary), *Grandmother Had No Worries* (35) (co-dir:

M. Waszinsky), *Ludzie Wisly/People of the Vistula* (37) (co-dirs: J. Zarzycki, Helena Boguszewska, J. Kornacki), *Maidenek* (44) (short, co-dir: J. Bossak), *Bitwa o Kolobrzeg/The Battle of Kolberg* (45) (short, co-dir: J. Bossak), *Ulica Graniczna/Border Street** (48), *Mlodosc Chopina/The Youth of Chopin* (52), *Piatka z ulicy Barskiej/Five Boys from Barska Street** (53), *Osmy dzien tygodnia/The Eighth Day of the Week* (GFR/Pol58), *Kryzacy/Knights of the Teutonic Order* (60), *Pierwszy dzien wolnosci/The First Day of Freedom* (64), *Der Arzt stellt fest* (Switz/GFR 66), *Good Morning Poland* (69) (documentary).

FORD, John (Sean Aloysius O'Fearna) DIR USA. (Cape Elizabeth, Maine Feb 1, 1895–) A titan of the American cinema, the director of over 125 films, whose works at their best have mirrored the vast saga of the West and the American Dream. Under the name, Jack Ford (John from 1923) he moved to Hollywood in 1913 as assistant to his bother, Francis. In 1917 he was hired by Universal to write and direct westerns featuring Harry Carey and made about thirty of these until 1921. He continued making westerns during the Twenties (notable among which is *The Iron Horse*) and established an international reputation in the early Thirties with *The Lost Patrol, The Whole Town's Talking,* and, especially, *The Informer.* After a bad period he reaffirmed his qualities with *Stagecoach The Grapes of Wrath,* and *How Green Was My Valley.* During the war he made several documentaries for the US Marines (including the patriotic *The Battle of Midway* with its tear-jerking commentary) and has since built up a solid reputation, mainly on the basis of his best westerns, from *My Darling Clementine, She Wore a Yellow Ribbon,* and *Wagonmaster* to *The Searchers,* and *Two Rode Together,* even though their style, atmosphere, and sense of authenticity are sometimes predictable. He is a powerful personality, though contradictory: an excellent artist, yet with a sharp sense of commercial appeal; a liberal who dislikes prejudice, yet paternalistic; sometimes critical of the army, sometimes ultramilitaristic — he often seems the heir of Thomas Ince. A common theme is evident in some of his best films: that of a group of people facing death or difficult perils. Concerning this, he told Jean Mitry in 1956: "I would think that it is for me a means of confronting individuals. The moment of tragedy allows them to define themselves, to take stock of who they are, to shake off their indifferences, inertia, conventions, their 'ordinariness.' To find the unusual in the commonplace, the heroic in the everyday, is a dramatic device that suits me. It's like finding comedy in tragedy." "A film maker can be identified through his manner of telling a story, his direction. The plot situations are only a starting point. One must go beyond them." He has said elsewhere: "I am of Irish origin but of Western culture. What interests me is the folklore of the West, to show the reality almost like a documentary. I have been a cowboy. I love the open air, the great spaces. Sex, obscenity, perversion, things like that don't interest me." And of film makers' commercial restrictions: "For a director there are commercial rules that it is necessary to obey. In our profession, an artistic failure is nothing; a commercial failure is a sentence. The secret is to make films that please the public and that also allow the director to reveal his personality . . . I can't count ten films among my work that I was able to carry out according to my own tastes and attitudes; even being one's own producer does not give greater freedom, because one must still submit to the distributors." Since 1947 he has produced most of his own films; many of his westerns feature John Wayne.

DIR: 1917–21, some 30 short and medium-length westerns, including *The Tornado* (17), *A Woman's Fool* (18), *Bare Fists* (19), *Marked Men* (19), *The Wallop* (21). From 1922: *Silver Wings* (22), *Cameo Kirby* (23), *The Face on the Barroom Floor* (23), *The Iron Horse* (24), *Hearts of Oak* (24), *Lightnin'* (25), *Kentucky Fair* (25), *The Fighting Heart* (25), *Thank You* (25), *The Shamrock Handicap* (26), *The Blue Eagle* (26), *Three Bad Men* (26), *Mother Machree* (27), *Four Sons* (28), *Hangman's House* (28), *Napoleon's Barber* (28) (short), *Riley the Cop* (28), *Strong Boy* (29), *The Black Watch* (29), *Salute* (30), *Men Without Women* (30), *Born Reckless* (30), *Up the River* (30), *The Seas Beneath* (31), *The Brat* (31), *Arrowsmith* (31), *Air Mail* (32), *Flesh* (32),

Pilgrimage (33), *Doctor Bull* (33), *The Lost Patrol** (34), *The World Moves On* (34), *Judge Priest* (34), *The Whole Town's Talking** (35), *The Informer** (35), *Steamboat Round the Bend* (35), *The Prisoner of Shark Island* (36), *Mary of Scotland* (36), *The Plough and the Stars* (36), *Wee Willie Winkie* (37), *The Hurricane* (37) (co-dir: Stuart Heisler), *Four Men and a Prayer* (38), *Submarine Patrol* (38), *Stagecoach** (39), *Young Mr. Lincoln* (39), *Drums Along the Mohawk* (39), *The Grapes of Wrath** (40), *The Long Voyage Home* (40), *Tobacco Road* (41), *How Green Was My Valley** (41), *The Battle of Midway* (42) (documentary), *December Seventh* (43) (documentary), *We Sail at Midnight* (43) (documentary), *They Were Expendable* (45) (co-dir: Robert Montgomery), *My Darling Clementine** (46), *The Fugitive* (47), *Fort Apache* (48), *Three Godfathers* (48), *Pinky* (49) (completed by Elia Kazan), *She Wore a Yellow Ribbon* (49), *When Willie Comes Marching Home Again* (50), *Wagonmaster* (50), *Rio Grande* (50), *This is Korea* (51) (documentary), *What Price Glory* (52) (remake), *The Quiet Man** (52), *The Sun Shines Bright* (53), *Mogambo* (53), *Hondo* (53) (probably only exteriors, dir: John Farrow), *The Long Gray Line* (55), *Mister Roberts* (55) (completed & co-dir: Mervyn LeRoy), *The Searchers* (56), *The Wings of Eagles* (57), *The Rising of the Moon* (57), *The Last Hurrah* (58), *Gideon's Day/Gideon of Scotland Yard* (Brit59), *The Horse Soldiers* (59), *Korea* (59) (documentary), *Sergeant Rutledge* (60), *The Alamo** (60) (assist only, dir: John Wayne), *Two Rode Together* (61), *The Man Who Shot Liberty Valance* (61), *How the West Was Won** (62) (one episode), *Donovan's Reef* (63), *Cheyenne Autumn* (64), *Young Cassidy* (64) (replaced by Jack Cardiff), *Seven Women* (65). Also PROD *Mighty Joe Young** and recently a documentary on Vietnam for the US Information Agency.

*FOREMAN, Carl SCEN USA SCEN/PROD/ DIR Britain. (Chicago July 23, 1914–) Scenarist who played an important role in the success of several early Stanley Kramer (*q.v.*) productions: Mark Robson's *Champion* and *Home of the Brave*, Zinnemann's *The Men** and *High Noon**. He refused to testify in 1951 for the

House Un-American Activities Committee and this brought his association with Kramer to an end. He moved to Britain, wrote the scripts of Losey's *The Sleeping Tiger* (54) (uncredited), David Lean's *The Bridge on the River Kwai** (57), Carol Reed's *The Key* (58), J. Lee Thompson's *The Guns of Navarone* (60) and *Mackenna's Gold* (67), and his own *The Victors* (63) — which revealed he had little directorial talent. In recent years he has concentrated his activities on production: *The Key, The Mouse That Roared* (59), *The Guns of Navarone, Born Free* (65), *Mackenna's Gold, The Virgin Soldiers* (69).

*FORMAN, Milos DIR Czechoslovakia. (Caslav Feb 18, 1932–) A young film maker of the Czechoslovakian "new wave" of the Sixties, who has a warmly intimate, gently ironic style and a talent for observing the quirks of everyday behavior, perhaps derived from *cinéma-vérité*. He studied drama at the Academy of Music and Dramatic Art in Prague and while still a student collaborated in the script of Martin Fric's comedy, *Leave It to Me* (55). Later he wrote the script and assisted Ivo Novak on *Puppies* (57) and assisted Alfred Radok (*q.v.*) on *Old Man Motorcar* (56). Radok took him away from the studios for some years to work on Laterna Magica (Magic Lantern) presentations. He shot his first film (medium-length on 16mm), *Audition/ Talent Competition*, in 1963 and followed this with the medium-length *The Glory of the Brass Bands/If There Were No Music*. His first feature, *Peter and Pavla*, a psychological exploration of the mind of the modern adolescent, won awards at Locarno and Venice, and Forman went on to develop his subtle behavioral studies in the highly successful *Loves of a Blonde* and *Fireman's Ball*. He left Czechoslovakia in 1968 and eventually moved to the USA to direct *Taking Off*. DIR: *Konkurs/Audition/Talent Competition* (63) (two films: *Audition* and *The Glory of the Brass Bands/If There Were No Music*), *Cerny Petr/Peter and Pavla/ Black Peter* (64), *Lasky jedne plavovlasky/The Loves of a Blonde/A Blonde in Love** (65), *Hori, ma panenko/The Fireman's Ball/Like a House on Fire/ Fire! Fire!* (67), *Taking Off* (USA71).

FORST, Willi (Willi Frohs) DIR Austria/Germany. (Vienna March 7, 1903–) A specialist in Viennese operettas and frilly period romances whose films have gobs of sentiment and numerous fashionable ladies and gentlemen waltzing about during the "good times" of Emperor Franz Joseph. His films seemed appealing during the Thirties but have quickly faded. A famous handsome lead in numerous films from 1922, he directed his first film in 1933.

DIR: *Leise Flehen meine Lieder* (Ger/ Aust33), *Maskerade* (Aust34), *Mazurka* (Ger35), *Burgtheater* (Aust36), *Allotria* (Ger36), *Serenade* (Ger37), *Ich bin Sebastian Otto* (Ger39) (co-dir: V. Becker), *Bel Ami/Der Liebling schöner Frauen* (Ger39), *Operette* (Ger40), *Wiener Blut* (Ger42), *Frauen sind keine Engel* (Ger43), *Wiener Mädeln* (Ger45, released 49), *Die Sünderin/The Sinner* (GFR50), *Es geschehen noch Wunder* (GFR51), *Dieses Lied bleibt bei Dir* (GFR54), *Kaiserjäger* (Aust56), *Die Unentschuldigte Stunde* (Aust57) (remake), *Wien, du Stadt meiner Träume* (Aust57) (remake). Also supervised *Die Drei von der Tankstelle* (GFR55) (dir: Hans Wolff, remake).

FOU SEN DIR China. (? – ?) Good film maker of the Shanghai school who directed two interesting films in 1947–48: *The Light of Thousands of Families* and *Humanity's Hope*.

FOX, William (William Friedman) PROD USA. (Hungary Jan 1, 1879–New York May 1, 1952) Originally in the garment industry in New York, he moved into exhibition in 1904 by establishing a flourishing chain of Nickelodeons, headed the battle of the independents against the Edison (*q.v.*) Trust, became a producer around 1914, and launched Theda Bara, Tom Mix, Buck Jones, Charles Farrell and Janet Gaynor. He took an early interest in sound as a means of acquiring more power and his Fox Movietone sound system (developed by Theodore Case from the De Forest system of sound photographed directly onto film) was a rival to Warner's (*q.v.*) Vitaphone system. [For a few months in 1929 he acquired controlling interest in Loew's Inc. (owners of MGM) but the stock market crash created financial difficulties for him and the US Justice Department instituted a suit against him for operating a trust. This began his downfall: he was forced to relinquish control of Fox Theaters Corporation and Fox Films to a board of trustees and was hounded by creditors. The Fox companies were eventually merged with Twentieth Century in 1935. William Fox thereafter had a checkered career and went to prison in 1942 for attempting to bribe a federal judge. He was one of the great power wielders of the industry and the ripples of his activities took decades to subside.]

FRANCIOLINI, Gianni DIR Italy. (Florence June 1, 1910–Rome May 1960) He made his debut with the interesting *Fari nella Nebria/Lighthouse in the Fog* (41) but thereafter had to work on many commissioned films, notable among which is the comedy, *Buon giorno elefante!* (52), from Zavattini's script.

*FRANCIS, Freddie PHOTOG/DIR Britain. (London 1917–) An outstanding British cameraman with a fine sense of composition. He began his film career in 1935 as an assistant and did his best work on the films of several of the new British directors of the Fifties and early Sixties: for Jack Clayton, *Room at the Top** (59), *The Innocents* (61); for Karel Reisz, *Saturday Night and Sunday Morning** (60); for Jack Cardiff, *Sons and Lovers* (60); for Joseph Losey, *Time Without Pity** (56). Began directing in 1962 with less successful results but has made several stylish horror films.
DIR: *Two and Two Make Six* (62), *Vengeance* (62), *Paranoiac* (63), *Nightmare* (63), *The Evil of Frankenstein* (64), *Hysteria* (64), *Dr. Terror's House of Horrors* (64), *Traitor's Gate* (64), *The Skull* (65), *The Psychopath* (66), *The Deadly Bees* (66), *They Came from Beyond Space* (66), *Torture Garden* (67), *Dracula Has Risen from the Grave* (68), *Mumsy, Nanny, Sonny, and Girly* (69).

FRANJU, Georges DIR France. (Fougères, Brittany April 12, 1912–) A film maker with a mocking sense of anarchic black humor and a feeling for unusual atmospheres. He was interested in the cinema from an early age, made a short, *Le Métro*, in 1934 with Henri Langlois (with whom he later founded the Cinémathèque française), was secretary of the International Federation of Film Archives from 1938–45, and from 1945–53 secretary of Jean Painlevé's (q.v.)

Institut de Cinématographie Scientifique. From 1948–58 he was one of the best French documentary directors (*Le Sang des bêtes, Hôtel des Invalides, Les Poussières*). He made his first fiction feature in 1958, the remarkable *La Tête contre les murs,* which he followed with the atmospheric *Eyes Without a Face,* excellent adaptations of *Thérèse Desqueroux* and *Thomas l'Imposteur,* a tribute to Feuillade (q.v.), *Judex,* and the poetic, passionate Zola adaptation, *La Faute de l'Abbé Mouret* (a film he had wanted to make for 20 years). He has said of himself: "I am a realist through the necessity of things. An image on the screen has an immediate presence. It is perceived as if it were actual. Whatever one does, a film is always in the present tense. Past time is spontaneously made actual by the spectator. That is why what is artificial ages badly and quickly. Dream, poetry, the unknown must all emerge out of reality itself. The whole of cinema is documentary, even the most poetic. What pleases is what is terrible, gentle, and poetic."
DIR (shorts): *Le Métro* (34) (co-dir: Henri Langlois), *Le Sang des bêtes** (49), *En passant par la Lorraine* (50), *Hôtel des Invalides** (52), *Le Grand Méliès* (52), *Monsieur et Madame Curie* (53), *Les Poussières* (54), *Navigation marchande/Marine marchande* (54), *A propos d'une rivière/Au fil d'une rivière/Le Saumon Atlantique* (55), *Mon chien* (55), *Le Théâtre National Populaire* (56), *Sur le pont d'Avignon* (56), *Notre-Dame, Cathédrale de Paris* (57), *La Première nuit* (58).
DIR (features): *La Tête contre les murs/The Keepers** (58), *Les Yeux sans visage* (59), *Pleins feux sur l'assassin* (61), *Thérèse Desqueroux* (62), *Judex** (63), *Thomas l'Imposteur* (65), *Les Rideaux blancs* (66) (TV), *Marcel Allain* (66) (TV), *La Faute de l'Abbé Mouret* (70).

*FRANKEN, Mannus DIR Netherlands/Indonesia. (189?–1953) Former collaborator of Joris Ivens (q.v.) on *Rain* and director of several documentaries, including *Redding* (29) and *De Trekschuit* (32), before leaving for what was then the Dutch East Indies. There he made the semi-documentary *Pareh, Song of the Rice** (35) with local nonprofessional actors, the first notably Indonesian film. He made numerous other documentaries in the Far East, including

Tanah Sabrang (38) and *'t Sal waarach-tig wel gaen* (39). After the war, he assisted J. C. Sol on newsreels and made a short film for Philips on musical instruments, *Slaet op ten trommle*.

FRANKENHEIMER, John DIR USA. (Malba, New York Feb 19, 1930–) Former TV director (*Studio One, Playhouse 90*) whose later films have never fulfilled the promise of his first feature, *The Young Stranger* (56), a violent and intense portrait of adolescence. He spent another three years in television before devoting himself entirely to feature films. Since then he has largely offered either conventional Hollywood melodrama (*The Birdman of Alcatraz*), or unbelievable fantasy (*The Manchurian Candidate*). Since 1963 he has produced his own films, including the large-budget *Grand Prix*.
DIR: *The Young Stranger* (56), *The Young Savages* (61), *All Fall Down* (61), *Birdman of Alcatraz* (61), *The Manchurian Candidate* (62), *Seven Days in May* (63), *The Train* (65) (begun by Arthur Penn), *Seconds* (66), *Grand Prix* (66) (begun by John Sturges), *The Extraordinary Seaman* (68), *The Fixer* (68), *The Gypsy Moths* (69), *I Walk the Line* (70), *The Horsemen* (71).

FRANKLIN, Sidney DIR/PROD USA. (San Francisco March 21, 1893–) Hollywood pioneer who made his first films for Triangle in 1915 and directed his best film in 1937, *The Good Earth**. After *Goodbye Mr. Chips* (39), he became a producer: *Waterloo Bridge* (40), *Mrs. Miniver* (42), *The Yearling* (46), *Young Bess* (54).

FREDA, Riccardo DIR Italy. (Alexandria Feb 24, 1909–) A specialist in Italian period spectaculars who is better than his colleague Cottafavi (*q.v.*), at these exploitation films.
DIR (notably): *Tutti la Città Canta* (42), *I Miserabli** (46), *The Black Eagle* (46), *Count Ugolin* (49), *Spartacus* (52), *Theodora, Slave Empress* (53), *I Vampiri* (54), *Beatrice Cenci* (56), *The Giant of Thessaly* (61), *The Terror of Dr. Hitchcock* (62), *The Spectre* (63), *Coplan FX18 casse tout/The Exterminators* (Fr/It65), *Tamar, Wife of Er* (Israel/It69).

*FREED, Arthur (Arthur Grossman) PROD USA. (USA Sept 9, 1894–) Lyricist on many musicals (all the songs of *Singin' in the Rain* are by him) who, as a producer at MGM, exercised considerable influence on the development of postwar musicals, notably those of Stanley Donen (*q.v.*), and Vincente Minnelli (*q.v.*).
PROD (notably): *The Wizard of Oz* (39), *For Me and My Gal* (42), *Dubarry Was a Lady** (43), *Meet Me In St. Louis** (44), *Yolanda and the Thief** (45), *Ziegfield Follies* (46), *The Pirate* (48), *Easter Parade* (48), *Take Me Out to the Ball Game* (49), *On the Town** (49), *Annie Get Your Gun* (50), *Royal Wedding* (51), *Show Boat* (51), *An American in Paris** (51), *Singin' in the Rain** (52), *Band Wagon* (53), *Brigadoon** (54), *It's Always Fair Weather* (55), *Kismet* (55), *Silk Stockings** (57), *Gigi* (58), *Bells are Ringing* (60).

FREND, Charles DIR Britain. (Pulborough Nov 21, 1909–) Former editor in the Thirties (Hitchcock's *Secret Agent, Sabotage*) who moved to Ealing under Michael Balcon (*q.v.*) and Cavalcanti (*q.v.*) and demonstrated a particular flair for forceful, semidocumentary action sequences in his early films: *The Foreman Went to France* (42), *San Demetrio, London* (43), and *Johnny Frenchman* (45). But, after the commercial failure of *Scott of the Antarctic** (48), he made no important films except *The Cruel Sea* (53).

FREUND, Karl PHOTOG Germany/USA DIR USA. (Königinhof, Bohemia Jan 16, 1890–Hollywood 1969) The greatest cameraman of the German silent cinema, whose contributions rank alongside those of Fritz Lang (*q.v.*) and Carl Mayer (*q.v.*) and who was equally at ease with expressionism or actuality. He joined the cinema in 1906 and originally (08) worked as a newsreel cameraman. He emigrated to the USA in 1930, photographed numerous films and even directed a few horror films, but his work in Hollywood was merely that of a good craftsman. After 1950 he confined his activities largely to TV, including the *I Love Lucy* series.
[PHOTOG (notably): in Germany for Urban Gad, *Engelein/Den Lille Engels* (Ger/Den13); for Murnau, *Satanas* (19), *Der Bucklige und die Tänzerin*

(20), *Der Januskopf* (20), *Marizza, gennant die Schmugglermadonna* (21), *Der Brennende Acker* (22), *Die Finanzen des Grossherzogs* (23), *Der Letzte Mann** (24), *Tartüff* (25); for Max Reinhardt, *Venezianische Nacht* (14); for Paul Wegener, *Der Golem** (20), *Der Verlorene Schatten* (21), *Lukrezia Borgia* (24); for Fritz Lang, *Die Spinnen, II* (20), *Metropolis** (26); for Carl Dreyer, *Michaël* (24); for E. A. Dupont, *Varieté** (25); for Ruttmann, *Berlin, die Symphonie einer Grosstadt** (27); for Paul Czinner, *Dona Juana* (27), *Fräulein Else* (29). In USA: for Mamoulian, *Dr. Jekyll and Mr. Hyde* (31), *Golden Boy* (39); for John Ford, *Air Mail* (32); for Tod Browning, *Dracula** (31); for Robert Florey, *Murders in the Rue Morgue* (32); for John Stahl, *Back Street* (32), *Parnell* (37); for Cukor, *Camille* (35); for Sidney Franklin, *The Good Earth** (37); for Clarence Brown, *Conquest/Marie Walewska* (37); for James Whale, *Green Hell* (40); for Jules Dassin, *A Letter for Evie* (44), *Two Smart People* (46); for Minnelli, *Undercurrent* (46); for Zinnemann , *The Seventh Cross* (44); for Huston, *Key Largo* (48).
DIR: *The Mummy* (32) (also photog), *Moonlight and Pretzels* (33), *Madame Spy* (33), *Mad Love* (35).]

FRIC, Martin DIR Czechoslovakia. (Prague March 29, 1902–) The dean of Czechoslovakian film makers, active in films for over 40 years (since 1928) and with more than 100 films to his credit. He is known abroad mainly for *Janosik* (36), *Past/The Trap* (50) and the two-part color period comedy based on the Golem legend, *The Emperor's Baker* and *The Baker's Emperor* (51).

FROELICH, Carl DIR/PROD Germany. (Berlin Sept 5, 1875–Berlin Feb 12, 1953) A pioneer of the German cinema who began to work in the industry in 1902, started producing newsreels in 1918, and founded his own production company in 1920. From 1908–1951 he directed many dozens of films, almost all mediocre. During the Nazi regime he was head of Reichsfilmkammer.

FUENTES, Fernando de DIR Mexico. (190?–) Though after 1945 he was a prolific commercial director, Fuentes has made several notable films: a portrait of the (then quite recent) Mexican Revolution, *Vamanos con Pancho Villa* (35); a remarkable satire set in the same period, *El Compadre Mendoza** (54), *Cruz Diablo* (34), and, later, *Doña Barbara* (43), a technically accomplished film in which Maria Felix had her first major role. He contributed to the commercial development of the Mexican film industry with *Alla en el Rancho Grande* (36), on which the cameraman, Figueroa (*q.v.*) made his debut.

FULLER, Samuel DIR USA. (Worcester, Mass Aug 12, 1911–) Former journalist and detective-story writer who became a scriptwriter (largely of thrillers) in 1936 and directed his first film in 1948. He has written all his own scripts and has produced many of them. Since 1948 he has directed numerous mediocre thrillers and adventure films, almost all imbued "with heavy anti-Communist propaganda or racist themes" (*Film Lexicon degli Autori*), or with apologies for militarist brutalities — but without any other bond than this "ideology" in their direction and their extremely incongruous styles. His career has been in difficulties since the early Sixties and he has worked on several abortive projects.
DIR: *I Shot Jesse James* (48), *The Baron of Arizona* (50), *The Steel Helmet* (50), *Fixed Bayonets* (51), *Park Row* (52), *Pickup on South Street** (53), *Hell and High Water* (54), *House of Bamboo* (55), *Run of the Arrow* (57), *China Gate* (57), *Forty Guns* (57), *Verboten!* (58), *The Crimson Kimono* (59), *Underworld USA* (61), *Merrill's Marauders* (62), *Shock Corridor* (63), *The Naked Kiss* (64), *Caine/Shark* (Mexico/USA67) (disowned by Fuller).

FULTON, John P. USA (1902–) Special effects cameraman responsible for the remarkable tricks in *The Invisible Man** (33). He has also worked, notably, on *The Werewolf in London* (35), *Scarlet Street** (45), *The Ten Commandments** (56), and *Vertigo** (58).

*FURTHMAN, Jules SCEN USA. (1888–1966) Hollywood scriptwriter of the Thirties and Forties, notable especially for his work with Sternberg (*q.v.*) and Hawks (*q.v.*). He had a deep sense of irony, of sophisticated, droll dialogue, and of the development of character within a given dramatic situation. Despite his talent for dialogue, his scripts are never mere repartee, nor are they theatrical, and several of Hawks's best films owe much to his contribution. Although he was active for some 40 years and wrote numerous famous scripts, he was not a prolific writer. In later years he also acted as producer on some of his films.

SCEN (notably): for Maurice Tourneur, *Treasure Island* (18); for Sternberg, *Underworld** (27), *The Dragnet* (28), *The Docks of New York** (28), *Morocco** (31), *Shanghai Express** (32), *The Blonde Venus* (32), *The Shanghai Gesture* (41), *Jet Pilot* (50, released 57) (completed by Howard Hughes); for Howard Hawks, *Come and Get It** (36) (co-dir: Wyler), *Only Angels Have Wings** (37), *To Have and Have Not*

(44), *The Big Sleep** (46), *Rio Bravo** (59); for Paul Fejos, *Broadway* (29); for Henry King, *Any Woman* (25), *Over the Hill* (31); for Raoul Walsh, *Body and Soul* (31), *Yellow Ticket* (31); for Howard Hughes, *The Outlaw* (43); for Edmund Goulding, *Nightmare Alley* (47); for Richard Fleischer, *The Girl in the Red Velvet Swing* (56).

FUSCO, Giovanni MUS Italy/France. (Sant Agata dei Goto Oct 10, 1906–) Antonioni's (*q.v.*) favorite composer, his atonal sounds have matched well many of Antonioni's films. He has also worked for Resnais, *Hiroshima mon amour** (co-mus: Delerue), *La Guerre est finie**; for Francesco Maselli, *I Delfini* (60); for Mauro Bolognini, *La Corruzione* (64).

GAD, Peter Urban DIR Denmark/Germany. (Copenhagen 1879–Copenhagen 1947) Notable Danish pioneer film maker who directed many of the films of Asta Nielsen (his wife until 1926) from the social drama *Afgrunden/The Abyss* (Den10) to *Hanneles Himmelfahrt* (Ger22). He went with her to Germany, then returned to Denmark and made *Likkehjulelet* (27). He usually wrote the scripts for these successful dramas, which anticipated many later Hollywood styles and genres.

*GADE, Sven(d) DIR Denmark/Germany/ USA. (Copenhagen Feb 9, 1877–Copenhagen June 25, 1952) Danish director and actor who began with *Maharejaens Yndlings hustru* (16), directed a pompously elegant version of *Hamlet** (20) with Asta Nielsen in Berlin, and 1922–29 was in Hollywood as an actor, as an art director (e.g., Lubitsch's *Rosita*), and as director on the mediocre *Siege* (25), *Peacock Feather* (25), *The Blond Saint* (26), *Watch Your Wife* (26), *Into Her Kingdom* (26), *Jazz Mad* (28). He then returned to Denmark, where he made *Balleten Danser* (38).

GAISSEAU, Pierre-Dominique DIR France (Mézières March 10, 1923–) Documentary film maker who has taken part in many expeditions (the Congo, the Amazon, New Guinea, Mali, etc.). He made the interesting *Forêt sacrée* (54) in Africa, but his *Le Ciel et la boue/ The Sky Above, the Mud Below*, which won an Oscar, sacrifices meaning for picturesqueness.
DIR: *Des hommes qu'on appelle sauvages* (50), *Pays bassari* (52), *Naloutai* (52), *Forêt sacrée* (54), *Survivants de la préhistoire* (55), *Le Ciel et la boue* (61), *New York sur mer* (63), *Flame and the Fire* (65), *Round Trip* (67).

*GALEEN, Henrik SCEN/DIR Germany. (Czechoslovakia ? – ?) Perhaps the most important single influence on the development of film expressionism in Germany, he is the scriptwriter and/or director of such notable films as *Der Golem, Nosferatu, Waxworks, The Student of Prague,* and *Unholy Love.* He was originally a journalist, then secretary to novelist Hans Heinz Ewers (author of the script of the first *Student of Prague,* the novel *Alraune,* and other fantasy stories). He began working in the cinema around 1910. He left Germany with the advent of Hitler and apparently settled in the USA.
DIR: *Der Golem** (14) (co-dir: Wegener), *Die Rollende Kugel* (19), *Judith Trachtenberg* (20), *Stadt in Sicht* (23), *Die Liebesbriefe der Baronin von S . . .* (24), *Der Student von Prag* (26), *Alraune/Mandrake/Unholy Love/A Daughter of Destiny* (27), *Sein grösster Bluff* (27) (co-dir: Harry Piel), *After the Verdict* (Brit29), *Salon Dora Green/ Die Falle* (33).
SCEN: *Peter Schlemil* (19) (dir: Stellan Rye), *Die Geliebte Roswolskys* (21) (dir: Felix Basch), *Der Golem, wie er in die Welt Kam** (20) (dir: Wegener), *Nosferatu** (23) (dir: Murnau), *Das Wachsfigurenkabinett** (24) (dir: Paul Leni), *Das Fraulein von Amt* (25) (dir: C.-H. Schroth), *Zigano, der Brigant vom Monte Diavolo* (25) (dir: Harry Piel), *Die Dame mit der Maske* (28) (dir: W. Thiele), *Schatten der Unterwelt* (31) (dir: Harry Piel), and all his own films.

GALINDO, Alejandro DIR Mexico. (1911–) A prolific director whose work is of variable quality, mostly mediocre but also including some of the best Mexican films: *Mientras Mexico Duerme* (38), *Campeon sin Corona* (45), *Esquina Bajan* (48) and, especially, *Espaldos*

Nojaldas (53) on the exploitation of migrant Mexican workers in the USA.

GALLO, Mario DIR Argentina. (Barletta, Italy July 31, 1878–Buenos Aires May 8, 1945) The father of the Argentinian cinema, he was originally a photographer and choir director in Buenos Aires before directing or producing (from 1908–23) films largely based on 19th-century Argentinian history, such as *El Fusillamiento de Dorrego* (08).

GALLONE, Carmine DIR Italy. (Taggia, Imperia Sept 18, 1886–) Prolific and versatile veteran Italian film maker who began with flamboyant "high life" melodramas with Lyda Borelli, *La Donna Nuda* (13), etc., or Soava Gallone, *Avatar* (15), *Maman poupée* (18), etc. He made one of the numerous versions of *Gli Ultimi Giorni di Pompei/The Last Days of Pompeii* (26) from Bulwer-Lytton's novel, worked in Berlin, London, and Paris — where he made some populist films, including *Un soir de rafle* (31) — before returning to Italy to sing the praises of fascism in *Scipio Africanus* (37), rumored to have been written by Mussolini, and *Odessa in Flames* (42). He also made one of the numerous versions of "The Two Orphans," *Le Due Orfanelle** (42), and several opera films, e.g., *The Dream of Butterfly* (39). After the war he switched to the side of the Italian partisans in *Davanti a lui Tremava Tutta Roma* (46) before returning to opera films — *Rigoletto* (47), *Il Trovatore* (47), *Madame Butterfly* (55), etc., and Roman spectaculars, *Messalina* (51), *Carthage in Flames* (59), etc.

GANCE, Abel DIR France. (Paris Oct 25, 1889–) One of the giants of the cinema, a man of monumental talents who moved mountains and was almost crushed by them, an innovator who suffered in France as Stroheim did in Hollywood. His roots were in Griffith (*q.v.*) and Thomas Ince (*q.v.*) but also in the French traditions of literature, theater, and film and in his own largely self-taught cultural knowledge. [Though intended by his bourgeois family for a professional career, he was passionately enamoured of the theater and in 1907 took a job acting in Brussels, where he wrote his first film script. He returned to Paris, acted in numerous films, and wrote short scripts for directors like Albert Capellani (*q.v.*) and Louis Feuillade (*q.v.*). In 1911 he formed his own production company and made his first film *La Digue (ou pour sauver la Hollande)*, a period drama. Then followed several routine dramas (but including a black comedy, *La Folie du Docteur Tube*, using experimental camera effects).] He flirted with film impressionism but his talents transcended this school and he incorporated its lessons into his own approach. With the sophisticated *Mater Dolorosa* (17) and *La Dixième Symphonie* (18) he established himself as a front-rank director. He then pushed intercutting as a metaphorical device to its extreme limits in *J'accuse* (19) and *La Roue* (22), both fevered, monumental epics, the former on the terrible wastage of war, the latter on love, suffering, and death among a family of railway workers. In the brilliant *Napoléon* (27) he made maximum use of camera mobility and rapid intercutting or superimpositions: "In certain shots of *Napoléon*, I superimposed up to 16 images. They played a 'potential' role like that of fifty instruments at a concert. This led me to Polyvision, to the triple screen presenting many dozens of images at the same time." His *Fin du monde,* which came at the beginning of sound, was taken out of his hands by the producers and he disclaimed responsibility for it. It almost marked the end of his career, even though he understood the importance of the sound cinema and was the first to use stereophonic sound in his sound version of *Napoléon* (34). Though he was able to continue working for some years, it was only on cheap, uninteresting productions that did not reflect his true talents. In the Fifties he rolled back the stone from the tomb in which he had been buried alive and once again revealed his abilities in the multiscreen short, *Quatorze juillet* (53) and in *Magirama* (56). His strange genius was marked by a single-minded determination that flung caution and restraint to the winds; according to Moussinac he was a torrent who swept pollutants along with him, while Delluc once told him he never stopped trying to exceed his own grasp. This great film maker has said of his strength and weakness: "I have been perpetually in unstable equilibrium on the rails of a small Decauville train. What good is a powerful locomotive if it cannot run quickly along somewhat solid rails?

Champing at the bit, I have had to leave the locomotive in the garage for some years, and it would be necessary to have strong rails in order to launch Polyvision, that supercharged locomotive of the future."

DIR: *La Digue* (11), *Le Nègre blanc* (12), *Il y a des pieds au plafond* (12), *Le Masque d'horreur* (12), *Les Morts reviennent-ils?/Un drame de Château d'Acre* (14), *La Folie du Docteur Tube* (14), *L'Enigme de dix heures* (16), *La Fleur des ruines* (16), *L'Héroïsme de Paddy* (16), *Strass et compagnie* (16), *Fioritures* (16), *Le Fou de la falaise* (16), *Ce que les flots racontent* (16), *Le Périscope* (16), *Barberousse* (16), *Les Gaz mortels* (16), *Le Droit à la vie* (17), *La Zone de la mort* (17), *Mater Dolorosa** (17), *La Dixième Symphonie** (18), *J'accuse** (19), *La Roue** (22), *Au secours!* (23), *Napoléon* (27), *Marines* (28) (short), *Cristeaux* (28) (short), *La Fin du monde* (30), *Mater Dolorosa** (32) (remake), *Le Maître de forges* (33), *La Dame aux camélias* (34), *Poliche* (34), *Napoléon** (34) (sound version), *Le Roman d'un jeune homme pauvre* (35), *Lucrèce Borgia* (35), *Un grand amour de Beethoven* (36), *Jérôme Perreau, héros des barricades* (36), *Le Voleur des femmes* (36), *J'accuse** (37) (remake), *Louise* (38), *Le Paradis perdu* (39), *La Vénus aveugle* (40), *Le Capitaine Fracasse* (42), *Manolette* (44), *Quatorze juillet* (53) (multiscreen short), *La Tour de Nesle/The Tower of Lust* (54), *Magirama** (56), *Austerlitz* (60), *Cyrano et D'Artagnan* (64), *Bonaparte et la révolution* (71) (new version of *Napoléon**).

SCEN: *Mireille* (08) (dir: Léonce Perret), *L'Infirmière* (15) (dir: Henri Pouctal), several for Feuillade and Capellani (08–15), *La Reine Margot* (54) (dir: Jean Dreville), and all his own films.

GARDIN, Vladimir DIR USSR. (Moscow 1877–1965) He was already famous in the theater as an actor for Fyodor Kommisarzhevsky and Vsevelod Meyerhold when he became a director in 1913 with *Klyuchi shchastya/Keys to Happiness* (co-dir: Protazanov). After the Revolution, he was a member of the Cinema Committee, directed some of the first Soviet fiction films (including a version of Jack London's *The Iron Heel*, 1919) in a typically "prewar" style, and in 1921 gave Pudovkin (*q.v.*) and Eduard Tisse

(*q.v.*) their first opportunities on *Serp i molot/Sickle and Hammer* (Pudovkin assist to Gardin) and *Golod . . . golod . . . golod/Hunger . . . Hunger . . . Hunger* (Pudovkin co-dir). In 1919 he founded the All-Union State Institute of Cinematography (VGIK). He later appeared as a lead actor in many notable films, e.g., *Counterplan**, *Peasants**.

GARMES, Lee PHOTOG USA. (Peoria May 27, 1898–) One of the great Hollywood cameramen, at his best in the Thirties when his atmospheric, baroque style and mood lighting marked several memorable romances and gangster films. [PHOTOG (notably): for Sternberg, *Morocco*, *Dishonored*, *Shanghai Express**, *An American Tragedy**; for Mamoulian, *City Streets**; for Ben Hecht and Charles MacArthur, *Crime Without Passion**, *The Scoundrel;* for Alexander Korda, *The Private Life of Helen of Troy*, *The Yellow Lily;* for Howard Hawks, *Scarface**, *Land of the Pharaohs*, for Paul Czinner, *Dreaming Lips;* for Julien Duvivier, *Lydia;* for King Vidor, *Duel in the Sun**; for Ophüls, *Caught;* for Norman Z. McLeod, *The Secret Life of Walter Mitty**; for William Wyler, *Detective Story*, *The Desperate Hours;* for Alfred Hitchcock, *The Paradine Case;* for Martin Ritt, *Adventures of a Young Man.* Also CO-DIR: *Angels Over Broadway* with Ben Hecht.]

GARNETT, Tay DIR USA. (Los Angeles 1898–) Former acrobat, cartoonist, aviator, and writer who became a scriptwriter for Hal Roach and directed his first film, *The Spieler*, in 1929. Many French critics accepted him as an important director after *Her Man* (30) and *One Way Passage* (32), but his consistently mediocre work has belied this. [The best of his later work: *Seven Sinners* (40), *The Postman Always Rings Twice** (46), *Wild Harvest* (47). Most of his work in the Sixties has been in TV: *The Untouchables*, *Wagon Train*, *Death Valley Days*, and so on.]

GASNIER, Louis J. DIR USA/France. (Paris Sept 26, 1882–?) Mediocre director of B-pictures and serials (100–200 films from 1909–14) who originally worked for Pathé in France (on many of Linder's films, 1905–09), moved to the USA as the first director of Pathé's American branch, and is best known as the director

97

of Pearl White serials, *The Perils of Pauline* and *The Exploits of Elaine**, made in the spirit of, and with several ideas from, the stories of Eugène Sue.

GATTI, Armand DIR France. (Monaco Jan 24, 1924–) Journalist, poet, and playwright who wrote the script of *Moranbong**, contributed a major work to the young French cinema with *L'Enclos* (61), a tragedy set in a concentration camp, and has since made *El Otro Cristobal* (63) in Cuba.

GAUDIO, Tony (Gaetano) PHOTOG USA. (Rome 1885–Hollywood 1951) A good American cameraman, one of the founders of his profession in Hollywood, notable especially for his work on period films, including *The Mark of Zorro** (20), *The Temptress* (both dir: Fred Niblo), *The Gaucho** (27) (dir: F. Richard Jones), *The Story of Louis Pasteur* (35), *The Life of Emile Zola** (36) (both dir: William Dieterle), *The Adventures of Robin Hood* (38) (dir: Michael Curtiz), *Juarez* (39) (dir: William Dieterle). [Also, notably: *Little Caesar** (30) (dir: Mervyn LeRoy), *Hell's Angels** (dir: Howard Hughes), *Anthony Adverse* (36) (dir: Mervyn LeRoy), *The Letter* (40) (dir: William Wyler), *High Sierra* (41) (dir: Raoul Walsh).]

GAUMONT, Léon INVENTOR/PROD France. (1863–1946) A major pioneer of the film industry in France, founder of the Gaumont Studios and the Gaumont theaters (later Odeon) in Britain, who took a great interest in perfecting technical developments in sound and color (Chronophone and Chronochrome, e.g.). The excellent productions from his studios in France, notably those of Louis Feuillade (*q.v.*), dominated the French cinema from 1910–20.

GAZIADIS, Dimitrios DIR Greece. (Athens 1897–1961) The most important pioneer of the Greek cinema who directed the first Greek features at the same time as Orestis Laskos (*q.v.*). He studied photography in German 1913–16, from 1916–24 worked as assistant cameraman on the films of Lubitsch, Korda, Dupont, etc., and made several comedy shorts in Berlin. In 1925 he returned to Greece and established the first major Greek production company. His work is marked by a

romantic expressionism derived from his German experiences. After 1933, he restricted his activities to newsreels and documentaries.
DIR: *The Greek Miracle* (21) (documentary), *Prometheus desmotis* (27), *Eros Ke Kimata* (28), *To Limani ton Dacrion/The Port of Tears* (28), *I Thiella/The Storm* (29), *Astero* (29), *I Apachides ton Athinon/The Apaches of Athens* (30), *Philise me, Maritsa/Kiss Me, Marisa* (31), *Exo ptochia/Be Happy* (32), *The End of Bad Luck* (33).

GEBEL, Bruno DIR Chile. (? – ?) The director of the only Chilean film of merit known outside Latin America, *La Caleta Olvidida/The Forgotten Cove* (58), the story of a poor fishing village.

GEESINK, Joop ANIM Netherlands. (La Haye May 28, 1913–) Puppet film maker who, since 1936, has produced at his Dollywood studios near Amsterdam some 100–200 short films (mostly publicity or sponsored films) in an appealing, but not particularly original, manner. [For Philips, he has made *Gala Concert, La Kermesse fantastique* (51), and *Light and Mankind*; for General Electric (US), *The Story of Light*; for *Life* magazine, *The World We Live In*; and such other films as *Cinderella, The Three Musketeers, A Visit to Bols*, and *The Four Masters*.]

GELABERT, Fructuoso DIR Spain. (Barcelona Jan 15, 1874–Barcelona Feb 27, 1955) Pioneer of the Spanish cinema who made numerous fiction films in Barcelona after his first, *Dorotea*, in 1897.

GELENBEVI, Baha DIR Turkey. (Istanbul 1902–) Turkish film maker who studied in France, was assistant to L'Herbier (*q.v.*) on *L'Argent*, and returned to Turkey in 1942, where he worked first as a cameraman then as a director. He is a versatile craftsman, has worked with many genres, and contributed to the postwar quantitative increase in production.
DIR (notably): *Dertli pinar* (43), *Deniz kizi* (44), *Yanik kaval* (46), *Cildiran kadin* (48), *Barbaros Hayrettin Pasa* (51), *Bos besik* (52), *Kaldirim cicegi* (53), *Balikci güzeli* (53).

GENINA, Augusto DIR Italy. (Rome Jan 28, 1892–Rome Sept 28, 1957) Highly professional but conventional director who made some 150 films in 40 years, moving readily from melodrama or costume dramas *La Gloria* (13), *Cyrano de Bergerac* (25), *Quartier Latin* (Ger29) to fascist propaganda, *Bengasi* (42), or the lives of saints *Cielo sulla Palude/Heaven Over the Marshes* (49). He returned to his origins with his later films, *Tre Storie Proibite* (52), *Maddalena* (54), *Frou Frou* (57).

GERASIMOV, Sergei DIR USSR. (Urals 1906–) Originally an actor closely involved with FEKS and the films of Kozintsev and Trauberg (*q.v.*), he directed his first film in 1934 and established his reputation with *Komsomolsk* (38), the story of the building of a socialist village in the Siberian taiga, and *Teacher* (39), one of his best films. After the war, his adaptation of Alexander Fadeyev's novel about Ukrainian partisans, *Young Guard* (47), was an undeniable success; he followed this with his three-part adaptation of Sholokhov's epic novel, *Quiet Flows the Don*. His *Men and Beasts* (62) is a summation of the experiences of his career and life.
DIR: *Do I Love You?* (34), *Semero smelykh/The Bold Seven* (36), *Komsomolsk* (38), *Uchitel/The Teacher* (39), *Maskarad/Masquerade* (41), *Fighting Film Album No. 1* (41), *Invincible* (42) (co-dir: Kalatozov), *Bolshaya zemlya/Mainland/The Great Earth* (44), *Molodaya gvardiya/The Young Guard* (47), *Liberated China* (50) (documentary, co-prod, China), *Selskii vrach/The Country Doctor* (52), *Nadezhda/Nadejda* (55), *Tikhi Don/Quiet Flows the Don/And Quiet Flows the Don* (57) (in 3 parts), *Lyudi i zveri/Men and Beasts/Menschen und Tiere* (GDR/USSR62) (co-dir: Lutz Köhlert), *Zhurnalist/The Journalist* (67), *V ozera/By the Lake* (69).

GERLACH, Arthur von DIR Germany. (c. 1877–1925) Worked mainly in the theater but directed two masterly films, both based on German ghost legends: the visually eloquent and most Stendhalian of films, *Vanina oder die Galgenhochzeit* (22), and the bleak *Zur Chronik von Grieshuus*, in which the natural setting of the Lüneberger Heide in Northern Germany plays a major role. He also apparently made two earlier films, now lost, for Fern Andra.

GERMI, Pietro DIR Italy. (Genoa Sept 14, 1914–) Although not one of the best

Italian neorealists, he depicted certain aspects of Sicilian life in *In the Name of the Law* (49) and *The Path to Hope* (50). He later turned to satirical comedy – at his best in the acerbic *Divorce, Italian Style*, at his worst in *The Birds, the Bees, and the Italians, Serafino,* and *Seduced and Abandoned*, all full of meaningless caricatures.
[DIR: *Il Testimone* (46), *Gioventu perduta* (47), *In Nome della Legge** (49), *Il Cammino della Speranza** (50), *Il Ferroviere* (56), *L'Uomo di Paglia* (57), *Un Maledetto Imbroglio/A Sordid Affair* (57), *Divorzio all'Italiana** (61), *Sedotta e Abbandonata* (63), *Signor e Signori/The Birds, the Bees, and the Italians* (65), *La Bomba* (66), *L'Immorale* (67), *Serafino* (68), *Le Castagne sono buone* (71).]

GERSHWIN, George MUS USA. (New York 1899–New York 1937) Famous American composer of popular songs and concert pieces whose music has been used in such films as *The King of Jazz* (30), *Shall We Dance?* (37), *The Goldwyn Follies* (38), *Funny Face** (57), *An American in Paris** (51), *Kiss Me, Stupid* (64), etc. His brother Ira (1896–), wrote lyrics for his songs and the lyrics for, e.g., Jerome Kern's music in *Cover Girl* (44). *Rhapsody in Blue* (45) is his film "biography."

GHAFFARY, Farrokh DIR Iran. (Teheran Feb 26, 1922–) After many years in France, this Iranian film maker returned to the difficult film industry of his own country in order to give it a new impetus. His first film, *Jonube Shahr/Southern Teheran* (59), was impounded by the authorities after one screening; his second, a comedy, *Arous Kodume?/Who is the Bride?* (60) was, he admitted, a mistake. He has since directed several documentaries and *Shabe Quzi* (63).

GHATAK, Ritwik DIR India. (Dacca, India, now Bangla Desh, 1924–) Remarkable Bengalese film maker, as indicated by his picaresque *Ajaantrik** (58). Also, notably, *Bari Thekey Pauye/The Vagrants* (59), *Meghey Dhaaka Taara/The Red Star Hidden by the Moon* (61), *Subarna Rekha* (64).

GHIONE, Emilio DIR Italy. (Turin 1879–Rome Jan 7, 1930) Major pioneer of the Italian cinema who made numerous "high

99

life" melodramas, then turned to thriller serials in the *Fantômas** manner, notably: *Za la Mort* (16), *I Topi Grigi* (18) (8 episodes), *Dollari e fraks* (19) (4 episodes), *Za la Mort contra Za la Mort* (21). He was also an actor, e.g., in Gallone's *The Last Days of Pompeii* (26).

*GIBBONS, Cedric ART DIR USA. (Dublin March 23, 1893–1960) The dean of Hollywood designers who worked on sets for Edison 1915–17, for Goldwyn 1918–24, and was chief art director for MGM 1924–56. His architectural approach is evident on many notable MGM films during these years, from Greta Garbo vehicles to literary adaptations to musicals: *The Wind** (28), *Susan Lennox, Her Fall and Rise* (31), *Private Lives* (31), *Grand Hotel* (32), *Mutiny on the Bounty* (36), *Romeo and Juliet* (36), *The Good Earth** (37), *Pride and Prejudice* (40), *Blossoms in the Dust* (41), *Gaslight** (44), *The Yearling* (46), *Little Women* (49), *An American in Paris** (51). He also co-directed one feature, *Tarzan and his Mate* (34), and is designer of the Oscar statuette.

GILLIAT, Sidney DIR/SCEN Britain. (Edgeley Feb 15, 1908–) Originally a scriptwriter in the Thirties (with his usual partner, Frank Launder) on such films as *The Lady Vanishes, Jamaica Inn, They Came By Night, Kipps, Night Train to Munich,* he began his directorial career with the likeable war film, *Millions Like Us* (43) (co-dir: Frank Launder), and the satirical *The Rake's Progress* (45), but has since made many (largely unremarkable) comedies, thrillers, and light dramas.

GODARD, Jean-Luc DIR France/Britain. (Paris Dec 3, 1930–) One of the strongest forces to come from the *nouvelle vague,* an intellectual, self-analytical, impatient film maker who is totally dedicated to his art and whose exploration of all the potentialities of cinematic language made him one of the strongest influences on the cinema of the Sixties. [Originally a critic, he wrote his first pieces in 1950, made his first short film in 1954, wrote continuously through the Fifties, and made several more shorts before directing his first feature in 1959, *A bout de souffle.* Since then he has directed numerous features and his style has become increasingly abstract. He works rapidly, often on a low budget and tends to improvise during shooting, however complete or sketchy his original scenario.] Though his films were originally socially and politically uncommitted, he began, almost in spite of himself, to ask questions about the anarchistic conception of life (*A bout de souffle*), the Algerian war (*Le Petit soldat*), and the feminine condition in the modern world (*Vivre sa vie, Une femme mariée*). His cynical nihilism has its positive aspect in the certain quality of spirit often found in his films. [After *Bande à part* (64), his original anarchism developed through philosophic social studies, which have been increasingly de-dramatized (*Une femme mariée, Masculin-féminin, Deux ou trois choses . . .*), to revolutionary political commitment pervaded by a deep sense of nihilism (*La Chinoise, Le Gai Savoir, Weekend, One Plus One*). His esthetic has become less concerned with plot and drama in the usual sense and more with dialectic and even with rhetoric — political in intent, phenomenological in its exploration of perception and communication. The following quotes from his writings or interviews suggest something of his development: "Editing, therefore, at the same time that it denies, announces and prepares the way for directing; they are interdependent. To direct is to plot, and one speaks of a plot as well or poorly knit" (1956). "I consider myself an essayist. I construct essays in novel form and novels in the form of essays: except that I film them rather than write them . . . To my mind, there is a profound continuity among the various modes of expressing oneself" (1962). "Basically (in *Vivre sa vie*), I would like to show what modern philosophy calls existentialism as opposed to essence. However, thanks to cinema, which can demonstrate that the two are not really in opposition to each other at all, I want to prove that existentialism presupposes essence and vice versa" (1962). "I believe I start more from the documentary, in order to give truth to fiction. That's why I've worked with excellent, professional actors — without them my films would not be as good . . . By being a realist one discovers the theater and by being theatrical . . . As in *The Golden Coach**: behind the theater is life and behind life, the theater . . . And why not make reconstructed newsreels like Méliès (*q.v.*) did? Today we should show Castro and Johnson, played by actors. . . . We would add real footage and people would love all that. I'm sure of it" (1962). "It seems to me that we have to discover everything about everything. There is only one solution and that is to turn one's back on the American cinema . . . We are now in a period of rupture. We must turn to life again. We must move into modern life with a virgin eye" (1966). "You could say that *Pierrot* is not really a film. It is an attempt at cinema. And the cinema, by forcing reality to unfold itself, reminds us that we must attempt to live" (1965). "(Cinema) belongs to the bourgeoisie, to the bourgeois mentality. Even in the countries of Eastern Europe. Cinema is capitalism in its purest form . . . And people don't ask questions when they are faced with a film, either. They say to themselves: cinema is for distraction . . . This is because we live and work without questioning the clichés, the taboos . . . My film, *Le Petit soldat*, was more or less true with regard to the cinema and more or less false with regard to everything else and was therefore a mediocre film . . . (The theory of cinema) does in fact enter into *La Chinoise* because cinema itself is called in question. I can't conceive of how its intervention in the film could be reduced — even though, paradoxically, this tends toward narcissism" (1967). Godard's practice is now to film *en groupe* (the Dziga Vertov Group) and he believes that "right ideas come from social practice," of which there are three modes — scientific experiment by film theorists, the struggle for production, and the class struggle. He now considers all his work prior to *Le Gai Savoir* to have been only on the first of these levels. "My idea of film hasn't changed. It has gone in its own direction and needs to find the right allies" (1969).]

DIR: *Opération Béton* (54) (short), *Une femme coquette* (55) (short), *Tous les garçons s'appellent Patrick* (57) (short), *Charlotte et son Jules* (58) (short), *Une histoire d'eau* (58) (short, co-dir: Truffaut), *A bout de souffle** (59), *Le Petit soldat* (60), *Une femme est une femme* (61), *Les Sept péchés capitaux* (61) (one episode), *Vivre sa vie** (62), *Rogopag* (62) (one episode), *Les Carabiniers** (63), *Les Plus belles escroqueries du monde* (63) (one episode), *Le Mépris** (63), *Paris vu par . . .* (64) (one epi-

sode), *Bande à part** (64), *Une femme mariée** (64), *Alphaville** (65), *Pierrot le fou** (65), *Masculin-féminin** (66), *Made in USA* (66), *Deux ou trois choses que je sais d'elle* (66), *Le Plus vieux métier du monde/L'Amour à travers les âges* (67) (one episode), *Loin de Vietnam* (67) (one episode), *La Chinoise* (67), *Vangelo 70* (67) (one episode), *Weekend* (67), *Le Gai Savoir* (68), *One Plus One/Sympathy for the Devil* (Brit 68), *Une film comme les autres/A Film Like All the Others* (68), *Pravda* (69, in Czechoslovakia), *British Sounds/See You at Mao* (Brit69), *Le Vent d'est/Vento dell'est* (Fr/It69), *Struggle in Italy* (Fr/It69), *Vladimir et Rosa* (Fr/GFR 70). Also, *One P.M./One Parallel Movie* (USA70), dir: D. A. Pennebaker) was derived from Godard's unfinished *One A.M.*

*GOLDWYN, Samuel B. (Samuel B. Goldfish) PROD USA. (Warsaw Aug 27, 1884–) Independent-minded Hollywood producer with a forceful personality and great ability who emigrated from Poland to the States as a youth, became an apprentice in a glove factory, prospered, and eventually owned a lucrative glove agency. He was enamoured of show business since he first met and married Blanche Lasky, a former vaudeville performer. With her brother, Jesse L. Lasky (*q.v.*), he produced his first film in 1913, *The Squaw Man*, directed by Cecil B. DeMille (*q.v.*). Soon after the Lasky company merged with Zukor's Famous Players, he resigned to set up his own company (1916) with Edgar and Archibald Selwyn (the "Goldwyn" name came from a merger of *Gold*fish with Sel*wyn*). The famous MGM Lion trademark was originally used by the Goldwyn company. Its first films, notably those with Geraldine Farrar, were successful, but after 1919 the company began to run into difficulties that eventually led to the removal of Samuel Goldwyn from an active role in the company. It was acquired by Loew's Inc. and on April 17, 1924 merged with Metro under Louis B. Mayer's direction, soon thereafter officially becoming Metro-Golwyn-Mayer. Samuel Goldwyn continued as an independent producer (usually releasing through United Artists), notably on: *Stella Dallas** (25 and 37), *Arrowsmith* (31), *Roman Scandals* (33), *Nana** (34), *The Dark Angel* (35), *Come and Get It** (36), *Hurricane* (37),

Dead End* (37), *The Goldwyn Follies* (38), *Wuthering Heights** (39), *The Westerner* (40), *The Little Foxes** (41), *North Star/Armored Attack* (43), *The Kid from Brooklyn* (46), *The Best Years of Our Lives** (46), *The Secret Life of Walter Mitty** (47), *A Song is Born* (48), *My Foolish Heart* (49), *Guys and Dolls* (55), *Porgy and Bess* (59).

GOLESTAN, Ebrahim PROD/DIR Iran. (Shiraz 1923–) The best Iranian film maker, with a background as a writer and intellectual, whose rigorously constructed documentaries, *Fire* (61), *Wave, Coral, and Rock* (64), and his first feature, *Darya* (64), reflect his keen perception. He is also the owner of a film studio.

GOLOVNYA, Anatoli N. PHOTOG USSR. (Simferopol 1900–) A masterly Soviet cameraman who worked with Protazanov (*q.v.*) and on all of Pudovkin's (*q.v.*) films, from *Mechanics of the Brain* to *Joukovsky*.

GOPO, Ion Popescu *see* POPESCU GOPO, ION

GOSHO, Heinosuke DIR Japan. (Tokyo Feb 1, 1902–) One of the greatest Japanese directors, the peer of his better-known contemporary, Kenji Mizoguchi (*q.v.*). He began as assistant director to Yasujiro Shimazu at Shochiku, directed his first films in 1925, and has since made many dozens of films. According to Iwasaki, Gosho's films since 1930 have considerably influenced the development of realism in Japanese films, notably, *The Dancing Girl from Izu* (33), *Bundle of Life* (35), and *Nameless People* (37). His films, except for *Where Chimneys are Seen, Behold Thy Son*, and *When a Woman Loves*, are largely unknown outside Asia. Donald Richie and J. L. Anderson wrote of him: "Gosho always tries to get the best possible script, sometimes writing it himself. In the same way, he likes to work closely with his art director, showing an almost fanatical concern over details . . . 'Goshoism,' now an accepted critical term often used by Japanese writers on film, has been defined as a style incorporating 'something that makes you laugh and cry at the same time' . . . Gosho's essential concern in both his life and films, has been the understanding of human life, the purpose of 'the film director's life (being) to describe the real life around him and create works which ex-

press the true feelings of human beings' . . . Thus Gosho, in perfecting the form of the *shomin-geki*, the drama of common people, raised it to the level of personal tragedy. His feelings made it impossible for him to create any war films acceptable to the government. He would turn any subject, no matter how military, into a simple love story or a *shomin-geki*. The poor health from which he has suffered all his life was all that saved him from official wrath . . . Gosho's belief in humanity is a very genuine thing. He seems to set the camera rolling by itself and then gently whispers to you that these people are worth saving . . . No one in Gosho's type of film is every really to blame for what happens."
DIR (notably): *Sabishii Rambo-mono/ The Lonely Roughneck* (27), *Karakuri Musume/Tricky Girl* (27), *Mura no Hanayome/The Village Bride* (28), *Madamu to Nyobo/The Neighbor's Wife and Mine* (31), *Izu no Odoriko/Dancing Girl from Izu* (33), *Hanayome no Negoto/The Bride Talks in Her Sleep* (33), *Ikitoshi Ikerumono/Everything that Lives* (34), *Jinsei no O-nimotsu/Bundle of Life* (35), *Nameless People* (37), *Mokuseki/ Wooden Head* (40), *Shinsetsu/New Snow* (42), *Ikite Iru Sugoroku/The Living Sugoroku* (43), *Izu no Musumetachi/The Girls of Izu* (45), *Ima Hitotubi/ Once More* (47), *Wakare Kumo/ Dispersing Clouds* (51), *Entotsu no Mieru Basho/Where Chimneys are Seen/ Three Chimneys** (53), *Ai to Shi no Tanima/The Valley Between Life and Death* (54), *Osaka no Yada/An Inn at Osaka* (54), *Niwatori wa Futataki Naku/ The Cock Crows Again* (54), *Takekurabe/Growing Up/Adolescence* (55), *Kiiroi Karasu/The Yellow Crow/Behold Thy Son* (57), *Banka/Dirge* (57), *Ari no Machi no Maria/Village Wife/Maria of the Ant Village* (58), *Hotarubi* (58), *Yoku* (58), *Hibari no Takekurabe* (59), *Waga Ai/When a Woman Loves* (60), *Ryoju* (61), *Elegy of the North* (61), *Kumo ga Chigireru Toki/As the Clouds Scatter* (61), *Kaachan Kekekon/You Must Marry* (62), *Hyakuman Nin no Musume Tachi/A Million Daughters* (63), *Osorezan no Onna/An Innocent Witch* (66), *Our Wonderful Years* (66), *Utage/Rebellion of Japan* (68), *Onna to Misoshiro* (68).

GOULDING, Edmund SCEN/DIR USA. (London March 20, 1891–Hollywood Dec 24,

1959) A former British actor who went to Hollywood in 1921 as a scriptwriter — e.g., on *Fury* (23) for Henry King and *Broadway Melody* (29) for Harry Beaumont — and became a director in 1927. He was a prolific director, sometimes of large-budget films — *Dawn Patrol** (38), *Of Human Bondage* (46), *The Razor's Edge* (46) — but his films are almost all mediocre, though his two for Greta Garbo, *Love* (27) and *Grand Hotel* (32), are worthy of note.

GRANGIER, Gilles DIR France. (Paris May 5, 1911–) A prolific but largely unexciting craftsman who has occasionally had good moments in comedy and has often worked with Jean Gabin. Notable films: *Le Cavalier Noir* (44), *L'Amour, Madame* (52), *Archimède le clochard* (58), *Les Vieux de la vieille* (60), *Le Cave se rebiffe* (61), *La Cuisine au beurre* (63), *Train d'enfer* (65), *L'Homme à la Buick* (67), *Fin de journée* (69).

GRAS, Enrico DIR Italy. (Genoa March 7, 1919–) After collaborating with Luciano Emmer (*q.v.*) on numerous films on art (41–49), he moved to Latin America, where he made several shorts before directing with Mario Craveri several pseudo documentaries such as *The Lost Continent** (54) and *Empire of the Sun* (56).

GREMILLON, Jean DIR France/Spain/Germany. (Bayeux Oct 3, 1902–Paris Nov 25, 1959) Grémillon is one of the great French film makers, despite forced periods of inactivity and a limited output of features (in a 35-year career). He studied music (and later wrote the scores for many of his own films) until a meeting with Georges Périnal (who photographed most of his early films) aroused his interest in the cinema. From 1923 to 1927 he made a number of industrial documentaries and an occasional experimental short before making a remarkable fiction film debut with *Maldone* (27) and *Gardiens de phare* (29). His first sound film was a failure and he was forced into the commercial wilderness for a decade, making films in Spain, then (in French) at the UFA Studios in Berlin. The production of his first serious film for some years, *Remorques,* was interrupted by the outbreak of war and completed in the studios in 1941. His brilliant *Lumière*

d'été and *Le Ciel est à vous* dominated the worst period of the Nazi Occupation but, unhappily, after the war the shortsightedness of producers prevented his giving full expression to his considerable talents as director, writer, and musician. [His moving, somber documentary, *Le Six juin à l'aube* was mutilated by the distributors; his commemoration of the 1848 Revolution, *Le Printemps de la liberté,* was eventually abandoned by its sponsors, the Ministry of Education; and other projects evaporated. He spent much time on administrative work as president of the Cinémathèque française (43–58) and of the Syndicat des Techniciens. His three features, none made in complete freedom, were again not the commercial successes Grémillon hoped and he turned to documentary. In the last decade of his life he made an extraordinary series of shorts, mostly films on art; *Les Charmes de l'existence* (49), *Au coeur de l'Île de France* (54), *La Maison aux images* (55), *Haute Lisse* (56), and his finest achievement in the genre, *André Masson et les quatre éléments* (58), a meditation on the mysteries of artistic creation. He also wrote the commentary and music for Pierre Kast's *Les Désastres de la guerre* (51).] He said of himself and his work: "Realism is the discovery of what the human eye cannot perceive directly, establishing harmonies, unknown relationships between objects and beings." "The nature of the cinema, like that of architecture, is not to restrict its audience. Its function and even its responsibility is to take stock of our times. It is a red herring to avoid encompassing reality or to turn back the hourglass in order to give the illusion that the times themselves have also been turned back."
DIR (features): *La Vie des travailleurs Italien en France* (26) (documentary), *Un tour au large* (27) (documentary), *Maldone** (27), *Gardiens de phare** (29), *La Petite Lise* (30), *Daïnah la métisse* (31), *Pour un sou d'amour* (32), *Gonzague/L'Accordeur* (33), *La Dolorosa* (Sp34), *Centinella Alerta!* (Sp35) *La Valse Royale* (Ger35) (French version of *Koenigs Waltzer*), *Pattes de mouches* (Ger36), *Gueule d'amour* (Ger 37), *L'Etrange Monsieur Victor* (Ger38), *Remorques** (41), *Lumière d'été** (43), *Le Ciel est à vous** (44), *Le Six juin à l'aube** (45) (documentary), *Pattes blanches* (49), *L'Etrange Madame X* (51), *L'Amour d'une femme** (53).

DIR (shorts): *Chartres, La Revêtement des routes* (both 23), *La Fabrication du fil, Du fil à l'Aiguille, La Fabrication du ciment artificiel, La Bière, Le Roulement à Bille, Les Parfums, L'Etirage des ampoules électriques, La Photogénie mécanique* (all 24), *L'Education professionelle des conducteurs de tramway, L'Electrification de la ligne Paris-Vierzon, L'Auvergne, La Naissance des cicognes, Les Aciéries de la Marine et d'Homecourt* (all 25), *La Croisière de l'Atalante* (26), *Gratuites* (27), *Bobs* (28), *Le Petit Babouin* (32), *Les Charmes de l'existence* (49) (co-dir: Pierre Kast), *Astrologie/Le Miroir de la vie* (52), *Alchimie* (in *Encyclopédie filmée* series) (52), *Au coeur de l'Île de France* (54), *La Maison aux images* (55), *Haute Lisse* (56), *André Masson et les quatres éléments* (58).

*GRIERSON, John PROD/DIR Britain/Canada. (Deanston Apr 26, 1898–Feb 1972) Although he only directed a handful of films and was mainly a producer, he has been justifiably called the "father of the British documentary" and was of considerable international influence as theoretician, proselytizer for the documentary film, and organizer. Among his numerous other achievements, he founded the National Film Board of Canada and the influence of his teachings was still evident there many years after he resigned as its head. He brought Cavalcanti (*q.v.*) and, briefly, Flaherty (*q.v.*) into the English documentary and encouraged the talents of Len Lye, Basil Wright, Norman McLaren, Paul Rotha, Harry Watt, Arthur Elton, Humphrey Jennings, and Edgar Anstey, among others. His influence continued to be evident in the postwar renaissance of the British cinema.

After graduating in philosophy he spent 1924–27 in the USA, where his interest was aroused in the cinema as a means of reaching public opinion — as a social force, not as an art form. In 1927 he became Films Officer to the Empire Marketing Board (EMB) and in 1929 directed his first film, *Drifters*. Its success enabled him to further his ideas and he devoted his time to building up a film unit and training its members. Over 100 films were produced by the unit 1930–33 and when the EMB was dissolved in 1933 the entire unit moved to the General Post Office (GPO). In 1938 he prepared a survey on the possibilities of film pro-

duction in Canada, and in 1939 the Canadian Government appointed him Film Commissioner, head of the new National Film Board. There, he again created a cadre of trained film makers able to continue his sociological approach to documentary when he resigned in 1945. He joined UNESCO in 1946 and in 1948, back in Britain, became Film Controller at the Central Office of Information. In 1951 he became the executive producer of Group Three and in 1957 produced his own weekly program for Scottish TV, *This Wonderful World*. He later returned to Canada to teach film at McGill University in Montreal. His influence on the documentary film ("the creative treatment of actuality") over some 40 years has been profound and while it is impossible to give an adequate indication of the power of his writings in a single quote, the following (1933) summarizes his approach to the cinema: "I have no great interest in films as such. Now and again, shapes, masses, and movements so disport themselves that I have a brief hope that something of the virtue of great painting may one day come into cinema . . . I look on cinema as a pulpit, and use it as a propagandist . . . Cinema is to be conceived as a medium, like writing, capable of many forms and many functions. A professional propagandist may well be interested in it. It gives generous access to the public. It is capable of direct description, simple analysis, and commanding conclusion, and may, by its tempo'd and imagistic powers, be made easily persuasive."
DIR: *Drifters** (29), *Industrial Britain* (32) (co-dir: Flaherty), *The Fishing Banks of Skye* (33), *So This is London* (34) (co-dir: Edgar Anstey).

GRIFFITH, David Wark DIR USA. (La Grange, Kentucky Jan 23, 1875–Hollywood July 23, 1948) A titan of the cinema, a director who, though he didn't invent film language, molded and shaped it — particularly editing — into the means of expression of a developing art form. Originally a stage actor (under the name Lawrence Griffith) and occasional playwright, he first entered the cinema as an actor in Edwin S. Porter's *Rescued from an Eagle's Nest* (07) and soon after joined the Biograph Company as actor and scriptwriter. He directed his first film *The Adventures of Dollie* in 1908 and from then until 1913 directed some 50–100 films a year, most of them photographed by the man who shot all his most famous later films, Billy Bitzer (*q.v.*). Griffith was largely self-educated, both in the traditional arts and in the new art he was helping create, but his Biograph films (though not as ambitious or famous as his features) quickly made their mark, surpassing the competing Vitagraph films produced by James Stuart Blackton (*q.v.*). His scripts were often based on literary works and in them he developed and perfected many varied techniques drawn from films around the world — close-ups, parallel action, suspense cross-cutting, etc. In late 1913 he joined Reliance-Majestic (which released through Mutual) as head of production, directing personally four 5–7 reel features and producing a dozen others. In 1915 came his first supreme achievement, *The Birth of a Nation,* a film whose dramatic and emotional impact has not diminished with time. In July 1915, Harry Aitken persuaded Thomas Ince (*q.v.*), Mack Sennett (*q.v.*), and Griffith to form the Triangle Film Corporation. There he produced several films of directors William Christy Cabanne, John Emerson, Allan Dwan (all *q.v.*), and Edward Dillon, until his new project *Intolerance* (produced on his *Birth of a Nation* profits) grew so ambitious that he had no time for Triangle films. This extraordinary film was a commercial disaster compared to *Birth of a Nation,* but its exploration of film techniques opened new paths of development for the cinema and exerted a worldwide influence on other directors. Griffith's contradictory personality is revealed in his first two major films, oscillating between the Southern racist attitudes of *Birth of a Nation* and the liberalism of *Intolerance.* With the advent of the war, Griffith made two war films, *Hearts of the World* and *The Great Love.* With the return of peace he turned to romantic dramas, notably with *True Heart Susie* and, what still remains his most perfect masterpiece, *Broken Blossoms.* His intimate and moving style transcended the old-fashioned melodrama of films like *Way Down East,* but not that of his large-budget spectacle, *Orphans of the Storm.* Once sensitive to the best in foreign influences, he finally turned to emulating the traditional Hollywood style and desperately searched for money-making films, but never truly suc-

ceeded. The success of his earlier features had helped establish Hollywood as the world's film capital; now, little by little, it crushed him. Though he lived another 17 years after *The Struggle* (31), he never made another film. His company went into receivership after *The Struggle* and though he made half-hearted attempts at other projects, nothing materialized. He lived his last years, forgotten and withdrawn from the world, in a room of the Hollywood Knickerbocker Hotel. Though his creative contribution gradually diminished after 1920, in his best period he unquestionably made major advances in the art of cinema, which Léon Moussinac summarized in 1924: "He is the cinema's first great name . . . a master wise enough to concentrate his ambition by a continuing effort, tenacious creative experimentation. This artist creates, every one of his productions reveals to us some noble truth. Thus his genius asserts itself in concern for serious emotions . . . His art has many analogies with the art of all the primitives. A concern for sometimes scrupulous exactitude; a passion for truth; brutality. Lyricism, the spirit that animates Thomas Ince (*q.v.*) and without which no work can become great and make its mark, is almost totally absent. He rarely rises to true power (except for the end of *Intolerance*) and his choice of means of expression is occasionally witness of a wearisome puerility. The theme presents the same characteristics. His art draws its force from its moderation. He concentrates the spectator's full attention on the chosen theme and on the emotions that are externalized. In *Broken Blossoms* and *Way Down East,* simple plots are raised to the level of tragedies . . . One finds in them the eternal contrast between beauty and ugliness, good and evil, which was used in the beginning of all the arts to exalt the masses . . . He submits his actors to the same discipline he imposes on himself. From this comes his concern for composition, his stylization of characters."

DIR (1908–13, notably): *The Adventures of Dollie, The Taming of the Shrew, The Song of the Shirt, For Love of Gold, After Many Years, The Call of the Wild* (all 08), *Edgar Allan Poe, The Lonely Villa, A Corner in Wheat**, *The Expiation* (all 09), *Ramona, The Thread of Destiny, In Old California* (all 10), *The Lonedale Operator, Enoch*

Arden, The Battle, The Last Drop of Water (all 11), An Unseen Enemy, The Musketeers of Pig Alley, The Massacre, The New York Hat*, Just Like a Woman, Man's Genesis, The Female of the Species (all 12), The Mothering Heart, The Battle of Elderbush Gulch, Judith of Bethulia (all 13).

DIR (all features): The Battle of the Sexes (14), The Escape (14), Home, Sweet Home (14), The Avenging Conscience (14), The Birth of a Nation* (15), Intolerance* (16), Hearts of the World* (18), The Great Love (18), A Romance of Happy Valley (18), The Greatest Thing in Life (18), The Girl Who Stayed at Home (19), True Heart Susie* (19), Scarlet Days (19), Broken Blossoms* (19), The Greatest Question (19), The Idol Dancer (20), The Love Flower (20), Way Down East* (20), Dream Street (21), Orphans of the Storm* (21), One Exciting Night (22), The White Rose (23), America (24), Isn't Life Wonderful? (24), Sally of the Sawdust (25), That Royle Girl (26), The Sorrows of Satan (26), Drums of Love (28), The Battle of the Sexes (28), Lady of the Pavements (29), Abraham Lincoln (30), The Struggle (31).

GRIMAULT, Paul ANIM France. (Neuilly-sur-Seine March 23, 1905–) The greatest French animator, a man of great artistic sensibility who began making commercials – with Carné (q.v.) and Aurenche (q.v.) – in the early Thirties and progressed into short and feature-length cartoons. His style, though fairly conventional, is highly imaginative and his themes have benefitted greatly from his collaboration with Aurenche, Leenhardt, and Prévert. From Prévert's (q.v.) script he made the feature, La Bergére et le Ramoneur (53), and, though he was not able to complete it as he wished, it remains one of the most remarkable cartoons in the history of the cinema. Thereafter, apart from one short, he had to return to the production of commercials.

DIR: Les Lampes Mazda (37), Go chez les oiseaux (39), Les Passagers de la Grande Ourse (41) (feature), Les Marchands des notes (42), L'Epouvantail (43), Le Voleur de paratonnerres (45), La Flûte magique (46), Le Petit Soldat (47), La Bergère et le Ramoneur/Mr. Wonderbird/The Shepherdess and the Chimney Sweep* (53), Le Faim du monde (58).

GRIMOIN-SANSON, Raoul INVENTOR France. (Elbeuf June 7, 1860–Oissel Nov 1941) The inventor of Cinéorama (also known as Cinecosrama), a projection technique that anticipated Abel Gance's triple screen, Cinerama, and Circlorama. It was demonstrated at the Paris Exposition 1900 and involved spectators sitting in the basket of a false balloon entirely surrounded by a circular screen on which 10 projectors threw a panoramic picture. Later, this spectacle toured France, Algeria, Belgium, Spain, and England. When his enterprise failed, Grimoin-Sanson lost interest in the cinema.

GRUEL, Henri ANIM France. (Mâcon Feb 5, 1923–) Animator who developed the idea of using children's drawings in cartoons also conceived by children (Martin et Gaston, Gitanes et Papillons, etc.). He achieved his first major success with La Joconde, a blend of live action and animation parodying Da Vinci's "Mona Lisa." He later worked with Lenica (q.v.), Monsieur Tête, and has made several sponsored films, notably, Un atome qui vous veut du bien. He directed his first, and to date, only live-action feature in 1963: Le Roi du village/Moise et l'amour.

ANIM: Martin et Gaston (53), Gitanes et papillons (54), La Rose et le radies (55), Le Voyage de Badabau (55), Le Voyageur (56), La Joconde (57), Coeur de cristal (57), Métropolitain (58), Un atome qui vous veut du bien (59), Douze mois (59), La Lutte contre le froid (59), Monsieur Tête (59) (co-dir: Jan Lenica), Notre Paris (61), Poêles d'aujourdhui, cuisinières de toujours (61), Etroits sont les vaisseaux (62), La Margarine Astra (62), Le Rendez-vous d'Asnières (63), Contes Zaghawa (65).

GRUNE, Karl DIR Germany PROD Britain. (Vienna Jan 22, 1890– Bournemouth, Britain Oct 2, 1962) Former actor in Vienna and Berlin who was a disciple of Reinhardt, became director of the Residenttheater, and entered the cinema in 1918. After some uninteresting first films, he became interested in Kammerspiel and social films and directed the first of the "street" films, and his best film, Die Strasse (23). After several more ventures into social realism, Ara-

bella (24), *Eifersucht/Jealousy* (25), *Die Brüder Schellenberg* (26), *Am Rande der Welt* (27), he fell back on conventional historical costume films, *Königin Luise* (27), *Waterloo* (28), etc. In 1931 he went to France and then to England, where he directed *Abdul the Damned* (35). He founded Capitol Films with Max Schach, directed *The Marriage of Corbal* (36) and *Pagliacci* (36), then concentrated on production.

GUAZZONI, Enrico DIR Italy. (Rome Sept 18, 1876–Rome Sept 24, 1949) The principal director of historical spectaculars in the Italian manner who established an international reputation with the success of his monumental *Quo Vadis?* (12). He was originally a painter and designer and designed the sets and costumes for all his own films. His costume dramas, such as *Madame Tallien* (16), exerted considerable influence on Lubitsch (*q.v.*) and Griffith (*q.v.*), on Hollywood, and even on some of the post-1945 Italian co-productions.

DIR: *Messalina* (09), *Il Sacco di Roma* (09), *La Nuove Mammina* (09), *Adriana di Berton* (10), *Bruto* (10), *I Maccabei* (10), *Agrippina* (10), *San Francisco* (11), *Quo Vadis?** (12), *La Gerusalemme liberata* (13), *Marcantonio e Cleopatra* (13), *Il Lettino Vuto* (13), *Scuola di Eroi* (13), *Caius Julius Caesar* (14), *Immolazione* (14), *L'Instruttoria* (14), *L'Amica* (15), *Madame Tallien* (16), *La Gerusalemme liberata* (17) (remake), *Il Sacco di Roma* (20) (remake), *Messalina* (23) (remake), *Miriam* (28), *La Sperduta di Allah* (28), *Il Dono del Mattino* (32), *Signora Paradiso* (34), *Re Burlone* (35), *Re di Denari* (36), *I Due Sergenti* (36), *Ho Perduto mio Marito* (36), *Il Dottor Antonio* (37), *Il Suo Destino* (38), *Ho Visto brillare le Stella* (39), *Antonio Meucci* (40), *La Figlia de Corsaro Verde* (40), *Oro Nero* (40), *I Pirati della Malesia* (41), *La Fornarina* (42).

*GUFFEY, Burnett PHOTOG USA. (Del Rio, Tennessee May 26, 1905–) Highly professional Hollywood cameraman who began as an assistant in 1923 and is notable for his chiaroscuro photography on several memorable films of the Forties and Fifties and more recently on *Bonnie and Clyde, The Madwoman of Chaillot,* and *The Great White Hope.*

PHOTOG (notably): for Wellman, *Gallant Journey* (46); for Robert Rossen, *Johnny O'Clock* (47), *All the King's Men* (49), *They Came to Cordura* (59); for Nicholas Ray, *Knock on Any Door* (48), *In a Lonely Place* (50); for Max Ophüls, *The Reckless Moment* (49); for Curtis Bernhardt, *Sirocco* (51); for Phil Karlson, *Scandal Sheet/Dark Page* (52), *Tight Spot* (55), *The Brothers Rico* (57), *Hell to Eternity* (60), *Kid Galahad* (62), *The Silencers* (66); for Dmytryk, *The Sniper* (52); for Zinnemann, *From Here to Eternity** (52); for Fritz Lang, *Human Desire** (54); for Don Siegel, *Private Hell 36* (54), *Edge of Eternity* (59); for Rudy Maté, *The Violent Men/ Rough Company* (55); for Mark Robson, *The Harder They Fall* (56); for Daniel Taradash, *Storm Center* (56); for Jacques Tourneur, *Nightfall* (56); for Jack Garfein, *The Strange One/End as a Man* (57); for Boetticher, *Decision at Sundown* (57); for Philip Leacock, *Let No Man Write My Epitaph* (59); for Frankenheimer, *The Bird Man of Alcatraz* (61); for Bryan Forbes, *King Rat* (65), *The Madwoman of Chaillot* (69); for Arthur Penn, *Bonnie and Clyde** (67); for Martin Ritt, *The Great White Hope* (70); for Paul Bogart, *Halls of Anger* (70).

GUITRY, Sacha (Alexandre-Pierre-Georges Guitry) DIR/SCEN France. (Saint Petersburg, Russia Feb 21, 1885–Paris July 24, 1957) The famous French comedy actor, author, and producer found in the cinema a device for conserving his own stage plays. Though he took an early interest in the cinema (his first film, *Ceux de chez nous,* in 1914, was a series of intimate portraits of characters from the artistic world), it was much less of a means of artistic expression than a mirror in which to contemplate himself, an echo through which he could savor his own jokes. His most veracious self-portrait was *Le Roman d'un tricheur/ Story of a Cheat* in which he used not interior monologue or commentary but a kind of running patter to vaunt his own personality. Many of his plays have been filmed by others, sometimes from his own scripts.

DIR: *Ceux de chez nous* (14), *Pasteur* (35), *Bonne chance* (35), *Le Nouveau testament* (36), *Le Roman d'un tricheur** (36), *Mon père avait raison* (36), *Faisons un rêve* (36), *Le Mot de Cambronne* (36), *Les Perles de la Couronne* (37) (co-dir: Christian-Jaque), *Désire* (37), *Quadrille* (37), *Remontons Les Champs-Élysées* (38), *Ils était neuf célibataires* (39), *Le Destin Fabuleux de Desirée Clary* (38), *Donne-moi tes yeux* (42), *La Malibran* (42), *Le Comédien* (47), *Le Diable boiteux* (48), *Aux deux colombes* (49), *Toa* (49), *Le Trésor de Cantenac* (49), *Tu m'as sauvé la vie* (50), *Deburau* (50), *La Poison* (51), *Je l'ai été trois fois* (52), *La Vie d'un honnête homme* (52), *Si Versailles m'était conté* (53), *Napoléon* (54), *Si Paris nous était conté* (55), *Assassins et voleurs* (56), *Les Trois font la paire* (57) (co-dir: Clément Duhour).

[SCEN (from his own plays): *Le Blanc et le noir* (31) (dir: Robert Florey, Marc Allégret), *Les Deux couverts* (35) (dir: Léonce Perret), *L'Accroche coeur* (38) (dir: Pierre Caron), *Adhemar/Le Jouet de la fatalité* (51) (dir: Fernandel), *La Vie à deux* (58) (dir: Clément Duhour). His play *Bonne chance* was used in *Lucky Partners* (USA40) (dir: Lewis Milestone).]

GUY-BLACHE, Alice (born Alice Guy, married Herbert Blaché) DIR France/USA. (Paris July 1, 1873–Brussels ?1965) Originally Léon Gaumont's (*q.v.*) secretary when he was still only making film equipment, she began making short films intended for use as demonstrations for potential clients. She made her first film, *La Fée aux choux* in 1896, some months before Méliès (*q.v.*), and thus became the first woman director in the world. She made several films for Gaumont (including an important *Vie du Christ*), helped establish Feuillade's (*q.v.*) career, married a Gaumont cameraman, Herbert Blaché, and went with him to the USA, where he headed Gaumont's American branch. In 1912 they founded Solax Studios and she continued her directorial career in the States until 1925, as did her husband.

DIR (notably): *La Fée aux choux* (1896), *Au bal de flore* (1900), *La Danse des saisons* (1900), *Hussards et grisettes* (01), *Sage-femme de première class* (02), *Le Voleur sacrilège* (03), *Les Petits Coupeurs de bois vert* (04), *Le Courrier de Lyon* (04), *Paris la nuit* (04), *Le Crime de la rue du Temple* (04), *Une noce au lac Saint-Fargeau* (05), *La Esmerelda* (05), *La Vie du Christ* (06), (co-dir: Jasset), *Beneath the Czar* (USA13), *Dick Whittington and His Cat* (USA13), *The Dream Woman* (USA14), *The Shadows of the Moulin Rouge* (USA14).

HAANSTRA, Bert DIR Netherlands. (Holten, Overijsel May 31, 1916–) The best postwar Dutch documentary film maker, a superb technician, he began by making amateur films, worked as cameraman on a feature, *Myrthe en de Demonen* (48) by Paul Bruno Schreiber, and made his first film the following year. He established an international reputation with the subtle visual experiments *Mirror of Holland* (50) and *Panta Rhei* (51), worked on many sponsored films (notably for Shell Oil), reaped a host of international prizes for *Glass,* and in 1958 made his first fiction film, *Fanfare,* an amusing but sometimes heavy-handed bucolic comedy. [He has since made two more features, the disastrous *The M. P. Case* (60) and the outstanding *Alleman* (63). The latter is a documentary feature using the "candid camera" technique, as in the early short *Zoo,* to pinpoint people's foibles, never maliciously, but tolerantly and with a gentle wit.
DIR: *De Muiderkring Herleft* (49), *Spiegel van Holland/Mirror of Holland* (50), *Nederlandse Beeldhouwkunst tijdens de late Middeleeuwen/Medieval Dutch Sculpture* (51), *Panta Rhei* (51), *Dijkbouw/Dike Builders* (52), *Aardolie/ The Changing Earth* (53), *The Search for Oil* (53), *The Wildcat* (53), *The Oilfield* (53), *The Rival World* (54), *God Shiva* (55), *En de Zee was niet meer/And There Was No More Sea* (56), *Rembrant, Schilder van der Mens/ Rembrandt, Painter of Men* (56), *Over Glas gesproken/Speaking of Glass* (57), *Glas/Glass* (58), *Fanfare* (58) (feature), *De Zaak M. P./the M. P. Case* (60) (feature), *Zoo* (62), *Delta Phase I* (62), *Alleman/The Human Dutch* (63) (documentary feature), the *Voice of the Water* (65) (feature).]

HALAS, John (Budapest April 16, 1912–) *and* **BATCHELOR, Joy** (London May 12, 1914–) ANIM Britain. The most consistently successful and prolific British animators, they followed in the train of Walt Disney in the Thirties and Forties, then modernized their graphics in the Fifties under the influence of UPA. [John Halas studied animation with George Pal (*q.v.*), came to England to work on an early British color cartoon, *Music Man,* and met Joy Batchelor, who was working on the same unit. After a period working as commercial artists, they founded the Halas and Batchelor cartoon company in 1940. They have made over 200 sponsored shorts (many of them models of their kind), 800 commercials, and several TV series. They made the first British cartoon feature, *Animal Farm,* in 1954. Notable among their work are the abstract *Magic Canvas* (51), *The History of the Cinema* (56), *Automania 2000* (63), and *The Hoffnung Symphony Orchestra.*
ANIM (notably): *The Pocket Cartoon* (41), *Dustbin Parade* (42), *Abu* series (43) (4 films), *Six Little Jungle Boys* (44), *Old Wives' Tales* (46), *Heave Away My Johnny* (47), *Charley* series (48) (7 films), *First Line of Defence* (49), *As Old as the Hills* (50), *Magic Canvas* (51), *Poet and Painter* series (51) (4 films), *Submarine Control* (51), *The Figurehead* (52) (puppets), *The Owl and the Pussycat* (53) (3D), *The Moving Spirit* (53), *Power to Fly* (54), *Animal Farm** (54), *Speed the Plough* (55), *The History of the Cinema* (56), *The Candlemaker* (56), *To Your Health* (56), *The World of Little Ig* (56) (TV), *All Lit Up* (57), *The Christmas Visitor* (58), *The Cultured Ape* (59), *The Insolent Matador* (59), *The Widow and*

the Pig (59), *The History of Inventions* (60), *Foo Foo* TV series (60) (33 films), *Snip and Snap* TV series (60) (26 films), *Dam the Delta* (60), *The Colombo Plan* (61), *For Better, For Worse* (61), *Hamilton, the Musical Elephant* (62), *Automania 2000* (63), *Hoffnung* TV series (65) (4 films), *Ruddigore* (67), *Children and Cars* (70). Other work includes: *Handling Ships* (45) (documentary), *The Monster of Highgate Ponds* (61) (live action, dir: Cavalcanti), *Is There Intelligent Life on Earth?* (63) ("Living Screen").]

*HALL, Charles D. ART DIR USA. (Britain 1899–) After working as a stage designer in Britain, he moved to Hollywood in 1931 and developed a reputation on the *Frankenstein** films directed by James Whale and for his extraordinary machinery in Chaplin's *Modern Times** (36). He also designed Whale's *By Candlelight* (33) and *Showboat* (36), several of John Stahl's romances, including *Magnificent Obsession* (35), and Robert Florey's *Vicious Years* (50).

*HALLER, Ernest PHOTOG USA. (Los Angeles 1896–Oct 1970) One of the greatest of Hollywood craftsmen, he began as an actor at Biograph in 1914, was cameraman on the serial, *Hazards of Helen*, in 1915, and photographed some 150 features. He was a complete professional without a unique style of his own and handled all genres — romance, comedy, drama, and horror — with equal facility.
PHOTOG (notably): for Ralph Ince, *Homeward Bound* (23); for Benjamin Christensen, *House of Horror* (29); for Howard Hawks, *The Dawn Patrol** (30); for Michael Curtiz, *Woman from Monte Carlo* (32), *The Key* (34), *British Agent* (34), *Mountain Justice* (36), *Four's a Crowd* (38), *Four Daughters* (38), *Mildred Pierce* (45), *My Dream is Yours* (49), *Jim Thorpe — All American/Man of Bronze* (51); for Robert Florey, *The House on 56th Street* (33); for William Wyler, *Jezebel** (38); for Raoul Walsh, *The Roaring Twenties* (39), *Manpower* (41); for Victor Fleming, *Gone With the Wind** (39); for Anatole Litvak, *All This and Heaven Too* (40), *Blues in the Night* (41); for Don Siegel, *The Verdict* (46); for Jean Negulesco, *Humoresque* (47); for Nicholas Ray, *Rebel Without a Cause** (55); for Anthony Mann, *Men in War* (57), *God's Little Acre* (58), *Man of the West* (58); for Robert Aldrich, *Whatever Happened to Baby Jane?* (62); for Ralph Nelson, *Lilies of the Field* (63); for Paul Henreid, *Dead Ringer/Dead Image* (64); for Phil Karlson, *A Time for Killing/The Long Ride Home* (67).

*HAMER, Robert DIR/SCEN Britain. (Kidderminster March 31, 1911–Dec 1963) A film maker who had a brief period of brilliance as writer and director with Ealing on *Dead of Night, It Always Rains on Sundays,* and the sardonic *Kind Hearts and Coronets.* He was originally an editor with Korda, and later Ealing, working on *Jamaica Inn, Ships with Wings, The Foreman Went to France.* He wrote his first script in 1943. Some of his work has European affinities (the "poetic realism" of *It Always Rains on Sundays* and the decided French flavor of many of his comedies). His films in the Fifties are of far less interest, the impeccable stylization and wit of his early films having degenerated into vacuous, self-indulgent "sophistication." He also worked as a TV producer after 1956.
DIR: *Dead of Night** (45) (one episode), *Pink String and Sealing Wax* (45), *It Always Rains on Sundays** (47), *Kind Hearts and Coronets** (49), *The Spider and the Fly* (49), *His Excellency* (51), *The Long Memory* (52), *Father Brown* (54), *To Paris with Love* (55), *The Scapegoat* (59), *School for Scoundrels* (60).
SCEN: *San Demetrio, London* (43) (dir: Charles Frend), *Dead of Night** (45) (co-dir: Hamer, Cavalcanti, etc.), *A Jolly Bad Fellow* (63) (dir: Don Chaffey), and his own *It Always Rains on Sundays, Kind Hearts and Coronets, His Excellency, The Long Memory.*

HAMMETT, Dashiell SCEN USA. (1891–1961) Major American writer of thrillers who exercised considerable influence on the development of the Hollywood *film noir* in the Thirties and Forties, both through film adaptations of his novels, *The Thin Man*, The Glass Key,* and *The Maltese Falcon*,* and through his activities as a scriptwriter, e.g., Mamoulian's *City Streets** (31). He was active in the antifascist movement in Hollywood prior to the war and consequently later suffered from the "witch hunts."

HARBOU, Thea von SCEN/DIR Germany. (Berlin Dec 12, 1888–Berlin July 2, 1954) Best known for her scripts for Fritz Lang (*q.v.*), to whom she was married 1924–33; she wrote all his scripts from *Der Müde Tod** (21) to *Das Testament des Dr. Mabuse** (33). She was a Nazi and continued her career in Germany after the advent of Hitler (and Lang's departure from Germany), became an official film maker of the regime, wrote numerous scripts for Richard Eichberg, Lamprecht (*q.v.*), Veit Harlan (*q.v.*) Von Baky (*q.v.*), etc., and directed two films. She wrote a few scripts in West Germany after the war.
SCEN (notably): for Joe May, *die Heilige Simplizia* (20); for Murnau, *Der Brennende Acker* (22), *Phantom* (22), *Die Austreibung* (23), *Die Finanzen des Grossherzogs* (23); for Dreyer, *Michael* (24); for Arthur von Gerlach, *Zur Chronik von Grieshus* (25); and all Fritz Lang's films 1921–33.
DIR: *Elisabeth und der Narr* (33), *Hanneles Himmelfahrt* (34).

HARLAN, Veit DIR Germany/German Federal Republic. (Berlin Sept 29, 1899–Capri 1964) Self-important, grandiloquent, pretentious director, notorious for his anti-Semitic and pro-Nazi films. He began in the theater, acted in films, 1927–34, and directed his first film in 1935. Goebbels appointed him a professor and state director. His *Jud Süss* (40) contributed to the Nazi persecution of Jews. He returned to film-making in the German Federal Republic in 1950 and made many mediocre films. He has scripted most of his own films.
DIR: *Krach im Hinterhaus* (35), *Der Müde Theodor* (36), *Kater Lampe* (36), *Alles für Veronika* (36), *Maria, die Magd* (36), *Mein Sohn, der Herr Minister* (37), *Die Kreutzersonate* (37), *Der Herrscher* (37), *Jugend* (38), *Verwehte Spuren* (38), *Die Riese nach Tilsit** (39) (new version of *Sunrise**), *Das Unsterbliche Herz* (39), *Jud Süss** (40), *Pedro soll hängen* (41), *Die Goldene Stadt* (Czech 42), *Der Grosse König* (42), *Immensee* (43), *Opfergang* (44), *Kolberg* (45), *Unsterbliche Geliebte* (50), *Hanna Amon* (51), *Die Blaue Stunde* (53), *Sterne über Colombo* (54), *Die Gefangene des Maharadscha* (54), *Verrat an Deutschland* (55), *Anders als Du und Ich/the Third Sex* (57), *Liebe kann wie Gift sein* (58), *Ich werde Dich auf Händen tragen* (58), *Die Blonde Frau des Maharadscha* (62).

HARMAN, Hugh (Pagosa Spring Sept 31, 1903–) *and* **ISING, Rudolf** (Kansas City Sept 7, 1903–) ANIM USA. Constant collaborators whose animal cartoons rivaled those of Disney (*q.v.*) in the Thirties. They began in 1923, made *Arabian Nights Cartoons*, and, after 1930, *Looney Tunes* (whose star was a loquacious Negro, "Bosko") for Vitaphone, one of the first cartoon series to adopt sound. They also made some of the *Happy Harmonies* series for MGM, which they joined in 1938. Their *Peace on Earth* (40) won a Nobel Peace Prize.

HATHAWAY, Henry DIR USA. (Sacramento March 13, 1898–) The director of a handful of memorable films, among numerous mediocre ones, during a prolific 40-year career. Though some have mistaken this artisan for an artist, he has failed to live up to the promise of two high points in his career: the first in the mid-Thirties with the enormous commercial success of *Lives of a Bengal Lancer* and the remarkable *Peter Ibbetson;* and the second in the postwar years, when, under Louis de Rochemont's (*q.v.*) tutelage, he contributed to the introduction of documentary realism into the thriller with *The House on 92nd Street, 13 Rue Madeleine, Call Northside 777,* and *Kiss of Death.* Other notable films: *14 Hours, The Bottom of the Bottle, Circus World, The Last Safari, True Grit.* He began his career as a child actor in 1907, became an assistant director in the Twenties, and in 1932 began directing B-westerns.
[DIR: *Wild Horse Mesa* (32), *Heritage of the Desert* (33), *Under the Tonto Rim* (33), *Sunset Pass* (33), *Men of the Forest* (33), *To the Last Man* (33), *Come on Marines* (34), *The Last Roundup* (34), *Thundering Herd* (34), *The Witching Hour* (34), *Now and Forever* (34), *Lives of a Bengal Lancer* (35), *Peter Ibbetson** (35), *Trail of the Lonesome Pine* (36), *Go West, Young Man* (36), *Souls at Sea* (37), *Spawn of the North* (38), *The Real Glory* (39), *Johnny Apollo* (40), *Brigham Young— Frontiersman* (40), *The Shepherd of the Hills* (41), *Sundown* (41), *Two Gentlemen from West Point* (41), *China*

Girl (42), *Home in Indiana* (44), *A Wing and a Prayer* (44), *Nob Hill* (45), *The House on 92nd Street* (45), *The Dark Corner* (46), *13 Rue Madeleine* (46), *Kiss of Death* (47), *Call Northside 777* (48), *Down to the Sea in Ships* (49), *The Black Rose* (49), *You're in the Navy Now* (51), *Rawhide* (51), *14 Hours* (51), *The Desert Fox/Rommel* (51), *Diplomatic Courier* (52), *White Witch Doctor* (53), *Niagara* (53), *Prince Valiant* (54), *Garden of Evil* (54), *The Racers* (55), *The Bottom of the Bottle* (56), *23 Paces to Baker Street* (56), *Legend of the Lost* (57), *From Hell to Texas/Man Hunt* (58), *Woman Obsessed* (59), *Seven Thieves* (60), *North to Alaska* (60), *How the West Was Won** (62) (co-dir: John Ford, George Marshall), *Circus World/The Magnificent Showman* (64), *Of Human Bondage* (64) (completed by Ken Hughes), *The Sons of Katie Elder* (65), *Nevada Smith* (66), *The Last Safari* (67), *5 Card Stud* (68), *True Grit* (69), *Airport* (70) (completed only).]

HAWKS, Howard   DIR USA. (Goshen, Indiana May 30, 1896–) "He is the embodiment of modern man. It is striking how his cinema anticipates his time. An American he certainly is, no more than a Griffith or a Vidor, but the spirit and physical structure of his work is born from contemporary America and enables us to better and more fully identify with it, both in admiration and criticism" (Henri Langlois). He was originally a racing pilot and then a fighter pilot in the First World War; in 1919 he joined Paramount as a prop man, became an editor in 1922, a scriptwriter in 1924 (e.g., *Tiger Love*), and directed his first film in 1926. He became famous in France as early as 1927 with *A Girl in Every Port*. He wrote many of his own early scripts and later worked often with Jules Furthman, Ben Hecht, and William Faulkner (all *q.v.*). He has worked successfully in many genres: action dramas, westerns, and "screwball" comedies. Aviation stories have often appeared in his work, *Dawn Patrol, The Air Circus, Ceiling Zero, Only Angels Have Wings, Air Force,* etc., with their common elements of a male fraternity, everyday courage without swagger or clarion calls, and relations between men and machines that are sometimes docile, sometimes hostile. Among his westerns (in the broadest sense) one could include *Barbary Coast, The Outlaw* (completed by Howard Hughes), the very American drama of conscience, *Sergeant York, Red River, The Big Sky, Rio Bravo, Rio Lobo,* and even *Hatari,* though it is set in Africa. Here also one finds the same male fraternity, the "iron fists with a heart of gold," often integrated with the natural magic of the landscapes. "The people I show," he has said, "don't dramatize crises, they deal with them quietly as is normal with these kinds of men. The average film has too much talk. You have to construct your scenes, set them up properly, then let the spectator do a little work so he feels involved. Scripts that are easily read are not good . . . You have to write what the character might think: he motivates your story. It is because a character believes in something that a situation develops, not because you decide on paper, that it must develop." He has also made several thrillers and screwball or other comedies. With *Scarface* he created an exemplary gangster film whose only peer is Sternberg's (*q.v.*) *Underworld**; and his *The Big Sleep* is a classic *film noir.* His greatest comedy period was in the Thirties: *Twentieth Century,* a dramatic and witty comedy through which one can trace the imprint of the American crisis of the Thirties, and the marvelous *Bringing Up Baby,* a film he prefers to all his other comedies — *His Girl Friday, I Was a Male War Bride, Gentlemen Prefer Blondes,* and even *Monkey Business.*

DIR: *The Road to Glory* (26), *Figleaves* (26), *The Cradle Snatchers* (27), *Paid to Love* (27), *A Girl in Every Port** (28), *Fazil* (28), *The Air Circus* (28), *Trent's Last Case* (29), *The Dawn Patrol** (30), *The Criminal Code* (31), *The Crowd Roars* (32), *Scarface: Shame of a Nation** (32), *Tiger Shark* (32), *Today We Live* (33), *Viva Villa!** (34) (completed by Jack Conway), *Twentieth Century** (34), *Barbary Coast* (35), *Ceiling Zero* (36), *Come And Get It** (36) (completed by William Wyler), *The Road to Glory* (36), *Bringing Up Baby** (38), *Only Angels Have Wings** (39), *His Girl Friday** (39), *The Outlaw* (40) (completed by Howard Hughes, released 43), *Sergeant York** (41), *Ball of Fire* (41), *Air Force** (43), *To Have and Have Not* (44), *The Big Sleep** (46), *Red River* (48), *A Song is Born* (48),

I Was a Male War Bride (49), *The Big Sky* (52), *O. Henry's Full House* (52) (one episode), *Monkey Business** (52), *Gentlemen Prefer Blondes* (53), *Land of the Pharaohs* (55), *Rio Bravo** (59), *Hatari!* (62), *Man's Favorite Sport?* (63), *Red Line 7000* (65), *El Dorado* (67), *Rio Lobo* (70).

HAYER, Nicolas PHOTOG France. (Paris May 1, 1902–) Talented cameraman, especially notable for his ability to create fantastic and exotic atmospheres: for Delannoy, *Macao* (39); for Becker, *Le Dernier Atout* (42), *Falbalas* (45); for Clouzot, *Le Corbeau** (43); for Daquin, *Patrie* (45), *Bel-Ami* (54); for Christian-Jaque, *La Chartreuse de Parma* (48); for Cocteau, *Othello;* for Duvivier, *Don Camillo* (52); for Melville, *Deux hommes dans Manhattan* (58), *Le Doulos* (63).

HAYS, Will H. (Sullivan Nov 5, 1879–New York March 8, 1954) The "Czar of Hollywood" as president of the Motion Picture Producers and Distributors Association of America from 1922–45, he was closely associated with the notorious Hollywood Code (drafted by a Jesuit, Father Lord, in 1930), which controlled the moral tone of Hollywood films and put many producers in fear of the "Hays Office." He was a lawyer and postmaster general in the Hoover administration before taking up his Hollywood job. He took his mission seriously. "Motion pictures, already the principal entertainment of most people, have unlimited possibilities for moral information and education. On this account we have to protect film just as we protect churches and schools."

HEARST, William Randolph PROD USA. (San Francisco 1863–Beverly Hills 1951) The most famous American newspaper magnate, the model for Welles's *Citizen Kane**, had a continuing interest in the cinema. He bought Eclectic Pictures, which produced some of the first serials (*The Exploits of Elaine**, *The Perils of Pauline*, etc.), the stories of which he published in his newspapers. He owned Hearst-Metrotone News and played a role in Hollywood (16–36) by buying Cosmopolitan Film Co. (a Goldwyn subsidiary) in 1920 in order to film vehicles for his mistress Marion Davies, but he failed in his attempts to push her to stardom.

HECHT, Ben SCEN/DIR USA. (New York Feb 28, 1894–April 18, 1964) An authentic screenwriter, one of the most significant Hollywood artists, whose scripts (usually in collaboration with Charles MacArthur) contributed much to the films of Sternberg, Lubitsch, Hawks, Milestone, etc. With MacArthur (*q.v.*) he attempted to establish an independent production center in New York and, though their work was a commercial disaster, made two important films: *Crime Without Passion* and *The Scoundrel*. [He was originally a journalist (1911), wrote his first novel in 1919, and during the Twenties made minor contributions to Hollywood scripts based on his knowledge of the underworld. He won an Academy Award for his story for *Underworld* (though Sternberg has said there was little left of Hecht's original story). He returned to Hollywood after the failure of his New York enterprise and continued writing scripts and occasionally directing. His association with MacArthur ended in the late Forties and his work in the Fifties was of much less interest. He spent most of his last years reminiscing about the "old days" and complaining about the Hollywood system. In addition to his scripts, several Hecht-MacArthur plays have been filmed: *Front Page Story** by Milestone and *His Girl Friday** (remake) by Hawks, *Nothing Sacred* (from *Hazell Flagg*) by Wellman.]
SCEN (notably): for Sternberg, *Underworld** (27); for James Cruze, *The Great Gabbo* (30); for Howard Hawks, *Scarface** (32), *Viva Villa!** (34) (completed by Conway), *Twentieth Century** (34), *Barbary Coast* (35), *Monkey Business** (52); for Lubitsch, *Design for Living* (33); for Louis Gasnier, *Topaze* (33); for George Marshall, *Goldwyn Follies* (38); for George Stevens, *Gunga Din* (39); for Wyler, *Wuthering Heights** (39); for King Vidor, *Comrade X* (40); for Duvivier, *Lydia* (41); for Henry King, *The Black Swan* (42); for Henry Hathaway, *China Girls* (42), *The Kiss of Death* (47), *Legend of the Lost* (57); for Hitchcock, *Spellbound* (45), *Notorious* (46); for Preminger, *Whirlpool* (49), *Where the Sidewalk Ends* (50); for André de Toth, *The Indian Fighter* (55); for Charles Vidor,

A Farewell to Arms (57); for Sidney Lanfield, *Hello Charlie* (60) (TV); and all his own films.
DIR: *Crime Without Passion** (34), *The Scoundrel* (35), *Once in a Blue Moon* (35), *Soak the Rich* (36), *Until I Die* (40) (all co-dir: MacArthur), *Angels Over Broadway* (40) (co-dir: Lee Garmes), *Specter of the Rose* (47), *Actors and Sin* (52).

HEGYI, Barnabas PHOTOG Hungary. (? –   ) Good cameraman, notable since 1940 for: *Somewhere in Europe** (47) (dir: Radvanyi), *Ludas Matyi* (49) (dir: Nadasdy), *Merry-go-round** (55) (dir: Fabri).

HEIFITZ, Josif DIR USSR. (Minsk Dec 17, 1905–   ) One of the best Soviet directors who, in collaboration with Alexander Zarkhi (*q.v.*), developed his reputation in the Thirties with a series of films that portrayed contemporary Soviet life. He achieved new international recognition in the Sixties for his adaptations of Chekhov stories. In the Thirties he and Zarkhi made *Baltic Deputy,* in which Cherkassov gave one of his most masterly performances, and *Member of the Government,* whose central character was a woman. After the war they again showed the problems and passions of their contemporaries through their *In the Name of Life.* After two more films they stopped working together, but the same qualities continued in the films Heifitz made alone: *The Big Family,* which portrayed the daily life of shipyard workers, and *The Rumiantsev Case,* one of his most well-known and admired works with a truck driver for a hero. With the subtle and melancholy *Lady with a Little Dog* (60) he began a series of exemplary adaptations of Chekhov stories whose style perfectly reflects the tone of the originals. Both Zarkhi and Heifitz were originally scriptwriters.
DIR (all until 1950, co-dir: Zarkhi): *Veter v litso/Facing the Wind* (29), *Poldien* (31), *Moi rodina/My Country* (32), *Gorjace d eneki* (35), *Deputat Baltiki/Baltic Deputy** (37), *Chlen pravitelstava/Member of the Government/ The Great Beginning* (40), *Yevo Zovut Sukhe-Bator/His Name is Sukhe-Bator* (42), *Malakov Hill* (44), *The Defeat of Japan* (46) (documentary), *Vo imya zhizni/In the Name of Life* (47), *Dragotsennye zerna/Precious Grain* (48),

Ogni Baku/Fires of Baku (50), *Vesna v Moskve/Spring in Moscow* (53), *Bolshaya semya/The Big Family** (54), *Delo Rumiantseva/The Rumiantsev Case* (55), *Dorogoi moi chelovek/My Dear Man* (58), *Dama s sobatchkoi/Lady with the Little Dog** (59), *Horizon* (61), *Den schastya/A Day of Happiness* (64), *V gorode "S"/In the Town of "S"* (66).

*HELLINGER, Mark PROD USA. (March 21, 1903–Dec 21, 1947) Former journalist who became a scriptwriter (Raoul Walsh's *The Roaring Twenties*), a producer in 1940 for Warner's and later for Universal, and developed the crime thriller to new levels of realism, notably in *The Killers, Brute Force,* and *The Naked City.*
PROD (notably): William Seiter's *It All Came True* (40), Raoul Walsh's *They Drive By Night* (40), *High Sierra* (41), *The Strawberry Blonde* (41), *Manpower* (41), *The Horn Blows at Midnight* (45), Archie Mayo's *Moontide* (42), Robert Siodmak's *The Killers** (46), Jules Dassin's *Brute Force** (47), *The Naked City** (48).

HELLMAN, Lillian SCEN USA. (New Orleans June 20, 1905–   ) Playwright who has also written screenplays and adapted several of her own plays. She is perhaps the principal author of three major films by Wyler: *These Three* (36), from her play *The Children's Hour, Dead End** (37), and *The Little Foxes** (41); she also wrote two antifascist scripts, *North Star* (43) (dir: Milestone) and *Watch on the Rhine* (43) (dir: Shumlin). [She was for a long time the companion of Dashiell Hammett (*q.v.*) and it is said he collaborated on some of her scripts. Like him she suffered under McCarthyism, being considered too "committed." Other scripts or adaptations include: for Dieterle, *The Searching Wind* (46); for Michael Gordon, *Another Part of the Forest* (48); for Wyler, *The Children's Hour* (62), for George Roy Hill, *Toys in the Attic* (63); for Arthur Penn, *The Chase* (65).]

HENNING-JENSEN Astrid (Copenhagen Dec 10, 1914–   ) **and Bjarne** (Copenhagen Oct 1, 1908–   ) DIR Denmark. A husband and wife team who are the best postwar Danish film makers. They work in close association, often co-directing or collaborating on the screenplays for each other's films; very rarely do they work separately. Their films in the Forties and Fifties were a credit to their country, even though the difficult conditions of the industry prevented their full development. CO-DIR (notably): *Christian IV som bygherre* (41) (short), *De Danske sydhavsöer* (44) (short), *Flyktingar finner en hamn* (Swed45) (short), *De Pokkers Unger* (47), *Kristinus Bergman* (48), *Vesterhavsdrenge* (50), *Solstik* (53), *Tivoligarden spiller* (54), *Ballet Girl* (54) (short), *Een blandt mange* (61), *Kort er sommaren* (62) (short). DIR (Astrid H.-J.): *Palle allene i verden/ Palle Alone in the World* (49) (with their son, Lars), *Kranes Konditori* (50), *Ukjent mann* (Nor52), *Kaerlighed pa kredit* (55), *Nye venner* (56) (short), *Paw* (59), *De Bla Undulater* (65), *Utro* (66), *Nille* (68), *Kald mig Miriam* (68). DIR (Bjarne H.-J.): *Cykledrengene i Törvegraven* (40) (short), *Ditte Menneskebarn** (46), *Where Mountains Float* (55), (documentary feature).

*HEPWORTH, Cecil M. DIR/PROD Britain. (London 1874–London 1953) Important British pioneer who entered the cinema via his father's magic lantern activities, wrote a book, *Animated Photography,* in 1897, took up cinematography in 1898, and founded his own company, Hepwix Films, in 1900. He directed all his own films until 1904, when he began hiring others to assist under his supervision — which became less personal as his volume of production increased. He returned to directing in 1913 and made some 50 features until 1923, when his company collapsed. His best remembered films are *Rescued by Rover** (05), with its extraordinary sense of rhythmic intercutting, *Blind Fate* (12), *Comin' Thro' the Rye* (16 and 22).

HERLTH, Robert (also Fritz Paul) ART DIR Germany/German Federal Republic. (Wriezen May 2, 1893–Munich Jan 6, 1962) Important German set designer whose style played a major role in expressionism and *Kammerspiel* in the Twenties but who applied himself to the typical UFA decorative style after 1930. He originally worked in the theater and collaborated with Walter Röhrig (*q.v.*) on most of his important films. ART DIR (notably): for Lupu Pick, *Das Lächende Grauen* (20); for Lang, *Der Müde Tod** (21); for Pabst, *Der Schatz*

(23); for Rochus Gliese, *Komödie des Herzens* (24); for Arthur von Gerlach, *Zur Chronik von Grieshus* (25); for Murnau, *Der Letzte Mann** (24), *Tartuff* (25), *Faust** (26), for Charell, *Der Kongress Tanzt** (31); for Gustav Ucicky, *Hokuspokus* (30), *Der Unsterbliche Lump* (30), *Yorck* (31), *Morgenrot/Red Dawn* (33); for Rudolf Jugert, *Film ohne Titel* (GFR48); for Harald Braun, *Der Letzte Sommer* (GFR54), *Der Letzte Mann** (GFR55), *Regine* (GFR55); for Alfred Weidenmann, *Buddenbrooks* (GFR59). Also responsible for technical designs for Riefenstahl's *Olympiad**.

*HERRMANN, Bernard MUS USA. (New York June 29, 1911–) One of the most important contemporary film composers with a remarkable ability to create psychological effects, mainly through the use of string instruments (*Psycho*). He joined CBS in 1933, was staff conductor starting in 1934, and was responsible for the music in Orson Welles's (*q.v.*) *The Mercury Playhouse Theater.* (His later development seems to have been influenced by his association with Welles.) He is perhaps best known for his contribution to the films of Alfred Hitchcock (*q.v.*) but his work for other directors is equally distinguished. He has also composed ballet, concert, and opera music (notably *Wuthering Heights*). MUS (notably): for Orson Welles, *Citizen Kane** (40), *The Magnificent Ambersons** (42); for Robert Stevenson, *Jane Eyre* (43); for William Dieterle, *All that Money Can Buy/The Devil and Daniel Webster** (41); for Robert Wise, *The Day the Earth Stood Still* (51); for Joseph L. Mankiewicz, *The Ghost and Mrs. Muir* (47), *Five Fingers* (52); for Alfred Hitchcock, *The Trouble with Harry** (55), *The Man Who Knew Too Much** (55), *The Wrong Man* (56), *Vertigo** (58), *North by Northwest** (59), *Psycho** (60), *The Birds** (63), *Marnie* (64); for Zinnemann, *A Hatful of Rain* (57); for Raoul Walsh, *The Naked and the Dead* (58); for François Truffaut *Fahrenheit 451* (66), *La Mariée était en noir* (67); for Pim de la Parra, *Obsessions* (69). Also music for TV: the Alfred Hitchcock programs, *The Twilight Zone, Kraft Suspense Theater,* and *The Virginian* series.

HERTZ, Aleksander DIR/PROD Poland. (Warsaw 1879–Warsaw 1928). The father of the Polish cinema who in 1911 founded the "Sfinks," the first Polish film production society, and from then until 1928 produced and/or directed some 170 films. He launched Pola Negri's career in *Bestia* (15). Also, directed, notably: *Antek cwaniak* (10), *Meir Ezofowicz* (11), *Arabella* (16), *Krysta* (19), *Ziema obiecana* (27).

HEUZE, André DIR France. (Paris 1880–Paris Aug 16, 1942) French primitive who from 1905–10 contributed much to the development of the cinema with his chase films (*Le Voleur de bicyclette, La Course des sergents de ville,* both 05), his comic *Boireau* series (06–07), and his dramas and adaptations (*L'Ange du coeur, A Biribi, Les Meurt-de-faim, Le Deserteur,* all 06).

HILL, George William DIR USA. (Douglas, Kansas April 25, 1895–Hollywood 1934) A former war cameraman, then assistant to D. W. Griffith (*q.v.*), he directed 11 (mostly adventure) films between 1924–34 but only one of note — *The Big House* (30). He committed suicide in 1934.
DIR: *Through the Dark* (24), *The Barrier* (26), *Tell It to the Marines* (26), *Buttons* (27), *The Cossacks* (28), *The Flying Fleet* (29), *Min and Bill* (30), *The Big House** (30), *Hell Divers* (31), *The Secret Six* (31), *Clear All Wires* (33).

HILLYER, Lambert DIR USA. (South Bend, Illinois July 8, 1889–) A major specialist in westerns who directed several of William S. Hart's films from 1919–21, worked with Tom Mix, and from 1924–54 was a prolific director of B-westerns and serials (including *Batman* in 1941).

HITCHCOCK, Alfred DIR Britain/USA. (London Aug 13, 1899–) Though undoubtedly "the master of suspense," his qualities as a director surpass this publicity slogan. He is passionately devoted to the cinema and has a marvelous talent for telling stories in film terms. His influence on other films makers, particularly French, has been considerable, though, for some, his films have been "Spanish inns" in which critics found only what they themselves brought with them. [He joined the British branch of Famous Players-Lasky in 1920 and worked successively as scriptwriter, art director, and assistant director (to Graham Cutts). His first feature, *Number 13* (21) was unfinished; in 1922 he collaborated in the direction of *Always Tell Your Wife.* His first completed feature, *The Pleasure Garden,* was made in Germany for Michael Balcon.] His visit to Germany brought him much under the influence of expressionism, a style especially evident in his early British films. He established his reputation with his first success, *The Lodger,* and further developed the style and approach of this film in his remarkable *Blackmail,* the first British sound film. He reached the peak of his art in the Thirties with a number of suspense thrillers that usually climaxed in a chase: *The Man Who Knew Too Much, The 39 Steps, The Lady Vanishes.* In 1939 he was hired by Selznick (*q.v.*) and moved to Hollywood, where he built on his earlier experiences by making several films with similar approaches and themes, such as *Foreign Correspondent* and *Saboteur. Shadow of a Doubt* (43), his own favorite in his American period, matches any of his best films in its exact sense of observation and sureness of touch. Later he followed the Hollywood fashion for psychological melodramas (*Spellbound*) and *films noir* (*Suspicion, Notorious, Rope*). After the highly accomplished *Under Capricorn* (49), he made several somber, suspenseful psychological dramas (*I Confess, The Wrong Man, Vertigo, Marnie, Strangers on a Train*), and some films of terror (*Psycho, The Birds*), but remained at his best in chase films (*To Catch a Thief, The Man Who Knew Too Much* (remake), *North by Northwest*). His best film in this latter period is *The Trouble with Harry,* with its black humor set against a marvelous, and natural, autumnal backdrop. Hitchcock has an undeniable feeling for images. He personally prepares in advance and in detail every aspect of each film. He has complete technical mastery of traveling shots, depth of field, and predesigned long camera takes (10 minutes in *Rope,* for example). He takes great delight in these techniques without ever losing sight of his commercial responsibilities: "There are a certain number of imperatives that a film maker has to respect, and with reason. It is useless to attribute profound intentions to me. I am not at all interested in the message or moral of a film. I am like, let us say, an artist who paints flowers . . . A production involves much money, other people's money. And my conscience tells me

*for full filmography see Truffaut.
Hitchcock pp. 351-63

it is necessary to play down my own feelings in order for them to regain their investment . . . A movie theater is like a screen facing a pile of seats that have to be filled. I have to create 'suspense.' Without it people would be disappointed. If I made *Cinderella,* they would be content only if I put a corpse in the coach. The audience screams and cannot bear the agony in some of my films. That gives me great pleasure; I am interested less in stories than in the manner of telling them." (1954–62)

DIR: *Number Thirteen* (Brit21) (unfinished), *Always Tell Your Wife* (22) (co-dir: Seymour Hicks), *The Pleasure Garden* (Brit/Ger25), *The Mountain Eagle* (26), *The Lodger* (26), *Downhill* (27), *Easy Virtue* (27), *The Ring* (27), *The Farmer's Wife* (28), *Champagne* (28), *The Manxman* (29), *Blackmail** (29), *Elstree Calling* (30), *Juno and the Paycock* (30), *Murder* (30), *The Skin Game* (31), *Rich and Strange* (32), *Number 17* (32), *Waltzes from Vienna* (33), *The Man Who Knew Too Much** (34), *The 39 Steps** (34), *The Secret Agent* (36), *Sabotage* (36), *Young and Innocent* (37), *The Lady Vanishes* (38), *Jamaica Inn* (Brit39), *Rebecca* (USA40), *Foreign Correspondent* (40), *Mr. and Mrs. Smith* (41), *Suspicion* (42), *Shadow of a Doubt** (43), *Lifeboat* (43), *Aventure Malgache* (Brit44) (short), *Bon Voyage* (Brit44) (short), *Spellbound** (45), *Notorious** (46), *The Paradine Case* (47), *Rope** (48), *Under Capricorn* (49), *Stage Fright* (50), *Strangers on a Train** (51), *I Confess* (52), *Dial M for Murder* (53), *Rear Window* (54), *To Catch a Thief** (55), *The Trouble with Harry** (55), *The Man Who Knew Too Much** (56) (remake), *The Wrong Man* (57), *Vertigo** (58), *North by Northwest** (59), *Psycho** (60), *The Birds** (63), *Marnie* (64), *Torn Curtain* (66), *Topaz* (69). Also, produced and occasionally directed the TV series, *Alfred Hitchcock Presents* (55–62), and produced The *Alfred Hitchcock Hour* (63–65).

HODATYEV, Nikolai *see* KHODATEYEV, NIKOLAI

HOLGER-MADSEN DIR Denmark/Germany (Copenhagen April 11, 1878–Copenhagen Nov 30, 1943) Imaginative Danish film maker, responsible for several unusually stylish (and somewhat decadent) dramas from 1913–20, who seems to have been the first to make systematic use of high- and low-angle photography and whose innovative and daring use of lighting, extreme close-ups, etc., in *The Life of the Lay Preacher* and *The Spiritualist* influenced the development of the German cinema. He was originally an actor, directed for Nordisk 1913–20, worked briefly in Germany, then returned to Denmark, where he acted in or directed several films until 1940.

DIR (notably): *Under Savklingens taender* (13), *Elskovmagt* (13), *Elskovsleg/Liebelei* (13), *Ned med Millionaerdrengen* (13), *Vabnene* (14), *Evangeliemandens Liv/The Life of the Lay Preacher** (14), *Spiritisten/The Spiritualist* (14), *Pax Aeterna* (16), *Himmelskibet* (17), *Folkets Ven* (18), *Gudernes Yndling/Digterkongen* (19), *Pömperly's Kampf mit dem Schneeschuh* (Ger22) (co-dir: Arnold Fanck), *Darskab, dyd od drivert* (23), *Ole Opfinders offer* (24), *Vester vov vov* (27), *Vask, Videnskab og Velvaere* (33), *Sol over Danmark* (35), *Alens livsmysterium* (40).

*HOLT, Seth (James Holt) DIR Britain. (Palestine 1923–London Feb 13, 1971) Talented former editor (*Lavender Hill Mob**, *Mandy, Saturday Night and Sunday Morning**) and producer (*Ladykillers*) who directed a handful of textured, off-beat thrillers and horror films, notably *Nowhere to Go* (58), *Taste of Fear* (61), the edgy *Station Six Sahara* (62), *The Nanny* (65), and the brutal *Danger Route* (67).

HOMOKI NAGY, István DIR Hungary. (1914–) Notable director of nature films who has made some interesting features, including *A Kingdom on the Waters* (52) and *From Blossom Time to Autumn Leaves* (54).

HONEGGER, Arthur MUS France. (Le Havre March 10, 1892–Paris Nov 18, 1955) This great modern composer was converted to the cinema in the silent days by Abel Gance (*q.v.*), for whom he wrote the music for *La Roue** and *Napoléon**. He later wrote a number of significant film scores that were far from being mere accompaniment, notably: *Rapt* (34) (dir: Kirsanoff, co-mus: Hoérée), *Les Misérables** (34) (dir: Bernard), *L'Idée* (34) (dir: Bartosch), *Crime et Châtiment* (35) (dir: Chenal), *L'Equipage* (35), *Mayerling* (36) (both dir:

Litvak), *Regain* (37) (dir: Pagnol), *Mademoiselle Docteur/Spies from Salonika* (36) (dir: Pabst), *La Citadelle du silence* (37) (dir: L'Herbier), *Pygmalion** (Brit38), *J'attendrai* (39) (dir: Moguy), *Mermoz* (42) (dir: Cuny), *Les Démons de l'aube* (46) (dir: Yves Allégret, co-mus: Hoérée), *Un revenant* (46) (dir: Christian-Jaque). *Giovanna d'Arco al Rogo/Joan at the Stake** (It 54) (dir: Rossellini) is based on his oratorio; *Pacific 231** (49) (dir: Jean Mitry) is based on a score he wrote for a silent film that was never made.

HOWE, James Wong (Wong Tung Jim) PHOTOG USA. (China Sept 28, 1889–) One of the greatest of all American cameramen who has been in Hollywood since 1917, worked with Herbert Brenon (*Peter Pan, Sorrell and Son*) in the Twenties, and has collaborated on many important films with Hawks, Walsh, Mackendrick, etc. He is equally excellent in black and white and color, studio sets, and natural landscapes. He directed one film, *Go Man Go* (52).
PHOTOG (notably): for Hawks, *The Criminal Code* (31), *Viva Villa** (34), *Air Force** (43); for Walsh, *Yellow Ticket* (31), *Strawberry Blonde* (41), *Objective Burma!* (45), *Pursued* (47); for Van Dyke, *The Thin Man** (34); for Tod Browning, *The Mark of the Vampire* (35); for W. K. Howard, *Fire Over England* (Brit36); for Victor Sjöström, *Under the Red Robe* (Brit36); for Lloyd Bacon, *The Oklahoma Kid* (39); for Sam Wood, *King's Row* (42); for Lang, *Hangmen Also Die* (42); for Milestone, *The North Star* (43); for Robert Rossen, *Body and Soul* (47), *The Brave Bulls* (51); for Daniel Mann, *Come Back, Little Sheba* (52), *The Rose Tattoo* (54); for Joshua Logan, *Picnic** (55); for Mackendrick, *The Sweet Smell of Success** (57); for John Sturges, *The Old Man and the Sea* (58); for Clifford Odets, *The Story on Page One* (60); for Martin Ritt, *Hud* (63), *The Outrage** (64), *Hombre* (67); for John Frankenheimer, *Seconds* (65).

HUBERT, Roger PHOTOG France. (Montreuil March 30, 1903–Paris Nov 28, 1964) Trained by Epstein, *L'Auberge rouge**, and Gance, *Napoléon**, *Le Fin du monde,* he developed into one of the best creators of imagery for French poetic realism, a cameraman with a sense of the picturesque and an ability to develop atmosphere, notably for Feyder, *Pension Mimosas** (35), *La Loi du nord* (42); for Carné, *Jenny* (36), *Les Visiteurs du soir** (42), *Les Enfants du Paradis** (45), *Thérèse Raquin** (53), *L'Air de Paris* (54); for Gance, *J'accuse** (37); for Duvivier, *La Femme et le Pantin* (59); for Cloche, *Cocagne* (61).

HUBLEY, John ANIM USA. (New York May 21, 1914–) One of the greatest modern animators whose drawings have the freedom of touch of Matisse, Bonnard, or Marquet in the early 20th century. He worked for Disney (*q.v.*) on *Snow White**, *Pinocchio*, "the Rite of Spring" sequence in *Fantasia**, *Dumbo,* and *Bambi*. In 1941 he joined UPA under Stephen Bosustow (*q.v.*) and is one of the co-creators of *Mr. Magoo**. At UPA he was responsible for, notably, *Flathatting* (45), *Robin Hoodlum* (48), *The Magic Fluke* (49), *Punchy de Leon* (49), *Rooty Toot Toot* (52), and several Magoo's. He left UPA in 1952 and has since worked independently after a sojourn in Europe: *The Adventures of ** (56), *The Tender Game* (58), *Harlem Wednesday* (58) *A Date with Dizzy* (58), *Seven Lively Arts* (59), *Moonbird** (60), *Children of the Sun* (61), *Of Stars and Men* (62) (feature), *The Hole* (62), *The Hat* (64), *Herb Alpert and the Tijuana Brass Double Feature* (66), *Gulliver's Troubles* (67).

HUGHES, Howard PROD/DIR USA. (Houston Dec 24, 1905–) This legendary multimillionaire, a kind of "Citizen Kane" 1930–60 model, made his money mainly from the manufacture of machine tools and airplanes, but had two complementary passions: the cinema and beautiful women. While often using the cinema to publicize his aviation interests, he never lost the ability to make the right choice of directors and stars. He owned RKO-Radio Studios from 1948 to 1955 when he finally liquidated it. He is credited with a few films as director (notably *Hell's Angels*) and has occasionally taken a film out of the assigned director's hands when it didn't match his own conception. [DIR: *Hell's Angels** (30), *The Outlaw* (43, released 46) (replaced Hawks), *Jet Pilot* (52, released 57) (additional scenes shot and film re-edited by Hughes after Sternberg completed).
PROD: *Two Arabian Nights* (27) (dir:

Milestone), *The Racket* (28) (dir: Milestone), *Scarface** (32) (dir: Hawks), *Sky Devils* (32) (dir: Edward Sutherland), *Vendetta* (46, released 50) (dir: Ophüls, then Preston Sturges, Stuart Heisler, and Mel Ferrer), *Montana Belle* (48, released 52) (dir: Dwan), *Two Tickets to Broadway* (51) (dir: J. Kern), *The Racket* (51) (dir: John Cromwell), *This Kind of Woman* (51) (dir: Richard Fleischer, then John Farrow), *Double Dynamite* (52) (dir: I. Cummings), *The Las Vegas Story* (52) (dir: R. Stevenson), *The French Line* (54) (dir: Lloyd Bacon), *Macao* (52) (dir: Sternberg, then Nicholas Ray), *Underwater* (55) (dir: John Sturges), *Son of Sinbad* (55) (dir: Tetzlaff).]

HUSNI, Kameran DIR Iraq. (? –) In the context of a still developing cinema he has directed at least one interesting film, *Said Effendi* (59), the story of a teacher in the poor section of Baghdad.

HUSTON, John DIR USA/Britain. (Nevada, Missouri Aug 5, 1906–) The most notable film maker of the Hollywood "lost generation," a director who established an immediate reputation (and set the style for the Hollywood thrillers of the Forties) on his first film, an intelligently faithful adaptation of Hammett's *The Maltese Falcon* (41), fell into mediocrity in the Fifties, and found a new maturity of style in the Sixties. [He is the son of actor Walter Huston and had a varied career as a boxer, member of the Mexican cavalry, actor and dialogue writer (*A House Divided, Murders in the Rue Morgue, Law and Order*) before finally settling in Hollywood as a script-writer in 1938. After three Hollywood features, he made three documentaries for the army during the war, including two of the most poignant portraits of war and its effects ever made, *The Battle of San Pietro* and *Let There Be Light*. His Hollywood reputation was re-established with the successful *Treasure of the Sierra Madre*. A constant theme in his films is the importance of a struggle despite the inevitability of failure. Thus one can consider as symbols the wind in *Treasure of the Sierra Madre* which blows away the gold dust wrested so painfully from the hills; the uselessness of the Cuban revolutionary struggle in *We Were Strangers;* the wretched end of an imaginative robbery in the *Asphalt Jungle;* and the absurd stubbornness of a middle-aged spinster trying to win the war single-handed in *The African Queen*. His masterpiece, *The Red Badge of Courage* (mutilated by the producers) is concerned less with endeavor and failure than with fear of fear at a time when McCarthyism was at its height. He moved to Europe, where he made, for Hollywood, several competent films (like *Moulin Rouge*) and where, after his lifeless *Moby Dick* adaptation, he quickly fell into an unconvincing and sometimes soulless academicism. He came close to betraying the promise of his great period in such abysmal productions as *Roots of Heaven* and *The Barbarian and the Geisha*. But he rediscovered himself in the *Misfits,* which seems to imply that it is vain to struggle and only failure is valid. [Since then his work has been extremely uneven, ranging from the depths of *The List of Adrian Messenger, Sinful Davie,* and (perhaps the worst spectacular of all time) *The Bible,* to the heights of *Freud, Night of the Iguana, Reflections in a Golden Eye,* and *A Walk with Love and Death*. In these films he seems to have found a maturity of artistic vision; his earlier preoccupations have given way to metaphysical explorations of the human spirit. His style has developed a subtlety that enables him to probe the hidden, latent emotions of his characters while avoiding psychoanalytic pretentiousness. Even the thriller, *The Kremlin Letter,* reflects his new-found maturity.]

SCEN: for Wyler, *Jezebel** (38); for Litvak, *The Amazing Dr. Clitterhouse* (38); for Dieterle, *Juarez* (39), *Dr. Ehrlich's Magic Bullet* (40); for Raoul Walsh, *High Sierra* (41); for Howard Hawks, *Sergeant York** (41); for Jean Negulesco, *Three Strangers* (46); and for several of his own films.

DIR: *The Maltese Falcon** (41), *In This Our Life* (42), *Across the Pacific* (42), *Report from the Aleutians* (43) (documentary), *The Battle of San Pietro* (44) (documentary), *Let There Be Light** (46) (documentary), *The Treasure of the Sierra Madre** (48), *Key Largo* (48), *We Were Strangers* (49), *The Asphalt Jungle** (50), *The Red Badge of Courage** (51), *The African Queen** (Brit51), *Moulin Rouge** (Brit52), *Beat the Devil* (Brit/It53), *Moby Dick* (USA56), *Heaven Knows, Mr. Allison* (USA57), *The Barbarian and the Geisha* (USA58), *The Roots of Heaven* (USA58), *The*

119

Unforgiven (USA60), *The Misfits** (USA61), *Freud — the Secret Passion* (USA62), *The List of Adrian Messenger* (USA63), *The Night of the Iguana* (USA64), *La Bibbia/The Bible: In the Beginning* (It66), *Casino Royale* (Brit66) (part only), *Reflections in a Golden Eye* (USA67), *Sinful Davie* (Brit68), *A Walk with Love and Death* (USA69), *The Kremlin Letter* (USA69).

IBERT, Jacques MUS France. (Paris Aug 15, 1890–1961) An excellent musician who had a great interest in the cinema and wrote several interesting scores, notably for Pabst's *Don Quichotte* and Welles's *Macbeth.* After the war he was for a long time director of the Villa Médicis. MUS (notably): for Duvivier, *Cinq Gentlemen maudits* (31), *Golgotha* (34), *La Charette fantôme/The Phantom Chariot** (39), *Panique* (46), *Marianne de ma jeunesse* (53); for Pabst, *Don Quichotte** (32); for Tourneur, *Les Deux orphélines** (33), *Justin de Marseille* (35), *Le Patriote* (38); for L'Herbier, *La Comédie du bonheur* (40), *La Vie de bohême* (44), *L'Affaire du collier de la reine* (46); for Welles, *Macbeth** (48). His ballet, *Invitation to the Dance,* was adapted as a film by Gene Kelly (56).

IBRAHIM-KHAN, Mitza DIR Iran (? – ?) Official photographer to the Shah of Persia, he directed the first Iranian films in 1900–1903 — intended for the exclusive use of the court.

ICHAC, Marcel DIR France. (Rueil Oct 22, 1906–) Documentary film maker who is the greatest specialist in mountaineering films in France (and undoubtedly in the world) and is especially famous for the scenes he shot on Annapurna.
DIR (notably: *Karakoram* (36), *A l'assaut des aiguilles du diable* (42), *Sondeurs d'abîme* (43), *Padirac* (48), *Groenland* (51) (co-dir: Languepin), *Victoire sur l'Annapurna* (53), *Nouveaux horizons* (54), *L'Aluminum* (55), *Tour du monde express* (56), *Les Etoiles de midi* (60).

*ICHIKAWA, Kon DIR Japan. (Uji Yamada, Mie Nov 20, 1915–) Idiosyncratic Japanese film maker with a superb sense of visual texture and a taste for black comedy and obsessional characters. He studied animation and made his film debut with a puppet film in 1946. His *Mr. Poo* and *A Billionaire* revealed the tone of his work, and *Harp of Burma, Enjo, Odd Obsession,* and *Fires on the Plain* confirmed his international stature. He has oftened worked with Kazuo Miyagawa (*q.v.*) and Setsuo Kobayashi as cameramen. The expressive visual designs that have resulted from their collaboration is evident particularly in the color films, *Bonchi, An Actor's Revenge, Alone in the Pacific,* and even in the documentary, *Tokyo Olympiad 1964.* His work has most consistently been concerned with spiritually abnormal behavior that characterizes the social environment of his characters, but it is the visual experiences of his films that are best remembered. His wife, Natto Wada, has worked on the scripts of most of his films.
DIR: *Musuhi Dojoji/A Girl at Dojo Temple* (46) (puppets), *Nana Hiraku/A Flower Blooms* (48), *Sanhyaku-roku-jugo ya/365 Nights* (48), *Ningen Moyo/Design of a Human Being* (49), *Hateshinaki jo-netsu/The Passion without Limit* (49), *Ginza Shanshiro/Sanshiro at Ginza* (50), *Netsudei-chi/The Hot Marshland* (50), *Akatsuki no Tsuiseki/Pursuit at Dawn* (50), *Ye-rai-shang/Nightshade Flower* (51), *Koibito/Lover* (51), *Mukokuseki-sha/The Man without Nationality* (51), *Nusumareta Koi/Stolen Love* (50), *Bungawan Solo* (51), *Kekkon Koshin-kyoku/Wedding March* (51), *Rakki-san/Mr. Lucky* (52), *Waki Hito/Young Generation* (52), *Ashi ni Sawatta Onna/The Woman Who Touched the Legs* (52) (remake), *Ano te, Kono te/This Way, That Way* (52), *Pu-san/Mr. Poo* (53), *Aoiro Kakumei/The Blue Revolution* (53), *Seishun Zenogata Heiji/The Youth of Heiji Zenigata* (53), *Aijin/The Lover* (53), *Watashi no Subete*

O/All of Myself (54), Okumanchoja/A Billionaire (54), Josei ni Kansura juni sho/Twelve Chapters about Women (54), Seishun Kaidan/Ghost Story of Youth (55), Kokoro/The Heart (55), Biruma no Tategoto/Harp of Burma* (56), Shokei no Heya/Punishment Room (56), Nihonbashi/Bridge of Japan (56), Manin/Densha/The Crowded Train (57), Ana/the Hole/The Lady Has No Alibi (57), Tohoku no Zummu Tachi/Man of the North/The Men of Tohoku (57), Enjo/Conflagration/The Flame of Torment* (58), Sayonara Konnichiwa/Goodbye, Good Day (59), Kaji/Odd Obsession/The Key (59), Nobi/Fires on the Plain* (59), Kankon Sosai/Earthly Rituals (59), Bonchi (60), Jokei/Code of Women/A Woman's Testament (60) (one episode), Ototo/Younger Brother/Her Brother (60), Ashi ni Sawatta Onna/The Woman Who Touched the Legs (60) (TV remake), Kuroi Junin no Onna/Ten Dark Women (61), Lemon (61) (TV), Hakai/The Sin (61) (TV), Hakai/The Sin/Outcasts (61), Watashi wa Nisai/Being Two Isn't Easy (62), Puro (62) (TV), Yukinojo Henge/An Actor's Revenge/the Revenge of Yukino-jo (63), Taiheiyo Hitoribotchi/Alone in the Pacific/My Enemy the Sea (63), Zeni no Odori/Money Talks (64), Tokyo Olympiad 1964 (65) (documentary), Genji Monogatari/Tale of Genji (65–66) (26 parts, TV), Aibo/Hey, Buddy! (66), Topo Gigio e i Sei Ladre (It67) (partly animated), Seishun/Tournament (69) (documentary), Kyoto (69) (documentary).

ILIU, Victor DIR Romania. (Nov 24, 1912–1968) Film maker with a special feeling for peasant life, captured notably in his major postwar films, In sat la noi/Our Village (51) (co-dir: Jean Georgescu), Mitrea Cocor (52) (from the novel by Mikhail Sadoveanu) and Moara cu noroc/The Mill of Luck and Plenty (56).

IMAI, Tadashi DIR Japan. (Tokyo Jan 8, 1912–) A liberal, forceful film maker with a feeling for the creation of atmosphere and a sense of documentary realism. He made, independently, And Yet We Live (51), the first major example of Japanese neorealism. He has always been deeply interested in politics, began his film career as a scriptwriter in 1934, and is considered very highly

in his own country. He has made several equally important films, such as Muddy Waters, Rice, A Story of Pure Love, Kiku and Isamu, and especially Darkness at Noon, based on a true judicial case.

DIR (notably): Numazu Hei-gakko/Numazu Military Academy (39), Warera ga Kyokan/Our Instructor (39), Tajinko Mura/Tajinko Village (40), Kakka/The General (40), Kekkon no seitai/Married Life (40), Boro no Kesshitai/The Suicide Troops of the Watchtower (42), Ikari no Umi/Cruel Sea (44), Minshu no Teki/An Enemy of the People (46), Aoi Sammyaku/Blue Mountains (47), Mata Au Hi Made/Until the Day We Meet Again (50), Dokkoi Ikiteru/And Yet We Live* (51), Yambiko Gakko/Echo School (52), Himeyuri no To/The Tower of Lilies/The Young Girls of Okinawa (53), Nigori/Muddy Waters (53), Koko ni Izumi Ari/Here is a Spring (54), Aisurebakoso/Because I Love (54) (episode), Yukiko (55), Mahiro no Ankoku/Darkness at Noon* (56), Kome/Rice/Men of the Rice Fields (57), Junai Monogatari/A Story of Pure Love (57), Yoru no Tsuzumi/The Adulteress/Night Drum (58), Kiku to Isamu/Kiku and Isamu* (59), Shiroi gake/The White Cliff (60), Are ga Minato no Hi da/Pan Chopali (61), Nippon no Obachan tachi/The Old Women of Japan (62), Bushido zanzoku Monogatari/The Oath of Obedience (63), Echigo Isutsuishi Oyashirazu/Oyashirazu in the Echigo Regime (64), Adauchi/Revenge (65), Satogashi ga Kawareru Toki/When the Cookie Crumbles (67), Fushin no Toki/The Time of Reckoning (68), Hashi no Nai Kawa/The River Without a Bridge (70) (two parts).

INAGAKI, Hiroshi DIR Japan. (Tokyo Dec 30, 1905–) A film maker who at the beginning of his career made left-wing "tendency" films but quickly established his reputation as a skilled and prolific director of conventional samurai films. His biggest foreign successes have been Samurai (54), which won an Academy Award, and The Rickshaw Man (58), which won the Golden Lion at Venice. He was originally an actor, became a director in 1927, and has made some 80 films.

DIR (notably): Tenka Taiheiki/Peace of the World (28), Ippon-Gatana Dohyoiri/A Sword and the Sumo Ring (31),

Yataro-gasa/Yataro's Sedge Hat (32), *Miyamoto Musashi/Musashi Myamoto* (40), *Edo Saigo no Hi/The Last Days of Edo* (41), *Umi o Wataru Sairei/Festival Across the Sea* (41), *Muho Matsu no Issho/The Life of Matsu the Untamed* (43), *Te o Tsunaga Kora/Children Hand in Hand* (48), *Wasurerareta Kora/Forgotten Children* (49), *Sasaki Kojiro/Kojiro Sasaku* (50–51) (3 parts), *Miyamoto Musashi/Musashi Myamoto/Samurai* (54) (remake), *Arashi/Storm* (57), *Muho Matsu no Issho/The Rickshaw Man* (58) (remake), *Soru Hiken/Ninjutsu* (58), *Fundoshi Isha/Country Doctor* (60), *Osaka-jo Monogatari/The Story of the Castle of Osaka* (61), *Chushingura/the 47 Ronin** (62), *Tatsu* (62), *Hiken/Young Swordsman* (63), *Daitatsumaki/Whirlwind* (64), *Abare Goemon/Rise Against the Sword* (66), *Sasaki Kojiro/Kojiro* (68), *Furin Kazan/Samurai Banners* (64).

INCE, Thomas Harper DIR/PROD USA. (Newport Nov 6, 1882–Hollywood Nov 19, 1924) A film maker of equal intertional importance to D. W. Griffith (*q.v.*), he was a self-taught man with experience in the popular American theater and music hall, who, between 1912–24, turned the western into an art. Though he directed several hundred films in the first years of his film career, he was also an extremely efficient organizer and, as an executive producer, developed the technique of writing what was later called the shooting script — usually in collaboration with C. Gardner Sullivan (*q.v.*), who wrote the majority of his plots. These shooting scripts were then shot by "directors" working directly under his guidance; once the footage was shot, he closely supervised the editing. Though credited as "supervisor" he was himself, to a great extent, creatively responsible for his productions; few of the directors who worked under him reached the same heights in their later careers. In 1918 Louis Delluc (*q.v.*) hailed his "lyrical power" and "poetry" and, although some have said Ince is a myth invented by Delluc, a kind of "Thomas the Imposter," he is one of the principal pioneers of cinematic art. Moussinac wrote in 1921: "He contributes a striking spirit, a power that revels in detail, a lyricism that makes one forget the relative perfection of the craft. With him, the cinema was no longer a fantastic toy but a creative instrument. The cowboy leaped on the back of the wild beast and imposed his audacious rule." Jean Mitry (responsible for the masterful compilation of Ince's filmography) wrote: "If Griffith was the first poet of an art whose basic syntax he created, one could say that Ince was its first dramaturgist. His experiments, in fact, were based on the composition of original themes, on the expression of ideas more than on perfecting formal aspects. He was able to guide and discipline his collaborators only because, like them, he was a director, and superior to them." From 1889–1908 he was an actor, often appearing in western melodramas; in 1906–09 he played several small parts in Edison and Vitagraph films. In 1910 he appeared in a film for Carl Laemmle's Imp Company and in one for Biograph (alongside his wife Alice Kershaw) befor returning to Imp in December as a director. His first film was *Little Nell's Tobacco;* in January 1911, he was assigned to direct all of Mary Pickford's films (*Their First Misunderstanding,* etc.). When Imp was forced to flee to Cuba because of legal action, Ince continued directing there. In late 1911, he joined the New York Motion Picture Company (Kay Bee) and began film-making in Los Angeles, where he persuaded the producers to hire the Miller Brothers 101 Ranch Circus to provide him with extras for "real" westerns. He directed a hundred films 1911–13, including a five-reel *The Battle of Gettysburg* in 1913. By the end of 1913 he stopped directing his productions himself (with a handful of exceptions in 1915 and 16) but continued to supervise closely the films of his directors, including Reginald Barker (*q.v.*), William S. Hart, Raymond B. West, Irvin Willat, Alfred Parker, Frank Borzage (*q.v.*), Henry King (*q.v.*), Lloyd Ingraham, Fred Niblo (*q.v.*), Rowland Lee, Lambert Hillyer (*q.v.*), Marshall Neilan, and Ralph Ince (his brother). By 1916 Inceville Studios had five shooting stages and Ince had given several notable stars their screen debuts: among his contracted actors were W. S. Hart (who quarreled continuously with Ince over his films), Sessue Hayakawa, H. B. Warner, Lew Cody, Lewis Stone, Billie Burke, and Charles Ray. In 1918 he left Triangle (which he had joined in 1915), built new studios at Culver City, and signed a distribution contract with Paramount-Artcraft; he formed Associated Producers

Inc. in the following year. In 1924, while spending a weekend on William Randolph Hearst's yacht, he became ill, dying soon after as a result of what would now be called thrombosis. Rumors of his having been poisoned have no basis in fact.

DIR (notably): *Little Nell's Tobacco* (11), *Their First Misunderstanding* (11), *The Silver Dollar* (11), *The New Cook* (11), *War on the Plains* (12), *Renegade* (12), *For Freedom of Cuba* (12), *Custer's Last Fight* (12), *The Shadow of the Past* (12), *The Ambassador's Envoy* (13), *The Battle of Gettysburg* (13), *The Pride of the South* (13), *The Despoiler* (15), *Civilization** (16) (co-dir). PROD (notably): *The Wrath of the Gods* (14), *The Typhoon* (14), *The Fugitive* (15), *The Coward* (15), *The Iron Strain* (15), *The Bargain* (15), *Hell's Hinges* (16), *The Aryan** (16), *Primal Lure* (16), *Honor's Altar* (16), *Moral Fabric* (16), *The Patriot* (16), *The Captive God* (16), *Flying Colors* (17), *Until They Get Me* (17), *The Wolf Women* (17), (17), *Golden Rule Kate* (17), *The Beggar of Cawnpore* (17), *Vive la France* (18), *Behind the Door* (18), *Carmen of the Klondyke* (18), *Human Wreckage* (23), *Anna Christie* (23).

INGRAM, Rex (Rex Fitchcock) DIR USA. (Dublin 1892–Hollywood June 21, 1950) A film maker with taste, but with a somewhat academic attitude to his materials, who discovered Rudolph Valentino and whose work was overestimated in the silent period after the enormous success of *The Four Horsemen of the Apocalypse** (21). After directing several Ramon Novarro vehicles, *Scaramouche* (23), etc., he moved to France in 1926 and established his own studios in Nice, where he continued to make films for Hollywood, *The Garden of Allah* (27), *Belladonna* (27), etc. He stopped directing when sound was introduced.

IPSEN, Bodil DIR Denmark. (Copenhagen Aug 30, 1889–Nov 1964) A former star of the Danish silent cinema, he began directing in 1942 and made several films in collaboration with Lau Lauritzen, Jr. (*q.v.*): *Afsporet* (42), *De Röde Enge Café Paradis* (50), *Det Sande Ansigt* (51) and, alone, *En Herre i Kjole og Hvidt* (42), *Basaettelse* (44).

IRANI, Ardeshir M. PROD India. (Bombay 1885– ?) Originally an exhibitor in Bombay, he became a partner in the Imperial Film Company in 1926 and in 1931 produced the first Indian talking films (in Hindi): *Alam Ara/Beauty of the World* and *Shirin Farhad*, which contained no less than 42 songs. Both were enormous commercial successes.

ISING, Rudolph ANIM USA *see* HARMAN, HUGH

ISMAI, Osman DIR Indonesia (? –) Talented young Indonesian film maker responsible, notably, for *Embun* (56).

ITO(H), Daisuke DIR Japan. (Tokyo Oct 13, 1898–) A film maker who was at his best in the silent period, when he was noted for the violent realism of his films – *Shuchu Nikki/The Diary of a Drunkard* (24), *Gero/The Servant* (27), *Chuji Tabinikki/Diary of Chuji's Travels* (27–28) (in 3 parts), *Ooka Seidan/Ooka's Trial* (28) (in 3 parts). These period films were forerunners of the "tendency" films, his *Zanjin Zamba Ken/Man-Slashing, Horse-Piercing Sword* (29) being an outspoken piece of social criticism against the exploiting classes. His talent did not long survive the introduction of sound, but he continued to make excellent, vigorous, and sometimes formally beautiful samurai melodramas, from his first sound film, *Tange Sazan* (33), through his remake of *The Servant*, and *Gero no Kubi/The Servant's Neck* (55), to *Hangyakuji/The Conspirator* (61), with its inspired use of color and scope.

IVENS, Joris (Georg Henri Anton Ivens) DIR Netherlands/France/USSR/USA/ German Democratic Republic, etc. (Nijmegen Nov 18, 1898–) One of the greatest documentary film artists, the peer of Robert Flaherty (*q.v.*), a kind of "Flying Dutchman" who has worked in many countries but whose work always reflect his basic concerns: men at work, men struggling against nature or social oppression. He is a great documentarist not only because of the poetry of his images and their rhythmic construction, but also because he has been, in every sense of the term, a man of his times. He has been a constant witness of passing events, a film maker who has always been present at decisive turning points in human history. Totally uninterested in depressive aspects, he is excited by mankind's struggles, constructions, and creations, and, as a masterly editor, he has been able to unite people and the world around them with a deep feeling for the poetry that is intrinsic in what he shows. He made his first film in 1911 at the age of 13 and in 1926 jointly established "Filmliga," one of the first film societies. His first significant film, *The Bridge* (28) contains the image of water (he was born beside the Rhine) he has returned to again and again ·in his work: *Rain; The Breakers,* which protect Holland against the sea; *New Earth,* which was wrested from the Zuyderzee; the problem of irrigation in *Spanish Earth* during the Civil War; the dockers' strike in *Indonesia Calling;* the unity of the world's workers in *Song of the Rivers;* and the poetical view of Paris and the Seine in *La Seine a rencontré Paris.* He is a committed partisan of a *cinéma-vérité* that expresses social reality and he has never refused to tackle quite humble films if he felt they would serve a just cause. He has continued the teachings of his master, Dziga Vertov, in the Western world and has stated that, for the camera to be truly a witness it must count less on powerful material resources than on the solidarity of the workers. This view is expressed most clearly in *Borinage,* a film made amid a bitter miners' strike and despite the Belgian police, and in *Indonesia Calling,* which centers on Australian dockers and seamen who refused to load arms intended for colonial reconquest. His whole approach to his art has made him not only one of the great classic directors but a man who has laid the foundations for the cinema of the future.

DIR: *De Brandende Straal/Flaming Arrow* (11), *Zeedijk Film Studie/Zeedyk Film Study* (27), *Der Brug/The Bridge** (28), *Regen/Rain** (29) (co-dir: Mannus Franken), *Branding/Breakers* (29) (co-dir: Franken), *Schaatsenrijden/Skating* (29), *Wij Bouwen/We are Building* (30), *Heien/Pile-Driving* (30), *Nieuwe Architectuur* (30), *Zuid Limburg* (30), *Caisson bornn Rotterdam* (30), *Philips Radio/Industrial Symphony* (31), *Creosoot/Creosote* (31), *Zuiderzee* (31–33),

Komsomol/Song of Heroes. (USSR32), *Borinage/Misère au Borinage** (Belg33), *Nieuwe Gronden/New Earth** (Neth 34), *The Spanish Earth** (USA37), *The 400 Million** (USA39), *Power and the Land* (USA40), *New Frontiers* (USA40) (abandoned), *Our Russian Front* (USA 41) (co-dir: Milestone), *Oil for Aladdin's Lamp* (USA42), *Action Stations!* (Canada42), *Know Your Enemy: Japan* (USA45) (abandoned), *Indonesia Calling* (Austral46), *Pierwsze Lata/The First Years** (Pol/Bulg/Czech49), *Poko j Zwyeciezy Swiat/Peace Will Win* (Pol 51) (co-dir: Bossak), *Naprozod Mloziezy swiata/Friendship Triumphs* (USSR/GDR52) (co-dir: Ivan Pyriev), *Friedensfahrt 1952/Friendship Tour 1952* (GDR/Pol52), *Das Lied der Ströme/The Song of the Rivers** (GDR54), *Die Windrose/The Wind Rose* (GDR56) (5 part film, supervised by Ivens, Cavalcanti), *Les Aventures de Till l'Espiègle/The Adventures of Till Eulenspiegel* (Fr/GDR56) (co-dir: Gérard Philipe), *La Seine a rencontré Paris** (Fr57), *Early Spring/Letters from China* (China 58), *600 Million People Are with You/The War of 600 Million People* (China 58), *L'Italia non e un Paesa Povere/Italy is Not a Poor Country* (It60) (TV), *Demain à Nanguila/Nanguila Tomorrow* (Mali60), *Carnet de Viaje* (Cuba60), *Cuba, Pueblo Armado* (Cuba61), . . . *A Valparaiso* (Chile/Fr63), *El Circo más Pequeño del Mundo/The Little Circus* (Chile/Fr63), *Le Train de la Victoire* (Chile64), *Le Mistral* (Fr65) (TV), *Le Ciel, la Terre/The Threatening Sky* (Fr/Vietnam65), *Rotterdam-Europoort* (Neth66), *17° Parallèle/17th Parallel* (Fr/Vietnam67), *Rotterdam-Europoort from Vietnam* (Fr67) (one episode).

"angston" china '72

IWERKS, Ub ANIM USA. (Kansas City March 24, 1901–July 1971) American cartoonist responsible for the original design of *Mickey Mouse** (later attributed to Disney) who began in 1920 as an artist in a commercial advertising firm and joined Disney in 1924. Iwerks also made *Flip the Frog* and *Little Negro* cartoons for his own Celebrity Pictures in the Thirties. He again joined Disney in 1935 as head of production services and has since specialized in trick work, such as the combination of live action and animation.

*JAENZON, Julius (also J. Julius) PHOTOG
Sweden. (Göteborg 1885–1961) The
greatest cameraman of the brilliant Swedish silent cinema and a pioneer in the
development of location photography.
His creation of atmosphere and feeling
for nature contributed much to the films
of Sjöström and Stiller (both *q.v.*):
Terje Vigen, The Outlaw and His Wife,
Sir Arne's Treasure*, The Phantom
Chariot*, Love's Crucible, Gunnar
Hede's Saga*, The Saga of Gösta Ber-
ling**. His brother, Henrik Jaenzon, also
photographed several notable silent films,
e.g., *Ingeborg Holm*, Karin, Daughter
Ingmar**. As an instructor at Svensk
Filmindustri, Julius Jaenzon exercised
considerable influence on the photographic style of the modern Swedish
cinema.

JAKUBOWSKA, Wanda DIR Poland. (Warsaw Nov 10, 1907–) A film maker of
key importance in the postwar development of the Polish cinema, notably
with her portrait of the Auschwitz death
camp *Ostatni etap/The Last Stage** (48).
She was a founding member of Start
and directed documentaries in the Thirties; her wartime sufferings are reflected
in several of her films.

*JANCSO, Miklos DIR Hungary. (Vac 1921–
) Individualistic film maker with a
masterful sense of the epic and a strongly
formal style, he established his international reputation with *The Round-Up*
(66) and paved the way for a more personal school of film makers in Hungary.
Many of his films reflect the bitterness
and weariness of war's aftermath. His
style relies heavily on long takes empha-
sizing the composition of characters in
a landscape, and approach that gives his
films their visual grandeur and epic
quality. He graduated from the Academy
of Dramatic and Film Art in 1950, made
newsreels from 1950–54, and then a
large number of shorts and documentaries before directing his first feature
in 1958.
DIR (shorts, notably): *Osz Badacsony-
ban/Autumn in Badacsony* (54), *Egg
Kiallitas Kepei/Pictures at an Exhibition*
(54), *Szinfoltok Kinabol/Colorful China*
(57), *Derkovitas* (58), *Halhatatlansag/
Immortality* (59), *Az Ido Kereke/The
Wheels of Time* (61), *Hej te Eleven
fa . . ./Living Tree . . .* (63), *Közel-
rol: a Ver/Close-up: The Blood* (66).
DIR (features): *A Harangok Romaba
Mentek/The Bells Have Gone to Rome*
(58), *Harom Csillag/Three Stars* (60)
(first part only), *Oldas es Kotes/Can-
tata* (63), *Igy Jöttem/My Way Home*
(64), *Szegenylegenyek/The Round-up/
Poor Outlaws** (66), *Csillagosok, Kan-
tonak/The Red and the White* (67),
Csend es Kialtas/Silence and Cry (68),
Fenyes szelek/The Confrontation (68),
Sirocco/Winter Wind (Fr/Czech69).

JARRE, Maurice MUS France/USA/Britain.
(Lyon 1924–) Former composer of
several remarkable scores for the Théâtre National Populaire who began in the
cinema writing music for short films by
Franju (*q.v.*) and Resnais (*q.v.*) [but
has more recently received wider exposure through his scores for epics like
Lawrence of Arabia and *Dr Zhivago*.
He tends to favor the guitar as a principal instrument] and has sometimes used
a compilation of natural sounds as a
symphonic element. His scores have contributed much to many notable films.
MUS (notably): for Franju, *Hôtel des
Invalides** (51), *Le Théâtre National
Populaire* (56), *Sur le Pont d'Avignon*
(56), *La Tête contre les murs** (58),
Les Yeux sans visage (59, *Pleins feux
sur l'assassin* (61), *Thérèse Desqueroux*

126

(62), *Judex** (63); for Resnais, *Toute la mémoire du monde* (56); for Jean-Pierre Mocky, *Les Drageurs* (59); for Richard Fleischer, *Crack in the Mirror* (60); for David Lean, *Lawrence of Arabia* (62), *Dr. Zhivago* (65); for Zanuck, *The Longest Day** (62); for Serge Bourguignon, *Les Dimanches de Ville d'Avray* (62); for Zinnemann, *Behold a Pale Horse* (63); for Letterier, *Un roi sans divertissement* (63); for Wyler, *The Collector* (65); for Frankenheimer, *The Train* (64), *Grand Prix* (66); for Clément, *Paris-brûle-t-il?* (66); for Richard Brooks, *The Professionals* (66); for Litvak, *Night of the Generals* (66); for Karel Reisz, *Isadora* (67); for Visconti, *Caduta degli Dei/The Damned** (69); for John Guillermin, *El Condor* (70).

JASNY, Vojtěch DIR Czechoslovakia. (Kelc, Moravia Nov 30, 1925–) The best of the first generation of new Czechoslovakian directors to emerge since the war, a film maker with a deep sense of poetry (*Desire*) and formal beauty who is not afraid of social polemic and is notable for the courage with which he has tackled contemporary themes. [He studied at the Prague film school (FAMU), first in the cinematographic section, then in direction. His graduation film (co-dir: Karel Kachyna) was a documentary on the Czech border regions, *The Clouds Will Roll Away* (50). He made several documentaries (*Towards a Joyful Life, Unusual Years, People of One Heart*, etc.) in the early Fifties before making his first feature in 1954.]
DIR: *Dnes vecer vsechno skonei/Everything Ends Tonight* (54) (co-dir: K. Kachyna), *Zarijove noce/September Nights* (57), *Touha/Desire* (58), *Prezil jsem svou smrt/I Survived Certain Death* (60), *Procesi k Panence/Pilgrimage to the Virgin Mary** (61), *Az prijde kocour/That Cat** (63), *Dymky/Pipes* (65), *Vsichni dobri rodaci/All Good Citizens/Our Countrymen* (68).

JASSET, Victorin DIR France. (Fumay 1862–Paris June 22, 1913) One of the best pre-1914 French directors, a man with a unique style and a sense of fantasy and of the bizarre. He made several episode films: *Nick Carter* (08), *Zigomar* (11), *Protea* (13) and published an excellent monograph on the theories and practice of directing in 1918.

JAUBERT, Maurice MUS France. (Nice Jan 3, 1900–Azerailles June 19, 1940) The greatest prewar French composer whose brilliant scores (popular and yet not facile) served to perfection the poetic realism of Vigo, Clair, Carné, and Prévert (all *q.v.*). He was killed on the front in 1940.
MUS (notably): for Cavalcanti, *Le Petit Chaperon rouge* (29); for Pierre Prévert, *L'Affaire est dans le sac** (32); for Clair, *Quatorze juillet* (33), *Le Dernier Milliardaire** (34); for Vigo, *Zéro de conduite** (33), *L'Atalante** (34); for Carné, *Drôle de drame* (37), *Hôtel du Nord* (38), *Quai des Brumes* (38), *Le Jour se lève** (39); for Duvivier, *Carnet de bal** (37), *La Fin du jour* (39).

JEANSON, Henri SCEN France. (Paris March 6, 1900–Nov 1970) Notable French writer who is at his best with sharp, biting dialogue and who excels in word plays and verbal jokes in the best *boulevardier* tradition. He was also a journalist and film critic, 1920–50.
SCEN (notably): for Korda, *La Dame de chez Maxim's* (33); for Duvivier, *Pépé le Moko** (37), *Carnet de bal** (37), *Pot-Bouille* (57); for Moguy, *Prison sans barreaux* (38); for Marc Allégret, *Entrée des artistes* (38); for Carné, *Hôtel du Nord* (38); for L'Herbier, *La Nuit fantastique* (42); for Christian-Jaque, *Carmen** (42), *Boule de suif** (48), *Fanfan la tulipe** (51), *Nana** (55), *Les Bonnes causes* (63); for Decoin, *Les Amoureux sont seuls au monde* (48); for Delannoy, *Au yeux du souvenir* (48); for Becker, *Montparnasse 19* (57); for Verneuil, *L'Affaire d'une nuit* (60).

JENKINS, Charles Francis INVENTOR USA. (Dayton 1868–Richmond, Indiana June 6, 1934) Co-inventor (in the summer of 1895) with Thomas Armat of the Phantoscope, a projector based on Jenkins's design of a revolving-light kinetoscopic machine and Armat's idea that intermittent motion of the strip of film was necessary. The first public presentation of the device (in mid-Sept 1895 at the Cotton States Exposition in Atlanta) preceded by some months that of the Lumière (*q.v.*) Cinématographe. Between 1896 and 1930 Jenkins took out some 400 patents, most of them to do with moving pictures and "broadcast transmission of motion pictures"; he wrote frequently of the possibilities of this latter development.

*JENNINGS, Humphrey DIR Britain. (Suffolk 1907–Greece 1950) Perhaps the greatest of the British documentary film makers and certainly the most poetic, he had a sensitivity to the power of images, a deep humanity, and a perception that enabled him to capture the emotional mood of wartime Britain. He was an intellectual, a man of broad culture, whose strongest early wish was to be a painter and who wrote poems full of visual imagery. During the Thirties he developed an interest in surrealism and in Charles Madge's sociological Mass-Observation, both of which were reflected in his films. He first worked in films as designer on Cavalcanti's *Pett and Pott* (34), then directed with Len Lye the stylized puppet film, *Birth of a Robot* (36). None of his prewar films have the sense of poetry, rhythm, and humanity of his best films during the war: *Listen to Britain* (with its impressionistic blend of sounds and images), *Fires Were Started,* and *A Diary for Timothy.* He died accidentally while filming in Greece.
DIR: *Birth of a Robot* (36) (co-dir: Len Lye), *The First Days* (39) (co-dir: Cavalcanti, Watt, etc.), *Spare Time* (39), *Spring Offensive/An Unrecorded Victory* (39), *Speaking from America* (39), *Her Last Trip/S.S. Jonian* (39), *London Can Take It* (40) (co-dir: Watt), *Welfare of the Workers* (40), *Words for Battle* (41), *Heart of Britain/This is England* (41), *Listen to Britain* (41), *The Silent Village* (43), *Fires Were Started** (43), *The Story of Lilli Marlene* (44), *A Diary for Timothy* (45), *A Defeated People* (45), *The Cumberland Story* (47), *Dim Little Island* (49), *Family Portrait* (50).

JOHNSON, Martin DIR USA. (Rockford, Illinois Oct 9, 1884–Hollywood 1937) He usually worked in collaboration with his wife, Osa, and together they formed the most famous team of explorer-film makers. Martin Johnson shipped (as cook) with Jack London on his round-the-world voyage and he and his wife later became inveterate travelers, largely in Africa and Polynesia, recording all their adventures on film. Their features and shorts enjoyed continuing popularity from 1912–35.

DIR (notably): *Jack London's Adventures in the South Seas* (08–12) (M. Johnson only), *Cannibals of the South Seas/ Head Hunters of Malekula* (12) (M. Johnson only), *On the Borderland of Civilization* (15?), *Head Hunters of the South Seas* (22), *Trailing Big Game in Africa/Hunting African Animals* (23), *Simba* (24–27), *Congorilla* (29–32), *Baboona* (35), *I Married Adventure* (40) (compilation) (O. Johnson only).

*JOHNSON, Nunnally SCEN/DIR/PROD USA. (Columbus, South Carolina Dec 5, 1897–) The perfect example of a talented Hollywood scriptwriter working under contract (mostly for 20th Century-Fox) and able to turn his hand to almost any subject. His best work was his adaptation of *The Grapes of Wrath* and Lang's exemplary thriller, *The Woman in the Window.* He had had a brilliant career as a journalist before moving to Hollywood in 1933 as a scriptwriter. Following 1935 he often worked as associate producer on the films he wrote and, after 1942, as producer. He become a director in 1954 but his work has been consistently uninteresting, from the anticommunist *Night People* to the routine comedies *Oh Men!, Oh Women!* and *The Man Who Understood Women.*
SCEN (notably): for Raoul Walsh, *Baby Face Harrington* (35); for Howard Hawks, *The Road to Glory* (36); for John Ford, *The Prisoner of Shark Island* (36), *The Grapes of Wrath** (40), *Tobacco Road* (41); for Henry King, *Jesse James* (39), *The Gunfighter* (50); for Fritz Lang, *The Woman in the Window** (44); for John Stahl, *The Keys of the Kingdom* (44); for Robert Siodmak, *The Dark Mirror* (46); for Jean Negulesco, *Three Came Home* (49), *The Mudlark* (50), *Phone Call from a Stranger* (52), *How to Marry a Millionaire* (53); for Hathaway, *The Desert Fox* (51); for Henry Koster, *My Cousin Rachel* (53), *Take Her, She's Mine* (63), *Dear Brigitte* (64); for Walter Lang, *There's No Business Like Show Business* (54); for Nicholas Ray, *The True Story of Jesse James* (57); for Don Siegel, *Flaming Star* (60); for George Roy Hill, *The World of Henry Orient* (64); for Robert Aldrich, *The Dirty Dozen* (67); and for his own films.
DIR: *Night People* (54), *The Black Widow* (54), *How to Be Very, Very Popular* (55), *The Man in the Gray*

Flannel Suit (56), *The Three Faces of Eve* (57), *Oh Men!, Oh Women!* (57), *The Man Who Understood Women* (59), *La Sposa Bella* (62).

JOHNSTON, Eric A. (Washington Dec 21, 1895–Hollywood August 1963) Successor in September 1945 to Will Hays (*q.v.*) as president of the Motion Picture Association of America and roving ambassador for the American cinema. Despite all his international activities, he saw the postwar decline of Hollywood and the big studios under his reign.

JONES, Chuck (Charles M. Jones) ANIM USA. (Spokane, Washington 1912–) Excellent American animator who, with Fritz Freleng and Robert McKimpson, created in the Warner Brothers studios the famous anthropomorphic cartoon characters of Bugs Bunny, Tweetie Pie, Daffy Duck, Speedy Gonzalez, Road Runner, and Coyote with their attendant gags (often brilliant) and stylized violence (less objectionable than in *Tom and Jerry*). [He had earlier been, successively or simultaneously, an animator, director, and scenario writer for Ub Iwerks (*q.v.*), Charles Mintz, Walter Lantz, and Walt Disney (*q.v.*). He was a leader of the famous strike at Walt Disney Studios that led to the formation of UPA. He directed the first UPA film, *Hell Bent for Election* (44), and wrote the script for UPA's first feature *Gay Purree*. His films have won eight Oscars and numerous other awards. His work in the Sixties has been particularly imaginative (though clearly influenced by European styles), especially the abstractions of *High Note,* the story line based on sound effects and free flowing visuals of *Now Hear This,* and the witty austereness of *The Dot and the Line.* In 1965 he founded his own production company, Tower Twelve Productions, and has worked for MGM on a somewhat unsatisfactory revival of the Tom and Jerry cartoons. His notable films include: *Private Snafu* (44), *Hell Bent for Election* (44), *Mississippi Hare* (47), *Mouse Wreckers* (47), *Frigid Hare* (49), *Rabbit Seasoning* (51), *Bully for Bugs* (52), *Claws for Alarm* (53), *Punch Trunk* (55), *Nightmare Hare* (55), *Gee Whiz-z-z* (56), *Robin Hood Daffy* (57), *Scrambled Aches* (57), *The Abominable Snow Rabbit* (61), *I Was a Teenaged Thumb* (63), *High Note* (63), *Now Hear This* (63), *Tom-ic Energy* (64), *The Cat Above, the Mouse Below* (64), *The Dot and the Line* (66), *Horton Hears a Who* (70), *The Phantom Tollbooth* (69–71).]

JUILLARD, Robert PHOTOG France. (Joinville Aug 24, 1906–) One of the best postwar French cameramen, notable for his temperate, precise style: for Rossellini, *Germania, Anno Zero** (48); for Clément, *Jeux interdits** (52), *Gervaise** (56); for Clair, *Les Belles de nuit** (52), *Les Grandes Manoeuvres** (55); for Gance, *Austerlitz* (60); for Delannoy, *Le Rendez-vous* (61).

JULIAN, Rupert DIR USA. (Auckland Dec 25, 1889– ?) Former stage and screen actor who became a director for Universal and was rated by Carl Laemmle (*q.v.*) as superior to Stroheim (*q.v.*), whom he replaced on *Merry-Go-Round* (23). He made the fascinating Lon Chaney vehicle, *Phantom of the Opera* (25), and several routine films before disappearing from Hollywood when sound was introduced.

JULIUS, J. *pseud see* JAENZON, JULIUS

JUNGHANS, Carl DIR Czechoslovakia. (Dresden Oct 7, 1897–) The director of the remarkable *Such is Life** at the end of the silent period in Czechoslovakia but of nothing else of note. He emigrated to the USA in the Thirties.

*JUTRA, Claude DIR Canada. (Montreal March 11, 1930–) Imaginative Canadian film maker who has made a number of individualistic shorts, a perceptive *cinéma vérité* documentary feature, *Niger 60,* and a remarkable semi-autobiographical feature, *A tout prendre* (63), whose style anticipated that of many films of the Sixties. He originally studied medicine, then theater at the Théâtre du Nouveau Monde in Montreal. He made his first films as an amateur before joining the National Film Board of Canada and collaborating with Norman McLaren (*q.v.*) on *A Chairy Tale.* He has also worked briefly with Jean Rouch (*q.v.*). Many of his films have been photographed by and/or co-directed with Michel Brault. He has worked often in TV, notably for the series *Images* *en boîte* for Radio-Canada, and has taken a further step in the use of "direct cinema" techniques in *Wow!* a 16-mm feature conceived collectively by "nine bourgeois adolescents expressing their interests and preoccupations."

DIR: *Mouvement perpétuel* (49), *Le Dément du lac Jean Jeune* (49), *Pierrot des bois* (54), *Jeunesses musicales* (56), *A Chairy Tale/Il était une chaise** (57), *Les Mains nettes* (58) (supervised: F. Dansereau), *Felix Leclerc, troubadour* (59), *Fred Barry* (59), *Niger 60* (60), *La Lutte* (61) (co-dir: M. Brault and others), *Anna la bonne* (61), *Québec-USA/Visit to a Foreign Country* (62) (co-dir: M. Brault), *Les Enfants du silence* (62) (co-dir: M. Brault), *A tout prendre/Take it all* (63), *Comment savoir* (66), *Rouli-roulant* (66), *Wow!* (69), *Le Québec vu par Cartier-Bresson* (69), *Marie-Christine* (70), *Mon oncle Antoine* (71).

JUTZI, Phil (Piel) DIR/PHOTOG Germany. (Rheinpfalz 1894–194?) Film maker whose reputation rests on a handful of realistic films on working-class themes that were made in the late Twenties. He was also a renowned cameraman before, during, and after his own most famous films (e.g., Fedor Ozep's *Der Lebende Leichmann*) and he photographed all his own silent films. He remained in Germany after the advent of Hitler and directed and/or photographed several mediocre films, the last in 1942.

DIR (notably): *Der Maskierte Schrecken* (20), *Klass und Datsch die Pechvögel* (26), *Kindertragödie* (27), *Die Machnower Schleusen* (27) (short), *Mutter Krausens Fahrt ins Glück/Mother Krausen's Journey to Happiness* (29), *Unser tägliches Brot/Hunger in Waldenburg/ Our Daily Bread** (29) (documentary), *Berlin-Alexanderplatz* (31), *Lockspitzel Asew* (35).

*KADAR, Ján DIR Czechoslovakia. (Budapest April 1, 1918–) Film maker whose best work in collaboration with Elmar Klos (*q.v.*) since 1952 reflects a deep concern for human rights (*Death is Called Engelchen, The Shop on the Main Street*). He studied at the Bratislava Film School and was imprisoned in a Nazi labor camp during the war. After the war he directed the documentary, *Life is Rising from the Ruins,* then became a scriptwriter and assistant at the Barrandov Studios in Prague and directed independently a comedy feature, *Katya* (50), before joining with Klos in 1952. Together they have worked on the Magic Lantern presentations and made the polyscreen *Youth* (58) and the documentary, *Spartakiade* (60), in addition to their features. They have invariably written their own scripts but stopped collaborating in 1970 when Kadar moved to the USA.

CO-DIR: *Unos/Kidnapped* (52), *Hudba z Marsu/Music from Mars* (54), *Tam na konecne/The House at the Terminus* (57), *Tri prani/Three Wishes* (58), *Smrt si rika Engelchen/Death is Called Engelchen* (63), *Obzalovany/The Defendant/The Accused* (64), *Obchod na korze/Shop on the High Street/Shop on Main Street** (65).

DIR: *Touha zvana Anada/Adrift* (Czech/USA69), *Angel Levine* (USA70).

KALATAZOV, Mikhail Konstantinovich DIR USSR. (Tiflis Dec 28, 1903–) Veteran Soviet film maker who began as an editor and cameraman and directed, at the end of the silent period, the remarkable *Salt for Svanetia.* He made several other less interesting films before and during the war and, for a time, was Soviet Consul in Los Angeles before influencing the Soviet feature film of the Fifties and Sixties with his romantic masterpieces *The Cranes Are Flying* (57) and *The Letter That Wasn't Sent* (60), both of which made a great new actress, Tatiana Samoilova, internationally famous.

DIR: *Sol Svanetia/Salt for Svanetia** (30) (documentary), *Nail in the Boot* (32) (unreleased), *Mut/Manhood* (39) (documentary), *Valeri Chkalov/Wings of Victory* (41), *Nepobedimyie/Invincible* (42) (co-dir: Gerasimov), *Zagavor obrechyonnikh/Conspiracy of the Doomed* (50), *Verniye druzya/True Friends/Close Friends* (54), *Pervi eshelon/The First Echelon* (66), *Letyat zhuravli/The Cranes are Flying** (57), *Neotpravlennoe pismo/The Letter that Wasn't Sent* (60), *Ya-Kuba/I am Cuba/Here is Cuba* (USSR/Cuba62), *Krasnaya palatka/The Red Tent* (USSR/It69).

KALMUS, Herbert T. INVENTOR USA. (Chelsea Nov 9, 1881–1963) American pioneer photographic expert, the inventor of Technicolor in 1914 and later president of the Technicolor Corporation. His wife, Natalie (1892–1965), was his faithful technical assistant and acted as adviser on all Technicolor films, 1933–50.

KAMEI, Fumio DIR Japan. (April 1, 1908–) Independent polemical Japanese film maker who studied films in Moscow 1928–33, became a documentary film maker, and was imprisoned for making a pacifist film during the war. After the war he played a major role in the development of the independent Japanese cinema, making, notably, as part of this movement, the touching *A Woman Walks the Earth Alone* (53). He later returned to documentaries.

DIR (notably): *Shanghai* (38) (documentary), *Tatakai Hettai* (40), *Shina no Fudok* (41) (banned), *Nichon no Higeki/A Japanese Tragedy** (45) (documentary, banned), *Senso to Hewai/ War and Peace** (47) (co-dir: Yamamoto), *Onna no Issho/A Woman's Life* (49), *Onna Hitori Daichi o Iku/A Woman Walks the Earth Alone** (53), *To Be a Mother, To Be a Wife* (53), *It is Better to Live* (56).

KAMEL MORSI, Ahmad DIR Egypt. (190?–   ) A friend and disciple of Kamel Salim (*q.v.*), he had directed numerous films, most memorably, *El Amel/The Worker* (43), *El Naeb el Am/The Public Prosecutor* (45).

KAMENKA, Alexandre PROD France. (Odessa May 18, 1888–France Dec 1969) Emigrated from Russia and established himself in Paris (with Mosjoukine and Ermolieff), where he headed Albatros Films and produced many important films (23–40) by Epstein, Clair, Feyder, L'Herbier, etc. Also produced for Jean Renoir (*q.v.*) in 1936 and Louis Daquin (*q.v.*) in 1947.

KANIN, Garson SCEN/DIR USA. (Rochester Nov 24, 1912–   ) A scriptwriter, director, playwright, and Broadway producer who made several remarkable prewar comedies (notably, *Tom, Dick, and Harry*) and was Cukor's favorite writer in the Forties and Fifties. [He was originally a musician and actor, was brought to Hollywood in 1936 by Sam Goldwyn (*q.v.*), and worked for two years in the cutting rooms before directing his first feature for RKO. He directed eight prewar films and several notable war documentaries (*Fellow Americans, The True Glory*) but after the war restricted his activities to Broadway and to scriptwriting. He has often worked in collaboration with his wife, the actress Ruth Gordon (who alone wrote the script for Cukor's *The Actress*), on Broadway plays, scripts and film adaptations of their plays. Recently, he has returned to film directing.]
DIR: *A Man to Remember* (38), *Next Time I Marry* (38), *The Great Man Votes* (39), *Bachelor Mother* (39), *My Favorite Wife* (40), *They Knew What They Wanted* (40), *Tom, Dick, and Harry* (41), *Fellow Americans* (42) (documentary), *German Manpower* (43) (documentary), *The True Glory* (USA/Brit45) (documentary, co-dir: Carol Reed), *Where It's At* (69), *Some Kind of Nut* (69), *Mr. Broadway* (TV series).

SCEN (notably): for George Cukor, *A Double Life* (47), *Adam's Rib* (49), *Born Yesterday** (51), *Pat and Mike* (52), *The Marrying Kind* (52), *It Should Happen to You** (54); for George Seaton, *Teacher's Pet* (58); for Blake Edwards, *High Time* (60); for Robert Mulligan, *The Rat Race* (60). Also, Tashlin's *The Girl Can't Help It** and Sidney Buchman's *Over 21* are based on his plays.

KAPLER, Alexei SCEN USSR. (Briansk Sept 15, 1904–   ) An excellent scriptwriter and a former member of FEKS, who has worked on, notably: Ermler's *She Defends Her Country** and Romm's *Lenin in 1918** and *Lenin in October**.

KAPOOR, Raj DIR/PROD India. (Bombay Dec 4, 1924–   ) [The most famous showman of the Indian film industry and the master of the Hindi film musical. He began as a clapper boy with Bombay Talkies but soon became famous as a matinée idol in numerous light comedies. After the war he established his own company, R. K. Films, and built his reputation on a series of sentimentalized treatments (with songs and dances) of social themes. His first film, *Aag/ Fire*, was about a young man rebelling against social conventions.] In 1951, he made the enormously popular *Awara**, a film that was highly praised in the USSR and whose theme song swept Asia. In 1955, he made *Shri 420/ Mister 420* and in 1957 *Jagte Raho**. These were typical of his approach: lavish settings, vigorous stories centering on the misadventures of a "little man," who was probably based on Chaplin, and who was played by Kapoor himself. [His most commercially successful film, *Sangam/Union*, has no overt social message, while *Jis Desh Men Ganga Behit/Where the Ganges Flows* (61) — which won a number of awards — is more typical of his later approach and makes no pretense at anything but action, drama, pathos, and lots of music.]

KARABASZ, Kasimierz DIR Poland. (1930–   ) Young documentary film maker with a personal, poetic style that involves the expressiveness of the human faces he photographs: "I want to capture my heroes in their everyday work by making them forget the camera." He received international attention with *Musicians*

132

but is best known for his lyrical *People on the Road*.

DIR (notably): *People from the Empty Area* (57) (co-dir: Slesicki), *A Day Without Sun* (59) (co-dir: Slesicki), *Musicians* (60), *People on the Road* (61), *Railway Junction* (61), *Where Do You Go?* (61), *Jubilee* (62), *The First Steps* (62), *The Birds* (63), *In the Club* (63), *Born 1944* (64), *A Year in Frank's Life* (67) (co-dir: Niedbalski).

KARDAR, Aaejay DIR/PHOTOG Pakistan. (? –) A film maker responsible for making in East Pakistan the remarkable *Day Shall Dawn**, worthy of note not only for its faithful portrait of life in a small fishing village but also for Walter Lassally's (*q.v.*) photography. Also: *Qasum us Waqt ki/No Greater Glory* (69).

KARLSON. PR.1.

KARMEN, Roman Lasarevich DIR USSR. (Odessa Nov 11, 1906–) One of the truly great film makers, a man who is perhaps less of a director of documentary films than a documentarist, an actuality cameraman, and film journalist. He was a cameraman in Spain during the Civil War and in 1938–39 in China where he recorded, often under bombardment, reel after reel of memorable sequences – many of which have been reproduced (without credit) in various newsreels and documentaries. During the Spanish Civil War he was the equal of, and influenced, the photographer, Robert Capa.

DIR/PHOTOG (notably): *Moscow* (32), *Parade in Red Square Moscow* (33), *Moscow – Kara Kum – Moscow* (33), *At Home* (34), *Salute to the Spanish Pioneers* (36), *Spain* (39) (compiled by Esther Shub from Karmen footage), *China Defends Herself* (39), *Sedov Expedition* (40), *A Day in the New World* (40), *In China* (41), *The Defense of Leningrad* (43), *Albania* (45), *Berlin* (45), *Judgment of the People/Nuremberg* (47), *Soviet Turkmenistan* (50), *Soviet Georgia* (51), *Caspian Oil Workers* (53), *Vietnam* (54), *How Broad is Our Country* (58) (first Soviet film in 70mm "Kinopanorama"), *Dawn of India* (59), *Cuba, Island in Flames* (60), *Our Indonesian Friend* (60), *A Guest from the Island of Freedom* (63), *The Great Patriotic War* (65), *Death of a Commissar* (66), *Granada, Granada,*

My Granada (67) (compilation of Spanish Civil War footage).

KASSILA, Matti DIR Finland. (Keuru Jan 12, 1924–) Good Finnish director who has made some 15 films since 1949 and who possesses a particular feeling for nature and landscape, best displayed in *Elokuu* (56).

KAST, Pierre DIR France. (Paris Dec 22, 1920–) A film maker who spent too many years for his liking directing short films before he made his first feature. He is a well-established film critic (*Action, Postif, Cahiers du Cinéma*, etc.), has also worked in the theater, as an editor for Emmer (*q.v.*) and as assistant to Grémillon, Clément, Renoir, and John Sturges (all *q.v.*). His features – ingenious, intelligent, intellectual, introspective, and intimate – are sometimes irritating but never lacking in feeling or in sincerity. He has said of his approach: "Handled in the right way, anything, even very personal things, can be communicated to others, even though some details might not be directly understood."

DIR (shorts): *Les Charmes de l'existence* (49) (co-dir: Grémillon), *Les Femmes du Louvre* (51), *Les Désastres de la guerre* (51), *L'Arithmétique* (in *Encyclopédie filmée*) (51), *La Guerre en dentelles* (52), *Je sème à tous vents* (52), *La Chasse à l'homme* (53), *A nous deux Paris* (53), *Monsieur Robida, prophète et explorateur du temps* (54), *Claude-Nicholas Ledoux, architecte Maudit* (54), *Nos ancêtres les explorateurs* (54), *Le Corbusier, l'architecte du bonheur* (56), *Des ruines et des hommes* (58), *Images pour Baudelaire* (58), *Une question d'assurance* (59), *Japan d'hier et d'aujourd'hui* (59), *Promenade quotidienne aux Indes* (59), *Regards sur le Pakistan* (58), *La Brûlure de mille soleils* (64), *Croquis bresiliens* (66) (TV).

DIR (features): *Un amour de poche* (57), *Le Bel âge* (59), *Merci, Natercia* (60), *La Morte – saison des amours** (60), *Vacances Portugaises/Les Sourires de la destinée* (63), *Le Grain de sable/Le Triangle circulaire* (64), *La Naissance de l'empire romain* (65) (TV), *Drôle de jeu* (68), *Le Drapeau blanc d'Oxala/Candomblé et Macumba* (69).

KAUFMAN, Boris Abramovich PHOTOG France/USA. (Bialystok, Poland 1906–) A great cameraman with a naturalistic, low-key style, indirectly trained by his brothers Dziga Vertov (*q.v.*) and Mikhail Kaufman (*q.v.*) and, more directly by his early work with Jean Lods (*q.v.*) and Jean Vigo (*q.v.*). He emigrated to France in 1927, to the USA in 1940, and worked on documentaries in Canada during the war. His work in the States is best characterized by his collaboration with Kazan and Lumet.

PHOTOG (notably): for Jean Lods, *Champs-Elysées* (28); for Jean Vigo, *A Propos de Nice** (30), *Taris* (31), *Zéro de conduite** (33), *L'Atalante** (34); for Willard van Dyke, *Journey into Medicine* (46), *Terribly Talented* (48); for Elia Kazan, *On the Waterfront** (54), *Baby Doll** (56), *Splendor in the Grass* (61); for F. Cook, *Patterns of Power* (56); for Sidney Lumet, *Twelve Angry Men** (57), *That Kind of Woman* (59), *The Fugitive Kind* (60), *Long Day's Journey into Night* (62), *The Pawnbroker** (63), *The Group* (66), *Bye Bye Braverman* (67); for George Roy Hill, *The World of Henry Orient* (64); for Jules Dassin, *Uptight* (68); for Preminger, *Tell Me That You Love Me Junie Moon* (69).

KAUFMAN, Mikhail Abramovich PHOTOG/DIR USSR. (Bialystok, Poland Sept 5, 1897–) Dziga Vertov's (*q.v.*) cameraman and close collaborator on *Kino-Eye*, *Kino-Pravda* (22–25), *A Sixth of the World** (26), *The Eleventh Year* (28), *Man with a Movie Camera** (29), etc., and a distinguished cameraman and documentary film maker in his own right. His *Moskva/Moscow* (27) was the first of a long line of films portraying a city from dawn to dusk, and *Vesnoy/Spring** (29) is an excellent lyrical documentary. Other documentaries include *The Great Victory* (33), *Air March* (36), *Our Moscow* (39), *Folk Dances of the USSR* (39), *The Tretyakov Gallery* (56).

KAUTNER, Helmut DIR German Federal Republic. (Düsseldorf Feb 25, 1908–) The best West German director, sensitive, intelligent and humanistic, despite the uneven quality of his work, which has varied from the brilliant to the mediocre (often because of his working conditions). He was an actor, then a scriptwriter, and finally a director in Nazi Germany, making his first major film, *Romanze in Moll*, in 1943. He has scripted most of his own films. According to Louis Marcorelles, his work, in a world full of intolerance, is "a message of purity and elegance; he is the last German romantic." In recent years he has confined his directing activities mainly to the stage and TV.

DIR: *Kitty und die Weltkonferenz* (39), *Kleider machen Leute* (40), *Frau nach Mass* (40), *Auf Wiedersehen, Franziska* (41), *Wir machen Musik* (42), *Anuschka* (42), *Romanze in Moll** (43), *Grosse Freiheit Nr. 7* (44), *Unter den Brücken* (45), *In Jegen Tagen** (47), *Der Apfel ist ab* (48), *Königskinder* (49) (remake), *Epilog* (50), *Weisse Schatten* (51), *Käpt'n Bay-Bay* (52), *Die Letzte Brücke** (54), *Bildis einer Unbekannten* (54), *Ludwig II* (55), *Des Teufels General** (55), *Himmel ohne Sterne* (55), *Ein Mädchen aus Flandern* (55), *Der Hauptmann von Köpenick* (56), *Die Zürcher Verlobung* (56), *Monpti* (56), *Der Schinderhannes* (58), *The Wonderful Years* (USA58), *Stranger in My Arms* (USA59), *Der Rest is Schweigen* (59), *Die Gans von Sedan* (59), *Das Glas Wasser* (60), *Schwarzer Kies* (60), *Der Traum von Lieschen Müller* (61), *Zu Jung für die Liebe* (61) (supervised only), *Die Rote* (62), *Das Haus in Montevideo* (63), *Lausbubengeschichten* (64).

KAWALEROWICZ, Jerzy DIR Poland. (Gwozdziec, Ukraine Jan 19, 1922–) An excellent director of the postwar Polish generation, he has a feeling for a romantic story and a sense of characterization, atmosphere, and precise detail. He became an assistant director and scriptwriter after his studies at Cracow after the war and directed his first film in 1950. "Each film I make reflects my current state of mind concerning life, art, people, and love. There are no more immutable truths in our often crazy world. I return constantly to the same motifs: the most intimate feelings that have only sometimes touched our awareness but whose importance has always pressed hard on the destiny of men."

DIR: *Gromada/The Village Mill/The Community* (50) (co-dir: K. Sumerski), *Celuloza/A Night of Remembrance** and *Pod Gwiazda Frygijiska/Under the Phrygian Star* (two part film) (54), *Cien/The Shadow* (56), *Prawdziwy koniec wielkiej wojny/The Real End of the Great War* (57), *Pociag/Night*

Train* (59), *Matka Joanna od Anio-low/Mother Joan of the Angels** (61), *Faraon/Pharaoh* (65), *Gra/The Game* (69).

KAZAN, Elia (Elia Kazanjoglou) DIR USA. (Istanbul Sept 7, 1909–) [A director whose films have been variously dismissed as "more excessive than expressive, more mannered than meaningful" (Andrew Sarris) and praised (most commonly by British critics) as intensely individual chronicles of the American way of life and of the life of Kazan himself.] His parents emigrated to the USA in 1913. He became an actor, then producer, with the Group Theater in the Thirties and has retained from his theatrical background a greater or lesser degree of grandiloquence in his imagery and in his direction of actors (many of whom have had an Actors Studio training). He acted in several films and made two documentaries before directing features, the first two of which were mediocre adaptations of novels. He turned to social themes; judicial error in *Boomerang!* (47), anti-Semitism in *Gentleman's Agreement* (47), blacks passing as white in *Pinky* (49). After 1950, and *Panic in the Streets*, panic seized him, and when faced with McCarthyism he preferred to yield. In 1952 he "named" his former friends (he had joined the Communist Party in 1934) to the House Un-American Activities Committee, placed an ad in the *New York Times* asking all "democrats" to denounce the "Reds," and "involved himself in depth in what he considered a kind of moral duty" (Marcorelles). In *Viva Zapata!* (52), he depicted the corruption of revolutionary leaders; he confirmed his political position with the portrait of criminal communism in *Man on a Tightrope* ("I don't blush for the film"); described unions as led by villains who had to be denounced in *On the Waterfront;* and showed the masses as stupidly following a charismatic personality in *A Face in the Crowd.* This second period is dominated by an academically functional, craftsmanlike style, inflated and pompous under an apparent sparseness and naturalism. His best film, *Baby Doll,* owes much to the author Tennessee Williams, another of whose plays he had earlier adapted in *A Streetcar Named Desire.* He gave James Dean his first major role in the impressive *East of Eden,* based on Steinbeck's novel. He went back to the stage for three years and returned to the cinema in 1960 with *Wild River,* a somewhat schematic portrait of the confrontation between progress and reaction in the Thirties, and *Splendor in the Grass.* [His films in the Sixties have become increasingly personal, more concerned with human motivations and obsessions in the social context of America. *America, America* and *The Arrangement* (both from his own novels) are partially autobiographical. The former portrays the odyssey of Kazan's uncle from the Old World to the New and is full of incisive characterizations; the latter, which shows a man breaking decisively with his former way of life, "an allegory of contemporary America . . . going through a terrible crisis," is hysterical in style, pretentious, and far less convincing than his original novel.]
DIR: *Pie in the Sky* (35) (an improvised film devised by Ralph Steiner, Kazan, Irving Lerner, etc.), *The People of the Cumberland* (37) (documentary), *It's Up to You* (41) (documentary feature), *A Tree Grows in Brooklyn* (45), *Sea of Grass* (47), *Boomerang!* (47), *Gentleman's Agreement** (47), *Pinky* (49), *Panic in the Streets* (50), *A Streetcar Named Desire** (52), *Viva Zapata!** (52), *Man on a Tightrope* (52), *On the Waterfront** (54), *East of Eden** (55), *Baby Doll** (56), *A Face in the Crowd** (57), *Wild River* (60), *Splendor in the Grass* (61), *America, America/The Anatolian Smile* (64), *The Arrangement* (69).

KEATON, Buster (Joseph Francis Keaton) DIR/SCEN USA. (Pickway, Kansas Oct 4, 1895–Hollywood Feb 1, 1966) This great comic genius, the only American comedian comparable to Chaplin, is also the true creator of all but his earliest and last films, since he always collaborated on their scripts and often on their direction. The following is a list of the main films (silent features complete) that exemplify his unique genius: *One Week** (20), *The Goat* (21), *The Boat* (21), *The Paleface* (21), *Cops** (22), *The Blacksmith* (22), *The Balloonatic* (23) (all shorts), *The Three Ages** (23), *Our Hospitality** (23), *Sherlock Junior** (24), *The Navigator** (24), *Seven Chances* (25), *Go West** (25), *Battling Butler* (26), *The General** (26), *College* (27), *Steamboat Bill, Jr.** (28), *The Cameraman** (28), *The Spite Mar-*

riage (29), *Free and Easy* (30), *Dough Boys* (30), *Parlor, Bedroom, and Bath* (31), *Sidewalks of New York* (31), *The Passionate Plumber* (32), *Le Roi des Champs-Élysées* (Fr34), *El Moderno Barba Azul* (Mex66), *Un Duel à mort* (Fr52), *Film* (USA65), *The Railrodder* (Canada65).

KEIGHLEY, William DIR USA. (Philadelphia Aug 4, 1889–) Prolific and mediocre Hollywood director (mostly for Warner Brothers) with a stage background who co-directed *Green Pastures** (36) with its real author, Marc Connelly (*q.v.*). [Also made, notably: *Bullets or Ballots* (36), *The Adventures of Robin Hood* (38) (exteriors only), *The Man Who Came to Dinner* (41), *Rocky Mountain* (50).]

KELBER, Michel PHOTOG France/Spain (Kiev April 9, 1908–) Trained by Marc Allégret (*q.v.*), he made his name mainly after the war with his superb images for Autant-Lara's *Le Diable au Corps** and was responsible for the delicate photography (in black and white or color) of Cocteau's *Ruy Blas* and *Les Parents terribles**, Renoir's *French Cancan**, Bardem's *Calle Mayor**, Nicholas Ray's *Amère Victoire**, Clair's *La Beauté du diable**.

KALETI, Marton DIR Hungary. (1905–) Prolific (over 40 films since 1937) director of popular features and musicals, including *Mickey Magnate* (49), *Singing Makes Life Beautiful* (50) and, most notably, *Tegnap/Yesterday* (59), a dramatic portrait of the Hungarian uprising of 1956.

***KENNEDY, Burt** SCEN/DIR USA. (Muskegon, Michigan 1923–) Budd Boetticher's (*q.v.*) favorite scriptwriter who was originally a radio writer. His first film as director (*The Canadians*) was a disaster and he worked in TV (*Combat* series) for three years before returning to the cinema with the personal and original *Mail Order Bride* (64). His westerns (in which he specializes) tend to use the traditional myths to bring out psychological tensions and characterizations, but are highly uneven, ranging from the intellectual complexities of *Welcome to Hard Times* to the routine *The War Wagon*.
SCEN (notably): for Boetticher, *Seven*

*Men from Now** (56), *The Tall T* (57), *Ride Lonesome* (59), *Comanche Station* (60); for Gordon Douglas, *Fort Dobbs* (58), *Yellowstone Kelly* (60); for Harry Keller, *Six Black Horses* (60), and for his own *The Canadians, Mail Order Bride, The Rounders, Welcome to Hard Times*.
DIR: *The Canadians* (61), *Mail Order Bride/West of Montana* (64), *The Rounders* (65), *The Money Trap* (65), *Return of the Seven* (66), *Welcome to Hard Times/Killer on a Horse* (67), *The War Wagon* (67), *Support Your Local Sheriff* (68), *The Good Guys and the Bad Guys* (68), *Young Billy Young* (69), *Dirty Dingus MaGee* (70), *The Deserter* (70), *Support Your Local Gunfighter* (70), *Hannie Calder* (71).

KERTESZ, Mihaly *see* CURTIZ, MICHAEL

KHACHATURIAN, Aram MUS USSR. (Tiflis May 6, 1904–) Famous Soviet composer who has also written several film scores, notably, for Romm's *Girl No. 217** (44) and Yutkevich's *Othello** (56).

KHAN, Ramjakhan Mehboob *see* MEHBOOB KHAN, RAMJAKHAN

KHODATEYEV, Nikolai (*also* N. Hodatyev) ANIM USSR. (1892–) Pioneer Soviet animator responsible for a curious cartoon in the futurist style, *Interplanetary Revolution* (24), and later for *Organchik/The Music Box* (33), a satire on militarism.

***KING, Henry** DIR USA. (Christiansburg, Virginia Jan 24, 1896?–) A Hollywood director who has tackled all subjects assigned to him, but in his feeling for images and for plot has sometimes been of comparable value to his contemporary, Raoul Walsh (*q.v.*). Originally a stage actor and producer, he began directing films for Pathé in 1916 and in 1918–19 came under the influence of Ince (*q.v.*), for whom he made several westerns. His masterpiece, *Tol'able David* (21), perhaps owes much to his southern background. His work in the Twenties is of special interest, notably for the warm sentiment of *The White Sister, Stella Dallas,* and *The Winning of Barbara Worth.* He was a director totally out of sympathy with modern themes and at his best with evocative, nostalgic American period films like *Alexander's Ragtime Band*, *Little Old New York*, *Wilson*, *Margie*, and *Wait Till the Sun Shines Nellie*, films that portrayed the period of his own younger days. However, his *Gunfighter*, with its pre-*High Noon* theme is a model of the genre.

DIR (notably, complete from 29) *Who Pays* (16), *23½ House Leave* (19), *A Sporting Chance* (19), *Help Wanted, Male* (20), *Tol'able David** (21), *The Bond Boy* (22), *Sonny* (22), *Fury* (23), *The White Sister* (23, in Italy), *Romola* (24, in Italy), *Stella Dallas** (25), *The Winning of Barbara Worth* (26), *The Magic Flame* (27), *She Goes to War* (29), *Hell's Harbor* (29), *Eyes of the World* (30), *Lightnin'* (30), *Merely Mary Ann* (31), *Over the Hill* (31), *The Woman in Room 13* (32), *State Fair* (33), *I Loved You Wednesday* (33), *Carolina* (34), *Marie Galante* (34), *Way Down East** (35) (remake), *One More Spring* (35), *Lloyd's of London* (36), *Ramona* (36), *The Country Doctor* (36), *Seventh Heaven* (37), *In Old Chicago* (37), *Alexander's Ragtime Band* (38), *Jesse James* (39), *Stanley and Livingstone* (39), *Little Old New York* (40), *Chad Hanna* (40), *Maryland* (40), *A Yank in the R.A.F.* (41), *Remember the Day* (41), *The Black Swan* (42), *The Song of Bernadette* (43), *Wilson* (44), *A Bell for Adano* (45), *Margie* (46), *Captain from Castile* (47), *Deep Waters* (48), *Prince of Foxes* (49), *Twelve O'Clock High* (49), *The Gunfighter* (50), *I'd Climb the Highest Mountain* (51), *David and Bathsheba* (51), *Wait Till the Sun Shines Nellie* (52), *The Snows of Kilimanjaro* (52), *O. Henry's Full House* (52) (one episode), *King of the Khyber Rifles* (53), *Untamed* (55), *Love is a Many Splendored Thing* (55), *Carousel* (56), *The Sun Also Rises* (57), *The Old Man and the Sea* (58) (completed by John Sturges), *The Bravados* (58), *This Earth is Mine* (59), *Beloved Infidel* (59), *Tender is the Night* (61).

KINOSHITA, Keisuke DIR Japan. (Hamamatsu Dec 5, 1912–) A film maker who established his reputation with lyrical comedy-satires (*The Blossoming Port, The Girl I Loved, Carmen Comes Home*) somewhat in the René Clair manner, he is one of the best Japanese directors to emerge from the war. He began his

career as assistant (36–43) to Yasujiro Shimazu at Toho and is totally dedicated to his work and the continual development of his style. He has worked equally with the neorealist approach of *Twenty-four Eyes* and the kabuki drama of *Ballad of the Narayama*. "In every picture I try to do something that hasn't been done before. I'm not like some directors who say: 'William Wyler tried it this way, so I'll have a go in the same manner.' Just because something has been done successfully by another doesn't interest me."

DIR (notably): *Hana Saku Minato/The Blossoming Port* (43), *Ikiteiru Magoroku/The Living Magoroku* (43), *Rikugun/Army* (44), *Kanko no Machi/ Jubilation Street* (44), *Osone-ke no Asa/A Morning with the Osone Family* (46), *Waga Koiseshi Otome/The Girl I Loved* (46), *Fujicho/Phoenix* (47), *Kekkon/Marriage* (47), *Hakai/Apostasy* (48), *Yabure Daiko/Broken Drum* (49), *O-josan Kampei/Here's to the Girls* (49), *Yotsuya Kaidan/The Yotsuya Ghost Story* (49) (3 parts), *Shonen-ki/ Youth* (50), *Zemma/Good Fairy* (51), *Karumen Kokyo ni Kaeru/Carmen Comes Home* (51), *Karumen Junjosu/ Carmen's Pure Love* (52), *Nihon no Higeki/A Japanese Tragedy** (53), *Onna no Sono/The Garden of Women* (54), *Nijushi no Hitomi/Twenty-four Eyes** (54), *Toi Kumo/Distant Clouds* (55), *Nogiku no Gotoki kimi Nariki/She Was a Wild Chrysanthemum* (55), *Taiyo to Bara/Sun and Rose* (56), *Yuyake Kumo/ Clouds at Twilight* (56), *Yorokobi mo Kanashimi mo Ikutoshitsuki/Times of Joy and Sorrow/The Lighthouse* (57), *Fuzen no Tomoshibi/Candle in the Wind/Danger Stalks Near* (57), *Narayama Bushi-ko/Ballad of the Narayama** (58), *Kono Ten no Niji/The Eternal Rainbow* (58), *Kazahana/Snow Flurry* (59), *Sekishun-cho* (59), *Eien no Hito/ The Bitter Spirit/Immortal Love* (61), *Fuefukigawa/The River Fuefuki* (61), *Kotoshi no Koi/New Year's Love* (62), *Futaride Aruita Iku-Shunju/Ballad of a Workman* (62), *Shito no Densetsu/A Legend . . . or Was It?* (63), *Koge/ The Scent of Incense* (66), *Natsukashiki Fue ya Taiko/Eyes, the Sea, and a Ball* (67).

KINUGASA, Teinosuke Kukame DIR Japan. (Mie Jan 1, 1896–) One of the artistic pioneers of the Japanese cinema, who,

137

with his contemporaries Mizoguchi (*q.v.*) and Tomu Uchida (*q.v.*), played a major role in the evolution of the cinema in the Far East, particularly during the silent period. From 1914 to 1922 he was an *oyama* actor (female impersonator) and in 1922 led a strike at the Nikkatsu Studios against the introduction of actresses in female roles. A firm believer in the cinema as an art form in its own right, he made his first film in 1922 and then joined the Japanese avantgarde with *A Crazy Page* (26), based on the theory of "neosensationalism." His *Crossroads* (28) is a work of great originality. Following its release, he left for a trip to Europe where he met Pudovkin (*q.v.*) and Eisenstein (*q.v.*). The influences of this visit were evident in his first film after his return, *Before the Dawn*, a film notable for its editing and for its polemic against feudalism. With *The 47 Ronin* he joined his friends Mizoguchi and Uchida in the "new realism" movement and its interest in ideological films. After the war he took part in the "democratization" of Japan, notably with *Lord for a Night* (46). Always interested in the stylistic possibilities of new technical developments, he made remarkable use of color in the award-winning *Gate of Hell* and of the split-screen in *The White Heron*. He has directed over 100 films, among which are many assigned productions.

DIR (notably): *Niwa no Kotori/Two Little Birds* (22), *Hibana* (22), *Koi/Love* (24), *Kiri no Ame/The Polownia Rains* (24), *Nichirin/The Sun* (25), *Kurutta Ippeiji/A Crazy Page** (26), *The Palanquin* (27), *Jujiro/Crossroads/ Shadows of Yoshiwara** (28), *Reimei Izen/Before Dawn** (31), *Genroku Chushingura/The 47 Ronin** (32), *Ikinokotta Shinsengumi/The Surviving Shinsengumi* (32), *Koina no Kimpei/ Kimpei from Koina* (33), *Futatsu Doro/ Two Stone Lanterns* (33), *Ippon Gatana Dohyoirii* (34), *Yukinojo Henge* (35) (3 parts), *Osaka Natsu no Jin/The Summer Battle of Osaka* (37), *Hebihimesama/The Serpent Princess* (38), *The Battle of Kanakajima* (41), *Susume Dokuritsu-ki/Forward, Flag of Independence* (43), *Aru Yo no Tono-sama/Lord for a Night* (46), *Joyu/Actress* (47), *Nichirin/The Sun* (50) (remake), *Daibutsu Kaigen/Dedication of the Great Buddha* (52), *Jigokumon/Gate of Hell** (53), *Shinkin Stones* (54), *Naruto Hicho/*

Naruto Fantasy (57), *Harukoro no Hana no En/Symphony of Love/Spring Bouquet* (58), *Shirasagi/The White Heron* (58), *Joen/The Affair/Tormented Flame* (59), *Kagero Ezu/Stop the Old Fox* (59), *Uta-Andon/The Lantern* (60), *Midaregami/Disheveled Hair* (60), *Okoto to Sasuke/Okoto and Sasuke* (61), *Uso/When Women Lie* (63) (one episode), *Yoso/The Bonze Magician* (63), *Chiisana Tobosha/The Little Runaway* (Jap/USSR67).

KIRCHER, Athanasius INVENTOR Italy. (Germany May 12, 1601–Rome Nov 28, 1680) A Jesuit priest who was the first to describe – if not to invent – the magic lantern in his book "Ars magnae lucis et umbrae" in 1646.

KIRSANOFF, Dimitri DIR France. (Dorpat, Russia March 6, 1899–Paris Feb 11, 1957) Russian emigré film maker whose remarkable *Ménilmontant** (26) was a precursor of French poetic realism and of Italian neo-realism. He continued his experiments for some years notably in *Brumes d'automnes* (28) and in the use of contrapuntal sound in *Rapt* (34), but eventually had to resign himself to working on commercial films and sponsored documentaries.

*KLINE, Herbert DIR USA, etc. (1909–) Former left-wing magazine editor in the Thirties who became involved in film-making through the Spanish Civil War. He photographed *Heart of Spain* and *Return to Life* for Frontier Films and in 1938–39 made two notable documentaries on the Fascist threat, *Crisis* and *Lights Out in Europe*. In Mexico he made the remarkable *The Forgotten Village* (41) from John Steinbeck's script and in Israel *My Father's House* (47), a dramatization of the Jewish struggle for nationhood. The first three of these were photographed by Czech-born Alexander Hackenschmied (Hammid) the last by Floyd Crosbie.

*KLOS, Elmar DIR/PROD Czechoslovakia. (Brno Jan 26, 1910–) Film maker who since 1952 has always worked in collaboration with Jan Kadar (*q.v.*). Before the war he founded the film studio run by the Bata shoe company in Zlin (Gottwaldov) and after the war worked in various administrative posts – including heading the Short Film

Studios (Kratky Film) — before joining Kadar.

KOBAYASHI, Ichizo PROD Japan. (Kofu Jan 3, 1873–Tokyo 1960?) Picturesque Japanese industrialist who founded the famous Toho production and distribution company. He made a fortune in real estate along his Osaka-Kobe railroad (part of the Mitsui Trust) by creating and developing the town of Takarazuka, a gigantic amusement park, and an all-girl "opera" troupe of the same name. In 1932 he organized the Tokyo Takarazuka Theater Corporation and began acquiring or building theaters for his troupes. In 1935 he gained control of P.C.L. Studios and the J.O. Company as well as a newsreel company and a year later formed the Toho Motion Picture Distributing Company to release films produced by the two studios he controlled. He became a minister in the second Konoye cabinet in 1940 and during the war contributed to the establishment of a super cinema trust dominated by Toho. After the war the American occupation authorities forced him to relinquish his interest in Toho, which came under the control of the unions. A series of strikes and labor problems led to Toho's financial collapse and, eventually, to court control and police and army intervention. Kobayashi became president of Toho again in 1951 and again tried to gain major control of the industry. He retired in 1955 but remained honorary president.

KOBAYASHI, Masaki DIR Japan. (Hokkaido Feb 4, 1916–) [One of the best of the postwar generation of film makers whose work has steadily increased in stature during the Sixties, e.g., *Harakiri*, *Kwaidan* and *Rebellion*.] He began as assistant to Kinoshita (*q.v.*) at the Shochiku studios and made his first films in the Fifties as one of the independent group of directors. From 1959–61 he directed his first major work, the eight-hour long trilogy of the horrors of war *Ningen no Joken*.
DIR: *Musuko no Seishun/My Son's Youth* (52), *Magokoro/Sincerity* (53), *Kabe Atsuki Heya/The Room with Thick Walls* (53, released 56), *Kono Hiroi Sora no Dotokani/Somewhere under the Broad Sky* (54), *Uruwashiki Saigetsu/ Beautiful Days* (55), *Izumi/The Fountainhead* (56), *Anata Kaimasu/I'll Buy You* (56), *Kuroi Kawa/Black River* (57), *Ningen no Joken/The Human Condition* (trilogy)* (*No Greater Love, Road to Eternity, A Soldier's Prayer*) (58–61), *Karami-ai/The Inheritance* (62), *Seppuku/Harakiri** (62), *Kaidan/ Kwaidan* (64), *Joi-uchi/Rebellion* (67), *Nippon no Seishun/Hymn to a Tired Man/The Youth of Japan* (68), *Inochi Bonifuro/At the Risk of My life* (70).

KONDOUROS, Nikos *see* KOUNDOUROUS, NIKOS

KONWICKI, Tadeusz DIR/SCEN Poland. (Lithuania 1926–) Prominent Polish author who worked as a film critic, then as a scriptwriter (e.g., Kawalerowicz's *Mother Joan of the Angels** and *Pharaoh*), and has written and directed the highly personal *Ostatni dzien lata/ The Last Day of Summer* (58) (co-dir: Laskowski), *Zaduszki/Halloween* (61), and *Salto* (65), films somewhat reminiscent of Antonioni (*q.v.*) and haunted by an emotional feeling of war.

KOPALIN, Ilya Petrovich DIR USSR. (Moscow Aug 2, 1900–) Veteran documentary film maker who collaborated with Dziga Vertov (*q.v.*) as one of the "kinoks" after 1924 and made his first independent film in 1927. He developed into a highly esteemed documentarist in the USSR. During the war he was leader of a camera group and made various documentary features with Varlamov.
DIR (notably): *The Berlin Conference* (45), *Liberated Czechoslovakia* (46), *The Day of the Victorious Country* (47) (co-dir: Setkino), *Transformation of the Land* (50), *The Glorious Road* (Albania51) (co-dir: Kekko), *Albania* (52) (co-dir: Schtichin), *The Unforgettable Years* (57), *City of Great Destiny* (60), *First Trip to the Stars* (61), *Pages of Immortality* (65).

KORDA, (Sir) Alexander (in Hungary, Sandor Korda; in Germany/Austria, Alexander Corda) DIR/PROD Hungary/Germany/ Austria/USA/France/Britain. (Turkeye, Hungary Sept 16, 1893–London Jan 13, 1956) Unarguably a major producer who exerted enormous influence on the development of the British film industry. After a long international career as a director (Hungary 16–19, Germany/ Austria 20–27, USA 27–30, France 30– 31) he settled in Britain, formed Lon-

139

don Films, and established his position with the successful *The Private Life of Henry VIII* (33). He built Denham Studios and made numerous cosmopolitan, lush, costume dramas (largely derivative of the Hollywood style) of which many were international commercial successes. He maintained complete control over his films, supervising them at each stage of production in the Ince (*q.v.*) manner. He brought many important directors from around the world (Feyder, Clair, Flaherty, etc.) to work for him but they ended up being buried under his ostentatious approach. Though he is not a great artist, his influence and his development of a commercial basis for the British film industry have earned him a place in film history.

DIR (notably): *Feher ejszakak/White Night* (Hung16), *Aranyember* (Hung 18), *Mary Ann* (Hung19), *Feher Rozsa/White Rose* (Hung20), *Seine majestät das Bettelkin* (Aust20), *Samson und Delilah* (Aust22), *Jedermanns Weib* (Ger24), *Der Tänzer meiner Frau* (Ger25), *Madame wünscht keine Kinder* (Ger26), *Stolen Bride* (USA27), *The Private Life of Helen of Troy* (USA27), *Yellow Lily* (USA28), *Night Watch* (USA28), *Love and the Devil* (USA29), *Lilies of the Field* (USA30), *Women Everywhere* (USA30), *The Princess and the Plumber* (USA30), *Rive gauche* (Fr 31), *Marius** (Fr 31), *Service for Ladies* (Brit31), *The Wedding Rehearsal* (Brit 32), *The Private Life of Henry VIII** (Brit33), *The Private Life of Don Juan* (Brit34), *Rembrandt* (Brit36), *Conquest of the Air* (Brit40), *That Hamilton Woman* (Brit41), *The Perfect Stranger* (Brit45), *An Ideal Husband* (Brit48). PROD (notably): *Men of Tomorrow* (33) (dir: Leontine Sagan), *Catherine The Great* (34) (dir: P. Czinner), *The Scarlet Pimpernel* (35) (dir: Harold Young), *The Ghost Goes West** (36) (dir: René Clair), *Things to Come* (36) (dir: William Cameron Menzies), *Knight without Armour* (37) (dir: J. Feyder), *The Four Feathers* (39) (dir: Zoltan Korda), *The Lion Has Wings* (39) (dir: Michael Powell and others), *The Thief of Bagdad* (40) (dir: Ludwig Berger, Michael Powell, Tim Whelan), *Lydia* (40) (dir: Duvivier), *To Be or Not to Be** (42) (dir: Lubitsch), *Anna Karenina* (48) (dir: Duvivier), *The Fallen Idol** (48) (dir: Carol Reed), *The Third Man** (49) (dir: C. Reed),

The Deep Blue Sea (55) (dir: Litvak), *Richard III* (56) (dir: Olivier).

KORDA, Vincent (Vincze Korda) ART DIR Britain/USA. (Turkeye, Hungary 1896–) A talented designer who collaborated often with his brothers Alexander and Zoltan and was best at creating sets and effects for spectaculars, e.g., *The Private Life of Henry VIII**, *Things to Come*, *Sanders of the River*, *The Four Feathers*, *The Thief of Bagdad*. Also designed, notably: *The Ghost Goes West**, *To Be or Not to Be**, *The Fallen Idol**.

KORDA, Zoltan DIR Britain/USA. (Turkeye, Hungary May 3, 1895–Hollywood 1961) The younger brother of Alexander (with whom he worked in several countries before settling in Britain in 1933) who directed several fairly good films and various spectaculars. He was in Hollywood from 1940–48. DIR (notably): *Cash* (32), *Sanders of the River* (35), *The Elephant Boy* (37) (interiors only, co-dir: Flaherty), *The Drum* (38), *The Four Feathers* (39), *The Jungle Book* (USA42), *Sahara* (USA43), *Counterattack* (43), *The Macomber Affair* (USA47), *A Woman's Vengeance* (USA47), *Cry the Beloved Country!/African Fury* (52), *Storm over the Nile* (55) (co-dir).

KOSMA, Joseph MUS France. (Budapest Oct 22, 1905–) Individualistic composer with an undeniable talent and a real feeling for popular music. He emigrated from Hungary to France in 1933 and has written there several memorable scores, notably for Renoir (*q.v.*) and Carné (*q.v.*); his style matched perfectly the poetry of Prévert (*q.v.*). He is also a composer of *chansons*. MUS (notably): for Renoir: *Le Crime de Monsieur Lange** (36) (with Jean Wiener), *Une Partie de campagne** (36), *La Grande Illusion** (37), *La Marseillaise** (38), *La Bête humaine** (38), *La Règle du jeu** (39) (arranged only), *Eléna et les hommes* (56), *Le Testament du docteur Cordelier* (56), *Le Déjeuner sur l'herbe* (59), *Le Caporal épingle* (62); for Carné, *Jenny* (36), *Les Visiteurs du soir** (42), *Les Enfants du Paradis** (45), *Les Portes de la nuit** (46), *La Marie du port* (50), *Juliette* (51); for Prévert, *Adieu Leonard* (43), *Voyage surprise** (46); for André Ca-

140

yatte, *Les Amants de Vérone* (48); for Franju, *Le Sang des bêtes** (49); for Le Chanois, *L'Ecole buissionière** (49), *Sans laisser d'adresse** (50), *Agence matrimoniale* (52); for Grimault, *La Bèrgere et le Ramoneur** (52); for Bardem, *Calle Mayor** (56); for J. Audry, *Huis clos* (54); for Buñuel, *Cela s'appelle l'aurore** (56); for Henri Decoin, *La Chatte* (58); for Marcel Hanoun, *Le Huitème jour* (59); for Jacques Baratier, *La Poupée* (62); for Robert Parrish, *In the French Style* (64).

KOSTER, Henry (Hermann Kosterlitz) DIR Germany/USA. (Berlin April 1, 1905–) Hollywood director of largely uninteresting comedies and costume dramas who began his career (under his own name) as a scriptwriter in Germany for UFA and became a director for the German branch of Universal (two films) in 1932. He moved in the mid-Thirties to Hollywood where he directed some lively prewar films, notably *Three Smart Girls* (36) with the young Deanna Durbin. In 1953 he was given the opportunity to make the first Cinema-Scope film, *The Robe**.

KOUNDOUROS, Nikos DIR Greece. (Crete 1926–) One of the best contemporary Greek directors, a sincere film maker with a fiery, direct style, portraying his characters as part of a disordered, chaotic world. He has expressed the soul of his people better than any other, most notably in *I Mayiki Polis/Magic City* (55), *O Dracos** (56), *I Paranomi/The Lawless* (58), *To Potami/ The River* (60), *Mikres Aphrodites/ Young Aphrodites** (62).

KOZINTSEV, Grigori DIR USSR. (Kiev 1905–) One of the greatest Soviet film makers, a director whose films with Trauberg (*q.v.*) in the Twenties and Thirties, though little known outside the USSR, stand far above most contemporaneous films. He studied at the Academy of Fine Arts and in 1922 (at the age of 17) founded, with Trauberg, the Factory of the Eccentric Actor (FEKS), a futurist theatrical movement to which Kapler, Yutkevich (*q.v.*), and, briefly, Eisenstein (*q.v.*) all belonged. FEKS believed in excess and incorporated into their work elements of the circus, cabaret, the music halls, and adventure films. Their 1922 staging of Gogol's *Marriage* in this manner brought them instant notoriety. Their first film, *The Adventures of Octyabrina* (24), was an experimental short delightfully parodying the typical elements of the adventure film. Their version of Gogol's *The Cloak* was much influenced by expressionism. They came close to creating a masterpiece with *New Babylon*, a film whose original visual design was intimately bound with a strongly felt emotion. They reached the peak of their art in the sound period with *Alone* and especially with the vast modern epic, the *Maxim* trilogy, a perfect example of socialist realism at its best. The characters they portrayed in these films, closely tied to Russian revolutionary history, evolved with the years, their experiences and the course of history. However, even *Maxim* retains elements from their FEKS background. The war interrupted their work and brought their collaboration to an end. Kozintsev worked as a stage director for some years (he is an expert on Shakespeare) before returning to the cinema in 1957 with his intelligent, sensitive, and somewhat melancholy adaptation of *Don Quixote*. His two recent Shakespeare adaptations have again brought him international pre-eminence. CO-DIR (with Trauberg): *Pokhozdeniya Octyabrini/The Adventures of Octyabrina** (24), *Chyortovo koleso/The Devil's Wheel* (26), *Shinel/The Cloak** (26), *Bratishka* (27), *S.V.D./The Club of the Big Deed** (27), *Novyi Vavilon/ The New Babylon** (29), *Odna/Alone** (31), *Yunost Maksima/The Youth of Maxim** (35), *Vozvrashcheniye Maksima/The Return of Maxim** (37), *Vyborgskaya storona/The Vyborg Side** (39), *Prostiye lyudi/Plain People/Ordinary People* (45, released 56). DIR: *Fighting Film Album No. 2* (41) (short), *Pirogov* (47), *Belinskii/Belinsky* (47), *Don Quixote** (57), *Gamlet/Hamlet** (64), *Karoli Lir/King Lear* (70).

KRAHLY, Hanns (also Hans Kraly) SCEN Germany/USA. (Germany 1885–Los Angeles Nov 11, 1950) Ernst Lubitsch's (*q.v.*) usual scriptwriter, both in Germany and in Hollywood, where he went with Lubitsch and where he continued to make a major contribution to his work based on the theatrical traditions of central Europe. In Hollywood he also wrote scripts, but less successfully, for

Henry Koster, Lewis Milestone, and William Wyler (all q.v.).

KRAMER, Stanley PROD/DIR USA. (New York Sept 29, 1913–) Courageous and intelligent producer/director whose principal aim has been to use the cinema as a means of "communicating a message to the conscience of humanity." He has always worked closely with the directors and writers of his films and is considered by some as the principal author of many excellent films directed by Zinnemann, Benedek, and Robson (all q.v.) As a director himself he has many successes (such as *Judgment at Nuremberg*) to his credit. He was one of the defenders of liberalism under the McCarthy era and later directed several polemical message films — against intolerance in *Inherit the Wind*, racism in *The Defiant Ones,* the peril of atomic war in *On the Beach,* and Nazism in *Judgment at Nuremberg.*
PROD (notably): Robson's *The Champion* (49), *Home of the Brave* (49); Zinnemann's *The Men** (50), *High Noon** (52), *Member of the Wedding* (52); Michael Gordon's *Cyrano de Bergerac* (50); Dmytryk's *The Sniper* (52); *The Caine Mutiny* (54); Benedek's *Death of a Salesman** (51), *The Wild One** (54), Hubert Cornfield's *Pressure Point* (62); John Cassavetes' *A Child is Waiting* (62); Richard Wilson's *Invitation to a Gunfighter* (64); and his own films.
DIR: *Not as a Stranger* (55), *The Pride and the Passion* (57), *The Defiant Ones** (58), *On the Beach* (59), *Inherit the Wind* (60), *Judgment at Nuremberg* (61), *It's a Mad, Mad, Mad, Mad World* (63), *Ship of Fools* (65), *Guess Who's Coming to Dinner* (67), *The Secret of Santa Vittoria* (69), *Bless the Beasts and Children* (71).

KRASKER, Robert PHOTOG Britain/USA/Italy. (Australia Aug 21, 1913–) One of the great cameramen, a master of color photography (and the first to use it artistically in Britain) [who began his training in France and has worked mainly in Britain and occasionally in Europe, usually on American films. He was assistant to Georges Périnal (q.v). His evocative photography in *The Third Man* is unforgettable.]
PHOTOG (notably): for Brian Desmond Hurst, *Dangerous Moonlight* (40); for Lawrence Olivier, *Henry V** (44); for David Lean, *Brief Encounter** (46); for Gabriel Pascal, *Caesar and Cleopatra** (45); for Carol Reed, *Odd Man Out** (47), *The Third Man** (49), *Trapeze* (56), *The Running Man* (63); for Zoltan Korda, *Cry the Beloved Country* (52); for Visconti, *Senso** (52) (cophotog: G. R. Aldo); for Castellani, *Romeo and Juliet* (53); for Rossen, *Alexander the Great* (55); for John Ford, *The Quiet American** (58); for Losey, *The Criminal** (60); for Ustinov, *Romanoff and Juliet* (61), *Billy Budd* (62); for Anthony Mann, *El Cid** (61), *The Fall of the Roman Empire* (63), *The Heroes of Telemark* (65); for Asquith, *Guns of Darkness* (62); for Wyler, *The Collector* (65).

KRUGER, Jules PHOTOG France/Spain/Britain. (Strasbourg July 12, 1891–) Excellent cameraman during the Thirties, with a feeling for atmosphere and a sense of the picturesque but somewhat addicted to oblique shots. He worked with Gance on *Napoléon* and *La Fin du monde* and his talents matched well those of Raymond Bernard (q.v.) in *Les Croix de bois** (32), *Les Misérables** (34), and those of Duvivier (q.v.) in *La Bandera** (35), *La Belle Equipe* (36), *Pépé le Moko** (37), *La Charette fantôme/The Phantom Chariot** (39), *Untel père et fils* (40). Also for Decoin, *Les Inconnus dans la maison* (42).

KUBRICK, Stanley DIR USA. (New York July 26, 1928–) A film maker who must be included among the best of his generation. He began as a journalist and his first film-making experience was on short documentaries and low-budget features. He established his reputation as a film maker with a harsh, bold, and often brutal style in *The Killing* (56) — which retained (from the documentaries) his feeling for exact observation — and followed this with the best of his early films, *Paths of Glory* (58), a film about French soldiers executed "in error" during the First World War. *Spartacus* is less his film than that of its producerstar Kirk Douglas, and his version of *Lolita* is extremely open to criticism. It is a pity he did not observe his own earlier rule: "I am resolutely opposed to the adaptation of good novels." However he was happier with the black comedy about atomic war, *Dr. Strangelove.* [With the ambitious *2001: A Space Odyssey,* a metaphysical epic that relinquished traditional visual forms and structures, he reached the peak of his art to date.] DIR: *Day of the Fight* (49) (documentary), *Fear and Desire* (53) (also scen and photog), *Killer's Kiss* (55) (also scen and photog), *The Killing* (56) (also scen), *Paths of Glory** (58), *Spartacus* (60), *Lolita* (62), *Dr. Strangelove or How I Learned to Stop Worrying and Love the Bomb** (Brit63), *2001: A Space Odyssey** (Brit68).

KULESHOV, Lev DIR USSR. (Tambov Jan 1, 1899–Moscow March 29, 1970) The founder of the Soviet cinema together with his opponent, Dziga Vertov (*q.v.*), and, like Vertov, both film maker and theoretician who, since he was twenty, propounded the theory that editing was the principal means of cinematic expression. He began his career in 1916 as a set designer for Yevgeni Bauer (*q.v.*) and in 1917 completed *After Happiness* after Bauer's death and then went on to direct his own first films. During the Civil War he was one of several film makers penetrating the combat zones in agit-trains in order to prepare polemical documentary films. Kuleshov's work culminated in *On the Red Front* (20), a two-reel short combining actuality and acted scenes. Since 1917 he had been interested in theoretical aspects of the cinema and in 1919 was active in organizing the first State Film School, the directors of which had little confidence in the bustling twenty-year-old film maker. He gathered around him a group of "bad pupils" like Pudovkin (*q.v.*), Khokhlova, Leonid Obolensky, Boris Barnet (*q.v.*), and Valeri Inkizhinov and in 1920 established the Kuleshov Workshop where he and his students experimented actively with the possibilities of editing. Ivan Mozhukhin's expressionless face was intercut with various shots (Pudovkin says they were a bowl of soup, a woman in a coffin, and a child with a toy bear) to create the famous "Kuleshov effect" in which an audience marveled at the actor's apparently sensitive performance. He developed "artificial landscape" or "creative geography" by intercutting shots of streets in different cities. He "synthesized" a woman filmically by combining shots of parts of different women. Because of the shortage of film stock, the students created "films without celluloid" in which everything was staged and directed exactly as if it were before a camera and in which "models" were used as actors — that is to say actors trained for the cinema and not for the theater. With his stock company, Kuleshov directed two detective-story satires, *The Extraordinary Adventures of Mr. West in the Land of the Bolsheviks,* and *The Death Ray,* both full of sophisticated cinematic effects. His team was disbanded after 1925, but Pudovkin and Barnet, notably, had drawn much from his teachings. In 1926 he made one of his two best films, *By the Law,* an intense tragedy based on the Jack London story, *The Unexpected.* It was poorly received by Soviet critics and his next three silent films were all failures. He made only one other film of note, *The Great Consoler* (33). [Starting in 1925 he had come under increasing ideological attacks and at the 1935 Congress of Film Workers was denounced and forced to confess to "formalistic" errors, to preferring form over content. He continued writing and in 1944 was appointed head of the Film Institute (VGIK), where he continued to lecture almost until his death. None of his later films is of particular merit. Regrettably, none of his several theoretical works from *Art of the Cinema* (29) to *Fundamentals of Film Direction* (41) have to date been published in English.] DIR: *After Happiness* (17) (completed after Bauer), *Proyekt inzhenera Praita/Engineer Prite's Project* (18), *Na krasnom fronte/On the Red Front* (20), *Neobychainiye priklucheniya Mistera Vesta v stranye bolshevikov/The Extraordinary Adventures of Mr. West in the Land of the Bolsheviks** (24), *Luch smerti/The Death Ray* (25), *Po zakonu/By the Law/Dura Lex** (26), *Vasha znakomaya/The Journalist/Your Acquaintance* (27), *The Gay Canary* (29), *Dva, Bouldej, dva/The Great Buldis* (30), *Electrification* (30) (documentary), *Horizon* (32), *Velikii uteshitel/The Great Consoler* (33), *The Siberians* (40), *Incident on a Volcano* (41) (co-dir: Khokhlova), *Timur's Oath* (42).

KULIDJANOV, Lev DIR USSR. (Tiflis March 19, 1924–) Good representative of the new Soviet generation with an individualistic, realistic, and sensitive style. DIR: *Damy/Ladies* (54) (co-dir: Oganisyan), *Eto nachinados tak . . . /It*

Started Like This (56) (co-dir: Y. Se-
gel), *Dom v kotorom ya zhivu/The
House I Live In* (57) (co-dir: Y. Segel),
Otchii dom/Our Father's House (59),
*Kogda derevya byli bolshimi/When the
Trees Grow Tall* (61), *Sinaya tetrad/
The Blue Notebook* (63), *Poteryannaya
fotografiya/The Lost Photograph* (67),
*Prestuplenie i nakazanie/Crime and Pun-
ishment* (69).

KUROSAWA, Akira DIR Japan. (Tokyo
March 23, 1910–) One of the greatest
contemporary directors, a film maker
of the postwar Japanese generation with
concerns different from those of his
elders Mizoguchi, Kinoshita, and Ozu
(all *q.v.*). He is above all a humanist
who has used his visual sensitivity, sense
of characterization, ability to direct actors, technical gifts for staging, and
vigorous editing to further his ideals.
Violence and furious battles may often
play a role in his films, but only as an
expression of his anger and revulsion
at social injustices of the past and
present. [He originally studied to be a
painter but relinquished this goal to
join P.C.L. (later Toho) as an assistant
director. He was partially responsible
for Kajiro Yamamoto's *The Horse* (41),
wrote several scripts, and directed his
first film in 1943.] Though he made several notable films in the Forties, he
established an immediate reputation in
the West when his *Rashomon* (50) won
first prize at Venice in 1951 and revealed to Europe the existence of a
totally unknown film industry. In this
connection he said: "When I received the
major award at Venice in 1951, I re-
marked that I would have been happier,
and the award would have had more
significance for me, if the festival had
given a prize to one of my works that
had depicted something of modern life
in Japan, as *Bicycle Thieves* had depicted Italy. In 1959 I still thought the
same, because Japan has produced some
modern films as good as that of De Sica
(*q.v.*) while continuing to produce historical films, excellent or not." For Toho
(then run by the film workers' unions)
after the war he made a series of films
portraying a modern Japan shattered by
bombings and defeat: *Drunken Angel,
The Silent Duel,* and especially, *Stray
Dog.* In these films he continued the

traditions of the "tendency" film of the
"new realism" of the mid-Thirties.
Rashomon, an attack on the samurai
tradition, was intended as a parenthesis
in this modern tableau, which he later
continued in his exceptional *Ikiru.* Then
came *The Idiot* and *I Live in Fear* —
films that are far better than the famous
Seven Samurai, but they in turn are not
better than his adaptation of Macbeth,
The Throne of Blood/Cobweb Castle.
[After several lightweight, but, as always,
technically accomplished samurai epics,
he returned to more contemporary
themes with the humanistic and unsentimental *Red Beard* and *Dodeskaden.*]
DIR: *Sanshiro Sugata/Judo Saga/The
Legend of Judo* (43), *Ichiban Utsuku-
shiku/Most Beautifully* (44), *Sanshiro
Sugata (Zoku)/Judo Saga (Sequel)*
(45), *Tora no O o Fumo Otoko Tachi/
The Men Who Tread on the Tiger's Tail/
Walkers on the Tiger's Tail* (45), *Asu o
Tsukuru Hitobito/Those Who Make To-
morrow* (46) (co-dir: K. Yamamoto,
H. Sekigawa), *Waga Seishun ni Koinashi
/No Regrets for Our Youth* (46), *Su-
barshiki Nichiyobi/Wonderful Sunday*
(47), *Yoidore Tenshi/Drunken Angel*
(48), *Shizuka Naru Ketto/The Silent
Duel* (48), *Nora Inu/Stray Dog** (49),
Shibun/Scandal (50), *Rashomon** (50),
Hakuchi/The Idiot* (51), *Ikiru/Living/
To Live** (52), *Shichi-nin no Samurai/
The Seven Samurai** (54), *Ikimono no
Kiroku/I Live in Fear** (55), *Kumonosu-
jo/Throne of Blood/Cobweb Castle**
(57), *Donzoko/The Lower Depths**
(57), *Kakushi Toride no San-Akunin/
The Hidden Fortress* (58), *Warui Yatsu
Hodo Yoko Nemuru/The Bad Sleep
Well* (60), *Yojimbo/The Bodyguard*
(61), *Tsubaki Sanjuro/Sanjuro* (62),
Tengoku to Jigoku/High and Low (63),
Aka Hige/Red Beard* (65), *Dodeskaden*
(70).

KUSHAN, Esmail PROD Iran. (? –) In
the late Forties he produced a dubbed
Persian version of *Premier rendez-vous*
with Danielle Darrieux and with the
profits built a film studio in Teheran,
produced *Tufane zendegi/The Tempest
of Life* and *Sharmsar/The Shame-
Stricken Man,* and laid the foundations
for a commercial development of the
Iranian film industry in the Fifties.

LA CAVA, Gregory DIR USA. (Towanda March 10, 1892–Malibu Beach, California May 1, 1949) Former cartoonist, animator, and director of Mack Sennett shorts who had a reputation as a director of delicate comedies in the Thirties, notably the excellent *My Man Godfrey* (36) with Carole Lombard and William Powell, and the curious satire, *Gabriel Over the White House* (33).

LACOMBE, Georges DIR France. (Paris Aug 19, 1902–) He began his career with a remarkable documentary, *La Zone** (27), encouraged the careers of Gérard Philipe in *Le Pays sans étoiles* (46), of Brigitte Bardot in *La Lumière d'en face* (56), and of Clouzot (*q.v.*) as a scriptwriter on *Le Dernier des six* (41). However, despite the undeniable qualities of *Jeunesse* (34), he was never able to raise himself above the craftmanship level.

Ernst ?

LAEMMLE, Carl PROD USA. (Laupheim, Germany Jan 7, 1867–Hollywood Sept 24, 1939) A typical example of the group of immigrants who established Hollywood as the movie capital. After working in various professions, he created the famous Nickelodeons in 1906, became a producer, and founded Universal Pictures in 1912. Though he was always a businessman, he contributed to the artistic development of the cinema, never lost his film intuition, and promoted Stroheim's (*q.v.*) career. [His son, Carl Laemmle, Jr. (April 28, 1908–), was an imaginative producer with Universal (*All Quiet on the Western Front**, *Frankenstein**, *Little Man, What Now?**, *The Bride of Frankenstein*) and later an executive producer with Universal for many years.]

LAINE, Edwin DIR Finland. (Iisalmi July 13, 1905–) Good Finnish director who began as an actor and is best known outside Finland for *Tuntematon Sotilas/The Unknown Soldier** (55).

LAKHDAR AMINA, Mohamed DIR Algeria (Msila Feb 26, 1934–) A contributor to the development of the Algerian cinema during the war of independence by directing (with Jamal Chanderli) two dramatized documentaries, *Yasmina* (61) and *Les Fusils de la liberté* (62).

LAMORISSE, Albert DIR France. (Paris Jan 13, 1922–June 1970) A specialist in documentary-type poetic fantasies who achieved international recognition and commercial success with *Crin blanc* and *The Red Balloon*. During the latter part of his career he developed an interest in exploring the visual possibilities of filming from helicopters.
DIR (notably): *Djerba* (47) (short), *Bim, le petit âne* (49), *Crin blanc, cheval sauvage** (53), *Le Ballon rouge** (56), *Le Voyage en ballon/Stowaway in the Sky* (60), *Fifi la plume* (64), *Versailles* (66) (short), *Paris jamais vu/Paris Rediscovered* (68).

LAMPRECHT, Gerhard DIR Germany/German Federal Republic (Berlin Oct 6, 1897–) A completely professional director, passionately devoted to the cinema, and an important historian on the early German cinema who has made only one really successful film in his long career: *Emil and the Detectives.* DIR (notably): *Der Friedhof der Lebenden* (21), *Die Buddenbrooks,* (23), *Die Unehelichen* (26), *Untere der Laterne* (28), *Emil und die Detektive** (31), *Prinzessin Turandot* (34), *Madame*

145

Bovary (37), *Clarissa* (41), *Kamerad Hedwig* (45), *Irgendwo in Berlin* (46), *Oberwachtmeister Borck* (55).

*LANG, Charles, Jr. *Photog* USA. (1902–) One of the great Hollywood cameramen, with a fine sense of atmospheric lighting of interiors and a fully professional control of color tones.
PHOTOG (notably): for Frank Borzage, *A Farewell to Arms* (32), *Desire* (36); for Hathaway, *Lives of a Bengal Lancer* (35), *Peter Ibbetson** (35); for Lubitsch, *Angel* (37); for Fritz Lang, *You and Me* (38), *The Big Heat* (53); for Cukor, *Zaza* (38), *It Should Happen to You* (53), *Wild is the Wind* (57); for Billy Wilder, *A Foreign Affair* (48), *Ace in the Hole/The Big Carnival** (51), *Sabrina* (54), *Some Like It Hot** (59); for David Miller, *Sudden Fear* (52); for Joseph Pevney, *Female on the Beach* (55); for Anthony Mann, *The Man from Laramie* (55); for Aldrich, *Autumn Leaves* (55); for John Sturges, *Gunfight at the O.K. Corral* (56), *The Last Train from Gun Hill* (57), *The Magnificent Seven* (60), *A Girl Named Tamiko* (62); for Delbert Mann, *Separate Tables* (58); for Marlon Brando, *One Eyed Jacks* (61); for Donen, *Charade* (63); for Wyler, *How to Steal a Million* (66); for Irvin Kershner, *The Flim-Flam Man/One Born Every Minute* (67); for Guy Green, *A Walk in the Spring Rain* (69); for Terence Young, *Wait Until Dark* (67); for Jacques Charon, *A Flea in Her Ear* (68).

LANG, Fritz DIR Germany/USA. (Vienna Dec 5, 1890–) A film maker who has made many monumental films and who, though he lost several battles in his career, never went into decline and always retained his seriousness of approach and sense of dignity. He was the son of an architect who hoped he would follow the same career and, though he early decided against it, his background and the artistic training he received helped determine the distinctive architectural style of especially his silent German films. In the hospital during the First World War he began writing scenarios, two of which were filmed by Joe May in 1917–18. [In 1919 he joined Decla, then headed by Erich Pommer (*q.v.*), as story editor and scriptwriter, and occasionally as editor, then served as Joe May's (*q.v.*) assistant on the eight-part episode film *Die Herrin der Welt* (19) before directing his first film the same year.] His early experience, both as scriptwriter and director, was on crime thrillers, exotic adventure stories, and macabre dramas and he never lost his taste for these genres. In 1925 he wrote: "I shall never forget what a French journalist, hardly a suspect Germanophile, wrote of *Destiny* – 'As though it were leaving a tomb, the German soul (which in other days we had loved so much but thought dead) has risen again in this film.' If there is anything that should bear witness of the German people, their soul, their vigor, their miseries, and hopes to all humanity it is certainly the film . . . The film has made us witnesses of the magic of the human face, it has taught us to read what lies behind the silence of this face and has shown us the reaches of the human soul. Likewise, a film creator is called for to unveil the face of an entire people to the world, to become the transmitter of its soul. Thus these films will be considered as witnesses of the period in which they were born and will become, in their way, documents of universal history." Lang was very much a witness both of the present and future of his country in the major films he created in 1920–33 with Thea von Harbou (*q.v.*), who was then his wife – *Dr. Mabuse,* a metaphorical portrait of the troubled postwar years; *The Nibelungen,* an exaltation of legendary German heroics prophesying (without intending to) the monumental Nuremberg parades and the downfall of Nazism in blood and flames; *Metropolis,* in which a master race rule the shadow people, the workers; *M,* the story of a murderer to whom the unemployed mete out justice; and *The Testament of Dr. Mabuse,* a fantasy-thriller that Lang later claimed was a metaphorical attack on Nazism. He was forced to leave Germany in 1933 (though Hitler was a great admirer of *The Nibelungen* and wanted to use him in the Nazi film industry) and finally settled in the USA. To his earlier obsession with blind destiny was now added the theme of guilt, a depiction of his belief that "the inexorability of the first mistake brings about the last atonement." Though he later exclaimed, "We are all children of Cain," he never set himself up as a believer in the judiciary – particularly in his first two American films, *Fury* and *You Only Live Once,* in which he took the side of the "guilty," the victims of society's errors. A series of commercial failures after 1945 led to his downfall in critical esteem. But, as he said, "We are born of men, not of gods," adding that though he had often had to work under the constraint of dictatorial producers he had always "tried to make each film his best work." After *M* much of the monumental, decorative quality of his work in silent films was sacrificed in favor of an interest in the psychology and development of character. He considers that *The Woman in the Window, Scarlet Street,* and *While the City Sleeps* are the best of his American films, which, since 1940, have been "based on social criticism," that is to say on "the criticism of our environment, laws and conventions." He sees the major theme of his work as: "the individual's struggle against circumstances, his struggle with the gods, the struggle of Prometheus. Today we are fighting laws, we are contending orders that seem to us neither just nor the right ones for our times."

SCEN: for Joe May, *Die Hochzeit im Excentricclub* (17), *Hilde Warren und der Tod* (17), *Das Indische Grabmal* (I: *Die Sendung des Yoghi,* II: *Der Tiger von Eschnapur*)/*The Indian Tomb* /*The Mysteries of India*/*Above the Law* (21); for Otto Rippert, *Die Frau mit den Orchideen* (19), *Die Pest in Florenz* (19), *Totentanz* (19); for Erich Kober, *Lilith und Ly* (Aust19), for *Carola Hauser* (21), *König Artus Tafelrunde* (22), and collaboration on most of his own German films.

DIR: *Halbblut* (Ger19), *Der Herr der Liebe* (19), *Harakiri* (19), *Die Spinnen* — I: *Der goldene See* (19), *Die Spinnen* — II: *Das Brillantenschiff* (20), *Das Wandernde Bild* (20), *Vier um die Frau*/*Kämpfende Herzen* (20), *Der Müde Tod*/*Destiny** (21), *Dr. Mabuse, der Spieler** (I: *der Grosse Spieler,* II: *Inferno*) (22), *Die Nibelungen** (I: *Siegfrieds Tod;* II: *Kriemhilds Rache*) (24), *Metropolis** (26), *Spione* (28), *Die Frau im Mond* (29), *M** (31), *Das Testament des Dr. Mabuse** (Ger33), *Liliom* (Fr33), *Fury** (USA36), *You Only Live Once** (37), *You and Me* (38), *The Return of Frank James* (40), *Western Union* (41), *Man Hunt* (41), *Confirm or Deny* (41) (completed by Archie Mayo), *Hangmen Also Die* (42),

The Ministry of Fear (43), *The Woman in the Window** (44), *Scarlet Street** (45), *Cloak and Dagger* (46), *The Secret Beyond the Door* (48), *House by the River* (50), *An American Guerrilla in the Philippines*/*I Shall Return* (50), *Rancho Notorious* (51), *Clash by Night* (52), *The Blue Gardenia* (53), *The Big Heat* (53), *Human Desire** (54), *Moonfleet* (55), *While the City Sleeps* (56), *Beyond a Reasonable Doubt* (USA56), *Der Tiger von Eschnapur* (GFR58), *Das Indische Grabmal* (GFR59) (latter two films released as one film in English: *The Tigress of Bengal*), *Die tausend Augen des Dr. Mabuse** (GFR 60).

LANGDON, Harry DIR USA. (Council Bluff June 15, 1884–Hollywood Dec 22, 1944) Former vaudeville actor who appeared in numerous short Sennett (*q.v.*) comedies and whose unique whimsical comic gifts make him at least part *auteur* of his own best films: *The Strong Man**, *Tramp, Tramp, Tramp**, and *Long Pants**, all three of which owe much to Frank Capra (*q.v.*). [He directed his own less successful *Three's a Crowd* (27), *The Chaser* (28), and *Heart Trouble* (28), but did not successfully survive the introduction of sound.]

LANGUEPIN, Jean-Jacques DIR France. (Paris Nov 12, 1924–) Good documentarist, specializing in aviation and mountain films, notably: *Terre des glaces* (49), *Groenland* (51) (co-dir: Ichac), *Des hommes et des montagnes* (53), *Neiges* (55), *La Route des cimes* (57), *Saint-Exupery* (57), *Des hommes dans le ciel* (59), *La Vitesse est à vous* (61).

LA PATELLIERE, Denys de DIR France. (Nantes March 8, 1921–) Diligent director who has made a number of commercially successful films since 1958. DIR (notably): *Les Aristocrates* (55), *Le Salaire du péché* (56), *Retour de manivelle* (57), *Thérèse Etienne* (58), *Les Grandes Familles* (58), *Rue des prairies* (59), *Un taxi pour Tobrouk* (61), *Le Bateau d'Emile* (62), *Tempo di Roma* (63), *Marco le Magnifique* (65), *Du Rififi à Paname* (66).

LAROCHE, Pierre SCEN France. (Paris May 7, 1902–Paris 1962) Spirited, stubborn and committed scriptwriter who, with

Jacques Prévert (*q.v.*), co-authored Grémillon's *Lumière d'été** and Carné's *Les Visiteurs du soir** before writing a number of scripts alone, largely for his wife Jacqueline Audry (*q.v.*): *Les Malheurs de Sophie* (45), *Gigi* (49), *Minne* (50), *Huis clos* (54), *La Garçonne* (57).

LASKOS, Orestis DIR Greece. (Eleusis 1908–) A pioneer of the Greek cinema who began as an actor and scriptwriter and made, notably, *Daphnis and Chloe* (30) before directing numerous commercial melodramas.

*LASKY, Jesse L. PROD USA. (San Francisco Sept 13, 1880–Hollywood Jan 13, 1958) One-time cornet player and then vaudeville impresario, he was persuaded to join the motion picture industry in 1913 with his brother-in-law Sam Goldwyn (*q.v.*) and formed the Lasky Feature Play Company, whose first film was Cecil B. DeMille's *The Squaw Man* (13). His company later merged with Zukor's (*q.v.*) Famous Players to form Famous Players–Lasky Corporation, which in turn acquired Paramount Pictures Corporation in 1916. Lasky remained as executive head of production. He went bankrupt in the Depression, left Paramount, and later produced for Warner Brothers, RKO, and 20th Century-Fox.

*LASKY, Jesse, Jr. SCEN USA. (New York Sept 19, 1910–) Son of the Hollywood pioneer (see above), who, in addition to writing novels and poetry, had a long collaboration with DeMille (*q.v.*) on many of his spectaculars, from *Union Pacific** (39), to *The Ten Commandments** (56) and *The Buccaneer* (58). He has sometimes worked in collaboration with his wife, the writer Pat Silver.

LASSALLY, Walter PHOTOG Britain/Greece. (Berlin Dec 18, 1926–) Former member of the British Free Cinema documentary group in the Fifties who later developed into one of the world's most imaginative and skillful cameramen. His feeling for natural sets, sense of atmosphere, and evocative photography of faces has contributed much to the Greek films of Cacoyannis (*q.v.*), to the exceptional Pakistani film, *Day Shall Dawn,* and to many of the British "new wave" films of the Sixties. His color work on *Tom Jones* was outstanding.
[PHOTOG (notably): for Lindsay Anderson, *Thursday's Children* (53), *Every Day Except Christmas* (57); for Gavin Lambert, *Another Sky* (54); for L. Mazzetti, *Together* (55); for Karel Reisz, *Momma Don't Allow* (55), *We Are the Lambeth Boys* (58); for Cacoyannis, *To Koritsi me ta mavra/A Girl in Black** (Gr55), *A Matter of Dignity* (Gr57), *Our Last Spring* (Gr58), *Elektra** (Gr61), *Zorba the Greek** (Gr64), *The Day the Fish Came Out* (Gr67); for Kardar, *Jago Hua Savera/Day Shall Dawn** (Pakistan58); for Edmond Gréville, *Beat Girl* (Brit60); for Tony Richardson, *A Taste of Honey** (61), *The Loneliness of the Long Distance Runner* (62), *Tom Jones** (63); for Alexander Singer, *Psyche 59* (USA63); for Philip Saville, *Oedipus the King** (Brit67); for Michael Sarne, *Joanna* (Brit67); for Jerome Epstein, *The Adding Machine* (Brit69); for George Stamboulopoulos, *Anihti Episoli/Open Letter* (Gr68–70), for Harold Prince, *Somebody for Everyone* (USA70).]

LATTUADA, Alberto DIR Italy. (Milan Nov 13, 1914–) Talented Italian director, despite the fact that he has had to accept various commercial assignments in his career and has occasionally lost himself artistically. His work is too little known abroad. He was originally a writer and, even before he took up directing, made a major contribution to the Italian cinema as founder of the Milan film archive, Cineteca Italiana, and by showing certain banned films (such as *La Grande Illusion*) in film clubs. He worked as assistant and scriptwriter on Soldati's *Piccolo Mondo antico* (40) and his first films as director were in the "decorative" style. Rather than serve the regime he directed refined, mannered films: *Giacomo l'idealista* (42) and *La Freccia nel fianco* (44). As soon as neorealism appeared in liberated Italy, he directed several notable films in this style: *The Bandit* (46), *Without Pity* (48), *The Mill on the Po* (49). He looked forward to the time when "film stock can be bought for the price of paper and a camera for the price of an electric razor," giving everyone the possibility of true freedom of expression. His best film, *Il Cappotto* (an adaptation of Gogol's *The Cloak*) is an evolution of neorealism into a kind of fantasy-realism.
DIR (notably): *Giacomo l'Idealista* (42), *La Freccia nel fianco* (44), *Il Bandito*

(46), *Il Delitto di Giovanni Episcopo* (47), *Senza Pietà** (48), *Il Mulino del Po* (49), *Luci del Varietà** (50) (co-dir: Fellini), *Anna* (51), *Il Cappotto/The Overcoat** (52), *La Lupa* (53), *Amore in città* (53) (one episode), *La Spiaggia* (53), *Scualo Elementare* (54), *Guendalina* (57), *La Tempesta* (58), *I Dolci Inganni* (60), *Lettera di una Novizia* (60), *Lo Imprevisto* (61), *Adolescenti* (61), *La Steppa* (61), *Mafioso* (63), *La Mandragola* (65), *L'Amante di Gramigna* (66), *Matchless* (66), *Don Giovanni in Sicilia* (67), *Fräulein Doktor* (Yug/It68), *Venga a prendere il caffè da noi* (70).

LAURITZEN, Lau DIR Denmark (Silkeborg March 18, 1878–Silkeborg July 2, 1938) The director of some 60–80 films between 1911 and 1936 but best known as director of the delightful comic series in the Twenties that featured "Fy og By" ("the Long and Short"), two characters played respectively by Carl Schenstrøm and Aage Bendixen.

LAURITZEN, Lau, Jr. DIR Sweden/Denmark (Vejle June 26, 1910–) Son of the Danish director (see above), he was originally an actor then a fairly prolific director in Scandanavia. In Denmark he collaborated with Bodil Ipsen (*q.v.*) on his two best films, *Afsporet* (42) and *De Röde Enge* (45), and in Sweden co-directed *Julia Jubilerar* (38) and *Västkustens Hjälter* (40) with Alice O'Fredericks and *Jag älskar dig, Karlsson* (47) with John Zacharias.

LAUSTE, Eugène INVENTOR USA/France. (Paris 1856–USA June 27, 1935) On the technical level he is perhaps the principal inventor of motion pictures in the USA since, as engineer, he developed and perfected the Edison Kinetoscope in 1893 and the W. K. L. Dickson Biograph projector in 1895–97. He also played a role in the development of sound on film. His work with Ruhmer in Germany on the optical recording of sound led to a demonstration of the technique in 1911 in the USA and to Lauste's later career at the Bell Laboratories in New Jersey.

LAWSON, John Howard SCEN USA. (New York Sept 25, 1886–) Former journalist in Rome and dramatist for the Group Theater who became a Hollywood scriptwriter and wrote the documentary *Heart of Spain* (37) (dir: Paul Strand, Leo Hurwitz), Zoltan Korda's *Sahara* (43) and *Counterattack* (43), John Cromwell's *Algiers** (38), Dieterle's *Blockade* (36), Heisler's *Smash-Up* (47), etc. He was politically active, first president of the Screen Writers Guild, and was one of the Hollywood Ten imprisoned for contempt of Congress. He also wrote the books, *Film in the Battle of Ideas* (1955), *Film: The Creative Process* (1964, second edition 1967), and several other books on playwriting and screenwriting.

LEACOCK, Philip DIR Britain/USA. (London 1917–) Former documentary film maker who has made many features, often with children, most notably *The Kidnappers* (53). His later work in Britain and the USA (including TV work) is mediocre.

LEACOCK, Richard DIR/PHOTOG USA. (London 1921–) Younger brother of the above, he began his film career as a documentary cameraman (most memorably on Flaherty's *Louisiana Story*) and graduated into making many sensitive and intelligent "direct cinema" journalistic films for TV, using lightweight hand-held cameras and portable sound equipment. Robert Drew has often collaborated with him and Albert Maysles (*q.v.*) worked as cameraman on several of the earlier films.
[PHOTOG (notably): for Willard Van Dyke, *To Hear Your Banjo Play* (40), *Mount Vernon* (49), *Years of Change* (50), *New York University* (52); for Robert Flaherty, *Louisiana Story** (48); for Don Pennebaker, *Monterey Pop* (68), and footage for *Quint City USA* (63).]
DIR and/or PHOTOG (notably): *Toby and the Tall Corn* (55), *F 100* (56), *Yanki No!* (60), *Primary** (60), *On the Pole/Eddie Sachs at Indianapolis* (61), *Pete and Johnnie* (61), *Kenya '61* (61), *Football* (61), *X-15* (61), *The New Frontier* (61), *David* (62), *Nehru* (62), *The Chair* (63), *Jane* (63), *Happy Birthday Blackie* (63), *Aga Khan* (63), *Happy Mother's Day* (64), *Republicans — the New Breed* (64), *Igor Stravinsky — a Portrait* (66), *Chiefs* (70).

LEAN, David DIR Britain. (Croydon March 25, 1908–) A conscientious, honest,

painstaking director who justifies the proverb, "Every soldier carries a field marshall's baton in his knapsack." Like many English directors he gained experience as an editor, first on newsreels in the early Thirties, then on, e.g., Czinner's *Escape Me Never* (35) and Asquith's *Pygmalion** (38) and *French Without Tears* (39). Noel Coward (*q.v.*) made him his co-director on the chauvinistic *In Which We Serve* (42) and wrote for him the equally chauvinistic *This Happy Breed* (43), as well as *Blithe Spirit* (44) and *Brief Encounter* (45). This latter film, an astute study of suburban mores, was improperly hailed as a masterpiece at the time. His two Dickens adaptations, *Great Expectations* (46) and *Oliver Twist* (47), were models of their kind, but his ensuing films, except for *The Sound Barrier* (52) and the entertaining comedy *Summer Madness* (55) were routinely handled. He regained his international stature with his decorously directed *The Bridge on the River Kwai* (57), retaining the sense and significance of Pierre Boulle's original moral fable. He has since turned to large-budget epics and romances, spending several years directing *Lawrence of Arabia,* to the glory of the famous spy and his colonialist intrigues in the Middle East, [and the portentous, if often elegant, *Dr. Zhivago* and *Ryan's Daughter*. British playwright Robert Bolt wrote the scenarios of these last three films.]
DIR: *In Which We Serve** (42) (co-dir: Noel Coward), *This Happy Breed* (43), *Blithe Spirit* (44), *Brief Encounter** (45), *Great Expectations* (46), *Oliver Twist* (47), *The Passionate Friends/One Woman's Story* (48), *Madeleine* (50), *The Sound Barrier/Breaking the Sound Barrier* (52), *Hobson's Choice* (53), *Summer Madness/Summertime* (55), *The Bridge on the River Kwai** (57), *Lawrence of Arabia* (62), *Doctor Zhivago* (64), *Ryan's Daughter* (70).

Le CHANOIS, Jean-Paul (J.-P. Dreyfus) DIR France. (Paris Oct 25, 1909–) Former member of the French avant-garde and an actor and producer with the October Group, whose postwar films with their simple, straightforward, and appealing themes were often major popular successes. During the Thirties he worked on scripts for, and as assistant to, Duvivier, Maurice Tourneur, Alexander Korda, Litvak, Jean Renoir, and Max Ophüls

(all *q.v.*). He has learned, he says "to restore the heart to its true place, that heart which is in all feelings and not least in the best" – a lesson amply justified in his best films, such as *L'Ecole buissonnière* and *Sans laisser d'adresse.*
DIR: *la Vie d'un homme* (38) (documentary), *Le Temps des cerises* (38), *Au coeur de l'orage* (47) (documentary feature on the Resistance), *L'Ecole buissonnière/I Have a New Master** (48), *Sans laisser d'adresse** (50), *La Belle que voilà* (51), *Agence matrimoniale* (52), *Le Village magique* (53), *Papa, maman, la bonne, et moi* (54), *Les Evades* (54), *Papa, maman, ma femme, et moi* (55), *Le Cas du docteur Laurent* (56), *Les Misérables** (58), *La Française et l'amour* (60) (one episode), *Par-dessus le mur* (61), *Mandrin* (63), *Monsieur* (64), *Le Jardinier d'Argenteuil* (66).

LEE, Jack DIR Britain. (Stroud 1913–) A quite good British director whose documentary background is evident in his best fiction films. He was originally an associate producer with the GPO Film Unit and edited Jennings' *London Can Take It* (40).
DIR (notably): *The Pilot is Safe* (41) (documentary), *Ordinary People* (42) (documentary), *Close Quarters* (43) (documentary), *Children on Trial* (46) (documentary), *The Woman in the Hall* (47), *Once a Jolly Swagman* (48), *The Wooden Horse* (50), *South of Algiers* (52), *Turn the Key Softly* (53), *A Town Like Alice* (56), *Robbery Under Arms* (57), *The Captain's Table* (58), *Circle of Deception* (60).

LEENHARDT, Roger DIR France. (Paris July 23, 1903–) Documentary film maker and influential critic and theoretician on several film magazines (notably, *Esprit* 1936–39 and *Lettres françaises* 1944–46) whose extreme circumspection and almost complete restriction to the short film form has not prevented his exerting a major influence on several *nouvelle vague* directors. His best feature film is the sensitive and individualistic *Les Dernières Vacances* (47), but he is equally well known for his shorts, which most often deal with art or literature and are largely produced and scripted by himself.
[DIR (shorts): *L'Orient qui vient* (34), *Le Vrai jeu* (34), *Métro* (34), *Le Pain de Barbarie* (34), *Le Père Hugo* (34),

R.N. 37 (38), *Revêtements routiers* (38), *Pavage moderne* (38), *Le Rezzou* (38), *Fêtes de France* (40), *A la poursuite du vent* (43), *Le Chant des ondes* (43), *Le Chantier en ruines* (45), *Lettre de Paris* (45), *Le Barrage de l'aigle* (46), *Naissance du cinéma* (in English as two films: *Animated Cartoons, The Toy That Grew Up* and *Biography of the Motion Picture Camera*) (46), *La Côte d'Azur* (48), *Le Pain de Barbarie* (48), *Entrez dans la danse* (48), *Métro* (50), *La Fugue de Mahmoud* (50), *Victor Hugo* (51), *Du Charbon et des hommes* (52), *La France est un jardin* (53), *François Mauriac* (54), *Louis Capet* (54) *Ordinations* (55), *La Conquête de l'Angleterre* (55), *Notre sang* (55), *Les Transmissions hydrauliques* (55), *Le Bruit* (55), *Paris et le désert français* (57), *Jean-Jacques* (58), *Bâtir à notre âge* (58), *En plein midi* (58), *Daumier* (58), *Paul Valéry* (59), *Le Maître de Montpelier* (60), *Entre Seine et mer* (60), *L'Homme à la pipe* (62), *Des Femmes et des fleurs* (63), *1989* (63), *Monsieur de Voltaire* (63), *George* (63), *Corrot* (65), *Naissance de la photo* (65), *Le Coeur de la France* (66), *Le Beatnick et le minet* (67).
DIR (features): *Les Dernières Vacances** (47), *Le Rendez-vous de minuit* (62), *Une fille dans la montagne* (64) (TV). SCEN: *L'Amour de la maison* (46) (dir: Pierre de Hérain), *Aubusson* (46) (dir: Jean Lods), his own features and most of his own shorts.]

LEE THOMPSON, John DIR Britain/USA. (Bristol 1914–) Former stage actor, playwright, and scriptwriter, who since 1950 has directed several lively, if routine, adventure films and comedies in a prolific directorial career in Britain and the USA. His best film is his portrait of behavior in *Woman in a Dressing Gown* (Brit57) rather than the stentorian *Guns of Navarone* (Brit61). Other notable films: *Yield to the Night* (Brit56), *No Trees in the Street* (59), *Tiger Bay* (59), *Mackenna's Gold* (USA68).

LE FEBVRE, Robert PHOTOG France. (Paris March 19, 1907–) After gaining experience in the Thirties (with, e.g., Gance on *Un grand amour de Beethoven* in 1936) he suddenly shot into prominence with his work on Becker's *Casque d'or** (52), whose images are among the most beautiful in the French cinema. He has since made sensitive and delicate photographic contributions on Clair's *Les Grandes Manoeuvres**, and *Porte des Lilas**; Buñuel's *Cela s'appelle l'aurore**; Astruc's *Les Mauvaises Rencontres**.

LEGER, Fernand (Argentan Feb 1881–Paris Feb 1955) Major 20th-century artist who throughout his career was greatly attracted to the cinema and came near to abandoning his paint brush for the camera after his *Ballet mécanique** film in 1924. Other work for the cinema includes an uncompleted animated film, *Charlot cubiste* (21); sets for L'Herbier's *L'Inhumaine** (24); posters for Gance's *La Roue**; set designs (never used) for Korda's production of *Things to Come* (36); one of the visual poems of Hans Richter's *Dreams That Money Can Buy* (47).

LEGOSHIN, Vladimir DIR USSR. (Baku 1904–Moscow 1955) Routine Soviet director who had one major achievement in his career: *Byeleyet parus odinoky/ The Lone White Sail** (37), a portrait of the 1905 Revolution in Odessa seen through the eyes of two children. He began his career as Donskoy's (*q.v.*) collaborator on *Song about Happiness* (34).

*LEGRAND, Michel MUS France. (France 1931–) Prolific French composer, closely associated with the *nouvelle vague*, who has written several atmospheric, and often catchy, scores, most notably for Jacques Demy (*q.v.*). His work established a fashion for French film composers and is often rather poorly imitated.
MUS (notably): for François Reichenbach, *L'Amérique insolite* (59); for Demy, *Lola** (61), *La Baie des Anges* (63), *Les Parapluies de Cherbourg** (64), *Les Demoiselles de Rochefort* (66); for Agnès Varda, *Cléo de 5 à 7** (62); for Godard, *Une femme est une femme* (61), *Les Sept péchés capitaux* (62) (episode), *Vivre sa vie** (62), *Les Plus belles escroqueries du monde* (64) (episode), *Bande à part** (64), *Le Plus vieux métier du monde* (66) (episode); for Joseph Losey, *Eva* (62); for Chris Marker, *Le Joli mai** (62); for J.-P. Rappeneau, *La Vie de château* (64); for John Sturges, *Ice Station Zebra* (USA 68); for Richard Brooks, *The Happy Ending* (69); for Anatole Litvak, *The*

Lady in the Car with Glasses and a Gun (70).

LEHRMAN, Henry (also "Pathé" Lehrman) DIR USA. (Vienna March 30, 1886– Hollywood Nov 7, 1946) Pioneer director of slapstick comedies who was Sennett's assistant (*q.v.*) and, in the opinion of some, responsible for much of the characteristic Keystone style. He is however best known now as the director of Chaplin's (*q.v.*) first films in 1914: *Making a Living, Kid Auto Races at Venice, Mabel's Strange Predicament* and *Between Showers*. He got his nickname because he obtained his first film job with Biograph by pretending to have worked with Pathé in Paris.

LEISER, Erwin DIR Sweden/Switzerland. (Berlin May 16, 1923–) Documentary film maker responsible for two remarkable anti-Nazi compilation films: *Den Blodiga Tiden/Mein Kampf* (Swed60), *Eichmann und das dritte Reich/Murder by Signature* (Switz61), and *Waehle das Leben* (Switz63).

*LELOUCH, Claude DIR/PHOTOG France. (1937–) Young film maker whose films have a lush visual style and somewhat plastic emotions but almost always reach their audiences. His *A Man and a Woman* was a world-wide commercial success. He began his career as an amateur film maker and made 16mm TV shorts before directing his first feature. He has photographed and produced many of his own films.
DIR (shorts): *Une ville pas comme les autres* (57), *USA en vrac* (57), *Quand le rideau se lève* (57), *Madame conduit* (61), *Jean-Paul Belmondo* (63), *Pour un maillot jaune* (65).
DIR (features): *Le Propre de l'homme* (60), *l'Amour avec des si . . .* (63), *La Femme spectacle* (64), *Une fille et des fusils* (64), *Les Grands moments* (65), *Un homme et une femme* (66), *Vivre pour vivre* (67), *Loin du Vietnam* (67) (episode), *13 jours en France* (68) (co-dir: F. Reichenbach), *La Vie, l'amour, la mort* (68), *L'Homme qui me plaît/Love is a Funny Thing* (69), *Le Voyou/Simon the Swiss* (70).

LENI, Paul DIR/ART DIR Germany/USA. (Stuttgart July 8, 1885–Hollywood 1929) An important figure in the German expressionist cinema, a director and art director with a fine sense of visual design who had worked with Max Reinhardt (*q.v.*) and Leopold Jessner on their famous stage productions. Though his *Kammerspiel* film, *Backstairs* (21), is more of a trailblazer than a complete success, his expressionistic *Waxworks* (written by Henrik Galeen) is an important work, both for its extravagant baroque style and for its portrait of tyrannical cruelty. Its worldwide success led to an invitation from Carl Laemmle (*q.v.*) to work in Hollywood, where Leni developed a new genre of horror films with *The Cat and the Canary* and *The Last Warning*. These involved macabre effects produced from ultra-mobile cameras and elaborately lighted and carefully designed décors set off against pleasant comic episodes. His early death cut short a promising career.
DIR: *Das Rätsel von Bangalore* (17), *Dornröschen* (17), *Platonische Ehe* (19), *Prinz Kuckuck* (19) (also script), *Patience* (20), *Die Verschwörung zu Genua/Fiesco* (20), *Das Gespensterschiff* (21), *Die Hintertreppe/Backstairs* (21) (co-dir: Leopold Jessner), *Komödie der Leidenschaften* (21), *Das Tagebuch des Dr. Hartl* (21), *Das Wachsfigurenkabinett/Waxworks** (24), *The Cat and the Canary** (USA27), *The Chinese Parrot* (27), *The Man Who Laughs* (28), *The Last Warning* (29).
[ART DIR: for Joe May, *Veritas vincit* (18); for E. A. Dupont *Der Weisse Pfau* (20), *Kinder der Finsternis* (22); for Karl Grune, *Frauenopfer* (22); for Richard Oswald, *Lady Hamilton* (22) (co-art dir: Hans Dreier), *Die Frau in vierzig Jahren* (25); for Alexander Korda, *Der Tänzer meiner Frau* (25); for Michael Kertesz (Curtiz), *Fiakr Nr. 13* (26), *Der Goldene Schmetterling* (26); for Arthur Robison, *Manon Lescaut* (26); and for all his own German films.]

LENICA, Jan ANIM Poland/France/German Federal Republic. (Poznan Jan 4, 1928–) Polish-born animator whose tragicomic, often surrealistic films generally combine simplified, heavy black-line animation, cut-out figures, engraved backgrounds, and collage. [He studied music before turning to art and played a major role (since 1950) in the development of designs for the Polish cinema posters. He has also illustrated books and worked as an exhibition designer.]
ANIM: *Once Upon a Time* (Pol57), *Love*

Requited (Pol57), *Dom/House* (Pol58) (all co-dir: Borowczyk), *Monsieur Tête* (Fr60) (co-dir: Henri Gruel), *Janko the Musician* (Pol61), *Italia 61* (Pol61) (co-dir: Zamecznik), *Labyrinth** (Pol 63), *Rhinoceros* (GFR63), *A* (GFR64), *The Flower Woman* (GFR65), *Adam II* (GFR68).

LEONARD, Robert Z(igler) DIR USA. (Denver Sept 7, 1889–1968) Hollywood director who had occasional bright moments in a long but mediocre career. In the Thirties he specialized, without much flair, in musical comedies and revues — of which the most famous is *The Great Ziegfield* (36) — and had the good fortune to direct Fred Astaire's first film, *Dancing Lady* (33). He was also known as a good director of actresses, especially his wife, Mae Murray, all of whose films he directed from 1916–23, and Marion Davies 1928–32, plus several vehicles for Garbo, Jeanette MacDonald, Greer Garson, Lana Turner, etc.

LEROY, Mervyn DIR USA. (San Francisco Oct 15, 1900–) A film maker of great stature and artistry in the Thirties who later became an impersonal, routine director of largely uninteresting films. His early films, like *Little Caesar* (30), *Five Star Final* (31), *I Am a Fugitive from a Chain Gang* (32) and *Gold Diggers of 1933* (33), probed American society during the Depression and he offered a vivid indictment of intolerance and mob brutality in *They Won't Forget* (37). Realism later gave way to romantic melodramas (*Waterloo Bridge*), routine theatrical adaptations, and lush spectaculars like *Quo Vadis?*
DIR (notably): *Little Caesar** (30), *Five Star Final* (31), *I Am a Fugitive from a Chain Gang** (31), *Three on a Match* (32), *Big City Blues* (32), *Two Seconds* (32), *Hard to Handle* (32), *Gold Diggers of 1933** (33), *Tugboat Annie* (33), *Oil for the Lamps of China* (35), *Anthony Adverse* (36), *They Won't Forget* (37), *The Wizard of Oz* (39), *Waterloo Bridge* (40), *Escape* (40), *Random Harvest* (42), *Madame Curie* (43), *The House I Live In* (45), *Little Women* (48), *Any Number Can Play* (49), *Quo Vadis?** (51), *Rose Marie* (53), *Mister Roberts* (54) (begun by John Ford), *The Bad Seed* (55), *Toward the Unknown* (56), *Moment to Moment* (65).

*LESTER, Richard DIR Britain. (Philadelphia 1932–) A film maker whose films have great pace and technical assurance and use a wide range of cinematic devices without merely being fashionable. He studied clinical psychology and television at the University of Pennsylvania, moving to Britain in 1955 where he worked on TV commercials. He made over 100 commercials, worked on several TV comedy programs (notably the BBC "Goon Show") and made a short "Goon" film in 1959 before directing his first feature. His two Beatles films, *A Hard Day's Night* and *Help!* have tremendous verve and an invigorating comic sense, traits evident also in his next three films. With *Petulia*, on the air-conditioned nightmare of American society in turmoil, his work took on new depth and assurance.
DIR: *The Running, Jumping, and Standing Still Film* (59) (short), *It's Trad, Dad!* (62), *The Mouse on the Moon* (63), *A Hard Day's Night** (64), *The Knack* (65), *Help!** (65), *A Funny Thing Happened on the Way to the Forum* (66), *How I Won the War* (67), *Petulia** (68), *The Bed-Sitting Room* (69).

LEVIN, Henry DIR USA. (Trenton June 5, 1909–) Mediocre Hollywood director (since 1944) credited with one good western, *The Lonely Man* (57).

LEVY, Raoul PROD/SCEN France. (Anvers April 14, 1922–Dec 31, 1966) A French producer in the grand Hollywood manner who built his extraordinary success on Brigitte Bardot's films, from *And God Created Woman** (which he also wrote) to *Babette Goes to War* and *La Vérité**. [He also produced, notably, Peter Brook's *Moderato Cantabile* (60) and directed, produced, and wrote *Je vous salue Mafia* (65) and *L'Espion/The Defectors* (66).]

*LEWIN, Albert PROD/DIR/SCEN USA. (Newark Sept 23, 1902–May 9, 1968) An MGM producer (*Cuban Love Song, China Seas, The Good Earth, Mutiny on the Bounty, Zaza, So Ends Our Night*), who became a director in 1942 with his adaptation of *The Moon and Sixpence* from Somerset Maugham, a film whose theme appeared in one film or another in all his later work: the marvelous evocation of the Oscar Wilde universe, *The Picture of Dorian Gray;*

the stylistic Maupassant world of *The Private Affairs of Bel Ami;* and the symbolic paean to feminine beauty, *Pandora and the Flying Dutchman.* Perhaps the most cultured of Hollywood film makers and a man of evident cinematic talents, he never quite fulfilled his own promise and his last two films are mediocre, dominated by a precious quality that lurks beneath the surface of his earlier work. DIR/SCEN: *The Moon and Sixpence* (42) (co-dir: Steve Sekeley), *The Picture of Dorian Gray* (44), *The Private Affairs of Bel Ami* (47), *Pandora and the Flying Dutchman* (51), *Saadia* (54), *The Living Idol* (57).

LEWTON, Val (Vladimir Ivan Lewton) PROD USA. (Yalta May 7, 1904–USA March 14, 1951) Imaginative Hollywood producer noted for his series of brilliant, low-budget horror films for RKO in the Forties: Jacques Tourneur's *Cat People** (42), *I Walked with a Zombie* (43), *The Leopard Man* (43); Mark Robson's *The Seventh Victim* (43), *The Ghost Ship* (43), *Youth Runs Wild* (44), *Isle of the Dead* (45), *Bedlam* (46); Robert Wise's *Curse of the Cat People** (44), *Mademoiselle Fifi** (44) (from Maupassant), *The Body Snatchers* (45). He produced three more films after he left RKO in 1946 (*My Own True Love, Please Believe Me, Apache Drums*), but none is distinctive. He died of a heart attack just after signing a contract with Stanley Kramer (*q.v.*).

L'HERBIER, Marcel DIR France. (Paris April 23, 1890–) The master of French film impressionism, a cultured, subtle and intelligent film maker who was much enamored of art and experiment and who contributed significantly to the development of the means of cinematic expression. He originally studied law and has been a poet and playwright. In 1917 he wrote scripts for Mercanton and Hervil, *Torrent* and *Bouclette,* and in 1919 he directed his first film, after serving with the Army's film unit during the war. His *Eldorado* (21) was hailed by Louis Delluc (*q.v.*) with his famous line, "That's real cinema!" There are faults in *L'Inhumaine* (23) and his ambitions for *Don Juan et Faust* (22) were not fulfilled, but his *Feu Mathias Pascal* (25) is a major achievement. His budget problems over *Don Juan et Faust* were met

again later when too large resources crushed *L'Argent* (29). He has said of his career: "For ten years — 1918–28 — I made the films I chose in the way I intended. The next ten years were years of misfortunes and commercial constraints." He has defined "the revolutionary art" of the cinema as "the most miraculous means of portraying man to other men, of educating man by other men, and of reconciling (an urgent task) man with other men." In 1943 he founded the Institut des Hautes Études Cinématographiques (IDHEC), the Paris film school whose international prestige has risen steadily over the years and of which he has remained president. He continued to make features, rather unsuccessfully, until 1954, when he became a TV producer. DIR: *Phantasmes* (17), *Rose France* (19), *Le Carnaval des vérités* (20), *L'Homme du large* (20) (from Balzac), *Villa destin* (21), *Prométhée banquier* (21), *Eldorado** (21), *Don Juan et Faust* (22), *L'Inhumaine** (23), *Feu Mathias Pascal** (25), *Le Vestige* (26), *L'Argent* (27) (from Zola), *Le Diable au coeur* (28), *Nuits de prince* (30), *L'Enfant de l'amour* (30), *La Femme d'une nuit* (30), *Le Mystère de la chambre jaune* (30), *Le Parfum de la dame en noir* (31), *L'Epervier* (33), *Le Scandale* (34), *L'Aventurier* (34), *Le Bonheur* (34), *La Route impériale* (35), *Veille d'armes* (35), *Les Hommes nouveaux* (35), *La Porte du large* (35), *La Citadelle du silence* (37), *Nuits defeu* (37), *Forfaiture/The Cheat** (37), *Adrienne Lecouvreur* (38), *Terre de feu* (38), *La Tragédie impériale* (38), *Entente cordiale* (39), *La Brigade sauvage* (39), *La Comédie du bonheur* (41), *Histoire de rire* (41), *La Nuit fantastique* (42), *L'Honorable Catherine* (42), *La vie de bohème* (43), *Au petit bonheur* (45), *L'Affair du collier de la reine* (46), *La Revoltée* (47), *Les Derniers jours de Pompéi* (49), *Le Père de mademoiselle* (53).

LIEBENEINER, Wolfgang DIR Germany/German Federal Republic. (Liebau Sept 5, 1905–) Facile director, both during the Nazi era — with the glorification of *Bismarck* (40) and the propaganda for the extermination of the mentally unfit in *Ich klage an* (41) — and in postwar years with such family entertainment films as *Die Trapp-Familie* (56). He was head of production at UFA 1942–45.

LINDER, Max (Gabriel Levielle) DIR/SCEN France/USA. (Saint Loubès, Gironde Dec 16, 1883–Paris Oct 30, 1925) The French genius of silent comedy, named by Charles Chaplin (*q.v.*) as a formative influence on his own work, who wrote and directed most of his own films from 1910 until his suicide in 1925. He appeared in some 200–300 films from his first supporting roles in 1905. Of those he wrote and/or directed the following are of special interest (features complete): *Max aeronaute* (10), *Les Débuts de Max au cinéma* (10), *Max se marie/ Le Mariage de Max* (10), *Max victime du quinquina** (11), *Max lance la mode* (11), *Max professeur de tango** (12), *Max toréador** (12), *Max à Monaco* (13), *Le Hasard et l'amour* (13), *Max pedicure* (14), *Max et l'espion* (15), *Max Comes Across* (USA17), *Max in a Taxi* (USA17), *Le Petit café* (19), *Le Feu sacré* (20), *Be My Wife* (USA21), *Seven Years Bad Luck** (USA21), *The Three Must-Get-Theres** (USA22), *Au Secours!* (23) (dir: Abel Gance), *Der Zirkuskönig/The Circus King* (Aust24).

LINDTBERG, Leopold DIR Switzerland. (Vienna June 1, 1902–) The director of dozens of minor or mediocre features — e.g., *Füsilier Wipf* (38), *Die Miss-brauchten Liebesbriefe* (40), the semi-documentary, *Marie Louise* (44), and *Die Vier im Jeep/Four in a Jeep* (51) — but justly famous for his best film, *Die Letzte Chance** (45).

*LIPMAN, Jerzy PHOTOG Poland. (1922–) Excellent Polish cameraman (he is a Lodz graduate) with a distinctive style, who is notable for his work with Wajda on *A Generation**, *Kanal**, *Lotna*, *Ashes;* with Kawalerowicz on *The Shadow, The Real End of the Great War;* with Aleksander Ford on *The Eighth Day of the Week;* with Passendorfer on *Zanach/ Answer to Violence* (58); with Munk on *Bad Luck;* with Polanski on *Knife in the Water;* with Mikhail Bogin on *Zozya* (USSR67); with Jerzy Hoffman on *Colonel Wolodyjowski* (69).

LITVAK, Anatole DIR USA/Germany/ France/Britain. (Kiev, Russia May 10, 1902–) Although entirely conscientious, technically well trained, professionally dedicated and with a special ability to select and direct actors, he has never been able to rise above the merely commercially successful level. [He worked in Germany, France, and Britain before settling in Hollywood in 1937 and has, in the Sixties, worked largely in Europe, though on American productions. During the war he collaborated with Frank Capra (*q.v.*) on the *Why We Fight** series.]
DIR (notably): *Dolly macht Karriere* (Ger30), *Nie Wieder Liebe* (Ger31), *Sleeping Car* (Brit33), *Coeur de lilas* (Fr33), *L'Equipage* (Fr35), *Mayerling* (Fr36), *The Woman I Love* (USA37) (remake of *L'Equipage*), *Tovarich* (38), *The Amazing Dr. Clitterhouse* (38), *The Sisters* (38), *Confessions of a Nazi Spy* (39), *All This and Heaven Too* (40), *Castle on the Hudson* (40), *City for Conquest* (40), *Out of the Fog* (41), *Blues in the Night* (41), *This Above All* (42), *The Nazis Strike** (42) (documentary, co-dir: Capra), *Divide and Conquer** (43) (documentary, co-dir: Capra), *The Battle of Russia** (44) (documentary), *The Battle of China** (44) (documentary, co-dir: Capra), *War Comes to America* (45) (documentary), *The Long Night** (47) (remake of *Le Jour se lève**), *The Snake Pit* (48), *Sorry, Wrong Number* (48), *Decision before Dawn* (51), *Act of Love* (54), *The Deep Blue Sea* (Brit55), *Anastasia* (56), *The Journey* (58), *Aimez-vous Brahms?/Goodbye Again* (61), *Le Couteau dans le plaie/Five Miles to Midnight* (62), *The Night of the Generals* (66), *La Dame dans l'auto avec des lunettes et une fusil* (Fr70).

LIU PAN DIR China. (Shanghai 190?–) Imaginative Chinese director of the Shanghai school who has made at least two important works: the romantic epic *New Heroes and Heroines* and the powerfully realistic *Gate No. 6*. (His pseudonym is derived from a street in the former French concession in Shanghai. His real name is not known.)
DIR (notably): *Tche Sen* (25), *Li Oke* (25), *New Heroes and Heroines* (50) (co-dir: Si Tung), *The Heroes of the Liulang Mountains* (50) (co-dir: Yi Lin), *Gate No. 6** (52), *Heroic Railway Engineers* (54), *When the New Director Arrives at His Post* (56).

LIZZANI, Carlo DIR/SCEN Italy. (Rome April 3, 1922–) As a film critic and later as a scriptwriter he played a role in the development of Italian neorealism but, as a director, he belonged to the somewhat ill-favored Fifties generation. In his first film, *Achtung! Banditi!* (51) — which also gave Gina Lollobrigida her first major role — he portrayed the Italian Resistance in some historical perspective; in *Chronicle of Poor Lovers* (54) he evoked not the gaiety of the 1925 period but a Florence struggling against Fascism.

SCEN (notably): for Vergano, *Il Sole Sorge Ancora** (46); for De Santis, *Caccia Tragica** (47), *Riso Amero** (49), *Non c'è pace tra gli ulivi** (50); for Rossellini, *Germania, Anno Zero** (48); for Lattuada, *Il Mulino del Po* (49); and for his own films. (All scripts in collaboration.)

DIR: *Nel Mezzogiorno qualcosa è cambiato* (50) (documentary), *Achtung! Banditi!* (51), *Ai Margini della Metropoli* (54), *Cronache di Poveri Amanti** (54), *Lo Svitato* (56), *La Muraglia Cinese* (58) (documentary feature), *Esterina* (59), *Il Gobbo/The Hunchback of Rome* (60), *L'Oro di Roma* (61), *Il Procesa di Verona* (62), *La Vita agra* (64), *La Celestina* (64), *Thrilling* (65) (one episode), *I Sette Fratelli* (66), *Svegliati e uccidi* (66), *Amore e Rabbia/Vangelo 70* (67) (one episode), *Requiescant* (67), *Assassinio a Sarajevo* (68), *Banditi a Milano* (69).

LLOYD, Frank DIR USA. (Glasgow, Scotland Feb 2, 1889–Hollywood 1960) Among the hundred or so films he directed from 1916 to 1956 are a number of careful adaptations of best-sellers and well-known literary works: *Les Miserables** (18), *Madame X* (20), *Oliver Twist* (22), *East Lynne* (30), *Cavalcade** (33), *Mutiny on the Bounty* (35).

*LLOYD, Harold DIR/SCEN USA. (Burchard, Nebraska April 20, 1893–March 8, 1971) One of the great creators of the silent comedy who, although not always credited as "director," was more artistically responsible for his films than Sam Taylor, Fred Newmeyer, etc. He began with Essanay and Hal Roach (*q.v.*), then made features for Roach and for his own company. He did not successfully survive the introduction of sound, his only good sound film being *Movie Crazy*. He appeared in some 200 films in his career, including the "Lonesome Luke" series. Features: *A Sailor-Made Man* (21), *Grandma's Boy* (22), *Dr. Jack** (22),

*Safety Last** (23), *Why Worry?** (23), *Girl Shy* (24), *Hot Water* (24), *The Freshman** (25), *For Heaven's Sake* (26), *The Kid Brother* (27), *Speedy* (28), *Welcome Danger* (29), *Feet First* (30), *Movie Crazy* (32), *The Catspaw* (34), *The Milky Way* (36), *Professor Beware* (38), *Mad Wednesday/The Sins of Harold Diddlebock* (47). Released two feature-length compilation films: *Harold Lloyd's World of Comedy* and *The Funny Side of Life*.

LODS, Jean DIR France. (Vesoul March 4, 1903–) Major French documentary film maker who played an important role in the avant-garde and pioneered the film on art in 1942 with *Maillol*.

DIR (notably): *24 heures en trente minutes* (27), *Champs-Elysées* (28), *La Vie d'un fleuve* (31), *Ladoumègue* (32), *Maillol* (42), *Aubusson* (46), *Mallarmé* (60).

LOEW, Marcus PROD USA. (New York May 8, 1870–New York 1927) Born of poor Austrian immigrants in the slums of New York's East Side, he became a fur salesman and through his friend Adolph Zukor (*q.v.*) invested in the developing Nickelodeons, which quickly grew into a nationwide chain of vaudeville and motion picture theaters. In 1920 Loew's Inc. purchased Metro Pictures Corporation, which a few years later was amalgamated with Goldwyn's to form Metro-Goldwyn-Mayer.

LOGAN, Joshua DIR USA. (Texarcana, Texas Oct 5, 1908–) The success of *Picnic** (55) and *Bus Stop** (56) led some to assume that Logan was a brilliant new film maker. But in fact he was an experienced theater director, well served by excellent scripts for his first two films, which he interpreted tastefully and intelligently. His admirers were disappointed with *Sayonara* (57), *South Pacific* (58), *Tall Story* (60), *Fanny* (61), *Ensign Pulver* (64), *Camelot* (67), *Paint Your Wagon* (69).

LOMNICKI, Jan DIR Poland. (1929–) The best of the younger generation of Polish documentary film makers, he has a sharp and sure touch and made striking use of images and sound to show how *A Ship is Born*. In 1963 he made his first feature, *The Dowry*, and has since made several others.

[DIR (notably): *Ziemia czeka* (54), **Mistrz Nikifor/Master Nikifor** (56), *Dom starych kobiet/The End of the Road* (58), *Huta 59* (59), *Stal/Steel* (59), *Narodziny miasta/The Birth of a Town* (59), *Koncert Wawelski/Wawel Concert* (60), *Narodziny statku/A Ship is Born* (61), *Suita Polska/Polish Suite* (62), *Wiano/ The Dowry* (63) (fiction feature), *Spotkania z Warszawa/Meetings with Warsaw* (65) (documentary feature), *Ab urbe condita* (65), *Kontrybucia/Contribution* (66) (fiction feature), *Cyrograf dojrzalosci/Compact of Maturity* (67) (TV fiction feature).]

LORENTZ, Pare DIR USA. (Clarksburg Dec 11, 1905–) Excellent American documentary film maker in the Thirties, most famous for *The Plow that Broke the Plains* (36), *The River** (37), *The Fight for Life* (41). [He was also a film critic and head of the short-lived US Government Film Service, for which he produced Ivens's *The Power and the Land* and Flaherty's *The Land**.]

LORENZI, Stellio DIR France. (Paris May 7, 1921–) The principal director of French TV, responsible for numerous documentary shorts from 1944 to 1957, who made his feature film debut by adapting *Climats* (62) from Maurois in his typical small-screen style.

*LOSEY, Joseph DIR Britain/USA. (La Crosse, Wisconsin Jan 14, 1909–) A film maker of great visual sensibility who has developed from the "socially committed" films of his Hollywood days to a broader concern with examining characters under moral or physical pressures, the pressures of an age molded by technology and in social turmoil. He began his career in 1930 as a dramatic critic in New York, then worked as a theater director for the Theater Guild and others. He traveled to Europe and was much influenced by the work of Brecht (*q.v.*), an influence that has continued throughout his film career, as he has often testified. In 1937 he began supervising documentaries and educational films for the Rockefeller Foundation, the State Department, and the National Youth Administration and directed his first film, a short puppet film, in 1939. He was under contract to MGM from 1943 to 1945, but it was not until 1948 that he broke completely with the theater

when he directed the morality fable *The Boy with Green Hair*, followed by the equally liberal *The Lawless*. His next three films revealed something of the style of his later work: *The Prowler*, *M* (remake), and *The Big Night* all emphasize character relationships in a sharp-edged, almost hysterical style. In 1950, hounded by the House Un-American Activities Committee, Losey left the USA and worked for some years in Europe under pseudonyms before re-establishing his reputation with the moral and social analysis of *Time without Pity* (57). Since then his work has increased in depth and assurance through the brilliant social thrillers, *Blind Date* and *The Criminal*, the bleak metaphysical fable *The Damned*, and the social tragicomedies, *The Servant* and *Accident. Eve* is perhaps his most personal film and, even in the mutilated version, intensely poetic and brilliant, arguably comparable to Mizoguchi's *Ugetsu**, though less affirmative. In recent years his work has gained much from his association with scriptwriter Harold Pinter (*q.v.*) as earlier it had from his collaboration with production designer Richard Macdonald (*q.v.*) on many of his American and British films. He sees film-making as a collaborative venture: "I believe that everybody should make his particular contribution: the designer, the writer, the composer, the cameraman. Everyone must be free and encouraged to make his own contribution within an overall framework and control and discipline which obviously comes from the director . . . the more one works with people, the more one establishes an artistic language, and the more one can deepen one's work . . . There are in general two kinds of writers who work on films as far as I'm concerned. One is very personal and contributive, like Pinter for instance . . ." Of his work in general he has said: "I don't regard my work as being particularly pessimistic because I think pessimism is an attitude that sees no hope in human beings or life in general, that has no compassion therefore; and to have compassion, I strongly believe you have to examine the worst, the most tragic, the most crucifying aspects of life as well as the beautiful ones, and also the things that corrupt life, distort it, destroy it."

DIR: *Pete Roleum and His Cousins* (USA 39) (puppet short), *A Child Went Forth*

157

(USA41) (short), *Youth Gets a Break* (USA41) (short), *A Gun in His Hand* (USA41) (short in series *Crime Does Not Pay*), *The Boy with Green Hair* (USA48), *The Lawless/The Dividing Line** (USA49), *The Prowler* (USA50), *M** (USA50) (remake), *The Big Night* (USA51), *Imbarco a Mezzanote/Stranger on the Prowl/Encounter* (It51) (under *pseud* Andrea Forzano), *The Sleeping Tiger* (Brit54) (credited to Victor Hanbury), *A Man on the Beach* (55) (short), *The Intimate Stranger/Finger of Guilt* (55) (under *pseud* Joseph Walton), *Time without Pity** (56), *The Gypsy and the Gentleman* (57), *Blind Date/Chance Meeting** (59), *The Criminal/Concrete Jungle** (60), *The Damned/These Are the Damned** (61), *Eva/Eve* (It62), *The Servant** (Brit63), *King and Country* (64), *Modesty Blaise* (66), *Accident* (67), *Boom* (68), *Secret Ceremony* (68), *Figures in a Landscape* (70), *The Go-between* (71).

LOTAR, Eli PHOTOG/DIR France. (Paris Jan 30, 1905–) Above all, a cameraman, responsible for the photography of Buñuel's *Las Hurdes** and Storck's *Les Maisons de la misère,* he directed an important short on the sordid life in Paris slums, *Aubervilliers* (46), from Jacques Prévert's script.

*LOW, Colin ANIM/DIR Canada. (Cardston, Alberta 1926–) After studying at the Calgary School of Fine Arts, he joined the National Film Board (NFB) of Canada in 1945 and collaborated with George Dunning (*q.v.*) on the animated *Cadet Rousselle* (47). He was named director of the animation department at NFB in 1950 and made his most popular cartoon in 1952, *The Romance of Transportation,* somewhat in the UPA style. He later turned to documentary and co-directed, with Roman Kroitor, the famous *Universe* (60). He was co-producer of *Labyrinth* at Expo '67 in Montreal and was responsible for the first participatory social film series, the *Challenge for Change* program in Newfoundland.
ANIM (notably): *Cadet Rousselle* (47), *Time and Terrain* (48), *Science Against Cancer* (48), *The Romance of Transportation* (52), *Jolifou Inn* (55), *It's a Crime* (57) (co: Grant Munro).
DIR (notably): *Corral* (54), *City of Gold* (57) (co-dir: Wolf Koenig), *City Out of Time* (59), *Universe* (60) (co-dir: Roman Kroitor), *Circle of the Sun* (61), *The Days of Whisky Gap* (61), *The Hutterites* (63).

LOY, Nanni DIR Italy. (Cagliari 1925–) Relatively new Italian director, best known for his portrayals of various events of the last war.
DIR (notably): *Il Marito* (55) (co-dir: G. Puccini), *Parola di Ladri* (56), *Audace Colpo dei Soliti Ignoti* (59), *Giorno da Leoni* (61), *La Battaglia di Napoli/ Four Days of Naples* (62), *Il Padre di Famiglia* (68).

LUBITSCH, Ernst DIR Germany/USA. (Berlin Jan 28, 1892–Hollywood Nov 30, 1947) An artful, clever film maker whose films, even the most vulgar, never lacked verve or craftsmanship. He worked in many genres, most notably spectaculars and sophisticated comedies, and had many successes. He was the son of a Berlin tailor and at an early age had acting ambitions. Through the actor, Victor Arnold, he met Max Reinhardt (*q.v.*) and joined his theater company in 1911. He played many stage roles and began appearing as an actor in films in 1912. He directed his first film, a short comedy, in 1914 and made numerous shorts (mostly one-reelers) until he established his international reputation in 1918 with *The Eyes of the Mummy Ma.* This spectacular, based on the traditions of the Italian spectaculars, established a formula that he followed with varying success in *Carmen, Madame Dubarry, Sumurun, Anna Boleyn,* and *The Loves of Pharaoh.* [At this time he also made his first sophisticated, satirical comedies derived from the traditions of central European vaudeville: *Die Austernprinzessin, Die Puppe, Kölhiesels Töchter, Die Bergkatze,* though these were then less well-known outside Germany than his historical spectaculars.] He was invited to the USA by Mary Pickford to direct her next film (*Rosita*) and in the USA during the silent period made a series of stylish comedies of manners, *The Marriage Circle, Three Women, Forbidden Paradise, Lady Windermere's Fan,* and *So This Is Paris,* in which, as a French critic of the time put it, "he set about bringing to the Americans the European comedy in all its charm, decadence, and frivolity." With the coming of sound, he developed a penchant for musical comedy with *The Love Parade, Monte Carlo, The Smiling Lieutenant, One Hour With You,* and even a version of *The Merry Widow.* He never lost his taste for comedy, or, more exactly, for central European vaudeville, and his brilliant films like *Trouble in Paradise* and *Design for Living* made him one of the founders of the Hollywood "screwball" comedies and the comedies of manners. He later turned to political propaganda with *Ninotchka* and used the background of Nazi-occupied Poland with great flair in *To Be or Not to Be.* During his career he gathered around him many collaborators of German extraction — like his scriptwriter Hans Kräly, set designer Hans Dreier, and in later years Billy Wilder and Otto Preminger (all *q.v.*), who were to inherit his mantle. Pierre Henry justly characterized him in 1926 as "a brilliant man but one who never completely lost his theatrical background."

DIR: *Fräulein Seifenschaum* (Ger14), *Blinde Kuh* (14), *Meyer als soldat* (14), *Aufs Eis geführt* (15), *Zucker und Zimt* (15) (co-dir: F. Matray), *Als Ich Tot War* (16), *Der Gemischte Frauenchor* (16), *Leutnant auf Befehl* (16), *Wo Ist Mein Schatz* (16), *Der Schwarze Moritz* (16), *Schuhpalast Pinkus* (16), *Der GmbH Tenor* (16), *Der Erste Patient* (16), *Ossis Tagebuch* (17), *Der Blusenkönig* (17), *Wenn Vier Dasselbe Tun (Machen)* (17), *Ein Fideles Gefängnis* (17), *Der Kraftmeyer* (17), *Prinz Sami* (17), *Der Letzte Anzug* (17), *Der Rodelkavalier* (18), *Ich Möchte Kein Mann Sein* (18), *Der Fall Rosentopf* (18), *Die Augen der Mummie Ma* (18), *Das Mädel vom Ballet* (18), *Carmen/Gypsy Blood** (18), *Führmann Henschel* (?) (18), *Marionetten* (18), *Meine Frau, Die Filmschauspielerin* (18), *Meier aus Berlin* (18), *Schabenmädle* (19), *Die Austernprinzessin** (19), *Rausch* (19), *Madame Dubarry/Passion** (19), *Die Puppe* (19), *Kölhiesels Totchter* (20), *Romeo und Julia im Schnee* (20), *Sumurun/One Arabian Night* (20), *Anna Boleyn/Deception* (20), *Die Tolle Rikschau* (?) (20), *Die Bergkatze* (21), *Vendetta* (?) (21) (18?), *Das Weib des Pharaoh/The Loves of Pharaoh* (22), *Die Flamme/Montmartre* (Ger22), *Rosita* (USA23), *The Marriage Circle* (24), *Three Women* (24), *Forbidden Paradise* (24), *Kiss Me Again* (25), *Lady Windermere's Fan* (25), *So This is Paris* (26), *The Student Prince/In Old Heidelberg* (27), *The Patriot* (28), *Eternal Love* (29), *The Love Parade** (29), *Paramount on Parade* (30) (in part), *Monte Carlo* (30), *The Smiling Lieutenant* (31), *The Man I Killed/Broken Lullaby* (32), *One Hour With You* (32), *Trouble in Paradise** (32), *If I Had a Million* (32) (one episode), *Design for Living* (33), *The Merry Widow** (34), *Desire* (36) (supervised only, dir: Frank Borzage), *Angel* (37), *Bluebeard's Eighth Wife* (38), *Ninotchka** (39), *The Shop Around the Corner* (40), *That Uncertain Feeling* (41), *To Be or Not to Be** (42), *Heaven Can Wait* (43), *A Royal Scandal* (45) (remake of *Forbidden Paradise,* supervised by Lubitsch, dir: Otto Preminger), *Cluny Brown* (46), *That Lady in Ermine* (48) (completed by Preminger).

LUKOV, Leonid DIR USSR. (Ukraine May 1909–Leningrad April 1963) Prolific film maker with an exuberant but often facile style, notable for *Bolshaya zhizn/A Great Life* (40) and *Ya Lyublyu/I Love* (36), a somewhat rosy portrait of the life of Donbas miners.

LUMET, Sidney DIR USA. (Philadelphia June 25, 1924–) Not a film maker in the true sense but a talented and conscientious technician with a passion for the theater and an ability to handle actors. His work is usually as good as the original play or novel on which it is based. He began his career as a child actor and after the war became interested in directing. He was responsible for over 250 teleplays in the Fifties.

DIR: *12 Angry Men** (56), *Stage Struck* (58) (remake of *Morning Glory*), *That Kind of Woman* (59), *The Fugitive Kind* (59), *A View from the Bridge/Vu du pont* (Fr/USA61), *Long Day's Journey into Night* (62), *Fail Safe* (63), *The Pawnbroker** (64), *The Hill* (Brit 65), *The Group* (66), *The Deadly Affair* (Brit67), *Bye Bye Braverman* (67), *The Sea Gull* (Brit68), *The Appointment* (69), *Blood Kin* (69), *The Last of the Mobile Hot Shots* (69), *The Anderson Tapes* (71).

LUMIERE, Antoine PHOTOG France. (Ormay, Haute-Saône 1840–Lyon 190?) The father of Auguste and Louis Lumière was originally trained as a painter and in 1860 became a photographer in Besançon, where his sons were born. In 1871 he moved to Lyon and in 1881 he opened a factory for photographic products in Lyon-Montplaisir. His business prospered and became a major industry. By 1894 he was taking less of an active role in the *Société Antoine Lumière et ses fils* (founded in 1893) but in that year he became enthusiastic over the Edison Kinetoscope, which he had seen in Paris. He purchased one of these and asked his sons to develop a means for projecting its pictures. In 1895 he took the apparatus his sons had patented and organized the first public screening in Paris at the Grand Café with his friend and former collaborator, Clément Maurice. In 1896–97 he refused to sell the Cinématographe equipment to Georges Méliès and arranged for Georges Hatot to direct some films for their company.

LUMIERE, Auguste INVENTOR France. (Besançon Oct 20, 1862–Lyon April 10, 1954) With his brother, Louis, he filed the original patents on the Cinématographe, in the invention of which he played a small part. He later devoted himself to medical research. He directed one film: *Mauvaises herbes/les Brûleurs d'herbe* (1896).

LUMIERE, Louis INVENTOR France. (Besançon Oct 5, 1864–Bandol, Var June 6, 1948) He is, first and foremost, the inventor of the Cinématographe, but he was also an excellent film maker. In 1895 the Cinématographe represented a major advance over all existing equipment (various parts of which he had adopted) because it could not only record moving pictures anywhere but could project them on a screen. Its worldwide success was such that it gave birth to a new form of entertainment and a new industry; the name he gave the equipment has been adapted into the languages of most countries as the term for the art and industry of film. Few countries have retained the names of rival equipment — Bioskop, Biograph, etc. As a film maker he was the first to record "life as it happened" in his first very short films, all of which reflect his feeling for visual qualities, background, and framing. He used "close-ups" in *Déjeuner de bébé*, depth of field in *Arrivée d'un train*, and devised the first "comedies" with *L'Arroseur arrosé* and *Le Faux Cul-de-jatte*. He trained numerous cameramen who traveled around the world and made major contributions to the development of documentaries, editing, and the film industry in various countries. His importance in the history of the cinema is considerable, even though he was eventually outstripped by his competitors in making commercial films and was indebted to the work of the Americans, Muybridge (*q.v.*), Armat, Jenkins (*q.v.*), and Latham and the German, Skladanowsky (*q.v.*), who first demonstrated his equipment before Lumière. 1882: Perfected Van Monckhoven's silver bromide on gelatin formula, creating the *Etiquette Bleue* photographic plates on which the Lumière factory's success was based. December 1894: Developed a process for moving film using two perforations per frame, abandoning the Marey chronophotographic camera and the Kinetoscope in the process. The first films were made on paper. January-February 1895: Developed the apparatus (prototype built by Charles Moisson) for making films on 35mm celluloid. February 13, 1895: Patent granted for an "apparatus used for obtaining and viewing chronophotographic prints." March 10, 1895: Additional patent granted for the perfected apparatus, now called Cinématographe. March 22, 1895: First projection of the film, *La Sortie des usines,* to the Société pour L'Encouragement à l'Industrie. Other presentations to the Congrès des Sociétés Françaises de Photographie (Lyon, June 10 and 12), to the Revue Générale des Sciences (Paris July 11) and at the Sorbonne (Paris Nov 16). Louis Lumière made some 30–40 films during 1895. December 28, 1895: First public presentation of the Lumière Cinématographe in the Salon Indien of the Grand Café, 14 boulevard des Capucines, Paris. 1896: Louis Lumière hires and trains many cameramen and operators (including A. Promio and Félix Mesguich) and sends them around the world. The Cinématographe is premiered in London (Feb 17), Brussels (Feb 29), Vienna and Madrid (April), Berlin (April 30), Geneva (May 1), Bombay (June 7), Belgrade (June 25), New York (June 28), Saint Petersburg (July 17), Bucharest (August), and later in Egypt, Japan, Australia, Canada, etc. 1897: Lumière's representative leaves New York. The Cinématographes are placed on sale. 1898–1900 Louis Lumière experiments with large screen cinematography for the Paris Exposition. May-November 1900: Projection of widescreen (21 meters by 16 meters) films photographed on 72mm film with 8 pairs of perforations per frame. November 3 1900: Lumière patent for stereoscopic cinema. December 29 1900: Lumière patent for Photorama, static, circular panoramic photography, which is exhibited in Paris in 1902. 1905: Last films made for the Société Lumière, which thereafter ceased the production and sale of films. 1920: Louis Lumière abandons his position with the Lumière factory. 1934: Makes his first stereoscopic films. May 1 1936: Premiere in Paris of stereoscopic films (which required special bicolored glasses for viewing).

DIR (in 1895, notably): *La Sortie des usines* (two versions), *L'Arroseur arrosé/ Le Jardinier, Forgerons, Pompiers* (four films), *Le Déjeuner de Bébé/Le Repas de Bébé, Pêche aux poissons rouges, Le Débarquement, Saute à la couverture/ Brimade dans una caserne, Lyon, place des Cordeliers, Characuterie mécanique, Atéliers de la Ciotat, Barque sortant du port/La Sortie du port, Arrivée d'un train en gare, Arrivée d'un train à La Ciotat, Partie d'écarté, Assiettes tournantes, Chapeaux à transformations, Photographe* (?1896), *Démolition d'un mur* (?1896), *Querelle enfantine, Aquarium, Partie de tric-trac, Le Déjeuner du chat, La Voltige, Départ en voiture, Enfants au jouets, Course en sac, Baignade en mer, Le Maréchal-ferrant, Lyon, place Bellecour,* *Récreation à la Martinière, Lancement d'un navire à La Ciotat.* See entry: *Lumière Films* in the companion *Dictionary of Films.*

LUPU-PICK *see* PICK, LUPU

LYE, Len ANIM/DIR Britain. (Christchurch, New Zealand 1901–) Imaginative pioneer animator who invented the technique of drawing and painting dynamic forms onto film (in *Colour Box*) and worked for Grierson (*q.v.*) at the GPO Film Unit in the Thirties. His work considerably influenced Norman McLaren, who took up and developed his techniques, but he himself was not able to make a career in the cinema and later, after he moved to the USA, turned to more traditional art forms. [He also worked on documentary and compilation films, most notably *Cameramen at War* and the photomontage *Trade Tattoo,* but not on *Germany Calling* (a trick film in which the Nazis are made to dance the Lambeth Walk), although he has been credited with this in Europe.]

ANIM/DIR (notably): *Experimental Animation* (33), *Colour Box* (35), *Birth of a Robot* (35) (with Humphrey Jennings), *Rainbow Dance** (36), *Kaleidoscope* (36), *Trade Tattoo* (37), *Musical Poster No. 1* (40), *Swinging the Lambeth Walk* (40), *Kill or Be Killed* (42), *Women at War* (43), *Cameraman at War* (44), *Bells of Atlantis* (52), *Colour Cry* (55), *Free Radicals* (57).

MABROOK, Hossein DIR Somalia. (? –)
He would appear to be the director of
the first Black African feature, *Love
Knows No Obstacle* (61), a film in the
Somali language, entirely conceived,
staged, and acted by Africans.

MACARTHUR, Charles SCEN/DIR USA.
(Cranton Nov 5, 1895–New York April
21, 1956) Playwright and excellent
American scriptwriter of the Thirties
who almost always worked in collaboration with Ben Hecht, both on scripts and
on the series of independently produced
films they co-directed. (See HECHT for
filmography.) A teleplay on his youth,
Hello Charlie, was written in 1960 by
Ben Hecht.

MCCAREY, Leo DIR USA. (Los Angeles
Oct 3, 1898–July 1969) From 1918–23
he was Tod Browning's (*q.v.*) assistant;
from 1923–28 he worked under Hal
Roach (*q.v.*) and scripted and directed
many notably Laurel and Hardy shorts.
In the Thirties he directed several "screwball" comedies, including *The Awful
Truth* (37) and *Ruggles of Red Gap*
(35), and worked for some excellent
comedians: for the Marx Brothers on
*Duck Soup** (33); for W. C. Fields on
Six of a Kind (34); for Harold Lloyd
on *The Milky Way* (36); for Eddie Cantor on *The Kid from Spain* (32). He
later gave his sentimental streak free
vein in the religious propaganda of *Going
My Way** (44) and *The Bells of St.
Mary* (45), the first of which won him
Oscars for both best script and direction. His later comedies and sentimental
melodramas are of little interest.

*MACDONALD, Richard ART DIR Britain.
(Banffshire, Scotland c. 1920–) Not
an art director in the traditional sense
but a "production designer" who designs
a film's whole visual style, even the composition of individual images. He studied
at the Royal College of Art in London
and began his film career as a sketch artist. It was in this capacity that he worked
with Losey (*q.v.*) on his first British
film, *The Sleeping Tiger.* For over ten
years he collaborated closely with Losey,
undoubtedly contributing much to the
characteristic Losey style of this period:
*Time without Pity** (56), *The Gypsy
and the Gentleman** (57), *Blind Date**
(59), *The Criminal** (60), *The Damned**
(61), *Eve* (62), *The Servant** (63),
King and Country (64), *Modesty Blaise*
(66), *Secret Ceremony* (69). Also, for
John Schlesinger, *Far From the Madding
Crowd* (67); for Dick Clement, *A Sev-
ered Head* (70).

MACHATY, Gustav DIR Czechoslovakia/
USA, etc. (Prague May 9, 1901–Munich
Dec 14, 1963) A film maker best remembered for *Erotikon* and *Extase,* films
whose worldwide success certainly
stemmed from their erotic themes but
which were, nevertheless, cinematically
admirable. [From 1920–24 he worked
in the USA as Stroheim's (*q.v.*), assistant. He also worked in the States from
1936–45.
DIR (notably): *Sonata Kreutzerova* (26),
*Erotikon** (29), *Ze Soboty na Nedeli*
(31), *Extase** (32), *Nocturno* (Aust34),
Ballerine (It36), *Within the Law* (USA
39), *Jealousy* (USA45), *Suchkind 312*
(GFR55).
SCEN: for Pabst, *Es Geschah am 20 Juli*
(Aust55), and for his own *The Kreutzer
Sonata, Erotikon, Extase, Jealousy.*]

**MACHIN, Alfred (Eugène Alfred Jean-Baptiste
Machin)** DIR France/Belgium/Nether-
lands. (Blandecques, Pas-de-Calais 1877–
1929) One of the most individual talents
of the early cinema and one of the few

pre-1914 French film makers concerned with social themes (*Au ravissement des dames, Le Moulin maudit*). He began in 1908 as a cameraman-director for Pathé on outdoor animal films and in 1911 directed comedies for Comica in Nice. He worked in the Netherlands and Belgium and during the war joined the French Army film service. He was Griffith's assistant on *Hearts of the World**. After 1920 he returned to directing mainly animal films.

[DIR (notably): *Chasse à l'Hippopatame sur le Nil bleu* (08), *Chasse à la panthère* (09), *Babylas a herite d'une panthère* (11), *Babylas explorateur* (11), *Le Devouement d'un gosse* (11), *Little Moritz soldat d'Afrique* (12, *La Fleur sanglante* (12), *Het Lidjen van der Scheepsjongen* (Neth12), *De Molens die Juichen en Weemen* (Neth12), *L'Histoire d'un p'tit gars* (Fr12), *De Strijd der Geuzen* (Neth12), *Histoire de Minna Claessens* (Belg12), *Un episode à Waterloo* (Belg13), *Le Moulin maudit/Maudite soit la guerre** (Belg13), *L'Agent Rijolo et son chien policier* (Belg13), *De Droppel Bloed* (Neth13), *La Ronde infernale* (Belg13), *Supreme sacrifice* (Belg13), *Au ravissement des dames** (Belg13), *Napoléon: du sacre à Sainte-Hélène* (Fr14), *La Tulipe d'or* (Belg14), *La Bataille de la Somme* (Fr16), *La Bataille de Verdun* (Fr17), *Une nuit agitée* (Fr20), *Pervenche* (Fr21) (5 episodes), *Bêtes . . . comme les hommes* (Fr23), *Moi aussi, j'accuse* (Fr23), *Le Manoir de la peur* (Fr27), *Le Retour* (Fr28), *De la jungle à l'écran* (Fr29) *Robinson Junior/Black and White* (Fr31).]

MACKENDRICK, Alexander DIR/SCEN Britain/USA. (Boston, USA 1912–) Undoubtedly the best British director to develop in the immediate postwar years, a film maker whose work retained and even increased in assurance after the demise of Ealing. He began in advertising and wrote documentary films before joining Ealing as a scriptwriter. He established his reputation with his first directorial effort, *Whisky Galore* (48), a truculent film in which his own Scottish ancestry served him well. Though *Mandy* is oversentimental and *The Ladykillers* is built on stereotypes and hackneyed themes from the Ealing heyday, *The Man in the White Suit* has the depth of a modern morality fable and *The Maggie* and

Whisky Galore are delightful satires. He made one of the best American films of the Fifties, the mordant *The Sweet Smell of Success,* while the underestimated *Sammy Going South, High Wind in Jamaica,* and *Don't Make Waves* have extremely subtle, delicate, and individualistic styles.

SCEN (notably): *The Pocket Cartoon* (41) (short), *Carnival in the Clothes Cupboard* (42) (short), *Fable of the Fabrics* (43) (short), *Abu* series (43) (4 shorts), and for Sinclair Hill, *Midnight Menace* (37); for Basil Dearden, *Saraband for Dead Lovers* (48), *The Blue Lamp* (50); for Charles Crichton, *Dance Hall* (50); and for his own *Whisky Galore, The Man in the White Suit.*

DIR: *Whisky Galore/Tight Little Island** (48), *The Man in the White Suit** (51), *Mandy/The Crash of Silence* (52), *The Maggie/High and Dry** (53), *The Ladykillers* (55), *The Sweet Smell of Success** (USA57), *Sammy Going South/A Boy Ten Feet Tall* (Brit62), *A High Wind in Jamaica* (Brit65), *Don't Make Waves* (USA67), *Mary Queen of Scots* (in preparation 71).

MCLAREN, Norman ANIM Canada/Britain. (Stirling, Scotland April 11, 1914–) Undoubtedly the greatest contemporary creator of animated films, a film maker who went back to the genre's roots, particularly to the work of Emile Cohl (*q.v.*). He has employed a wide range of techniques — drawing and painting directly onto film (see Len Lye) and making use of crayons, synthetic sound, pixilation (animation of objects and people), stereoscopy, etc. [He studied at Glasgow Art School and made his first films as an amateur after seeing the films of Oskar Fischinger (*q.v.*). In 1935 John Grierson (*q.v.*) offered him a position with the GPO Film Unit, where he worked on both animated films and documentaries. In 1939 he went to the USA and made several films there before joining the National Film Board of Canada in 1941. He has worked at the NFB ever since, except for several months in China, 1949–50, and in India, 1953, training students in animation techniques.] He has said: "Animation is not the art of putting designs into motion but of designed motion. What happens between two images is more important than a single image. Animation is the art of knowing properly how to treat the invisible spaces that exist between images."

ANIM/DIR: *Seven Till Five* (33) (documentary), *Camera Makes Whoopee* (35), *Color Cocktail* (35), *Hell Unlimited* (36), *Book Bargain* (37) (documentary), *News for the Navy* (37) (documentary), *Money a Pickle* (37), *Love on the Wing* (37), *The Obedient Flame* (39), *Allegro* (USA39), *Rumba* (USA 39), *Stars and Stripes* (USA39), *Dots* (USA40), *Loops* (USA40), *Boogie Doodle* (USA40), *Spook Sport* (USA40) (collab: Mary Ellen Bute), *Mail Early for Christmas* (Canada41), *V for Victory* (41), *Hen Hop* (42), *Five for Four* (42), *Dollar Dance* (43), *Keep Your Mouth Shut* (44), *Chants populaires* series (44–46) (supervised all and directed *Alouette*, 44, *C'est l'Aviron*, 45, *Là-haut sur ces montagnes*, 46), *A Little Fantasy on a 19th Century Painting* (46), *Hoppity Pop* (46), *Fiddle De Dee* (47), *La Poulette grise* (47), *Begone Dull Care* (49), *Pen Point Percussion* (50) (documentary on the making of synthetic sound), *Around is Around* (50) (3D film produced in collaboration with the British Film Institute), *Now is the Time* (51) (3D film prod: in collaboration with the British Film Institute), *A Fantasy* (52), *Neighbors** (52), *Two Bagatelles* (52), *Blinkity Blank* (54), *Rythmetic* (54), *A Chairy Tale** (57) (collab: Claude Jutra), *Le Merle* (58), *Serenal* (59), *Short and Suite* (59), *Mail Early for Christmas* (59), *Lines Vertical* (60), *Opening Speech* (60), *New York Lightboard* (60), *Lines Horizontal* (62), *Canon* (64), *Mosaic* (65), *Pas de deux* (67), *Spheres* (69). Other work includes: photography for Ivor Montagu's *Defense of Madrid* (Brit36), credit titles for *The Wonderful World of Jack Paar* (USA59, TV series), credit titles for the animation compilation, *Christmas Crackers* (Canada63).

MCLEOD, Norman Z(enos) DIR USA. (Graylong Sept 20, 1898–1964) An unpretentious Hollywood craftsman whose name will always be associated with several outstanding burlesque comedies in the early Thirties, [though he is hardly the creative genius behind the Marx Brothers or W. C. Fields. He began as an animator, then became a scriptwriter. In the Forties he directed Danny Kaye in his most famous film, *The Secret Life of Walter Mitty,* and also directed several Bob Hope comedies.]

DIR (notably): *Monkey Business** (31), *Horse Feathers* (32) (both with the Marx Brothers), *Alice in Wonderland* (33), *It's a Gift* (34) (both with W. C. Fields), *Topper* (37), *Lady Be Good* (41), *The Kid from Brooklyn* (46) (remake of *The Milky Way*), *The Secret Life of Walter Mitty** (47) (both with Danny Kaye), *Road to Rio* (48), *The Paleface* (48), *My Favorite Spy* (51) (all with Bob Hope).

*MADDOW, Ben (David Wolff) SCEN/DIR (? –) Imaginative scriptwriter with an often potent style, though it is somewhat elusive since he has worked under various pseudonyms. In the Thirties, under his real name, he was a poet, left-wing writer, and a member of Frontier Films, for whom he wrote the commentary for *Native Land** (42). He moved to Hollywood under the name Ben Maddow and wrote several notable scripts, including *The Asphalt Jungle* and *Intruder in the Dust,* before being blacklisted during the McCarthy era. It has been suggested that he wrote several uncredited scripts for Huston (*q.v.*) and under commission to Yorden (*q.v.*). He has returned to scriptwriting, under the name Maddow, in the Sixties. He co-directed the documentary, *The Bridge,* and directed the ferocious portrait of a decadent society, *The Savage Eye,* and the mediocre *An Affair of the Skin.*

SCEN (notably): for Richard Wallace, *Framed* (47); for Norman Foster, *Kiss the Blood off My Hands* (48); for Henry Levin, *The Man from Colorado* (48); for Huston, *The Asphalt Jungle** (50), *The Unforgiven* (60); for Clarence Brown, *Intruder in the Dust** (49); for Fred Wilcox, *Shadow in the Sky* (51); for Charles Walters, *Two Loves/Spinster* (61); for Joseph Strick, *The Balcony* (63); for J. Lee Thompson, *The Most Dangerous Man in the World* (Brit69), for Kramer, *The Secret of Santa Vittoria* (69), for Paul Wendkos, *The Mephisto Waltz* (70).

DIR: *The Bridge* (44) (co-dir: W. Van Dyke), *The Savage Eye* (59) (co-dir: Sidney Meyers, Joseph Strick), *An Affair of the Skin* (63), *Storm of Strangers* (69) (short).

MAETZIG, Kurt DIR German Democratic Republic (Berlin Jan 25, 1911–) Co-founder of DEFA, the East German film production company, in 1945, he established his reputation as one of the new postwar talents with the sincere and somewhat melancholic *Ehe im Schatten* (47) and *Die Buntkarierten* (49), both better than his ambitious *Roman einer jungen Ehe* (51) and the two *Ernst Thälmann* films (53, 55).

MAGDALENO, Maurico SCAN Mexico. (Villa de Refugios May 13, 1906–) He was Emilio Fernandez's (*q.v.*) usual script-writer and contributed much to such major successes of this director as *Maria Candelaria** and *Rio Escondido**.

MAGGI, Luigi DIR Italy. (Turin Dec 21, 1867–Turin Aug 22, 1946) An important pioneer of the Italian cinema who began his career as an actor in Piedmontese dialect theater and was the first in Italy, before Martoglio (*q.v.*), to use the cinema for descriptive realism. He used flashbacks in *La Lampada della nonna* (12) and parallel action in *Satana* (12) and might have influenced Griffith (*q.v.*) and perhaps Dreyer (*q.v.*). Also, notably: *Gli Ultimi giornii di Pompei* (08), *Galileo Galilei* (08), *La Fiaccola sotto il Moggio* (11), *Nozze d'oro* (11), *Il Ponte dei Fantasmi* (12).

MAKK, Karoly DIR Hungary. (1925–) Gifted and intelligent Hungarian film maker who emerged as a major talent in the Fifties after serving as an assistant since the end of the war. DIR: *Liliomfi* (54), *9-es korterem/Ward No. 9* (55), *Mese a tizenket talalatrol/Tale on the Twelve Points* (56), *Haz a sziklak alatt/The House Under the Rocks* (58), *A 39-es dandar/Brigade No. 39* (59), *Fure lepni szabad/Don't Keep off the Grass* (60), *Megszallottak/The Fanatics* (61), *Elveszett paradicsom/The Last Paradise* (62), *Az Utolso elotti ember/The Last But One* (63), *Mit csinalt felseged 3-5-ig/His Majesty's Dates* (64), *Isten es ember elott/Before God and Man* (68).

MALLE, Louis DIR France. (Thumeries, Nord Oct 30, 1932–) Former *nouvelle vague* film maker who established an international reputation with *Les Amants* (58) and has continued to make worth-while films. Though he has not yet made a masterpiece, he has at least been concerned with making each new film a development in both mastery of technique and of subject, moving from the stylistic exercise of the commercial thriller, *Ascenseur pour l'échafaud,* to the elegant treatment of sexual passion in *Les Amants,* to zaniness verging on tragedy in *Zazie dans le Métro* and to the extension of narrative method in the portrait of a film star's life in *Vie privée*. [With *Le Feu follet* he reached a new level of assurance but, regrettably, his later features have been largely vivid, colorful confections. Since he made a TV documentary in Thailand in 1963 he has shown increasing interest in a kind of subjective TV journalism, most notably in his curious series on India. He graduated from IDHEC, served as Cousteau's (*q.v.*) assistant from 1953, and was Bresson's (*q.v.*) assistant on *Un condamné à mort s'est échappé**.] DIR: *Fontaine de Vaucluse* (53) (short), *Station 307* (55) (short), *Le Monde du silence** (56) (co-dir: Cousteau), *Ascenseur pour l'échafaud* (57), *Les Amants** (58), *Zazie dans le Métro** (60), *Vie privée* (61), *Le Feu follet** (63), *Twiste encore* (63) (short, in *Vive le Tour*), *Bons baisers de Bangkok* (63) (TV short), *Viva Maria* (65), *Le Voleur* (66), *Loin de Vietnam* (67) (in part), *Histoires extraordinaires/A Tre Passi del Delirio* (67) (one episode), *Calcutta* (69), *India* (70) (7 TV shorts), *Le Souffle au coeur* (71)

MALRAUX, André DIR France. (Paris Nov 3, 1901–) Famous French novelist, essayist, philosopher of art and former revolutionary militant, who, more recently, was prominent in the Gaullist movement and was Minister of State for Cultural Affairs in the Fifth Republic. He has, since his youth, retained a deep interest in the cinema. He wrote his famous essay *Sketch for a Psychology of the Moving Pictures* in 1940 (reprinted in English in *Reflections on Art,* 1958, edited by Susanne K. Langer) and made the feature film *Espoir** (38–45) in Spain during the Civil War.

MALTZ, Albert SCEN USA. (New York Oct 28, 1908–) Excellent American scriptwriter, one of the Hollywood Ten imprisoned in 1949 for contempt of Congress. [He was blacklisted for many years: in 1957 he was hired by Frank Sinatra to write *The Execution of Private Slovick,* but the pressure of anti-Communist groups, and even of John F. Kennedy, forced Sinatra to withdraw his offer. He has recently returned to scriptwriting in his own name. He is also the author of several novels. His scripts had an occasional tendency to rather wordy sermonizing.]

SCEN (notably): for Archie Mayo, *Black Legion* (36); for W. S. Van Dyke, *They Gave Him a Gun* (37); for Frank Tuttle, *This Gun for Hire* (42), *Moscow Strikes Back* (42) (English adaptation of *The Defeat of the German Armies Near Moscow,* USSR 42, dir: I. Kopalin, L. Varlamov); for Delmer Daves, *Destination Tokyo* (43), *Pride of the Marines* (45); for Fritz Lang, *Cloak and Dagger* (46); for Jules Dassin, *Naked City** (48); for Don Siegel, *Two Mules for Sister Sara* (69).

MAMOULIAN, Rouben DIR USA. (Tiflis, Armenia Oct 8, 1898–) Undeniably a film maker of enormous talent who contributed many innovations both to Broadway and to the American cinema. Originally a stage director (best remembered for his *Porgy and Bess*), his imaginative Hollywood films — from the revolutionary *Applause* (29) to the first three-color Technicolor film, *Becky Sharp* (35) — marked him as one of the great individual talents, but his later work, mainly remakes and theatrical adaptations, is largely routine.

DIR: *Applause* (29), *City Streets** (31), *Dr. Jekyll and Mr Hyde* (31), *Love Me Tonight* (32), *The Song of Songs* (33), *Queen Christina* (33), *We Live Again* (34), *Becky Sharp* (35), *The Gay Desperado* (36), *High, Wide, and Handsome* (37), *Golden Boy* (39), *The Mark of Zorro** (40), *Blood and Sand* (41), *Rings on Her Fingers* (42), *Summer Holiday* (48), *The Wild Heart* (51), (replaced Michael Powell but uncredited), *Silk Stockings** (57), *Porgy and Bess* (59) (replaced by Otto Preminger), *Cleopatra* (63) (replaced by Joseph L. Mankiewicz).

MANKIEWICZ, Herman SCEN USA. (New York Nov 7, 1897–New York March 7, 1953) Good American scriptwriter (brother of Joseph Mankiewicz) in Hollywood from 1926, best known for his close collaboration with Orson Welles (*q.v.*) on the script of *Citizen Kane**. [His son, Don Mankiewicz (1922–) is also a scriptwriter, e.g., Mark Robson's *Trial* (55), Robert Wise's *I Want to Live* (58).]

MANKIEWICZ, Joseph Leo DIR/SCEN/PROD USA. (Wilkes-Barre, Pennsylvania Feb 11, 1909–) A skillful, cultivated, and intelligent film maker who has worked in many genres — thrillers, melodramas, theatrical adaptations, musical comedies, and social comedies — and has above all excelled in such comedies of social mores as *A Letter to Three Wives* and *All about Eve,* films that continued the Lubitsch tradition. The studied extravagance of *The Barefoot Contessa* brought him many admirers. [He began his career in Berlin in 1928 writing English subtitles for UFA and in 1929 joined Paramount (through his brother Herman) in Hollywood, where he became a dialogue writer. In 1933 he became a scriptwriter and later a producer for MGM. He directed his first film in 1946 and, until 1953, when he formed his own company, Figaro, made all his films for 20th Century-Fox. His contract with Fox to make *Cleopatra* involved the sale to Fox of Figaro. He has scripted and produced most of his own films.] His later films leaned heavily on the star system, though his excessively costly *Cleopatra* played a part in the crisis of this system, and the search for new, less expensive actors.

[SCEN (notably): for Edward Sutherland, *Fast Company* (29); for James Cruze, etc., *If I Had a Million* (32); for Eddie Cline, *Million Dollar Legs** (32); for Norman Z. McLeod, *Alice in Wonderland* (33); for W. S. Van Dyke, *Manhattan Madness* (34), *Forsaking All Others* (34), *I Live My Life* (35), *Love on the Run* (36); for Robert Leonard, *After Office Hours* (35); for Frank Borzage, *Mannequin* (38), *Strange Cargo* (40); for John Stahl, *The Keys of the Kingdom* (44); and most of his own films.]

DIR: *Dragonwyck* (46), *Somewhere in the Night* (46), *The Late George Apley* (47), *The Ghost and Mrs. Muir* (47), *Escape* (48), *A Letter to Three Wives** (49), *House of Strangers* (49), *No Way Out* (50), *All About Eve** (50), *People Will Talk* (51), *Five Fingers* (52), *Julius Caesar* (53), *The Barefoot Contessa**

166

(54), *Guys and Dolls* (55), *The Quiet American* (58), *Suddenly Last Summer* (59), *Cleopatra** (63) (replaced various directors), *Carol for Another Christmas* (64) (TV), *The Honey Pot* (67), *There Was a Crooked Man* (70).
[PROD *The Three Godfathers* (36), *Fury** (36), *The Gorgeous Hussy* (36), *Love on the Run* (36), *The Bride Wore Red* (37), *Double Wedding* (37), *Mannequin* (37), *Three Comrades* (38), *The Shopworn Angel* (38), *The Shining Hour* (38), *A Christmas Carol* (38), *The Adventures of Huckleberry Finn* (39), *Strange Cargo* (40), *The Philadelphia Story** (40), *The Wild Man of Borneo* (41), *The Feminine Touch* (41), *Woman of the Year* (42), *Cairo* (42), *Reunion in France* (42), *The Keys of the Kingdom* (44), *I Want to Live* (58), and most of his own films.]

MANN, Anthony (Emil Bundsmann) DIR USA. (San Diego June 30, 1906–April 29, 1967) Although not the equal of a director such as Howard Hawks (*q.v.*), he is, like him, an excellent example of all that is best in the American cinema: a feeling for character and story, an efficient style, and an intelligent use of landscape and background. Originally a Greenwich Village actor, director, and stage manager, he was hired by Selznick (*q.v.*) in 1938 as a talent scout. From 1938–42 he was a casting director and assistant, notably to Preston Sturges (*q.v.*) on *Sullivan's Travels*. He began his directorial career with mediocre B-pictures (including the worst kind of pseudo historical melodramas like *Reign of Terror*) and established his reputation in the Fifties with a series of brilliant, classical westerns: *Winchester 73, The Naked Spur, The Man from Laramie, The Far Country, Man of the West,* and *Cimarron*. His sense of style allowed him to make *El Cid* one of the most notable of epics without falling victim to the enormous financial resources at his command.
DIR: *Dr. Broadway* (42), *Moonlight in Havana* (42), *Nobody's Darling* (43), *My Best Gal* (43), *Strangers in the Night* (44), *The Great Flamarion* (45), *Two O'Clock Courage* (45), *Strange Impersonation* (45), *Sing Your Way Home* (45), *Bamboo Blonde* (46), *Desperate* (47), *Railroaded* (47), *T-Men* (48), *Raw Deal* (48), *He Walked By Night* (48) (completed by Alfred Werker), *Reign of Terror* (49), *Border Incident* (49), *Side Street* (49), *Devil's Doorway* (50), *The Furies* (50), *Winchester 73* (50), *Quo Vadis** (50) (2nd unit, dir: LeRoy), *The Tall Target* (51), *Bend of the River/Where the River Bends* (52), *The Naked Spur* (53), *Thunder Bay* (53), *The Glenn Miller Story* (54), *The Far Country* (55), *Strategic Air Command* (55), *The Man from Laramie* (55), *The Last Frontier* (56), *Serenade* (56), *Men in War* (57), *The Tin Star* (57), *God's Little Acre* (57), *Man of the West** (58), *Cimarron* (60) (completed by Charles Walters), *Spartacus* (60) (replaced by Stanley Kubrick after directing the opening), *El Cid** (61), *The Fall of the Roman Empire* (64), *The Heroes of Telemark* (Brit65), *A Dandy in Aspic* (Brit67) (completed by Laurence Harvey after Mann's death).

MANN, Daniel DIR USA. (New York Aug 8, 1912–) His moving adaptation of William Inge's play *Come Back Little Sheba* (52) could have led to his being taken for a film maker, but in fact he has remained true to his theatrical background, photographing Broadway successes (and occasionally novels) for the Hollywood screen: *The Rose Tattoo* (55), *Teahouse of the August Moon* (56), *Hot Spell* (58), *Butterfield 8* (60), *Judith* (65), etc.

MANN, Delbert DIR USA/Britain. (Lawrence Jan 30, 1920–) Like Daniel Mann, he is more of a conscientious adaptor of stage and literary successes than a film maker, though his background is more as a producer in TV (47–55) than in the theater. His first (and best) films, *Marty** (55), *Bachelor Party** (57), and *The Middle of the Night* (59), owe much, if not all, to Paddy Chayevsky (*q.v.*). [Also directed, notably, *Separate Tables* (58), *Desire under the Elms* (58), *The Dark at the Top of the Stairs* (60), *The Outsider* (62), *That Touch of Mink* (62), *Quick Before It Melts* (65), *Fitzwilly* (67), *David Copperfield* (Brit69), *Jane Eyre* (Brit70).]

MAREY, Etienne Jules INVENTOR France. (Beaune March 5, 1830–Paris May 16, 1904) Brilliant French physiologist whose pioneering work on the development of photographic techniques for the study of animal locomotion directly influenced the invention of cinematography. His

Chronophotographe (1888), at first used with opaque film then with transparent, was the first piece of equipment that had the characteristics of a modern camera — apart from the use of sprockets and sprocket holes to guide the film. His communication of his work to the French Academy of Sciences in 1888 was reported around the world and seems to have influenced Edison, Le Prince, Skladanowsky, Friese-Green, Le Roy, Lumière, and others working on the development of the projection of moving pictures on a screen. He was more interested in analyzing movements through slow speed and high speed studies than in synthesizing movement for exhibition purposes, but his work was seminal to the invention of the cinema.

1859: Doctoral thesis on animal locomotion. 1865–67: First experiments with a graphic method for studying locomotion, using a pen that traced curves to record movement. 1869: Experiments in recording schematically the movements of a galloping horse. 1872–77: In California, Leland Stanford hears of Marey's work and asks Muybridge (*q.v.*) to develop Marey's photographic techniques to settle a bet. 1882: Muybridge travels to Paris and meets Marey, who is impressed by his photographs. 1882–1888: Muybridge's work and the invention of the dry gelatino-bromide plate convince Marey to use photography. He first used a *fusil photographique* (the photo-gun) derived from the French astronomer Janssen's *revolver photographique*. He began work on the *Chronophotographe*, originally on a fixed photographic plate, then on a moving plate, and finally, in 1888, on Kodak roll film. 1890–96: Imperfect projections onto a screen in the laboratory.

MARIASSY, Félix DIR Hungary. (1919–) Good Hungarian film maker with a lyrical style and a special talent for family comedies in a working-class background. He has worked in films since 1939 and was Radvanyi's assistant on *Somewhere in Europe**.
DIR: *Szabone/Ann Szabo* (49), *Kis Katalin hazassaga/Catherine's Marriage* (49), *Teljes gozzel/Full Steam Ahead* (51), *Rokonok/Relatives* (54), *Egy pikolo vilagos/A Glass of Beer* (55), *Budapest/Spring in Budapest* (55), *A Legend of the Suburbs* (57), *Csempeszek/Smugglers* (58), *Almatlan evek/Sleepless*

Years (59), *Fapados szerelem/A Simple Love/Third-class Love* (59), *Hosszu az ut hazaig/It's a Long Way Home* (60), *Probaut/Test Trip* (60), *Pirosbetus hetkoznapok/Every Day Sunday* (Hung/Czech62), *Karambol/Goliath* (64), *Fugefalevel/Fig Leaf* (66), *Kotelek/Bondage* (68).

MARION, Frances SCEN USA. (San Francisco Nov 18, 1888– ?) Hollywood scriptwriter who provided several notable scripts for some of the best directors of the Twenties and furnished Garbo and Valentino with some excellent roles. Though she worked on many routine commercial vehicles, her work with Henry King, Sjöström, King Vidor, Cukor, and George Hill testifies to her talents.
SCEN (notably): for Frank Borzage, *Humoresque* (20); for Paul Powell, *Pollyanna* (20); for Frances Marion, *The Love Light* (20); for Frank Lloyd, *The Eternal Flame* (22), *Within the Law* (23); for Henry King, *Stella Dallas** (25), *The Winning of Barbara Worth* (26); for Sjöström, *The Scarlet Letter** (26), *The Wind** (28); for Edmund Goulding, *Love* (27); for Clarence Brown, *Anna Christie* (30); for George Hill, *The Big House** (30); for King Vidor, *The Champ* (31); for George Cukor, *Dinner at Eight** (33); for Jacques Feyder, *Knight Without Armor* (Brit37); for James Whale, *Green Hell* (40).

MARISCHKA, Ernst DIR Austria. (Vienna Jan 2, 1893–) After long experience in Viennese operetta with his brother Hubert (Vienna 1882–Vienna 1959), he directed *Sissi/Forever My Love* (56) and the ensuing continuations.

MARKER, Chris (Christian François Bouche-Villeneuve) DIR France. (Neuilly sur Seine July 29, 1921–) A leader of the Left Bank group of film makers who has made numerous brilliant, personal, socially committed, often witty documentaries: *Dimanche à Pekin, Lettre de Siberie, Cuba Si.* [He began his career as a writer (Chris Marker is only one of several pseudonyms) and a journalist who traveled around the world before making his first film in 1952. He has been described as the cinema's first essayist, making films in a variety of styles but always on a subject of concern to him.] André Bazin wrote: "He is a member of that new generation of writers who feel that the era of the image has arrived but that it is not, however, necessary to sacrifice language . . . For him, the commentary is not something added onto the images but almost the primary, fundamental element." However, it should not be forgotten that he used *cinéma-vérité* techniques in *Le Joli Mai,* a film in which the commentary is subordinate to the interrelationship of images and interviews.

DIR: *Olympia 52* (52), *Les Statues meuren taussi* (53) (co-dir: Resnais), *Dimanche à Pekin* (55), *Le Mystère de l'atelier 15* (57) (co-dir: Resnais, A. Heinrich), *Lettre de Siberie* (57), *Les Astronautes* (59) (co-dir: W. Borowczyk), *Description d'un combat* (60), *Cuba Si!** (61), *La Jetée** (62, released 64), *Le Joli mai** (63), *Le Mystère Koumiko* (65), *Si j'avais 4 dromadaires* (66), *Loin de Vietnam* (67) (in collab), *Rhoudiacéta* (69), *La Bataille des 10 millions* (70).

[COMMENTARY: for Ruspoli, *Les Hommes de la Baleine* (56); for Paviot, *Django Reinhardt* (57); for Languepin, *Des Hommes dans le ciel* (58); for Vogel, *Ce siècle a soif* (58), *La Mer et les jours* (58); for Ivens, *A Valparaiso* (63); for Haroun Tazieff, *Le Volcan interdit* (66).]

MARTELLI, Otello PHOTOG Italy. (Rome May 10, 1903–) An assistant in the silent days, he developed a reputation after World War II for his often somber photography, particularly for the films of Fellini (*q.v.*) and De Santis (*q.v.*).

[PHOTOG (notably): for Blasetti, *Vecchia Guardia* (34); for Rossellini, *Paisa** (46), *Amore* (47), *Stromboli* (49); for De Santis, *Caccia Tragica** (47), *Riso Amero** (49), *Roma Ore 11** (52); for Fellini, *Luci del Varieta** (50), *I Vitelloni** (53), *La Strada** (54), *Il Bidone** (55), *La Dolce Vita** (59), *Boccaccio '70* (62) (also De Sica episode); for Mario Soldati, *La Donna del Fiume* (55); for Réné Clément, *La Diga sul Pacifico* (58); for Dassin, *La Loi* (58); for Emmer, *La Ragazza in Vetrina* (60); for Bolognini, *La Mia Signora* (64), *I Tre Volti* (64), *La Donna è una cosa meravigliosa* (65).

MARTIN-DUNCAN, F. DIR Britain. (? – ?) A professional biologist and the most important pioneer of the science film with his series of microscopic studies for Charles Urban: *Natural History* series (03), *Unseen World* series (03), *Marine Studies* series (05), etc. He later worked on the *Secrets of Nature* series (1924 on) as consulting editor.

MARTOGLIO, Nino DIR Italy. (Catania Dec 3, 1870–Catania Sept 13, 1920) With a background in naturalistic Sicilian dialect drama, he made two masterpieces *Sperduti nel Buio** (14) and *Teresa Raquin** (15), both precursors of Italian neorealism.

MARX Brothers: Groucho (Julius) (New York 1895–), **Chico (Leonard)** (New York 1891–1961), **Harpo (Adolph)** (New York 1893–1964) These three masters of anarchic comedy and zaniness were largely responsible for their own films, though they were, in fact, "directed" by other hands: *Cocoanuts* (29), *Animal Crackers** (30), *Monkey Business** (31), *Horse Feathers* (32), *Duck Soup** (33), *A Night at the Opera** (35), *A Day at the Races* (37), *Room Service* (38), *At the Circus* (39), *Go West** (40), *The Big Store* (41), *A Night in Casablanca* (46), *Love Happy* (50). [They also appeared, separately, in other films. Originally there were two other brothers: Gummo, who left the act at an early date, and Zeppo (New York 1901–) who left after playing romantic supporting roles in their first five films.]

MASELLI, Francesco DIR Italy. (Rome Dec 9, 1930–) After working as Antonioni's (*q.v.*) assistant (47–50) and making two shorts, he made a remarkable debut in feature films, at the age of 23, with his episode in *Amore in Città* (53), and then confirmed his talents and vision of the world in *Gli Sbandati* (55). However, his youthful spirit was not evident in his later films, *La Donna del Giorno* (56), *I Delfini* (60), *Gli Indifferenti* (63), etc.

MATE, Rudolf (also Rudolph, Rudy) (Rudolf Mathéh) PHOTOG Germany/France/USA DIR USA. (Cracow 1898–Hollywood Nov 1964) The famous cameraman on Dreyer's *Passion de Jeanne d'Arc* and *Vampyr,* he began his career as assistant to Alexander Korda (*q.v.*) in Hungary, became assistant cameraman to Karl Freund in Germany in 1925, and might be considered as merely a conscientious technician for Dreyer if his work for other directors were not often equally remarkable, e.g., *Le Dernier Milliardaire, Gilda, Foreign Correspondent.* He began directing in 1947, but his work, mostly adventure films, is almost totally mediocre.

[PHOTOG (notably): for Dreyer, *La Passion de Jeanne d'Arc** (Fr28), *Vampyr** (Fr/Ger31); for A. Genina, *Prix de beauté* (Fr29); for Clair, *Le Dernier Milliardaire** (Fr34); for Fritz Lang, *Liliom* (Fr34); for Wyles, Hawks, *Come and Get It** (USA36); for King Vidor, *Stella Dallas** (USA37); for Leo McCarey, *Love Affair* (USA39); for Hitchcock, *Foreign Correspondent* (40); for Tay Garnett, *Seven Sinners* (40); for Lubitsch, *To Be or Not to Be* (USA42); for Charles Vidor, *Cover Girl* (USA44), *Gilda** (USA46).

DIR (notably): *The Dark Past* (48), *No Sad Songs for Me* (50), *Union Station* (50), *When Worlds Collide* (51), *Mississippi Gambler* (53), *The Violent Men/Rough Company* (55), *The Rawhide Years* (56), *Three Violent People* (56), *Serenade einer Grossen Liebe* (GFR58), *For the First Time* (59), *The 300 Spartans* (It62), *Seven Seas to Calais* (It62).]

MATHIS, June SCEN/ED USA. (Leadville 188?–New York July 27, 1927) Commercially successful Hollywood scriptwriter and sometime editor in the Twenties — *The Four Horsemen of the Apocalypse** (21), *Ben Hur** (26), and others — who was also responsible for the final mutilated version of Stroheim's *Greed**.

MATRAS, Christian PHOTOG France. (Valence Dec 29, 1903–) Masterly French cameraman who drew on his early experience in documentaries and newsreels when he shot Epstein's *L'Or des mers* and Renoir's *La Grande Illusion.* He later developed a fluid, impressionistic style and a use of color to which Ophüls postwar French period films owe much. [PHOTOG (notably): for Epstein, *L'Or des mers** (32); for Renoir *La Grande Illusion** (37); for Marc Allégret, *Entrée des artistes* (38); for Georges Lampin *L'Idiot** (46); for Christian-Jaque, *Boule de suife** (45), *Fanfan la tulipe** (52); for Jean Dellanoy, *Les Jeux sont faits* (47); for Cocteau, *L'Aigle à deux têtes* (47); for Ophüls, *La Ronde** (50), *Le Plaisir** (52), *Madame De . . .** (53),

Lola Montès* (55); for Becker, *Montparnasse 19* (57); for Clouzot, *Les Espions* (57); for Franju, *Thérèse Desqueroux* (62); for Clair, *Les Fêtes Galantes* (65); for Buñuel, *La Voie lactée* (68).]

MATTSSON, Arne DIR Sweden. (Uppsala Dec 2, 1919–) A director whose best period was in the early Fifties, when he made not only the extraordinary portrait of adolescent passion, *One Summer of Happiness** (51), but also several dramas, notably, *Woman in White* (49) and *Salka Valka* (54). His later work suffers from poor scripts but is often visually imaginative, e.g., his remake of *The Phantom Chariot** (58).

MAURO, Humberto DIR Brazil. (Volta Grande April 30, 1897–) A pioneer of Brazilian cinema and an important film maker with a profoundly cinematic vision, ingenuous but not naive, whose work is unfortunately little known outside Brazil. As a self-taught former electrician, he was drawn to the cinema by his delight in westerns, serials, and the films of Stroheim (*q.v.*) and as an amateur made his first film, *Valadiao o Cratera* (25) in tribute to them. He was soon discovered and supported by the film society movement in Brazil and directed a series of unique features that are indebted to no one: *Tesouro Perdido, Brasa Dormida,* and *Sangre Mineiro.* Though the plots of his society dramas are often clichéd, he had a remarkable feeling for images and backgrounds, a highly original conception of filmic space, and an impassioned feeling for people and the landscapes of his country. *Ganga Bruta* (33) is his best film and a landmark in the history of the Brazilian cinema. Mauro's use of erotic symbolism in the film earned him the name "the suburban Freud." *Argila* was his last major work: the difficulties of the Brazilian film industry forced him after that to restrict his activities mainly to directing short documentaries. He is, nevertheless, a great film maker who will inevitably one day receive the international reputation he deserves.

DIR: *Valadiao o cratera* (25) (amateur documentary), *Na Primavera da Vida* (26), *Tesouro Perdido* (28), *Sangre Mineiro* (28), *Brasa Dormida** (28), *Labios sem Beijos* (30), *Mulher* (32), *Ganga Bruta** (33), *Voz do Carnaval*

170

(34), *Favela dos Meus Amores* (34), *Cidade Mulher* (37), *O Descobrimento do Brasil* (37), *Argila** (40) (co-dir: Carmen Santos), *Os Bandeirantes* (40), *Licao de Taxiderma* (50), *O Canto de Sandade* (52), *Joao de Barro* (55).

MAY, Joe (Joseph Mandel), DIR Germany/ USA. (Vienna Nov 7, 1880–Hollywood May 5, 1954) A pioneer of the German cinema (which he saw mainly as an entertainment industry), he began directing in 1911, founded his own company in 1914, and directed the first German serials and thrillers — *Stuart Webb* series (13–14), *Veritas vincit* (18), etc. He gave Fritz Lang (*q.v.*) his first opportunities as scriptwriter on *Hilde Warren und der Tod* (17), *Das Indische Grabmal*, I and II/*The Mysteries of India/ Above the Law* (21), etc. Under the influence of *Kammerspiel* and New Objectivity he directed his two best films, *Heimkehr/Homecoming* (28) and *Asphalt** (29). He moved to Hollywood in 1934 and directed mainly B-pictures: *The Invisible Man Returns** (40), *The House of Seven Gables* (40), *Johnny Doesn't Live Here Any More* (44), etc.

MAY, Paul (Paul Ostermayr) DIR German Federal Republic. (Munich May 9, 1909–) Talented West German director best known for his trilogy — *08/15* (54), *08/15, II teil* (55), *08/15 In der Heimat* (55) — based on Hans-Helmuth Kirst's novels about an ordinary soldier in the war.

MAYER, Carl SCEN Germany. (Graz Feb 20, 1894–London July 1, 1944) The most original scriptwriter during the most creative period of the German cinema, 1920–30, [who "had the soul and eyes of a poet — a poet who wrote in visual images rather than in words" (Gabriel Pascal). He was not a voluminous writer, as Ivor Montague wrote: "We have only to run over the record of Mayer's work to see how many original conceptions it includes, to see how often in their realization good directors, good cameramen, good actors and actresses achieved each the outstanding performances of their careers, to realize what a powerful original force in the team was there at work. His influence pervaded and moulded all his colleagues." He was originally an actor and literary manager.] His first script (with Hans Janowitz), *The Cabinet*

of *Dr. Caligari* (19) was the first expressionist masterpiece but, after *Genuine* he abandoned the fantastic and grotesque to concentrate primarily on the everyday life of ordinary people in their usual surroundings. These *Kammerspiel* films (he was also the principal theoretician of *Kammerspiel*) are distinguished by their strict unity of time, place, and action, their naturalistic, spare style, their air of finality and social destiny, their "typical" characters, their avoidance of explanatory titles, and the significance of their sets and objects as symbols or metaphors. After *Backstairs,* his first, somewhat unsuccessful, attempt at this approach, he created the brilliant "trilogy" of *Scherben, Sylvester,* and *The Last Laugh.* He was also a brilliant adaptor, most notably in his fluent treatment of Stendhal's *Vanina Vanini* for Arthur von Gerlach (*q.v.*). New Objectivity also benefited from his work, since Ruttmann's *Berlin, The Symphony of a Great City* was based on his original ideas. [When Murnau left for Hollywood in 1927, Mayer was invited to accompany him. He declined, but nevertheless wrote for Murnau perhaps his most poetic screen ballad, *Sunrise.* He worked on two films for Czinner, left Germany in January 1933 when Hitler rose to power, and settled in England. He wrote no more scripts but was associated with Gabriel Pascal on *Pygmalion** (38) and *Major Barbara* (40), worked with documentarist Paul Rotha (*q.v.*), and was adviser to the Two Cities production company.]
SCEN: for Robert Weine, *Das Cabinett des Dr. Caligari** (19) (co-scen: Janowitz), *Genuine* (20), *Tragikomödie* (22), *Der Puppenmacher von Kiang-Ning* (23); for Hans Kobe, *Brandherd* (20); for Murnau, *Der Bucklige und die Tänzerin* (20), *Der Gang in die Nacht* (20), *Schoss Vogelöd* (21), *Phantom* (22), *Der Letzte Mann** (24), *Tartuffe* (25), *Sunrise** (USA27), *Four Devils* (USA 28); for Karl Gerhardt, *Johannes Goth* (20); for Lupu Pick, *Das Lachende Grauen* (20), *Grausige Nächte* (21), *Scherben** (21), *Sylvester** (23); for Leopold Jessner and Paul Leni, *Die Hintertreppe* (21); for Arthur von Gerlach, *Vanina oder die Galgenhochzeit* (22); for Leopold Jessner, *Erdgeist* (23); for Carl Boese, *Die Letzte Droschke von Berlin* (26) (?); for Paul Czinner, *Ariane* (31), *Der Träumende Mund* (32) (and remake, 1953). Also: ideas for Karl

171

Grune's *Die Strasse** (23), *Am Rande der Welt* (27), and for Walther Ruttman's *Berlin – die Symphonie einer Grosstadt** (27); "consultant" on Paul Rotha's *The Fourth Estate* (Brit40).

*MAYER, Louis B[urt] PROD USA. (Russia 1885? 1882?–Hollywood Oct 29, 1957) A typical example of a Hollywood tycoon, he was for many years the production chief of MGM. He emigrated with his parents from Russia (original Christian names and birthdate uncertain) to New Brunswick, Canada, and was at first a scrap-metal dealer before becoming involved in show business as a theater owner and the owner of a film exchange in Boston. In 1915 he formed Metro Pictures Corporation with three partners, sold out in 1917, worked for various companies, and finally established his own Louis B. Mayer Production Company. When Loew's Inc. acquired Metro and, later, Goldwyn, Mayer was named vice-president and general manager of the new production company – which eventually became MGM. He was a great believer in the star system and built up the fortunes of MGM in the Thirties with a wide range of talented actors, directors, and technicians. After an internal company struggle, he was forced to resign in 1951.

MAYSLES, Albert (1933–) and **David** (1931–) DIR USA. Sensitive, intelligent *cinéma vérité* film makers. Former cameramen for Leacock (*q.v.*) – Drew – Pennebaker on, e.g., *Primary**, *Yanki No!**, they have made a number of shorts together, a portrait of the American producer Joseph E. Levine, *Showman* (62), and *The Beatles in New York* (64), *Salesman* (69), *Gimme Shelter* (70).

`WORKED IN LO'S IN FRANCE w`
MEERSON, Lazare ART DIR France/Britain. (Russia 1900–London June 1938) The most influential art director of the Twenties and Thirties, a designer whose studio-built street scenes and sets for Feyder (*q.v.*) and Clair (*q.v.*) broke completely away from expressionism, impressionism, and conventional studio "naturalism" to create an ambience at once realistic and poetic. He is undoubtedly one of the major contributors to the development of French poetic realism. His early death ended a remarkable career, but even in the Sixties many French designers (some of them his

former assistants) were still profiting from his lessons.
ART DIR (notably): for Feyder, *Gribiche* (25), *Carmen** (26), *Les Nouveaux Messieurs** (28), *Le Grand jeu** (34), *Pension mimosas** (35), *La Kermesse heroïque** (35), *Knight without Armour* (Brit37); for L'Herbier, *Feu Mathias Pascal** (25), (co: Cavalcanti), *L'Argent* (29), *Le Parfum de la dame en noir* (31); for Clair, *La Proie du vent* (26), *Un chapeau de paille d'Italie** (27), *Les Deux timides* (28), *Sous les toits de Paris** (30), *Le Million** (31), *A nous la liberté** (31), *Quatorze juillet* (32), *Break the News* (Brit37); for Richard Oswald, *Cagliostro* (29); for Duvivier, *David Golder* (30); for W. Thiele, *Le Bal* (31); for J. Choux, *Jean de la lune* (31); for Autant-Lara, *Ciboulette* (33); for Fedor Ozep, *Amok* (34); for Marc Allégret, *Les Beaux jours* (35); for Czinner *As You Like It* (Brit36); for King Vidor, *The Citadel* (Brit38).

MEHBOOB KHAN, Ramjakhan DIR/PROD India. (Bilimora 1907–Bombay 1964) Originally an actor, he began directing in 1935 and established his own production company in Bombay in 1942. His early films – *Bread, The Only Life* – have social themes but it was his spectacular *Aan* that brought him the greatest success; its popularity in the Middle East, Asia, and Africa gave the Indian film industry new access to the large international market. His *Mother India* had equal success. Although adventure films, they are not devoid of power and beauty in their imagery.
DIR (notably): *Roti/Bread* (36), *Watan* (36), *We Three* (39) (a version of *Devdas**), *Aurat/Woman* (40), *Mannohan* (40), *Ekhi Rosta/The Only Life* (41), *Jadirdar* (42), *Andaz* (42), *Huma Gun Anmogaldi* (46), *Amar* (48), *Aan/ Savage Princess** (52), *Mother India* (57), *Son of India* (60).

MELIES, Georges DIR France. (Paris Dec 8, 1861–Paris Jan 21, 1938) He is the father of the narrative cinema, the first director of story films and the first man in the world to decide consciously that he wanted to make films; he is the Giotto and Ucello of the seventh art, the artist who guided its initial development. Originally an itinerant conjuror, in 1888 he purchased the Théâtre Robert Houdin, where he staged many illusionist spec-

172

tacles. He attempted to purchase a Lumière Cinématographe from Antoine Lumière (*q.v.*) for 10,000 francs and when this was refused, he purchased a Bioscope from William Paul in London and installed it in his theater. The first presentation was on April 5, 1896 and soon thereafter Méliès established his Star Film company and began production of simple films. The following year he constructed on his property at Montreuil-sous-Bois a film studio with a stage and theatrical machinery and there made films using not only all the usual theatrical resources — actors, costumes, sets, scripts, make-up, etc. — but also new cinematic tricks that he invented. In this, his approach was radically different from that of Lumière, who was busy recording "life as it happened." Though he very soon abandoned the use of natural sets in favor of carefully designed studio re-creations, he did not totally abandon reality for fantasy. His first long film (about 650 ft.), *L'Affaire Dreyfus* (1899), is also the first film committed to expressing a particular sociopolitical viewpoint, while one of his last films, *La Civilisation à travers les âges* (08), is a tract directed against war, violence, and intolerance. His greatest speciality was fantasy films (*Cendrillon, Barbe-Bleue, Le Royaume des fées, L'Ange de Noël, La Fée Carabosse*) and his amusing science fiction films in the Jules Verne manner (*A la conquête du Pôle, 20,000 lieues sous les mers, Le Voyage à travers l'impossible, Le Voyage dans la lune*). This latter film, made in 1902, brought him international fame and, for a time, a financial fortune. Its worldwide success also assured the international future of the story film and so marks the true birth of the motion picture art and industry. For some years Méliès was able to devote himself to his delight in fantasy, tricks, and illusions. He gave free rein to his mischievous imagination in dozens of films, all marked by their rhythm, visually inventive designs, and marvelous sense of detail — though he never completely abandoned his identification of stage with screen. However, the formidable machine he had set in motion soon became bigger than the individual artist. Better businessmen than he plagiarized his ideas and built up monopolies and trusts that overran his modest Montreuil company. Techniques he had developed were

adopted everywhere and, after 1908, he lost touch with the rapid evolution of the cinema. Once a rich man, he was completely bankrupt at the end of the First World War and was reduced to selling toys and candies in a Paris Métro station. His talents were unwanted, his films forgotten. But, before he died in a rest home, several young film enthusiasts (including Henri Langlois) rediscovered some of his masterpieces and restored them and the artist who made them to their rightful place in the annals of film history.

DIR: some 500 films, of which the following is a selection: *Une partie de cartes* (first film), *Séance de prestidigitation, Plus fort que le maître, Un bon petit diable, Escamotage d'une dame chez Robert Houdin, Le Fakir Mystère Indien, Sauvetage en rivière, Une nuit terrible, Cortège du Tzar allant à Versailles* (all 1896); *Paulus chantant* (3 films), *Le Malade imaginaire, Episode de guerre, Le Cabinet de Mephistophélès, Après le bal/Le Bain de la Parisienne, Vente d'esclaves au harem, Magie diabolique, La Cigale et la Fourmi, En cabinet particulier, L'Auberge ensorcelée* (all 1897); *Le Cuirassé Main, Pygmalion et Galatée, Damnation de Faust, La Caverne maudite, Rêve d'artiste, L'Homme de tête, La Tentation de Saint Antoine, La Lune a un mètre* (all 1898); *Un vol dans la tombe de Cléopâtre, La Danse de feu, L'Affaire Dreyfus*, Le Coucher de la mariée, Le Diable au couvent, Le Christ marchant sur les eaux, Le Miroir de Cagliostro, Cendrillon, L'Homme Protée* (all 1899); *L'Exposition de 1900, L'Homme orchestre, Jeanne d'Arc*, Le Livre magique, Le Rêve de Noël, Le Déshabillage impossible, L'Homme qui a des roues dans la tête, Une maison tranquille* (all 1900); *Le Petit Chaperon rouge, Barbe-bleue, L'Homme à la tête de caoutchouc, Le Diable géant/Le Miracle de la Madone, L'Oeuf magique prolifique, La Danseuse microscopique* (all 01); *L'Eruption du mont Pelé, Le Voyage dans la lune*, Le Voyage de Gulliver à Lilliput et chez les géants, Les Adventures de Robinson Crusoe* (all 02); *Le Cake-Walk infernal, Le Mélomane, Le Royaume des fées, La Lanterne magique, Faust aux enfers, Le Rêve du maître de ballet* (all 03); *Benvenuto Cellini/Curieuse évasion, Damnation du Dr. Faust, Le Barbier de Seville, Le Voyage à travers l'impossible** (all

173

04); *L'Ange de Noël, Le Palais des Mille et une nuits, La Tour de Londres, Le Raid Paris-Monte Carlo en deux heures, La Legènde de Rip Van Winkle* (all 05); *Jack le ramoneur, La Magie à travers les âges, Les Incendiaires, Les 400 farces du diable, La Fée carabosse, Les Affiches en goguette, Les Bulles de savon animées* (all 06); *20,000 lieues sous les mers, Le Tunnel sous la Manche, Hamlet*, Shakespeare écrivant 'Jules César', Eclipse du soleil en pleine lune* (all 07); *Le Tambourin fantastique, La Civilisation à travers les âges, Le Génie du feu, La Prophétesse de Thèbes, L'Habit ne fait pas le moine, La Rêve d'un fumeur d'opium, La Curiosité punie Lulli, Tartarin de Tarascon, Rivalité d'amour, La Fée Libellule, L'Ascension de la rosière, Conte de la grand-mère et rêve de l'enfant, Pochardiana, Le Génie des cloches, La Poupée vivante* (all 08); Hydrothérapie fantastique, *Les Illusions fantaisistes, Les Papillons fantastiques, Si j'étais roi, L'Homme aux mille inventions, Le Mousquetaire de la reine* (all 09–10), *Les Hallucinations du baron de Munchhausen** (11), *A la conquête du Pole** (12), *Le Chevalier des neiges* (13), *Le Voyage de la famille Bourrichon* (13).

MELVILLE, Jean-Pierre (Jean-Pierre Grunbach) DIR France. (Paris Oct 20, 1917–) Interested in the cinema from an early age, he made many amateur films as an adolescent, founded his own production company in 1945, and made a good debut on his first feature, *Le Silence de la mer* (47), notable for its exemplary fidelity to the original story. His next film, *Les Enfants terribles,* was of lesser quality, and *Deux hommes dans Manhattan* was a failure. *Quand tu liras cette lettre* (53) allowed him to construct his own film studio and achieve commercial success with Belmondo in *Léon Morin, prêtre* and *le Doulos.* [Melville is fascinated by the dark, urban universe of crime, which has dominated his work since his first underworld film, *Bob le Flambeur* (55), except for *Léon Morin.* Even his austere lament for the French Resistance, *L'Armée des ombres,* reveals his interests; its taut, economical, unflamboyant style is a continuation of that developed in his masterly trio of gangster films, *Le Doulos, Le Deuxième souffle,* and *Le Samouraï,* in which he ritualized the gangster genre to create deep tragedies of love and loyalty, betrayal and deceit. He has scripted all his own films except *Quand tu liras cette lettre* and has worked on the photography and editing of some of them. He has also appeared as an actor in several films, including his own *Deux hommes dans Manhattan,* Cocteau's *Orphée*,* and Godard's *A bout de souffle*.*]

DIR: *Vingt-quatre heures de la vie d'un clown* (45) (short), *Le Silence de la mer** (47), *Les Enfants terribles* (49), *Quand tu liras cette lettre* (53), *Bob le Flambeur* (55), *Deux hommes dans Manhattan* (58), *Léon Morin, prêtre** (61), *Le Doulos/The Fingerman* (62), *L'Aîné des Ferchaux* (63), *Le Deuxième souffle* (65), *Le Samouraï* (67), *L'Armée des ombres* (68), *Le Cercle rouge* (70).

*MENZEL, Jiří DIR Czechoslovakia. (1938–) The youngest member of the new Czechoslovak cinema of the Sixties, a film maker with a delicious sense of wry comedy drawn from everyday situations. He graduated from the state film school in 1963 and directed his first professional feature in 1965. He enjoys acting and has appeared in many films, including his own.

DIR: *The Death of Mr. Foerster* (63) (graduation film), *Perlicky na dne/Pearls at the Bottom* (65) (one episode), *Zlocin v divci skole/Crime at the Girl's School* (65) (one episode), *Ostre sledovane vlaky/Closely Watched Trains** (66), *Rozmarne Leto/Capricious Summer* (68), *Zlocin v santanu/Crime at the Nightclub* (69), *Skrivanci na nitich/ Larks on a String* (70).

MENZIES, William Cameron ART DIR/DIR USA. (New Haven, Connecticut July 29, 1896–Hollywood March 5, 1957) Perhaps the most famous of Hollywood art directors and certainly one of the most imaginative, he was a designer with a baroque and abundantly lavish style influenced by German expressionism. His work as a director is of far less interest, except for his famous *Things to Come* — memorable more for his set designs than his direction.

ART DIR (notably): for Lubitsch, *Rosita* (23); for Raoul Walsh, *The Thief of Bagdad* (24); for Howard Hawks, *Fig Leaves* (26); for Sam Taylor *The Tempest* (27); for Norman Z. McLeod, *Alice in Wonderland* (33); for Norman Taurog, *The Adventures of Tom Sawyer*

(38); for Victor Fleming, *Gone With the Wind** (39); for Hitchcock, *Foreign Correspondent* (40); for Milestone, *Arch of Triumph* (48); for Anthony Mann, *Reign of Terror* (49); for Michael Anderson, *Around the World in 80 Days* (56); and for his own *Things to Come, Chandu the Magician, Drums in the Deep South.*
[DIR (notably): *Chandu the Magician* (32) (co-dir: M. Varnel), *Things to Come* (Brit36), *The Green Cockatoo* (Brit40), *Address Unknown* (44), *Drums in the Deep South* (51), *Whip Hand* (51), *Invaders from Mars* (53), *The Maze* (53).]

*MESSTER, Oskar Eduard INVENTOR/PROD/ DIR Germany. (Berlin Nov 21, 1866– Tegernsee Dec 7, 1943) Pioneer of the German cinema who, after taking over his father's optical laboratory in 1895– 96, patented his own *Kinematograph* system for transporting film through a camera without jerking. He established his own production company in 1896 and released 84 of his own films the following year. He produced all his company's films until 1913 and directed many until 1910. The first German film star, Henry Porten, began under his aegis, as did Emil Jannings, Lil Dagover, Conrad Veidt, etc. His various companies for production, distribution, and the manufacture of film equipment came under UFA control in 1917, but he continued as a producer until 1924.

*METZNER, Ernö ART DIR Germany/USA DIR Germany. (Hungary 1892–) One of the most important German designers of the naturalist school, notable for his association with Pabst (*q.v.*) on *Diary of a Lost Girl, Westfront 1918*, and *Kameradschaft.* He also directed several silent German films and his *Der Ueberfall* was a major contribution to the naturalistic movement. He left Germany in 1933, worked briefly in France and Britain, then settled in Hollywood.
ART DIR (notably): for Lubitsch, *Sumurun* (20), *Das Weib des Pharao* (21); for Hans Behrendt, *Alt-Heidelberg/The Student Prince* (23); for Anton von Cserepy, *Fridericus Rex* (23) (co: Hans Dreier); for Karl Grune, *Arabella* (24); for Friedrich Feher, *Hotelgeheimnisse* (28), *The Robbery Symphony** (Brit36); for Pabst, *Tagebuch einer Verlorenen** (29), *Die Weisse Hölle vom Piz Palü*

(29), *Westfront 1918** (30), *Kameradschaft** (31), *Die Herrin von Atlantis/ L'Atlantide** (32), *Du haut en bas* (Fr 33); for Walter Forde, *Chu Chin Chow* (Brit34); for René Clair, *It Happened Tomorrow* (USA43); for Zoltan Korda, *The Macomber Affair* (USA47), and for most of his own films.
DIR (notably): *Salome* (22) (co-dir: L. Kozma), *Man Steigt Nach* (27), *Der Ueberfall/Polizeibericht Ueberfall/Accident* (28), *Rivalen im Weltrekord* (32).

MEYER, George pseud MUNDVILLER, Joseph-Louis (*q.v.*)

MEYER, Paul DIR Belgium. (Limal Sept 29, 1920–) Excellent Belgian film maker notable for a very beautiful cinematic short story, *Klinkart* (57), and a feature on the miners of the Borinage, *Déjà s'envole la fleur maigre** (60).

*MEYERS, Sidney (also Robert Stebbins) DIR/ ED/SCEN USA. (1906–1969) Best known as director of *The Quiet One** (48), but also a major contributor to the independent, realist school of film-making over some 30 years. He entered films in 1934 as a film critic under the name, Robert Stebbins, and under that name was a founder member of Frontier Films in 1936. With Frontier Films he worked as writer-producer on *China Strikes Back*, as co-director on *People of the Cumberland* (38), *The White Flood* (39–40) and *The History and Romance of Transportation* (41), and as sound editor on *Native Land**. During the war he was American editor for British Information Services and then chief film editor for the Office of War Information (*The Cummington Story*, etc.). He directed and produced independently *The Quiet One* and later worked as an editor in Hollywood, e.g., Ritt's *Edge of the City** (56). In 1959 he directed (with Joseph Strick and Ben Maddow) *The Savage Eye*, a ferocious portrait of a decadent society. His last work was as editor on Joseph Strick's *Tropic of Cancer* (69).

MICHEL, André DIR France. (Paris Nov 7, 1910–) Sensitive, intelligent, individualistic film maker who began his career with two successes — the short, *La Rose et le Réséda* (45), and the feature, *Trois femmes* (52) — but found himself out of favor with the French film industry of

175

the Fifties, which was not propitious to newcomers.

MILER, Zdenek ANIM Czechoslovakia. (Kladno Feb 21, 1929–) He made a remarkable debut with the strange and powerful *The Man Who Stole the Sun* (48) and then made numerous children's cartoons before regaining his originality in *The Red Stain* (63).

MILESTONE, Lewis DIR USA. (Russia Sept 30, 1895–) In the early sound period he was one of the best American directors, but his work since has never quite matched this earlier promise. He made, one after another, the beautiful classic war film, *All Quiet on the Western Front* (30), and the extraordinary cinematic comedy-thriller adaptation, *Front Page* (31). [He emigrated to the USA in 1913, started working in 1918 as assistant to King, Ince, and Sennett (all *q.v.*) and as an editor, and directed his first film in 1925. He has also worked as stage and TV producer.]
DIR: *Seven Sinners* (25), *The Cave Man* (26), *The New Klondike* (26), *Two Arabian Nights* (27), *The Garden of Eden* (28), *The Racket* (28), *Betrayal* (29), *New York Nights* (29), *All Quiet on the Western Front** (30), *Front Page** (31), *Rain* (32), *Hallalujah, I'm a Bum* (33), *The Captain Hates the Sea* (34), *Paris in the Spring* (35), *Anything Goes* (36), *The General Died at Dawn* (36), *Night of Nights* (39), *Of Mice and Men* (39), *Lucky Partners* (40), *My Life with Caroline* (41), *Edge of Darkness* (43), *North Star/Armored Attack* (43), *The Purple Heart* (44), *A Walk in the Sun/Salerno Beachhead** (45), *The Strange Love of Martha Ivers* (46), *Guest in the House* (46), (replaced John Brahm), *No Minor Vices* (48), *Arch of Triumph* (48), *The Red Pony* (49), *The Halls of Montezuma* (50), *Kangaroo* (52), *Les Miserables** (52), *Melba* (53), *They Who Dare* (Brit54), *The Widow* (55), *Pork-Chop Hill* (59), *Ocean's Eleven* (60), *Mutiny on the Bounty* (62), (remake, replaced Carol Reed), *PT-109* (63) (completed by Leslie Martinson), *The Dirty Game* (66) (replaced by Terence Young).

MILHAUD, Darius MUS France. (Aix-en-Provence Sept 4, 1892–) This great French composer has been interested in the cinema since the Twenties and has written several distinguished film scores. MUS (notably): for L'Herbier, *L'Inhumaine** (23), *La Citadelle du silence* (37), *La Tragédie impériale* (38); for Cavalcanti, *La P'tite Lilie* (28); for Buñuel, *Las Hurdes** (32); for Jean Painlevé, *L'Hippocampe** (34); for Renoir, *Madame Bovary* (34); for Curtis Bernhardt, *The Beloved Vagabond* (Brit 38); for Robert Siodmak, *Mollenard* (38); for Malraux, *Espoir** (39); for Hans Richter, *Dreams That Money Can Buy* (USA46); for Nicole Vedrès, *La Vie commence demain* (50); for Albert Lewin, *The Private Affair of Bel Ami* (USA47); for Resnais, *Gauguin* (50).

MILLER, Arthur SCEN USA. (New York Oct 17, 1915–) Distinguished American playwright who has written one original film script, *The Misfits** (61), for his ex-wife, Marilyn Monroe, and contributed to the script of Cukor's *Let's Make Love* (60). Several of his plays have been adapted for the cinema: *All My Sons* (48) (dir: Irving Reis), *The Death of a Salesman** (52) (dir: L. Benedek), *Les Sorcières de Salem* (Fr/GDR56), *A View from the Bridge* (61) (dir: Sidney Lumet).

***MILLER, Arthur C.** PHOTOG USA. (c.1895– July 1970) Professional craftsman in Hollywood since the early Twenties, a winner of several Oscars and best known for his contributions to *How Green Was My Valley** (41), *The Ox-Bow Incident** (42), *The Song of Bernadette* (43), *The Razor's Edge* (46), *Anna and the King of Siam* (46), *A Letter to Three Wives** (48), *The Gunfighter* (50).

MIMICA, Vatroslav ANIM/DIR Yugoslavia. (Dalmatia 1923–) A leading light of the Zagreb school, a highly original animator with an acid sense of comedy and a somewhat mannered graphic style. [He began his career as an art director, then directed three features before turning to animation for nine years. He has since returned to directing features.]
ANIM (notably): *The Storm* (55), *The Scarecrow* (57), *Alone/The Lonely Man* (58), *Happy Ending* (58), *At the Photographer's* (58), *The Egg* (60), *The Inspector Goes Home* (60), *A Little Story* (62), *Typhoid* (63), *Perpetual Motion* (63).
[DIR: *U oluji/In the Storm* (52), *Jubilej G. Ikla/Mr. Ikla's Jubilee* (55), *Soli-*

mano il Conquistare (It61), *The Telephone* (62) (short), *Mr. Marzipan's Marriage* (63) (short), *Prometej sa otoka Visevice/Prometheus from Visevica Island* (65), *Ponedeljak ili utorak/Monday or Tuesday* (66), *Kaja, ubit cu te/ Kaya, I'll Kill You* (67).]

MINNELLI, Vincente DIR USA. (Chicago Feb 28, 1913–) Former set and costume designer of Earl Carroll's *Vanities* and the *Ziegfeld Follies,* whose films at their best have an excellent, sometimes exhilarating, sense of visual design and color, but at their worst are far less baroque than mid-Thirties Hollywood rococo. His specialty has always been musical comedy and, in this genre, he has made several excellent films, largely in the florid MGM tradition — with Fred Astaire, *Yolanda and the Thief, Ziegfeld Follies,* and *The Band Wagon;* with Gene Kelly, *The Pirate, An American in Paris,* and *Brigadoon;* with Judy Garland, *Meet Me in Saint Louis.* He has been less at home with literary adaptations and failed to capture the French atmosphere in *Madame Bovary, Gigi,* and *The Four Horsemen of the Apocalypse* because he drew on Hollywood stereotyped effects rather than on his own experiences of the country that he likes and knows quite well. Deprived of musical support, his films often end up as mere melodramas or statically photographed theater. He considers that "the search for an appropriate style is as important for a dramatic comedy as for a dramatic film. A story must be told in the most stylistic way to allow the introduction of a little magic. It isn't always easy to capture shades of meaning."
DIR: *Cabin in the Sky* (42), *I Dood It* (43), *Meet Me in Saint Louis** (44), *The Clock/Under the Clock* (45), *Ziegfeld Follies* (45), *Yolanda and the Thief** (45), *Undercurrent* (46), *The Pirate* (47), *Madame Bovary* (49), *Father of the Bride* (50), *An American in Paris** (51), *Father's Little Dividend* (51), *The Bad and the Beautiful* (52), *The Band Wagon* (53), *The Story of Three Loves* (53) (one episode), *The Long, Long Trailer* (54), *Brigadoon** (54), *Kismet* (55), *The Cobweb* (55), *Lust for Life* (56), *Tea and Sympathy* (56), *Designing Woman* (57), *Gigi* (58), *The Reluctant Debutante* (58), *Some Came Running** (58), *Home from the Hill* (60), *Bells Are Ringing* (60), *The Four Horsemen of the Apocalypse** (62) (remake), *Two Weeks in Another Town* (62), *The Courtship of Eddie's Father* (63), *Goodbye Charlie* (64), *The Sandpiper* (65), *On a Clear Day You Can See Forever* (69). Also directed some sequences of *The Seventh Sin* (57), dir: Ronald Neame, during the latter's illness.

*MIRISCH, Walter M. PROD USA. (Nov 8, 1921–) After ten years (1947–57) as a producer of cheap B-films he joined with his brothers, Harold (1907–1968) and Marvin (1918–), in founding Mirisch Brothers, the most successful of the independent production companies in the Sixties, under whose banner many popular successes appeared. Walter Mirisch has continued to play an active role as producer on the company's films, notably: *Man of the West** (58), *The Magnificent Seven** (60), *West Side Story** (61), *Two for the Seesaw* (62), *The Children's Hour* (62), *The Great Escape* (63), *Toys in the Attic* (63), *The Pink Panther* (64), *Hawaii* (66), *The Russians Are Coming, the Russians Are Coming* (66), *The Fortune Cookie* (66), *In the Heat of the Night* (67), *The Hawaiians* (70), *The Landlord* (70), *They Call Me "Mister" Tibbs!* (70).

MISRAKI, Paul MUS France. (Istanbul Jan 28, 1908–) Composer with an often mystical, Middle-Eastern style, at his best creating atmosphere music for psychological thrillers and poignant tragedies.
MUS (notably): for Decoin, *Retour à l'aube* (38), *Battement de coeur* (39); for Clouzot, *Manon* (48); for Yves Allégret, *Les Orgueilleux* (53); for Orson Welles, *Confidential Report/Mr. Arkadin** (55); for Vadim, *Et Dieu créa la femme** (56); for Buñuel, *Le Mort en ce jardin* (56), *La Fièvre monte à El Pao* (59); for Becker, *Montparnasse 19* (57); for Chabrol, *Les Cousins** (58), *A double tour* (59), *Les Bonnes femmes** (59); for Godard, *Alphaville** (65).

*MIYAGAWA, Kazuo PHOTOG Japan. (Kyoto 1908–) One of the most distinguished Japanese cinematographers, especially skilled in tracking shots, who has made important contributions to the work of Mizoguchi (*q.v.*) and Ichikawa (*q.v.*).
PHOTOG (notably): for Kurosawa, *Rasho-*

177

mon* (50), *Yojimbo* (61); for Mizoguchi, *Ugetsu Monogatari** (53), *Gion Festival Music* (53), *Sansho Dayu** (54), *Uwasa no Onna* (54), *Chikamatsu Monogatari* (54), *Shin Heike Monogatari* (55), *Akasen Chitai* (56); for Ichikawa, *Enjo** (58), *Kagi* (59), *Bonchi* (60), *Ototo* (60), *Hakai* (61), *Zeni no Odori* (64), *Tokyo Olympiad* (64); for Ito, *The Gay Masquerade* (58), *The Woman and the Pirates* (59), *Kirare Saburo* (60); for Ozu, *Floating Weeds* (59); for Mori, *A Certain Killer* (67); for Kenji Misumi, *Devil's Temple* (69).

*MIZOGUCHI, Kenji DIR Japan. (Tokyo May 16, 1898–Kyoto Aug 24, 1956) One of the great artists of the Japanese cinema, a director whose film career spanned 34 years and some 90 films. His style involved the distillation of the essence of a situation with the minimum of images, incorporating all the elements of design, composition, and fluid camera movements. Throughout his career he had a deep interest in feminine psychology and, since the Thirties, his films tended to follow a unified thematic pattern: an elucidation of the conflicts in past and present societies, usually centered on portraits of the feminine condition within that society. Like most directors, he had his share of "imposed" commercial films, especially in the first years of his career and under the militarist regime. But those on which he was a completely free agent, and especially those on which he worked with scriptwriter Yoshikata Yoda (from 1936), reveal his interests: a basic humanism and a concern for an absolute social good and evil. He designed his scripts carefully in advance, often polishing and repolishing for months until he was satisfied, before filming quickly in a short period of time. In 1954 he said: "It is important to reflect for five or six years before beginning a film." He studied as a painter, drifted into film acting, and, after the introduction of female actresses and the ensuing strike of female impersonators, became a director's assistant and then a director in 1922. From then on he was a very prolific film maker. His first films were routine thrillers and melodramas, but in films like *Harbor in the Fog* (23) his concern for pictorial qualities was already evident. In 1925 he became interested in the social "tendency" film and made *Street Sketches*

in the "slice of life" technique. The following year he made in a similar style, *A Paper Doll's Whisper of Spring*, of which he said, "it was at this time I began to find my voice." In 1929 he made not only his first *Meiji-mono* film set in the Meiji period (1868–1912), but two of his most famous films, both concerned with contemporary social issues, *Tokyo March* and *Metropolitan Symphony*. This latter film (long disappeared and never shown outside Asia) used dynamic montage in the Russian manner and seems to have anticipated in some way French poetic realism, Italian neorealism, and the work of the postwar Japanese independents. After 1930 and *Nevertheless, They Go On* (31) — a sympathetic film about the proletariat that suffered severe censorship difficulties — he turned increasingly to period films in an attempt to avoid the restrictions imposed on contemporary themes, though he occasionally had to make patriotic "policy" films. In 1936 he made his first two masterpieces, *Naniwa Elegy* and *The Sisters of Gion:* "It was at this time that I began to use my technique of never changing a set-up during a sequence, leaving the camera immobile at a certain distance from the action. . . . I have tried to use it very spontaneously as the most precise and specific expression for intense psychological moments. . . ." After the war he made a series of impassioned films that he characterized as "barbarous . . . I think at that time I had been accumulating a sense of resentment during the long war period that I wanted to work off on something. You could call this 'Mizoguchi's postwar style' or else the misplaced bravura of an old man." The last six years of his life contained a succession of brilliant films, including his greatest films, *O'Haru, Gion Festival Music* (a remake of *Sisters of Gion*), *Sansho the Bailiff, Chikamatsu Monogatari*, and, above all, *Ugetsu Monogatari*, of which he said: "I'm not happy with the result. Personally, I think the original novel has a more lasting quality. For example, the man played by Ozawa shouldn't change his mind at the end but continue his ambitious social climb regardless. But Daiei didn't want this ending and forced me to change it." *O'Haru* (52) can lay justifiable claim to being his most perfect film; it is certainly the most characteristic example of his work, both as a portrait of social predes-

178

tination seen through the eyes of a woman and in its simple, perfectly constructed and controlled style, with extensive use of the moving camera. In 1950 he spoke of his life and work: "To tell you the truth I have not yet made a film that pleases me . . . It was only when I passed forty that I began to understand the human truths I want to express in my films. And since then, the cinema has become an extremely difficult art for me . . ."
DIR: *Ai ni Yomigaeru Hi/Resurrection of Love* (22), *Furusato/Home Town* (22), *Seishun no Yumeji/Dream of Youth* (22), *Joen no Chimata/Harbor of Desire* (22), *Haizan no Uta Wa Kanashi/The Song of Failure* (22), *813/Rupimono/The Adventures of Arsène Lupin* (22), *Chi to Rei/Blood and Soul* (22), *Kiri no Minato/Harbor in the Fog/Foggy Harbor* (23), *Yoru/The Night* (23), *Haikyo no Naka/In the Ruins* (23), *Toge no Uta/The Song of the Mountain Pass* (23), *Kanashiki Hakuchi/The Sad Idiot* (24), *Gendai no Jo-on/The Queen of Modern Times* (24), *Josei wa Tsuyoshi/Strong is the Female* (24), *Jin-kyo/This Dusty World* (24), *Shichimencho no Yukue/The Trace of a Turkey/Turkeys in a Row/Turkeys: Whereabouts Unknown* (24), *Samidare Zoshi/Chronicle of the May Rain* (24), *Kanraku no Onna/Woman of Pleasure* (24), *Aka-tsuki no Shi/Death in the Dawn* (24), *Kyokubadan no Jo-O/Queen of the Circus* (24), *Musen Fusen/No Money, No Fight* (25), *Gakuso o Idete/Out of College* (25), *Shirayuri wa Nageku/The White Lily Laments* (25), *Akai Yuhi ni Terasarete/Under the Crimson Sunset* (25), *Daichi wa Hohoemu/The Earth Smiles* (25), *A-a Tokumukan Kanto/Ah, the Special Service Vessel* (25) (one episode), *Furusato no Uta/The Song of Hometown* (25), *Ningen/The Human Being* (25), *Gaijo no Suketchi/A Sketch on the Road/Street Sketches/Street Scenes* (25) (one episode), *Nogi Taisho to Kuma-San/General Nogi and Kuma-San* (25), *Doka-o/The Copper Coin King* (26), *Kami Ningyo Haru no Sasayaki/A Paper Doll's Whisper of Spring* (26), *Shin Onoga Tsumi/It's My Fault* (26), *Kyoren no Onna Shisho/The Passion of a Woman Teacher/The Love-Mad Tutoress* (26), *Kaikoku Danji/The Boys from the Sea/The Boy from the Navy* (26), *Kane* (or *Kin*)*/Money/Gold* (26), *Ko-on/*

The Imperial Grace (27), *Jihi Shincho/The Cuckoo* (27), *Hito no Issho/A Man's Life* (27) (in 3 parts), *Musume Kawaiya/My Loving Daughter* (28), *Nihon Bashi/The Nihon Bridge* (29), *Tokyo Koshin-Kyoku/Tokyo March* (29), *Asahi wa Kagayaku/The Morning Sun Shines* (29), *Tokai Kokyogaku/Metropolitan Symphony/Symphony of the Metropolis/City Symphony** (29), *Tojin Okichi/Okichi, Mistress of a Foreigner* (30), *Furusato/Hometown* (30), *Shikamo Karera wa Iku/Nevertheless, They Go On/And Yet They Go On* (31), *Manmo Kenkoku no Reimei/Dawn in Manchuria/The Dawn of the Founding of Manchuko* (32), *Toki no Ujigami/The Man of the Right Moment/Timely Mediator* (32), *Taki no Shiraito/The White Threads of the Waterfall* (33), *Gion Matsuri/Gion Festival* (33), *Shimpu-Ren/The Shimpu Group* (also known as *Kamikaze-Ren/The Kamikaze Group*) (33), *Aizo to Ge/The Mountain Pass of Love and Hate* (34), *Orizuru O-Sen/The Downfall* (34), *Maria no O-Yuki/O'Yuki, the Virgin* (35), *Gubijinso/The Poppies* (35), *Naniwa Ereji/Naniwa Hika/Naniwa Elegy/Osaka Elegy** (36), *Gion no Shimai/The Sisters of Gion** (36), *Aienkyo/The Straits of Love and Hate* (37), *A-a Furusato/A-a Kokyo/Ah, My Hometown* (38), *Roei no Uta/The Song of the Camp* (38), *Zangiku Monogatari/The Story of the Late Chrysanthemums* (39), *Naniwa Onna/Woman of Naniwa/The Woman of Osaka* (40), *Geido Ichidai Otoko/The Life of an Actor* (41), *Genroku Chushingura (Part I)/The 47 Ronin/The Loyal 47 Ronin of the Genroku Era** (41), *Genroku Chushingura (Part II)/The 47 Ronin** (42), *Danjuro Sandai/Three Generations of the Danjuro Family/Three Danjuros* (44), *Hissyo ka/Song of Victory* (45), *Musashi Miyamoto/Miyamoto Musashi, the Swordsman* (45), *Meito Bijo-Maru/Bijo-Maru, the Noted Sword* (45), *Josei no Shori/The Victory of Women/Women's Victory* (46), *Utamaro o Meguru Gonin no Onna/Utamaro and His Five Women* (46), *Joyu Sumako no Koi/The Love of Sumako, the Actress* (47), *Yoru no Onnatachi/Women of the Night* (48), *Waga Koi wa Moenu/My Love Has Been Burning/Flame of My Love* (49), *Yuki Fujin Ezu/Picture of Madame Yuki/Sketch of Madame Yuki* (50), *Oyu-Sama/Miss Oyu* (51), *Musashino Fujin/Lady Mushashino* (51), *Sai-*

179

*kaku Ichidai Onna/The Life of O'Haru/
The Life of a Woman by Saikaku/
O'Haru** (52), *Ugetsu Monogatari/Tales
of the Pale and Silvery Moon After the
Rain** (53), *Gion Bayashi/Gion Festival
Music** (53), *Sansho Dayu/The Super-
intendent Sansho/Sansho, the Bailiff**
(54), *Uwasa no Onna/The Woman of
Rumor/The Crucified Woman* (54),
*Chikamatsu Monogatari/A Story from
Chikamatsu/The Crucified Lovers** (54),
*Yokihi/The Empress Yang Kwei-Fei/
The Princess Yang** (55), *Shin Heike
Monogatari/New Tales of the Taira
Clan/Saga of the Taira Clan/The Sacri-
legious Hero* (55), Akasen Chitai/Street
of Shame/Red-Light District (56), Osaka
Monogatari/An Osaka Story* (56) (com-
pleted by Kimisaburo Yoshimura (*q.v.*)
after Mizoguchi's death).

MOCKY, Jean-Pierre (Jean Mokiejewski) DIR
France. (Nice July 6, 1929–) Former
actor (e.g., Franju's *La Tête contre les
murs**) who turned full time director
after the commercial success of his first
film, *Les Drageurs* (59), and has since
made *Un couple* (60), *Les Snobs* (61),
Les Vierges (63), *Un drôle de paroissien*
(63), *La Grande frousse* (64), *La Bourse
et la vie* (65), *Les Compagnons de la
Marguerite* (66), *La Grand lessive* (68),
L'Etalon (69), *Solo* (69), *L'Albatros*
(70).

MOGUY, Leonide (Leonide Maguilevsky)
DIR France/USA/Italy. (St. Petersburg
July 14, 1899–) Former director of
newsreels and shorts who emigrated to
France in 1929 and worked as an editor,
technical supervisor, and journalist before directing his first feature. He spent
the war years in the USA. As a director,
he was much involved in the themes he
handled and made several successful
films, including: *Prison sans barreaux,
Je t'attendrai,* and *Domani e troppo
Tardi.*
[DIR: *Le Mioche* (Fr36), *Prison sans
barreaux* (38), *Conflict* (38), *Je t'attendrai* (39), *L'Empreinte du Dieu* (40),
I'll Wait for You (USA41) (remake, ?
under name, Robert B. Sinclair), *Paris
After Dark* (44), *Action in Arabia* (44),
Whistle Stop (45), *Bethsabee* (Fr46),
Domani e troppo Tardi (It49), *Domani
e un altro Giorno* (It49), *Les Enfants
de l'amour* (Fr53), *Le Long des troit-
toirs* (56), *Donnez-moi ma chance* (57),
Les Hommes veulent vivre (67).]

MOLANDER, Gustaf DIR/SCEN Sweden.
(Helsinki Nov 18, 1888–) Though
not the equal of Stiller (*q.v.*) or Sjöström (*q.v.*), he started his career alongside them – first as a stage actor, then
as a scriptwriter, and later as a director
– during the great period of the Swedish
cinema. He was able to continue something of their tradition during the low
period, 1925–40, and thus laid the
groundwork for the renaissance of the
Swedish cinema. He directed most of
Ingrid Bergman's Swedish films (*Sweden-
hielms, On the Sunnyside, Intermezzo,
Dollar, A Woman's Face*) and Ingmar
Bergman's second script (*Woman With-
out a Face*) was written for him.
[SCEN (notably): for Konrad Tallroth,
Millers dokument (16); for Sjöström,
Terje Vigen (17); for Stiller, *Thomas
Graal's Best Film* (17), *Thomas Graal's
First Child* (18), *Song of the Scarlet
Flower* (19), *Sir Arne's Treasure** (19),
*Gunnar Hede's Saga** (23); and for
many of his own films.]
DIR: *Bodakungen/King of Boda* (20),
*Thomas Graals myndling/Thomas Graal's
Ward* (22), *Amatörfilmen/The Amateur
Film* (22), *33.333* (24), *Polis Paulus
paskasmäll/Constable Paulus's Easter
Bomb* (25), *Ingmarsarvet/The Ingmar
Inheritance*(25), *Till Österland/To the
Orient* (26), *Hon, den enda/She the Only
One* (26), *Hans engelska fru/His En-
glish Wife* (27), *Förseglade läppar/
Sealed Lips* (27), *Parisskor/Woman of
Paris* (28), *Synd/Sin* (28), *Hjärtats
triumf/Triumph of the Heart* (29), *Fri-
das Visor/Frida's Song* (30), *Charlotte
Löwensköld* (30), *En natt/One Night*
(31), *Svarta rosor/Black Roses* (32),
Kärlek och kassabrist/Love and Deficit
(32), *Vi som gar köksvägen/We Go
Through the Kitchen* (32), *Kära Släkten/
Dear Relatives* (33), *En stille flirt/A
Quiet Affair* (33), *Fasters Millioner/
My Aunt's Millions* (34), *Ungkarspap-
pan/Bachelor Father* (34), *Swedenhielms*
(35), *Under falsk flagg/Under False
Colors* (35), *Bröllopsresan/The Honeymoon Trip* (36), *Pa solsidan/On the
Sunny Side* (36), *Intermezzo* (36),
Familjens hemlighet/The Family Secret
(36), *Sara lär sig folkvett/Sara Learns
Manners* (37), *Dollar* (38), *En Kvinnas
ansikte/A Woman's Face* (38), *En enda
natt/One Single Night* (38), *Ombyte
förnöjer/Variety is the Spice of Life*
(39), *Emilie Hogquist* (39), *En, men ett
Lejon/One, But a Lion* (40), *Den Lju-*

sande framtid/Bright Prospects (41), *I natt eller aldrig/Tonight or Never* (41), *Striden gar vidare/The Fight Goes on* (41), *Jacobs stege/Jacob's Ladder* (42), *Rid i natt/Ride Tonight* (42), *Det Brinner en eld/There Burned a Flame* (43), *Älskling, jag ger mig/Darling, I Surrender* (43), *Ordet/The Word** (43), *Den Osynliga muren/The Invisible Wall* (44), *Kejsarn av Portugallien/The Emperor of Portugal* (44), *Galgamannen/Mandragora* (45), *Det Är min modell/It's My Model* (46), *Kvinna utan ansikte/Woman Without a Face* (47), *Nu börjar livet/Life Begins Now* (48), *Eva* (48), *Kärleken segrar/Love Will Conquer* (49), *Kvartetten som Sprängdes/The Quartet That Split Up* (50), *Fästmö Uthyres/Fiancée for Hire* (51), *Franskild/Divorced* (51), *Trots/Defiance* (52), *Kärlek/Love* (52), *Glasberget/Unmarried* (53), *Herr Arnes penningar* (sic)/*Sir Arne's Treasure** (54) (remake), *Enhorningen/The Unicorn* (55), *Sangen om den eldröda blomman/The Song of the Scarlet Flower* (56) (remake), *Stimulantia* (65, released 67) (one episode).

MOLINARO, Edouard DIR France. (1928–) A film enthusiast, intelligent and cultured, who began by making short films but in his feature films has rarely been able to break away from commercial considerations, specializing in routine thrillers and comedies. [DIR: *Chemins d'avril* (53) (short), *L'Honneur est sauf* (54) (short), *La Mer remonte à Rouen* (55) (short), *Les Biens de ce monde* (56) (short), *Appelez le 17* (56) (short), *Les Alchimistes* (57) (short), *Los Dos au mur/Evidence in Concrete* (57), *Des femmes disparaissent* (58), *Un témoin dans la ville* (59), *Une fille pour l'été* (59), *La Morte de Belle* (60), *Les Ennemis* (61), *Les Sept péchés capitaux* (61) (one episode), *Arsène Lupin* (62), *Une ravissante idiote* (63), *La Chasse à l'homme/The Gentle Art of Seduction* (64), *Quand paissent les faisans* (65), *Peau d'espion/To Commit a Murder* (66), *Oscar* (67), *Hibernatus* (69), *Mon oncle Benjamin* (69), *La Liberté en croupe* (70), *Les Aveux les plus doux* (70).

MONCA, Georges DIR France. (187?–1940) Originally an actor, he became, together with Capellani (*q.v.*), one of the directors of SCAGL 1908–14, and there made the majority of the Prince Rigadin comedies. He made numerous mediocre films until 1920.

MONICELLI, Mario DIR Italy. (May 15, 1915–) After some years as an assistant (from 1935) and later as a scriptwriter, he made a modest debut as a director on a series of minor comedies (co-directed and scripted by S. Steno) often featuring the comedian, Toto. He later confirmed his own talents and ability, making two notable comic successes, *I Soliti Ignoti* and *Le Grande Guerra*, but after the excellent *The Organizer* he has tended to concentrate on minor episode films.
CO-SCEN: for Pietro Germi, *In Nome della Legge** (49); for De Santis, *Riso Amaro** (49); and for most of his own films.
CO-DIR (with S. Steno, notably): *Totò Cerca Casa* (49), *Totò e i re di Roma* (51), *Guardie e Ladri/Cops and Robbers* (51), *Totò e le Donne* (52), *Le Infedeli* (52).
DIR (notably): *Proibito* (54), *Totò e Carolina* (55), *Padri e figli* (57), *I Soliti Ignoti/Persons Unknown* (58), *Le Grande Guerra* (59), *Risate di Gioia* (60), *Boccaccio '70* (62) (one episode), *I Compagni/The Organizer* (63), *Alta Infedeltà* (64) (one episode), *Casanova '70* (64) (one episode), *L'Armata Brancaleone* (65), *Le Streghe* (66) (one episode), *Le Fata* (66) (one episode), *La Ragazza con la Pistola* (67), *Il Frigorifero* (70) (co-dir: L. Comencini).

MONTAZEL, Pierre PHOTOG/DIR France. (Senlis 1911–) He began brilliantly during the war with his impressionist-inspired images for *Le Lit à colonnes*. After his excellent photography for Becker's *Antoine et Antoinette* (47), he turned to directing, but never achieved the quality of his earlier work.

MONTUORI, Carlo PHOTOG Italy. (Casacalenda Aug 3, 1885–) The doyen of Italian cameramen and one of the best, he developed a technique for artificial lighting, worked on many of the extravagant Italian melodramas from 1912 on. He also worked on part of the 1926 *Ben Hur**, on the bittersweet comedies of Camerini (*q.v.*) in the Thirties, on "white telephone" films of the war period and, above all, on De Sica's *Bicycle Thieves**.

MORLHON, Camille de DIR France. (? –c. 1945) A pre-1914 Pathé director, responsible for several brazen society dramas: *L'Ambitieuse* (12), *Sacrifice surhumain* (13), *Sous l'uniforme* (14), *Une brute humaine* (14).

MORSI, Ahmad Kamel *see* KAMEL MORSI, AHMAD

MOSKVIN, Andrei PHOTOG USSR. (Saint Petersburg 1901–Leningrad 1961) One of the most distinguished of Soviet cameramen, he began his career in FEKS in the Twenties and collaborated for many years with Kozintsev (*q.v.*) and Trauberg (*q.v*): [*The Devil's Wheel* (26), *The Cloak** (26), *The Club of the Big Deed** (27), *Bratishka* (27), *The New Babylon** (29), *Alone** (31), *Maxim trilogy**, *Ordinary People* (45); with Kozintsev alone: *Pirogov* (47), *Belinsky* (53), *Don Quixote** (57), and *Hamlet** (64) (died during shooting). Also, notably, for Ermler, *Katka's Reinette Apples** (27); for Yutkevich, *Stories About Lenin* (57); for Heifitz, *Lady With a Little Dog** (60), and for Eisenstein, the unforgettable images of *Ivan the Terrible**.]

MUNDVILLER, Joseph-Louis (also, in Russia, George Meyer) PHOTOG France/Russia. (Mulhouse April 10, 1886–) [After a year at the Pathé studios in Paris, he was appointed chief cameraman in the Russian Pathé studio and was there 1908–14, shooting, e.g., *Cossacks of the Don* (08), *Peter the Great* (10), *Romance with Double Bass* (11), *1812* (12), *God of Vengeance* (12), *Keys to Happiness* (13).] On his return to France he contributed many skillful and polished images to the French cinema, especially in the Twenties. From 1944–60 he was a professor at IDHEC.
PHOTOG (notably): for Volkoff, *La Maison du mystère* (22), *Kean* (23); for Mosjoukine, *Le Brasier ardent* (23); for Epstein, *Le Lion des Moguls* (24); for Gance, *Napoléon** (27) (as Jean-Paul Mundviller?); for Bernard, *Le Jouer d'échecs* (27); for Renoir, *Le Tournoi dans la cité* (29), *Le Bled* (29).

MUNK, Andrzej DIR Poland. (Cracow Oct 16, 1921–Sept 25, 1961) The most gifted film maker, together with Wajda (*q.v.*), of the group of new Polish directors who reached international prominence in the Fifties. He was trained as a cameraman and director at the Lodz film school and made several outstanding documentaries before turning to features. He was one of the first to use an orchestration of exclusively natural sounds as an accompaniment to his documentaries. His probing style continued in his features as he tackled various social taboos in a manner that was characteristically tinged with bitter irony: pointless heroism in *Eroica*, the career of an opportunist under various regimes in *Bad Luck*, unjustified suspicion of political unreliability in his best film, *Man on the Track*. These, and his unfinished but potentially brilliant *Passenger*, illustrate perfectly his own observation: "I consider it impossible to judge men in too schematic a manner, everything black or everything white, as happened during the period when people were almost denying the existence of gray." His premature death (in a car crash) was a major loss to the Polish cinema.
DIR (documentaries): *Zaczelo sie w Hiszpanii/It Began in Spain* (50), *Kierunek Nowa Huta/Direction Nowa Huta* (51), *Nauka blizej zycia/Science Closer to Life* (51), *Bajka w Ursusie/Tale at Ursus* (52), *Pamietnniki chlopow/Diaries of the Peasants* (53), *Kolejarskie slowo/ A Railwayman's Word* (53), *Gwiazdy musza plonac/Stars Must Shine* (54) (co-dir: W. Lesiewicz), *Niedzielny poranek/On a Sunday Morning* (55), *Spacerek staromiejski/A Walk in the Old City* (58), *Kronika jubileuszowa/Jubilee Story* (59).
DIR (features): *Blekitny Krzyz/Men of the Blue Cross* (55), *Czlowiek na torze/ Man on the Track** (57), *Eroica** (58), *Zezowate szczescie/Bad Luck* (60), *Pasazerka/Passenger** (63) (completed by W. Lesiewicz).

MURNAU, Friedrich Wilhelm (Friedrich Wilhelm Plumpe) DIR Germany/USA. (Bielefeld Dec 28, 1888–California March 11, 1931) Murnau and Fritz Lang are the two greatest directors of the German silent cinema. Murnau studied art and literature, was a pupil of Max Reinhardt (*q.v.*), and an assistant director and stage director in Berlin before making his first feature in 1919. After *Burning Soil* in 1922 his individualistic approach kept him from being identified with any of the characteristic schools of the German cinema. *Nosferatu*, which established his international reputation, is more expressionistic in its script and theme than in its sets, often uncharacteristically realistic. Even *The Last Laugh*, despite its Carl Mayer script, is only on the outer fringe of *Kammerspiel*. He said then: "The designers who made *Caligari** didn't imagine the importance their film would have, and yet they discovered some astonishing things. Simplicity, greater simplicity, and greater simplicity still, that must be the nature of the films of the future . . . All our efforts must be directed toward abstracting everything that isn't true cinema, toward sweeping away everything that isn't the true domain of the cinema, everything that is trivial and acquired from other sources — all the tricks, devices, and clichés inherited from the stage and from books. This is what happens when certain films reach the level of great art." In *The Last Laugh,* a film hailed in the USA at the time as the best film in the world, Murnau made extensive use of the subjective camera, expressing through its movements what the expressionists had through their distortions and lighting. The sets and ancillary objects played a similar role: "On account of the way they (objects) were placed or photographed, their image is a visual drama. In their relationship with other objects or with the characters, they are units in the symphony of the film" (Murnau). After a somewhat ponderous *Tartuffe*, he undertook a version of *Faust* for which he was given almost unlimited financial resources; it was, however, a financial failure. He signed a contract with William Fox (*q.v.*) to work in Hollywood on condition he could make one film of his own choice. That film was *Sunrise*, one of the last great silent films, masterfully expressive, and one that again dealt with the loss and redemption of love, a theme as recurrent in his work as his obsession with death — usually through the intervention of a divine malediction, as that which kills the Maori lovers in *Tabu*. [His other two films for Fox were much less successful: *Four Devils* was routine melodrama and *Our Daily Bread,* intended as a lyrical epic of peasant life, was mutilated by Fox and released as *City Girl*.] *Tabu* is far from the ethnographic documentary envisaged by Flaherty (*q.v.*) but is a visually evocative, modern tragedy and a characteristic Murnau film. This was his last film: he died in a car crash a week before its premiere.

DIR: *Der Knabe in Blau* (19), *Satanas* (19), *Abend . . . Nacht . . . Morgen* (20), *Der Bucklige und die Tänzerin* (20), *Der Gang in die Nacht* (20), *Der Januskopf/Janus-Faced* (20), *Sehnsucht/Bajazzo* (20), *Marizza, gennant die Schmugglermadonna* (21), *Schloss Vogelöd/Vogelöd Castle* (21), *Der Brennende Acker/Burning Soil* (22), *Nosferatu-Eine Symphonie des Grauens** (22), *Phantom* (22), *Die Austreibung* (23), *Die Finanzen des Grossherzogs/The Grand Duke's Fiancées* (23), *Der Letzte Mann/ The Last Laugh** (24), *Tartüff* (25), *Faust** (26), *Sunrise** (27), *Four Devils* (28), *Our Daily Bread/City Girl** (29, released 30), *Tabu** (31).

MUSTAFA, Niazi DIR Egypt. (1903–)
Since 1938 he has been a very prolific and widely popular director of musical comedies, of "Bedouin Westerns" *Rahba* (45), and of thrillers, comedies, and such traditional legends as *Antar wa Abla* (45), etc.

MUYBRIDGE, Eadweard INVENTOR USA. (Kingston-upon-Thames April 4, 1830– Kingston-upon-Thames May 8, 1904) English-born photographer working in San Francisco, who, according to legend, was asked by California's Governor Leland Stanford to settle a wager about whether all four of a horse's legs are off the ground at once as it trots. After five years of work, he succeeded in 1877 (using an idea by John D. Isaacs, an engineer) in analyzing the motion of a horse by using 24 cameras, each attached to a trip wire. His work was a great success and, after joining the University of Pennsylvania, he took sequence photographs of all manner of animals and of man in every conceivable movement, publishing them in eight volumes that contained 20,000 photographs in 1887. In 1881 he traveled to Europe and met Marey (*q.v.*), who was much impressed by his photographs. [He also took over a machine invented in Paris by Jean Louis Meissonier, the Zoopraxinoscope, which resynthesized the movements of his photographs, renamed it the Zoopraxoscope, and used it to exhibit his pictures during personal lectures. His fame as an inventor rests on the ideas of two other men and there is no evidence to suggest he had any conception of "motion pictures." Nevertheless, as his published work testifies, he was a remarkable photographer.]

183

NARUSE, Mikio DIR Japan. (Tokyo Aug 20, 1905–1969) Distinguished Japanese director, though not the equal of Mizoguchi, Ozu, Gosho, Kinoshita, or Kurosawa (all *q.v.*). His films have a real sense of everyday life, behavior, and feelings and of the family in its social contest — qualities that made *Okaasan/ Mother* his best film. His career began in 1926 as assistant to Yoshinobu Ikeda at Shochiku. His first films as director were largely comedies and routine melodramas until he established his reputation as a director of *Shomin-geki* films dealing with the lower middle-classes.

DIR (notably): *Chambara Fufu/Mr. and Mrs. Swordplay* (29) (short comedy), *Junjo/Pure Love* (29), *Shinkon-ki/ Record of Newlyweds* (30), *Ne Kofun Shicha Iyayo/Now Don't Get Excited* (31), *Uwaki wa Kisha ni Notte/Fickleness Gets on the Train* (31), *Kimi to Wakarete/Apart from You** (32), *Yo Goto no Yume/Everynight Dreams* (33), *Otome Gokoro San-nin Shimai/Three Sisters with Maiden Hearts* (34), *Uwasa no Musume/The Girl in the Rumor* (35), *Tsuma yo Bara no yo ni/Wife! Be Like a Rose!/Kimiko* (35), *Tsuruhachi Tsurujiro* (38), *Urashima Taro no Koe/The Descendants of Tara Urashima* (46), *Ishinaka Sensei Gyojoki/ Conduct Report on Professor Ishinaka* (50), *Shiroi Yaju/White Beast* (50), *Meshi/Repast* (51), *Okaasan/Mother** (52), *Inazuma/Lightning* (52), *Ani Imoto/Older Brother, Younger Sister* (53), *Fufu/Husband and Wife* (53), *Tsuma/The Wife* (53), *Bangiku/Late Chrysanthemums* (54), *Yama no Oto/ Sounds from the Mountains* (54), *Shuu/ Sudden Rain* (54), *Tsuma no Kokoro/ A Wife's Heart* (55), *Ukigomo/Floating Clouds* (55), *Nagareru/Flowing* (56), *Arakure/Untamed Woman* (57), *Anzukko* (58), *Iwashi Gumo/Herringbone Clouds/Summer Clouds* (58), *Kotan no Kuchibue/A Whistle in My Heart* (59), *Onnaga Kaidao Agaru Toki/When a Woman Climbs the Stairs* (60), *Yoruno Nagare/The Lovelorn Geisha* (60), *Musume, Tsuma, Haha/Daughters, Wives, and a Mother* (60), *Aki Tachinu/The Approach of Autumn* (60), *Tsuma Toshite, Onna Toshite/Like a Wife, Like a Woman* (61), *Horoki/Lonely Lane* (62), *Onna no rekishi/A Woman's Story* (63), *Midareru/Yearning* (64), *Onna no Naka ni Iru Tanin/The Thin Line* (65), *Hit and Run* (66), *Hikinige/Moment of Terror* (67), *Midare-gumo/ Two in the Shadow* (67).

NASR, Georges M. *see* NASSER, GEORGES M.

NASSER, Georges M. (also Nasr) DIR Lebanon. (Tripoli 191?–) Lebanese director responsible for the interesting *Ila Ayn/ Whither?** (56) in the neorealist manner. His later attempt to "internationalize" his style in the quasi-French *new wave Al Gharib Al Saghir/The Small Stranger* (62) was abortive.

NAUMOV, Vladimir DIR USSR. (1921–) *see* ALOV, ALEXANDER with whom he has collaborated.

NEAME, Ronald DIR/PHOTOG/PROD Britain/ USA. (London 1911–) Former cameraman (*Major Barbara, In Which We Serve*, Blithe Spirit*, etc.) who turned producer after the war and developed into a solid director of major commercial successes that did not have much flair but often had excellent acting performances.

DIR: *Take My Life* (47), *The Golden Salamander* (49), *The Card/The Promoter* (52), *The Million Pound Note* (53), *The Man Who Never Was* (55), *Windom's Way* (57), *The Seventh Sin*

(USA57), *The Horse's Mouth* (58), *Tunes of Glory* (60), *I Could Go on Singing* (62), *The Chalk Garden* (63), *Mister Moses* (64), *A Man Could Get Killed* (USA66) (co-dir: Cliff Owen), *Gambit* (USA66), *The Prime of Miss Jean Brodie* (68), *Scrooge* (70).

PROD (notably): David Lean's *Brief Encounter** (45), *Great Expectations* (46), *Oliver Twist* (48), *The Passionate Friends* (49); John Boulting's *The Magic Box* (51).

NEGRONI, (Comte) Baldassare DIR Italy. (Rome 1877–Rome 1948) Cultured, knowledgeable, Italian film pioneer who specialized in typical Italian society dramas and literary adaptations and whose *Histoire d'un pierrot* (13) might have been an important precursor of neorealism.

*NEMEC, Jan DIR Czechoslovakia. Prague July 12, 1936–) Young Czech director obsessed with exploring memory and the tensions created by physical and psychological stress who has evolved a characteristic staccato, aloof style that reflects undercurrents of anguish. He has said: "My aim was to portray man as he is. Through his destiny I want to find out more about him than I already know. I am concerned with man's reactions to the drastic situation in which, through no fault of his own, he may find himself. After all, so many people's fates rest in the hands of others. I want to interpret the emotions a man goes through in such situations, to assess the meaning of his striving." Though said in relation to his first feature, *Diamonds of the Night* (64), this statement could equally apply to his episode, "The Liars," in *Pearls at the Bottom,* which dealt with the self-cheating memories of two old men, and to his allegory of social and political conformism, *Report on the Party and the Guests,* a film which brought him official displeasure. He has scripted or co-scripted all his own films.

DIR: *Sousto/The Loaf of Bread/A Bite to Eat* (59) (short), *The Memory of Our Day* (63) (short), *Demanty Noci/ Diamonds of the Night** (64), *Perlicky na dne/Pearls at the Bottom* (64) (one episode), *Life After Ninety Minutes* (65) (short, co-dir: Jan Schmidt), *O Slavnostia Hostech/ Report on the Party and the Guests* (66), *Mucednici Lasky/*

The Martyrs of Love (66), *Mother and Son* (Neth/GFR67) (short).

*NEWMAN, Alfred MUS USA. (Connecticut 1901–Los Angeles Feb 1970) The most prolific (some 200 films) of Hollywood composers, highly skilled in creating "mood" music in a classical symphonic manner for every kind of film. He began his career as a child pianist, became a conductor, and moved to Hollywood in the early years of sound. As examples of their kind, his music for *The Grapes of Wrath, How Green Was My Valley, My Darling Clementine, The Gunfighter,* and *The Razor's Edge* could hardly be bettered.

MUS (notably): for John Ford, *Arrowsmith* (31), *The Hurricane* (37), *Young Mr. Lincoln* (39), *Drums Along the Mohawk* (39), *The Grapes of Wrath** (40), *How Green Was My Valley** (41), *My Darling Clementine** (46); for King Vidor, *Cynara* (32), *Our Daily Bread** (33), *Stella Dallas** (37); for Raoul Walsh, *The Bowery* (33); for Dorothy Arzner, *Nana** (34); for William Wyler, *Dodsworth* (36), *Dead End** (37); for Henry King, *Alexander's Ragtime Band* (38), *The Song of Bernadette* (44), *The Gunfighter* (50), *Love is a Many Splendored Thing* (55); for George Stevens, *Gunga Din* (39), *The Diary of Anne Frank* (58); for William Wellman, *Call of the Wild* (35), *Yellow Sky* (48), *The Iron Curtain* (48); for Hitchcock, *Foreign Correspondent* (40); for Fritz Lang, *Man Hunt* (41); for Edmund Goulding, *The Razor's Edge* (46); for Elia Kazan, *A Tree Grows in Brooklyn* (44), *Gentleman's Agreement** (47), *Pinky* (49), *Panic in the Streets* (50); for Joseph L. Mankiewicz, *Dragonwyck* (46), *A Letter to Three Wives** (48), *All About Eve** (50), *People Will Talk* (51); for Preston Sturges, *Unfaithfully Yours* (48); for Walter Lang, *Call Me Madame* (53), *The King and I* (56); for Billy Wilder, *The Seven Year Itch** (55); for George Seaton, *The Counterfeit Traitor* (61) *Airport* (69); for Henry Hathaway, *How the West Was Won** (62), *Nevada Smith* (66).

NIBLO, Fred (Federico Nobile) DIR USA. (Nebraska Jan 6, 1874–New Orleans Nov 11, 1948) Famous Hollywood director of the Twenties after starting his career with stage and vaudeville experience and working for Thomas Ince (*q.v.*), notable for *The Mark of Zorro** (20) and *The Three Musketeers* (21) (both with Douglas Fairbanks), *Blood and Sand* (22) (with Valentino), *The Red Lily* (23), *Thy Name is Woman* (24), *The Temptress* (26), *The Mysterious Lady* (28) (both with Garbo), *Camille* (27), and especially *Ben Hur** (26). He left Hollywood in the early Thirties to return to the stage.

NICHOLS, Dudley SCEN/DIR USA. (Wapakoneta, Ohio April 6, 1895–Los Angeles 1960) Perhaps the best Hollywood scriptwriter of the Thirties and Forties and one of the most prolific (47 films 1936–56), he is best known for his long and fruitful collaboration with John Ford (*The Informer, Stagecoach*), but he wrote with equal brilliance for Hawks (*Bringing Up Baby, Air Force*), Lang (*Man Hunt, Scarlet Street*), Clair (*It Happened Tomorrow*), Renoir (*Swamp Water*), and Mann (*The Tin Star*).
[SCEN (notably): for John Ford, *Men Without Women* (30), *Born Reckless* (30), *Seas Beneath* (31), *Pilgrimage* (33), *The Lost Patrol** (34), *Judge Priest* (34), *The Informer** (35), *Steamboat Round the Bend* (35), *The Plough and the Stars* (36), *Mary of Scotland* (36), *The Hurricane* (37), *Stagecoach** (39), *The Long Voyage Home* (40), *The Fugitive* (47); for Cecil B. DeMille, *The Crusades* (35); for George Marshall, *Life Begins at Forty* (35); for Hawks, *Bringing Up Baby** (38), *Air Force** (43), *The Big Sky* (52); for Mark Sandrich, *Carefree* (38); for Fritz Lang, *Man Hunt* (41), *Scarlet Street** (45); for Renoir *Swamp Water* (41), *This Land is Mine* (42); for Clair, *It Happened Tomorrow** (43), *And Then There Were None/Ten Little Indians* (45); for Sam Wood, *For Whom the Bell Tolls* (43); for Leo McCarey, *The Bells of St. Mary's* (45); for Elia Kazan, *Pinky* (49); for Hathaway, *Rawhide* (51), *Prince Valiant* (54); for Delmer Daves, *Return of the Texan* (52); for Roy Boulting, *Run for the Sun** (55); for Anthony Mann, *The Tin Star* (57); for Michael Curtiz, *The Hangman* (59); for Cukor, *Heller in Pink Tights* (60), and for his own films. DIR: *Government Girl* (43), *Sister Kenny* (46), *Mourning Becomes Electra* (47).]

*NICHOLS, Mike (Michael Igor Peschkowsky) DIR USA. (Germany 1931–) Former cabaret performer who made an excellent directorial debut on the well-staged adaptation of *Who's Afraid of Virginia Woolf?** (66) and the often brilliant *The Graduate** (67), but flopped badly with the large-budget *Catch 22* (70). Also, *Carnal Knowledge* (71).

NIEPCE, Joseph Nicéphore INVENTOR France. (Chalon-sur-Saône 1765–1833) The true inventor of photography who first succeeded in recording an image in 1820 after 12 hours exposure to a silver-iodide-coated metal plate. He later worked with Daguerre (*q.v.*), who marketed the process. His cousin, Niepce de Saint-Victor (1805–1870), later developed the technique of negatives on glass and positive prints on paper.

NILSSON, Leopoldo Torre *see* TORRE NILSSON, LEOPOLDO

NIOUN, Mahoun Tien DIR Burma. (? –) The director of a somewhat saturnine Burmese melodrama, *The Ratanapoum House* (56).

*NORDGREN, Erik MUS Sweden. (1913–) The most distinguished, versatile, and prolific of Swedish composers, with an ascetic, economical style that often incorporates baroque elements, most notably in his long collaboration with Bergman (*q.v.*), 1944–64: *Thirst*, This Can't Happen Here, Summer Interlude*, Waiting Women, Summer with Monika*, Smiles of a Summer Night*, The Seventh Seal*, Wild Strawberries*, The Face, The Virgin Spring*, Now about These Women*. Also, notably: for Erik Faustman, *Crime and Punishment* (45); for Gustaf Molander, *Woman without a Face* (47), *Life Begins Now* (48), *Eva* (48), *Love Will Conquer* (49), *Divorced* (51), *Defiance* (52), *Unmarried* (53); for Lars-Eric Kjellgren, *Vald/Violence* (55), *Leg pa regnbagen/Playing on the Rainbow* (58), *Brott i paradiset/Crime in Paradise* (59); for Hasse Ekman, *Gabrielle* (54), *Private Entrance* (56), *Ratataa* (56), *The Decimals of Love* (60), *On the Bench in the Park* (60); for Alf Kjellin, *Lustgarden/Pleasure Garden* (61), for Vilgot Sjöman, *Klänningen/The Dress* (64); for Torbjörn Axelman, *Ojojoj/Well Well Well* (65); for Jan Troell, *4x4* (65) (one episode),

Har har du ditt liv/Here is Your Life (66), *Ole dole doff* (68).

*NYKVIST, Sven PHOTOG Sweden. (Moheda 1922–) Bergman's (*q.v.*) regular cameraman in the Sixties and unquestionably one of the world's greatest cinematographers, particularly skillful in conveying the bleakly beautiful Swedish landscape and in giving a translucent clarity to his images. The realistic yet otherworldly images of *The Silence* were due to his use of specially treated film stock. He joined Sandrews in 1941 as an assistant and shot his first film in 1945.
PHOTOG (notably): for Alf Sjöberg, *Barabbas* (53), *Karin Mansdotter* (54), *The Judge* (60); for Bergman, *Sawdust and Tinsel** (53) (interiors only), *The Virgin Spring** (60), *Through a Glass Darkly** (61), *Winter Light** (62), *The Silence** (63), *Now about These Women* (64), *Persona* (66), *Hour of the Wolf** (68), *Shame* (68), *The Rite* (69), *A Passion* (69); for Arne Mattson, *Storm over Tjurö* (54), *Salka Valka* (54), *Girl in a Dress Coat* (56), *Lady in Black* (58); for Gunnar Hellström, *Nattbarn/Children of the Night* (56), *Synnöve Solbakken* (57); for Rolf Husberg, *Laila* (GFR/Swed58); for Vilgot Sjöman, *Klänningen/The Dress* (64); for Mai Zetterling, *Älskande par/Loving Couples* (64); for Jorn Donner, *Att Älskar/To Love* (64); for Hans Abramson, *Roseanna* (67), *Bränt barn/The Sinning Urge* (67); for Arne Skouen, *An-Magritt* (Norway69).
DIR/PHOTOG: *Gorilla* (56), *Lianbron/Vine Bridge* (65).

1989 Scorses part of "New York Stories"

187

*OBOLER, Arch DIR/SCEN/PROD USA. (Chicago 1909–) Independent producer-director-writer (who finances his own films) with a long and famous radio career as a committed writer-producer ("This Precious Freedom," "To the President," "Plays for Americans," "Oboler Omnibus," "Free World Theater"). His film career has been rather mixed, ranging from often well-written but pointlessly mannered B-films (*Bewitched, Strange Holiday*) to his brilliant science-fiction drama staged like a piece of reportage, *Five*. He made a fortune out of the first 3-D feature, the mediocre *Bwana Devil,* and made another stereoscopic film, *The Bubble,* in 1966, apparently using a new process, but this has mysteriously disappeared and has never had a general public release.
DIR/SCEN: *Bewitched* (45), *Strange Holiday* (46), *The Arnelo Affair* (47), *Five* (51), *Bwana Devil** (53), *The Twonky* (53), *One Plus One/Exploring the Kinsey Report* (Canada61), *The Bubble* (66).

*ODETS, Clifford SCEN/DIR USA. (Philadelphia July 18, 1906–New York 1963) Famous American playwright (*Waiting for Lefty, Awake and Sing, Paradise Lost, Golden Boy, Clash By Night, The Big Knife, Country Girl*) who influenced many writers and film directors through his collaboration with them at the Group Theater. He wrote two brilliant scripts: Milestone's *The General Died at Dawn* and Mackendrick's *The Sweet Smell of Success.* Also: Negulesco's *Humoresque* (46), Harold Clurman's *Deadline at Dawn* (46), Philip Dunne's *Wild in the Country* (61). His plays were adapted in Mamoulian's *Golden Boy* (39), Seaton's *The Country Girl* (54), and Aldrich's *The Big Knife.*
DIR/SCEN: *None But the Lonely Heart* (44), *The Story on Page One* (59).

OFUGI, Naburo ANIM Japan. (? –1960) Pioneer Japanese animator who worked with both a shadow-theater technique and multiplanar *chiyogami* (transparent colored paper), notably in *The Whale* (two versions, 27 and 52).

OKHLOPKOV, Nikolai DIR USSR. (Irkutsk 1900–) Former film actor who directed only three films (all comedies), including the highly original *The Sold Appetite,* before returning to the stage as a director at the Krasnaya Presnoya (Realistic) Theater, where his imaginative work exercised considerable influence.
DIR: *Mitya* (27), *Prodannyi appetit/The Sold Appetite* (28), *Put entuziastov/Way of the Enthusiasts* (30, not released).

OLIVEIRA, Manuel de DIR/PROD Portugal. (Passamarinas Dec 12, 1905–) The best Portuguese director, sensitive, enamored of art, and knowledgeable, who began by making experimental documentaries (*Douro Faina Fluvial*) and later made, outside of the official industry, *Aniki Bobo* (42), a precursor of Italian neorealism.
DIR (notably): *Douro Faina Fluvial* (29), *Estatuas de Lisboa* (32), *A Cancao de Lisboa* (33), *Miramar* (39), *Praia de Rosas* (39), *Aniki Bobo** (42), *Opintor ea Citade* (56) (prod/photog only, dir: Lopez Fernandez) *O Coracao* (58), *O Pao* (59), *Acto de Primavera* (60), *A Caça* (61).

OLIVIER, (Sir) Laurence DIR Britain. (Dorking, Surrey May 22, 1907–) The most distinguished figure in modern British theater, a consummate stage actor who has also appeared in many film roles. He drew on his stage experience in his important trio of Shakespeare films: *Henry V** (45), *Hamlet** (48), and *Richard III*

(56). Though one might argue with his interpretations of the plays and his manner of adaptation, these are not merely photographed theater but films in which Olivier used visual means to amplify and expand the original text. Also directed: *The Prince and the Showgirl* (57) and the Chekhov adaptation, *Three Sisters* (70).

*OLMI, Ermanno DIR Italy. (Bergamo 1931–) Young Italian film maker, former stage producer and documentarist, whose sympathetic films are largely concerned with the routines of everyday life in modern, industrialized society. He normally uses nonprofessional actors and has a precise feeling for gesture and the comedy inherent in everyday situations. He established his international reputation with the appealing *The Job* and *The Fiancés* and after a somewhat moribund period confirmed his position as one of the major Italian film makers with *One Fine Day* and with the oblique look at the aftermath of war, *The Scavengers*.
DIR (shorts, notably): *La Pattuglia di Passo San Giacomo* (54), *Buongiorno Nature* (55), *La Mia Valle* (55), *Manon: finestra 2* (56), *Tre fili fino a Milano* (58), *Il Pensionato* (58), *Venezia, Città Modernà* (58), *Alto Chiese* (59), *Le Grand Barrage/Time Stood Still* (61).
DIR (features): *Il Tempo si è fermato* (59), *Il Posto/The Job** (61), *I Fidanzati/The Fiancés* (62), *E Venne un Uomo/A Man Named John* (64), *Beata Gioventù* (67) (TV), *Un Certo Giorno/One Fine Day* (69), *I Recuperanti/The Scavengers* (70) (TV).

OPHULS, Max (Max Oppenheimer) DIR Germany/France/USA. (Saarbrücken May 6, 1902–Hamburg March 26, 1957) A totally dedicated film maker, enamored of the cinema and its techniques, even though his experience was as a stage actor and producer (1919–32). He began working in films in 1930 as an assistant and dialogue director for Anatole Litvak (*q.v.*) on *Dolly macht Karriere*. After directing three routine dramas he established his reputation with the lavish, rhythmic *The Bartered Bride* (32) and especially with *Liebelei* (32), whose evocative style and bittersweet quality prevented it from being merely routine Viennese froth. He left Germany when Hitler came to power and for the en-

suing seven years worked in France, Italy, and the Netherlands; he became a French citizen in 1938. According to him, "This was a real rupture; it was difficult to find in France themes that were, let us say, poetic. I had an opportunity with *Werther* but I bungled it." His difficult position as an exile forced him to accept routine commissions such as *Yoshiwara*, but his personal touch was evident in the charming *La Tendre ennemie, Divine,* and *Sans lendemain.* After the fall of France he went to Switzerland, where he worked briefly on the unfinished *Ecole des femmes,* leaving, in 1941, for Hollywood, where he spent four years out of work. He was rediscovered by Preston Sturges (*q.v.*), worked abortively on Howard Hughes's (*q.v.*) *Vendetta,* then made four characteristically stylish films, including *Letter From an Unknown Woman.* He returned to France in 1949 and made his four last, and unquestionably best, films, founded on his 30 years of theatrical and cinematic experiments and the misfortunes of his life and career. In the bittersweet sexual comedies, *La Ronde, Madame de. . . ,* and *Le Plaisir,* and especially in the ironic *Lola Montès,* he transcended the scripts with his elaborately fluid visual style and with the sense of nostalgia and of love betrayed that runs through them. According to François Truffaut and Jacques Rivette: "He was as subtle as he was thought ponderous, as profound as he was thought superficial, as pure as he was thought vulgar. He was considered old-fashioned, out-of-date, antiquated though he dealt with eternal themes: passion without love, pleasure without love, love without reciprocation. Luxury and insouciance only provided a favorable framework for this savage painter." He was obsessed less by "baroque" than by a passion for decor (especially staircases, chandeliers, mirrors, gauzes, cages) and for tracking shots and crane shots that he used to create an often intoxicatingly fluid style. His style is sometimes reminiscent of expressionism, of French pictorial impressionism, and even of the UFA decorative style of the Thirties.
DIR: *Dann schon lieber Lebertran* (Ger 30), *Die Lachende Erben* (Ger31), *die Verliebte Firma* (Ger31), *die Verkaufte Braut/The Bartered Bride* (Ger32), *Liebelei** (Ger33), *Une histoire d'amour* (Fr33) (French version, with new close-

ups, of *Liebelei*), *On a volé un homme* (Fr33), *La Signora di Tutti* (It34), *Divine* (Fr35), *Komedie om Geld/The Trouble with Money* (Neth36), *Ave Maria de Schubert* (Fr36) (short), *La Valse Brillante* (Fr36) (short), *La Tendre ennemie** (Fr36), *Yoshiwara* (Fr37), *Werther* (Fr38), *Sans lendemain* (Fr39), *De Mayerling à Sarajevo* (Fr40), *Vendetta* (USA46) (completed by Mel Ferrer and Howard Hughes), *The Exile* (USA47), *Letter from an Unknown Woman* (USA48), *Caught* (USA48), *The Reckless Moment* (USA49), *La Ronde** (Fr50), *Le Plaisir** (Fr51), *Madame de . . .** (Fr/It53), *Lola Montès** (Fr/GFR55).
NOTE His son Marcel Ophüls (Frankfurt am Main 1927–) is a well-established French TV and film director.

ORKIN, Ruth DIR USA. Independent New York film maker who works in collaboration with her husband, Morris Engel (*q.v.*) on, e.g., *The Little Fugitive**.

*OSHIMA, Nagisa DIR Japan. (Kyoto March 31, 1932–) Independent Japanese film maker with a highly personal style who is somewhat the obverse of Ozu (*q.v.*): where Ozu affirms the values of family and traditional social values, Oshima rejects them. Very much a member of the postwar Japanese generation who grew up during the period of industrialization and urbanization in the Western manner, his films are vigorous explorations of the personal and social implications of the values of modern Japanese society. He joined Shochiku in 1954 as an assistant and directed his first film in 1959. His early films, notably *The Sun's Burial,* were quasi-documentary portraits of adolescent crime, an approach he maintained in his first major film, *The Catch* (61), a violent denunciation of the nationalistic values of the older generation. His later films abandoned traditional narrative realism in favor of a complex style that uses illusion and fantasy to interpret events that inevitably exist on varying levels of reality and to query traditional moral and social assumptions. *Double Suicide, Diary of a Shinjuku Thief, The Boy,* and *Death by Hanging* have confirmed him as one of the most original and searching of contemporary film makers.
DIR: *Ai to Kibo no Machi/A Town of Love and Hope* (59), *Seishun Zankoku Monogatari/Cruel Story of Youth/Naked Youth* (60), *Taiyo no Hakaba/The Sun's Burial* (60), *Nihon no Yoru to Kiri/ Night and Fog in Japan* (60), *Shiku/The Catch* (61), *Amakusa Shiro Tokisada/ The Revolutionary* (62), *Chiisana Boken Ryoko/A Small Child's First Adventure* (64), *Watashii wa Bellett/It's Me Here, Bellett* (64), *Etsuraku/ Pleasures of the Flesh* (65), *Yunbogi no Nikki/The Diary of Yunbogi* (65), *Hakuchu no Torima/ Violence at Noon* (66), *Ninja Bugeicho/ Band of Ninja* (67), *Nihon Shunka-Ko/ Sing a Song of Sex/A Treatise on Japanese Bawdy Songs* (67), *Muri Shinju Nihon no Natsu/Japanese Summer: Double Suicide/Night of the Killer* (67), *Koshikei/Death by Hanging* (68), *Shinjuku Dorobo Nikki/Diary of a Shinjuku Thief* (68), *Kaettekita Yopparai/A Sinner in Paradise* (68), *Shonen/The Boy* (69), *Tokyo Senso Sengo Hiwa — Eigade Ishoo no Koshite Shinda Otokono Monogatari* (70).

OTANI, Takejiro PROD Japan. (Kyoto Dec 13, 1877–?) A Japanese executive producer in the Hollywood manner who co-founded, with Matsujiro Shirai, the Shochiku Cinema Company, a dominant influence on the Japanese cinema in the Twenties that has continued to be one of the major production-releasing companies. He began his career as a peanut vendor, initially developed Shochiku into a theatrical monopoly owning Kabuki troupes and many theaters, and became interested in films after observing the tremendous box-office success of *Intolerance**.

OTSEP, Fyodor *see* OZEP, FEDOR

OZEP, Fedor (*also, in USSR, Fyodor Otsep*) DIR USSR/Germany/France/USA. (Moscow Feb 9, 1895–Hollywood 1948) An active force in the Soviet cinema as scriptwriter and artistic supervisor of the Russ film cooperative (1918) who directed some interesting films, including *The Yellow Pass*. He made a somewhat pedantic adaptation of *The Living Corpse* in Berlin, remained there to make sound films, and later made a number of mediocre films in France and North America. [SCEN (notably): Protazanov's *The Queen of Spades* (16), Sanin's *Polikushka* (19), and his own *Miss Mend* (26).

DIR (notably): *Miss Mend* (USSR26) (co-dir: B. Barnet), *Zemlya v plenu/ Earth in Chains/The Yellow Pass* (USSR 28), *Zhivoi trap/Der Lebende Leichman/ The Living Corpse* (USSR/Ger29), *Mörder Dimitri Karamasoff/Karamazov/ Murder of Karamazov* (Ger31), *Amok* (Fr34), *Tarakanova* (Fr37), (co-dir: M. Soldati), *Gibraltar* (Fr38), *She Who Dares* (USA44), *La Forteresse/Whisper-ing City* (Canada47). It is said that Brecht wrote, uncredited, the script of the latter film, whose plot resembles that of Hitchcock's later *Stranger on a Train*.]

OZU, Yasujiro DIR Japan. (Tokyo Dec 15, 1903–Tokyo Dec 15, 1963) One of the great artists of the cinema, a film maker the Japanese themselves consider the most Japanese but one whose work was until recently little known in the West. He joined Shochiku at the age of twenty and four years later made his first film. Apart from his early nonsense-comedy films he specialized throughout his 40-year film career and 54 films in *shomin-geki*, social comedies and dramas about the lower middle-class — especially office workers — their family life and the tra-ditional ways of life. He was much more interested in character and observation than in action or plot: "Pictures with obvious plots bore me now. Naturally, a film must have some kind of structure or else it is not a film, but I feel that a picture isn't good if it has too much drama or too much action." Donald Richie wrote: "With little or no interest in plot movement, Ozu concerns himself with character development, and all of his better films represent a leisurely dis-closure of character, the like of which is rare in the films of any director . . . Ozu's characters and his tempo are in perfect synchronization with this time system he has created. His is time as it actually is. It is psychological time and so clock time has no meaning. Critic Tsuneo Hazumi's remark that 'Ozu's world is one of stillness' is accurate only if one realizes that this stillness, this re-pose, is the surface which is presents and that, beneath this world, lies the thwarted yet potential violence found in the Jap-anese family system." His style is eco-nomic and sparse in the extreme yet completely rigorous. He eschewed most accepted cinematic and editing devices and almost never moved the camera during shooting. Continuing scenes were almost always shot in one take and from the same viewpoint, about three feet from floor level, the level of someone seated in traditional fashion on *tatami:* "It is the attitude of a haiku master (with whom Ozu shares much) who sits in utter silence and with an occasionally painful accuracy observes cause and ef-fect, reaching essence through an ex-treme simplification. Inextricable from Buddhist precepts, it puts the world at a distance and makes the spectator a recorder of impressions which do not personally involve him" (Donald Richie). He took great pains preparing his scripts (usually in collaboration with Kogo Noda), selecting the right actors for the roles he was evolving and choosing carefully the properties used on the sets so that they played a role in re-vealing the personalities of his charac-ters. "Ozu's attitude to the films has always been that of a perfectionist . . . In everything that Ozu does in films, the parts fit so perfectly that one is never conscious of the virtuosity with which it is done. His pictures are so subtle — the precise opposite of Kuro-sawa's (*q.v.*) that one never thinks to praise the skill with which his effects are achieved" (Donald Richie). DIR: *Zange no Yaiba/Sword of Penitence* (27), *Wakodo no Yume/Dreams of Youth* (28), *Nyobu Funshitsu/Wife Lost* (28), *Kabocha/Pumpkin* (28), *Hikkoshi Fufu/A Couple on the Move* (28), *Niku-taibi/Body Beautiful* (28), *Takara no Yama/Treasure Mountain* (29), *Waka-kihi/Days of Youth* (29), *Wasei Kenka Tomodachi/Fighting Friends* (29), *Dai-gaku wa Deta Keredo/I Graduated, But . . .* (29), *Kaishain Seikatsu/Life of an Office Worker* (30), *Tokkan Kozo/ A Straightforward Boy* (30), *Kekkon-Gaku Nyumon/Introduction to Marriage* (30), *Hogaraka ni Ayume/Walk Cheer-fully* (30), *Rakudai wa Shita Keredo/ I Failed, But . . .* (30), *Sono yo no Tsuma/That Night's Wife* (30), *Erogami no Onryo/The Revengeful Spirit of Eros* (30), *Ashi ni Sawatta Koun/Luck Touched My Legs* (30), *Ojosan/Young Miss* (30), *Shukujo to Hige/The Lady and Her Favorites* (30), *Bijin Aishu/ The Beauty's Sorrows* (31), *Tokyo no Gassho/The Chorus of Tokyo** (31), *Haru wa Gofujin Kara/Spring Comes from the Ladies* (32), *Umarete wa Mita*

Keredo/I Was Born, But . . .* (32), Seishun no Yume Ima Izuko/Where Are the Dreams of Youth? (32), Mata Au Hi Made/Until the Day We Meet Again (32), Tokyo no Onna/Woman of Tokyo (33), Hijosen no Onna/Women on the Firing Line (33), Dekigokoro/Passing Fancy (33), Haha o Kowazuya/A Mother Ought to Be Loved (34), Ukigusa Monogatari/The Story of Floating Weeds (34), Hakoiri Musume/The Young Virgin (35), Tokyo Yoi Toko/Tokyo's a Nice Place (35), Tokyo no Yada/An Inn in Tokyo (35), Daigaku Yoi Toko/College is a Nice Place (36), Hitori Musuko/The Only Son (36), Shukujo wa Nani o Wasuretaka/What Did the Lady Forget? (37), Toda-ke no Kyodai/The Toda Brothers (41), Chichi Ariki/There is a Father (42), Nagaya Shinshi Roku/The Record of a Tenement Gentleman (48), Kaze no Naka no Mendori/A Hen in the Wind (48), Banshun/Late Spring (49), Munakata Shimai/The Munakata Sisters (50), Bakushu/Early Summer (51), O-chazuke no Aji/The Flavor of Green Tea over Rice (52), Tokyo Monogatari/Tokyo Story* (53), Soshun/Early Spring (56), Tokyo Boshoku/Tokyo Twilight (57), Higanbana/Equinox Flower (58), Ohayo/Good Morning/Too Much Talk (59), Ukigusa/Floating Weeds (59), Akibiyori/Late Autumn (60), Kohayagawa-ke no Aki/The Autumn of the Kohayagawa Family/Early Autumn/The Last of Summer (61), Samma no Aji/An Autumn Afternoon/The Taste of Mackerel* (62).

(√)

"I Lived But ..." Two hours docu on Ozu's career, made by his longtime associate Kazuo Inoue. Rvwd. by V. Canby NYT 1 Apr. 87.

Ozu's films are a cinema of character. He was not interested in Freud.

Inoue follows this lead — avoids any analysis. Good — no reduction; film clips — a meditation on Ozu.

Apr. 10, 1987

PABST, Georg Wilhelm DIR Germany/
France/Austria. (Raudnitz, Bohemia
Aug 27, 1885–Vienna May 30, 1967) A
film maker who, during his best years
(1925–32), brought a fresh vision to the
German cinema with his naturalistic
films that had much in common with
Neue Sachlichkeit (New Objectivity). He
began his career (1905) as a stage actor,
began film acting in 1921, and the following year was scriptwriter and assistant to Carl Froelich (*q.v.*) on *Der
Taugenichts* and *Luise Millerin*. His first
film was the somewhat expressionist
Der Schatz (25) but he revealed his
penchant for realism on the film that
established his reputation: *The Joyless
Street* (25), in which he forcefully portrayed the tragic disarray of the Viennese middle classes after the war. Although he said in 1927, "What need is
there for romantic treatment? Real life is
too romantic, too ghastly," he himself
used romanticism most pointedly in *Pandora's Box* (29) (a paean to the fascinating beauty of Louise Brooks),
Diary of a Lost Girl (29), and *The Love
of Jeanne Ney* (27). "Isn't it in raising
social and erotic questions," he said in
1930, "that we will find the essential
material for all our films? But public
taste has been corrupted by the banal-
ity of American stories. And the censor
undertakes to shun intellectual concerns
when considering themes. And yet we
are no longer children." His sound films,
Westfront 1918, Threepenny Opera, and
Kameradschaft, are part of an adult
cinema, socially committed films that
took him to the peak of the international
cinema. Then came decline. After *L'Atlantide* (32) and *Don Quichotte* (33) in
France and a brief sojourn (and one
film) in the USA, he returned to France
and made several mediocre films. [In
1939 he returned to Austria to liquidate

his property and settle his affairs but the
outbreak of war prevented his departure
for the USA. He made two uninteresting
(and nonpolitical) historical films during the war and after the war directed
several, largely routine films.] He had
only seven creative years before his decline but many directors would consider
themselves favored by as much.

DIR: *Der Schatz* (23), *Gräfin Donelli*
(24), *Die Freudlose Gasse/The Joyless
Street** (25), *Geheimnisse einer Seele/
Secrets of a Soul* (26), *Man spielt nicht
mit der Liebe!/Don't Play with Love*
(26), *Der Liebe de Jeanne Ney/The
Love of Jeanne Ney** (27), *Abwege/
Crisis* (28), *Die Büchse der Pandora/
Pandora's Box** (28/29), *Tagebuch
einer Verlorenen/Diary of a Lost Girl**
(29), *Die Weisse Hölle vom Piz Palü/
The White Hell of Pitz Palu* 29, sound
version 35) (co-dir; Arnold Fanck),
*Westfront 1918/Four from the Infan-
try** (30), *Skandal um Eva* (30), *Die
Dreigroschenoper/Threepenny Opera**
(31), *Kameradschaft** (31), *L'Atlantide/
Die Herrin von Atlantis** (Fr/Ger32),
*Don Quichotte** (Fr33), *De haut en bas*
(Fr33), *A Modern Hero* (USA34),
*Mademoiselle Docteur/Spies from Salon-
ika* (Fr36), *Le Drame de Shanghai*
(Fr38), *Jeunes filles en détresse* (Fr39),
Komödianten (Ger41), *Paracelsus* (Ger
43), *Der Fall Molander* (Ger44, un-
finished), *Der Prozess/The Trial** (Aust
47), *Duell mit dem Tod* (Aust49) (su-
pervised only, dir: Paul May), *Ge-
heiminisvolle Tiefe* (Aust51), *Ruf aus
dem Aether* (Aust53) (supervised only,
dir: Georg C. Klaren), *La Voce del
Silencio* (It52), *Cose da Pazzi/Droll
Stories* (It53), *Das Bekenntnis der Ina
Kahr/Afraid to Love* (GFR54), *Der
Letzte Akt/Ten Days to Die* (Aust55),
*Es geschah am 20. Juli/The Jackboot
Mutiny* (GFR55), *Rosen für Bettina*

(GFR56), *Durch die Wälder, durch die Auen* (GFR56).

PAGE, Louis PHOTOG France. (Lyon March 16, 1905–) French cameraman responsible for the exceptional and poetic photography in Malraux's (*q.v.*) *Espoir** and Gremillon's (*q.v.*) *Lumière d'été** (43) and *Le Ciel est à vous** (44) whose almost newsreel style was a precursor of Italian neorealism.

PAGLIERO, Marcello (*also,* **Marcel Pagliero**) DIR Italy/France. (London Jan 15, 1907–) An actor (he played the Resistance leader in *Rome, Open City**) who was also a talented director in the Forties with, at his best, a style derived from both Italian neorealism and French poetic realism: *Roma, Città Libera* (It46), *Un homme marche dans la ville** (Fr49), *Les Amants de Bras-Mort* (Fr50). [His later films, e.g., *La P . . . respecteuse* (Fr52), *Vergine Moderna* (It54), *Walk into Paradise* (Austra156), are of little interest. Since 1964 he has worked for TV.]

PAGNOL, Marcel SCEN/DIR France. (Aubagne Feb 25, 1895–) Above all a playwright and theatrical producer who advocated in 1930 that the sound film become "canned theater" and had his *Marius* and *Fanny* directed by Alexander Korda (*q.v.*) and Marc Allégret (*q.v.*), respectively. He himself became a director whose films were often extremely popular abroad. He brought to the French cinema in the Thirties a robust realism, not far from populism, that contributed to the style in which Renoir's *Toni** (which he produced) is included. He had a special gift with actors — who most often came from the *caf'conc'* of Marseilles.

SCEN (notably): for Korda, *Marius** (31); for Marc Allégret, *Fanny** (32); for Louis Gasnier, *Topaze* (32); for Raymond Bernard, *Tartarin de Tarascon* (34); for Bernard Deschamps, *Le Rosier de Madame Husson* (32); and for his own films.

DIR (notably): *Un direct au coeur* (33), *Joffroy* (33), *Angèle** (34), *Merleusse* (35), *Cigalon* (35), *César** (36), *Regain* (37), *La Femme du boulanger** (38), *Le Schpountz* (38), *La Fille du puisatier* (40), *Naïs* (45), *La Belle meunière* (48), *Topaze* (51), (remake), *Manon*

des sources (53), *Lettres de mon moulin* (54).

PAINLEVE, Jean DIR France. (Paris Nov 20, 1902–) Scientist and documentary film maker whose research studies and popular science films (about 100, mostly on marine animals) over some forty years were major contributions to the field and influential on its development. The rigorous scientific attitude of his films and their often striking visual beauty followed the path laid down by Jules Marey (*q.v.*), the inventor and founder of the scientific cinema.

The son of the famous mathematician and politician, Paul Prudent Painlevé, he made his first film in 1922 as part of a scientific paper to the French Academy of Sciences. He aims to portray nature "from the scientific and photogenic viewpoint," avoiding as much as possible, "the twin blinkers of anthropomorphism and anthropocentrism." He said in 1930: "Whatever the chosen subject, the artistic aspect must always be shown to as much advantage as the scientific. This is considerably easier to achieve with a more abstract subject or when the magnifications used or the manner of recording (high speed, time lapse) make the unusual and wonderful aspects more evident. Very pleasingly, in this way, one is undoubtedly moving toward a form of absolute cinema." He founded the Institut de Cinéma Scientifique in 1930 and was co-founder of the International Scientific Film Association.

DIR (notably): *Oeuf d'épinoche* (22), *Bernard l'ermite* (27), *La Pieuvre* (28), *Les Oursins* (28), *La Daphnie* (29), *Le Hyas* (29), *Reviviscence d'un chien* (29), *Les Crevettes* (30), *Caprelles et Pantopedes* (30), *Ruptures de fibres* (31), *Mouvements intraprotoplasmiques de l'elodea canadensis* (31), *Électrophorèse du nitrate d'argent* (32), *L'Hippocampe** (34), *Corethre* (35), *Microscopie à bord d'un bateau de pêche* (36), *Voyage dans le ciel* (36), (co-dir: A.-P. Dufour), *Culture des tissus* (37), *Barbe-Bleue* (37), (cor-dir René Bertrand), *Images mathématiques de la lutte pour la vie* (38), *Solutions Françaises* (39–45), *Le Vampire* (45), *Assassins d'eau douce* (47), *Notre planète la terre* (47), *l'Oeuvre scientifique de Pasteur* (47) (co-dir: Rouquier), *Ecriture de la danse* (48), *Les Oursins* (53), *Comment naisent les Méduses* (60), *Danseuses de la* *mer* (62), *Histoire de crevettes* (64), *Les Amours de la pieuvre* (67).

PAL, George ANIM Netherlands/Britain ANIM/DIR/PROD/SPECIAL EFFECTS USA. (Hungary Feb. 1, 1900–) Former puppeteer in the Netherlands and Britain, *Aladdin* (36), *Sinbad* (36), *On Parade* (36) *What Ho, She Bumps* (37), *Sky Pirates* (38) *Love on the Range* (39) (all using wooden marionettes), he moved to the USA in 1940, made a series of "Puppetoons" and later became a special effects technician, producer, and occasionally director of films combining live action, animation, and trick work (for which he won six Oscars), e.g.: *Destination Moon* (50) (dir: I. Pichel), *When World Collide* (51) (dir: Maté), *War of the Worlds* (53) (dir: B. Haskin), *The Conquest of Space* (55) (dir: Haskin). He himself directed *Tom Thumb* (58), *The Time Machine* (60), *Atlantis, the Lost Continent** (61), *The Wonderful World of the Brothers Grimm* (62), *The Seven Faces of Dr. Lao* (64).

PALSBO, Ole DIR Denmark. (Copenhagen Aug 13, 1909–Copenhagen June 11, 1952) Documentarist and film maker almost completely unknown outside his own country, who seems to have been, with the Henning-Jensens (*q.v.*), the best Danish director of the postwar period with liberal ideals and a racy, satiric style.
DIR (notably): *Spild er Penge* (42), *Kommunerne i vore dage* (43), *Vibringer en advarsel* (44), *Kartofler* (45), *Stop tyven* (45), *Livsfare-Miner!* (46), *Diskret ophold* (46) (fiction), *Ta' hvad du vil ha'* (47) (fiction), *Kampen mod uretten* (48) (fiction), *Familien Schmidt* (50), (fiction), *Vi arme syndere* (52) (fiction), *Man hurde ta' sig af det* (52).

PANIJEL, Jacques DIR France. (Paris 1921–) Apart from *La Peau et les os/The Mazur File* (60) (co-dir: J.-P. Sassy) which won the Prix Jean Vigo, he has directed (anonymously) *Octobre à Paris* (62), on the demonstrations in Algeria and the repercussions in Paris, one of those films that Delluc said "go beyond art, being life itself."

*PASOLINI, Piero Paolo DIR/SCEN Italy. (Bologna 1922–) Novelist, poet, theorist, and essayist who has developed in the Sixties into one of the most potent forces of a new generation of Italian film makers; his films and articulate theoretical writings have influenced both Bertolucci (*q.v.*) and Bellochio (*q.v.*). His first contact with the cinema was as scriptwriter, notably as consultant on Fellini's *Le Notti di Cabiria* and collaborator on Bolognini's *La Notte Brava* and *Il Bell'Antonio;* he directed his first film, *Accattone*, in 1961. He is a convinced Marxist and humanist, attitudes evident in all his work, from the pitiless attack on materialism in *Accattone,* through the historical dialectic of *The Gospel According to St. Matthew* and the satirical comedy of *The Hawks and the Sparrows* and his sketch films, to the blend of myth and realism in *Oedipus Rex* and *Teorema*. His literary background has contributed much to his work, but not at the expense of seeking an aesthetic peculiar to the cinema: "I made my first film simply in order to express myself in a different medium — a medium that I knew nothing about and whose technique I had to learn with that first film. And for each subsequent picture, I have had to learn a different technique . . . I am always trying out new means of expression." "I now find that the meaningfulness of images is analogous to the meaningfulness of words, that content achieves the same power of communication . . . an image can have an allusive force equivalent to that of a word, since it represent the culmination of a series of analogies selected aesthetically."
CO-SCEN: for Soldati, *La Donna del Fiume* (54); for Luis Trenker, *Il Prigioniero della Montagna* (55); for Fellini, *Le Notti di Cabiria** (56); for Bolognini, *Marisa la Civetta* (57), *Giovanni Mariti* (58), *La Notte Brava* (59), *Il Bell'Antonio* (59), *La Giornata Balorda* (60); for Franco Rossi, *Morte di un Amico* (60); for Cecilia Mangini, *La Canta della Marane* (60) (short; commentary based on a chapter of his novel, *Ragazza di Vita*); for Florestano Vancini, *La Lunga Notte del '43* (60); for Gianni Puccini, *Il Carro Armato dell'8 Settembre* (60); for Luciano Emmer, *La Ragazza in Vetrina* (61); for Bertolucci *La Commare Secca* (62); and for all his own films.
DIR: *Accattone** (61), *Mamma Roma* (62), *Rogopag* (62) (one episode), *La Rabbia* (63) (one episode, not released),

195

Comizi d'Amore (64), *Sopraluoghi in Palestina* (64) (documentary), *Il Vangelo Secondo Matteo/The Gospel According to St. Matthew** (64), *La Streghe/The Witches* (66) (one episode), *Uccellacci e Uccellini/The Hawks and the Sparrows* (66), *Amore e Rabbia/Vangelo '70* (67, released 69) (one episode), *Edipo Re/Oedipus Rex** (67), *Teorema* (68), *Porcile/Pig Sty* (69), *Medea* (70), *Il Decamerone* (71).

PASTRONE, Giovanni (also Piero Fosco) DIR Italy. (Asti Sept 13, 1882–Turin June 29, 1959) A pioneer film maker of rare skill and intelligence, originally a technician and founder of Itala Film, who was the first to launch himself into directing spectacular costume dramas — *The Fall of Troy* (10) — after making numerous comedies and dramas. His ambitions reached full fruition in *Cabiria,* a masterpiece of the genre, a key film in the history of the cinema, and unquestionably an influence on D. W. Griffith (*q.v.*). He abandoned the cinema after 1919.
DIR (notably): *La Caduta de Troia* (10) (sets by Romagnon Borgnetto), *Cabiria** (14), *Maciste* (15), *Il Fuco* (15), *Maciste Alpino* (16), *Tigre reale* (16), *Maciste Atleta* (19), *Hedda Gabler* (19).

PATHE, Charles PROD France. (Chevry-Cossigny 1863–Monte-Carlo Dec 26, 1957) The Napoleon of the film industry, a pioneer industrialist who started with a fun fair and erected, first from the phonograph then from the cinema, an empire that soon spread across the entire world and monopolized the industry from raw stock and cameras to projectors, theaters and films themselves. In 1909 he sold in the USA twice as many films as all the American companies combined and in 1913 the Germans said of him: "He has taken from our country far more than the 5 billions paid by France after the Franco-Prussian war." The cameramen, producers, and distributors of Pathé Frères were pioneers of the industry in Australia, Japan, Brazil, and the East Indies. After the First World War, amenable to the financiers who ruled him, he allowed his empire to be dismembered and the parts sold to the highest bidder. He retired after 1930 and exploded the Nathan scandal around the French company he was leaving — but he chose Monaco rather than Elba for his last years.

PAVIOT, Paul DIR France. (Paris March 11, 1925–) Originally a documentary film maker and director of parodic medium-length fiction films whose first feature, *Pantalaskas* (59), was a robust and sensitive film.
DIR: *Terreur en Oklahoma* (50) (co-dir: A. Heinrich), *Chicago Digest* (51), *Torticola contre Frankensberg* (52), *Saint-Tropez, devoir de vacances* (52), *Lumière* (53), *Pantomimes* (54), *Un jardin public* (55), *La Parade* (55), *Mam'zelle Souris* (58) (TV series), *Django Reinhardt* (58), *Pantalaskas* (59) (feature), *Portrait-robot* (60) (feature).

***PECKINPAH, Sam** DIR USA. (Madera County, California 1926–) Maker of westerns with a personal vision, a perfectly controlled style, and a concern for using the form to explore moral conflicts. His work has continued that of Boetticher (*q.v.*) in rejuvenating the western. He studied drama at the University of Southern California and began film work as dialogue director with Don Siegel and later as writer/director on several TV western series. His first two features, *The Deadly Companions* and *Ride the High Country,* leisurely exposés of moral conflict and character, immediately established his reputation, but until the success of *The Wild Bunch* (69) he suffered extensively from producer interference. He was replaced by Norman Jewison on *The Cincinnati Kid* (64) after only a few days shooting, and his *Major Dundee,* with its ironic use of western mythology, was re-edited by the producers. Many projects failed to materialize and he returned to TV directing. He has said: "Most of my work has been concerned one way or another with outsiders, losers, loners, misfits, rounders — individuals looking for something besides security . . . (Pretentiousness) is what I really resent in a picture more than anything else, that fatal weakness of so many astonishingly good directors." Unfortunately, after the masterly *The Wild Bunch,* he himself fell prey to this weakness in *The Ballad of Cable Hogue.*
DIR: *Gunsmoke* (57) (TV series, directed 13), *The Riflemen* (58) (TV series, wrote only), *The Westerner* (60–61) (TV series, directed most), *The*

Deadly Companions/Trigger Happy (61), *Ride the High Country/Guns in the Afternoon** (61), *Pericles on 34th Street* (62) (TV), *The Losers* (63) (TV), *Major Dundee* (65), *Moon Wine* (67) (TV), *The Wild Bunch** (69), *The Ballad of Cable Hogue* (70), *Straw Dogs* (Brit71).

PEIXOTO, Mario DIR Brazil. (Rio 1912–) A strange character who made *Limite** (30) when he was 18 years old, a film considered in his own country and in Europe as a masterpiece but which, since 1940, he has not allowed anyone to see. He did not make any other contributions to the cinema apart from two or three scripts.

***PENN, Arthur** DIR USA. (Philadelphia Sept 27, 1922–) A talented film maker, former TV and stage producer, with a succession of individualistic films to his credit: *The Left-Handed Gun*, *The Chase*, *Bonnie and Clyde*, *Little Big Man*, films whose impulsive, instinctive characters try to cope, frustratedly, with destiny. He said: "I think that there is very little that one can do about one's fate. I mean in term of external realities — how much effect one has upon what happens in one's life. How one *lives* with it is quite another matter." The penchant for excessive symbolism in his earlier work (*The Left-Handed Gun*, *Mickey One*) has matured into an eloquent use of metaphorical imagery.
DIR: *The Left-Handed Gun** (58), *The Miracle Worker* (62), *Mickey One* (64), *The Chase* (65), *Bonnie and Clyde** (67), *Alice's Restaurant* (69), *Little Big Man* (70).

PEON, Ramón DIR Cuba/Mexico. (Cuba 190?–) His best work was in Cuba, where he made *La Virgen de la Caridad** (30), a film of undeniable quality for his country at the time. He later settled in Mexico and made films that are undistinguishable from those of other prolific directors of the 1935–60 period.

PEREIRA DOS SANTOS, Nelson *see* SANTOS, NELSON PEREIRA DOS

***PERIES, Lester James** DIR Ceylon. (1921–) Excellent Sinhalese film maker, sometimes dubbed "Ceylon's Satyajit Ray," not only because of his intimate, elegaic style and sense of rhythm and characterization, but also because of his impact on the cinema in Ceylon and his giving it an international prominence. A former journalist and amateur film maker, he made several documentaries before achieving an immediate international reputation with his first feature, *Rekava*.
DIR (shorts): *Farewell to Childhood* (50), *A Sinhalese Dance* (51), *Soliloquy* (51), *Conquest of the Dry Zone* (54), *Be Safe or Be Sorry* (55), *Too Many, Too Soon* (61), *Home from the Sea* (62), *Forward into the Future* (64), *Steel* (69), *Forty Leagues from Paradise* (70), *A Dream of Kings* (70).
DIR (features): *Rekava/Line of Destiny** (56), *Sandesaya/The Message* (60), *Gamperilaya/The Changing Countryside* (64), *Delovak Athara/Between Two Worlds* (66), *Ran Salu/The Yellow Robe/Golden Shawl* (67), *Golu Hadawatha/The Silence of the Heart* (68), *Akkara Paha/Two Acres of Land* (69).

PERINAL, Georges PHOTOG France/Britain. (Paris 1897–London April 1965) A brilliant and talented cameraman who contributed much to the films of Grémillon (*q.v.*) and René Clair (*q.v.*) from 1927– 33 and in London was one of the principal talents behind the success of Korda's *The Private Life of Henry VIII*. However, he later rarely found a director to match his own talents.
PHOTOG (notably): for Grémillon, *Maldone** (27), *Gardiens de phare** (29), *Daïnah la métisse* (31); for Clair, *La Tour* (28), *Sous les toits de Paris** (30), *Le Million** (31), *A nous la liberté** (31), *Quatorze juillet* (32); for Feyder, *Les Nouveaux messieurs** (28); for Cocteau, *Le Sang d'un poète** (30); for Alexander Korda, *The Girl from Maxim's* (Brit33); *The Private Life of Henry VIII** (Brit33), *Rembrandt* (Brit36), *Perfect Strangers* (Brit45); for Duvivier, *Maria Chapdelaine* (Fr34); for Paul Czinner, *Catherine the Great* (Brit34); for William Cameron Menzies, *Things to Come* (Brit36); for Michael Powell, *The Thief of Bagdad* (Brit40), *The Life and Death of Colonel Blimp* (Brit43), *Honeymoon* (Brit58); for Leslie Howard, *The First of the Few/Spitfire* (Brit 42); for Cavalcanti, *Nicholas Nickleby* (Brit47); for Carol Reed, *The Fallen Idol** (Brit48); for Marc Allégret, *L'Amant de Lady Chatterley* (Fr55); for Chaplin, *A King in New York** (Brit

57); for Preminger, *Saint Joan** (Brit 57), *Bonjour Tristesse* (USA57); for Stanley Donen, *Once More with Feeling* (USA59); for Gregory Ratoff, *Oscar Wilde* (Brit60).

PERRET, Léonce DIR France/USA. (Niort May 13, 1880–Niort 1935) Unexacting in his choice of scripts and often accepting the worst melodramas and chauvinistic propaganda, he had, nonetheless, a real narrative sense and a feeling for visual design. His *Enfants de Paris* (13), was a model of cinematic writing, much in advance of its time, and even better than Griffith's (*q.v.*) scripts at the time. He was originally an actor (notably for Feuillade), began directing in 1908 for Gaumont, and made over 200 films in his career. He was in the USA from 1916–21.
DIR (notably): *Noël d'artiste, Le Roi de Thulé, Molière, Main de fer, Rival de Chérubin, La Dentellière, Les Blouses blanches, La Bonne Hôtesse*, etc. (08–12), *Léonce* series (10–16), *L'Enfant de Paris** (13), *Le Roi de la Montagne* (14), *Les Mystéres de l'ombre* (14), *La Voix de la patrie* (15), *Le Héros de l'Yser* (15), *Les Poilus de la revanche* (15), *The Silent Master* (USA17), *Lest We Forget* (18), *Million Dollar Dollies* (18), *The Thirteenth Chair* (19), *Soul Adrift* (19), *Lifting Shadows* (19), *Twin Pawns* 20), *Tarnished Reputations* (20), *A Modern Salome* (20), *The Money Maniac* (USA21), *Koenigsmark* (Fr23), *Madame Sans-Gêne* (25), *La Femme nue* (26), *Morgane la sirène* (28), *Quand nous étions deux* (29), *Après l'amour* (31), *Enlevez-moi* (32), *Sapho* (34), *Les Précieuses ridicules* 35).

*PETRI, Elio DIR/SCEN Italy. (Rome Jan 29, 1929–) A member of the Pasolini-Bertolucci-Bellochio (all *q.v.*) generation of Italian film makers who are dedicated to exploring the structure of society, he has evolved an individualistic, elliptical style, at his best in *The Assassin* (60), *A Quiet Day in the Country* (68), and *Investigation of a Citizen Above Suspicion* (69). He has been very active in left-wing politics, was film critic for the communist paper *L'Unità*, and began his film career as scriptwriter for De Santis, Lizzani, Casadio, etc. He made many documentaries, including *I Sette Contadini* (49) before his first film in 1960.

CO-SCEN: for De Santis, *Roma Ore 11** (51), *Un Marito per Anna Zacheo* (53), *Giorni d'Amore* (54), *Uomini e Lupi* (56), *La Strada Lunga un Anno/The Road a Year Long** (Yug/It59), *La Garconière* (60); for Amato, *Donne Proibite* (53); for G. Brignone, *Quando Tramenta il Solle* (56); for A. Casadio, *Un Ettaro di Cielo* (57); for E. Provencale, *Vento del Sud* (59); for Puccini, *L'Impiegato* (59); for Lizzani, *Il Gobbo* (60); for Schott-Schöbinger, *Le Notti dei Teddy Boys* (60); for Risi, *I Mostri* (63).
DIR: *L'Assassino/The Assassin* (60); *I Giorni Contati* (61), *Il Maestro di Vigevano* (63), *Alta Infedeltà* (64) (one episode), *La Decima Vittima* (65), *A Ciascuno il Suo/We Still Kill the Old Way* 66), *Un Tranquillo Posto di Campagna/ A Quiet Day in the Country* (68); *Indagine su un Cittadino al di sopra di Ogni Sospetto/Investigation of a Citizen Above Suspicion* (70), *Il Premio della Bonta'* (71), *La Classe Operaia va in paradiso/ The Working Class Goes to Heaven* (71).

PETROV, Vladimir DIR USSR. (Saint Petersburg 1896–) Former theater director and routine Soviet film maker who made his film debut with an adaptation of Ostrovosky's 1859 play, *Groza/The Thunderstorm* (34). His best film is the two-part film, *Pyotr Pervyi/Peter the Great* (37 and 39), whose earthy good humor prevented it from merely reflecting the personality cult — as occurred in his grandiloquent portrait of Stalin in the two-part *Stalingradskaya bitva/ The Battle of Stalingrad* (50).

PHALKE, Dhundiraj Govind DIR/PROD India. (Trimbkeshwar 1870–Bombay Feb 16, 1944) The father of the Indian cinema. Trained originally as a Sanskrit scholar, he became a skilled photographer and printer. In 1911 he developed a passionate interest in the cinema and visited Pathé (*q.v.*) in Paris and Cecil Hepworth (*q.v.*) and others in London to obtain guidance in film production. He completed his first film, *Rajah Harischandra/King Harischandra* late in 1912 and from its premiere in 1913 it was a phenomenal success. In 1913 he moved his company to Nasik, where he started what was later to be a highly developed film studio employing about 100 workers. [He delighted in magical trick effects in the Méliès (*q.v.*) manner and often explored their use as he did with models, animation, and color. His historical and mythical costume dramas were such a continuing success that in 1914, on a second visit to London, he was welcomed as a film maker of stature. In 1917, as productions became more costly, Phalke joined with five partners and in 1927 withdrew from the company. He made two more films (including one with sound) but public taste had passed him by and they were not a success. As with so many of the cinema's pioneers, Phalke died a pauper and almost forgotten.]

DIR (notably): *Rajah Harischandra* (12), *Bhasamur Mohini/The Legend of Bhasamur* (13), *Savitri* (14), *Chandraha, Tukaram Malvika,* and 16 others (15–17), *Lanka Dahan/The Burning of Lanka* (18), *Krishna Janma/The Birth of Krishna* (18), *Kaliya Mardan/The Slaying of the Serpent* (19), *Sati Manahanda* (23), *Setu Bandhan/Bridge Across the Sea* (31), *Gangavataren/The Desert of Ganga* (32).

PHILLIPS, Alex PHOTOG Mexico/USA. (Ontario, Canada 190?–) Excellent cameraman who has given some very beautiful images to the Mexican cinema, images that match those of Figueroa (*q.v.*) and that have contributed to the renaissance of the art of the Mexican cinema. He has worked notably with Buñuel (*q.v.*), Fernandez (*q.v.*), Roberto Galvadon, and Yves Allégret and has occasionally shot Hollywood westerns. He worked on the uncompleted Mexican sequence of Welles's *It's All True.*

PICASSO, Pablo Ruiz y (Malaga 1881–) It is commonly known that Picasso appeared in Clouzot's *Mystère Picasso** (56) but it is far less commonly known that he made a 16mm color feature in the summer of 1950 that has never been released.

PICK, Lupu (also Lupu-Pick) DIR Germany. (Jassy, Romania Jan 2, 1886–Berlin March 7, 1931) An actor and director who made many mediocre films but was also responsible for two masterpieces, *Scherben* (21) and *Sylvester* (23), both of which he directed from Carl Mayer's (*q.v.*) scripts. The esthetic of *Kammerspiel* reached its apogee in these two modern tragedies in which ordinary people are trapped by destiny.

DIR: *Der Liebe des Van Royk* (18), *Die Tolle Heirat von Lalo* (18), *Der Herr über Leben und Tod* (19), *Kitsch* (19), *Misericordia* (19), *Seelenverkäufer* (19), *Marionetten der Leidenschaft* (19), *Mein Wille ist Gesetz* (19), *Der Dummkopf/ The Idiot** (20), *Das Lachende Grauen* (20), *Niemand weiss es* (20), *Oliver Twist* (20), *Tötet nicht mehr* (20), *Grausige Nächte* (21), *Scherben/Shattered** (21), *Zum Paradies der Damen* (22), *Sylvester/New Year's Eve** (23), *Weltspiegel* (23), *Das Haus der Lüge/ Arme, kleine Hedwig* (25), *Das Panzergewölbe/The Armored Vault* (26), *Eine Nacht in London* (28), *Napoleon auf St. Helena* (29), *Gassenhauer* (31).

PIERCE, Jack MAKE-UP USA. (New York 1889–Hollywood 1968) Hollywood make-up artist who worked for Universal for many years as a specialist on horror films and who was responsible for the faces of Bela Lugosi in *Dracula**, Boris Karloff in *Frankenstein** and *The Mummy,* and Karloff and Elsa Lanchester in *Bride of Frankenstein.*

*PINTER, Harold SCEN Britain. (1930–) Major modern English playwright whose social comedies are allied to the Theater of the Absurd and who has recently turned to scriptwriting, most brilliantly in his collaboration with Joseph Losey (*q.v.*) on *The Servant** (65), *Accident* (67), *The Go-Between* (71). Also: for Jack Clayton, *The Pumpkin Eater* (63); for Michael Anderson, *The Quiller Memorandum* (66). His play, *The Caretaker,* was filmed as *The Guest* by Clive Donner in 1963 and *The Birthday Party* by William Friedkin in 1968.

PINTOFF, Ernest ANIM/DIR USA. (New York Dec 15, 1931–) One of the best contemporary American cartoonists whose original style involves an extreme economy in graphic design and a rich, often satirical, use of sound. He lectured at the University of Syracuse before joining UPA in 1956 as scriptwriter, animator, and producer. In 1957 he created the delightful character of "Flebus" for Terrytoons. In 1959 he set up his own studios, where he made numerous TV commercials and the highly original and witty *The Violinist, The Interview,* and *The Critic.* He has since turned to directing live-action films.

ANIM (notably): *The Wounded Bird* (56), *Aquarium* (56), *Good Ole Country Music* (56), *Fight on for Old* (56), *Martians Come Back* (56), *Performing Painter* (56), *Blues Pattern* (56), *The Haunted Night* (57), *Flebus* (57), *The Violinist* (59), *The Interview* (61), *The Critic* (63), *The Old Man and the Flower* (63).
DIR: *The Shoes* (61) (short), *Harvey Middleman, Fireman* (64) (feature), *This is Marshall McLuhan: The Medium is the Massage* (67) (documentary).

PISCATOR, Erwin DIR Germany/USA. (Ulm Dec 17, 1893–West Berlin 1966) A major figure in the German theater of the Twenties whose stage productions greatly influenced Brecht (*q.v.*). He often used film in his productions and while director of the International Theater in Moscow made an important experimental film: *Vostaniye rybakov/The Revolt of the Fishermen* (34). He later went to New York as teacher and director and returned to Germany in 1951.

PIZZETTI, Ildebrando MUS Italy. (Parma Sept 20, 1880–) Musician of some repute who was interested in the cinema since 1914, when he wrote a score to accompany *Cabiria**. He wrote several film scores after the introduction of sound, e.g., Camerini's *I Promessi Sposi* (40), Lattuada's *Il Mulino del Po* (49).

PLATEAU, Joseph INVENTOR Belgium. (Brussels 1801–Gand 1883) The inventor of animated pictures — a credit he shares with Stampfer (*q.v.*) — who demonstrated that in a machine with two independently rotating discs it was possible to produce the appearance of motion in a sequence of drawings on the lower disc seen in succession through slots in the upper one. In his device, originally called *Fantascope* and later (1832) *Phénakistiscope,* the "moving pictures" were viewed through a rotating polygon of mirror faces in the center of a circular strip of drawings. This apparatus later became a well-known family toy and was described by Baudelaire. Plateau began his work on the presistence of vision in 1829 and his imprudent viewing of the midsummer sun eventually cost him his eyesight in 1843. In 1849 he planned to use photographs in his device, but, already blind, he had to leave this work to others.

POGACIC, Vladimir DIR Yugoslavia. (Zagreb 1918–) One of the best Serbo-Croatian directors whose work is of key importance in the postwar development of the Yugoslav cinema. He is also director of the Yugoslav film archive, Jugoslovenska Kinoteka. His greatest achievement was on *Big and Small*.
DIR (notably): *Prica o fabrica/Story of a Factory* (48), *Poslednji dan/The Last Day* (51), *Nevjera/Equinox* (53), *Anikina vremena/Legends about Anika* (54), *Nicola Tesla* (56) (documentary), *Veliki i mali/Big and Small* (56), *Subotom uvece/Saturday Evening* (57), *Sam/Alone* (59), *Pukotina raja/Heaven with No Love* (61), *Covek sa fotografie/The Man from the Photography Department* (63).

POIRIER, Léon DIR France. (Paris 1876 or 1884–1968) An academic who was originally interested in the theater, he was nonetheless a dedicated film maker who established his reputation after the First World War and did his best work on documentaries after 1925.
DIR (notably): *Cadette* (13), *Le Nid* (14), *Ames d'Orient* (19), *Le Penseur* (19), *Narayana* (20), *L'Ombre déchirée* (21), *Le Coffret de jade* (21), *Jocelyn* (22), *Geneviève* (23), *L'Affaire de courrier de Lyon* (23), *La Brière* (24), *Croisière noire* (26) (documentary feature), *Amours exotiques* (27) (documentary), *Verdun, visions d'histoire* (28), *Caïn* (30), *Madagascar* (30), *Verdun, visions d'histoire* (31) (sound version), *La Folle Nuit* (32), *Chouchou poids plume* (32), *La Voie sans disque* (33), *L'Appel du silence* (36), *Soeurs d'armes* (37), *Brazza* (40), *Jannou* (43), *La Route inconnue* (47).

POJAR, Bretislav ANIM Czechoslovakia. (Sufice Oct 7, 1923–) Excellent Czech animator who specializes in puppet films and is Trnka's (*q.v.*) best disciple.
ANIM (notably): *The Gingerbread Cottage* (51), *A Drop Too Much* (54), *Speibl on the Trail* (56), *The Little Umbrella* (57), *The Lion and the Song* (58), *Bomb Mania* (59), *How to Furnish an Apartment* (59), *A Midnight Adventure* (60), *A Cat's Word of Honor* (60), *Cat School* (61), *Painting for Cats* (61), *The Orator* (62), *Billiards* (62), *Romance* (63), *Ideal* (64), *Come and Play, Sir* (65–67) (three films), *Hold onto Your Hats* (67).

*POLANSKI, Roman DIR Poland/Britain/ USA. (Paris Sept 18, 1933–) Volatile, original, Polish film maker whose ironic studies of sexual obsessions have roots in Kafka, Ionesco, and Samuel Beckett. He began his career (1947) as an actor in both plays and films and then studied for five years at the Lodz film school, where he assisted Munk (*q.v.*) on *Bad Luck* and made several shorts before directing his first feature, *Knife in the Water* (62). However, his short, wry fable about nonconformity, *Two Men and a Wardrobe* (58), had already won him an international reputation. He later left Poland and has since worked mainly in Britain. His best films, *Repulsion*, *Cul-de-sac*, and *Rosemary's Baby* (his first major commercial success) capture the perverse, the grotesque, and the sadomasochistic sides of human nature, but his acidulous vision is tempered by a gift for telling imagistic metaphors and a mischievous sense of irony and parody. DIR (shorts): *Rozbijemy Zabawa/Break Up the Party* (57), *Dwaj ludzie z szafa/ Two Men and a Wardrobe* (58), *Gdy spadaja anioly/When Angels Fall* (59), *Lampa/The Lamp* (59), *Le Gros et le maigre* (Fr61), *Ssaki/Mammals* (62). DIR (features): *Noz w Wodzie/The Knife in the Water* (Pol62), *Les Plus belles escroqueries du monde* (Fr63) (one episode), *Repulsion** (Brit65), *Cul-de-sac** (Brit66), *The Dance of the Vampires/The Fearless Vampire Killers* (Brit67), *Rosemary's Baby* (USA68), *Macbeth* (Brit71).

*POMMER, Erich PROD Germany/Britain/ USA. (Hildesheim July 20, 1889–Hollywood May 11, 1966) A key producer in the German silent cinema, he founded Decla in 1915 (later Decla-Bioscop, taken over by UFA in 1923) and played a role in encouraging the work of Lang (*q.v.*), Murnau (*q.v.*), and others, e.g., *The Cabinet of Dr. Caligari**, *Dr. Mabuse der Spieler**, *Die Nibelungen**, *Varieté**, *Metropolis**, *Der Letzte Mann**, *The Blue Angel**, *Liliom* (France), *Die Drei von der Tankstelle**, *Der Kongress tanzt**. He worked in Hollywood 1934–37, Britain 1937–40, Hollywood (for Paramount and RKO) 1940– 46, Germany 1946–56, then returned to Hollywood.

*PONTECORVO, Gillo DIR Italy. (Pisa 1919–) Former documentary film maker and assistant to Ivens, Allégret, and Monicelli (all *q.v.*), his four fiction films reflect a continuing quest for the reconstruction of actuality using nonprofessional actors. He believes in spending considerable time on research and preparation in order to be able to build up a persuasive "reportage" atmosphere, seen at its best in *Kapò*, the story of a young Jewess in Auschwitz who collaborates with the Nazis, and the striking *The Battle of Algiers*. He is the brother of nuclear scientist, Bruno Pontecorvo. DIR (shorts): *Missione Timiriazev* (53), *Porta Portese* (54), *Uomini di marmo* (55), *Cani dietro le Sbarre* (55), *Pane e solfo* (60). DIR (features): *Die Windrose* (GDR56) (Italian episode, supervised: Joris Ivens, Cavalcanti), *La Grande Strada azzurra* (58), *Kapò* (60), *La Battaglia di Algeri/ Maarakat Madinat al Jazaer/The Battle of Algiers* (Algeria/It65), *Queimada!/ Burn!* (70).

PONTI, Carlo PROD Italy. (Milan Dec 11, 1913–) Munificent Italian producer who once collaborated with De Laurentiis (*q.v.*) and has produced the films of Lattuada, Camerini, Comencini (all *q.v.*), Toto, etc. — and of his wife, Sophia Loren.

*PONTING, Herbert George DIR/PHOTOG Britain. (Wiltshire 1870–1935) The director and cameraman of the ancestor of all documentary films, *With Captain Scott, R.N., to the South Pole/The Great White Silence**, which he made in 1910–11 as official photographer to the ill-fated Scott expedition to the Antarctic. He had been seriously interested in photography since about 1900 and although he then knew nothing of film making he was determined to take motion pictures of the expedition and bought two cameras before leaving. As he described it, filming under the conditions of extreme cold was very difficult: the camera had to be lubricated with graphite and even loading the camera made his fingers frostbitten. He processed his own film in the Antarctic and often took great risks to get good shots. The results, even 60 years later, are impressive, with a real sense of composition that conveys the terrible beauty of that polar region. He did little photographic work after 1920 and spent his time re-editing versions of his film, lecturing with it, and working on non-photographic inventions.

POPESCU-GOPO, Ion ANIM/DIR Romania. (Bucharest 1923–) One of the greatest European animators, he established his international reputation with three shorts, *A Short History, The Seven Arts* and *Homo Sapiens*. All three were whimsical accounts of various historical or cultural events that featured a kind of nude, bald, Archetypal Adam and are full of gentle poetry and ingenious and ingenuous gags. He has now largely abandoned animation in favor of live-action fantasy and science-fiction films.

ANIM (notably): *The Naughty Duck* (51), *The Bee and the Dove* (51), *Two Rabbits* (53), *Marinica* (54), *Marinica's Bodkin* (55), *A Short History* (56), *The Seven Arts* (58), *Homo Sapiens* (60), *Allo! Hallo! Alo!* (63, for UNESCO).
DIR: *Fetita mincinoasa/The Little Liar* (53), *O Musca cu bani/A Fly with Money* (54), *S-a furat o bomba/A Bomb was Stolen* (61), *Pasi spre luna/Steps to the Moon* (63), *De-as fi Harap Alb/ The White Moor* (65), *Faust XX/ Faustus XX* (66), *Orasul meu/My City* (67), *Sancta Simplicitas* (68).

PORTER, Edwin Stratton DIR USA. (Pittsburg 1870–New York April 30, 1941) The most important pioneer of the American cinema. He joined the Edison (*q.v.*) Company in 1896 as mechanic and handyman and by 1900 had become a cameraman and director, making short films from real life and comedy series. His first important film was *The Life of an American Fireman* (02), whose construction reveals that Porter had studied the work of British (e.g., Williamson's *Fire!*, 1901) and other European pioneers. The following year he made the first western, *The Great Train Robbery*, a film that marks the start of the rise of the American film. His *Uncle Tom's Cabin* (03) has the charm of primitive paintings, and *The Dream of a Rarebit Fiend* (06) makes delightful use of trick effects. In 1907, he gave D. W. Griffith (*q.v.*) his first film role in *Rescued from an Eagle's Nest*. [He left the Edison Company in 1909 and formed his own production company, Rex. He joined Adolph Zukor (*q.v.*) in 1912 and as production manager helped establish Famous Players. He directed his last film (shot in Rome) in 1915 and retired, wealthy, from the industry only to have his investments wiped out in the crash of 1929.]

DIR (notably): *The America's Cup Race* (1899), *The Life of an American Fireman* (03), *Uncle Tom's Cabin* (03), *The Great Train Robbery** (03), *The Ex-Convict* (04), *White Caps* (04), *The Miller's Daughter* (04), *Jack and the Beanstalk* (04), *The Kleptomaniac* (05), *The Night Before Christmas* (05), *Dream of a Rarebit Fiend* (06), *The Seven Ages* (06), *A Tale of the Sea* (06), *Rescued from an Eagle's Nest* (07), *The Prisoner of Zenda* (13), *In the Bishop's Carriage* (13), *Hearts Adrift* (13), *A Good Little Devil* (13), *Tess of the Storm Country* (14), *Such a Little Queen* (14) (co-dir: Hugh Ford), *The Dictator* (15), *The Eternal City* (15) (co-dir: Hugh Ford). Porter also photographed many of his own films.

POTTER, H. C. DIR USA. (New York Nov 13, 1904–) Routine Hollywood director, mainly of comedies, who is credited as director of the famous masterpiece of zaniness, *Hellzapoppin** (41).

POUCTAL, Henri DIR France. (La Ferté-sous-Jouarre 1856–Paris Feb 3, 1922) Characterized by Louis Delluc as "one of the best directors" of the prewar years for his "meritorious endeavors in which French taste, prudence, and briskness played a marvelous part." *Travail* and his episode film, *Monte-Cristo*, made him, with Feuillade (*q.v.*), the best French film maker of the time. As head of Film d'Art he gave the young Abel Gance (*q.v.*) his first creative opportunity (script of *L'Infirmière*) and was one of the influences on his development. He made some 50 films in his career.

DIR (notably): *Vitellius* (11), *Werther* (11), *Madame Sans-Gêne* (11), *La Dame aux camélias* (12) (with Sarah Bernhardt), *Les Trois Mousquetaires* (13), *Un fil à la patte* (14), *La Fille du Boche* (15), *Alsace* (15), *L'Infirmière* (15), *Chantecoq* (16), *Monte-Cristo* (17–18) (episode film), *Le Dieu au hasard* (18), *Travail* (19), *Gigolette* (20), *Le Crime du bouif* (21), *La Résurrection du bouif* (22).

POULENC, Francis MUS France. (Paris Jan 7, 1899–Paris March 1963) Distinguished French musician who wrote original scores for several features: Baroncelli's

La Duchesse de Langeais (42), Anouilh's *Le Voyageur sans bagages* (43), Lavorel's *Le Voyage en Amérique* (52).

POWELL, Michael DIR/PROD/SCEN Britain. (Canterbury Sept 30, 1905–) Former editor, assistant director, scriptwriter, and director of B-films (1931–37) whose first notable film, *Edge of the World* (37), visibly influenced by Flaherty's *Man of Aran**, was part of the documentary movement. But, apart from *The 49th Parallel* (41), he quickly abandoned this approach in favor of sumptuous spectaculars, first as co-director of *The Thief of Bagdad* (40), then in his long partnership with Emeric Pressburger (*q.v.*) from 1942–57: *The Life and Death of Colonel Blimp* (43), *I Know Where I'm Going* (45), *A Matter of Life and Death* (46). *The Red Shoes** (48) was an imaginative attempt to expand the bounds of the film-ballet form, but the occasional tastelessness of this film became dominant in *The Tales of Hoffman* (61). He has since made only mediocre films, apart from *Peeping Tom* (60). ✔

POZNER, Vladimir SCEN USA/France/Austria/GDR. (Paris Jan 5, 1905–) Well-known author who has contributed, as scriptwriter, his authentic talent and a robust sense of reality to several directors, including Louis Daquin.
SCEN (notably): for Jean Negulesco, *The Conspirators* (USA44); for Siodmak, *The Dark Mirror* (USA46); for Bert Gordon, *Another Part of the Forest* (USA48); for Daquin, *Le Point du jour** (Fr49), *Bel Ami* (Aust55); for Ivens, *Lied der Ströme** (GDR54), *Die Windrose* (GDR56); for Cavalcanti, *Herr Puntila und sein Knecht Matti** (Aust 55) and his own *Mein Kind* (GDR56) (co-dir: Alfons Michalz, supervised by Joris Ivens).

PREMINGER, Otto Ludwig DIR USA. (Vienna Dec 5, 1906–) A skillful, engaging film maker who is more interested in revealing character than in comic simplification or visual jokes but who, like Lubitsch (*q.v.*), has worked successfully in a variety of genres: thrillers (*Laura,* his first successful film, *The Thirteenth Letter*), costume dramas (*Forever Amber*), musical comedy (*Carmen Jones, Porgy and Bess*), literary adaptations (*Saint Joan, Bonjour tristesse*), satiric comedies (*A Royal Scandal, The Moon is Blue*), westerns (*The River of No Return*). After his best film, *The Man with a Golden Arm,* he became interested in "social" themes and adapted three best-sellers: *Anatomy of a Murder, Exodus,* and *Advise and Consent.* [His work since has become increasingly mediocre, portentously conceived and pretentiously executed. One French critic feels he has become "the man with the leaden arm." He was originally an actor and stage director for the Max Reinhardt troupe in Vienna and was responsible for some fifty productions (and one film) before leaving for the USA in 1934. He was very active on Broadway 1935–40, the period when he made his first Hollywood films. He has also appeared as an actor most often as a German officer or spy in several 1941–43 films and as the camp commandant in Wilder's *Stalag 17.* He has disowned all his films before *Laura* (44) and has produced most of his own films since then.] Considered by his colleague Cukor as principally "a very adroit and perspicacious businessman," Preminger has said: "I like to have a basis, generally provided by a novel or stage play. But if someone brought me a really good idea, I would buy it very willingly . . . I don't seek out problems, but — it's my nature — they crop up in my path. And these problems are complex. It's from this that the ambiguity of my films comes."
DIR: *Die Grosse Liebe* (Aust32), *Under Your Spell* (USA36), *Danger, Love at Work* (36), *Margin for Error* (43), *In the Meantime, Darling* (44), *Laura** (44), *A Royal Scandal* (45) (remake of *Forbidden Paradise,* replaced Ernst Lubitsch), *Fallen Angel* (45), *Centennial Summer* (46), *Forever Amber* (47), *Daisy Kenyon* (47), *That Lady in Ermine* (48) (completed after Lubitsch's death), *The Fan* (49), *Whirlpool* (49), *Where the Sidewalk Ends* (50), *The Thirteenth Letter** (51) (remake of *Le Corbeau**), *Angel Face* (52), *The Moon is Blue* (53), *River of No Return* (54), *Carmen Jones** (54), *The Court Martial of Billy Mitchell/One Man Mutiny* (55), *The Man with the Golden Arm** (56), *Saint Joan** (Brit57), *Bonjour tristesse* (57), *Anatomy of a Murder* (58), *Porgy and Bess* (59), *Exodus** (60), *Advise and Consent* (62), *The Cardinal* (63), *In Harm's Way* (65), *Bunny Lake is Missing* (Brit65), *Hurry Sundown* (67),

Skidoo (68), *Tell Me that You Love Me, Junie Moon* (69).

PRESSBURGER, Emeric DIR/SCEN Britain. (Hungary Dec 5, 1902–) Former scriptwriter for UFA in Berlin who has worked since 1935 in Britain, first as a scriptwriter then in partnership with Michael Powell (*q.v.*) 1942–57 as The Archers production company. His only solo film as director is *Twice Upon a Time* (53).

PREVERT, Jacques SCEN France. (Paris Feb 4, 1900–) Poet and at one time a surrealist, he was one of the creative forces behind the development of French poetic realism of the Thirties; his films collectively form a metaphorical but realistic portrait of France and its concerns 1935–47. His forceful personality is imprinted on the films he wrote for Renoir (*Le Crime de Monsieur Lange, Une partie de campagne*), Grémillon (*Lumière d'été*), Grimault (*La Bergère et le Ramoneur*), his brother, Pierre Prévert (*L'Affaire est dans le sac, Adieu Léonard, Voyage surprise*), and, above all, on his long and fruitful collaboration with Marcel Carné (*q.v.*): *Jenny, Drôle de drame, Quai des brumes, Le Jour se lève, Les Visiteurs du soir, Les Enfants du Paradis, Les Portes de la nuit.* In these films are the elements of his poetry — the lyricism, the delight in words, the obsession with fate, and the use of the absurd to develop social criticism. In the Prévertian universe, goodness struggles against evil, honest people against black villains and it is "evil, evil with a gold watch that wins almost every trick. Almost." His sources might be found in his youthful admirations: Hawks, Sternberg, King Vidor (all *q.v*), and German *Kammerspiel,* but he also drew greatly on his native Paris. "The brilliance of his film dialogue," noted Roger Leenhardt in 1935, "is composed of a thousand pearls of the human language: its words are commonplaces." Above all, he was a moralist who conceived his fables for the moral they suggested.

SCEN: for Marc Allégret and Eli Lotar, *Téneriff* (32) (commentary only); for Pierre Prévert, *L'Affaire est dans le sac** (32), *Adieu Léonard* (43) (co-scen: Pierre Prévert), *Voyage surprise** (46), *Paris mange son pain* (58) (commentary), *Paris la belle* (60) (commentary);

for Autant-Lara, *Ciboulette* (33) (adaptation of opera and dialogue), *The Mysterious Mr. Davis* (Brit37), *L'Affaire du Courrier de Lyon* (37) (dialogue, not credited); for Marc Allégret, *L'Hôtel du libre échange* (34); for Richard Pottier, *Un oiseau rare/L'Éternel enfant/Les Deux gagnants* (35); for Jean Stelli, *Jeunesse d'abord* (35); for Renoir, *Le Crime de Monsieur Lange** (36), *Une partie de campagne** (36); for René Sti, *Moutonnet* (36); for Carné, *Jenny* (36), *Drôle de drame* (37), *Quai des brumes** (38), *Le Jour se lève** (39), *Les Visiteurs du soir** (41), *Les Enfants du paradis** (43–45), *Les Portes de la nuit** (46), *La Fleur de l'âge* (47) (unfinished), *La Marie du port* (50) (uncredited); for Léo Joannon, *Vous n'avez rien à déclarer* (36); for Christian-Jaque, *Les Disparus de St-Agil* (38) (uncredited), *Ernest le rebelle* (38), *Sortilèges* (45), *Souvenirs perdus* (50) (dialogue on first two episodes); for Grémillon, *Remorques** (39) (uncredited), *Lumière d'été** (42); for E. T. Gréville, *Une femme dans la nuit* (41); for Pierre Billon, *Le Soleil a toujours raison* (41); for Eli Lotar, *Aubervilliers* (45) (documentary, commentary); for Henry Jacques, *L'Arche de Noé* (46); for André Cayatte, *Les Amants de Vérone* (48); for Grimault, *Le Petit soldat* (49), *La Bergère et le Ramoneur** (released 53) (both animated films); for Albert Lamorisse, *Bim le petit âne* (51), (documentary, commentary); for Delannoy, *Notre-Dame de Paris* (56); for Joris Ivens, *La Seine a rencontré Paris** (57) (documentary, commentary); for Pierre Guilbaud, *Les Primitifs de XIII*ᵉ (58) (documentary). The short, *Les Feuilles mortes* (50), is based on his famous song, with music by Joseph Kosma.

PREVERT, Pierre DIR France. (Paris May 26, 1906–) Originally assistant to Cavalcanti (*q.v.*) and Renoir (*q.v.*), he collaborated with his brother, Jacques, on his first fiction film, *L'Affaire est dans le sac,* a masterful film in which he created a new comic style but one that only reached cinephiles and not the general public. He was mistrusted by the producers and had to wait some years before being allowed to direct features.
DIR: *Souvenirs de Paris/Paris Express* (28) (documentary; co-dir: Marcel Duhamel; supervision: Cavalcanti; photog: Mann Ray, etc.), *L'Affaire est dans le*

sac* (32); *Le Commissaire est bon enfant* (34) (short; co-dir: Jacques Becker), *Adieu Léonard* (43), *Voyage surprise* (46), *Paris mange son pain* (58) (short), *Paris, la Belle* (59) (documentary using material from *Souvenirs de Paris*, 1928, and new 1959 footage).

PROKOFIEV, Sergei MUS USSR. (Sontskova Aug 23, 1891–Moscow March 8, 1953) Major Soviet composer who collaborated with Eisenstein (*q.v.*) in creating a kind of cinematographic opera with the aural-visual counterpoint of *Alexander Nevsky** (38) and *Ivan the Terrible** (44–46). He had anticipated this development in an interview with Nino Frank in 1932: "I imagine a collaboration with the author of lyrical moving pictures. For a film with actors, a close collaboration with the composer will be necessary, timing the length of scenes, the dialogue, and, as with ballet, the music will describe the action or accompany it in counterpoint." [Also, notably: Alexander Feinzimmer's *Poruchik Kizhe/Lieutenant Kije/The Tsar Wants to Sleep* (34), A. Gendelstein's *Lermontov* (43), Leo Arnstam's and L. Lavrosky's *Romeo and Juliet* (55) (from his ballet). His *Lieutenant Kije* music was used in Neame's *The Horse's Mouth* (Brit59).]

PROMIO, Alexandre PHOTOG France. (c. 1870–Paris 1927) The principal cameraman trained by Louis Lumière (*q.v.*), he seems to have been the first to take "moving camera" shots — from a gondola in Venice in 1896.

PROTAZANOV, Yakov *(also, in France, Jacques Protozanoff)* DIR USSR/France. (Moscow 1881–Moscow 1945) Pioneer Soviet director who began his career before the Revolution directing period dramas and melodramas that often featured Ivan Mozhukhin. He left Russia after the Revolution in 1917 and directed in Paris until 1923, when he accepted an invitation to return. He made the science-fiction film, *Aelita*, notable for its constructivist sets, and directed numerous lively and well-acted films in a sound but somewhat old-fashioned style.
DIR (notably): *Pesnya katorzhanina/The Prisoner's Song* (11), *Anfisa* (12), *Ukhod velikovo startza/The Departure of a Grand Old Man/The Life of Tolstoy* (12), *Kak khoroshi, kak svezhi byli rozi/How Fine, How Fresh the Roses Were*

(13), *Razbitaya vaza/The Shattered Vase* (13), *Klyuchi shchastya/Keys to Happiness* (13) (co-dir: Vladimir Gardin), *Drama by Telephone* (14), *Voina i mir/War and Peace** (15) (co-dir: Gardin), *Peterburgskiye trushchobi/Petersburg Slums* (15) (co-dir: Gardin), *Plebei/Plebeian* (15) (from Strindberg's *Fröken Julie**), *Nikolai Stavrogin* (15), *Pikovaya dama/The Queen of Spades* (16), *Grekh/Sin* (16) (co-dir: G. Azagarov), *Prokuror/Public Prosecutor* (17), *Andrei Kozhukhov* (17), *Ne nado krovi/Blood Need Not Be Spilled* (17), *Prokliatiye millioni/Cursed Millions* (17), *Satana likuyushchii/Satan Triumphant* (17), *Otets Sergii/Father Sergius* (18), *Taina korolevy/The Queen's Secret* (19), *Une nuit d'amour* (Fr19), *Justice d'abord* (Fr19), *Le Sens de la Mort* (Fr22), *L'Ombre du péché* (Fr22), *L'Angoissante aventure* (Fr23), *Aelita** (USSR24), *Yevo prizyv/His Call/Broken Chains* (25), *Protsess o troyokh millyonakh/The Three Million Case* (26), *Sorok pervyi/The Forty-First** (27), *The Man from the Restaurant* (27), *Don Diego and Pelageya* (27), *Byeli orel/The White Eagle* (28), *Chiny i liudi/Ranks and People* (29), *Prazdnik svyatovo Iorgene/The Holiday of St. Jurgen* (30), *Tommy* (31), *Marionettes* (34), *Bespridannitsa/Without Dowry* (36), *Salavat Yalayev* (41), *Nasreddin v Bukhare/Nasreddin in Bukhara* (43).

PTUSHKO, Alexander ANIM/DIR USSR. (Ukraine 1900–) Former puppet film maker, 1927–32, whose films have sometimes had the Méliès (*q.v.*) touch, especially in *Novyi Gulliver/A New Gulliver** (35), a film whose main actors are puppets. He later turned to directing films with large numbers of extras: *Kamenni tsvetok/The Stone Flower* (46), *Sadko* (53), *Ilya Murometz* (56), *Sampo* (59), *The Tale of the Tsar Sultan* (66), etc.

PUDOVKIN, Vsevolod Ilarionovich DIR USSR. (Penza, Saratov Feb 6, 1893–Riga June 30, 1953) One of the four masters of the Soviet silent cinema, along with Eisenstein, Dovzhenko, and Vertov (all *q.v.*). Trained as a chemist, he abandoned his profession in 1920 after seeing *Intolerance** and joined the State Film School, where two years later he was a member of the Kuleshov (*q.v.*) Workshop. He was originally an actor, scriptwriter, and

assistant before making his first solo feature, *Mother* (26), which was an immediate success in the USSR and abroad. Thereafter, his romanesque films were marked by an approach at once lyrical, psychological, and social, showing the evolution of characters in a social environment, characters who were individualistic yet selected for their value as social types. It was with this style, using carefully detailed scripts and strictly directed actors, that he made his trilogy on the theme of a "crisis of conscience": of an old worker-mother (*Mother*), of a young peasant who became a worker and soldier (*The End of St. Petersburg*), of an Asiatic nomad (*Storm Over Asia*). At the same time, drawing on the teachings of Kuleshov, he developed and published a series of principles on the art of the cinema (*Film Technique, Film Acting*) that his friend Léon Moussinac summarized: "Editing is the foundation of cinematic art, the creative element of this new reality. Cinematic space and cinematic time, which have nothing to do with the real time and space of the action, are determined by the photography and the editing. A film is not 'shot,' it is built up from images. The isolated shot has only an analogous significance to that of the word for the poet." "A take is not the simple recording of a piece of action, but a representation of a particular, selected, form of that action. Whence the difference between the action in itself and the form one gives it on the screen, a difference that makes the cinema an art." Dominant both in the theory and practice of the silent film, he met a crisis with the advent of sound. He was not able to apply in *A Simple Case* the theory of audio-visual counterpoint that he and Eisenstein had propounded and though *Deserter* was more successful, it did not come close to matching his silent classics. After a long illness from 1934–38 he was forced to work in the then fashionable historical recreations: *Minin and Pozharsky, Suvorov, Joukovsky,* a genre for which he had no gift. Just before his death and during a depressed period in the Soviet cinema, he was able to return to something of his old form in *The Return of Vassili Bortnikov* (53) which, though not a masterpiece, is a very worthwhile achievement.
SCEN/ASSIST: *Serp i molot/Sickle and Hammer* (dir: V. Gardin), *Slesar i*

kantzler/*Locksmith and Chancellor* (23) (dir: V. Gardin), *The Extraordinary Adventures of Mr. West in the Land of the Bolsheviks** (24) (dir: Kuleshov; also acted), *Luch smerti/The Death Ray* (25) (dir: Kuleshov; also art dir).
DIR: *Golod . . . golod . . . golod/Hunger, Hunger Hunger* (co-dir/scen: V. Gardin), *Shakhmatnaya goryachka/Chess Fever* (25) (short: co-dir: N. Shpikovsky), *Mat/Mother** (26), *Mekhanikha golovnovo mozga/The Mechanics of the Brain* (26) (documentary), *Konyets Sankt-Peterburga/The End of St. Petersburg** (27), *Potomok Chingis-Khan/ Storm Over Asia/The Heir to Genghis Khan** (28), *Prostoi sluchai/A Simple Case/Life is Very Good* (32), *Deserter* (33), *Pobeda/Victory* (38), *Minin i Pozharsky/Minin and Pozharsky* (39), *Twenty Years of Cinema* (40) (documentary; co-dir: E. Shub), *Pir v Zhirmunke/Feast at Zhirmunka* (*Fighting Film Album,* No. 6) (41) (co-dir: Mikhail Doller), *Suvorov* (41) (co-dir: M. Doller), *Ubitzi vykhodyat na dorogu/Murderers are on Their Way* (42) (co-dir: Yuri Tarich; unreleased), *Vo imya rodini/In the Name of the Fatherland* (43) (co-dir: Dmitri Vasiliev), *Admiral Nakhimov* (46), *Tri vstrechi/Three Encounters* (48) (co-dir: Yutkevich and Ptushko), *Joukovsky* (50), *Vozvrashchenie Vassiliya Bortnikova/The Return of Vassili Bortnikov/The Harvest** (53). Pudovkin acted in several films, notably in Perestiani's *V dni borbi/In the Days of the Struggle* (20), Kozintsev's and Trauberg's *New Babylon** (29), Otsep's *A Living Corpse* (29), Eisenstein's *Ivan the Terrible, Part I** (44).

PURKINE, Jan Evangelista INVENTOR Czechoslovakia. (1787–1869) Distinguished Czech physiologist who projected animated drawings, first in the laboratory (1852) then in public (1865), with an apparatus called Forolyt and later Kinesiscop. Around 1850–60 he also set in motion a sequence of photographs taken in successive poses.

PYRIEV, Ivan DIR USSR. (Kamen 1901–1968) Originally an actor in experimental theater (notably for Eisenstein at the Proletkult Theater, 1923) and assistant to Yuri Tarich (e.g., *Krylya kholopal/Ivan the Terrible**, (26), he had a particular talent for directing lively, appealing musical comedies: *Strange Woman, The Rich Bride, They Met in Moscow, Song of Siberia, Kuban Cossacks,* films that made him a popular director in the USSR. He also specialized in naturalistic dramas about contemporary Soviet life, such as *Party Card, Tractor Drivers,* and *Secretary of the District Committee,* though these are largely unknown outside the USSR. Later, after spending some years as head of production at Mosfilm, he returned to directing with a series of literary adaptations, notably from Dostoyevsky: *The Idiot, White Nights, The Brothers Karamazov.*

DIR (notably): *Strange Woman* (29), *State Official* (30), *Conveyor of Death* (34), *Party Card* (36), *Bogataya nevesta/the Rich Bride* (38), *Trakoristi/ Tractor Drivers* (39), *Svinyarka i pastukh/Swineherd and Shepherd/They Met in Moscow* (41), *Sekretar raikon/Secretary of the District Committee* (42), *V shest chasov vechera posle voiny/At 6 p.m. after the War* (44), *Skazaniye o zemlye Sibirskoi/Tales of Siberian Land/Songs of Siberia* (47), *Kubanskie Kazaki/Kuban Cossacks* (49), *My za mir/We Are for Peace/Friendship Triumphs* (USSR/GDR52) (co-dir: Joris Ivens), *Ispystanie vernosti/Test of Fidelity* (54), *Nastasia Filipovna/The Idiot, Part I** (58), *Belye nochi/White Nights** (59), *Nash obschii drug/Our Mutual Friend* (61), *Svev dalekoi zvesdy/Light of a Distant Star* (65), *Bratya Karamazovy/The Brothers Karamazov* (68) (completed by Mikhail Ulyanov after Pyriev's death).

QUEENY, Mary PROD Egypt. (190?–)
Former actress who played an important
role as producer in the commercial development of the Egyptian cinema after
1930.

QUENEAU, Raymond SCEN France. (Le
Havre Feb 21, 1903–) French poet
and novelist who, since his days as a
surrealist, has been deeply interested in
the cinema — which in turn has influenced his writings. He has collaborated
in several films, including the dialogue
for the French version of Clément's
Knave of Hearts* (Brit53) and a commentary in verse for Resnais's documentary, *Le Chant du Styrène* (58). His
novel, *Zazie dans le Métro**, was the
basis of a film by Malle (60) and *Le
Dimanche de la vie* of a film by J. Herman (67). [*Also,* commentary for Kast's
Arithmétique; Théron's and Carènes,
Champs-Elysées; Pagliero's *Paradis ter-
restres, Saint Germain-des-Près;* Tabély's
Teuf-Teuf; dialogue for Buñuel's *La
Mort en ce jardin;* and script for Mocky's
Un Couple.]

QUILICI, Folco DIR Italy. (Ferrara April
9, 1930–) The director of "documentary" features using the most outrageous
trick effects and the originator of a de-
testable genre of pseudo-educational
travelogues whose natural heir was
Mondo Cane: Sesto Continente (54),
L'Ultimo Paradiso (57), *Dagli Appen-
nini alle Ande* (59). Also directed the
fictional *Tico e il suo Pescecane* (62)
and many shorts, including an interesting
Gauguin (57).

QUINE, Richard DIR USA. (Detroit Nov
12, 1920–) Second rank Hollywood
director, former actor and scriptwriter,
at his best with light comedy and musicals — *My Sister Eileen* (55), *The Solid
Gold Cadillac* (56), *Full of Life* (57),
Bell, Book, and Candle (58) — rather
than with dramatic comedies or melodramas such as *The World of Suzie
Wong* (60), *Strangers When We Meet*
(61), *Hotel* (67).

RABENALT, Arthur Maria DIR Germany/
German Federal Republic. (Vienna May
17, 1905–) Routine commercial di-
rector whose work is characterized by
the titles of his films alone: *Ein Kind,
ein Hund, ein Vagabond/A Child, a
Dog, a Vagabond* (34), *Die Liebe des
Maharadscha/The Maharaja's Love* (36),
Liebespremier/Love's Premiere (43),
Zirkus Renz/The Renz Circus (43),
Chemie und Liebe/Chemistry and Love
(48), *Der Zigeunerbaron/Gypsy Baron*
(54), *Für zwei Groschen Zartlichkeit/
Call Girls* (57), *Der Held meiner
Traume/The Hero of My Dreams* (60).

*RADOK, Alfred DIR Czechoslovakia.
(Kolodeje Dec 17, 1914–) Although
he has directed only three films, he is
one of the most influential figures in
the modern Czechoslovak cinema, particularly as mentor to the younger directors such as Milos Forman (*q.v.*).
His original and poetic portrait of a
Jewish family in an extermination camp,
Distant Journey (49), has only increased
in stature with the years. His major
activity has been in the theater, before,
during and after his three films as director. He is also the creator of the
famous "Magic Lantern" show, combining film, slide, and live action, which
was an outstanding success at the Brussels (58) and Montreal (67) World's
Fairs.
DIR: *Daleka cesta/Distant Journey** (49),
Divotvorny klobouk/The Magic Hat
(52), *Dedecek automobil/Old Man Motorcar* (56).

RADVANYI, Geza (von) DIR Hungary/Ger-
man Federal Republic/France. (Hungary Sept 26, 1907–) He has directed
only one worthwhile film, *Valahol Euro-
paban/Somewhere in Europe** (47), depicting the aftermath of the recent war.

He later directed routine commercial
films in Paris, Rome, and Munich, comparable to the "lemonade films" he had
directed in Budapest before 1945.

RAIK, Etienne ANIM France. (Hungary
July 14, 1904–) An excellent animator
specializing in pixilation who has had to
confine himself mainly to commercials,
ingeniously concentrating gags and lyricism into 90 seconds.

RAIZMAN, Yuli Yakovlevich DIR USSR.
(Moscow Dec 15, 1903–) One of the
best Soviet directors, too little known
outside his own country, he is, with
Frank Borzage (*q.v.*), one of those rare
film makers who have been able to communicate effectively and movingly the
warmth and empathy of human love.
His heroes were everyday people whose
characters and role in Soviet society he
portrayed with a certain freedom. Since
he avoided fashionable effects it is perhaps his restrained, economical style that
led to his being underestimated. However,
one of his first films, the semidocumentary, *The Earth Thirsts* (30), which
describes the changes in a central Asian
Soviet republic, was noted outside the
USSR. He has continued to make documentaries, most notably his feature-length
Berlin on the Red Army's capture of
that city. For the 20th anniversary of
the Russian Revolution he made the
sensitive, gentle *The Last Night,* a melancholy love story about a modern Romeo
and Juliet set in the romantic framework of an October night. During the
war his touching *Mashenka* was warmly
human, without any of the usual stereotyped heroics. In the entertaining postwar comedy, *The Train Goes East* (based
on the *It Happened One Night** formula), he portrayed the Soviet Union
from Vladivostok to Moscow. And,

though he was forced to adapt a novel strongly influenced by the cult of personality in *Cavalier of the Golden Star,* his very beautiful imagery gave it a certain sensitivity. Later, his *Lesson of Life* was one of the first films to offer criticism of some aspects of Soviet society, though in the end the film's attitude is positive. He was Protazanov's (*q.v.*) assistant on, e.g., *The Three Million Case* (26), *The Forty-First** (27).

DIR: *Circle* (27), *Katorga/Penal Servitude/Convict Labor* (28), *Zemlya zhazhdyot/The Earth Thirsts* (30, sound version 31), *Rasskaz ob Umare Hapsoko* (32), *Lyotchiki/Flyers* (35), *Poslednaya noch/The Last Night** (37), *Podnyataya tzelina/Virgin Soil Upturned* (40) (from Sholokhov's novel), *Mashenka* (42) (co-dir: Dmitri Vasiliev), *Nebo Moskvy/Moscow Sky* (44), *Berlin** (45), *Poezd idet na Vostok/The Train Goes East* (47), *Rainis* (49), *Kavaler zolotoi zvezdy/The Cavalier of the Golden Star/Dream of a Cossack** (50), *Urok zhizni/Lesson of Life* (55), *Kommunist/The Communist* (58), *A esli eto lyubov/If This Be Love* (61), *Tvoi sovremennik/Your Contemporary* (67).

RAMNOTH, K. DIR/PHOTOG/PROD India. (Trivandrum 1912–) Director, cameraman, and producer from the Madras region who was artistic director of Gemini Studios, owned by S. S. Vasan (*q.v.*), during its period of growth from 1942–48. In 1950 he directed a Tamil language version of *Les Misérables**, *Ezai padam padu.*

RANK, J. Arthur (later, Lord Rank) PROD Britain. (Hull Dec 23, 1888–) A dominant figure in the British film industry after the Second World War, he formed or took over companies in all branches of the industry, from equipment, studios, and production to distribution and exhibition, and is principally responsible for the industry's artistic stagnation. A former flour magnate and a Presbyterian, he became interested in films in 1933 as a means of religious education. He founded British National Pictures in 1935 and purchased a 25% interest in Universal; he set up a distribution outlet and founded a newsreel. In 1936 he created General Finance Cinema Corporation and in 1941 purchased Gaumont British and Odeon Theatres, thus gaining control of 750 first-run theaters, the largest single unit in Britain. In 1944 he owned or controlled a major share of British film studios. He purchased the Odeon theater chain in Canada in 1945 and set up Eagle Lion Distributors in the USA and Canada. In 1947 he compelled the major Hollywood companies to agree to distribute his films in their 3,000 theaters; he acquired Universal, bringing to 70 the number of companies under his control. He owned distribution agencies in 60 countries, all under the aegis of the Rank Organization, which he had set up in 1946. In the Fifties he was forced to abandon his conquest of the USA and relinquish Universal. [As attendances dropped, he retrenched his interests, closed many theaters and invested in bowling alleys, hotels, bingo, dance halls, and Xerox. The film interests of the Rank Organization are now of less importance than these other interests, but Odeon and Gaumont theaters still monopolize (with Associated-British Theatres) commercial film exhibition in Britain.]

RAY, Man PHOTOG/DIR France. (Philadelphia 1890–) Famous dadaist then surrealist painter, inventor of "objects," photographer, "memorialist," and creator of Rayograms (photographs taken without a lens) who also used film as a means of continuing his visual experiments and made a series of notable avant-garde films in the Twenties.

DIR: *Le Retour à la raison* (23), *Emak Bakia* (27), *L'Étoile de mer* (28), *Les Mystères du Château du Dé* (29), and one episode in Hans Richter's feature, *Dreams That Money Can Buy* (USA46). Also photographed *Souvenirs de Paris* (29) (dir: Pierre Prévert, Marcel Duhamel), reused in Pierre Prévert's *Paris, la Belle* (59).

RAY, Nicholas (Raymond Nicholas Kienzle) DIR USA. (La Crosse, Wisconsin Aug 7, 1911–) At his best, he is a true artist (though his work is of variable quality) whose films are most often concerned with socially maladjusted, sometimes doomed characters, misfits, and rebels. This concern is seen at its best in his dramatic, compassionate portrait of a confused youth and society, *Rebel without a Cause,* a film in which he drew from that quintessential rebel, James Dean, his best characterization. He was a student of architecture, a radio producer, and an assistant to John Houseman on Broadway productions before directing his first film, the remarkable ❯ *They Live by Night,* a film whose stark conflict, violence, and probing of human behavior served as a kind of preface to his later brilliant work. Unfortunately, its qualities were not to be found in such films as his studio-assigned *Born to Be Bad* and *Flying Leathernecks.* He fully recovered himself in the intellectual western *Johnny Guitar,* and in *Rebel without a Cause,* but *Bigger Than Life* and *Wind across the Everglades* were far from equaling them. Despite some weaknesses, *Bitter Victory* is a major work in which Ray expressed his distaste for war and his feeling for environment and human behavior. Some scenes of *The Savage Innocents* (in which Eskimos were played by American and Japanese actors) are effective and moving, but he collapsed under the weight of the multi-million dollar remake of *King of Kings* and the spectacular *55 Days at Peking.* Since then, none of his projects (in London or Paris) have reached fruition.

DIR: *They Live by Night* (47, released 49), *A Woman's Secret* (48), *Knock on Any Door* (48), *In a Lonely Place* (50), *Born To Be Bad* (50), *On Dangerous Ground* (50), *Flying Leathernecks* (51), *The Lusty Men* (52), *Johnny Guitar** (54), *Run for Cover* (54), *Rebel without a Cause** (55), *Hot Blood* (55), *Bigger Than Life* (56), *The True Story of Jessie James/The James Brothers* (56), *Amère victoire/Bitter Victory** (Fr57), *Wind across the Everglades* (58), *Party Girl* (58), *The Savage Innocents* (59), *King of Kings* (61), *55 Days at Peking* (63).

CO-SCEN: Hathaway's *Circus World* (63), and his own *They Live By Night, Rebel without a Cause, Amère victoire, The Savage Innocents.*

RAY, Satyajit DIR India. (Calcutta May 2, 1921–) The greatest contemporary Indian director whose most important work is the trilogy *Pather Panchali, Aparijito, The World of Apu* (adapted from an autobiographical novel), films that must be included among the world's best films in the Fifties. Originally a commercial artist much interested in the cinema, he dedicated himself to it after watching Jean Renoir shoot *The River** in Bengal. Following the traditions of the Bengali

cinema (the best in India), his films have a perfect visual style and an unusual warmth that fulfill his own statement: "Art wedded to truth must in the end have its reward." His characters are always integrated into their social background, whether that of a modern metropolis or a traditional village. Using a story by the Nobel Prize-winning author Rabindranath Tagore, he delivered a bold attack on religious superstition in *Devi,* a film whose noble beauty and classic, spare style (like that of *The Music Room*) perhaps surpass the qualities of the trilogy.

DIR: *Pather Panchali** (55), *Aparijito** (56), *Parash Pathar/The Philosopher's Stone* (57), *Apur Sansar/The World of Apu** (58) *Jalshagar/The Music Room* (58), *Rabindranath Tagore* (60) (documentary), *Portrait of a City* (61) (short), *Devi/The Goddess* (61), *Teen Kanya/Two Daughters* (61), *Kanchenjungha* (62), *Abhijan/Expedition* (62), *Mahanagar/The Big City* (63), *Charulata/The Lonely Wife* (64), *Kapurush o Mahapurush/The Coward and the Holy Man* (65), *Nayak/The Hero* (66), *Chidiakhana/The Zoo* (67), *Goopi Gyne o Baghi Byne/The Adventures of Goopi and Baghi* (69), *Aranyer Din Raatri/Days and Nights in the Forest* (70), *Sikkim* (70) documentary), *Pratiwandi/The Rival* (71).

MUS: James Ivory's *Shakespeare Wallah* ↰ (65) and all his own films from *Teen Kanya.*

REED, (Sir) Carol DIR Britain. (Putney, Dec 30, 1906–) Former actor, stage manager, and assistant to Basil Dean, he established his reputation in the late Thirties and early Forties, notably with *The Stars Look Down* (39) and *The Way Ahead* (44), and later achieved justified international renown with *Odd Man Out* (47), a film that recalls the themes of *Quai des brumes** and *Pépé le Moko**. His best film is the drama of a solitary child, *The Fallen Idol* (48). After the worldwide commercial success of *The Third Man* (49), he directed increasingly mediocre films, at his worst when he tried to be "poetic" in *A Kid for Two Farthings.* His musical *Oliver!* won an Academy Award.

DIR: *Midshipman Easy* (34), *Laburnum Grove* (36), *Talk of the Devil* (36), *Who's Your Lady Friend* (37), *Bank Holiday* (38), *Penny Paradise* (38),

Climbing High (38), *A Girl Must Live* (39), *The Stars Look Down** (39), *Night Train to Munich* (40), *The Girl in the News* (40), *Kipps* (41), *A Letter from Home* (41) (short), *The Young Mr. Pitt* (41), *The New Lot* (43) (documentary), *The Way Ahead* (44), *The True Glory* (45) (documentary; co-dir: Garson Kanin), *Odd Man Out/Gang War** (47), *The Fallen Idol** (48), *The Third Man** (49), *Outcast of the Islands* (51), *The Man Between* (53), *A Kid for Two Farthings* (55), *Trapeze* (USA 56), *The Key* (58), *Our Man in Havana* (59), *The Running Man* (63), *The Agony and the Ecstasy* (USA65), *Oliver!* (68), *The Last Warrior* (USA70).

REICHENBACH, François DIR France. (Paris July 3, 1922–) A human "camera-eye" with the ability to search out, especially in the USA, numerous unusual, unknown, and curious aspects of life, but not always with the commensurate ability to develop and build up a story. He often photographs his own films.
DIR: (shorts): *Impressions de New York* (55), *New York ballade* (55), *Visages de Paris* (55), *Houston-Texas* (56), *Novembre à Paris* (56), *Le Grand Sud* (56), *Au pays de Porgy and Bess* (57), *L'Américain se détend* (57), *Les Marines* (57), *Carnaval à la Nouvelle-Orléans* (57), *L'Eté indien* (57), *Weekend en mer* (62), *Retour à New York* (62), *A la memoire du rock* (62), *L'Amérique lunaire* (62), *Le Paris des photographes* (62), *Le Paris des mannequins* (62), *Jeux* (63), *Histoire d'un petit garçon devenu grand* (63), *La Douceur du village* (63), *L'Enterrement de Kennedy* (63) (TV), *Les Chevaux d'Hollywood/ Hollywood through a Key Hole* (64), *Mexico nuevo* (64), *L'Oeil neuf* (64) (12 TV films), *Bardot en Amérique* (65) (TV), *Mireille Mathieu* (66) (TV), *Orson Welles* (66) (TV), *Von Karajan* (66) (TV), *El Cordobes* (66) (TV), *Manitas de Plata* (66) (TV), *Olivier Gendebien* (66) (TV), *Aurora* (66), *Impressions de Paris* (67), *Brigitte Bardot* (67) (TV show).
DIR (features): *L'Amérique insolite/ L'Amérique vu par un Français* (60), *Un coeur gros comme ça* (61), *Les Amoreux du "France"* (63) (co-dir: P. Grimblat), *Tout reste à découvrir* (64), *Mexico, Mexico* (67) (co-dir: C. Fuentos), *13 jours en France* (68) (co-dir: C. Lelouch), *Arthur Ruben-*

stein: l'Amour de la vie (68) (co-dir: S. Gérard Patris), *L'Indiscret* (69), *La Caravane d'amour* (71).

REINHARDT, Max (Maximilian Goldmann) DIR Germany/USA. (Baden, Austria Sept 8, 1873–New York Oct 31, 1943) The most important name in the 20th-century German theater and the single most significant influence on the classic German silent cinema. Many of the actors (Krauss, Veidt, Jennings, etc.) and directors (Murnau, Leni, Lubitsch, Wegener, etc., all *q.v.*) were trained by him at the Deutsches Theater, Berlin; expressionism, *Kammerspiel,* and the UFA period dramas were in large measure derived from his theatrical experiences.
DIR: *Sumurun* (08), *Das Mirakel* (12), *Die Insel der Seligen* (13), *Venezianische Nacht* (14), *A Midsummer Night's Dream** (USA35) (co-dir: W. Dieterle).
NOTE: Gottfried Reinhardt (1911–), the Hollywood and German producer/ director, is his son.

REINIGER, Lotte ANIM Germany/Britain. (Berlin June 2, 1899–) The director of marvelously imaginative black and white silhouette films in an almost 18th-century rococo style. Unfortunately, no one has followed up her pioneering work. [Her first silhouette work was for the titles of Wegener and Gliese's *The Pied Piper of Hamelin* (18). She then made a series of shorts before making, in 1926, her first and only feature, the delightful *The Adventures of Prince Achmet.* Her work came to a halt at the end of the Thirties (she was in London 1936–39 and Rome during the war) until she moved to Britain in 1949 and was able to take up her experiments again, mostly for television. Her latest two films were in color.]
ANIM: *Das Ornament des verliebten Herzens* (20), *Der Amor und das standhafte Liebespaar* (22), *Der Fliegende Koffer* (22), *Der Stern von Bethlehem* (22), *Aschenputte/Cinderella* (22), *Die Abenteuer des Prinzen Achmed* (23–26), *Dr. Dolittle* (27–28) (3 shorts), *Die Jagd nach dem Glück* (30) (silhouette film as part of feature; dir: Rochus Gliese, Karl Koch), *Zehn Minuten Mozart* (30), *Harlekin* (31), *Sissy* (32), *Carmen** (33), *Das Rollende Rad* (34), *Das Gestohlene Herz* (34), *Der Graf von Carabas/Puss in Boots* (Switz34), *Papageno* (Switz35), *Galathea* (Switz35),

Der Kleine Schornsteinfeger (Switz35), La Marseillaise* (Fr37) (silhouette film as part of feature; dir: Jean Renoir), [The King's Breakfast (Brit37), The Daughter (Brit49), Mary's Birthday (49), The Frog Prince (50), Snow White and Rose Red (53), Aladdin (53), Puss in Boots (53), The Gallant Little Tailor (55), The Star of Bethlehem (56), Jack the Giant Killer (56), La Belle Hélène (58), Seraglio (58).]

REISZ, Karl DIR/PROD Britain. (Czechoslovakia 1926–) Former film critic and one of the most brilliant film makers of the Free Cinema group who demonstrated in his two documentaries his ability to capture the essential aspects of everyday acts and behavior. [He made a notable first feature, Saturday Night and Sunday Morning, but, apart from Morgan, his infrequent work has not fulfilled his early promise.]
DIR: Momma Don't Allow (55) (documentary; co-dir: Tony Richardson), We Are the Lambeth Boys (58) (documentary), March to Aldermaston (59) (documentary in collaboration), Saturday Night and Sunday Morning* (60), Night Must Fall (64), Morgan, a Suitable Case for Treatment (66), Isadora (67).
PROD: Lindsay Anderson's Every Day Except Christmas (57), This Sporting Life* (63).

RENOIR, Claude PHOTOG France. (Paris Dec 4, 1914–) Exceptionally talented and cultured cameraman in the great French tradition of his grandfather Auguste Renoir and his uncle Jean Renoir. His color work is especially remarkable. He is the son of actor Pierre Renoir and began his career as assistant to Boris Kaufman (q.v.).
PHOTOG (notably): for Jean Renoir, Toni* (34), Une partie de campagne* (36), La Grande Illusion* (37), The River* (50), Le Carosse d'or* (52), Elena et les hommes (56); for M. Cloche, Monsieur Vincent (47); for Clément, Le Père tranquille (46); for Becker, Rendez-vous de juillet* (49); for Dréville, Prélude à la gloire (50); for G. Lefranc, Knock (50); for Diamant-Berger, Monsieur Fabre (51); for Rouleau, Les Sorcières de Salem (56), Les Amants de Teruel (62); for Clouzot, Le Mystère Picasso* (56); for Marcel Carné, Les Tricheurs (58), Terrain vague (60); for

Astruc, Une vie* (58); for Vadim, Et mourir de plaisir (60), La Curée (66), Barbarella (67); for J. Deray, Symphonie pour un massacre (63); for Alain Cavalier, L'Insoumis (64); for Bryan Forbes, The Madwoman of Chaillot (Brit69).

RENOIR, Jean DIR France/USA. (Paris Sept 15, 1894–) The most French of prewar film makers, the greatest creator of poetic realism, who in 1938 said of his first films: "Naïvely and laboriously, I did my best to imitate my American teachers; I had not understood that a Frenchman living in France, drinking red wine and eating Brie cheese in front of a grisaille of Paris, could only create works of quality by following the traditions of people like himself." The younger son of impressionist painter Auguste Renoir, his first interest was in ceramics, but he soon fell in love with the cinema. He wrote the script for Albert Dieudonné's Catherine/Une vie sans joie (24) before directing his first features, La Fille de l'eau (24), a work full of nostalgic poetry, and Nana (26), the best silent adaptation from Zola, a writer who exercised a profound influence on him. The financial failures of these films forced him to accept routine commercial assignments: Le Tournoi dans la cité, Le Bled, and his little appreciated Tire-au-flanc. Apart from La Petite Marchande d'allumettes, he could have been classed among the commercial directors of the time. But in the sound period, he began with the brilliant La Chienne, which, like Boudu sauvé des eaux, La Nuit de carrefour, and Madame Bovary, was an unmerited financial failure. Toni (34) marked the start of his greatest period, followed by Le Crime de Monsieur Lange and the remarkable, enthusiastic contribution to the success of the Front populaire, La Vie est à nous. Though he was unable to complete his vibrant homage to Maupassant and impressionism, Une partie de campagne, and though he faltered with Les Bas-Fonds, he achieved international fame with La Grande Illusion. He was then at "the peak of his artistry," according to Alexandre Arnoux, who also said of him: "When he is working, he opens himself out, he eats nothing, he gives of himself unstintingly. I give myself up to the marvelous image of a masterful man, without cleverness, who has ideas and convictions, who has forged a language that fits his expression and who is not 'social' because it's fashionable but because a social approach is the inevitable outcome of his reflective, stubborn, and patient nature." After *La Marseillaise,* which was attacked by partisan critics, he created a remarkable Zola adaptation, *La Bête humaine,* then launched his corrosive satire of the French ruling classes in *La Règle du jeu.* "Now I am beginning to be aware of how I must work. I know that I am French and that I must work in an absolutely national sense. I know also that, by doing this, and only by doing this, I can reach the people of other countries and create works of international standing." But *La Règle du jeu* was a commercial disaster (see *Dictionary of Films* for an account of its mutilation and reconstruction) and this and the outbreak of war shattered his development. He was forced into exile in Hollywood, where he twice attempted to re-create his country in the studio: *This Land Is Mine* and *The Diary of a Chambermaid.* But in *Swamp Water* and especially in *The Southerner* he touched the heart of American realities. On his return to the Old World, his work continued to evidence his belief in universal good will but a certain acerbity was introduced. He took above all as pictorial "motifs," India in *The River,* Commedia dell'Arte in *The Golden Coach,* and turn-of-the-century Paris in *French Cancan.* Though his later work is not exempt from serious failures, as in *Le Testament du Dr. Cordelier,* he has nonetheless remained one of the great masters of world cinema, justly admired and venerated.

DIR: *La Fille de l'eau* (24), *Nana** (26), *Charleston* (27), *Marquitta* (27), *La Petite Marchande d'allumettes** (28), *Tire-au-flanc** (28), *Le Tournoi dans la cité* (29), *Le Bled* (29), *On purge bébé* (31), *La Chienne** (31), *La Nuit de carrefour* (32), *Boudu sauvé des eaux** (32), *Chotard et Cie* (33), *Madame Bovary* (34), *Toni** (34), *Le Crime de Monsieur Lange** (36), *La Vie est à nous** (36), *Une partie de campagne** (36, released 46), *Les Bas-Fonds** (36), *La Grande Illusion** (37), *La Marseillaise** (38), *La Bête humaine** (38), *La Règle du jeu** (39), *La Tosca* (It40) (unfinished), *Swamp Water* (USA41), *This Land Is Mine* (USA43), *Salute to France* (USA44) (in collaboration), *The Southerner** (USA45), *The Diary of a Chambermaid** (USA46), *The Woman on the Beach* (USA47), *The River** (India51), *Le Carosse d'or* (Fr/It52), *French Cancan** (54), *Elena et les hommes* (56), *Le Déjeuner sur l'herbe* (59), *Le Testament du Dr. Cordelier/Experiment in Evil* (TV, 59, released 63), *Le Caporal épinglé* (62), *Le Petit théâtre de Jean Renoir* (71) (TV drama series).

RESNAIS, Alain DIR France. (Vannes June 3, 1922–) The best film maker of the former *nouvelle vague,* exacting, thorough, obsessed with the themes of time and memory who, despite his sometimes excessive respect for his scriptwriters, imprints his own style on every film he makes. He spent a year at IDHEC, was a stage actor, and from 1946–48 made a number of short 16mm films, some of which were silent. He began his career as a director of 35mm shorts in 1948. The condition of the French film industry obliged him to restrict his activities for some ten years to the short film field — with occasional work as an editor for other directors. One might have taken him as a specialist in films on art after the success of the somewhat anecdotal *Van Gogh* (48) and *Gauguin* (50), but *Guernica* (50) was something else again, a kind of opera that blended the work of Picasso, the lyricism of Paul Eluard, the music of Guy Bernard, and the reality of Spain. Since then the art of the cinema has been for him principally one of construction — the choice of images, their framing and rhythm, the organization from sometimes disparate elements — of an audio-visual counterpoint that is as taut as a vibrating string and that treats time and space as physical matter and uses them as objects in his creation. Ever since his short film days he has had a keen sense of "contemporaneity" — which brought censorship interference with *Night and Fog* and the banning of *Les Statues meurent aussi* for its indictment of colonialism. His first feature, *Hiroshima mon amour,* centers on the most important of modern problems, the atomic bomb and war and peace, and is dominated by the cry, "How could anyone do that to people!" Though his particular intellectualism places him among the modern cinema's avant-garde, he constantly draws on the popular traditions of novelettes, serials, and strip cartoons that are scorned by the elite. Perhaps this is why *Hiroshima* and *Marienbad,* films one might have thought would appeal only to cinéphiles, reached an extremely wide public in many countries. His universe is far from being as closed in as the baroque palace of *Marienbad.* Even this apparently atemporal film was ultimately a reflection of contemporary French reality as were later, more openly, *Muriel* and *La Guerre est finie.*

[ED Nicole Védrès' *Paris 1900** (47) (assist to Myriam), *Aux frontières de l'homme* (56); Paul Paviot's *Saint-Tropez, Devoir de vacances* (52); Agnès Varda's *La Pointe Courte** (55); Reichenbach's *Novembre à Paris* (56); Jacques Doniol-Valcroze's *L'Oeil du maître* (57); William Klein's *Broadway by Light* (57); and most of his own shorts.]

DIR (shorts): *Schéma d'une identification* (46), *Ouvert pour cause d'inventaire* (46), *Visite à Lucien Coutaud* (47), *Visite à Félix Labisse* (47); *Visite à Hans Hartnung* (47), *Visite à Oscar Dominguez* (47) (unfinished), *Visite à César Domela* (47), *Portrait d'Henri Goetz* (47), *La Bague* (47) (Marcel Marceau mime), *Journée naturelle/Visite à Max Ernst* (47), *L'Alcool tue* (47, released 50), *Les Jardins de Paris* (48), *Châteaux de France* (48), *Malfray* (48), *Van Gogh* (48) (first in 16mm, then remade in 35mm), *Gauguin* (50), *Guernica** (50), *Les Statues meurent aussi* (50–53) (co-dir: Chris Marker), *Nuit et Brouillard** (55), *Toute la mémoire du monde* (56), *Le Mystère de l'atelier 15* (57) (co-dir: André Heinrich), *Le Chant du Styrène* (58).

DIR (features): *Hiroshima mon amour** (59), *L'Année dernière à Marienbad** (61), *Muriel ou le Temps d'un retour** (63), *La Guerre est finie** (66), *Loin de Vietnam* (67) (episode, in collaboration), *Je t'aime, je t'aime* (68).

REY, Florian DIR Spain. (189?–1961) The best of the Spanish directors during the silent period; his best film, *La Aldea Maldita* (29), was much admired in France, where it was presented by Juan Piqueras, "the Spanish Delluc."

REYNAUD, Emile INVENTOR/ANIM. France. (Montreuil Dec 8, 1844–Ivry Jan 8, 1918) Imaginative creator of precinema animated cartoons who was the first to organize regular showings of animated images (in color and with sound accompaniment) at the Musée Grévin in Paris in 1892. An artisan of genius and a marvelous "painter on film," which he drew and painted in gouache frame by frame, he died in poverty after destroying most of his film reels. Luckily, *Pauvre Pierrot* and *Autour d'une cabine* have been preserved. The first of these *pantomimes lumineuses,* still quite theatrical, abounds in tricks and gags, while the second moves into nature, showing the waves of the sea, birds in flight, and bathers on the beach as acutely observed as Jacques Tati later observed them in *Les Vacances de M. Hulot**. His progenitive cartoons reveal a marvelous ability to capture typical human behavior, a talent that his successors in the "eighth art" have never quite been able to match. 1876 — Praxinoscope, a toy with sequential drawings animated by rotating mirrors. 1878 — Projecting Praxinoscope. 1889 — Patent for his "optical theater" using perforated film, presented at the Exposition Universelle. 1892–1900 — Many thousands of performances of his *pantomimes lumineuses* at the Musée Grévin, with the reels: *Un bon bock* (1891), *Clown et ses chiens* (1891), *Pauvre Pierrot** (1891), *Rêve au coin du feu* (1894), *Autour d'une cabine** (1894), *Guillaume Tell* (1896), *Le Premier Cigare* (1896). These last two were *photos-scènes,* drawings based on photographs, the first featuring Footit and Chocolat, the second Galipaux. 1903 — Attempts at stereoscopic cinema using sets of praxinoscopic mirrors.

RICHARDSON, Tony (Cecil Antonio Richardson) DIR Britain. (Shipley, Yorkshire 1928–) With Lindsay Anderson (*q.v.*) and Karel Reisz (*q.v.*) he entered films via the Free Cinema movement and the revival of British drama in the Fifties (he was a stage and TV producer from 1949) and was one of the hopes for the British cinema in the Sixties. But his work has been extremely uneven: *Sanctuary* was a disastrous American experience, but he brilliantly and sensitively portrayed the realities of certain aspects of English life in *Look Back in Anger* and the excellent *A Taste of Honey,* films with a certain touch of poetry. [After *The Loneliness of the Long Distance Runner* he abandoned provincial drama in favor of the witty, ironic, and stylish *Tom Jones.* Its enormous commercial success led to his being given a completely free hand for the adaptation of *The Loved One* in the USA, but he turned out one of the most disappointing and disastrous films of the Sixties. He seems never to have recovered fully from this experience, for his subsequent films have hovered between the pretentious and the pointless – though *The Charge of the Light Brigade* stands out in comparison to the surrounding mediocrity.]

DIR: *Momma Don't Allow* (55) (documentary; co-dir: Karel Reisz), *Look Back in Anger* (59), *The Entertainer* (60), *Sanctuary* (USA60), *A Taste of Honey** (61), *The Loneliness of the Long-Distance Runner* (62) *Tom Jones** (63), *The Loved One* (USA64), *Mademoiselle* (Brit/Fr65), *The Sailor from Gibraltar* (66), *Red and Blue* (67), *The Charge of the Light Brigade* (68), *Laughter in the Dark* (Brit/Fr69), *Hamlet** (69), *Ned Kelly* (70).

RICHTER, Hans DIR Germany/USA/Switzerland. (Berlin 1888–) Important film maker of the European avant-garde of the Twenties and a theoretician on abstract films. He joined the dada movement in Zurich in 1916; his friendship with Viking Eggeling (*q.v.*) led to his making his first "Rollenbild" (scroll painting) in 1919 and eventually to his first abstract films in 1921. He later made surrealist essays, e.g., *Ghosts Before Breakfast*, and social studies, *Inflation* and *Rennsymphonie*. [He worked throughout Europe on industrial shorts and commercials until 1941, when he moved to the USA and was film professor at the City College of New York. He returned to Europe in 1952 and settled in Switzerland, where he has continued to collaborate with Duchamp, Calder, Ernest, etc. on experimental films. He has continued to work also as a painter.]

DIR: *Rhythmus 21* (21), *Rhythmus 23* (23), *Rhythmus 25* (25), *Filmstudie* (25), *Inflation* (27) (originally intended as prelude to W. Thiele's *Die Dame mit der Maske*), *Vormittagspuk/Ghosts Before Breakfast* (28), *Rennsymphonie* (29) (prelude to Robert Dinesen's *Ariadne in Hoppegarten*), *Zwischengroschenzauber* (29), *Alles drecht sich, alles bewegt sich* (29), *Everyday* (Brit 29), *Neues Leben* (Switz30), *Europa Radio* (Switz31), *Hallo Everybody*

(Neth33), *Metall* (31–33) (unfinished), *Vom Blitz zum Fernsehbild* (Neth36), *Eine kleine Welt im Dunkeln* (Switz38), *Die Enstehung der Farbe* (Switz38), *Die Eroberung des Himmels* (Switz38), *Hans im Glück* (Switz38), *Die Börse* (Switz 39), *The Movies Take a Holiday* (USA 44) (compilation), *Dreams That Money Can Buy* (USA44–46) (sequences in collaboration with Léger, Ernst, Man Ray, Duchamp, Calder, etc.), *Thirty Years of Experiments* (USA51) (anthology of his own films and those of Eggeling and Ruttmann, *Dadascope I* (Switz56), *Chesscetera/Passionate Pastime* (Switz57), *Acht mal acht/8 x 8* (Switz57), *Forty Years of Experiment, Parts I and II* (61) (reworking and updating of earlier anthology), *Alexander Calder: From the Circus to the Moon* (63) (episodes from *Dreams That Money Can Buy* and *8 x 8*), *Dadascope II* (Switz67).

RIEFENSTAHL, Leni (Bertha Amalie Helene R.) DIR Germany. (Berlin Aug 22, 1902–) An actress in the mountain films of Fanck (*q.v.*) and Pabst (*q.v.*) who directed the mammoth documentary to the glory of Hitler and the Nazis, *The Triumph of the Will*, a film that often reveals, in spite of itself, the vainglory and cruelty of the Fascists. She was given almost unlimited technical resources and financial backing to create an epic propaganda film of the Olympic Games in Berlin in 1936. [She was accused of Nazi collaboration after the war but was cleared of all charges in 1952. She has since made various attempts to complete a documentary on Africa, *Schwarze Fracht*, but has largely abandoned the cinema.]

DIR: *Das Blaue Licht* (32), *Der Sieg des Glaubens* (33) (documentary), *Triumph des Willens** (34), *Tag der Freiheit — unsere Wehrmacht* (35) (documentary), *Olympische Spiele 1936/The Olympiad** (38) (in two parts: *Fest der Völker, Fest der Schönheit*), *Tiefland* (45) (preparation began 1934, released 1954). She also acted in Fanck's *Der Heilige Berg* (26), *Der Grosse Sprung* (27), *The White Hell of Pitz Palu* (29), *Stürme über dem Montblanc* (30), *Der Weisse Rausch* (31), *S.O.S. Eisberg* (33), and her own *The Blue Light* and *Tiefland*.

RIM, Carlo *see* CARLO-RIM

RISKIN, Robert SCEN USA. (New York 1897–New York 1955) Hollywood scriptwriter, famous mainly for his scripts in the Thirties for Frank Capra's (*q.v.*) best films.

[SCEN (notably): for Capra, *The Miracle Woman* (31), *Platinum Blond* (31), *American Madness* (32), *Lady for a Day** (33), *It Happened One Night** (34), *Broadway Bill* (34), *Mr. Deeds Goes to Town** (36), *Lost Horizon* (37), *You Can't Take It With You** (38), *Meet John Doe* (41), *Riding High* (51) (remake of *Broadway Bill*); for John Ford, *The Whole Town's Talking** (35). His other work is uninteresting.]

RITT, Martin DIR USA. (New York March 2, 1920–) Like Delbert Mann (*q.v.*) and others, he graduated from TV-producing to film-making and began with two interesting low-budget films, *Edge of the City* and *No Down Payment*. Later, recognized by Hollywood as a "quality" director, he made only mediocre, craftsmanlike films, though *Hud*, *The Spy Who Came in from the Cold*, and *Hombre* stand out above the rest.

DIR: *Edge of the City/A Man is Ten Feet Tall** (56), *No Down Payment* (57), *The Long Hot Summer* (57), *The Sound and the Fury* (58), *The Black Orchid* (59), *Five Branded Women* (60), *Paris Blues* (61), *Adventures of a Young Man* (62), *Hud* (63), *The Outrage** (64) (remake of *Rashomon**), *The Spy Who Came in from the Cold* (65), *Hombre* (67), *The Brotherhood* (68), *The Molly Maguires* (69), *The Great White Hope* (70).

RITTAU, Günther PHOTOG Germany/German Federal Republic. (Königshütte 1893–Aug 1971) Major cameraman during the classic German silent period, who began his career working on scientific documentaries before collaborating on the photography of Lang's *Die Nibelungen** and *Metropolis**, Joe May's *Heimkehr* and *Asphalt**, and Sternberg's *The Blue Angel**. He photographed numerous mediocre films during and after the Nazi period and himself directed several mediocre films: *U-Boote westwärts* (41), *Der Strom* (42), *Der Ewige Klang* (43), *Vor uns liegt das Leben* (48), etc.

RIVETTE, Jacques DIR France. (Rouen March 1, 1928–) Former film critic and editor, a film maker of high intellectual sensibility, who, despite the importance of *Paris nous appartient*, has had difficulty establishing himself and has had little commercial success with any of his films.

[DIR: *Aux quatre coins* (50) (16mm short), *Le Quadrille* (50) (16mm short), *Le Divertissement* (52) (16mm short), *Le Coup de berger* (56) (short), *Paris nous appartient** (60), *Suzanne Simonin, la religieuse de Diderot/La Religieuse* (65), *Jean Renoir, le patron* (66) (TV), *L'Amour fou* (68), *Out One* (71).

ROACH, Hal PROD USA. (Elmira Jan 14, 1892–) Mack Sennett's (*q.v.*) nearest rival as a producer of comedy films, less creatively involved with his films but a better businessman than Sennett. He launched Harold Lloyd (*q.v.*), Laurel and Hardy, and Our Gang. A former truck driver and cowboy actor, he produced for Pathé the profitable series of *Lonesome Luke* comedies (14–22) with Harold Lloyd; in 1919 he established his own studios; in 1921 made the first of the *Our Gang* film with a group of children (which changed with the years); in 1925 he formed the team of Laurel and Hardy; in 1937 he produced the first of the *Topper* series (dir: Norman Z. McLeod). Also produced, notably, Milestone's *Of Mice and Men* (39), *One Million B.C./Man and His Mate* (40) (also dir).

ROBBE-GRILLET, Alain SCEN/DIR France. (Brest Aug 18, 1922–) Famous author of the French *nouveau roman* who wrote the script of *L'Année dernière à Marienbad** (61) and later developed his literary approach as director of *L'Immortelle* (62), *Trans-Europ Express* (66), *L'Homme qui ment/Muz ktory luze* (Fr/Czech67), *L'Eden et l'après* (69).

ROBERT, Yves DIR France. (Saumur June 19, 1920–) One-time cabaret (La Rose rouge) and stage actor who turned film maker and achieved great success with *La Guerre des boutons* (62), followed by *Bébert et l'omnibus* (63), *Copains* (64), *Monnaie de singe* (Fr/Sp65), *Alexandre le bienheureux* (67), and *Clérambard* (69).

ROBISON, Arthur (also A. Robinson) DIR Germany. (Chicago June 25 1888–Berlin? 1935) Born in the USA of German parents, he was a stage actor early in his career and directed only one memorable film, *Schatten/Warning Shadows** (22), a curious blend of the theatrical, expressionism, and *Kammerspiel.* [Other films include: *Natch des Grauens* (16), *Pietro der Korsa* (24), *Manon Lescaut* (26), *Der Letzte Walzer* (27), *The Informer** (Brit29), *Des Jungen Dessauers grosse Liebe* (33), *Fürst Woronzeff* (34), *Der Student von Prag* (35) (remake).]

ROBSON, Mark DIR USA/Britain. (Montreal, Canada Dec 4, 1913–) In a standard commercial career he has had the good fortune to direct several good scripts: *Champion* (49), *Home of the Brave* (49), *Phfft* (54), *The Harder They Fall* (56). [Like Robert Wise (*q.v.*), he began his career (1933) as an editor at RKO (Wise's *Cat People**) and directed several films for Val Lewton (*q.v.*) – *The Seventh Victim* (43), *The Ghost Ship* (43), *Youth Runs Wild* (44), *Isle of the Dead* (45), *Bedlam* (46) – before joining Stanley Kramer (*q.v.*) for the boxing film, *Champion,* and the antiracist war film, *Home of the Brave.* His work since has been increasingly facile: *My Foolish Heart* (50), *Edge of Doom* (50), *Bright Victory* (51), *I Want You* (51), *Return to Paradise* (53), *Hell below Zero* (Brit54), *The Bridges of Toko-Ri* (54), *A Prize of Gold* (55), *Trial* (55) (a mixture of antiracism and anticommunism), *The Little Hut* (57), *Peyton Place* (58), *The Inn of the Sixth Happiness* (Brit58), *From the Terrace* (59), *Nine Hours to Rama* (Brit63), *The Prize* (63), *Von Ryan's Express* (65), *Lost Command* (66), *Valley of the Dolls* (67), *Daddy's Gone A-hunting* (69).]

*ROCHA, Glauber DIR Brazil. (Bahia 1938–) Young Brazilian film maker, one of the most powerful forces behind the development of Brazilian *cinema novo,* first as journalist and film critic in the late Fifties, then as film maker, spokesman, and theorist for the movement. At the age of 23 he made his first feature, *Barravento,* and since then his work, like that of other members of the group, has turned away from European influences to return to the roots of his country, its tradition, conflicts and violence, its mysticism and primitivism. His *The Black God and the White Devil* (64), with its violent, lyrical, almost baroque style and its concern for Brazilian social reali-

ties, introduced *cinema novo* to the outside world; *Terra em transe* analyzed the urban political situation and the role of the Brazilian intellectuals, while the more conventional *Antonio das Mortes* returned to mythology and the agrarian situation.

DIR: *O Patio* (58) (short), *A Cruz na Praca* (59) (short), *Barravento** (61), *Deus e o Diabo na terra do sol/The Black God and the White Devil** (64), *Amazonas* (65) (short), *Maranhao* (66) (short), *Terra em transe** (66), *Antonio das Mortes/O Dragão da Naldada contra o Santo Guerreiro* (69), *Cabezas cortadas* (Sp70), *Der Leone Have Sept Cabecas* (Fr/It/Brazil70).

ROCHEMONT, Louis de *see* DE ROCHEMONT, LOUIS

*ROEG, Nicholas PHOTOG/DIR Britain. (1928–) One of the most brilliant of the new generation of cameramen, seen at his best in the fluent images of *Far from the Madding Crowd, Petulia,* and *Fahrenheit 451,* who made a striking debut as director of *Performance,* a "difficult" film whose release was held up for two years by its distributor.

PHOTOG (notably): Clive Donner's *The Caretaker* (63), *Nothing But the Best* (63); Robert Lynn's *Dr. Crippen* (64), *Victim 5* (GFR/Brit64); Roger Corman's *Masque of the Red Death* (64); Daniel Mann's *Judith* (Israel/USA65); Richard Lester's *A Funny Thing Happened on the Way to the Forum* (66), *Petulia** (67); Truffaut's *Fahrenheit 451* (66); John Schlesinger's *Far from the Madding Crowd* (67), and his own films.

DIR: *Performance* (68, released 70) (co-dir: Donald Cammel), *Walkabout* (71), *The Strange Voyage of Donald Crowhurst* (project). Also scenario for Cliff Owen's *A Prize of Arms* (61) and Lawrence Huntington's *Death Drums along the River* (64).

ROGOSIN, Lionel DIR USA. (New York 1924–) One of the best of the independent New York film makers who has used the "camera eye" to make two courageous and brilliant feature documentaries, *On the Bowery* (55) and *Come Back Africa** (59), the second shot in secret in South Africa. Also: *Good Times, Wonderful Times* (65).

ROHRIG, Walter ART DIR Germany. (189?–) Major set designer of German expressionist films, a style that he helped establish by his collaboration (with Warm and Reimann) on *The Cabinet of Dr. Caligari*. [He was originally a painter and stage designer. From 1920–36 he usually worked in collaboration with Robert Herlth (*q.v.*). His later work is typical of the heavy decorative UFA style of the Nazi regime.]
ART DIR (notably): for Wiene, *Das Cabinet des Dr. Caligari** (19); for Otto Rippert, *Die Pest in Florenz* (19); for Wegener and Boese, *Der Golem, Wie er in die Welt kam** (20); for Lang, *Der Müde Tod** (20); for Murnau, *Der Letzte Mann** (24), *Tartüff* 25), *Faust** (26); for Arthur von Gerlach, *Zur Chronik von Grieshuus* (25); for Erik Charrell, *Der Kongress tanzt** (31); for Gustav Ucicky, *Hokuspokus* (31), *Morgenrot* (33), *Heimkehr* (41); for Karl Ritter, *Unternehmen Michael* (37), *Patrioten* (37), *Pour le mérite* (38), *Capriccio* (39), *Die Hochzeitsreise* (39), *Bal paré* (40), *Ueber alles in der Welt* (41); for Hans Steinhoff, *Rembrandt* (42).

ROMM, Mikhail Ilych DIR USSA. (Irkutsk Jan 24, 1901–Oct 1971) Veteran Soviet director who began his directorial career with the remarkable *Boule de suif*, the best film adaptation ever made of a Maupassant story. His two lively biographical portraits of the great revolutionary, *Lenin in October* and *Lenin in 1918*, were well-merited successes, and his *Girl No. 217* was a moving tableau of the suffering endured by Russian women deported to Germany. But later, in *The Russian Question* and *Murder on the Rue Dante*, he tried unsuccessfully to re-create a foreign atmosphere that he understood poorly; and he was hampered by an excessive budget and the dictates of the "cult of personality" in *Admiral Ushakov*. However, his work returned to its original power in the personal and courageous *Nine Days of One Year* and *Ordinary Fascism*. Both as film maker and professor at the Moscow film school, (VGIK) he has contributed to the training of many contemporary Soviet directors, particularly Grigori Chukrai (*q.v.*). He began his film career (1930) as scriptwriter and was assistant to Alexander Macheret on *Dela y lyudi/Men and Jobs* (32).
DIR: *Pyshka/Boule de suif** (34), *Trinad-stat/The Thirteen* (37), *Lenin v Oktyabre/Lenin in October** (37), *Lenin v 1918/Lenin in 1918** (39), *Dream* (43), *Chelovek No. 217/Girl No. 217** (44), *Ruskii vopros/The Russian Question* 47), *Lenin** (48) (documentary; co-dir: V. Belyaev), *Sekretnaya missiya/Secret Mission* (50), *Admiral Ushakov* (53), *Korabli shturmuyut bastiony/The Ships Storm the Bastions* (53), *Ubiistvo na utilitze Dante/Murder on the Rue Dante* (56), *Devyat' dney odnogo goda/Nine Days of One Year** (61), *Obiknovennii Fashizm/Ordinary Fascism* (65), *Lost Letters* (66) (short), *A Night of Thought* (66).

ROOM, Abram DIR USSR. (Vilno 1894–) Good Soviet film maker, at his best in the silent period, he has an excellent visual sense and a feeling for psychological characterizations. He is most famous for *Bed and Sofa* (27), which depicts the daily life of a Moscow family and their lodger during the New Economic Policy (NEP), but directed at least one other worthwhile film, *The Ghost That Will Not Return* (30). He originally worked in the theater and was later a pupil of Kuleshov (*q.v.*) and an assistant director.
DIR (notably): *Bukhta smerti/Death Bay* (26), *Predatel/Traitor* (26), *Tretya Meshchanskaya/Bed and Sofa/Third Meshchanskaya* (27), *Ruts* (28), *Privideniye, kotoroye ne vozvrashchayetsa/The Ghost That Will Not Return* (30), *Plan velikh rabot/Plan of Great Works* (30) (documentary), *A Stern Young Man* (36), *Wind from the East* (41), *Nashestiviye/Invasion* (45) (co-dir: Oleg Zhakov), *In the Mountains of Yugoslavia* (46), *Court of Honor* (50).

ROOS, Jørgen DIR/PHOTOG Denmark. (Gilleleje Aug 14, 1922–) The best Danish documentarist and one of the best in Europe: sharp, perceptive, and often humorous, he has retained from his interest in surrealism a taste for poetic parody and curious interrelationships. He was a cameraman 1939–47, occasionally for his brother, Karl Johannes Roos (April 14, 1914–April 7, 1951); 1942–47 he co-directed several shorts with Albert Mertz, including *Flugten* (42), *Historien om en mand* (44), *Goddag Dyr!* (47).
DIR: *Isen brydes* (47) (co-dir: Poul Bang), *Opus 1* (Fr48), *Mikkel* (48),

Paris pa to mader (49), *Jean Cocteau* (Fr49), *Tristan Tzara, père du dadaïsme* (Fr49), *Det Definitiv afslag pa anmodningen om et kys* (49) (co-dir: W. Freddie), *Spiste horisonter* (50) (co-dir: W. Freddie), *Shakespeare og Kronborg* (50), *Historien om et slot* (51), *J. F. Willumsen* (51), *Den Stromlinjede gris* (52), *Slum* (52), *Ferieborn* (52), *Lyset i natten* (53), *Spaedbarnet* (53), *Goddag Børn* (53), *Skyldig-Ikke Skyldig* (53), *Kalkmalerier* (54), *Inge bliver voksen* (54), *Avisen* (54), *Martin Andersen Nexøs sidste rejse* (54), *Mit live eventyr* (55), *Solt* (56), *Ellehammer/ The Flying Dane* (57), *Johannes Larsen* (57), *Magie du diamant* (Belg58), *6-Dageslobet* (58), *Friluft* (59), *Den Sidste Vinter* (60), *En by ved navn København* (60), [*Danish Design* (60), *Staphylokokfaren* (60), *Forayar-Faeroerne* (61), *Vi haenger i en trad* (62), *Jørgen Roos zeigt Hamburg* (62), *Oslo* (63), *Nikita Krustjev* (64), *Stoj* (65), *Carl Th. Dreyer* (66), *Knud* (66), *Sisimilut* (66), *Kaerligheden varer laengt* (67), *En fangerfamilie i Thuledistriktet* (66), *Grønlandske dialektoptagelser og trommedanse fra Thuledistriktet* (67), *Sytten minutter Grønland* (67), *Et ar med Henry* (67), *Jeg skal ha' briller* (68), *Ultima Thule* (68), *Gustav Vigeland* (68).

PHOTOG (notably): for Karl Roos, *Copenhagen Calling* (47); for Dreyer, *De Naede Faergen* (48), *Krogen og Kronborg* (52); and many of his own films.]

ROSAS, Enrique and COS, Joachim DIR Mexico. The authors in 1919 of an admirable Mexican episode film, *El Automovil gris**, which re-created a series of crimes during the Mexican Revolution.

ROSHAL, Grigori DIR USSR. (Ukraine 1898–) Good Soviet director who has worked in many genres and has made many films of an appealing vitality, most memorably, *Petersburg Night* (34) and one of the most interesting films during the low period of the Soviet cinema, 1946–54, *Academician Ivan Pavlov* (49).

DIR (notably): *Gospoda Skotinini* (26), *Yevo prevoshoditielstvo/Your Excellency* (27), *Salamandra* (28), *Chelovek 12 mestietka* (30), *Petersburgskaya noch/ Petersburg Night* (34) (co-dir: V. Stroyeva), *Zori Parischa/Dawn in Paris* (37), *Semla Openheim/The Oppenheim Family* (38), *Delo Artamonovich/The*

Artamanov Affair (41), *Pesni Abaya/ Song of Abaya* (45), *Akademik Ivan Pavlov/Academician Ivan Pavlov** (49), *Musorgsky* (50), *Rimsky-Korsakov* (52), *Aleko* (53), *Volnitsa* (55), *Sestri I, II, III* (57, 59, 60) (from Tolstoy), *Karl Marx* (63). Also co-scripted Ptushko's *A New Gulliver** (35).

*ROSI, Francesco DIR Italy. (Naples Nov 15, 1922–) Excellent film maker of the younger generation whose aggressive, rigorous films concentrate on social problems. More than any other Italian film maker he has remained faithful to the challenges of neorealism and gave the movement a new impetus with, notably, *Salvatore Giuliano, Le Mani sulla Città,* an *Il Momento della Verità.* After a brief spell in radio he served his apprenticeship under Visconti (*q.v.*) and Antonioni (*q.v.*) and co-wrote several scripts before directing his first feature.

ASSIST (notably): to Visconti, *La Terra trema** (48), *Bellissima* (51), *Senso** (54); to Luciano Emmer, *Domenica d'Agosto* (50), *Parigi è sempre Parigi* (51); to Antonioni *I Vinti* (52).

CO-SCEN (notably): Zampa's *Processo alla Città* (52); Monicelli's *Proibito* (54); Risi's *Il Sorpasso* (62); and all his own films.

DIR: *Camicie Rosse* (51) (completed only; begun by G. Allessandrini), *Kean* (54) (technical dir only: dir: V. Gassman), *La Sfida* (58), *I Magliari* (59), *Salvatore Giuliano** (61), *Le Mani sulla Città** (63), *Il Momento della Verità* (65), *C'era una volta/More Than a Miracle/Happily Ever After/Cinderella Italian Style* (67), *Uomini contro* (70).

*ROSSELLINI, Renzo MUS Italy. (Rome 1908–) Italian composer partial to impressive symphonic themes, his best work has been for his elder brother, Roberto: *Un Pilota Ritorna, Roma, Città Aperta*, Paisà, Francesco Guiliare di Dio, Stromboli, Europa 51*, Viaggio in Italia*, Angst, Il Generale della Rovere.*

ROSSELLINI, Roberto DIR Italy. (Rome June 8, 1906–) For many, he is the best of the postwar Italian film makers. His *Rome, Open City*, made at the end of the war and based on the experiences of the Italian underground, established neorealism as the most important and influential postwar style and won him a worldwide reputation. His work, especially that in the Fifties, considerably influenced many of the French new-wave film makers. He was originally a technician, editor, and scriptwriter and made several short films before turning, in collaboration with F. De Robertis (who had preceded him in this approach), to the quasi-documentary fiction of *La Nave Bianca* (41), a film that didn't show "novelettish characters but real people." However, "documentary objectivity" was a pipe dream under fascism in wartime and he was forced into the worst propaganda with *L'Uomo della Croce*. But he quickly took hold of himself, and his involvement with the Italian underground led him to become the spokesman for the Italian people after the war. His second postwar film, *Paisà*, was an expensive production in which he was able to exploit freely the new approach of having people live out their actual experiences for the camera. With his scriptwriters, Fellini (*q.v.*) and Amidei (*q.v.*), he built up a fresco of various episodes in the liberation of Italy. *Germany, Year Zero* was another attempt at lyrical reportage but its near-failure commercially made him doubt his methods and the role he had played since the war. He tried new themes — the fantastic in *La Macchina ammazzacattivi* and Christian mythology in *Flowers of St. Francis* — before Ingrid Bergman came into his life. The attendant scandal marked a turning point in his work. During his "Bergman period" he depicted his beliefs and concern in the sincere Stendhalian, but little known *Europa 51*, better even than *Viaggia in Italia*. Though his work gained him many admirers in certain film circles, commercial success escaped him. After an absence of some years from the cinema, he visited India to recapture his documentary roots and made the brilliant, provocative *India*, of which he said: "What matters to me is man. I have tried to express the soul, the light that shines inside people, their reality, which is an absolutely personal, unique reality, secured by an individual, with a sense of the things around them. These things have a meaning since there is someone observing them." This statement could also be a summation of the best of his work and of the methods of filming that he has continued to advocate: "Begin by an investigation, a docu-

mentation, and then pass to dramatic motives, but in such a way as will represent things as they are, as will retain their integrity. Yes, it is necessary for the cinema to teach men to know themselves, to recognize themselves in others instead of always telling the same stories." Though he could not always follow his own advice after returning from India, he had commercial successes with *Generale Della Rovere* and *Era Notte a Roma*, both based on stories of the war. After those films, he came close to abandoning the cinema for the pen, but in the latter part of the Sixties found new possibilities in directing for television and has since created a brilliant series of intellectually rigorous, dramatized historical documentaries.

DIR: *Dafné* (36) (short), *Prélude à après-midi d'un faune* (37–38) (short), *Fantasia Sottomarina* (39) (short), *Il Tacchino Prepotente* (39) (short), *La Vispa Teresa* (39) (short), *Il Ruscello di Ripasottile* (40) (short), *La Nave Bianca* (41), *Un Pilota Ritorna* (41), *L'Uomo della Croce* (42), *Desiderio* (43) (co-dir: M. Pagliero), *Roma, Città Aperta** (45), *Paisà** (46), *Germania, Anno Zero/Evil Street** (Fr/It47), *L'Amore* (in two parts: *Una Voce Umana*, 47, and *Il Miracolo*, 48), *La Macchina Ammazzacattivi/The Infernal Machine* (48), *Francesco Giullare di Dio/The Flowers of St. Francis* (49), *Stromboli, Terra di Dio* (49–50), *Les Septs péchés capitaux* (Fr52) (episode, "Envy"), *Europa 51/The Greatest Love** (52), *Dov'è la Liberta?* (52), *Siamo Donne/We Are the Women* (53) (one episode), *Viaggio in Italia/The Lonely Woman/Strangers** (It/Fr53), *Amori di Mezzo Secolo* (54) (one episode), *Giovanna d'Arco al Rogo/Jean au bûcher/Joan at the Stake** (54), *Angst/La Peura/Fear* (GFR/It54), *L'India visita da Rossellini* (58) (10 TV shorts), *India* (58), *Il Generale della Rovere* (59), *Era Notte a Roma* (60), *Viva Italia!* (60), *Torino nei centi'anni* (61) (TV short), *Vanina Vanini* (61), *Anima Nera* (62), *Rogopag* (62) (one episode), *L'Eta del Ferro* (64) (TV, 5 episodes), *La Prise de pouvoir par Louis XIV* (Fr66) (TV), *Idea di Un'Isola* (67) (documentary for US TV), *La Lotta dell' Uomo per la Sua Sopravvivenza* (It/Rum/Fr/Egypt 67) (TV, 12 episodes; supervised only; dir: Renzo Rossellini, Jr.), *Gli Atti degli Apostoli* (It/Fr/Sp/

* Bosley Crowther, Fifty Films (1978) - "a powerful film in the Neo-realist Tradition."

GFR68) (TV, 5 episodes), *Socrate* It/
Sp/Fr70) (TV).

ROSSEN, Robert DIR/SCEN USA. (New
York March 16, 1908–Hollywood Feb
18, 1966) Good postwar American film
maker who, though he undoubtedly
worked on various routine commercial
films, was completely professional and
possessed great integrity — qualities he
evidenced on themes worthy of them:
*All the King's Men, Island in the Sun,
The Hustler,* and above all, his brilliant
Lilith. After stage experience, he worked
in Hollywood as a scriptwriter from
1937–47.
[SCEN: for Mervyn LeRoy, *They Won't
Forget* (37); for Lloyd Bacon, *Marked
Woman* (37), *Racket Busters* (38), *A
Child is Born* (40); for Lewis Seiler,
Dust Be My Destiny (39); for Raoul
Walsh, *The Roaring Twenties* (39); for
Litvak, *Out of the Fog* (41), *Blues in
the Night* (41); for Michael Curtiz,
The Sea Wolf (41); for Milestone, *Edge
of Darkness* (42), *A Walk in the Sun**
(45), *The Strange Love of Martha Ivers*
(46); for Lewis Allen *Desert Fury* (47);
and for all his own films except *Body
and Soul, The Brave Bulls.*
DIR: *Johnny O'Clock* (47), *Body and
Soul* (47), *All the King's Men* (49), *The
Brave Bulls* (50), *Mambo* (54), *Alexander the Great* (56), *Island in the Sun*
(57), *They Came to Cordura* (59), *The
Hustler* (61), *Lilith** (64).]

ROSSIF, Frédéric DIR France. (Montenegro
Aug 14, 1922–) Well-known French
TV documentary producer/director who
has also made several notable compilation films of historical events.
[DIR: *Une histoire d'éléphants* (58)
(short), *Vel' d'Hiv'* (59), (short), *Le
Monde instanté* (60) (short), *Le Temps
du ghetto* (61), *Imprévisible nouveauté*
(61) (short), *De notre temps* (62)
(short), *Mourir à Madrid* (63), *Pour
Espagne* (63) (short), *Les Animaux*
(64), *Révolution d'octobre* (67), *Un mur
à Jerusalem* (68) (co-dir: A. Knobler).]

ROTA, Nino MUS Italy. (Milan Dec 3,
1911–) Italian composer who is constantly in demand for the cinema and
whose simple and effective scores are
often very popular. His catchy melodies
for *In Nomme della Legge, La Strada,*
and *Rocco and His Brothers* themselves
became popular hits.

[MUS (notably): for Zampa, *Vivere in
Pace* (46); for Castellani, *E Primavera*
(49), *Il Brigante* (61), *Mare Matto*
(63); for Germi, *In Nomme della Legge**
(49); for Lattuada, *Anna* (51), *Mafioso*
(63); for Fellini, *Lo Sceicco Bianco**
(52), *I Vitelloni** (53), *La Strada** (54),
Le Notti di Cabiria* (57), *La Dolce
Vita** (59), *8½** (63), *Giulietta degli
Spiriti** (65), *Fellini Satyricon* (69);
for Franco Rossi, *Amici per la Pelle*
(55); for King Vidor, *War and Peace**
(55); for Visconti *Le Notte Bianche**
(57), *Rocco e i suoi Fratelli** (60), *Il
Gattopardo** (62); for Petri, *Il Maestro
di Vigevano* (63); for Bondarchuk, *Waterloo* (70).]

ROTHA, Paul DIR Britain. (London June 3,
1907–) One of the founders, with
Grierson (*q.v.*), of the British documentary movement at the Empire Marketing Board, 1931–33. He later became
an independent and is also a well-known
film historian and critic.
DIR (notably): *Contact* (32), *Shipyard*
(33), *The Rising Tide* (33), *The Face
of Britain* (34), *Death on the Road* (35),
The Future's in the Air (36), *Peace of
Britain* (36), *Statue Parade* (37), *New
World's for Old* (38), *The Fourth Estate*
(40), *World of Plenty* (43), *Soviet Village* (44), *Total War in Britain* (45),
Land of Promise (46), *A City Speaks*
(47), *The World is Rich* (48), *No Rest-
ing Place* (50) (feature), *World without End* (52) (part only; dir: Basil
Wright), *Cat and Mouse* (57) (feature),
The Life of Adolf Hitler (60) (compilation feature), *The Silent Raid* (62)
(feature).

ROTUNNO, Giuseppe PHOTOG Italy. (192?–
) A camera operator for some years
(on Visconti's *Senso** and several Carmine Gallone films), he developed in
the Fifties and Sixties into one of the
world's great cameramen, particularly in
his association with Visconti, to whom
he has contributed some evocative imagery.
PHOTOG (notably): for Dino Risi, *Pane,
Amore e . . .* (56); for Visconti, *Le
Notti Bianche** (57), *Rocco e i suoi
Fratelli** (60), *Boccaccio '70* (62) (episode), *Il Gattopardo** (63); for Stanley
Kramer, *On the Beach** (USA59), *The
Secret of Santa Vittorio* (69); for Monicelli, *La Grande Guerra* (59), *I Com-
pagni* (63); for Henry Koster, *The*

Naked Maja (USA59); for Martin Ritt, *Five Branded Women* (USA60); for Zurlini, *Cronaca Familiare* (62); for De Sica, *Ieri, Oggi, Domani* (63), *I Girasoli* (69); for Huston, *La Bibbia* (66); for Monicelli, De Sica, Rossi, Visconti, *Le Streghe* (66); for Pasolini, *Edipo Re** (67); for Dmytryk, *Anzio* (68); for Fellini, *Fellini Satyricon* (69).

ROUCH, Jean DIR France. (Paris May 31, 1917–) A professional ethnographer who, after making *Jaguar* and *Moi, un noir,* became in the Sixties, the apostle of *cinéma-vérité.* He aimed to avoid dramatic trickery and to bring life directly to the screen by using nonprofessional actors recreating their own lives for the camera in the Flaherty (*q.v.*) manner. He is also one of the first to give black Africans a voice on international screens. Since 1961 he has employed the "living camera" technique, using extremely portable silent cameras with synchronous sound that enabled him to capture life as it was being lived with a minimum of involvement on the "director's" part. But in *Chronique d'un été,* far from capturing "life as it was lived," he used the camera and the sociologist Edgar Morin as the principal characters in a drama in which he sought to provoke a "psychodrama" in the people interviewed in order to draw from them their deepest feelings and attitudes. Even in the earlier *La Pyramide humaine* he used fiction to try to reveal racism or antiracism in white and black students. He moved further in the direction of drama with *La Punition,* more of an exercise in the "living camera" than in *cinéma vérité,* and his later films have continued the development up to the free fusion of fiction and documentary in *Petit à petit.* His exploration of new techniques in an unbroken succession of profoundly humanistic films opened new perspectives for the cinema and have had a wide influence.
DIR (shorts): *Chasse à l'hippopotame* (46), *Au pays des mages noirs* (47) (co-dir: P. Ponty, J. Sauvy), *Initiation à la danse des possédés* (50), *Circoncision* (50), *Hombori* (50), *Les Magiciens de Wanzerbe* (50), *Bataille sur le grand fleuve* (51), *Cimetière dans la falaise* (51), *Les Hommes qui font la pluie* (51), *Les Gens du Nil* (51), *Les Maîtres fous* (55), *Mammy Water* (53–56), *Moro-Naba* (57), *Goumbé* (57, completed

63), *Hampi* (60), *Monsieur Albert, prophète* (62) (co-dir: J. Ravel), *Abidjan, port de pêche* (62), *Urbanisme africaine* (62), *Le Nil* (62), *Les Pêcheurs du Niger* (62), *Rose et Landry* (Canada 63; co-dir: J. Godbout), *Les Cocotiers* (63), *Le Plamier à huile* (63), *Le Lion* (60–64), *L'Afrique et la recherche scientifique* (64), *Tambours de pierre/Les Tambours des dogons/Eléments pour une étude de rhythme* (64–66).
DIR (features): *Jaguar* (53, completed and released 67), *Les Fils de l'eau* (55) (compilation of five of his short films), *Moi, un noir/Treichville** (56, released 58), *La Pyramide humaine* (60), *Chronique d'un été** (61) (co-dir: E. Morin), *La Punition* (62), *Paris vu par . . .* (64) (one episode), *Les Adolescentes* (64) (one episode), *La Chasse au lion à l'arc* (65), *La Goumbé des jeunes noceurs* (66), *Petit à petit* (70).

ROUQUIER, Georges DIR France. (Lunel June 23, 1909–) Masterly documentarist, the best French representative of the Flaherty (*q.v.*) approach, concerned with people in their daily lives and in their work. His masterpiece is *Farrebique* (46), a lyrical tableau of peasant family life during four seasons. He intended it to be the first of a series of similar documentary features but unfortunately he was not able to continue as planned.
DIR (shorts): *Vendanges* (29), *Le Tonnelier* (42), *Le Charron* (43), *Le Part de l'enfant* (43), *Pasteur* (47), *Le Chaudronnier* (49), *Le Sel de la terre* (50), *Lourdes et ses miracles* (54) (three shorts in a feature length film), *Arthur Honegger* (55), *La Bête noire* (56).
DIR (features): *Farrebique** (46), *Sang et lumière* (53), *S.O.S. Noronha* (57).

ROVENSKI, Josef DIR Czechoslovakia. (189?–1936) Good prewar Czech film maker, the author of the sensitive and moving *Rekka/Young Love* (33).

ROY, Bimal DIR/PHOTOG India. (Dacca, East Bengal July 12, 1912–Bombay Jan 1966) Undoubtedly the best Indian film maker to establish himself in the Forties. He trained at a photography school and in 1933 was hired by Nitin Bose (*q.v.*) as his assistant at New Theatres in Calcutta. He photographed *Devdas** (35) for P. C. Barua and remained with New Theatres until 1950, when he moved to Bombay. In 1952 he founded Bimal Roy

Productions and the following year made his best film, *Two Acres of Land*, a film whose impact on the Indian cinema was similar to that of *Bicycle Thieves* on the Italian. Its story of a Bengali peasant struck a responsive chord among millions of Asians. Roy's work at its best reflects the New Theatres tradition, with its sense of popular life, national feeling, and stories carefully selected to reach the enormous Asian public. His later work, like *Devdas, Sujata*, and *Biraj Baha*, was often based on the works of popular Bengali writers of the early 20th century and has a touching simplicity; however, they cannot be fully appreciated if they are measured against the norms of western narrative films.

DIR (notably): *Udahir Path* (43), *Battarcherjee* (43), *Anjangarb, Montra Mughdo, Hamrahi, Pahela Admi* (44–50), *Baap Beti* (51), *Parineeta* (52), *Do Bigha Zamin/Two Acres of Land** (53), *Devdas** (55), *Biraj Bahu* (56), *Sujata* (59), *Parakh* (61), *Prem Patra* (62), *Pandini* (63).

ROZIER, Jacques DIR France. (Paris 1926–) Trained at IDHEC, he has made numerous shorts (mostly for TV) but only one feature – the remarkable portrait of Parisian youth in the Sixties, *Adieu Philippine** (62).

RUSPOLI, Mario DIR France. (Rome 1925–) Leading French *cinéma-vérité* film maker, inactive for some years, who made effective use of the "living camera" with sympathy and prudence.

DIR: *Rennaissance* (55–56) (16mm feature), *Les Hommes de la baleine* (56), *Campagne Romaine* (58–59), *Ombre et lumière de Rome* (59), *Les Inconnus de la terre* (61), *Regards sur la folie* (62), *La Fête prisonnière* (62), *Le Dernier verre* (64), *Baath Omar/Rebirth of a Nation* (Tunisia65).

RUTTEN, Gerard DIR Netherlands. (?–) Dutch director of the Thirties, best known for his dramatized documentary feature, *Dood Wasser* (34).

RUTTMANN, Walther DIR Germany. (Frankfurt Dec 28, 1887–Berlin July 15, 1941) Documentary film maker who played a determinant role in the development of the documentary in the late Twenties with *Berlin, Symphony of a Great City* and *World Melody*, films that had a worldwide influence. He himself had been much influenced by the theories of Dziga Vertov (*q.v.*) on the camera-eye – capturing life as it was being lived – and adopted this approach in these films. He studied architecture and painting and was already a successful poster designer when he became interested in the work of Viking Eggeling (*q.v*). He made several experimental abstract films (the *Opus* series) animating geometric forms before turning to documentary in 1927 and establishing an immediate reputation with *Berlin*, a rigorously and ingeniously constructed portrait of life in the city from dawn to midnight – an idea already exploited by Mikhail Kaufman (*q.v.*) in *Moscow* (27). He was identified with the political left after making *World Melody*, which was based on the idea that everyone in the world, whatever their color, shares the same feelings and participates in the same basic daily routine. Again based on Vertov's theories (on the radio-ear), he directed *Weekend*, a sound "film without images," one of the first radiophonic montages. After directing several more short documentaries and then going to Italy to direct *Acciaio* (33) from a script by Pirandello, he collaborated with the Third Reich and agreed to direct several documentaries that served the purposes of Dr. Goebbels. He was adviser to Leni Riefenstahl (*q.v.*) on *Olympia** and in 1940 directed *Deutsche Panzer*, glorifying the triumphant Nazi conquest in France. He was working on a similar film in the east when he was mortally wounded.

DIR: *Die Tönende Well* (21), *Opus, I, II, III, IV* (21–24), *Der Falkentraum* (24) (animated sequence in Lang's *Die Nibelungen**), *Berlin, die Sinfonie der Grosstadt** (27) (documentary feature), *Hoppla wir Leben* (27) (co-dir: Piscator; film sequence used in theatrical production of a play by E. Töller), *Deutscher Rundfunk* (28), *Melodie der Welt** (29) (documentary feature), *Weekend* (30) ("film without images"), *In der nacht* (31), *Feind im Blut* (31) (documentary feature), *Acciaio/Arbeit macht frei/Steel* (It33) (feature), *Altgermanische Bauernkultur* (34), *Metall des Himmels* (34), *Kleiner Film einer grossen Stadt: Düsseldorff* (35), *Stuttgart, Grossstadt zwischen Wald und Reben* (35), *Schiff in Not* (36), *Mannesmann* (37), *Hamburg – Weltstrasse, Welthafen* (38), *Im zeichen des Vertrau-*

ens (38), *Im Dienste der Menschlichkeit* (38), *Henkel — ein deutsche Werk in seiner Arbeit* (38), *Die Deutsche Waffenschmiede* (40), *Deutsche Panzer* (40), *Aberglaube* (40).

Other work: Collaborated with Lotte Reiniger on *Die Abenteuer des Prinzen Achmed* (23–26); collaborated with Abel Gance on editing of *La Fin du monde* (31); adviser to Leni Riefenstahl on *Olympische Spiele 1936/Olympiad** (36).

RYBKOWSKI, Jan DIR Poland. (1912–)
Prolific and popular Polish director who has worked on many types of film in a characteristic, somewhat immoderately enthusiastic manner. His best films are *Pierwsze dni/The First Days* (51) and *Dzis w nocy umrze miasto/A Town Will Die Tonight* (61), an account of the saturation bombing of Dresden, which killed more people than the atomic bomb at Hiroshima.

SALIM, Kamel DIR Egypt. (191?–1945) The best Egyptian film maker of the 1930–45 period and the only one who was then tackling social themes, as in *El Azima*, his best film.

DIR: *Warra' el Setar/Behind the Curtain* (37), *El Azima/The Will** (40), *Ilal Abad/Forever* (41), *Ahlam el Chabab/ Dreams of Youth* (43), *El Bouassa/Les Misérables** (44), *Hanane Kadiet el Yom/The Problem of the Day* (44), *Shuhaddaa el Gharam/Romeo and Juliet* (44), *Lailat el Jumaa/Friday Evening* (45), *El Mazaher/Appearances* (45), *Kasset gharam/Story of Love* (46) (completed by Ahmed Abdel Jawad).

SAMSONOV, Samson DIR USSR. (1921–) Soviet director of the Fifties generation, assistant to Gerasimov (*q.v.*) on *The Young Guard** (48), who began his directorial career with an excellent Chekhov adaptation, *Poprigunya/The Grasshopper* (55), but whose later work, even *Optimisticheskaya tragediya/The Optimistic Tragedy* (64), never lived up to the promise of this first film.

SANDBERG, Anders Wilhelm DIR Denmark. (May 22, 1887–March 27, 1938) Film maker who, during the low period of the Danish cinema in the Twenties, kept it alive by directing skillful adaptations of foreign novels, particularly those of Dickens. He made his first film in 1914 for Nordisk, after working for a time as a press photographer and film cameraman. DIR (notably): *Klovnen/Clown* (17), *Vor faelles ven* (19–20), *Pigen fra Sydhavsoen* (20), *Store forventninger/Great Expectations* (21), *David Copperfield* (22), *Little Dorrit* (24), *Fra Piazza del Popolo* (25), *Klovnen* (26) (remake), *Revolutionsbryllup* (28), *Tuborgfilm* (30), *Fem raske piger* (33), *7-9-13* (34), *København* (35), *A Real Danish*

Lunch (35), *Millionaerdrengen* (36), *Indvielse af storstromsbroen* (37).

SANDRICH, Mark DIR USA. (New York Oct 26, 1900–March 5, 1945) One-time director of Lupino Lane shorts whose reputation rests on his work in musicals, notably those starring Fred Astaire and Ginger Rogers: *The Gay Divorcee* (34), *Top Hat** (35), *Follow the Fleet* (36), *Shall We Dance?* (37), *Carefree* (38).

*SANTOS, Nelson Pereira dos DIR/ED Brazil. (Sao Paolo Oct 26, 1928–) The father of the Brazilian *cinema novo*, his films and writings have consistently been a seminal influence on the movement. A former lawyer and journalist, he began his career as an assistant and has made several social and political shorts (*Juventude*, etc.). His first feature, *Rio 40°*, was the first to explore the thematic concerns of *cinema novo* and he later made a major contribution to the movement's international success with *Vidas Secas*.

DIR (shorts): *Juventude* (49), *Atividades politicas em Sao Paolo* (50), *Soldados de Fogo* (58), *Ballet do Brazil* (62), *Um Moco de 74 Anos* (63), *Rio de Machado de Assis* (65), *Abastecimento nova Politica* (68).

DIR (features): *Rio 40°** (55), *Rio, Zona Norte* (57), *Mandaracura Vermelho* (61), *O Bocca de Ouro* (62), *Vidas Secas** (63), *El Justiciero* (67), *Fome de Amor* (68), *Un Asilo Muito Louco* (70), *Como Era Gostoso e Meu Francês* (71).

ASSIST: to Rodolfo Nanni, *O Saci* (51); to Alex Viany, *Agulha no Palheiro* (53); to P. Vanderlei, *Balanca Mas Nao Cai* (53).

ED: I. Rozemberg's *A Barragem de Tres Marias* (59); Glauber Rocha's *Barravento** (61); S. Ricardo's *O Menino da Calca Branca* (62); Leon Hirszman's

Cinco Vevez Favela (62) (episode) and *Maioria Absoluta* (64); Jean Manzon's *A Forcade Furnas* (65) (short).
PROD: Roberto Santos's *O Grande Momento* (58); Arnaldo Jabor's *A Opiniao Publica* (66) (documentary feature).

SASLAVSKY, Luis DIR Argentina/France. (Santa Fe April 24, 1908–) One of the artisans of the renaissance of the Argentinian cinema, 1938–45, when he directed several tasteful and delicate dramas (though with sometimes conventional themes) such as *La Dame duende* (45). He directed several films in France in the Fifties, then returned to Argentina.

SAGUET, Henri MUS France. (Bordeaux May 18, 1901–) Excellent French composer who has often written for the cinema and always created interesting scores.
MUS (notably): for L'Herbier, *L'Epervier* (33), *Péchés de jeunesse* (41), *L'Honorable Catherine* (42); for Daquin, *Premier de cordée* (44); for Rouquier, *Le Charron* (43), *Farrebique** (46); for Boisrond *Lorsque l'enfant paraît* (56); for Rouleau, *Les Amants de Teruel* (62).

SAVCHENKO, Igor DIR USSR. (Ukraine Sept 15, 1906–Moscow Dec 14, 1950) Good Ukrainian director with a feeling for the spectacular (*Bogdan Khmelnitsky*) who showed much sensitivity in his best, and last, film, *Taras Shevchenko*, dedicated to the famous Ukrainian poet.
DIR (notably): *People without Hands* (33) (short), *Garmon/Accordion* (34), *Unexpected Meeting* (36), *The Song of the Cossack Golota* (37), *Vsadniki/ Guerilla Brigade* (39), *Bogdan Khmelnitsky* (41), *Youthful Years* (41), *Partisans in the Ukrainian Steppes* (42), *Ivan Nikulin, Russian Sailor* (43), *Love Polka* (46), *Taras Shevchenko** (51).

SCEMANA CHIKLY DIR Tunisia. (Tunis Jan 24, 1872–c. 1950) The first film maker of Maghreb who directed an interesting early Tunisian dramatic feature, *Ain el Ghezal/The Girl from Carthage** (24).

SCHAEFFER, Pierre MUS France. (Nancy Aug 14, 1911–) The founder and director of the research branch of ORTF (French state radio and television organization) and the creator of *musique concrète*, he has both instigated and partici-

pated in several interesting cinematographic experiments.

*SCHARY, Dore PROD USA. (Newark, New Jersey 1905–) Former actor and journalist who joined Columbia as a scriptwriter in 1932, then worked as a freelance writer (*Boys' Town*, 38) until heading his own low-budget production unit at MGM in 1942. He left the following year, produced for David O. Selznick (*q.v.*) and RKO and became head of production at RKO in 1947. A dispute with Howard Hughes (*q.v.*) led to his departure and he rejoined MGM as vice-president in charge of production in 1948. He became MGM studio head in 1951 after Mayer's (*q.v.*) demise and was himself forced out in a studio upheaval in 1956. He has since worked independently on Broadway and as an independent producer: *Lonelyhearts* (59), *Sunrise at Campobello* (61), *Act One* (63).

SCHENK, Joseph M. PROD USA. (Russia Dec 25, 1877–1961) A typical example of the poor immigrants who became Hollywood magnates after building up financial resources in unrelated activities. [He came to the USA with his brother, Nicholas; together they acquired amusement parks in Manhattan and New Jersey and leased film concessions to Marcus Loew (*q.v.*), which led to their joining Loew's Consolidated. After running the group's theaters, he left in 1917 to produce his own films and played a role in developing Buster Keaton's (*q.v.*) career. By 1924, he was president of United Artists and organized its theater circuit. He founded Twentieth Century in 1933 with Darryl Zanuck (*q.v.*) and, after the merger with Fox, became chairman. He left Fox in 1952 and joined Mike Todd (*q.v.*) in the Magna Corporation to explore widescreen techniques.]

*SCHENCK, Nicholas M. PROD USA. (Russia 1881–1969) Brother of Joseph, he became secretary of Loew's Consolidated in 1910 and in 1927 succeeded Loew (*q.v.*) as president, in which capacity he controlled the finances of MGM and was involved in many battles with Louis B. Mayer (*q.v.*). He was eased out of Loew's in 1955.

*SCHLESINGER, John DIR Britain. (London 1926–) A talented film maker, former

TV director, and documentarist, with an occasional unfortunate propensity toward fashionable stylistic effects. At his best he has a real feeling for characterization and situations.

DIR (shorts, notably): *The Starfish* (52), *Monitor: The Class* (57), *The Innocent Eye* (58), *Terminus* (60).

DIR (features): *A Kind of Loving* (62), *Billy Liar* (63), *Darling . . . ** (65), *Far from the Madding Crowd* (67), *Midnight Cowboy* (USA69), *Sunday, Bloody Sunday* (71).

SCHOEDSACK, Ernest Beaumont DIR/PROD USA. (Council Bluffs, June 8, 1893–) Former newsreel cameraman (from 1914) who collaborated with Merian C. Cooper (*q.v.*) on two somewhat Flaherty-like dramatized documentaries, *Grass* and *Chang*, before turning to adventure films involving trick effects that sometimes reached the poetic, as in his famous *King Kong*.

DIR (notably): *Grass** (25), *Chang** (27), *The Four Feathers* (29), (all co-dir: Cooper), *Rango* (31), *The Most Dangerous Game** (32), *King Kong** (33) (co-dir: Cooper), *Son of Kong** (33), *Blind Adventure* (33), *Long Lost Father* (34), *The Last Days of Pompeii* (35), *Outlaws of the Orient* (37), *Dr. Cyclops* (40), *Mighty Joe Young** (49).

*SCHORM, Evald DIR Czechoslovakia. (Prague Dec 15, 1931–) Though his films have attracted less attention than those of his compatriots, Forman, Menzel, Kadar, and Klos (all *q.v.*), he has gradually emerged as the most significant member of the Czechoslovak new wave of the Sixties. He is a film maker of uncompromising moral integrity and has sometimes been referred to as the "conscience of the new wave." He studied at the Prague Film School (FAMU), mainly in the documentary department, and directed several documentary shorts before making his first feature, *Courage for Everyday* (64). One of the key films of the Czechoslovak cinema of the Sixties, it portrays the reactions of a politically active young man when events prove his image of society false. He continued his probing of contemporary spiritual and moral values in *The Return of the Prodigal Son*, concerned with why a man attempts suicide, *Saddled with Five Girls*, on the critical age of adolescence, and the tragicomedies *End of a Priest* and *The Seventh Day, the Eighth Night.*

His work reflects his statement: "In the eternal search for the meaning of things, for the message of truth, we usually meet with failure. But it is necessary to search incessantly, not only for the aim itself, but also for the means to attain it. It is without end, without limit."

DIR (shorts): *Too Much to Carry* (59), *Block 15* (60), *The FAMU Newsreel* (61), *The Tourist* (62) (all student films), *Helsinki* (62), *Trees and People* (62), *The Country of Countries/The Land* (62), *Chamber Harmony* (63) (TV), *Railwaymen* (63), *To Live One's Life* (63), *Proc?/Why?* (64), *Zrcadleni/ Reflections* (65), *Dialogue* (66) (TV), *Zalm/Psalm* (66), *The Legacy* (66), *Carmen nejen podle Bizeta/Carmen — Not Only by Bizet* (67).

DIR (features): *Kazdy den odvahu/ Courage for Everyday/Everyday Courage* (64), *Perlicky na dne/Pearls of the Deep* (65) (one episode), *Navrat ztraceneho syna/The Return of the Prodigal Son* (66), *Pet holek na krkv/Saddled with Five Girls/Five Girls Like a Millstone Round One's Neck* (67), *Fararuv konec/ Pastor's End/The End of a Priest* (68), *Prazske noci/Prague Nights* (68) (one episode), *Sedmy den, osma noc/The Seventh Day, the Eighth Night* (69–71), *Zabijet je snadne/Killing is Easy* (project).

SCHUB, Esther *see* SHUB, ESTHER

SCHUFFTAN, Eugen (*also, in USA and France,* **Eugene (Eugène) Schuftan)** PHOTOG Germany/France/USA. (Breslau July 21, 1893–) One of the world's greatest cameramen, he has contributed memorable images over some 40 years of activity and is notable especially for his carefully modulated and atmospheric high-key lighting effects on films like Carné's *Quai des brumes* and Franju's *La Tête contre les murs* and *Les Yeux sans visage.* In 1924 he also invented the "Schuftan process," first used in *Die Nibelungen** and *Metropolis**, in which mirror images of miniature sets are blended with real backgrounds or action to create a monumental effect. He originally studied painting, design, and architecture and his first film activities were as an optical effects designer. He was in the USA from 1939–49 but found it difficult to get work.

PHOTOG (notably): for Siodmak and Ulmer, *Menschen am Sonntag** (Ger29); for Ophüls, *Dann schon lieber Lebertran*

(Ger30), *Komoedie om Geld* (Neth36), *La Tendre ennemie* (FR36), *Yoshiwara* (Fr37), *Werther* (Fr38), *Sans lendemain* (Fr39); for Pabst, *L'Atlantide** (Fr32), *De haut en bas* (Fr34), *Mademoiselle Docteur* (Fr37), *Le Drame de Shanghai* (Fr39); for Feher, *The Robber Symphony** (Brit36); for Carné, *Drôle de drame* (Fr37), *Quai des brumes** (Fr39), *Trois chambres à Manhattan* (Fr65); for Clair, *It Happened Tomorrow** (USA43); for Astruc, *Le Rideau Cramoisi** (Fr52); for Pagliero, *La P . . . respecteuse* (Fr53); for Camerini, *Ulisse* (It53); for M. Clavel and M. Barry *Mina de Vanghel* (Fr53); for Duvivier, *Marianne de ma jeunesse* (Fr 55); for Franju, *La Première nuit* (Fr 58), *La Tête contre les murs** (Fr58), *Les Yeux sans visage* (Fr59); for Jack Garfein, *Something Wild* (USA61); for Robert Rossen, *The Hustler* (USA61), *Lilith** (USA64); for Mocky, *Un couple* (FR60), *Les Vierges* (Fr63); for Aleksander Ford, *Der Arzt stellt fest* (Switz/ GFR66).

SCHULBERG, Budd SCEN USA. (New York 1914–) American writer who was at one time director of publicity for Paramount and wrote *What Makes Sammy Run?*, a novel based on his Hollywood experiences. He wrote Kazan's *On the Waterfront** (53) and *A Face in the Crowd** (57) and Nicholas Ray's *Wind Across the Everglades* (58); Robson's *The Harder They Fall* (56) was based on his novel. He is the son of Hollywood producer, B. P. Schulberg (1892–1957).

SCOTTO, Vincent MUS France. (Marseilles 1876–Paris Nov 15, 1952) Famous composer, responsible for such successes as "Ma Tonkinoise," who also wrote several film scores, most notably for Pagnol's *Joffroy*.
MUS (notably): for Pagnol, *Joffroy* (33), *Merlusse* (35), *La Fille du puisatier* (40), *Naïs* (45); for Duvivier, *L'Homme du jour* (35), *Pépé le Moko** (36); for Dréville, *Les Cadets de l'océan* (42–45); for Daniel Norman, *Le Diamant de cent sous* (47); for Grémillon, *L'Étrange Madame X* (50).

SEASTROM, Victor *see* SJÖSTRÖM, VICTOR

SEATON, George DIR/SCEN USA. (South Bend, Indiana April 18, 1911–) Former stage producer and actor who was a scriptwriter for MGM, 1933–43 (*A Day at the Races, The Song of Bernadette*, etc.) and developed into a second-rank director with musicals (*Coney Island* (43), *The Shocking Miss Pilgrim* (47)), propaganda films (*The Big Lift* (50)), religious fantasy (*The Miracle on 34th Street* (47)), and inane melodramas (*Little Boy Lost* (53), *Airport* (69)). He scripts most of his own films.

SECHAN, Edmond PHOTOG/DIR France. (Montpellier Sept 20, 1919–) Good IDHEC-trained cameraman with a taste for portraying little known countries, he shot numerous short documentaries between 1947–55. He has taken up directing in the Sixties and enjoyed considerable international success with his two shorts, *Le Poisson rouge* (60) and *Le Haricot* (63).
PHOTOG (notably): for Jacques Dupont, *Pirogues sur l'Ogoué* (46); for Albert Lamorisse, *Crin blanc** (53); for Cousteau and Malle, *Le Monde du silence** (56); for Camus, *Mort en fraude* (57); for Jacques Becker, *Les Aventures d'Arsène Lupin* (56); for Berry, *Tamango* (58); for Mocky, *Les Drageurs* (59); for Yves Ciampi, *Le Ciel sur la tête* (64); for Broca, *Les Tribulations d'un Chinoise en Chine* (65); for Jean Giraux, *Le Gendarme à New York* (65); for Jean Becker, *Le Tendre voyou* (65); for Bourguignon, *A coeur joie* (66); for Norbert Carbonneaux, *Toutes folles de lui* (67).
DIR (notably): *Niok, le petit éléphant* (57), *Le Poisson rouge* (60) (short), *L'Ours* (60), *Le Haricot* (63) (short), *Pour un amour lointain* (67).

SEEBER, Guido (Conrad-Guido) PHOTOG Germany. (Chemnitz June 22, 1879–1940) One of the most important cameramen of the German silent period, together with Fritz-Arno Wagner (*q.v.*) and Karl Freund (*q.v.*), he made major contributions to the films of Pabst, Pick, and Wegener (all *q.v.*).
PHOTOG (notably): for Reinhardt, *Sumurun* (08); for Urban Gad, *Komödianten* (Ger/Den12); for Stellan Rye, *Der Student von Prague* (13); for Galeen and Wegener, *Der Golem** (14); for Arsen von Cserépy, *Fridericus Rex* (23); for Lupu Pick, *Sylvester** (23); for Pabst, *Die Freudlose Gasse** (25), *Geheinisse einer Seele* (26); for Bruno Rahn, *Dirnentragödie* (27). He later photographed many mediocre films.

*SELZNICK, David Oliver PROD USA. (Pittsburgh May 10, 1902–June 22, 1965) Independent-minded producer who impressed his stamp on the work of various directors: he is far more creatively responsible for *Gone With the Wind* than its credited director, Victor Fleming. The son of movie pioneer Lewis J. Selznick, he started by producing cheap documentaries, became a Hollywood producer with MGM (26–30), RKO (31–32 as head of production), then as vice-president at MGM until 1936, when he founded his own company, Selznick International Pictures.

PROD (notably): *Topaze* (33), *Dinner at Eight** (33), *Little Women* (33), *Viva Villa!** (34), *David Copperfield* (35), *Anna Karenina* (35), *A Tale of Two Cities* (35), *A Star is Born* (37), *Nothing Sacred* (37), *The Prisoner of Zenda* (37), *Intermezzo* (39), *Gone With the Wind** (39), *Rebecca* (40), *Jane Eyre* (44), *The Keys of the Kingdom* (44), *Spellbound* (45), *Notorious* (46), *Duel in the Sun** (46), *The Paradine Case* (48), *The Third Man** (Brit49) (co-prod: Korda), *Gone to Earth/The Wild Heart* (52), *A Farewell to Arms* (57).

SENNETT, Mack (Michael Sinnott) PROD/DIR USA. (Richmond, Canada Jan 17, 1880–Richmond Nov 5, 1960) The American "king of comedy" who had a prodigious sense of the absurd, of zany, nonsense humor that burlesqued everything and everybody, and who, with Ince (*q.v.*) and Griffith (*q.v.*), is one of the three great pioneers who fashioned the art of the American cinema. Like Ince he was less of a director himself than an artistic head of production, supervising each film closely from script (often based on his own ideas) to the final editing. But whereas Ince's approach stemmed from preparation of a detailed shooting script, Sennett's was based on the essential nature of editing. He discovered and made the first films of Chaplin, Keaton, Langdon (all *q.v.*), Fatty Arbuckle, Mabel Normand, Chester Conklin, Mack Swain, Al St. John, Gloria Swanson, Carole Lombard, Louise Fazenda, Wallace Beery, and even Bing Crosby. In 1913 he created the famous Keystone Cops (*The Bangville Police*), burlesque cops involved in crazy chases, and later the Sennett Bathing Girls dressed in mock-enticing bathing costumes that never got wet. From his first Keystone films —

Cohen Collects a Debt and *The Water Nymph* (Sept 23, 1912) — until 1920, his films were a dazzling succession of wild action, slapstick, and inspired burlesque. Then his work gradually became less inspired. The coming of sound and the Wall Street crash of 1929 reduced him to routine commercial shorts. In 1933 he filed a petition for voluntary bankruptcy and ceased production after 1935. Through the ensuing 25 years until his death, he waited vainly for an opportunity to direct again. Ironically, since his death, his films (often mutilated versions) have made vast sums of money from TV for those who bought the rights to them. Louis Delluc wrote of him in 1923: "He is perhaps the inventor, but at least the greatest virtuoso of that science without which a film isn't worthy of being called a film: the rhythm of images. I have often referred to Igor Stravinsky in relation to him. The rhythm of his productions is of the highest and boldest quality, not composed of an arbitrary baroque but derived from simple classical themes as old as the world, which he daringly syncopates like the master Russian symphonic composer. With the genius of a juggler's precision, he frolics with the Bathing Girls and finds in them not charm but movement. If his ideas are good, if his partners are good, if the rhythm is good, the charm will be there — that is his secret." 1902 — Stage actor. 1908–12 — Film actor at Biograph with D. W. Griffith. 1911 — Directed first films: *Comrades, Snookie's Flirtation* (with Ford Sterling), *The Diving Girl* (with Mabel Normand) and many others. 1912 — Keystone Company established in January with capital from Charles O. Bauman and Adam Kessel; Sennett officially joined company in the summer; directed 30 films — including *Cohen Collects a Debt, The Water Nymph, At Coney Island, Stolen Glory* — with Mabel Normand, Fred Mace, Ford Sterling. 1913 — Produced (and directed a few) 140 shorts (of which 30–40 were documentaries) including *The Bangville Police, Mabel's Awful Mistake, Barney Oldfield's Race for a Life* (dir: Sennett), *The Gangster* (first Fatty Arbuckle), *His New Beau* (dir: Sennett), *Their First Execution, Fatty's Day Off, Red Hot Romance, Mabel's Dramatic Career, A Quiet Little Wedding*. 1914 — Chaplin, hired at the end of 1913, began filming at Keystone, replacing Ford

Sterling as star of the troupe, which included Fatty Arbuckle, Mabel Normand, Mack Swain, Harry McCoy, Alice Davenport, Chester Conklin, Minta Durfee, Phyllis Allen, Hank Mann, Al St. John, Charley Chase, Slim Summerville, and Charles Murray; 150 Keystone shorts directed by Henry "Pathé" Lehrman, Robert Thornby, and Chaplin; films include *Tillie's Punctured Romance* (feature), *Kid Auto Races at Venice, In the Clutches of the Gang, Mabel's Strange Predicament, Leading Lizzie Astray, The Alarm,* and other Chaplin (*q.v.*), Fatty Arbuckle, and Mabel Normand shorts. 1915 — from July the Keystone films are produced for Triangle; 100 shorts, including "Mabel" and "Fatty" films — *Ambrose* (with Mack Swain), *Hogan* (with Charles Murray), *Gussle the Golfer* (with Syd Chaplin), *Wabrus* (with Chester Conklin), and *Mabel and Fatty's Married Life, Love, Speed and Thrills, Hogan out West, Love in Armor, The Little Teacher, My Valet, Saved by Wireless, A Village Scandal, The Great Vacuum Robbery, Submarine Pirate.* 1916 — 66 films with Normand, Arbuckle, Swain, Ford Sterling, St. John etc., augmented by Louise Fazenda, Wallace Beery, Gloria Swanson, Mae Busch; films include *The Mystery of the Leaping Fish* (with Douglas Fairbanks), *Teddy at the Throttle, Wife and Auto Trouble, A Modern Enoch Arden, The Great Pearl Tangle, Perils of the Park, Bucking Society, A Movie Star, A Village Vampire, His Last Laugh, Gipsy Joe, Snow Cure, Bathtub Peril, Moonshiner,* directed by, e.g., Dick Jones, Charles Avery, Clarence Badger, Eddie Cline, Frank Griffin. 1917 — Sennett gains absolute control of Keystone; 40 films, of which 30 were for Triangle and the rest for Paramount release, films include *The Butcher Boy** (first Keaton and Fatty), *A Bedroom Blunder, A Pullman Bride, Roping Her Romeo* (with Polly Moran, Ben Turpin), *Dangers of a Bride, Whose Baby?, A Royal Rogue, Oriental Love, Her Nature Dance, Secrets of a Beauty Parlor,* directed by E. Cline, Clarence Badger, Fred Fishback, etc. 1918 — 25 films, including *Mickey* (feature; dir: R. Jones, with Mabel Normand, Minta Durfee, George Nichols, Laura La Varnie), *Watch Your Neighbor.* 1919 — 25 films with Ben Turpin, Phyllis Haver, Louise Fazenda, Chester Conklin, Marie Prevost, Ford Sterling, Charles Murray,

etc., directed by Malcolm St. Clair, Dick Jones, Eddie Cline, Erle Kenton, etc., including *Yankee Doodle in Berlin, Uncle Tom without a Cabin, Salome versus Shenan Doach.* 1920 — 23 films, including the features, *Down on the Farm* and *Married Life* (dir: E. Kenton, with Louise Fazenda), and *Love, Honor, and Behave* (dir: R. Jones, with Ford Sterling, Charles Murray). 1921 — 13, films, including the feature, *Small Town Idol* (dir: E. Kenton, with Ben Turpin, Billy Bevan, Jimmy Finlayson, Charles Murray). 1922 — 13 films directed by Mal St. Clair, Roy Del Ruth, Fred Jackman. 1923 — 13 films, including the features, *Suzanna* and *The Extra Girl* (dir: R. Jones, with Mabel Normand); several shorts with Ben Turpin, Billy Bevan, Andy Clyde. 1924 — 33 films, including *Lizzies of the Field* and Harry Langdon's first films: *Picking Peaches* (dir: E. Kenton), *The First Hundred Years* (dir: R. Jones), *All Night Long* (dir: Harry Edwards), etc. 1925 — 40 films, directed and/or scripted by Lloyd Bacon, Frank Capra, Eddie Cline, Harry Edwards, Arthur Ripley, Tay Garnett including nine Langdon shorts. 1926 — 50 films, including Langdon's *Saturday Afternoon, Fiddlesticks, Soldier Man* (all dir: Harry Edwards). 1927 — 30 films, including *The Campus Vamp* (with Carole Lombard): apart from Turpin and Andy Clyde, the troupe had few real talents left. 1928 — 30 films, including the uninspired *Smith Family* series (with Raymond McKee). 1929 — About 15 films. 1930 — 20 films; Sennett began directing again. 1931 — 25 films directed by W. Beaudine, Eddie Cline, and Sennett, with Andy Clyde, Harry McCoy, and Bing Crosby. 1932 — 27 films. 1933 — three W. C. Fields shorts: *The Fatal Glass of Beer, The Pharmacist, The Barbershop.* 1934 — no films. 1935 — About six, then ceased production.

SHANDOFF, Zachari *see* ZHANDOV, ZAHARI

SHAHIN, Youssef DIR Egypt. (Alexandria 1926–) The best Egyptian film maker of the Fifties, he has a great sense of imagery, of editing, and of suspense, and has created some important works, *The Blazing Sun* (53), *Cairo Station* (57). He studied in the USA after the war.
DIR: *Baba Amine/Father Amine* (50), *Ibn el Nil/The Son of the Nile* (51),

El Muharrajel Kabir/The Great Clown (51), Sayidat el Katar/The Lady of the Train (51), Nessaa bala Rajal/ Women without Men (52), Seraa fil Wadi/The Blazing Sun* (53), Shaitan el Sahara/The Devil of the Desert (54), Seraa fil Minaa/Struggle in the Port (55), Inta Habibi/You Are My Love (56), Wadaat Hubak/Farewell to Your Love (56), Bab el Hadid/Cairo Station* (57), Jamila el Gazairia/Jamila, the Algerian Girl (58), Hub ilal Abad/Forever Yours (58), Bayen Idek/Between Your Hands (59), Nedaa el Ochak/Lover's Call (60), Rajul fi Hayati/The Man in My Life (61), El Nasser Salah-el-dine/ The Leader Saladin (62), Fajr Yom Jadid/Dawn of a New Day (64), Auliban (65).

SHANKAR, Uday DIR India. (Udaipur Dec 8, 1900–) Famous Indian dancer and choreographer who is notable in the Indian cinema for one film, Kalpana/Imagination (48), a fascinating experiment, made independently by Shankar, whose story was told entirely through choreography.

*SHANTARAM, Rajaram Vanakudre DIR/ PROD India. (Kolhapur Nov 18, 1901–) The best Indian director of the Bombay region in the Thirties and Forties and one of the most influential. He began in films as a general assistant in a local film company headed by Barburao Painter (q.v.) and founded his own company, Prabhat, in 1929 with four others. After making a few silent films, the company produced a great number of sound films in the Marathi language, some in the Hindi language, and later only films in Hindi. Though he began by directing mythological spectaculars, in 1937 he turned towards social themes in The Unexpected, on the child-bride problem; later he examined prostitution in Life is for Living (39) and the Moslem-Hindu problem in Neighbors (41). His Eternal Light (36) was shown at the Venice Festival and his Sant Tukaram (37) was the first Indian film to win a Venice Festival award. His Shakuntala (43) was, in 1947, the first Indian film to break into the American market. He was also an actor and played leading roles in many of his own films.
DIR (notably): Nethaji Palkar (26), Adomi (29), Amar (29), Bhoopali (30),

Parchain (30), Ayodhyecha Raja/The King of Ayodhya (32), Amar Jyoti/ Eternal Light (36), Sant Tukaram (37), Duniya Na Mane/The Unexpected (37), Admi/Life is for Living (39), Pardosi/ Neighbors (41), Shakuntala (43), The Journey of Dr. Kotnis (46), Jhanak, Jhanak, Payal Baje/Jangle, Jangle, Sound the Bells (55), Stree/Woman (62).

SHEIKH, Kamal el see EL SHEIKH, KAMAL

SHENGELAYA, Nikolai DIR USSR. (Tiflis 1901–Tiflis 1943) Excellent Georgian film maker, a disciple of Eisenstein (q.v.), best known for Eliso (28), Dvadtsat shest komissarov/26 Commissars (36). [His son, Eldar Shengelaya (1933–), is also a successful director of legendary fantasies: Legenda o ledyanom/Legend of the Ice Heart (57), Snezhnaya skazka/Snow Fairy Tale (59) (both co-dir: Sakharov), Belyi karavan/The White Caravan (64) (co-dir: Melyava), On ubivat ne khotel/He Did Not Want to Kill (67).]

SHINDO, Kaneto DIR/SCEN Japan. (Hiroshima 1912–) One of the best postwar Japanese film makers whose work is distinguished by its honesty and social commitment, and by a delicate style that depends more on allusion than forceful expressiveness. He entered films in 1934 as an assistant art director and later became a highly esteemed scriptwriter, notably for Yoshimura (q.v.), many of whose best films he has written. In 1950, with Yoshimura, he established his own independent company, Kindai Eiga Kyokai, and in 1951 he directed his first film. He was assistant to Mizoguchi on O'Haru* (52) and Ugetsu Monogatari* (53), having earlier worked on scripts for him. He created a harrowing portrait of the horrors of war in Children of Hiroshima (52), and later made the international successes, The Island (61) (a tableau of his own childhood) and Onibaba (64). His recent work has tended to concentrate on sexual or romantic themes.
DIR/SCEN: Aaisai Monogatari/The Story of a Beloved Wife (51), Nadare/Avalanche (52), Genbaku no Ko/Children of Hiroshima* (52), Shukuzu/Epitome/ Ginko the Geisha (53), Onna no Issho/ A Woman's Life (53), Dobu/Gutter (54), Ookami/Wolves (55), Shirogane

Shinju (56), *Ryuri no kishi* (56), *Umi no Yarodomo/Harbor Rats* (57), *Kanashimi wa Onna Dakeni/Only Women Have Trouble* (58), *Daigo Fukuryo Maru/The Lucky Dragon No. 5* (59), *Hanayome-san wa Sekai Ichi/The Bride from Japan* (59), *Hadaka no Shima/ The Island** (60), *Ningen/Man* (62), *Haha/Mother* (63), *Onibaba** (64), *Akuto/The Conquest* (65), *Honno/Lost Sex* (66), *Sei no Kigen/Libido/The Origins of Sex* (67), *Kuroneko* (68), *Tsuyomushi Onna to Yowamushi Otoko/ Operation Negligé* (68), *Shokkaku/Odd Affinity* (69), *Kagero/Heat-Wave Island* (70), *Hadaka no Jukyusai/Nineteen-Year-Old Misfit* (70).

[SCEN (notably): for Yoshimura, *A Ball at the Anjo House* (47), *Clothes of Deception* (51), *A Tale of Genji* (51), *Violence* (52), *Thousand Cranes* (53), *Desires* (53), *Before Dawn* (53), *The Beauty and the Dragon* (55), *On This Earth* (57), *The Naked Face of Night* (58), *Women of Kyoto* (60), *A Design for Dying* (61), *Their Legacy* (62), *A Fallen Woman* (67), *The House of Sleeping Virgins* (68); for Mizoguchi, *The Victory of Women* (46), *My Love Has Been Burning* (49); for Kinoshita, *Here's to the Girls* (49), *When Women Lie* (63) (episode); for Ichikawa, *Pursuit at Dawn* (50); for Kamei, *A Woman Walks the Earth Alone** (53); for Masamura, *The Precipice* (58), *The Lowest Man* (58), *Stolen Pleasure* (62), *Passion* (64), *Seisaku's Wife* (65), *The Spider Girl* (65), *Two Wives* (67), *The Wife of Seishi Hanaoka* (67), *Thousand Cranes* (69); for Imai, *The Adulteress* (58); for Kenji Misumi, *Destiny's Son* (62), *Dynamite Doctor* (66), *Devil's Temple* (69).]

SHOSTAKOVICH, Dmitri MUS USSR. (Saint Petersburg Sept 25, 1906–) The most famous Soviet composer, he was once a pianist for silent films and has written many notable film scores.
MUS (notably): for Kozintsev and Trauberg, *The New Babylon** (29), *Alone** (31), *The Maxim Trilogy** (35–39), *Plain People* (45); for Yutkevich, *Golden Mountains** (31), *Counterplan** (32) (co-dir: Ermler), *The Man with a Gun* (58); for Arnstam, *The Girl Friends** (36), *Zoya* (40); for S. and G. Vasiliev, *Volochayevsk Days* (38); for Ermler, *A Great Citizen** (38–39); for Ivens, *Our Russian Front* (USA41)

(co-mus: Eisler), *Lied der Ströme** (GDR54); for Kozintsev, *Pirogov* (47), *Bielensky* (53), *Hamlet** (64), *King Lear* (70); for Dovzhenko, *Michurin** (47); for Gerasimov, *The Young Guard** (47); for Alexandrov, *Meeting on the Elbe* (49); for Chiaureli, *The Fall of Berlin** (49), *The Unforgettable Year, 1919* (52); for Kalatozov, *The First Echelon* (56); for M. Shapiro, *Katerina Ismailova* (65).

SHUB, Esther Ilyanichna (Esther Schub) DIR/ ED USSR. (Ukraine 1894–Moscow Oct 21, 1959) The originator of the compilation film using existing newsreel and actuality material. With a strong sense of rhythm and tempo, she constructed her selected material into a series of brilliant features that marked her as a major individual talent. She proved that editing itself could be a means of artistic creation, even though using material filmed by others. She joined Goskino in 1922 to work on the re-editing and titling of foreign films for Soviet audiences: Pearl White serials, Chaplin's *Carmen**, Lang's *Doctor Mabuse** (on which Eisenstein also worked). She edited some new Soviet films, including Tarich's *Wings of a Serf/Ivan the Terrible** (26), before discovering the possibilities of using newsreel material as a means of re-creating the revolutionary past. Her first feature was a great success and she followed it with two others. Later, however, she used her analytical techniques successfully only in the remarkable *Spain*. She published her memoirs in *Krupnym planom* (*In Close-Up*), 1959.
DIR/ED: *Padeniye dinasti Romanovikh/ The Fall of the Romanov Dynasty** (27), *Veliky put/The Great Road* (27), *Rossiya Nikolai II i Lev Tolstoy/The Russia of Nicholas II and Lev Tolstoy** (28), *Sevodnya/Today* (30), *K. SH. E./Komsomol, Leader of Electrification* (32) (short), *The Metro at Night* (34) (short), *Strana sovietov/Country of the Soviets* (37) (short), *Ispaniya/Spain* (39) (from Karmen's footage), *Twenty Years of Soviet Cinema* (40) (co-dir: Pudovkin), *Faschism budet rasbyt/The Face of the Enemy* (41) (short), *Across the Arak* (47) (short).

SIDNEY, George DIR USA. (New York 1916–) Quite good director of musicals, often based on Broadway successes;

233

however, his best films, *Anchors Aweigh* (45) and *The Three Musketeers* (48), owe more to Gene Kelly than to him. His highly successful *Bathing Beauty* (44) was a typical MGM dance film of the period. He was still in form with *Bye, Bye Birdie* (63) and *Half a Sixpence* (67). Oother notable films include: *Annie Get Your Gun* (50), *Showboat* (51), *Scaramouche* (52), *Kiss Me Kate* (53), *Pal Joey* (57), *Love in Las Vegas/Vive Las Vegas* (63)

*SIEGEL, Donald DIR USA. (1912–) Skillful, and occasionally brilliant, director who started his career (1933) as a film editor and began directing B-films after the war. His two shorts both won Academy Awards. He is at his best creating elliptical thrillers dominated by psychopathic tensions: *Baby-Face Nelson, The Line Up, Crime in the Streets, The Killers*. His best film, *Invasion of the Body Snatchers*, could also lay justifiable claim to being one of the best science-fiction films, along with *The Incredible Shrinking Man*.

DIR: *Hitler Lives* (45) (short), *Star in the Night* (45) (short), *The Verdict* (46), *Night unto Night* (48), *The Big Steel* (49), *Duel at Silver Creek* (52), *No Time for Flowers* (52), *Count the Hours* (53), *China Venture* (54), *Riot in Cell Block Eleven* (54), *Private Hell 36* (54), *An Annapolis Story* (55), *Invasion of the Body Snatchers** (56), *Crime in the Streets* (56), *Baby-Face Nelson* (57), *Spanish Affair* (58), *The Line Up* (58), *The Gun Runners* (58), *Hound-Dog Man* (59), *Edge of Eternity* (59), *Flaming Star* (60), *Hell is for Heroes* (62), *The Killers** (64), *The Hanged Man* (65), *Madigan* (67), *Coogan's Bluff* (68), *Two Mules for Sister Sara* (69), *The Beguiled* (70), *Dirty Harry* (71).

SIODMAK, Robert (also Robert Siodmark) DIR USA/Germany/France. (Memphis Aug 8, 1900–) A director of undeniable skill who began as co-director of *Menschen am Sonntag** (Ger29) and many times almost touched brilliance — *Mister Flow* (Fr36), *The Killers** (USA 46), *Die Ratten* (Ger55) — but never quite managed to maintain this level. [Other notable films include: *Quick* (Ger32), *Mollenard* (Fr38), *Pièges* (Fr 39), *Son of Dracula* (USA43), *Phantom Lady* (USA44), *The Suspect* (USA44), *The Dark Mirror* (USA46), *Crisscross* (USA49), *The Crimson Pirate* (USA 52), *Le Grand jeu** (Fr/It53) (remake), *L'Affaire Nina B* (Fr61), *Escape from East Berlin/Tunnel 28* (GFR/USA62). His brother, Kurt (Curt) Siodmak (Dresden 1902–), also worked on *Menschen am Sonntag*, wrote a number of Hollywood horror films (*Frankenstein Meets the Wolf Man, Son of Dracula, The Beast with Five Fingers*, etc.) and has directed several mediocre horror films.]

SIRK, Douglas (Detlef Sierk) DIR USA/Germany. (Skagen, Denmark April 26, 1900–) Though not a creative film maker, he is a completely honest adaptor whose films are usually as good as their literary origins or the scripts based on them. His best film is *Written on the Wind* (56). He moved to Hollywood after scripting for UFA and directing eight films in Germany. He retired to Germany in 1960.

SJOBERG, Alf DIR Sweden. (Stockholm June 21, 1903–) Though not the equal of the "three Swedish masters," Sjöström, Stiller, and Bergman (all *q.v.*), he is a film maker of great talent. Like Bergman, he has also been a stage producer (since 1930) and has an instinctive feeling for the cinema. His failures, like *Barabbas* and *The Judge*, do not outweigh his at least three major works: *The Road to Heaven*, a fantasy, and the first film of the Forties to recall the great Swedish silent tradition; the oppressive *Torment/Frenzy*, which gave the young Bergman his first major chance as a scriptwriter; and especially his perfect Strindberg adaptation, *Miss Julie*.

DIR: *Den starkaste/The Strongest One* (29) (co-dir: Axel Lindholm), *Med livet som insats/They Staked Their Lives* (40), *Den blomstertid/Blossom Time* (40), *Hem fran Babylon/Home from Babylon* (41), *Himlaspelet/The Road to Heaven** (42), *Kungajakt/The Royal Hunt* (43), *Hets/Torment/Frenzy** (44), *Resan bort/Journey Out* (45), *Iris och Löjtnantshjärta/Iris and the Lieutenant* (46), *Bara en mor/Only a Mother* (49), *Fröken Julie/Miss Julie** (51), *Barabbas* (53), *Karin Mansdotter* (54), *Vildfagler/Wild Birds* (55), *Sista paret ut/Last Pair Out* (56), *Domaren/The Judge* (60), *On/The Island* (64, released 66), *Fadern/Father* (69).

SJOSTROM, Victor (also, in USA, Victor Seastrom) DIR Sweden/USA. (Silbodal, Värmland Sept 20, 1879–Stockholm Jan 3, 1960) He was the greatest Swedish director, surpassing his contemporary Stiller (*q.v.*) and also Bergman (*q.v.*), for whom he appeared in one last magnificent role — Professor Isak Borg in *Wild Strawberries**. As an actor, he resembled the films he directed: perhaps a little awkward and gauche, but profound, powerful and virile, impregnated with a deep and varied sense of humanity. A former stage actor and stage manager, he joined Svenska Bio in 1912 and made his acting debut in Stiller's *The Black Masks*. He had an instinctive feel for the cinema and, after *Ingeborg Holm* in 1913 (which could not then have been influenced by Ince), proved his mastery through his characterizations and his way of using sets and landscapes with an absolute stylistic economy. His individuality blossomed in 1916 with *Terje Vigen*, based on Ibsen's novel, and *Dödskyssen*, with its structured use of flashbacks. He then made a suite of epic Nordic sagas dominated by *The Outlaw and His Wife* (17), which Delluc praised as "the most beautiful film in the world." Selma Lagerlöf provided the basis for *The Girl from the Stormy Croft* (17), *Ingmarsönerna* (18), *Karin Ingmarsdotter* (19) and his most famous (though not his best) film *The Phantom Chariot* (20), in which he made masterful use of superimpositions, flashbacks, and the intermingling of fantasy and reality. At that time Léon Moussinac wrote: "He has attained an encompassing lyricism, unknown until now on the screen: tragic stillness, noble and potent serenity of some scenes. Though he tries to hypnotize us with the tragic dream of his *Phantom Chariot* or to move us with the grandeur and mystique of *Love's Crucible*, he never fails to draw out the gentle, pervasive force of familial intimacy and of the nuances of feelings externalized through a gesture or an illuminating expression. His films are for the most part freely elaborated etchings." He later accepted a gilded exile in Hollywood from 1923–30 and, though he had to accept several mediocre subjects, he took his inspiration from American realities for *The Scarlet Letter* (26) and *The Wind* (28), films that matched his greatest Swedish successes. He returned to Sweden but directed only one more film there and one in England; he spent the remainder of his life as an actor.
DIR: *Trädgardsmästern/The Gardener* (12), *Ett hemligt Giftermal/A Secret Marriage* (12), *Löjen och tara/Smiles and Tears* (12), *Blodets röst/Voice of the Blood* (12), *Lady Marions sommarflit/Lady Marion's Summer Flirtation* (12), *En sommarsaga/A Summer Tale* (12), (unreleased), *Äktenskapsbryan/The Marriage Agency* (12), *Ingeborg Holm** (13), *Prasten/The Priest* (13), *Halvblod/Half-Breed* (13), *Det var i Maj/It Was in May* (13), *Miraklet/The Miracle* (13), *Kärlek starkare än hat/Love Stronger Than Hate* (13), *Pa livets ödesvägar/On the Fateful Roads of Life* (13), *Dömen Icke/Do Not Judge* (14), *Bra flicka reder sig själv/A Clever Girl Takes Care of Herself* (14), *Gatans barn/Children of the Street* (14), *Högfjällets dotter/Daughter of the Mountain* (14), *Hjärtan som mötas/Meeting Hearts* (14), *Strejken/The Strike* (14), *En av de manga/One of the Many* (14), *Sonad oskuld/Expiated Guilt* (14), *Skomakare bliv vid din läst/Cobbler Stick to Your Last* (15), *Judaspengar/Traitors Reward/Judas Money* (15), *Landshövdingens dottrar/The Governor's Daughters* (15), *Rösen pa tistelön/The Rose of Thistle Island* or *Hausgammar/Sea Vulture* (15), *I prövningens stund/Hour of Trial* (15), *Skepp som mötas/Ships That Meet* (15), *Hon segrade/She Conquered* (15), *Thérèse* (16), *Dödskyssen/The Kiss of Death** (16, released 17), *Terje Vigen/A Man There Was* (16, released 17), *Berg-Ejvind och hans hustru/The Outlaw and His Wife** (17), *Tösen fran stormytorpet/The Girl from the Stormy Croft/The Girl from the Marsh Croft* (17), *Ingmarsönerna*, Parts I and II/*The Sons of Ingmar* (18), *Hans nads testamente/His Grace's Will* (19), *Klostret i Sendomir/The Monastery of Sendomir* (19), *Karin Ingmarsdotter/Karin, Daughter of Ingmar** (20), *Körkarlen/The Phantom Chariot/Thy Soul Shall Bear Witness/Clay** (20), *Mästerman/Master Samuel* (20), *Vem dömer/Love's Crucible* (20, released 22), *Eld ombord/Fire on Board/The Hell Ship* (22), *Det omringade huset/The Surrounded House* (22), *Name the Man* (USA23), *He Who Gets Slapped* (24), *Confessions of a Queen* (25), *The Tower of Lies* (25), *The Scarlet Letter** (26), *The Divine Woman* (27), *The Wind** (28), *Masks of the Devil* (28), *A Lady to Love* (USA30),

Markurells fran wadköping (Swed30) (also German version *Väter und Söhne*), *Under the Red Robe* (Brit37).

SKLADANOWSKY, Max INVENTOR Germany. (Berlin April 30, 1863–Berlin Nov 30, 1939) Inventor and pioneer whose elaborate system of projection, the *Bioskop*, was given its first public presentation as part of a music hall performance at the Berlin Wintergarten on February 1, 1895 – long before that of Lumière's (*q.v.*) *Cinématographe* – but it was too complicated and cumbersome to be generally adopted.

*SKOLIMOWSKI, Jerzy (Yurek) DIR Poland/ Belgium/Britain, etc. (Warsaw May 5, 1938–) Undoubtedly one of the most significant film-making talents to emerge in the Sixties, a director with an idiosyncratic vision of the pressures of modern urban life. He is also a poet, playwright, scriptwriter, and actor, was a boxer at his university, and studied at Lodz after graduation. His first films, *Rysopsis* and *Walkover*, seemed derivative of Godard (*q.v.*), but in the symbolic fantasy, *Barrier*, his individuality was evident; its surrealist streak was developed further in *Le Départ*. Apart from this, however, his extra-Polish work has been disappointing, though *Deep End* has something of his earlier touch. He has recently returned to Poland.
DIR: *Boxing* (61), *Rysopsis/Identification Marks: None* (64), *Walkover* (65), *Bariera/Barrier** (66), *Le Départ* (Belg 67), *Rece do gory/Hands Up!* (Pol-67, not released 71), *Dialog 20-40-60* (Czech68), *The Adventures of Gérard* (Brit/It/Switz70), *Deep End* (GFR/USA70).
SCEN: Wajda's *Innocent Sorcerers,* Polanski's *Knife in the Water,* and all his own films.

SKOURAS, Spyros P. PROD USA. (Skourohorian, Greece March 28, 1893–1971) Poor immigrant who built his fortune through a chain of theaters, joined Paramount in 1931 to supervise its theaters, and the following year moved to Fox. In 1942 he became president of 20th Century-Fox and is most famous for his introducing CinemaScope in 1953. Unable to maintain the studio's prosperity, he was removed from power in 1962 after the extravagance of the *Cleopatra** production. Thus he himself became a victim of the star system on which he had once built his power. He was replaced as president by Darryl F. Zanuck (*q.v.*).

*SLOCOMBE, Douglas PHOTOG Britain. (1913–) Excellent British cameraman who shot many of the most notable Ealing films and has more recently collaborated on Losey's (*q.v.*) *The Servant* and several films on which his color work is admirable.
PHOTOG (notably): for Cavalcanti, *et al. Dead of Night** (45); for Charles Crichton, *Hue and Cry** (47), *The Lavender Hill Mob** (51), *The Titfield Thunderbolt* (53); for Robert Hamer, *It Always Rains on Sunday** (47), *Kind Hearts and Coronets** (51); for Basil Dearden, *Saraband for Dead Lovers* (48), *Cage of Gold* (50); for Mackendrick, *The Man in the White Suit** (51), *A High Wind in Jamaica* (65); for Sidney Furie, *The Young Ones* (61); for Bryan Forbes, *The L-Shaped Room* (62); for John Huston, *Freud* (62); for Losey, *The Servant** (63), *Boom* (68); for Polanski, *Dance of the Vampires* (67); for Anthony Harvey, *The Lion in Winter* (68); for Ken Russell, *The Music Lovers* (70); for Peter Yates, *Murphy's War* (71).

SMITH, George Albert INVENTOR/DIRECTOR Britain. (Brighton 1864–Brighton 1959) The most remarkable pioneer film maker of the Brighton school, who was, with James Williamson (*q.v.*), the first to make systematic use of inserted close-ups in a complete sequence in at least four films between 1900 and 1903 (*Grandma's Reading Glass, The Little Doctor, At Last That Awful Tooth,* etc.), long before James Stuart Blackton (*q.v.*) and D. W. Griffith (*q.v.*). [He was originally a portrait photographer, built his first film camera in 1896, and in 1897 patented double exposure and began making trick films. In 1900 he built a studio in St. Anne's Well Garden. He began developing the Kinemacolor two-color system in 1902 and patented it in 1906, though it was not exploited commercially – by Urban (*q.v.*) – until 1909–14. It failed to become fully established because it required a special projector running at 32 f.p.s. By 1910 both Smith and Williamson found it impossible to compete with the expanding production in London and went out of business.]

DIR (notably): *Hanging Out the Clothes* (1897), *The Miller and the Sweep* (1897), *X-Rays* (1897), *Tipsy Topsy Turvey* (1897), *The Haunted Castle* (1897), *The Baker and the Sweep* (1898), *The Corsican Brothers* (1898), *Cinderella* (1898), *Faust and Mephistopheles* (1898), *Photographing a Ghost* (1898), *Santa Claus* (1898), *Comic Faces* (1898), *The Legacy* (1899), *A Good Joke* (1899), *The Haunted Picture Gallery* (1899), *Aladdin and the Wonderful Lamp* (1899), *Let Me Dream Again* (00), *Grandma Threading Her Needle* (00), *The Two Old Sports* series (00), *The House That Jack Built* (00), *Grandmas's Reading Glass* (00), *The Old Maid's Valentine* (00), *At Last This Awful Tooth* (02), *After Dark* (02), *The Little Doctor/The Sick Kitten* (03), *Mary Jane's Mishap* (03), *John Bull's Hearth* (03), *Dorothy's Dream* (03), *The Free Trade Branch* (04), *The Little Witness* (05), *A Visit to the Seaside* (08), *Natural Color Portraiture* (09), *Kinemacolor Puzzle* (09).

SOFFICI, Mario DIR Argentina. (Florence May 14, 1900–) The best Argentinian film maker of the 1935–45 period, notable for *Viento Norte* (37), *Prisioneros de la Terra** (39), and *Heroes sin Fama* (40), films portraying Argentinian realities with an authenticity and a particular social sense unusual in his country.

SOLDATI, Mario DIR Italy. (Turin Nov 17, 1906–) Although he was one of the most notable "decorative" directors, he made a major contribution to the renaissance of the Italian cinema with *Picolo mondo antico* (40) and *Malombra* (42). Since then he has not always made films that reflect his lively intelligence, his talents as a writer (he is also a novelist), and his love of the cinema, but *La Provinciale* (52) was a real achievement. He was second unit director on Vidor's *War and Peace** and scripted several of Mario Camerini's (*q.v.*) films in the Thirties.

***SOLTNTSEVA, Yulia** DIR USSR. (1901–) Widow of Dovzhenko (*q.v.*) who collaborated closely with him and has filmed several of his scripts since his death.

SPAAK, Charles SCEN France. (Brussels April 25, 1903–) Scriptwriter who, with Jacques Prévert (*q.v.*), contributed the most to the development of French poetic realism in writing for Feyder, *Le Grand jeu, La Kermesse héroïque, Pension Mimosas;* for Renoir, *La Grande Illusion;* for Grémillon, *La Petite Lise;* for Duvivier, *La Bandera, La Belle équipe.* He has said: "I have worked with more than 40 different directors. I have worked on a hundred completed films and forty that were not produced. That gives you the proportion of subjects that are abandoned. I reget that no film history has devoted a chapter to works that were not made. I assure you that these are the best that Prévert, Jeanson, Aurenche (all *q.v.*), and I conceived." "I have always maintained that scripts should be original and not adaptations. We consider there are neither secrets nor theories. Only critics and bad film makers have those. Everyone reacts according to his emotions. It's a game that takes place between authors, directors, actors and, in the end, the public. There are people who play well, people who play badly, people who cheat." "I have written no films about love. I have always been concerned with a man of good will facing problems that outstrip him: *La Grande Illusion* is typical."
SCEN (notably): for Feyder, *Les Nouveaux Messieurs** (28), *Le Grand jeu** (34), *Pension Mimosas** (35), *La Kermesse héroïque** (35); for Grémillon, *La Petite Lise* (30), *Gueule d'amour* (37), *L'Etrange Monsieur Victor* (38), *Le Ciel est à vous** (43); for Duvivier, *La Bandera** (35), *La Belle équipe** (36), *La Fin du jour* (39), *Un tel père et fils* (40), *Panique* (46); for Renoir, *Les Bas-Fonds** (36), *La Grande Illusion** (37); for Christian-Jaque, *L'Assassinat du Père Noël* (41), *D'homme à hommes* (48), *Adorables créatures* (52); for Daquin, *Patrie* (45); for Georges Lampin, *L'Idiot* (46), *Crime et châtiment* (56); for Cayatte, *Justice est faite** (50), *Nous sommes tous des assassins** (52), *Avant le déluge** (54), *Le Dossier noir* (55); for Carné, *Thérèse Raquin** (53), *Les Tricheurs* (58); for Henri Decoin, *Charmants garçons* (57); for Jean Dréville, *Normandie-Niémen* (60); for Philippe de Broca, *Cartouche* (61); for Nicolas Gessner, *Un milliard dans un brilliard/Diamonds Are Brittle* (65).

STAHL, John M. DIR USA. (New York Jan 21, 1886–1950) The director of several dozen films in a Hollywood career that started in 1914. He specialized in sentimental "women's pictures" and made many weep with the star vehicles *Back Street* (32), *Imitation of Life* (34), and *Magnificent Obsession* (35) – all remade recently. He made an equal number yawn with his adaptations, *The Keys of the Kingdom* (44), *The Foxes of Harrow* (47), and *The Walls of Jericho* (48).

STAMPFER, (General) Simon Ritter von INVENTOR Austria. (? – ?) Geometrician who developed an apparatus for viewing moving images – the *Stroboscope* – at the same time as, but independently of, Plateau (*q.v.*).

STAREVITCH, Ladislas (Wladyslaw Starewicz) ANIM USSR/France. (Poland Aug 6, 1892–Paris March 1965) Maker of puppet films who began his career in pre-Revolutionary Russia using stop motion to animate modeled figures (almost always jointed reproductions of insects) and later in France upheld the art of the puppet film although Disney-type cartoons dominated the market between the two wars. His films, made with perfect competence and much ingenuity, had characters and backgrounds that were somewhat mannered and involved.
ANIM (notably): *The Beautiful Leukanida* (USSR12), *Happy Scenes from Family Life* (12), *Aviation Week among the Insects* (12), *The Cameraman's Revenge* (12), *The Christmas at the Fox's Boarding House* (12), *The Dragonfly and the Ant* (USSR13), *Les Grenouilles qui demandent un roi* (Fr23), *La Petite chanteuse des rues* (23), *La Voix du rossignol* (23), *Le Rat de ville et le Rat des champs* (24), *La Cigale et la Fourmi* (24), *Les Griffes d'Araignée* (25), *L'Epouvantail* (25), *L'Horloge magique* (26), *Amour noir et blanc* (26), *La Reine des papillons* (27), *La Lion et le Moucheron* (27), *Les Yeux du dragon* (27), *Le Mariage de Babylas* (28), *La Petite Parade* (29), *Fétiche* (33) (live action and puppets), *Le Roman de Renart* (28–39) (feature), *Zanzabelle à Paris* (49), *Fleur de Fougère* (50).
DIR (live action): *Strashnaya mest/A Terrible Revenge* (USSR13), *Ruslan i ludmila* (USSR14), *Zhitel nyeobitayemovo ostrova/Inhabitant of a Desert Isle* (USSR15), *Na varshavskom trakte/On the Warsaw Highway* (USSR16), *Jola* (USSR20).

STAUDTE, Wolfgang Georg DIR German Democratic Republic/German Federal Republic. (Saarbrücken Oct 9, 1906–) One of the most important postwar German directors, with Käutner (*q.v.*) and Dudow (*q.v.*), and the first to make an impact after the war with his famous *Murderers Are Among Us* (46), a study of the problem of de-Nazification, and *Rotation* (49), the story of a Berlin worker during Nazism and the war, 1930–45. His films are often socially committed with a forceful style. He has a feeling for satire (but less for comedy) as he demonstrated in the GDR with *Der Untertan* and in the GFR with *Roses for the Prosecutor*. His work is not all of equal quality, but he is nonetheless a notable film maker. He began his career as a stage actor under Reinhardt (*q.v.*) and Erwin Piscator (*q.v.*), began film acting in 1931 (including *Jud Süss**) and scripted and/or directed commercials and shorts before making his first feature in 1943. He has scripted many of his own films.
DIR: *Akrobat schö-ö-ön* (43), *Ich hab' von Dir geträumt* (44), *Frau über Bord/Kabine* 27 (45) (not released), *Die Mörder sind unter Uns* (GDR46), *Die Seltsamen Abenteuer des Herrn Fridolin B.* (GDR48), *Rotation* (GDR49), *Schicksal aus zweiter Hand* (GDR49), *Der Untertan/The Kaiser's Lackey* (GDR51), *Die Geschichte des kleinen Muck* (GDR53), *Leuchtfeuer* (GDR54), *Ciske – Ein Kind braucht Liebe* (GFR/Neth55), *Rose Bernd* (GFR57), *Kanonen – Serenade* (GFR/It58), *Madeleine und der Legionär* (GFR58), *der Maulkorb* (GFR58), *Rosen für den Staatsanwalt* (GFR59), *Kirmes* (GFR60), *Der Letzte Zeuge* (GFR60), *Die Glücklichen Jahre der Thorwalds* (GFR62) (co-dir: John Olden), *Die Dreigroschenoper** (GFR/Fr63) (remake), *Herrenpartie* (GFR/Yugos64), *Das Lamm* (GFR64), *Ganovenehre* (GFR66), *Heimlichkeiten* (GFR68).

STAWINSKI, Jerzy Stefan SCEN/DIR Poland. (1921–) Scriptwriter and popular novelist most closely associated with the Ford-Wajda-Munk (all *q.v.*) school of the Fifties; he is also a popular novelist and began his directing career in the Sixties.

[SCEN (notably): for Munk, *Man on the Track** (57), *Eroica** (57), *Bad Luck* (60); for Wajda, *Kanal** (56); for Witold Lesiewicz, *The Deserter* (58); for Passendorfer, *Answer to Violence* (58), *Signals* (59); for Ford, *Knights of the Teutonic Order* (60); for Wanda Jakubowska, *It Happened Yesterday* (60); for Wojciech Has, *How To Be Loved* (62); and for all his own films. DIR: *Rozwodow nie bedzie/No More Divorces* (63), *Pingwin/The Penguin* (64), *Przedswiateczny wieczor/Christmas Eve* (66) (co-dir: H. Amiradzibi).]

STEBBINS, Robert pseud Meyers, Sidney (*q.v.*)

STEINER, Max MUS USA. (Vienna May 10, 1888–1972) Prolific Hollywood composer who was already well known as a concert pianist and composer when he became musical director of RKO in 1929. He is a typical Hollywood composer, both for his ability to create "tuneful" music in an imitative style and as a "Mickey Mouser" whose scores were linked closely with every minor action on the screen (as in cartoons). Jaubert (*q.v.*) characterized this in referring to *The Informer:* "Harmonic glug-glugs imitated the descent of the whisky down the hero's throat every time he took a drink."
[MUS (notably): for Cooper and Schoedsack, *King Kong** (33); for Ford, *The Lost Patrol** (34), *The Informer** (35), *The Searchers* (56); for Michael Curtiz, *The Charge of the Light Brigade* (36), *Casablanca** (42); for Wellman, *A Star is Born* (37); for Victor Fleming, *Gone With the Wind** (39); for Dieterle, *Dr. Ehrlich's Magic Bullet* (40); for John Cromwell, *Since You Went Away* (44); for Hawks, *Sergeant York** (41), *The Big Sleep** (46); for Florey, *The Beast with Five Fingers* (46); for Huston, *The Treasure of Sierra Madre** (47), *Key Largo* (48); for Vidor, *The Fountainhead* (48); for Rapper, *The Glass Menagerie* (50); for Dmytryk, *The Caine Mutiny* (54); for Raoul Walsh, *Battle Cry* (55), *Band of Angels* (57); for Delmar Daves, *The Hanging Tree* (59), *Parrish* (62), *Youngblood Hawke* (64).]

STEINHOFF, Hans DIR Germany. (Pfaffenhofen March 10, 1882–died in a plane crash 1945) A stage actor and director for many years, he began film directing in 1922; in 1933, at Goebbels's request, he attempted, unsuccessfully, to give the Nazi cinema its *Potemkin* with *Hitlerjunge Quex*. He was much in demand during the Nazi years and had more talent than his rival Veit Harlan (*q.v.*) as he demonstrated in his grandiloquent, but nonetheless relatively sound, films: *Robert Koch, der Bekämpfer des Todes* (39), *Die Geierwally* (40), *Ohm Krüger* (41). This latter film dealt with the Boer War and stigmatized the British for their concentration camps, which were on the lines of those Hitler himself was building.

*STEKLY, Karel DIR Czechoslovakia. (Prague Oct 9, 1903–) Veteran Czech director and prewar scriptwriter (from 1933), he directed the first postwar Czech feature and won the Grand Prix at Venice for his *Sirena/The Strike* (47). His later work, often literary adaptations, never attained the standard of this success.

STERN, Kurt Berlin Sept 18, 1907–) *and* **Jeanne** (Paris Aug 20, 1908–) SCEN German Democratic Republic. The best scriptwriters of the GDR cinema, notable especially for Dudow's *Stärker als die Nacht* (54) and a feature documentary on the Spanish Civil War, *Unbändiges Spanien* (62).

STERNBERG, Josef von (Josef Stern) DIR USA. (Vienna May 29, 1894–Hollywood Dec 22, 1969) One of the strongest individual talents of the cinema from 1925–35 whose muse was the angel of the bizarre: "The artist is the officiating priest who proffers beauty and his sense of beauty can manifest itself in a bizarre way." Certain of his films were paeans to femininity, to a reborn Nana, to a divinity enshrined in the alluring Marlene Dietrich and viewed against backgrounds as frenzied in their designs as a 17th-century Austrian baroque chapel dedicated to the Virgin Mary. [Though born in Vienna (without the "von"), he was brought to the USA at the age of seven; he spent his school years in Vienna and returned to the USA to work for the World Film Company. During the First World War he made training films for the Army Signal Corps; from 1921–24 he was, variously, technical assistant, scenarist, and cameraman in New York, London, and Hollywood, notably on Roy William Neill's *By Divine Right* (24),

and *Vanity's Price* (24).] His directorial debut was on the independent, experimental *The Salvation Hunters* (25), a film based on the principles of *Kammerspiel*. After several abortive projects, including the unreleased *The Sea Gull* for Chaplin, he achieved international fame with *Underworld* (27) and its new kind of antihero, the gangster. The *Kammerspiel* influence apparent in this film was even more evident in *The Docks of New York* (28), recounting the encounter of a stevedore and a prostitute. His only German film, *The Blue Angel* (30), marked a turning point in his career, for it was while working on this film about the downfall of a high-minded teacher that he discovered an obscure actress, Marlene Dietrich, and transformed her into a new kind of temptress. But, as with Frankenstein, the creator was gradually taken over by what he had created. He abandoned the everyday, sometimes populist, world that had earlier interested him in order to transform her into an adventuress, spy, *femme fatale,* Venus, or empress — but always a woman who played with men like puppets: *Morocco, Dishonored, Shanghai Express, The Blond Venus, The Scarlet Empress, The Devil is a Woman.* His visually elegant dramas ended by not being profitable; his star was put in the care of other directors and he himself practically eliminated from film-making. However, the spectre of the eternal seductress continued to haunt him in *The Shanghai Gesture* (41) and *The Saga of Anatahan.* Apart from these, several of his films were interfered with by producers, others were routine commercial assignments; various projects were abandoned, including the ambitious *I, Claudius.* "When I became aware," the stylist has said, "that the best intentions of a film maker were thwarted by human beings, I told myself I was chary of using the cinema, a means of expression involving human beings, in place of colors the painter uses in his palette, the director's materials not being malleable and often even rebellious. My background was in another world than that of films: that of literature and the plastic arts, which I have tried to transpose into my work."
DIR: *The Salvation Hunters** (25), *The Sea Gull/Women of the Sea** (26) (unreleased), *Underworld** (27), *The Last Command* (28), *The Dragnet* (28), *The Docks of New York** (28), *The Case of Lena Smith* (28), *Thunderbolt* (29), *Der Blaue Engel/The Blue Angel** (Ger 30), *Morocco* (30), *Dishonored* (31), *An American Tragedy** (31), *Shanghai Express** (32), *The Blond Venus* (32), *The Scarlet Empress* (34), *The Devil is a Woman** (35), *Crime and Punishment* (35), *The King Steps Out* (36), *Sergeant Madden* (39), *The Shanghai Gesture* (41), *The Town* (43–44) (short), *Jet Pilot* (50, released 57) (largely re-edited by Howard Hughes), *Macao* (52) (largely reshot by Nicholas Ray), *The Saga of Anatahan* (53).
[Other work: *Heaven on Earth/Exquisite Sinner* (25) (reshot by Phil Rosen from Sternberg's script), *The Masked Bride* (25) (abandoned; completed by W. Christy Cabanne); directed some scenes of *It* (27) (dir: Clarence Budger), *Children of Divorce* (27) (dir: Frank Lloyd); scenario for *The Street of Sin* (28) (dir: Stiller; completed by Ludwig Berger); recut Stroheim's *The Wedding March** (28); directed *I, Claudius* (37) (abandoned); consultant and director on some scenes of Vidor's *Duel in the Sun** (46).]

STEVENS, George DIR USA. (Oakland, California Dec 18, 1904–) Some American critics include him among the greatest modern directors; many French critics consider him worthless. Between these two extremes lies a real assessment of his talents as a director with probity and social conscience. Though his work in the Thirties and Forties is relatively minor, an undeniable talent is evident in *A Place in the Sun, Shane,* and *Giant.* Though he failed badly in his conception of Europe in *The Diary of Anne Frank,* he offered a series of accurate social portraits of his own country in the aforementioned films and in *The Only Game in Town.* [He began his career in 1910 as a child actor in the father's troupe, moved to Hollywood in 1923, and around 1928 became a cameraman and scriptwriter for Hal Roach (q.v.), working on several Laurel and Hardy shorts. He disowns all his films before *Alice Adams.*]
DIR: *The Cohens and the Kellys in Trouble* (33), *Bachelor Bait* (34), *Kentucky Kernels* (34), *The Nitwits* (35), *Alice Adams* (35), *Annie Oakley* (35), *Swing Time* (36), *Quality Street* (37), *A Damsel in Distress** (37), *Vivacious*

Lady (38), *Gunga Din* (39), *Vigil in the Night* (40), *Penny Serenade* (41), *Woman of the Year* (42), *The Talk of the Town* (42), *The More the Merrier* (43), *I Remember Mama* (47), *A Place in the Sun** (51), *Something to Live For* (52), *Shane** (53), *Giant** (56), *The Diary of Anne Frank* (59), *The Greatest Story Ever Told* (65), *The Only Game in Town* (69).

STIGLIC, France DIR Yugoslavia. (Ljubljana 1919–) Slovenian film maker with a lyrical approach to war themes, his international reputation as one of the best modern Yugoslav directors rests on *The Valley of Peace* and *The Ninth Circle*. A former journalist and actor, he directed several postwar documentaries before making his first feature in 1948. DIR: *Na svoji zemlji/On His Own Ground* (48), *Svet na Kajzarju/People of Kajzarje* (52), *Volca noc/Living Nightmare* (55), *Dolina Miru/The Valley of Peace** (56), *Viza na zloto/The False Passport* (58), *Deveti krug/The Ninth Circle** (60), *Balada o trobenti i oblaku/The Ballad of the Trumpet and the Cloud* (61), *Tistega lepega dne/That Fine Day* (63), *Ne joci Petre/Don't Cry, Peter* (65), *Amandus* (66).

STILLER, Mauritz (Mosche/Mowscha Stiller) DIR Sweden/USA. (Helsinki July 17, 1883–Stockholm Nov 8, 1928) Great Swedish film maker of the silent period, second only to Sjöström, and his equal in creating (though with a different style) epic national sagas: *Sir Arne's Treasure, Gunnar Hede's Saga,* and *The Saga of Gösta Berling,* all adapted from the novels of Selma Lagerlöf. His adaptations from the novels of Lagerlöf and others were particularly brilliant, with their subtly individualized yet typical heroes playing out their dramas against landscapes that themselves became characters in the drama. [Born in Finland of Russian-Jewish parents, he moved to Sweden in 1904 in order to avoid being drafted into the Russian army, became an actor, and then a director of the Lilla Teatern in Stockholm. He joined Charles Magnusson's Svenska Biograf studios around 1912 and directed, wrote, and acted in his first film in the same year. He directed some forty short films between 1912–18, mostly sensational thrillers and comedies that were often based on inferior novels or folksy peasant dramas.

Many of them, however, were visually imaginative. International recognition came first with *The Song of the Scarlet Flower* (18), a characteristic Stiller film in its use of landscape, epic qualities, and physical action.] *Sir Arne's Treasure* (19), with its ship trapped in the ice and its round tower, *Gunnar Hede's Saga,* with its reindeer herd in the snowy landscape and its Lady of Grief, and *The Saga of Gösta Berling,* with its estate and 1820 atmosphere, placed him in the front rank of the world's directors. He was equally masterful on sophisticated erotic comedies with elegant sets and costumes. Most notable of these was *Erotikon* (20), a brilliant witty comedy about love, influenced both by central European risqué stage dramas and the Hollywood films of Cecil B. DeMille (*q.v.*) and Douglas Fairbanks. In its turn it influenced the development of Hollywood sophisticated comedies and particularly the films of Ernst Lubitsch (*q.v.*). In 1924 Louis B. Mayer (*q.v.*) invited him and his protegé, Greta Garbo, to Hollywood. But the film capital destroyed him. [From his arrival in July 1925 until mid-1926, MGM gave him no work; he was assigned to direct Garbo in *The Temptress,* then removed; he left MGM for Paramount and made his only worthwhile Hollywood film, the elegant *Hotel Imperial* (27) with Pola Negri. Then his health failed and after the uninteresting *Woman on Trial* and the abortive *Barbed Wire* (on which he was replaced), his illness forced him to abandon *Street of Sin* (written by Sternberg) and return, sick and disappointed, to Sweden, where he died some months later.] Stiller's work was as delicate as Sjöström's was massive: "He plays with black and white with the subtle concentration of a troubadour. He is to the silent art something of what Charles d'Orléans and Louise Collet were to the art of verse. At times one fancies him playing arpeggios with lights softly echoing I know not what melodious chords" (Delluc). DIR: *Mor och dotter/Mother and Daughter* (12), *De Svarta Maskerna/The Black Masks* (12), *Den Tyraniske Fästmannen/The Despotic Fiancé* (12), *Vampyren/The Vampire* (12), *Barnet/The Child* (13), *När kärleken dödar/When Love Kills* (13), *När larmlockan ljuder/When the Tocsin Calls* (13), *När svärmor regerar/When Mother-in-Law Dictates*

(13, released 14), *Livets konflikter/Life's Conflicts* (13), *Moderna suffragetten/ The Modern Suffragette* (13), *Den Okända/The Unknown Women* (13), *Mannekängen/The Fashion Model* (13), *Bröderna/The Brothers* (13, released 14), *Gränsfolken/Frontier People* (14), *För sin körleks skull/Because of Love* (14), *Kammarjunkaren/The Chamberlain* (14), *Stormfaglen/Stormy Petrel* (14), *Skottet/The Shot* (14), *Det Röda Tornet/The Red Tower* (14), *När konstnärer älska/When Artists Love* (14), *Lekkamraterna/Playmates* (15), *Hans Hustrus förflutna/His Wife's Past* (15), *Dolken/The Dagger* (15) (banned by censors), *Mästertjuven/The Master Thief* (15), *Madame de Thebes* (15), *Hämnaren/The Revenger* (15), *Minlotsen/The Mine-Pilot* (15), *Hans Bröllopsnatt/Äventyret/His Wedding Night/ The Adventure* (16), *Lyckonalen/The Lucky Brooch* (16), *Kärlek och jorunalistik/Love and Journalism* (16), *Vingarna/Wings* (16), *Kampen om hans hjärta/The Fight for His Heart* (16), *Balettprimadonnan/Wolo/The Ballerina* (16), *Thomas Graals bästa film/Thomas Graal's Best Film/Wanted — an Actress* (17), *Alexander den store/Alexander the Great* (17), *Thomas Graals bästa barn/Thomas Graal's First Child* (18), *Sangen om den eldröda blomman/Song of the Scarlet Flower/The Flame of Life* (18, released 19), *Fiskebyn/The Fishing Village/The Vengeance of Jacob Vindas* (19, released 20), *Herr Arnes Pengar/ Sir Arne's Treasure** (19), *Erotikon** (20), *Johan* (20), *De Landsflyktige/ the Emigrants/The Exiles* (21), *Gunnar Hedes Saga/The Old Mansion/The Judgement** (22, released 23), *Gösta Berlings Saga/The Saga of Gösta Berling** (23, released 24), *The Temptress* (USA26) (replaced by Fred Niblo), *Hotel Imperial* (26), *The Woman on Trial* (27), *Barbed Wire* (27) (replaced by Rowland Lee), *The Street of Sin* (28), (abandoned; continued by Lothar Mendes; completed by Ludwig Berger). SCEN: for Sjöström, *The Gardener* (12), *On the Fateful Roads of Life* (13).

STORCK, Henri DIR Belgium. (Ostend Sept 5, 1907–) The best Belgian documentarist over the whole of his career, from the Vertovian *L'Histoire du soldat inconnu** (30), the reportages, *Idylle à la plage* (31), *Images d'Ostende* (32), *Borinage** (33) (co-dir: Ivens), *Les*

Maisons de la misère (38), and the dramatized *Les Carrefours de la vie* (49), to his films on art, *Le Monde de Paul Delvaux* (46) and *Rubens* (48). He also edited John Fernhout's *Easter Island* (34) and has worked on fiction films.

*STRADLING, Harry PHOTOG USA/France/ Britain. (Newark, New Jersey Sept 1, 1901–Hollywood Feb 1970) Accomplished Hollywood cameraman whose career spanned fifty years and many dozens of films, especially notable for his work in Europe in the Thirties and his color work in Hollywood in later years on such films as *Auntie Mame, Guys and Dolls, My Fair Lady, Funny Girl,* and *Hello Dolly.* He began as assistant cameraman at the age of 16 and shot his first films in 1920. In 1929 he went to France to assist in the introduction of sound there and worked both as cameraman and occasional director. He worked for Alexander Korda (*q.v.*) for four years before returning to Hollywood in late 1939. He is the nephew of Hollywood pioneer cameraman, Walter Stradling.

PHOTOG (notably): for Kenneth Webb, *The Devil's Garden* (20), *The Great Adventure* (20), for Feyder, *Le Grand jeu** (Fr34), *La Kermesse héroïque** (Fr35), *Knight without Armour* (Brit37), for Asquith, *Pygmalion** (Brit38), for Thornton Freeland, *Over the Moon* (Brit 39), for Vidor, *The Citadel* (Brit38), for Hitchcock, *Jamaica Inn* (Brit39), *Mr. and Mrs. Smith* (41), *Suspicion* (42), for Charles Vidor, *My Son, My Son* (40), *Hans Christian Andersen* (52), for Garson Kanin, *They Knew What They Wanted* (40), for Gregory Ratoff, *Intermezzo* (39), *The Corsican Brothers* (41), *Song of Russia* (43), for Richard Thorpe, *White Cargo* (42), for Clarence Brown, *The Human Comedy* (43), *Song of Love* (47), for Albert Lewin, *The Picture of Dorian Grey* (45), for Kazan, *Sea of Grass* (47), *A Streetcar Named Desire** (51), *A Face in the Crowd** (57), for Minnelli, *The Pirate* (48), *On a Clear Day You Can See Forever* (69), for Charles Walters, *Easter Parade* (48), *The Barkleys of Broadway* (49), *Walk, Don't Run* (66), for Robert Z. Leonard, *In the Good Old Summertime* (49), for Mark Robson, *I Want You* (51), for Preminger, *Angel Face* (52), for Irving Rapper, *Forever Female* (53), *Marjorie Morningstar*

(58), for Ray, *Johnny Guitar** (54), for Mankiewicz, *Guys and Dolls* (55), for Donen and George Abbott, *The Pajama Game* (57), for Morton da Costa, *Auntie Mame* (58), for Delmer Daves, *A Summer Place* (59), *Parrish* (61), for Delbert Mann, *The Dark at the Top of the Stairs* (60), for Mervyn LeRoy, *A Majority of One* (61), *Gypsy* (62), *Mary, Mary* (63), *Moment to Moment* (66), for Daniel Mann, *Five Finger Exercise* (62), for Cukor, *My Fair Lady** (64), for Richard Quine, *How to Murder Your Wife* (65), *Synanon/Get Off My Back* (65), for Wyler, *Funny Girl* (68), for Gene Kelly, *Hello Dolly* (69), for Herbert Ross, *The Owl and the Pussycat* (70) (completed by Andrew Laszlo).

*STRADLING, Harry, Jr. PHOTOG USA. (Yonkers, New York Jan 7, 1925–) Son of the preceding who began his career as his father's assistant and shot his first films in the late Sixties. He has tended to specialize in westerns (he is Burt Kennedy's favorite cameraman) and his work on *Little Big Man* especially is evidence of a major talent.
PHOTOG: for Burt Kennedy, *Welcome to Hard Times/Killer on a Horse* (67), *Support Your Local Sheriff* (68), *The Good Guys and the Bad Guys* (68), *Young Billy Young* (69), *Dirty Dingus Magee* (70), *Support Your Local Gunfighter* (70), for Jerry Paris, *How Sweet It Is* (68), for Howard Morris, *With Six You Get Egg Roll* (68), for Mankiewicz, *There Was a Crooked Man* (69), for Arthur Penn, *Little Big Man* (70).

STRAND, Paul DIR/PHOTOG USA. (New York Oct 16, 1890–) Brilliant still photographer with an acute sense of reality, a disciple of Alfred Stieglitz, who became in the Thirties one of the founders and leading figures in the independent New York film-making school. In 1921, with Charles Scheeler, he made the experimental hymn to New York, *Manhatta* (21), and throughout the Twenties worked as a freelance cameraman on newsreels and educational films. He was responsible for two works of major importance: *Native Land** (42) (co-dir: Leo Hurwitz; photog: Strand), an impassioned plea for workers' rights, and *Redes/The Wave** (Mex35) (prod/scen/photog: Strand; dir: Zinnemann,

Muriel), a dramatized documentary on the exploitation of fishermen and the first of an uncompleted series of films on Mexican life. In his proposal to the Mexican Government, Strand wrote: "We assume that these films are being made for the great majority of rather simple people to whom elementary facts should be presented in a direct and unequivocal way, a way that might bore more complicated sensibilities — though we believe otherwise." This approach was equally valid for Frontier Films, which Strand founded in 1936 as a cooperative with the poet David Wolff, Sidney Meyers, John Howard Lawson (all *q.v.*), Leo Hurwitz, and Irving Lerner. Others involved to a greater or lesser degree included Zinnemann, Herbert Kline, Willard Van Dyke, Elia Kazan (all *q.v.*) and Ralph Steiner. The group produced many notable films, but its efforts were interrupted by the war and later by McCarthyism; however, its influences were still evident after 1955, often in the work of other film makers. Strand himself co-photographed Lorentz's *The Plow That Broke the Plains* (36) (with Hurwitz and Steiner), co-directed *The Heart of Spain* (37) (with Leo Hurwitz) and *China Strikes Back* (39), and collaborated on *People of the Cumberland* (38) and *Return to Life* (38). He abandoned the cinema and left the USA after 1948 in order to devote himself to still photography.

STROHEIM, Erich von (Erich Oswald Stroheim) DIR USA. (Vienna Sept 22, 1885–Maurepas, France May 12, 1957) One of the greatest film makers of all time, although he rarely had the opportunity to direct as he wished. Independent, nonconformist, and legitimately proud of his creative talents, he was the victim of his own legend, slandered and bitterly hated; at the apogee of his talents he was forced to abandon directing entirely and earn his living by acting. A few years before his death he asked bitterly: "Am I really the most beloved and loathed director in the world?" [Born in Vienna, but the son of a Silesian Jewish hat manufacturer not (as he claimed) of an aristocratic father whose mother was lady-in-waiting to the Empress of Austria, he joined the Austrian Army (as a private soldier, not, as he claimed, as an officer), then apparently deserted and emigrated to the USA around 1906. (This debunking of the legend he carefully nurtured throughout his life rather increases one's admiration for the skill of his own films and the numerous roles he played that reflected his legendary youth.) Nothing is known of his first years in the USA, but in 1914 he began appearing as an extra in Hollywood films (Conway's *Captain McLean*) and in 1915 was an extra in Griffith's *Birth of a Nation* and John Emerson's *Ghosts* and *Old Heidelberg*.] John Emerson gave him his first opportunity as assistant director and military adviser and he later became Griffith's assistant. His early career as an actor quickly made him famous. Carl Laemmle (*q.v.*) gave him his directorial debut after the war on *Blind Husbands,* followed by *The Devil's Passkey* and the internationally successful *Foolish Wives,* all of which deal with the eternal triangle of obtuse husband, dissatisfied wife, and continental seducer. *Foolish Wives* was the first of his films to create problems for him with his producer: though made in 21 reels, the young producer, Irving Thalberg (*q.v.*), then with Universal, had it reduced to 14 for general release. A year later, Thalberg removed Stroheim from *Merry-Go-Round* and gave Rupert Julian the task of completing it. Then the Metro-Goldwyn Company engaged him to direct *Greed,* a major turning point in his career. At this time he considered: "The biggest handicap of the American cinema is its moral narrow-mindedness. Nevertheless, we are perfectly well aware that each of us is driven by ambition and failure, by temptation and dreams, by illusion and disillusion, which are the very framework of life" (1921). "The public at large is not as spiritually poor as the producers imagine. It wants to be shown life as real as it actually is for people: harsh, unexpected, hopeless, fatalistic. I intend to tailor my films in the rough fabric of human conflicts. Because to make films with the regularity of a sausage machine forces you to make them neither better nor worse than a string of sausages" (1925). But the "sausage machine" was more powerful than he. Irving Thalberg again stepped in, took the final cut of *Greed* out of Stroheim's hands, and turned it over to the pork butcher, June Mathis, to chop into pieces. His next film, *The Merry Widow,* was a box-office triumph, but he said in an interview: "When I saw how the cen-sors multilated my picture *Greed,* which I did really with my entire heart, I abandoned my ideals to create real art pictures . . . So I have to quit realism entirely . . . (the reason I make such pictures is) only because I do not want my family to starve." However, this film's commercial success enabled him to make the acerbic, ironic *The Wedding March.* This, too, was taken out of his hands and reduced by other hands (Sternberg's, with Stroheim's agreement), then split into two parts and further cut. His last major opportunity was *Queen Kelly,* a film of which only the first part was completed before talkies were introduced and Gloria Swanson abandoned the production. His only sound film, *Walking Down Broadway,* was largely reshot by another as *Hello Sister* and almost nothing of Stroheim is evident in it. That was the end of his directorial career; thereafter he returned to acting, creating many memorable roles in France and Hollywood. Before making *Greed* he wrote: "It is possible to tell a great story in motion pictures in such a way that the spectator . . . will come to believe that what he is looking at is real . . . Even as Dickens and Maupassant and Zola and Frank Norris catch and reflect life in their novels" — a statement that characterizes the qualities of the 19th-century novel intrinsic in his work. It is in this connection that André Bazin described him a "the creator of the virtually continuous cinematic story, tending to the permanent integration of the whole space . . . (he) rejects photographic expressionism and the tricks of montage . . . He has one simple rule for direction. Take a close look at the world, keep doing so, and in the end it will lay bare for you all its cruelty and its ugliness." Though his films contain sadomasochistic elements, they are nonetheless humanistic. If he showed crime, vice, misery, it was because it angered him that men could fall into these. His work is a continual indictment of society, particularly that of the "high society" of the Austro-Hungarian Empire. He denounced oppression, cynicism, and greed and the most typical symbol of these attitudes is that of the pseudo aristocrat thrown into the sewer at the end of *Foolish Wives.*

DIR: *Blind Husbands** (18), *The Devil's Passkey* (19), *Foolish Wives** (21), *Merry-Go-Round* (22) (replaced by

Rupert Julian), *Greed** (23–24), *The Merry Widow** (25), *The Wedding March** (26–28) (released in two parts: *The Wedding March, The Honeymoon*), *Queen Kelly** (28), *Walking Down Broadway/Hello Sister* (33) (remade by Sol Wurtzel).
[ASSIST: to John Emerson, *Old Heidelberg* (15), *The Social Secretary* (16), *Macbeth* (16), *Lesser Than the Dust* (16); to Griffith, *Intolerance** (16), *Hearts of the World** (18); to Allan Dwan, *Panthea* (17); to George Fitzmaurice, *Sylvia of the Secret Service* (17).]

STROYEVA, Vera DIR/SCEN USSR. (Kiev 1903–) Good Soviet director who has often scripted for, or collaborated with, her husband, Grigori Roshal (*q.v.*). After, notably, *Pokoleniye pobediteli/Generation of Conquerors* (36) and *Marite* (47), she tended to specialize in opera and dance films: *Bolshoi Koncert/Great Concert* (51), *Boris Godunov* (55), *Kovanchina* (59).

STURGES, John DIR USA. (Oak Park 1911–) Certainly not the more interesting of the two Sturges, but when working with a good script he has made several notable western, *Bad Day at Black Rock* (54), *Backlash* (56), *Gunfight at the O.K. Corral* (57), *The Law and Jake Wade* (58), and his best film, *The Magnificent Seven** (60). His other westerns are uninspired and, outside the western spaces, he has often fallen into complete mediocrity, as in *The Old Man and the Sea* (58). He was an editor and producer during 1932–42 period and directed several army documentaries during the war.

STURGES, Preston (Edmond P. Biden) DIR/SCEN USA. (Chicago Aug 29, 1898–New York Aug 6, 1959) Talented director of sharp, cynical satires incorporating something of the Mack Sennett (*q.v.*) tradition of broad visual burlesque, he revitalized the American comic tradition in the Forties. His films had nothing of the naïveté of Capra's (*q.v.*) and often pointedly satirized significant elements in American life: politics (*The Great McGinty*), the cult of riches (*Christmas in July*), small-town life (*The Miracle of Morgan's Creek*), the cult of heroism (*Hail the Conquering Hero*). His best film, *Sullivan's Travels,* was something

of a self-justification in its argument that comedy did more good than absolute social realism. In any case, after the end of the Roosevelt era, his talent seemed to fade away, apart from the stylish *Unfaithfully Yours*. He made only three Hollywood films after the end of the war before moving to France, where he directed one (mediocre) film and made "guest appearances" in two films. He had had a varied career (inventor, actor, song editor, playwright, etc.) before writing scripts and becoming, in 1933, staff writer for Paramount. Many of his films featured the same acting troupe.
DIR: *The Great McGinty** (40), *Christmas in July** (40), *The Lady Eve* (41), *Sullivan's Travels** (41), *Palm Beach Story* (42), *The Great Moment* (43), *The Miracle of Morgan's Creek* (43), *Hail the Conquering Hero** (44), *Mad Wednesday/The Sin of Harold Diddlebock* (47), *Unfaithfully Yours* (48), *The Beautiful Blonde from Bashful Bend* (49), *Les Carnets du Major Thompson* (Fr55).
[SCEN (notably): for W. K. Howard, *The Power and the Glory* (33); for Mamoulian, *We Live Again* (34); for Wyler, *The Good Fairy* (35); for M. Leisen, *Easy Living* (37); for James Whale, *Port of Seven Seas* (38) (adaptation of *Marius**); for Norman Taurog, *The Birds and the Bees* (56) (remake of *The Lady Eve*); and for most of his own films.]

SUCKSDORFF, Arne DIR Sweden. (Stockholm Feb 3, 1917–) One of the greatest modern documentarists, he has scripted, photographed and edited all his own shorts and features and is memorable above all for *Rhythm of a City* and *The Great Adventure*. He has a deep love of nature and, like his best compatriots (whether film makers or writers), he is a lyrical poet of nature, enchanted by the countryside, forests, the sea, towns, and the behavior of wild animals, birds, and people. Even more than his undoubted feeling for beautiful imagery, he has an instinctive sense of rhythm, both of art and of life.
DIR (shorts): *En Augustirapsodi/An August Rhapsody* (39), *Din tillvaros land/Your Own Land* (40), *Em sommarsaga/A Summer's Tale* (41), *Vinden fran vaster/Wind from the West* (43), *Sarvtid/Reindeer Time* (43), *Trut/The Gull* (44), *Gryning/Dawn* (45), *Skuggor*

over snon/Shadows on the Snow (45), *Manniskor i Stad/Rhythm of a City/ People of the City* (47), *Den Drömda dalen/Dream Valley* (47), *Uppbrott/ The Open Road/Moving On* (48), *En kluver warld/A Divided World* (48), *Strandhugg* (50), *Ett horn i norr/The Living Stream* (50), *Indisk by/Indian Village* (51), *Vinden och floden/The Wind and the River* (51).
DIR/PROD (features): *Det Stora äventyret/The Great Adventure** (53), *En djungelsaga/The Flute and the Arrow* (57), *Pojken i trädet/The Boy in the Tree* (61), *Mitt hem är Copacabana/ My Home is Copacabana* (65).

SUKARDI, Kotot DIR Indonesia. (? –) Film maker who contributed to the developing Indonesian cinema a sincere and authentic portrait of the aftermath of the colonial war: *Si Pitjang** (52).

SULLIVAN, C. Gardner SCEN USA. (Still Water, Minnesota Sept 18, 1879–Hollywood 1965) Notable pioneer Hollywood scriptwriter who made major contributions to the films of Thomas Ince (*q.v.*) and was one of the creators of the art of the western. According to his first biographer, Pierre Henri, he was responsible for "the mud in *Carmen of the Klondyke,* the prison in *Painted Soul,* the dead baby in *He Who Pays,* the bell in *Unlucky Star.* He had the advantage of having been a journalist; he knew how to live with his characters, to combine anecdote with images before writing the first word, to use the minimum possible characters and complications, to awaken the public's interest in the characters and the events of the story."
He wrote his first script in 1911 – *Her Polished Family* for Edison (*q.v.*) – and joined Ince in 1913. From 1914–17 he was head of Ince's scenario department, e.g., *The Battle of Gettysburg, The Typhoon, The Passing of Two-Gun Hicks, The Anger of the Gods, The Cup of Life, The No-Good Guy, Peggy, The Iron Strain, Hell's Hinges, Civilization*, the Aryan*, The Coward, Love's Torments, Expiation, Painted Soul, Carmen of the Klondyke, Lieutenant Danny, He Who Pays, Unlucky Star, Midnight Patrol, Between Men.*
[Also: for Fred Niblo, *Happy Though Married* (19), *Dangerous Hours* (20); for John Griffith Wray, *Hail the Woman* (22), *Human Wreckage* (23); for Sidney Franklin, *Dulcy* (23); for Rupert Julian, *Three Faces East* (26); for W. Beaudine, *Sparrows* (26); for Sam Taylor, *The Tempest* (28); for W. S. Van Dyke, *Cuban Love Song** (31); for Robert Z. Leonard, *Strange Interlude* (32); for DeMille, *The Buccaneer* (38), *Union Pacific** (39), *Northwest Mounted Police* (42).

TASHLIN, Frank DIR/SCEN USA. (Weehawken, New Jersey Feb 19, 1913–)
Good director of comedies, a former cartoonist who has retained in his live-action films something of the cartoon's sense of simplification and efficacious, fast pace. [He began as a cartoonist for Paul Terry (*q.v.*) in 1930 (*Aesop's Fables* series) and became a gag writer and scriptwriter for Hal Roach (*q.v.*) in 1933. He was the author of the "Van Boring" newspaper-strip cartoon, 1934–37. From 1935 to 1939 he scripted and/or directed Warners *Merry Melodies* and *Looney Tunes* cartoons and from 1939 to 1945 he was a story director at the Walt Disney (*q.v.*) studios. He scripted his first feature in 1945 and wrote some 15 films until 1950, when he directed his first film.] He has often worked with such major comedians as Bob Hope (*Lemon-Drop Kid, Son of Paleface, The Private Navy of Sgt. O'Farrell*), the Dean Martin–Jerry Lewis team (*Artists and Models, Hollywood or Bust*), Robert Cummings (*The First Time, Marry Me Again*), and especially Jerry Lewis until he began directing his own films (*Rock-a-bye Baby, The Geisha Boy, Cinderfella, It's Only Money, Who's Minding the Store, The Disorderly Orderly*). He has rarely touched satire, but with the ample Jayne Mansfield he offered delightful caricatures of the blonde as star in *The Girl Can't Help It* and *Will Success Spoil Rock Hunter?* However, he is more of a "court jester" with a gift for basic comedy and amusing tricks.
[SCEN (notably): for Arthur Lubin, *Delightfully Dangerous* (45); for Norman Z. McLeod, *The Paleface* (48); for W. Seiter, *One Touch of Venus* (48); for Lloyd Bacon, *Miss Grant Takes Richmond* (49), *The Fuller Brush Girl* (50);

for David Miller, *Love Happy* (49), and for many of his own films.]
DIR: *The Lemon-Drop Kid* (50) (co-dir: Sidney Lanfield), *The First Time* (51), *Son of Paleface* (52), *Marry Me Again* (53), *Susan Slept Here* (54), *Artists and Models* (55), *The Lieutenant Wore Skirts* (56), *Hollywood or Bust* (56), *The Girl Can't Help It** (56), *Will Success Spoil Rock Hunter?/Oh, For a Man!** (57), *Rock-a-bye Baby* (58), *The Geisha Boy* (58), *Say One for Me* (59), *Cinderfella* (60), *Bachelor Flat* (62), *It's Only Money* (62), *The Man from the Diner's Club* (63), *Who's Minding the Store?* (63), *The Disorderly Orderly* (64), *The Alphabet Murders* (65), *The Glass Bottom Boat* (66), *Caprice* (67), *The Private Navy of Sgt. O'Farrell* (68).

TATI, Jacques (Jacques Tatischeff) DIR France. (Pecq Oct 9, 1908–) The best French comedian since Max Linder (*q.v.*) whose distinctive Frenchness has contributed significantly to his world-wide success; he has a rare sense of observation and comedy and a feeling for atmosphere and the poetic. Though the dialogue is at a minimum in his films, the sound tracks are almost always as important as the images, blending music, natural sounds, and occasional words. Like Linder, he has taken for his heroes "average Frenchmen" – in a village in *Jour de fête*, in a seaside resort in *Les Vacances de M. Hulot*, in a Parisian suburb in *Mon Oncle*, in the hurly-burly of a complex, modern urban society in *Playtime*. Though their wit is largely gentle and almost surreptitious, they are not in the least "detached" and often have a biting ferocity. He has said of his comedy: "At heart, Hulot is never aware of what's going on. Chaplin, faced with a difficulty, something that impedes him, has ideas, finds a way out, modifies and interprets the impediment. Hulot never does anything intentionally, assumes nothing, constructs nothing. In the cemetery sequence in *Vacances,* he arrives in his car and has a puncture. He opens his car's trunk, takes out an inner tube, lets it fall, the leaves stick to it and it is transformed into a wreath. The funeral procession arrives, someone gathers up the inner tube and thanks him for the wreath. Hulot had not intended to do that. If Chaplin had agreed to do that gag, he himself would have collected the leaves and presented the wreath as he twirled his cane. The audience would have found the intention funny. Hulot, however, leaves the cemetery without even knowing why the leaves stuck; he invents nothing." Though he has never written his own feature scripts single-handed, he collaborates closely in their preparation, working out all the gags in minute detail before filming begins. He needs many years to conceive, shoot, and edit a film; no French director is more exacting than he, except for Bresson (*q.v.*). "I can't manufacture films like bread rolls. I'm not a baker. I consider how people live, I walk about. I listen to conversations, I observe mannerisms, details, the ways of behaving that reveal the personality of each individual . . . Without seeking a message, I would like to express what is leading to the suppression of personality in an increasingly mechanized world." [He began his career as a pantomimist in cabarets, music halls, and circuses. During the Thirties he made several short films incorporating aspects of his act, which was largely made up of sports mimes. The most successful of these films was *Soigne ton gauche,* in which he played a country boy who wants to be a champion boxer. After the war he made a short sketch, *L'Ecole des facteurs,* whose theme he soon after expanded in his first feature, *Jour de fête.*]

CO-SCEN: *Oscar, champion de tennis* (32) (short, unfinished), *On demande une brute* (34) (short; dir: Charles Barrois), *Gai dimanche* (35) (short; dir: Jacques Ber), *Soigne ton gauche* (36) (short; dir: René Clément), *Cours de soir* (67) (short; dir: Nicolas Ribowski), and his own films.

DIR: *Retour à la terre* (38) (short), *L'Ecole des facteurs* (47), *Jour de fête** (48), *Les Vacances de M. Hulot** (53),

Mon Oncle* (58), *Playtime* (67), *Trafic* (71).

TAUROG, Norman DIR USA. (Chicago Feb 23, 1899–) Veteran Hollywood director, in films since 1917, who has directed many comedies, including some of the early Larry Semon and Harold Lloyd shorts and, much later, the films of Dean Martin and Jerry Lewis (*The Caddy, Living It Up, You're Never Too Young, Pardners, The Stooge, Jumping Jacks*) and two with Lewis alone (*Don't Give Up the Ship, Visit to a Small Planet*). [He has also made many musicals: *Rhythm on the Range* (36) with Bing Crosby, *Mad about Music* (38) with Deanna Durbin, *Girl Crazy* (43) with Judy Garland and Mickey Rooney, and later several Mario Lanza films and many of Elvis Presley's.] Occasionally he has tackled more "serious" themes, e.g., *Boys' Town* (38) and the panegyric to the dropping of the Hiroshima atomic bomb, *The Beginning of the End* (47). He also evoked quite well the atmosphere of 19th century America in *Huckleberry Finn* (33), *The Adventures of Tom Sawyer* (38), *Young Tom Edison* (39).

TAZIEFF, Haroun DIR France. (Warsaw May 11, 1914–) Celebrated volcanologist and explorer who has often used the camera in his work and had considerable success with his two features: *Les Rendez-vous du Diable/Volcano* (56–58), *Le Volcan interdit* (66). [Earlier shorts: *Records au gouffre de la Pierre Saint Martin, Stromboli, L'Eruption de l'Etna, Au milieu des cratères en feu* (all 16mm), *Grêle de feu* (52), *Eaux souterraines* (57).]

TEDESCO, Jean PROD/DIR France. (London March 24, 1895–Paris 1959) The founder in 1924 of Le Vieux-Colombier, the first avant-garde film theater in Paris, producer and co-director of Renoir's *La Petite marchande d'allumettes** (28), editor (1923–30) of *Cinea-Ciné pour tous,* he was totally dedicated to the cinema and directed some dozen short films.

TERRY, Paul ANIM/PROD USA. (San Mateo Feb 19 1887–Nov 1971) Former cartoonist who founded Terrytoons studios in New York in the Thirties. His films, released by Twentieth Century-Fox, featured the characters of Mighty Mouse (from 1944), Heckle and Jeckle (from 1946), Little Roquefort (from 1951). Terry retired in the Fifties and the studios were taken over by CBS and headed by Gene Deitch (*The Juggler of Our Lady, Flebus*).

*TESHIGAHARA, Hiroshi DIR Japan. (Tokyo 1927–) Young, independent Japanese film maker, notable for the compelling *Woman of the Dunes* and *The Man without a Map*. He originally studied painting and worked on short documentaries before founding his own company in 1961 and making the experimental fantasy *Pitfall*.
DIR: *Hokusai* (53) (short), *José Torres* (59) (short), *Otoshi Ana/Pitfall/Cheap Sweet and a Kid* (62), *Suna no Onna/ Woman of the Dunes** (64), *La Fleur de l'age* (Fr/Jap65) (episode), *Tanin no Kao/The Face of Another* (66), *Bakuso* (67) (short), *Moetsukita Chizu/ The Man without a Map* (68).

THALBERG, Irving PROD USA. (Brooklyn 1899–Hollywood 1936) Hollywood's "boy wonder" producer, he went to Hollywood in 1919 as Carl Laemmle's (*q.v.*) secretary, ended up running the studio, joined Louis B. Mayer (*q.v.*) in 1923 and became second-in-command of MGM, responsible for the ponderous literary flavor of some of MGM's productions. An Oscar for "distinguished production" was instituted in his memory in 1937. However, when René Clair wrote of Hollywood's "ignorant and tyrannical producers" he was undoubtedly thinking of Thalberg. He considers the debut of a new Hegira as taking place that day in 1922 when Thalberg (then only 23, but Laemmle's right-hand man) bodily threw Stroheim (*q.v.*) out of the Universal Studios and forbade him, though he was at the peak of his fame, to finish *Merry-Go-Round*. Earlier, he had been responsible for butchering Stroheim's *Foolish Wives** and two years later was the principal force behind the dismemberment of *Greed** after Mayer's merger with Metro-Goldwyn. To punish him, he forced Stroheim to make *The Merry Widow**. [He never doubted his own judgment and, commercially, he was usually right, but his heavy hand and dedication to "prestige" pictures rarely gave birth to Hollywood's better films. His stultifying professionalism is evident in the loss of much of

the Marx Brothers zany spontaneity after they moved from Paramount to MGM.]

THIELE, Rolf DIR/PROD German Federal Republic. (Redlice, Czechoslovakia March 7, 1918–) Postwar producer who established his own company in 1945 and began directing in 1951. He has made numerous commercial films, often with sexual themes (including a version of Frank Wedekin's *Lulu**), among which is one lucky achievement – the ironic *Das Mädchen Rosemarie* (58), based on a notorious true story.

THIELE, Wilhelm (also, in USA, William T.) DIR/SCEN Germany DIR USA. (Vienna May 10, 1890–) Former stage actor and director who wrote scripts in Austria and Germany from 1923 to 1926, directed his first film in 1927, and was responsible for one major success: *Die Drei von der Tankstelle** (30). In 1933 he moved to Hollywood, where he directed many Tarzan films. He has occasionally directed in Germany since the war.

THIRARD, Armand PHOTOG France. (Mantes Oct 25, 1899–) An excellent cameraman, imbued with a feeling for the great painters, who has made masterful use of color in his later films.
PHOTOG (notably): for Grémillon, *Remorques** (41); for Christian-Jaque, *L'Assassinat du Père Noël* (41), *La Symphonie fantastique* (42), *Si tous les gars du monde* (56); for Clouzot, *Quai des Orfèvres** (47), *Manon* (49), *Miquette et sa mère* (49), *Le Salaire de la peur** (53), *Les Diaboliques* (55), *La Verité** (60); for Vadim, *Et Dieu créa la femme** (56), *Sait-on jamais* (57), *Les Bijoutiers de la clair de lune* (58), *Le Repos du guerrier* (62).

THIRIET, Maurice MUS France. (Meulan May 2, 1906–) Initiated by Jaubert (*q.v.*) into composing film music, he has collaborated on a number of films. Though not all excellent, some are notable: L'Herbier's *La Nuit fantastique* (42), Yves Allégret's *Une si jolie petite plage** (48), and especially Carné's *Les Visiteurs du soir** (42), *Les Enfants du paradis** (45) (both co-mus: Joseph Kosma), *Thérèse Raquin** (53), *L'Air de Paris* (54).

THOMPSON, J. Lee *see* LEE THOMPSON, J.

*THORNDIKE, Andrew DIR German Democratic Republic. (Berlin Aug 30, 1909–) Brilliant East German documentarist, specializing in compilation films using methods developed by Shub, Vertov, and Capra (all *q.v.*). He began his film career in the Thirties making industrial shorts for UFA and was sent to the eastern front as a result of his anti-Nazi activities. He began directing documentaries for DEFA in 1948 and made his first compilation film, *Wilhelm Pieck,* in 1951. Since 1955 he has concentrated on compilation films in collaboration with his wife, Annelie (Klützow 1925–), most notably on *The German Story, The Archives Testify* series, and *The Russian Miracle*.
DIR: *Der 13. Oktober* (49), *Von Hamburg bis Stralsund* (49) (in *Aus unseren Tagen* series), *Der Weg nach oben* (50), *Wilhelm Pieck — das Leben unseres Präsidenten* (51), *Freundschaft Siegt* (51), *Die Prüfung* (52), *Sieben vom Rhein* (54), *Du und mancher Kamerad . . . / The German Story/You and Other Comrades* (56), *Urlaub auf Sylt* (57) (in *The Archives Testify* series), *Unternehmen Teutonenschwert/Operation Teutonic Sword* (58) (in *The Archives Testify* series), *Das Russische Wunder* (63) (in 2 parts), *Tito in Deutschland* (65), *Du bist mein, ein Deutsches Tagesbuch* (69).

TIOMKIN, Dimitri MUS USA. (Russia 1899–) Versatile and undeniable skillful composer able to integrate his scores into the dramatic action but who is occasionally prey to superficial displays of style.
MUS (notably): for Norman Z. McLeod, *Alice in Wonderland* (33); for Capra, *Lost Horizon* (37), *You Can't Take It With You** (38), *Mr. Smith Goes to Washington** (39), *Meet John Doe* (41), *Why We Fight* series* (43–45), for Wyler, *The Westerner* (40), *Friendly Persuasion* (56); for Hitchcock *Shadow of a Doubt** (43), *Strangers on a Train** (51), *I Confess* (52), *Dial M for Murder* (54); for Vidor, *Duel in the Sun** (46); for Mark Robson, *Champion* (49); for Zinnemann, *The Men** (50), *High Noon** (52); for Hawks, *Red River* (48), *The Big Sky* (52), *Land of the Pharaohs* (55), *Rio Bravo* (58); for Wellman, *The High and the Mighty* (54); for George

Stevens, *Giant** (56); for John Sturges, *Gunfight at the O.K. Corral* (57), *The Old Man and the Sea* (58), *The Last Train from Gun Hill* (59); for Cukor, *Wild is the Wind* (57); for Huston, *The Unforgiven* (59); for J. Lee Thompson, *The Guns of Navarone* (61); for John Wayne, *The Alamo** (60); for Anthony Mann, *The Fall of the Roman Empire* (63); for Nicholas Ray, *55 Days at Peking* (62); for B. Kennedy, *The War Wagon* (67). Also produced *Tchaikovsky* (USSR/USA69) (dir: Igor Talankin).

TISSE, Eduard Kasimirovich PHOTOG USSR. (Lithuania April 1, 1897–Moscow 1961) Incomparable Soviet cameraman, Eisenstein's (*q.v.*) closest collaborator throughout his career. His first experiences, after studying painting (1914–16), were on the rough training ground of newsreels after the Revolution and during the Civil War (1917–21). It was here that he learned to give the most effective and striking form to actuality through his composition and framing. This experience served him well when he shot Eisenstein's *Strike, Potemkin, October,* and *The General Line,* films that Eisenstein had conceived in some respects as recreated actualities. However, this approach did not exclude the kind of rigorous visual stylization that reached its height in *Que Viva Mexico!* and that later led them to the operatic imagery of *Alexander Nevsky.* Tisse never reached the same perfection when he worked with other directors. (NOTE: Tisse was not Swedish; this was a joke invented by Eisenstein.)
PHOTOG (notably): for Alexander Arkatov, *Signal* (18) (short); for Vladimir Gardin, *Sickle and Hammer* (21), *Hunger, Hunger, Hunger* (21), *The Bear's Wedding* (26); for Cheslav Sabinsky, *Elder Vasili Gryaznov* (24); for Eisenstein, *Strike** (25), *The Battleship Potemkin** (25), *October** (27–28), *The General Line** (29), *Que Viva Mexico!** (Mex31) (unfinished), *Bezhin Meadow* (36) (abandoned), *Alexander Nevsky** 38), *Ivan the Terrible** (44–46) (exteriors only; co-photog: Andrei Moskvin), for Alexandrov, *Romance sentimentale* (Fr31) (short), *Woman's Weal, Woman's Woe* (Switz31) (short also co-dir), *Meeting on the Elba* (49), *Glinka* (52); for Alexei Granovsky, *Jewish Luck* (25); for Roman Karmen,

Moscow-Karakum-Moscow (33) (documentary; also co-dir), *Comrade Dimitrov in Moscow* (34) (documentary); for Shub, *Country of the Soviets* (37) (documentary); for Dovzhenko, *Aerograd** (35) (co-photog: M. Gindin).
CO-DIR: (with Z. Agranenko): *Bessmertnyi garnizon/The Immortal Garrison* (56).

TODD, Mike (Avrom Goldenborgen) PROD USA. (Minneapolis June 22, 1907–died in plane accident March 21, 1958) One of the most extraordinary and dynamic men to enter the cinema. A former producer of Broadway spectaculars, he formed Magna Productions in 1953 with Joseph Schenck (*q.v.*) and launched the widescreen 70mm process "Todd-AO." His company produced *Oklahoma!* (55) and he personally produced his magnum opus, *Around the World in Eighty Days* (56). He made a fortune, married Elizabeth Taylor, and died as spectacularly as he had lived.

TOLAND, Gregg PHOTOG USA. (Charleston May 29, 1904–Hollwood Sept 28, 1948) The greatest Hollywood cameraman, he began his career in the early Twenties as an assistant, worked mainly for Goldwyn (*q.v.*) through the Thirties, and affirmed his talents on Ford's *The Grapes of Wrath*, Welles's *Citizen Kane*, and Wyler's *Dead End* and *The Little Foxes*. He made especially brilliant use of chiaroscuro and deep-focus photography. A little before his premature death he said: "The cameraman should always work in close collaboration with the scriptwriter and director before production. Each film should have its own particular style. A comedy and a tragedy should not be photographed in the same way: *The Grapes of Wrath*, a harsh film; *The Long Voyage Home*, a character film; *Citizen Kane*, a psychological story in which the external realities were very important. It was marvelous to produce with Orson Welles. I made suggestions to him and tried out things I had wanted to try for a very long time. Camera movements should not be apparent because they distract attention from the actors and from what's happening."
PHOTOG (notably): for Leo McCarey, *The Kid from Spain* (32); for Frank Tuttle, *Roman Scandals* (33); for Dorothy Arzner, *Nana** (34); for Mamoulian, *We Live Again* (34); for King Vidor,

The Wedding Night (34); for Karl Freund, *Mad Love* (35); for Richard Boleslawsky, *Les Misérables** (35); for Wyler, *Come and Get It** (36), *These Three* (36), *Dead End** (37), *Wuthering Heights** (39), *The Westerner* (40), *The Little Foxes** (41), *The Best Years of Our Lives** (46); for Hawks, *The Road to Glory* (36), *The Outlaw* (40), *Ball of Fire* (41), *A Song is Born* (48); for Frank Borzage, *History Is Made at Night* (37); for George Marshall, *The Goldwyn Follies* (38); for Gregory Ratoff, *Intermezzo* (39); for Sam Wood, *Raffles* (39); for John Ford, *The Grapes of Wrath** (40), *The Long Voyage Home* (40); for Orson Welles, *Citizen Kane** (41); for Norman Z. McLeod, *The Kid from Brooklyn* (47); for Irving Reis, *Enchantment* (48).

TONTI, Aldo PHOTOG Italy. (Rome March 2, 1910–) He has photographed numerous mediocre films but made a major contribution to the germination of Italian neorealism on Visconti's *Ossessione** and has done his best work on Rossellini's *Europa 51**, *India*; Lattuada's *Il Banditi*, *Senza Pieta**, *Il Mulino del Po*, *La Lupa*; Fellini's *Le Notte di Cabiria**; Vidor's *War and Peace**, and Huston's *Reflections in a Golden Eye*.

TORRE NILSSON, Leopoldo DIR Argentina. (Buenos Aires May 5, 1924–) The best Argentinian director of his generation whose finest films have a strange and very personal ambience and are intelligently and carefully staged, lit, and composed. [The son of Argentinian director, Leopoldo Torre Rios, he began his career (1939) as assistant on 16 of his father's features, scripted ten features in the late Forties, and made one short before co-directing (with his father) his first feature in 1950. After several routine films, he reached full maturity and won international recognition with his first script collaboration with novelist Beatriz Guido (whom he later married), *House of the Angel* (57).] Since this film, he has excelled in portraying the social and political life of the Argentinian bourgeoisie, who live shut away from everyday realities, trapped by remorse, amorality, corruption, obsessions, passions, and illicit affairs: *The Fall, The Kidnapper, Fin de Fiesta, The Hand in the Trap, The Roof Garden* (all scripted or adapted from literary works by Beatriz

251

Guido). [He has made attempts to abandon his habitual universe with *Seventy Times Seven, Four Women for One Hero, The Eavesdropper*, etc., but these later works have tended to collapse into hysterical melodrama.]

DIR: *El Muro* (47) (short), *El Crimen de Oribe* (50), (co-dir: Torre Rios), *El Hijo del Crack* (53), *Dias de Odio* (54), *La Tigra* (54), *Para vestir Santos* (55), *Graciela* (56), *El Protegido* (56), *La Casa del Angel** (57), *Precursores de la Pintura Argentina* (57) (short), *Les Arboles de Buenos Aires* (57) (short), *El Sequestrador/The Kidnapper* (58), *La Caida/The Fall* (59), *Fin de Fiesta** (60), *Un Guapo del 1900* (60), *La Mano en la Trampa/The Hand in the Trap* (61), *Piel de Verano/Summer Skin* (61), *Setenta veces Siete/Seventy times Seven* (62), *Homenaje a la Hora de la Siesta/Four Women for One Hero* (62), *La Terraza/The Roof Garden/The Terrace* (63), *El Ojo de la Cerradura/ The Eavesdropper* (64), *Monday's Child* (66) (in English), *Cavor un Foso/To Dig a Pit* (66), *Los Traidores de San Angel* (USA/Argentina67), *Martin Fierro* (68).

TORRE RIOS, Leopoldo DIR Argentina. (Buenos Aires 189?–Buenos Aires April 4, 1960) Pioneer of the Argentinian cinema during the Twenties who made many modest, sensitive films. He is the father of Torre Nilsson, whom he trained as his assistant and to whom he gave his feature debut on *El Crimen de Oribe* (50).

TOSCANO BARRAGAN, Salvador DIR/PHOTOG Mexico. (Zapotlan March 24, 1873– Mexico City April 13, 1947) Pioneer Mexican film maker whose remarkable footage showing the daily life and political events of his country 1897–1920 (Porfirio Diaz, Zapata, Villa, Madero, armed peasants, the battles of the Mexican Revolution, etc.) was collected and edited into the striking compilation film, *Memorias de un Mexicano* (50), by his daughter, Carmen Toscano.

*TOSI, Piero COSTUMES Italy. (Florence 1928–) Fashion historian and brilliant costume designer with an exact sense of period, he has worked with Visconti (*q.v.*) in both theater and films: *Senso**, *Rocco and His Brothers**, and most notably, *The Leopard**, *The Damned**, and *Death in Venice*. Also scenario, art

director, and costumes for the episode film *I Tre Volti* (65), and costumes for *Fellini Satyricon* (69) and Pasolini's *Medea* (70).

*TOURNEUR, Jacques DIR USA. (Paris Nov 12, 1904–) The son of Maurice Tourneur, he has had a checkered career, mostly in Hollywood, and has made numerous mediocre films. However, he had a special gift for the macabre and directed for Val Lewton (*q.v.*) the brilliant *Cat People* (42), *I Walked with a Zombie* (43), and *The Leopard Man* (43) (films that revitalized the horror genre), the nightmarish thrillers, *Out of the Past* (47) and *Nightfall* (56), and the original *Night of the Demon* (57). In addition he has to his credit two notable westerns, *Canyon Passage* (46) and *Way of a Gaucho* (52), plus the individualistic *Stars in My Crown* (50). The rest of his work is largely undistinguished, though occasional sequences reveal his talents. Though raised in California, he began his film career in France, first as an editor (1928–32), then as director, before moving back to Hollywood, where he worked initially on shorts and as second unit director.

DIR: *Tout ça ne vaut pas l'amour* (Fr32), *Toto* (Fr32), *Pour être aimer* (Fr33), *Les Filles de la concierge* (Fr34), *They All Come Out* (USA39), *Nick Carter, Master Detective* (39), *Phantom Raiders* (40), *Doctors Don't Tell* (41), *Cat People** (42), *I Walked with a Zombie* (43), *The Leopard Man* (43), *Days of Glory* (44), *Experiment Perilous* (44), *Canyon Passage* (46), *Out of the Past* (47), *Berlin Express* (48), *Easy Living* (49), *Stars in My Crown* (50), *The Flame and the Arrow* (50), *Circle of Danger* (51), *Anne of the Indies* (51), *Way of a Gaucho* (52), *Appointment in Honduras* (53), *Stranger on Horseback* (55), *Wichita* (55), *Great Day in the Morning* (56), *Nightfall* (56), *Night of the Demon/ Curse of the Demon** (Brit58), *The Fearmakers* (58), *Timbuktu* (59), *The Giant of Marathon* (59), *The Comedy of Terrors* (63), *War Gods of the Deep/ City Under the Sea* (65).

TOURNEUR, Maurice (Maurice Thomas) DIR USA/France. (Paris Feb 2, 1876–Paris Aug 4, 1961) Imaginative film maker with a rich, atmospheric visual style whose work is too little known but who made significant contributions to the

development of film art, influenced many Hollywood directors, and was considered in 1920 as the peer of D. W. Griffith (*q.v.*). Originally an artist, a stage director with André Antoine (*q.v.*), and a pupil of Rodin and of Pierre Puvis de Chavannes, he began acting and then directing films for Eclair in Paris and went to the USA in 1914 to run the Eclair studios in Tucson. He made some 60 films in the USA, the best of which reflect his theatrical culture and training in the plastic arts: *The Whip, Trilby,* the picturesque *Poor Little Rich Girl* (with Mary Pickford), *The Bluebird, A Doll's House, Prunella, The Last of the Mohicans, Lorna Doone* and the spectacular *Woman.* In 1920 he said to Robert Florey: "The cinema is a different medium for hieroglyphically expressing human thoughts using images in place of words and with a savagery no one means of expression possesses. It is no more of an art than the printing press or the alphabet. It is the most significant instrument for bringing together nations and classes because it shows us in the most rapid and forceful way how human beings resemble each other, how the color of their skin or their language does not prevent their hearts from beating in a similar manner. More through the cinema than through the efforts of diplomats, men will realize their needs, aspirations and joys and will stop considering others as strangers." Delluc characterized him as: "a sincere and thoughtful craftsman who fashions for himself that kind of atmosphere that gives form, style, and superior quality to a work. He does not transform a given theme. He rises above it. Its merits only shine the more." He left Hollywood in 1927 rather than accept the system of "supervisors" at MGM and returned to Paris. He directed there until the late Forties, making a series of films, largely forgotten today but often remarkable achievements: *L'Equipage, Accusée, levez-vous, Les Gaîtés de l'escadron, Au nom de la loi, Le Main du diable* and even his last film, *Impasse des deux anges.*
[DIR (notably): *Rouletabille* (Fr13), *Le Dernier pardon* (Fr13), *Soeurette* (Fr14), *Mother* (USA14), *Man of the Hour* (14), *The Wishing Ring* (14), *Club* (15), *Trilby* (15), *The Ivory Snuff-Box* (15), *The Whip* (15), *Alias Jimmy Valentine* (15), *The Closed Road* (16), *The Rail Rider* (16), *The Pride of the Clans*

(16), *Poor Little Rich Girl* (17), *Barbary Sheep* (17), *Law of the Land* (17), *The Exile* (17), *The Bluebird* (18), *A Doll's House* (18), *Sporting Life* (18), *Woman* (18), *Prunella* (19), *The Broken Butterfly* (19), *Treasure Island* (20), *The Bait* (20), *The Last of the Mohicans* (20) (co-dir: Clarence Brown), *Lorna Doone* (22), *The Christian* (23), *Jealous Husbands* (23), *The Brass Bottle* (23), *Torment* (24), *Never the Twain Shall Meet* (25), *Aloma of the South Seas* (26), *Mysterious Island* (USA26) (replaced by B. Christensen, then by Lucien Hubbard), *L'Equipage* (Fr28), *Accusée, levez-vous* (30), *Partir* (31), *Maison des danses* (31), *Les Gaîtés de l'escadron* (32), *Au nom de la loi* (32), *Obsession* (33), *Les Deux orphelines** (34), *Le Voleur* (34), *Koenigsmark* (34), *Justin de Marseilles* (35), *Samson* (36), *Avec le sourire* (36), *Le Patriote* (38), *Katia* (38), *Volpone* (39–41), *La Main du diable* (42), *Cecile est morte* (43), *Après l'amour* (47), *Impasse des deux anges* (48).]

TRAUBERG, Ilya Zakharovich DIR USSR. (Odessa 1905–Berlin 1948) Notable Soviet director, younger brother of Leonid Trauberg, with a strong sense of rhythm and composition. He directed his first film in 1927, the documentary, *Leningrad Today,* and was Eisenstein's assistant on *October**. He made a remarkable feature debut on *Goluboi ekspress/Blue Express** (29) whose Far East setting he recaptured in *Syn Mongolii/Son of Mongolia** (36). His later films, such as *Concert Valse* and *Actress,* are of less interest.

TRAUBERG, Leonid Zakharovich DIR USSR. (Odessa 1902–) Co-founder with Grigori Kozintsev (*q.v.*) of FEKS and his close collaborator until 1947. He appears to have been mainly the scriptwriter on the remarkable series of films the two made together. Perhaps less artistic and refined than Kozintsev, he would seem to have contributed to their films a particular emotional tone and his sense of observation of everyday life. For filmography, see KOZINTSEV. Alone, Trauberg scripted Rappaport's *Zhizn v tsitadel/Life in the Citadel* (47) and Roshal's *Volnitsa* (55), and directed *Pirogov* (47), *Sli soldati/The Soldiers March* (57) and *Mortviye dushi/Dead Souls* (60) (from Gogol).

TRAUNER, Alexandre (also, Alexander T.) ART DIR France/USA. (Budapest Sept 3, 1906–) Talented designer with an international reputation who was trained by Lazare Meerson (*q.v.*) and has continued his tradition of poetic realism. [Like Meerson, he has specialized in the creation of evocative studio-built sets of cities, from that of Paris for many of Carné's (*q.v.*) films and Wilder's *Irma la Douce*, to that of London for Wilder's *Private Life of Sherlock Holmes*.]

ASSIST: to Meerson, *Le Million**, *Le Grand jeu**, *La Kermesse heroïque*, etc. ART DIR: for Marc Allégret, *Gribouille* (37), *Entrée des artistes* (38), *L'Amant de Lady Chatterley* (55), *En effeuillant la marguerite* (56); for Carné, *Drôle de drame* (37), *Quai des brumes** (38), *Hôtel du nord* (38), *Le Jour se lève** (39), *Les Visiteurs du soir** (42), *Les Enfants du paradis** (44–45) (in collab), *Les Portes de la nuit** (46), *La Marie du port* (50), *Juliette ou la clef des songes* (51); for Grémillon, *Remorques** (41), *Lumière d'été** (42); for Prévert, *Voyage surprise** (46); for Yves Allégret, *Manèges* (49), *Les Miracles n'ont lieu qu'une fois* (51), *Les Sept péchés capitaux* (51) (episode), *La Jeune folle* (52); for Orson Welles, *Othello** (52); for Howard Hawks, *Land of the Pharaohs* (55), for Litvak, *Act of Love* (54), *Aimez-vous Brahms?/Goodbye Again* (61), *Le Couteau dans la plaie/Five Miles to Midnight* (62), *The Night of the Generals* (66); for Billy Wilder, *Love in the Afternoon* (57), *Witness for the Prosecution* (58), *The Apartment* (60), *One, Two, Three* (61), *Irma la Douce* (63), *Kiss Me Stupid* (64), *The Private Life of Sherlock Holmes* (70); for Donen, *Once More with Feeling* (59); for Zinnemann, *The Nun's Story* (59); for Martin Ritt, *Paris Blues* (61); for Wyler, *How to Steal a Million* (66); for Jules Dassin, *La Promesse de l'aube* (70).

TRENKER, Luis DIR Germany/German Federal Republic. (St. Ulrich, Südtirol Oct 4, 1893–) Muscular mountaineer who began his career as an actor in Arnold Fanck's (*q.v.*) mountain films, directed some of these himself, and continued directing under the Nazis. After the war he made several features and founded his own production company.

DIR: *Berg in Flammen* (31) (co-dir: K. Hartl), *Der Rebell* (32) (co-dir: Kurt Bernhardt), *Der Verlorene Sohn* (34), *Der Kaiser von Kalifornien* (36), *Condottieri* (It/Ger37), *Der Berg ruft* (37), *Liebesbriefe aus dem Engadin* (38), *Der Feuerteufel* (40), *Germanin im Banne des Monte Miracolo* (45), *Flucht in die Dolomiten/Il Prigioniero della Montagna* (GFR/It55), *Von der Liebe besiegt* (56), *Wetterleuchten um Maria* (57), *Sein bester Freund* (62).

TRIVAS, Viktor DIR/SCEN/ART DIR Germany/USA. (Russia 1896–New York April 1970) Routine scriptwriter, designer, and director who was responsible for one significant film in his career, the pacifist *Niemandsland*. He emigrated to France and then to the USA, where he wrote and/or directed several mediocre films and later worked again as an art director.

DIR (notably): *Aufruhr des Blutes* (29), *Niemandsland** (31).

SCEN (notably): for Ozep, *Der Mörder Dimitri Karamasoff* (31), *Grossstadtnacht* (33); for Alexis Granowsky, *Das Lied vom Leben* (31); for Orson Welles, *The Stranger* (USA46).

ART DIR (notably): for Pabst, *Die Liebe der Jeanne Ney** (27).

TRNKA, Jiří ANIM Czechoslovakia. (Pilsen Feb 24, 1912–Dec 1969) Former painter, book illustrator, graphic artist, and puppeteer, he took up film production in 1945 and in the ensuing years revitalized animation throughout the world with his cartoons, paper cut-outs, and most especially with his puppet films. He made his first puppet films in 1946, later combining several of these that dealt with themes of Bohemian folklore into the feature-length *The Czech Year* (47). The epic qualities of this film were continued in his later work, in which his carved puppet characters were animated in complex sets with an expressive use of lighting. In this manner he has been able to realize the dream of Czech baroque sculptors to set their sculptures in motion. His work often recalls their style: the somewhat mannered *The Emperor and the Nightingale*, the very architectural *Prince Bayaya*, and, above all, the veritably operatic, noble epic, *Old Czech Legends*. About 1955, he said of his experiences: "The desire came to me to invade the screen, where everything is possible, with three-dimensional figures that would not play their parts in the frame like animated drawings, but in space. And since my beginnings as a film maker I have pursued this aim: the lyrical film. Puppet films are truly unlimited in their possibilities: they can express themselves with the greatest force precisely when the realistic expression of the cinematographic image often faces insurmountable obstacles. The greatest successes of the puppet film have been, on the one hand, satires, on the other, poignantly lyrical subjects and also where the theme has to be expressed through piercing pathos. They can retain their poetic character when allied to opera and ballet, since their lyricism is so akin to their means of expression. In this way it would be possible to accentuate properly their dramatic side, which has been neglected up to now." On this basis he was able to develop the "eighth art" of animation, creating ciné-operas and ciné-ballets such as *Old Czech Legends* and *A Midsummer Night's Dream*. In his early years he was a pupil of the distinguished puppeteer, Professor Skupa. He studied graphic arts from 1929–35 and then went on to do cartoons and establish his own puppet theater. During the war he designed stage sets and illustrated children's books.

ANIM (puppets, except where noted): *Zasadil dedek repu/Grandma Planted a Beet* (45) (cartoon), *Zviratka a Petrovsti/The Animals and the Brigands* (46), *Perak a SS/The Devil on Springs* (46) (cartoon), *Darek/The Gift* (47), *Spalicek/The Czech Year** (47) (compilation, short puppet films), *Cisaruv slavik /The Emperor and the Nightingale** (48), *Arie prerie/Song of the Prairie* (49), *Roman s bason/The Story of the Bass-Cello* (49), *Bajaja/Prince Bayaya** (50), *Veseley cirkus/Circus** (51) (paper cut-outs), *The Devil's Mill* (51), *Rybar a zlata rybka/The Golden Fish* (51) (cartoon), *Jak starecek menil az vymenil/How Grandpa Changed Till Nothing Was Left* (52) (cartoon), *Stare povesti ceske/Old Czech Legends** (53), *Dva mra zici/The Two Frosts* (54) (cartoon), *Osudy dobreho vojaka Svejka /The Good Soldier Schweik* (54), *Cirkus Hurvinek* (55), *Proc UNESCO?/Why UNESCO?* (58) (cartoon), *Sen noci svatojanske/A Midsummer Night's Dream** (59), *Vasen/Obsession* (62), *Kyberneticka babicka/The Cybernetic Grandmother* (62), *The Archangel Gabriel and Mother Goose* (64) (cut-outs, pup-

pets), *The Hand* (65) (cut-outs, puppets).

Trnka also designed Pojar's *A Drop Too Much* (54) and *The Little Umbrella* (57).

*TRUFFAUT, François DIR France. (Paris Feb 6, 1932–) With Godard, Resnais, and Franju (all *q.v.*), he is the most important figure to emerge from the French *nouvelle vague,* a film maker who has maintained his independence (through his own production company) throughout his career. He has a profound concern for satisfying an audience: "If you like, you could call my cinema one of compromise in that I think constantly about the public, but not one of concessions, since I never put in a comic effect that I haven't laughed at, nor a sad one that hasn't moved me." Apart from his first feature, the autobiographical *Les 400 coups,* with its sympathetic insight into adolescence, he has never been at ease with intellectualism and his weakest film, *Fahrenheit 451,* is his only film of direct social comment. What is evident is a disarming gentleness, a sympathetic handling of characters (usually focusing on a diffident hero who is a born loser), a belief in the value of friendship and the impossibility of abiding love, and a lyrical nostalgia for a world where these might have been possible. These elements are present in his best work: the brilliant (and underestimated) tragicomedy, *Tirez sur le pianiste,* the nostalgic exploration of the impossibility of a *ménage à trois, Jules et Jim,* the compelling and sympathetic study of adultery, *La Peau douce,* and the poetic evocations of lost (though different) innocences, *Baisers volés* and *L'Enfant sauvage.* Even the less interesting *The Bride Wore Black* and *Mississippi Mermaid* are captivating and full of vivid characterizations. He has said of his work: "I don't tackle the 'problems of our time' in my films and if I did try to tackle them I would be incapable of adopting an attitude . . . The characters in a film interest me more than the story, so I can't make a film of ideas . . . (fiction) doesn't exclude ideas about life, about the world, about our society. But I like everything that muddles the trail, everything that sows doubts . . . I enjoy unexpected details, things that prove nothing, things that show how vulnerable men are." He began his career as a critic for *Cahiers du Cinéma* and *Arts*.

DIR: *Une visite* (54) (16mm short), *Les Mistons* (57) (short), *Histoire d'eau* (58) (short, completed by Godard), *Les 400 Coups** (59), *Tirez sur le pianiste** (60), *Jules et Jim** (61), *L'Amour à vingt ans* (62) (episode), *La Peau douce* (64), *Fahrenheit 451* (Brit66), *La Mariée était en noir* (67), *Baisers volés* (68), *La Sirène de Mississippi/Mississippi Mermaid* (69), *L'Enfant sauvage* (69), *Domicile conjugal* (70).

TRUMBO, Dalton SCEN USA. (Montrose Dec 9, 1905–) The most talented scriptwriter of the "Hollywood Ten," imprisoned for refusing to testify before the House Un-American Activities Committee and later blacklisted. During the blacklist period he wrote some 30 scripts under various pseudonyms and even won an Oscar (*The Brave One*). Preminger (*q.v.*) broke the blacklist by allowing him a credit for the script of *Exodus*.

SCEN (notably): for Garson Kanin, *A Man to Remember* (38); for Sam Wood, *Kitty Foyle* (40); for Dmytryk, *Tender Comrade* (43); for Victor Fleming, *A Guy Named Joe* (43); for Mervyn LeRoy, *Thirty Seconds over Tokyo* (44); for Roy Rowland, *Our Vines Have Tender Grapes* (45); for Gustav Machaty, *Jealousy* (45); for Losey, *The Prowler* (50); for Rossen, *The Brave Bulls* (51); for Irving Rapper, *The Brave One* (56); for Preminger, *Exodus** (60); for Kubrick, *Spartacus** (60); for Aldrich, *The Last Sunset* (61); for David Miller, *Lonely Art the Brave* (62); for Minnelli, *The Sandpiper* (65); for George Roy Hill, *Hawaii* (66); for Frankenheimer, *The Fixer* (68).

DIR: *Johnny Got His Gun* (71).

TSAI, Tsou-sen DIR China. (190?–) The best Chinese director of the Thirties whose prewar films, in the technique of the avant-garde, were both satiric and compassionate and often contained a vital element of social polemic. After the war his epic *The River Flows East in the Spring* was an enormous success throughout the Far East, with its attack on the corrupt regime of the Kuomintang (even though it had been made under this regime). After 1950 he became one of the directors of the Chinese state cinema.

DIR (notably): *Southern Spring* (32), *Morning in the Town* (33), *Song of the Fisherman* (34), *New Women* (35), *Stray Lamb** (36), *Wang Lao Wou* (37–38), *Diabolical Paradise* (Hong Kong39), *The Great Experience* (40), *The River Flows East in the Spring** (48).

TSOU, Se-ling see CHU, Shih-ling

TUCKER, George Loane DIR USA/Britain. (Hollywood 1881–Chicago 1921) Pioneer film maker who began with Biograph and had a great success with *Traffic in Souls* (13). [That same year he moved to Britain and directed several films, some with his wife Elisabeth Risdon: *The Difficult Way* (14), *England Expects* (14), *The Revenge of Mr. Thomas Atkins* (14), *The Middleman* (15), *The Prisoner of Zenda* (15), *Sons of Satan* (15), *The Christian* (15), *The Morals of Weybury* (16), *The Manxman* (16), *Arsene Lupin* (16), *The Man without a Soul* (16), *I Believe* (17), *Mother* (17), *The Hypocrites* (17), etc.] He returned to the USA for his most famous film, and one that Delluc admired, *The Miracle Man* (19), with Lon Chaney in his first major role.

TURIN, Victor DIR USSR. (1895–1945) Film maker notable for only one film, the remarkable documentary, *Turksib** (29).

TYRLOVA, Hermina ANIM Czechoslovakia. (Pribram Dec 11, 1900–) Pioneer, with Zeman, of animation in Czechoslovakia, she began in the Twenties on trick films and animated commercials and after the war specialized in puppet films for children, [e.g., *Ferda the Aunt* (44), *Revolt of the Toys* (47), *Lullaby* (48), *The Taming of the Dragon* (53), *Goldilocks* (56), *The Inquisitive Letter* (61), *The Woolly Tale* (64), *The Snowman* (66), *Dog's Heaven* (67). Several of her later films combine puppets and child actors.]

TZAVELLAS, Georges (Gheorghiou) DIR Greece. (Athens 1916–) One of the three major postwar Greek directors, with Cacoyannis (*q.v.*) and Kondouros (*q.v.*). All three made their films under modest and sometimes difficult conditions but gave their country's cinema an international reputation. He is also a dramatist (over 26 plays) and has scripted all his own films, which reflect his sense of fantasy and imagination. He has excelled in comedy (*Marinos Kontaros*), drama (*O Methystakas*), and, like Cacoyannis, has tackled classical Greek tragedy in *Antigone*.

DIR: *Ta Chirrokkrotimata/Applause* (43), *Lismonimena prossopa/Forgotten Faces* (46), *Marinos Kontaros* (48), *O Methystakos/The Drunkard* (50), *Agni tou limaniou/Agnes of the Port* (52), *O Chroussousis/The Susceptible* (52), *To Soferaki/Taxi Driver* (53), *I Kalpiki lira/The False Coin** (55), *O Erastis erchete/The Lovers Arrive* (56), *Mia zoi tin echome/We Only Live Once* (58), *Antigone* (61).

UCHATIUS, (Lieutenant Baron) Franz von IN-
VENTOR Austria. (? – ?) Artillery officer in the Austrian army, famed for
his aerial bombing (from balloons) of
rebellious Venice in 1848, who devised
a technique for combining Stampfer's
(*q.v.*) Stroboscopic discs and the magic
lantern, thus enabling moving drawings
to be projected onto a wall for viewing.
This *Kinesistiskop* was constructed in
1853 by Prokesch, an optician in Vienna.

UCHIDA, Tomu DIR Japan. (Okayama April
26, 1897–August 1970) With his friends
Mizoguchi (*q.v.*) and Kinugasa (*q.v.*),
one of the founders of cinematic art in
Japan. After being an actor, he joined
Nikkatsu in the early Twenties as an
assistant (to Mizoguchi and Minoru
Murata) and directed his first films in
1926. Though he originally specialized
in farces and period satires, he was one
of the prime movers in the *shomin-geki*
genre, his first attempt being a Marxian
adaptation of Maeterlinck's *Blue Bird*
that was banned by the censors before
production. His best period was from
1936 to 1939, when he made several
"new realism" films — *Theater of Life,
Unending Advance, The Naked Town* —
and, above all, the semidocumentary
Earth, a realistic chronicle of the life of
a poor farmer. He was sent to Manchuria
in 1942 and later joined the armies of
Mao Tse-Tung, assisting in the organization of their film division. He returned
to Japan in 1954 after the Korean War
but never quite found his earlier strength,
specializing mainly in period dramas,
e.g, a curious Kabuki adaptation, *Love
Not Again;* a Japanese *William Tell,
Disorder by the Kuroda Clan,* in which
the peasants rise against tyrannical over-
lords; and a five-part *Mushashi Miyamoto.*
He has, however, occasionally tackled
contemporary themes, as in the pan-

oramic cross-section of postwar Japanese
life, *Twilight Beer Hall.*
[DIR: *Kyoso Mikka-kan* (26), *Kutsu/
Pain* (26), *Mirai no Shusse/Rising in the
World* (27), *Soteio* (27), *Toyo Bukyo-
den* (27), *Namakemono/Idler* (27),
Kechinbo Nagaya (27), *Hoen Danu/
Cannon Smoke and Rain of Shells* (27),
Nomisuke Kinshu Undo (28), *Chikyu
wa Mawaru/Spinning Earth,* Part II
(28), *Hikari/A Ray* (28), *Shabe no
Kaze/Wind of This World* (28), *Ikeru
Ningyo/A Living Doll* (29), *Nikkat-
su Koshinkyoku — Supotsu-hen/Nikkatsu
Sports Parade* (29), *Taiyoji/The Sea-
Loving Son Sails Away* (29), *Ase/Sweat*
(29), *Tengoku Sonohi-gaeri/Return to
Heaven* (30), *Rensen Rensho/Succes-
sive Victories* (30), *Jan Barujan/Jean
Valjean* (31) (in two parts), *Sanmen
Kaji/Stories of Human Interest* (31),
Miss Nippon (31), *Adauchi Sensho/
The Revenge Champion* (31), *Ai wa
Doko Mademo* (32), *Daichi no Tatsu/
Mother Earth Rises* (32), *Sakebu Azia/
Asia Calling* (33), *Keisatsu-kan* (33),
Kawa no Ue no Taiyo (34), *Neppu/
Hot Wind* (34), *Hakugin no Oza/The
White Man's Throne* (35), *Jinsei Gekijo/
Theater of Life* (36), *Kagirinaki Zen-
shin/Unending Advance* (36), *Seimei
no Kanmuri* (36), *Hadaki no Machi/
The Naked Town* (37), *Tokyo Senichi-
ya/A Thousand and One Nights in
Tokyo* (38), *Tsuchi/Earth* (39), *Rekishi
/History* (40) (only Part I completed),
Suneemon Tori (42), *Chiyari Fuji/ A
Bloody Spear at Mount Fuji* (55),
Tasogare Sakaba/Twilight Beer Hall
(55), *Jibun no Ana no Nakade/Each
within His Shell* (55), *Kuroda Soda/
Disorder by the Kuroda Clan* (56),
Abarenbo Kaido (57), *Dotanba/They
Are Buried Alive/The Eleventh Hour*
(57), *Daibosatsu Toge/The Great Bod-
hisattva Pass/Moonlit Swords,* Part I

(57), *Senryo Jishin/The Thief is Shogun's Kin* (58), *Daibosatsu Toge*, Part II (58), *Mori to Mizuumi no Matsuri/ The Outsiders* (58), *Daibosatsu Toge*, Part III (59), *Naniwa no Koi no Monogatari/Their Own World* (59), *Sake to Onna to Yari/Saki, Woman, and a Lance* (60), *Hana no Yoshiwara Hyakuningiri/Murder in Yoshiwara* (60)], *Miyamoto Musashi* Part I */Untamed Fury* (61), *Koiya Koi Nasuna Koi/Love Not Again* (61), *Miyamoto Musashi* Part II */Duel without End* (62), *Miyamoto Musashi* Part III */The Worthless Duel* (63), *Miyamoto Musashi* Part IV */The Duel at Ichijoji Temple* (64), *Kiga Kaikyo/Fugitive from the Past/Hunger Straits* (64), *Miyamoto Musashi* Part V */The Last Duel* (65), *Jinsei Gekijo: Hishakaku to Kiratsune/Kaku and Tsune* (68), *Shinken Shobei/Real Sword Fight* (69).

*ULMER, Edgar Georg DIR USA. (Vienna Sept 17, 1900–) Film maker with a love of the cinema and great taste and sensibility. After collaborating on *Menschen am Sonntag** (29), he settled in Hollywood and had to work on second features and exploitation films in which, nonetheless, his talent and individuality are apparent: *The Black Cat* (34), *Isle of Forgotten Sins* (43), *Bluebeard* (44), *Her Sister's Secret* (46), *Beyond the Time Barrier* (60), and his best film, *The Naked Dawn* (55). His version of *L'Atlantide** (61) is of little interest. Earlier, in Germany, he had collaborated with Max Reinhardt in the theater and was a set designer for films in the Twenties. He was Murnau's (*q.v.*) assistant on *Der Letzte Mann**, *Tartüff*, and *Faust**, and Murnau's influence is evident in his work.

*URBAN, Charles PROD Britain. (Cleveland, Ohio 1870?–Brighton Aug 29, 1942) Pioneer entrepreneur and producer who originally moved to Britain in 1894 as a representative for Edison's (*q.v.*) Kinetoscope, formed his own producing-releasing company – notably for the films of Smith (*q.v.*) and Williamson (*q.v.*) after 1900 – and was associated with Smith on the marketing of Kinemacolor. He was responsible for many early newsreels and travel, interest, and scientific documentaries, including those of F. Martin-Duncan (*q.v.*). In 1912 he sent a team of cameramen to India to make the spectacular color film, *Delhi Durbar*. He returned to North America after 1914 to produce and market newsreels and documentaries for the US and Canadian governments.

URRUETA, Chano DIR Mexico. (189?–) Mexican director who made two or three good films among a prolific output of 50–100 films, including *Noche de los Mayas* (39) and *Los de abajo* (40).

URUSEVSKY, Sergei PHOTOG/DIR USSR. (Moscow 1908–) Excellent Soviet cameraman who has contributed his splendid imagery and agile camera movements to the films of Kalatozov, Donskoy, Pudovkin, and Chukrai (all *q.v.*) and is one of the craftsmen responsible for the major international success, *The Cranes are Flying*. He photographed his first film in 1940 and has recently turned to directing.
PHOTOG (notably); for Dovzhenko and Solntseva, *The Fight for Our Soviet Ukraine* (43); for Vladimir Legoshin, *Poyedinok/Duel* (45); for Erast Garin, *Sinegoriya/The Land of the Blue Mountains* (45); for Donskoy, *Selskaya uchitelnitsa/A Village Schoolteacher** (47), *Alitet ukhodit v gory/Alitet Leaves for the Hills* (49); for Raizman, *Kavaler zolotoi zvezdy/Cavalier of the Golden Star** (50), *Urok zhizni/Lesson of Life* (55); for Pudovkin, *Vozvrashchenie Vasiliya Bortnikova/The Return of Vassili Bortnikov** (53); for Kalatozov, *Pervi eshelon/The First Echelon* (56), *Letyat zhuravli/The Cranes are Flying** (57), *Neotpravlennoe pismo/The Letter That Wasn't Sent* (60) (also co-dir), *Ya-Cuba/I Am Cuba* (62), for Chukrai, *Sorok pervyi/The Forty-First** (56).
DIR: *Prashnai gulsara/The Ambler's Race* (69).

VADIM, Roger (Roger Vadim Plemmianikov)
DIR France. (Paris Jan 26, 1928–)
Former stage actor, journalist (for *Paris-Match*), scriptwriter, and assistant director, whose first film, the sincere *Et Dieu créa la femme* (56), contributed to the germination of the *nouvelle vague*, although it was "commercial" in parts. It was a great international success because of its bold theme and its revealing shots of Brigitte Bardot, but also perhaps because of its commercialism. This aspect continued to appear in his always stylistically mannered films — *Sait-on jamais?*, *Les Bijoutiers du clair de lune* — and soon was dominant: *Les Liaisons dangereuses*, *Et mourir de plaisir*, *Le Repos de guerrier*, *La Ronde*, *La Curée*, *Barbarella*. From his original ambitions he has retained a taste for carefully calculated eroticism and for striking color imagery. "When a film maker dies," said Delluc, "he becomes a photographer."
[ASSIST: to Marc Allégret, *Blanche Fury* (47), *Maria Chapdelaine* (50), *La Demoiselle et son revenant* (51), *Juliette* (53), *Femina* (54), *Futures vedettes* (55), *En effeuillant la marguerite* (56). SCEN: for M. Allégret, *Blackmailed* (51), *Futures vedettes* (55), *En effeuillant la marguerite* (56); for Boisrand, *Cette sacrée gamine* (55); and for his own films.]
DIR: *Et Dieu créa la femme** (56), *Sait-on jamais?* (57), *Les Bijoutiers de la clair de lune* (58), *Les Liaisons dangereuses 1960** (59), *Et Mourir de plaisir/Blood and Roses* (60), *La Bride sur le cou* (61) (replaced Jean Aurel), *Les Sept péchés capitaux* (62) (episode), *Le Repos du guerrier* (62), *Le Vice et la Vertu* (62), *Château en suède/ Nutty, Naughty Chateau* (63) (from Sagan's play), *La Ronde** (64), *La Curée/The Game is Over* (66), *His-toires extraordinaires* (67) (episode), *Barbarella* (68), *Peryl* (70), *Pretty Maids All in a Row* (USA71).

VAILLAND, Roger SCEN France. (1907–May 1965) One of the best postwar scriptwriters, he wrote Louis Daquin's *Les Frères Bouquinquant**, *Le Point du jour**, and *Bel-Ami* and collaborated on many of Vadim's commercial successes: *Les Liaisons dangereuses**, *Et mourir de plaisir*, *Le Vice et le vertu*. He also wrote Clément's *Le Jour et l'heure*.

VAJDA, Ladislao (also Laszlo V., Ladislas V.)
DIR Hungary/France/Spain, etc. (Budapest Aug 18, 1905–1965) The director of numerous mediocre films in almost every European country; his crude *Marcellino Pan y Vino* (Sp55) was a great commercial success.
[His father, Ladislaus (Laszlo) Vajda (Budapest 188?–Budapest 1933), was a well-established scriptwriter in Germany in the Twenties, best known for his work for Pabst on *Die Liebe der Jeanne Ney**, *Abwege, Die Büchse der Pandora**, *Die Weisse Hölle vom Piz Palü, Die Dreigroschenoper**, *Kameradschaft**, *L'Atlantide**. He also wrote several scripts for Michael Curtiz in Hungary, Austria, and Germany.]

VAN DYKE, W. S. (Woodbridge Strong Van Dyke) DIR USA. (1887–1944) One time actor who became assistant to Griffith (*q.v.*) on *Intolerance** (16) and later established a reputation between the two wars as a reliable director at MGM. He is famous for his "collaboration" with Flaherty on *White Shadows in the South Seas** (27) (which he completed and was credited with) and made several interesting films: *Cuban Love Song** (31), *Eskimo/Mala the Magnificent* (33), *The Thin Man** (34) (and others in the series). He also made the first sound film with Tarzan, *Tarzan the Ape Man* (32), and several Nelson Eddy-Jeanette MacDonald musicals.

VAN DYKE, Willard DIR/PHOTOG USA. (Denver Dec 5, 1906–) Good independent documentarist of the New York school, famous for his classic documentaries *The City, Valley Town, The Bridge.* Originally a student of Edward Weston's in still photography, he was a cameraman for a while before becoming a director. In the Fifties he worked in Puerto Rico, where he developed a remarkable group of documentarists led by Amilcar Tirado. Since 1965 he has been Director of the Department of Film at the Museum of Modern Art in New York, but he has occasionally produced TV documentaries.
[PHOTOG (notably): for Pare Lorentz, *The River** (37); for Losey, *Youth Gets a Break* (41); and for several of his own films, including *The City.*
DIR (notably): *The City* (39) (co-dir: Ralph Steiner), *Valley Town* (40), *The Children Must Learn* (40), *To Hear Your Banjo Play* (40), *The Bridge* (42) (co-dir: Ben Maddow), *Steeltown* (43), *Northwest U.S.A.* (44), *San Francisco* (45), *Journey into Medicine* (46), *The Photographer* (47), *Terribly Talented* (48), *Mount Vernon* (49), *Years of Change* (50), *New York University* (52), *Cabos blancos* (Puerto Rico54), *Skyscraper* (59) (co-dir: Irving Jacoby, Shirley Clarke), *Land of White Alice* (59), *Ireland, the Tear and the Smile* (60), *Search into Darkness* (61), *Harvest* (62), *Depressed Area* (63), *Rice* (64), *Frontiers of News* (64), *Frontline Cameras 1935–1965* (65).]

VAN GASTERN, Louis DIR Netherlands. (1922–) After working on newsreels, he founded his own company in 1950 and has made many documentaries, although he is best known for the interesting fiction short, *The House* (62). [He has continued to work in documentaries, including the remarkable *cinéma-vérité, Do You Get It Now, Why I'm Crying?* (70), and has made the feature, *There's No Plane for Zagreb* (71).]

VAN PARYS, Georges MUS France. (Paris June 7, 1902–Jan 1971) An excellent composer of songs and appealing light music, he has written over 120 scores for French features, but his style has best matched the films of René Clair, of Christian-Jaque on *Fanfan la Tulipe,* and of Becker on *Casque d'or.*
MUS (notably): for Clair, *Le Million** (31), *Le Silence est d'or** (47), *Les Belles de nuit* (52), *Les Grandes manoeuvres** (55), *Tout l'or du monde* (61), *Les Fêtes galantes* (65); for Lacombe, *Jeunesse* (34); for Henri Decoin, *Abus de confiance* (37), *Le Bienfaiteur* (42), *Charmants garçons* (57); for M. Achard, *Jean de la lune* (48); for Carlo-Rim, *L'Armoire volante* (48); for Christian-Jaque, *Fanfan la Tulipe** (52); for Becker, *Casque d'or** (52), *Rue de l'estrapade* (53); for Ophüls, *Madame de . . .** (53); for Cayatte, *Avant le déluge** (54); for Clouzot, *Les Diaboliques* (55); for Siodmak, *Le Grand jeu** (54); for Renoir, *French Cancan** (54); for Preston Sturges, *Les Carnets du Major Thompson* (56); for Le Chanois, *Les Misérables** (58); for La Patellière, *Rue des prairies* (59).

VARDA, Agnès DIR France. (Brussels May 30, 1928–) Independent and original, she is one of the most important film makers of the *nouvelle vague,* with a sharp, highly personal vision of both people and life, a feeling for the eternal drama reflected in the most direct actuality (*La Point courte, Cléo de 5 à 7*) and a gentle irony (the shorts *O saisons, O château, Opera Mouffe*). [Her background as a photographer is evident in the formal visual pattern of her work, her ability to capture atmosphere and telling detail: "In my films I always wanted to make people see deeply. I don't want to show things, but to give people the desire to see." Her films, even the warm, decorative *Le Bonheur,* with its symbolic use of color, reveal her theatrical interest in spectator alienation, in non-identification, in forcing the spectator to sit outside the drama and judge it esthetically and intellectually. In this, she shows her kinship to Resnais, Jean Cayrol, Henri Colpi, and Marker (all *q.v.*), all members of the so-called "Left Bank group": "We have in common a certain way of thinking, a certain complicity . . . I often have the impression that I share with Resnais the same kind of plastic vocabulary and occasionally with Marker a similar desire to amuse myself, a particular way of seeing funny things." She was originally a photographer and was official photographer for the Théâtre National Populaire from 1951.]

DIR: *La Pointe courte** (55), *O saisons, O châteaux* (57) (short), *Opéra Mouffe* (58) (short), *Du côté de la côte* (58) (short), *La Cocotte d'Azur* (59) (short), *Cléo de 5 à 7** (61), *Salut les Cubains* (63) (short; montage of still photos), *Le Bonheur** (65), *Elsa* (66) (TV short), *Les Créatures* (66), *Loin de Vietnam* (67) (in collaboration), *Huey* (68) (short), *Lion's Love* (USA69).

VARMALOV, Leonid Vassilievich DIR USSR. (July 13, 1907–Sept 3, 1962) Soviet documentarist best known for several interesting feature-length battle films during the war.

[DIR (notably): *Komsomoliia* (29), *Pilots* (38), *Arctic Journey* (40), *Defeat of the German Armies Near Moscow* (42) (co-dir: I. Kopalin), *Stalingrad* (43), *Caucasus* (44), *Victory in the South* (44), *Yugoslavia* (46), *Poland* (48), *Victory of the Chinese People* (50), *Circus Arena* (51), *Through India* (52), *The Romanian People's Republic* (53), *A Hundred Days in Burma* (57), *Meeting in America* (60), *Conflict in the Congo* (60), *The Suez Canal* (62), *Port Said* (62), *Our "Pravda"* (62).]

VASAN, S. S. (S. Srinivasan) DIR/PROD India. (Tiruthiraipandu 1900–) A Madras producer-director who as head of Gemini Studios produced many films in the Tamil language and in 1948 created a spectacular with mammoth sets, *Chandralekha* (in both Tamil and Hindi versions), a film whose great success opened up Hindi areas to films from southern India. He later became a powerful figure in the Indian film industry and president of the Film Federation of India.

VASILIEV, Georgi DIR USSR. (Nov 25, 1899–June 18, 1946) Former editor, friend, and collaborator of Sergei Vasiliev, with whom he co-directed all his films except *Unlikely But True* (32).

VASILIEV, Sergei DIR USSR. (Moscow Nov 4, 1900–Moscow Dec 16, 1959) A Red Army soldier during the Civil War and a film editor, he made a relatively late directorial debut in collaboration with his friend, Georgi Vasiliev (who together were often called "the Vasiliev brothers," though they were not related). They had both attended Eisenstein's (*q.v.*) first seminars for directors, and Alexandrov (*q.v.*) provided the script for their first fiction film, *The Sleeping Beauty*. This and their next film attracted little attention, but their famous *Chapayev* (34) marked a turning point in the development of Soviet cinema that has not always been fully understood. Sergei Yutkevich (*q.v.*) described the hero of this important film as "an interesting and complex character, but not a hero mounted on a pedestal nor a speechifier. He was presented as a courageous revolutionary, but one who was not perfect. And the film offered a typical aspect of the conflicts of the civil war because the hero was in opposition against the government representative who told him he didn't fully understand the interests of the state." They did not have equal success with their *Volochayevsk Days*, set in the Far East and portraying the end of the war against Japanese interventionists around 1922. But later, their *Defence of Tsaritsin*, completed only shortly before another battle around the town (later renamed Stalingrad), was a noble and ample work that did not have fully the career it deserved. After three abortive years during which various projects were blocked by the authorities, Georgi died. Sergei was involved for many years in the direction of the Leningrad studios but later rediscovered his epic vitality in *The Heroes of Shipka*. He died while still fully creative.

CO-DIR (with Georgi): *Podvig vo Idach/ Exploit on the Ice/The Ice-Breaker Krassnin* (28) (documentary), *The Sleeping Beauty* (29), *A Personal Matter* (31), *Chapayev** (34), *Volochayevskiye dni/Volochayevsk Days* (38), *Oborona Tsaritsina/The Defence of Tsaritsin* (42), *Front* (43).

DIR: *Geroite na Shipka/Heroes of Shipka* (Bulg55), *Octiabr' dni/October Days* (58).

VAUTIER, René DIR France. (Camaret Jan 15, 1928–) A contributor to the development of the cinemas of Black Africa with *Afrique 50* made in the Ivory Coast, *Algérie en flammes* (58), a documentary made with the FLN at the height of the civil war, and *Les Anneaux d'or de Mahdia* (60), made in Tunisia.

VAVRA, Otakar DIR Czechoslovakia. (Feb 28, 1911–) Experienced, prolific, and somewhat academic Czech director who has specialized in literary adaptations. He made several experimental shorts, *Light Penetrates Darkness* (31), *We Live in Prague* (34), *November* (35), and was a scriptwriter and assistant before his directorial debut in 1937. His best film is *The Silent Barricade* (49).

DIR (notably): *Gaudeamus Igitur* (37), *Virginity* (37), *Cech panem Kutnohorskych/The Guild of the Virgins of Kutna Hora* (38), *Humoresque* (39), *The Enchanted House* (39), *May Fairy Tales* (40), *The Turbine* (41), *Rozina sebranec/Rosina the Foundling* (45), *Nezbedny bakalar/The Mischievous Tutor* (46), *Predtucha/Presentiment* (47), *Krakatit* (48), *Nema barikada/The Silent Barricade* (49), *Nastup/Fall In!* (52), *Jan Huss* (55), *Jan Zizka* (56), *Proti vsem/All Our Enemies* (57), *Srpnova nedele/A Sunday in August* (60), *Nocni host/Night Guest* (61), *Horouci srdce/ The Passionate Heart* (62), *Romance pro kridlovku/Romance for Trumpet* (66), *Trinacta komnata/The Thirteenth Room* (69).

VEDRES, Nicole DIR France. (Paris Sept 4, 1911–1965) French writer whose personality and unusually keen perception are evident in her compilation feature, *Paris 1900,* a film at once acerbic and compassionate, picturesque and polemical. Before abandoning the cinema for television and literature, she said: "One must not explain or describe. Quite the contrary. One must go, as it were, through the outer appearance of the selected shot to feel and, without insistence, make felt that strange and unexpected 'second meaning' that always hides behind the surface of the subject."

DIR: *Paris 1900** (47), *La Vie commence demain* (50) (with André Gide, Picasso, Le Corbusier, Jean-Paul Sartre, André Labarthe, etc.), *Amazone* (51), *Aux frontières de l'homme.* (53).

VELLE, Gaston DIR France. (? – ?) A pioneer French film maker for Pathé who was originally a conjuror. From 1903 he made numerous fantasy and trick films in the Méliès (*q.v.*) manner: *L'Amant de la lure* (05), *Le Petit Jules Verne* (07), etc. He made his last film in 1914.

VELO, Carlos DIR Spain/Mexico. (Galicia 1905–) Documentary film maker, orig-

inally in Spain, he emigrated to Mexico in 1937 because of his Republican convictions and there made the remarkable dramatized documentary, *Torero!* (55), and several notable TV films. He also scripted *Raices/Roots** and is probably more creatively responsible for its success than the credited director.

[DIR/SCEN: *Castillos de Castilla* (Sp33), *Tarraco Augusto* (33), *Galicia y Compostela* (33), *Almadrabas* (34), *Infinitos* (35), *Felip II y el Escorial* (35), *La Ciudad y el Campo* (35), (co-dir: F. Mantilla), *Saudade* (36), *En un Lugar de Castilla* (36), *Romancero Marroqui* (36) *Noticiaro Espana-Mexico-Argentina* (Mex41–56), *Cine-selecciones* series (53–55), *Pintura mural Mexicana* (53), *Telerevista* series (54–55), *Cine Verdad* series (54–), *Tierra Caliente* (54), *Cinerevista* series (55–58), *Torero!** (55), *Noticiero Emma* series (56–), *Camera* series (57–), *Mexico Mio!* series (58–59). All shorts except *Torero!*]

VERGANO, Aldo DIR Italy. (Rome Aug 27, 1894–Rome Sept 21, 1957) Former scriptwriter (e.g., Blasetti's *Sole,* 29) who, although he was not able to direct many films under the Fascist regime, laid the groundwork for neorealism and gave the movement one of its first masterpieces, *Il Sole Sorge Ancora** (46).

VERMOREL, Claude DIR France. (Villié-Morgan 1909–) Dramatist who has not been able to assert his talents in the cinema, despite the quality of the two films he directed in Black Africa: *Les Conquérants solitaires* (52), *La Plus Belles des vies* (56).

VERTOV, Dziga (Denis Arkadyevich Kaufman) DIR/ED USSR. (Bialystok, Poland Jan 12, 1896–Moscow Feb 12, 1954) Creator of the "Kino-eye," film poet, theorist, and prophet of *cinéma-vérité,* whose significance in the history of the cinema has only increased with the years. He created, by his own estimate, "counting the smaller ones, not less than 150 works." He turned to the cinema in 1918 after having created in 1916 a rudimentary "Laboratory of Hearing," where he experimented with recorded sound and "musical-thematic creations of word-montage." He worked on a film journal (*Cinema Weekly*) between 1918 and 1919 and his first films were films of everyday life and historical compilation films. In the early Twenties, after having formed the Kinoks group, he issued a series of manifestos (*Kinoks-Revolution*, published in 1922) that called for the renunciation of the theatrical film, actors, sets, studios, and scripts. In the series of *Kino-Pravda* films (from 22) and the experimental *Kino-Glaz/The Kino Eye* (24) he demonstrated his approach: ["The *kino-eye* is a means of making the invisible visible, the obscure clear, the hidden obvious, the disguised exposed, and acting not acting. But it is not enough to show bits of truth in the screen, separate frames of truth. These frames must be thematically organized so that the whole is also truth."] He believed that the *kino-eye* had to be allied to the "radio-ear," the editing of images with the editing of sound. In issues 12 and 14 of *Kino-Pravda* he showed that it was possible to create a coherent narrative out of fragments of daily life photographed in different places and at different times. One of the first Soviet film makers to make use of trick photography and animation, he considered the cinematic manipulation of space and time essential: ["*Kino-eye* offers the possibility of seeing the living processes in a temporally arbitrary order and following a chosen rhythm . . . *Kino-eye* avails itself of all the current means of recording: ultra-high speed, microcinematography, reverse motion, multiple exposure, foreshortening, etc., and does not consider these as tricks, but as normal techniques of which wide use must be made. *Kino-eye* makes use of all the resources of montage, drawing together and linking the various points of the universe in a chronological or anachronistic order as one wills."] In *Kino-Glaz*, with his brother Mikhail Kaufman (*q.v.*), he developed "candid camera" techniques, "life caught unaware" in order to ["show people without their make-up on; to catch them through the camera's eye at some moment when they are not acting; to capture their thoughts by means of the camera."] His feature, *Stride, Soviet!* (26), is a cinematic discourse whose commentary, in titles, is fully integrated into, and as essential as, the images. *A Sixth of the World* (26) is a "lyrical film poem," a "universal song" uniting, through montage, life in various regions of the USSR and abroad. After *The Eleventh Year* (28), he created with Mikhail Kaufman the brilliant *Man with*

a Movie Camera (29), a portrait of urban life and a film that both used and analyzed his "candid camera" and *kino-eye* techniques and employed a number of expressive photographic tricks. The introduction of sound allowed him to make *Enthusiasm* ("a symphony of sounds" that Chaplin much admired) and *Three Songs of Lenin* (34) ("a symphony of thought"), in both of which he was able to integrate the "film-eye" with the "radio-ear." His international influence throughout the Twenties and Thirties was considerable, both on the French and German avant-gardes and on the British and New York documentarists. Everywhere, his work instigated experiments based on the montage of images and sounds and directed towards the portrayal of social themes. In his own country, however, he came under increasingly virulent critical attacks for his "formalist" approach. His creativity gradually dried up and his earlier work was largely forgotten. But in the Sixties, technical progress made more practical many of the ideas he had advanced; lightweight cameras, both "film-eye" and "radio-ear" at the same time, allowed documentarists to photograph "life caught unaware"; the phrase "cinéma-vérité" (an expression Vertov himself used only later in a direct sense) was adopted as a banner by a group of film makers and Vertov's theories and predictions found new life. Also brother of Boris Kaufman (*q.v.*).

DIR (notably): *Weekly Reels* (18–19), *Calendars of Goskinof* (19), *Anniversary of the Revolution* (19) (compilation feature), *Battle at Tsaritsyn* (20), *Prozess Mironova/The Action at Mironov* (20), *Discovery of Sergei Radonezhsky's Remains* (20), *The VTIK Train* (20), *Istoriya grazhdenskoi voini/History of the Civil War* (21), (compilation feature), *Kino-Pravda/Film-Truth* series (22–25) (23 numbers), *Kino-Glaz/Kino-Eye** (24), *Leninskaya kino-pravda/Leninist Film-Truth* (25), *October Without Ilyich* (25), *Radio kino-pravda* (25), *Shagai, Soviet!/Stride, Soviet!** (26), *Shestaya chast mira/A Sixth of the World** (26), *Odinnadtsati/The Eleventh Year* (28), *Chelovek s kinoapparatom/The Man with a Movie Camera** (28), *Entuziazm/Enthusiasm/Symphony of the Don Basin** (31), *Tri pesni o Leninye/Three Songs of Lenin** (34), *Kolibelnaya/Lullaby* (37), *Sergei Ordjonikidze*

(37) (co-dir: J. Bliokh), *Tri geroini/ Three Heroes* (38), *Krov za krov, smert za smert/Blood for Blood, Death for Death* (41), *V linii ognia/In the Front Line* (41), *V gorach Ala-Tau/In the Mountains of Ala-Tau* (44), *Kliatva molodych/Youth's Oath* (44).

VIDOR, Charles DIR USA. (Budapest July 27, 1900–Vienna June 5, 1959) Honest Hollywood technician who since 1932 directed, conscientiously but without much artistic success, 30–40 films, sometimes with large budgets — such as the mediocre *A Farewell to Arms* (57) — and is credited as director of the remarkable thriller, *Gilda** (46).

VIDOR, King DIR USA. (Galveston, Texas Feb 8, 1894–   ) An important American film maker despite the uneven quality of his work. After working as a newsreel cameraman, prop boy, and assistant, and making a series of shorts (*Judge Brown*) for Universal, he made his feature debut in 1918. His first films (often produced by himself in his own studios) were unremarkable and mainly vehicles for their stars, but he suddenly established his talents with *The Big Parade* (25). He said at that time: "It is obvious that a film must be the visual translation of the thoughts of the author. If his idea passes through the intermediary of many other minds and receives the imprint of various persons, it would come to the screen very different from what it was in the beginning. In fact I submit that it is a serious error to compose a film with pen and paper. The thing is simply impossible. A film has to be composed with the camera. The greatest source of disappointment comes from a film being envisaged as a novel or a play, when it is neither one nor the other." In order to apply his theories he financed and produced independently *The Crowd,* a film whose characters were ordinary people, "human beings with their failings and qualities in their relationships with other human beings." He gave the sound film its first masterpiece, *Hallelujah!,* a film entirely acted by blacks that was a revelation despite certain conventionalities in the characterizations. Later, another attempt at independent production, *Our Daily Bread,* did not match the quality of *The Crowd.* After this, commercialism dominated his work (*Stella Dallas, The Citadel*) and a quite brutal, almost sadistic

violence began to appear in his work — *Northwest Passage, Duel in the Sun, Ruby Gentry.* Then, after a worthy adaptation of *War and Peace,* came his final film. For him, every man, whether consciously or not, knows that his life's work cannot simply end in oblivion. That is why the Bible has always headed the list of best-sellers. Vidor's last film, *Solomon and Sheba,* was based on a Biblical episode.

DIR: *The Turn in the Road* (18), *Better Times* (19), *The Other Half* (19), *Poor Relations* (19), *The Jack-Knife Man* (19), *The Family Honor* (20), *The Sky Pilot* (21), *Love Never Dies* (21), *Conquering the Woman* (21), *Woman, Wake Up* (21), *The Real Adventure* (22), *Dusk to Dawn* (22), *Alice Adams* (22), *Peg O'My Heart* (22), *The Woman of Bronze* (23), *Three Wise Fools* (23), *Wild Oranges* (23), *Happiness* (23), *Wine of Youth* (24), *His Hour* (24), *Wife of the Centaur* (24), *Proud Flesh* (25), *The Big Parade** (25), *La Bohème* (25), *Bardelys the Magnificent* (26), *The Crowd** (28), *The Patsy/The Political Flapper* (28), *Show People* (28), *Hallelujah!** (29), *Not So Dumb* (30), *Billy the Kid* (30), *Street Scene* (31), *The Champ* (31), *Bird of Paradise* (32), *Cynara* (32), *The Stranger's Return* (33), *Our Daily Bread** (34), *The Wedding Night* (35), *So Red the Rose* (35), *The Texas Rangers* (36), *Stella Dallas** (37), *The Citadel* (Brit38), *Northwest Passage* (40), *Comrade X* (40), *H. M. Pulham Esq.* (41), *An American Romance* (44), *Duel in the Sun** (46), *On Our Merry Way* (48) (co-dir: Leslie Fenton), *The Fountainhead* (49), *Beyond the Forest* (49), *Lightning Strikes Twice* (50), *Japanese War Bride* (51), *Ruby Gentry* (52), *Man without a Star* (54), *War and Peace** (55), *Solomon and Sheba* (59).

*VIERNY, Sacha PHOTOG France. (1919–   ) One of the most distinguished of modern French cameramen, a master at capturing the details of a shot. He had a close collaboration with Resnais (*q.v.*) for many years: *Nuit et Brouillard** (55), *Le Chant du styrène* (58), *Hiroshima mon amour** (59) (French scenes), *L'Année dernière à Marienbad** (61), *Muriel** (63), *La Guerre est finie** (66). Also notably, for Marker, *Lettre de Sibérie* (57); for Varda, *Opéra Mouffe* (58); for Buñuel, *Belle de jour** (67).

VIEYRA, Paulin DIR Senegal. (Dahomey Jan 30, 1923–) Principal pioneer of the Senegal cinema, he directed *Afrique-sur-Seine* while studying at IDHEC in Paris then in Dakar, *Un homme, un idéal, une vie,* a dramatization of the life of a fisherman.

VIGO, Jean (Jean Bonaventure de Vigo) DIR France. (Paris April 26, 1905–Paris Oct 5, 1934) The cinema's Rimbaud, not only because of his brief career but also because of his peculiarly personal mode of expression, the vividness of his imagery, his compelling lyricism, and the directness of his language. [The son of Eugène Bonaventure de Vigo (better known as the militant anarchist, Miguel Almereyda), who died in jail, he was educated in various boarding schools, started his career in a photographer's studio, and later became an assistant cameraman. He met the Russian emigré, Boris Kaufman (*q.v.*)] and, with him, planned his documentary about Nice: *A propos de Nice,* a kind of *kino-eye* social documentary that Vigo characterized as *point de vue documenté* and that was, in effect, a bitterly ironic portrait of middle-class decadence. "I don't know whether the result will be a work of art," he said at the time, "but I am sure it will be cinema. Cinema in the sense that no other art, no science, can take its place. The maker of social documentaries is a man thin enough to squeeze through a Romanian keyhole and shoot Prince Carol getting up in his nightshirt — granted the spectacle would be worthy of interest. He is a small enough fellow to squat under the chair of the croupier — the Great God of the Casino at Monte Carlo . . . Social documentary is distinct from the ordinary short film and the weekly newsreel in that its creator will establish his own point of view . . . It will dot its own i's. If it doesn't involve an artist it involves at least a man. Conscious acting cannot be tolerated; the character must be surprised by the camera . . . We shall achieve our aim if we can reveal the hidden reason for a gesture, if we can extract from an ordinary person, quite by chance, his interior beauty — or a caricature of him — if we can reveal his complete inner spirit through his purely external manifestations." After the beautiful and whimsical short study of a swimmer, *Jean Taris,* he turned to drama with *Zéro de conduite.*

This short feature, drawn from Vigo's own childhood experiences, was at once realistic, poetic, and symbolic, a film of delicate and profound psychological and sociological overtones. It so shocked bourgeois sentiments that it was banned without appeal by the French censor. "It had to await the Liberation (1945) in order to be liberated. He was said to be a rebel, an anarchist. On the contrary, he was a revolutionary, a builder. But in order to build he had first to destroy" (Claude Aveline). His next, and last, film *L'Atalante* was a commissioned, commercial film, but he radically transformed the story of the life of a barge sailor into a poem about love, blending lyrical passages with scenes of daily life on the barge, comedy with insight into feelings and tenderness. Vigo wrote: "We were intoxicated by the admirable landscape of the Parisian canals and developed the action against a backdrop of locks, steep banks, *guingettes,* and waste ground." After the film's completion, he fell seriously ill and his film was mutilated by its distributors and re-edited; a theme song was added and its title became the release title *Le Chaland qui passe.* He died at 29, just before the film's premiere, having briefly but magnificently demonstrated his creative genius. DIR: *A propos de Nice** (29–30), *Jean Taris, champion de natation/Taris, roi de l'eau* (30–31), *Zéro de conduite** (33), *L'Atalante/Le Chaland qui passe** (34).

VISCONTI, Luchino (Luchino Visconti de Modrone) DIR Italy. (Milan Nov 2, 1906–) One of the most brilliant of modern film makers whose work has ranged from the first neorealist masterpiece, *Ossessione,* to *Death in Venice.* Born into an ancient and noble family he has never let himself be dominated by his background nor his enthusiasm for breeding race horses. He is a committed communist (though opposed to the Party) and a Christian (though often anticlerical). From 1936–40 he was Renoir's (*q.v.*) assistant in France: ["His was a human influence not a professional one. To be with Renoir, to listen to him, that opened my mind."] This influence is evident in his first film, *Ossessione,* a film that forced the realities of Italy into a cinema then dominated by propaganda and "white telephones" — much to the irritation of the Fascists. Soon after Mussolini's fall, he wrote: "I was impelled toward the cinema by, above all, the need to tell stories of people who were alive, of people living amid things and not of the things themselves. The cinema that interests me is an anthropomorphic cinema. The most humble gestures of man, his bearing, his feelings, and instincts are sufficient to make the things that surround him poetic and alive. The significance of the human being, his presence, is the only thing that could dominate the images. The ambience that it creates and the living presence of its passions give them life and depth. And its momentary absence from the luminous rectangle gives to everything an appearance of dead nature" (1943). After the war he began making a vast three-part fresco of Sicilian life, *La Terra trema,* but was only able to complete the first part, the episode of the sea, a neorealist film totally different from *Bicycle Thieves.* For some years thereafter he restricted his activities to the theater and opera, in which he established a reputation as the greatest Italian director. After the interlude of *Bellissima* he returned to the cinema in full creative force with *Senso,* a romantic and romanesque evocation of the Risorgimento, a lyric melodrama whose tone was set by the music of Guiseppe Verdi as that of *La Terra trema* had been set by the novels of Giovanni Verga. "It has been said that my films are a little theatrical and my theater a little cinematic. Every means of expression is good. Neither the theater nor the cinema should avoid whatever serves it. It is possible that I have exaggerated by using techniques not typical of the cinema. But avoidance of the theatrical is not a rule, especially if one considers the beginnings, Méliès for example." After the Stendhalian, romantic adaptation of Dostoevski, *White Nights,* he created *Rocco and His Brothers,* a film that in some ways recalls a Greek tragedy, but is mainly a film-novel in the great realist tradition. Its theme of the disintegration in urban life of a peasant family from the south is something of a continuation of *La Terra trema.* [Since then Visconti has turned completely away from traditional concepts of "realism," his work reaching new heights in a series of brilliant period films and symbolic social dramas marked by their claustrophobic atmospheres of corruption and despair. Visconti once described himself as "very German" and the embryonic German Romanticism of his earlier films has since reached full flowering in the powerful adaptation of Lampedusa's *The Leopard,* the lurid vision of fatalistic passion, *Sandra,* and the brilliant, extravagant portrait of society trapped by destiny and decadence, *The Damned.* His attempt to capture the quality of Camus's *The Stranger* was less successful. Unquestionably his most perfect film is *Death in Venice* from Mann's novella, a richly textured, obsessional study of passion and social putrefaction whose use of musical association recalls the use of a César Franck theme as a reminder of the past in *Sandra.* He said: "I think of *Death in Venice* as essentially the search by an artist for perfection in art and the impossibility of achieving it. When he achieves it, that's death. There is a second theme: the dualism between bourgeois respectability and the corruption within the artist — the seeds of genius and self-destruction . . . The boy (is) a sort of angel of destiny, a fatal presence; he knows, instinctively, that he will lead Aschenbach to his death."]

ASSIST: to Jean Renoir, *Les Bas-Fonds** (36), *Une partie de campagne** (36), *La Tosca* (It40, completed by Carl Koch). DIR: *Ossessione** (42), *Giorni di Gloria* (45) (co-dir: De Santis) (compilation film), *La Terra trema** (48), *Bellissima* (51), *Appunti su un Fatto di Cronaca* (51) (short), *Siamo Donne* (52) (episode), *Senso** (53), *Le Notti Bianche** (57), *Rocco e i suoi Fratelli** (60), *Il Gattopardo** (62), *Boccaccio '70* (62) (episode), *Vaghe Stelle dell'Orsa/Sandra /Of a Thousand Delights** (65), *La Streghe* (66) (episode), *Lo Straniero* (67), *La Caduti degli Dei/The Damned** (69), *Morte a Venezia* (71).

VISHNEVSKY, Vsevolod Vital'evich SCEN USSR. (St. Petersburg 1900–Moscow 1951) Soviet dramatist, best known for *Optimisticheskaya tragediya/the Optimistic Tragedy,* 1932 (filmed by Samsonov in 1964), and the Stalinist *Nezabyvayemi 1919 god/The Unforgettable Year 1919,* 1949 (filmed in 1952 by Chiaureli from Vishnevsky's script); he also wrote the original script of the remarkable *My iz Kronstadt/We from Kronstadt** (36) (dir: Yefim Dzigan).

VON STERNBERG, Josef see STERNBERG, Josef von

VON STROHEIM, Erich *see* **STROHEIM, Erich von**

*VORKAPICH, Slavko SPECIAL EFFECTS/DIR USA. (Dobrinci, Serbia March 17, 1894–) Renowned advocate of "purely cinematic expression" who has been restricted for most of his film career to designing special "montage" effects for features such as *Crime Without Passion** (34), *Viva Villa** (34), *The Good Earth** (37), *Broadway Melody of 1938* (37), *Mr Smith Goes to Washington** (39), *Joan of Arc** (48). He studied painting in Belgrade, Budapest, and Paris, and in 1921 went to Hollywood, where he appeared in supporting roles in several films, including Rex Ingram's *Scaramouche* (23). Although he did not abandon painting, he became deeply interested in film esthetics and wrote for *American Cinematographer* and *Film Mercury* in the Twenties. He co-directed, designed, photographed, and edited the famous experimental short, *Life and Death of a Hollywood Extra*. This led to his being engaged by the Hollywood studios (Paramount, RKO, etc.) as a special-effects technician and montage specialist. During the war he worked on sponsored government documentaries and then made two experimental shorts, striking impressionistic interpretation of Wagner's *Forest Murmurs* and Mendelssohn's *Fingal's Cave*. Parallel with his filmmaking activities he continued to teach film at the University of Southern California and write essays on film theory. He returned to Yugoslavia in 1952, taught film direction for four years at the Belgrade Academy of Dramatic Art and was artistic consultant to Avala Film. He directed his first solo feature, *Hanka,* a story of love and revenge among gypsies in 1955. He gave a series of lectures in New York in 1964–65.
DIR: *The Life and Death of 9413 a Hollywood Extra* (28) (co-dir: Robert Florey), *The Past of Mary Holmes* (33) (co-dir: Harlan Thompson), *Fingal's Cave* (46), *Forest Murmurs* (47), *Hanka* (Yug55).

VUKOTIC, Dusan ANIM Yugoslavia. (1927–) One of the best modern animators, founder of the "Zagreb school" and one of the first to break away from the Disney (*q.v.*) style. He has a remarkable sense of zany humor. His work has won numerous international awards, including an Oscar for *Ersatz*.
[ANIM (notably): *How Kico was Born* (51), *The Enchanted Castle in Dudinci* (52), *The Playful Robot* (56), *Cowboy Jimmy* (57), *Abracadabra* (58), *Great Fear* (58), *Concerto for Submachine Gun* (59), *The Cow on the Moon* (59), *My Tail's My Ticket* (59), *Piccolo* (60), *Ersatz* (61), *Play* (62), *The Seventh Continent* (Czech/Yug66) (feature), *A Stain on the Conscience* (68), *Opera Cordis* (68).]

VULCHANOV, Rangel DIR Bulgaria. (1928–) Individualistic and talented film maker of the new Bulgarian cinema, his first film, which dealt with an episode in the revolutionary struggle of the Twenties, not only established his reputation but was germinal to the development of the Bulgarian cinema in the Sixties.
[DIR: *Na malkia ostrov/On the Little Island* (58), *Parvi urok/First Lesson* (60), *Slantseto i syankata/Sun and Shadow* (62), *Inspectorat i noshta/ The Inspector and the Night* (63), *Valchitsata/ The She-Wolf* (65), *Between Two Worlds* (68) (documentary feature), *Esop/Aesop* (Bulg/Czech69).]

WAGNER, Fritz Arno PHOTOG Germany/
German Federal Republic. (Schmiedefeld
am Rennsteig Dec 5, 1894–Göttingen
Aug 18, 1958) Brilliant cameraman of
the classic German period who contributed unforgettable images both to the
expressionist films of Murnau (*q.v.*),
Lang (*q.v.*). and others, and later to the
realist films of Pabst (*q.v.*). He began his
film career as an apprentice working
for Pathé in Paris and was later a
newsreel cameraman during the war and
in New York and Mexico. He returned
to Berlin in 1919 as cameraman for
Decla-Bioscop. He continued to work in
Germany under the Nazis and afterwards
in West Germany. He collaborated on
some 200 films in his career, but his
contributions after 1933 were of lesser
importance.
PHOTOG (notably): for Murnau, *Schloss
Vogelöd* (21), *Der Brennende Acker*
(22), *Nosferatu** (33); for Lang, *Der
Müde Tod** (21), *Spione* (28), *M**
(31), *Das Testament des Dr. Mabuse**
(33); for Robison, *Schatten** (22); for
Gerlach, *Zur Chronik von Grieshus* (25);
for Pabst, *Die Liebe der Jeanne Ney**
(27), *Westfront 1918** (30), *Skandal
um Eva* (30), *Die Dreigroschenoper**
(31), *Kameradschaft** (31); for Gustav
Ucicky, *Flüchtlinge* (33); for Reinhold
Schünzel, *Amphitryon* (35); for Hans
Steinhoff, *Robert Koch* (39), *Ohm
Krüger* (41); for Arthur Pohl, *Die Brücke*
(GDR49); for Erik Ode, *Ohne Mutter
geht es nicht* (58) (last film).

WAHBY, Youssef DIR Egypt. (1899–)
Successful actor and dramatist, founder
of the Ramses troupe, and author and
director of very many film melodramas.
The successful adaptation of his play,
Zeinab, contributed to the development
of the Egyptian cinema. He collaborated
with his friend Muhammed Karim on

the production of film versions of his
plays, *Zeinab* (30) and *Awlad el zawat/
Spoiled Children* (31), then himself took
to directing melodramas with songs and
dances, such as *Jawhara* (42), *Berlanti*
(43), *Gharam wa Intikam/Passion and
Revenge* (44), *Safir Gehannam/The Ambassador of Hell* (44), *Banat el Rif/The
Country Girls* (45), *Awlad el Shareh/
Children of the Streets* (51), *Bint el
Hawa/Daughter of Love* (53), etc.

WAIMON, Seto DIR China. (Shanghai
191?–) Chinese film maker of the
Shanghai school who was responsible for
many interesting, sometimes pre-neorealist, films between 1933–45. In 1955 he
became director of the Chinese State
cinema.
DIR (notably): *The Statue of Liberty*
(35), *The Players at the Gate of Love*
(37), *Yellow Flowers through a Rainy
Day* (37), *The Battle of Pao Shan* (38),
The Song of the Partisans (38) (documentary), *The Nation's Appeal* (40).

WAJDA, Andrzej DIR Poland. (Suwalki
May 9, 1926–) Together with Munk
(*q.v.*), the best Polish film maker of his
generation. After studying at the film
school at Lodz, he assisted Ford on
Five Boys from Barska Street* (53) and
revealed his sincerity, forceful style, and
typical preoccupation with social issues
and heroism in his first feature, *A Generation.* Soon after, though barely 30, he
created *Kanal,* an important work of the
Fifties that portrayed the Battle of Warsaw, brutally setting against each other,
love and death, heroism and stupidity, ra-
tionality and traditional patriotism. *Ashes
and Diamonds,* the third part of the
trilogy, was even better, despite certain
baroque overtones. [With *Samson,* he
escaped from the themes of his earlier
work to attempt, largely successfully, a

deeper, introspective examination of character. But his work through most of the Sixties was disappointing and not always successful. All these films, except for the excellent episode in *Love at Twenty*, and the austere *Innocent Sorcers*, were period films ranging from the frenetic *Siberian Lady Macbeth* to the mediocre *Gates of Paradise*. Then with *Everything for Sale, Hunting Flies, Landscape after Battle*, and *The Birch Wood* he found new perspective and maturity, a wide-ranging stylistic and thematic assurance, and a greater concern with the "esthetic, psychological experiences of man" (Wajda).] He considers himself a "violent romantic" but feels that "this way of life and of thinking has become difficult in a stabilized society. Munk and I attempted to illustrate this crisis of conscience, that one cannot accomplish heroic or liberal acts if they are useless, but that there is in every man an aspiration to be better."

[DIR (shorts): *Kiedy ty spisz/While You're Asleep* (50), *Zly chlopiec/Evil Boy* (50), *Ceramika Ilzecka/Ilza Ceramics* (51), *Ide ku sloncu/I Go Toward the Sun* (55), *Przekladaniec/Roly-Poly* (68) (TV).]

DIR (features): *Pokolenie/A Generation** (55), *Kanal** (56), *Popol i diament/ Ashes and Diamonds** (58), *Lotna* (59), *Niewinni czarodzieje/Innocent Sorcerers* (60), *Samson** (61), *Sibirska Ledi Magbet/Siberian Lady Macbeth* (Yugos 62), *L'Amour à vingt ans* (Fr62) (episode), [*Wywidd z Ballmayerem/The Ballmayer Interview* (62) (TV), *Cudza zona i maz pod lozkiem/Another's Wife and Husband under the Bed* (62) (TV), *Popioly/Ashes* (65), *Gates to Paradise/ Vrata raja* (Brit/Yugos67), *Wszystko na sprzedaz/Everything for Sale* (68), *Polowanie na muchy/Hunting Flies* (69), *Magbet/Macbeth* (69) (TV), *Krajobraz po bitwie/Landscape after Battle* (70), *Brzezina/The Birch Wood* (71).

SCEN: *Trzy opowiesci/Three Stories* (53) (episode film; dir: C. Petelski, K. Nalecki, E. Petelska), *Apel poleglych/Roll Call* (56) (documentary; dir: B. Poreba), and his own *Ashes and Diamonds, Lotna, Samson, Everything for Sale, Landscape after Battle*.]

WAKHEVITCH, Georges ART DIR France. (Odessa, Russia Aug 18, 1907-) Designer with a subtle, delicate, and exuberant style, particularly gifted on period films. He is also a painter and, since 1927, a stage designer.

ART DIR (notably): for Rex Ingram, *Baroud* (32); for Jean Epstein, *L'Homme à l'Hispano* (32); for Renoir, *Madame Bovary* (34), *La Grande Illusion** (37), *La Marseillaise** (38); for Robert Siodmak, *Pièges* (39); for Carné, *Les Visiteurs du soir** (42); for Delannoy, *L'Éternel retour** (43); for Yves Allégret, *Dedée d'Anvers* (47); for Pierre Billon, *L'Homme au chapeau rond* (46), *Ruy Blas* (47); for Cocteau, *l'Aigle à deux têtes* (47); for Clouzot, *Miquette et sa mère* (49); for Peter Brook, *The Beggar's Opera* (Brit53), *King Lear* (Brit/ Den70); for Becker, *Ali Baba et les quarante voleurs* (54); for Duvivier, *Marie-Octobre* (58); for Gérard Oury, *Le Crime ne paie pas* (62); for Buñuel, *Le Journal d'une femme de chambre** (64); for Clair, *Les Fêtes galantes* (65).

WALLER, Fred INVENTOR USA. (Brooklyn 1886–New York May 18, 1954) The inventor of Cinerama (three electronically synchronized projectors) and a research technician for many years, he originally worked on special effects for Paramount in the Twenties and was one of the inventors of water skiing. At the New York World's Fair in 1939, he presented a spectacle on a hemispheric screen and during the war used multiscreen projections in shows for the armed forces. His triple projector–triple screen technique with multitrack stereophonic sound was finally premiered commercially in New York in November 1952 and had considerable success. [*How the West Was Won** was the first fiction film in Cinerama. The three-camera system, abandoned in the Sixties in favor of a single lens system using wide film for increased definition, is now indistinguishable from other wide-screen systems.]

WALSH, Raoul DIR USA. (New York March 11, 1889-) One of the great Hollywood veterans, with a 52-year film career spanning both silent and sound periods. Like Henry King, Clarence Brown, and Allan Dwan (all *q.v.*) he is an honorable director of great technical skill whose film career began in the great days of Griffith (*q.v.*) — whose assistant he was — and Ince (*q.v.*) — the feeling of whose films is sometimes found in Walsh's work. He was originally a "heavy" in westerns, became Griffith's assistant in 1912, and directed his first (short) films in 1914 and his first features for Fox in 1915. His early films reveal his gift for handling narrative in the most forceful way, though he has never been as skilled as his contemporaries, John Ford, Frank Borzage, and Howard Hawks (all q.v.). He has worked in every genre, moving with ease from thrillers (notably They Drive By Night) to biblical spectaculars, from melodramas to costume dramas, but this typically American director has naturally excelled in westerns (Pursued, Silver River, Cheyenne, Colorado Territory, The Sheriff of Fractured Jaw) and has made many war films (What Price Glory? Battle Cry, The Naked and the Dead, Objective Burma).

[DIR (shorts, notably): The Double Knot (14), The Gunman (14), The Death Dice (15), The Buried Hand (15), The Celestial Code (15).
DIR (features): The Regeneration (15), Carmen* (15), The Serpent (16), Blue Blood and Red (16), The Honor System (17), The Conqueror (17), Betrayed (17), This Is the Life (17), The Pride of New York (17), The Silent Lie (17), The Innocent Sinner (17), The Woman and the Law (18), The Prussian Cur (18), On the Jump (18), Every Mother's Son (19), Evangeline (19), The Strongest (19), Should a Husband Forgive? (20), From Now On (20), The Deep Purple (20), The Oath (21), Serenade (21), Lost and Found (22), Kindred of the Dust (22), The Thief of Bagdad (24), East of Suez (25), The Spaniard (25), The Wanderer (25), The Lucky Lady (26), The Lady of the Harem (26), What Price Glory? (26), The Monkey Talks (27), The Loves of Carmen* (27), Sadie Thompson (28), The Red Dance (28), Me, Gangster (28), Hot for Paris (29), In Old Arizona (29), The Cock-Eyed World (29), The Big Trail (30), The Man Who came Back (31), Women of All Nations (31), Yellow Ticket (31), Wild Girl (32), Me and My Gal (32), Sailor's Luck (33), The Bowery (33), Going Hollywood (33), Under Pressure (35), Baby-Face Harrington (35), Every Night at Eight (35), Klondike Annie (36), Big Brown Eyes (36), Spendthrift (36), You're in the Army Now (37), When Thief Meets Thief (Brit37), Artists and Models (37), Hitting a New High (37), College Swing (38), St. Louis Blues (39), The Roaring Twenties (39), Dark Command (40), They Drive By Night (40), High Sierra (41), Strawberry Blond (41), Manpower (41), They Died With Their Boots On (41), Desperate Journey (42), Gentleman Jim (42), Background to Danger (43), Northern Pursuit (43), Uncertain Glory (44), Objective Burma! (45), Salty O'Rourke (45), The Horn Blows at Midnight (45), The Man I Love (46), Pursued (47), Cheyenne (47), Silver River (48), Fighter Squadron (48), One Sunday Afternoon (48), Colorado Territory (49), White Heat (49), Along the Great Divide (51), Captain Horatio Hornblower (Brit51), Distant Drums (51), Glory Alley (52), The World in His Arms (52), The Lawless Breed (52), Blackbeard the Pirate (52), Sea Devils (53), A Lion is in the Streets (53), Gun Fury (53), Saskatchewan/ O'Rourke of the Royal Mounted (54), Battle Cry (55), The Tall Men (55), The Revolt of Mamie Stover (56), The King and Four Queens (56), Band of Angels (57), The Naked and the Dead (58), The Sheriff of Fractured Jaw (59), A Private's Affair (59), Esther and the King (60), Marines, Let's Go (61), A Distant Trumpet (64). He has scriped many of his own films.]

WALTERS, Charles DIR/CHOREOG USA. (Pasadena, California Nov 17, 1911–) Former dancer who has specialized in Hollywood musicals and contributed to the genre's revitalization at MGM in the Forties, first as choreographer, e.g., Girl Crazy (43) (co-choreog: Berkeley), Meet Me in St. Louis* (44), Ziegfeld Follies (46), then as director of the delightful, if slightly syrupy, Easter Parade (48), The Barkleys of Broadway (49), Summer Stock (50), The Belle of New York (52), Lili (52). Then, with lesser means and less success he evolved toward sophisticated comedy with High Society (56) (a mediocre remake of The Philadelphia Story*), Ask Any Girl (59), and Please Don't Eat the Daisies (60), and finally fell into mediocrity — except for the curious Two Loves (61).

*WALTON, William MUS Britain. (Oldham, Lancashire 1902–) Apart from Benjamin Britten and Ralph Vaughan Williams, the most famous of modern English composers whose sweeping rhythms and aural sensuality are evident in his

271

few films scores, notably: for Olivier, *Henry V** (45), *Hamlet** (49), *Richard III* (56); for Leslie Howard, *The First of the Few* (42); for Charles Frend, *The Foreman Went to France* (42); for Gabriel Pascal, *Major Barbara* (41).

WANG, Tso-lin DIR China. (19? –) In Shanghai after the war he directed several excellent "neorealist" films (though he had never heard of the Italian movement) that continued the tradition of the avant-garde Chinese cinema of the Thirties.
DIR: *Hairdresser No. 3* (47), *The Lower Depths** (48) (from Gorky), *The Watch* (49), *The Ideological Problem* (50) (co-dir: Ting-Li), *Corruption* (50), *The Window of America* (52) (co-dir: Shih Hueh).

*WANGER, Walter (Walter Feuchtwanger) (San Francisco July 11, 1894–1968) Independent Hollywood producer who worked with Paramount, MGM, and Columbia in the Thirties and with Allied Artists in the Fifties, and ended his career with the debacle of *Cleopatra**. He worked with many notable film makers (Lang, Ford) and on many excellent films, including *The Cocoanuts* (29), *Gabriel over the White House* (33), *Queen Christina* (33), *The President Vanishes* (34), *Sabotage* (36), *You Only Live Once** (37), *Algiers** (38), *Stagecoach** (39), *Foreign Correspondent* (40), *Scarlet Street** (45), *The Last Moment* (47), *Joan of Arc** (48), *The Reckless Moment* (49), *Riot in Cell Block 11* (54), *The Invasion of the Body Snatchers** (56), *The Quiet American* (56), *I Want To Live!* (58).

*WARM, Hermann ART DIR Germany/France/German Federal Republic (Berlin 1889–) One of the greatest European designers whose distorted set perspectives were a basic contribution to the development of German film expressionism (*Caligari, Destiny, The Student of Prague,* etc.), but who also, unlike many of his colleagues of the same period, maintained a high level of creativity in later years — from Dreyer's *Passion of Joan of Arc* and *Vampyr* to *Le Corbeau, Wozzeck,* and *Love Now, Pay Later.* He was originally a stage designer and in the Thirties worked as a freelance architect and designer throughout Europe. He spent the war years in Switzerland and returned to Germany in 1947.

ART DIR (notably): for Max Mach, *Die Blaue Maus* (12), *Der Andere* (13), *Der König* (13); for Richard Oswald, *Die Geschichte der stillen Mühle* (15), *Dreyfus* (30); for Robert Wiene, *Das Cabinett des Dr. Caligari** (19); for Otto Rippert, *Die Pest in Florenz* (19), *Totentanz* (19); for Lang, *Die Spinnen* I, II (19–20), *Kämpfende Herzen* (21), *Der Müde Tod** (21); for Murnau, *Schloss Vogelöd* (21), *Phantom* (22); for Henrik Galeen, *Der Student von Prag* (26); for Pabst, *Gräfin Donelli* (24), *Die Liebe der Jeanne Ney** (27); for Lupu Pick *Eine Nacht in London* (28); for Dreyer, *La Passion de Jeanne d'Arc** (28), *Vampyr** (31); for Fritz Wendhausen, *Peer Gynt* (34); for Arthur Robison, *Der Student von Prag* (35); for Willi Forst, *Mazurka* (35); for Clouzot, *Le Corbeau** (43); for Georg C. Klaren, *Wozzek* (47); for Kurt Hoffmann, *Hokuspokus* (52); for Franz Peter Wirth, *Helden* (58); for Victor Trivas, *Die Nackte und der Satan/The Hand* (59); for Rudolf Jugert, *Die Wahrheit über Rosemarie/Love Now, Pay Later* (59).

WARNER BROTHERS: Harry M. (Kraznashiltz, Poland 1881–1958), **Albert** (Baltimore 1884–1967), **Samuel** (Baltimore 1888–1927), **Jack L.** (London, Ontario 1892–) PROD USA.The sons of a Polish immigrant cobbler and peddler, they began by buying a film projector in 1904 and giving traveling shows. From 1905 to 1907 they ran a theater in Newcastle, Pennsylvania, and then moved into film distribution. Jack and Sam failed in several unsuccessful attempts at production, only making their first successful film in 1919. Warner Brothers Pictures Inc. was established in 1923 and the company absorbed Vitagraph in 1924. They soon ran into financial difficulties, but Sam convinced his brothers to collaborate in developing the patent on a process for synchronizing recorded musical and vocal accompaniment with films. Their gamble was a great success and first *Don Juan* (26) and then *The Jazz Singer** (27) revolutionized the industry. In 1929 they absorbed the once powerful First National, together with its numerous theaters and distribution outlets. Warner Brothers became one of the Hollywood "Big Five," producing during the Thirties a hundred features a year and controlling 360 theaters in the USA and 400 abroad. [Jack was vice-president in charge of production, Harry was president and Albert was treasurer. Albert retired in 1956 and Harry died two years later. Jack remained as head of production until the take-over by Seven Arts in 1965, when he became president of the Warner-7 Arts Studio, retaining his own independent production unit (*My Fair Lady**, *Camelot*). He retired in 1969, the same year Warner-7 Arts merged with Kinney National Services Inc.]

WATT, Harry DIR Britain. (Edinburgh Oct 10, 1906–) British documentarist and film maker who joined Grierson (*q.v.*) at the Empire Marketing Board Film Unit in 1931 and was Flaherty's (*q.v.*) assistant on *Man of Aran**. He then made several notable documentaries before turning to fiction. He retained in his features a feeling for locations (Britain, Australia, Africa) and made them all with great integrity, maintaining as far as possible the ideals of his documentary background. His best film is *The Overlanders,* the odyssey of a cattle drive across the Australian outback.

DIR (shorts, notably): *Six-thirty Collection* (34), *Night Mail** (36) (co-dir: Basil Wright), *The Saving of Bill Blewitt* (37), *Big Money* (37), *North Sea* (38), *Squadron 992* (39), *The First Days* (39) (in collaboration with Cavalcanti, Jennings, Pat Jackson, etc.), *London Can Take It* (40) (co-dir: Jennings), *The Front Line* (40), *Britain at Bay* (40), *Christmas under Fire* (41), *Dover Revisited* (42), *21 Miles* (42).

DIR (features): *Target for Tonight* (41) (documentary), *Nine Men* (42), *Fiddlers Three* (44), *The Overlanders* (46), *Eureka Stockade* (48), *Where No Vultures Fly/Ivory Hunter* (51), *People Like Maria* (53) (UN documentary), *West of Zanzibar* (54), *The Siege of Pinchgut* (58).

WEGENER, Paul DIR/SCEN Germany. (Bischdorf, East Prussia Dec. 11, 1874– Berlin Sept 13, 1948) A famous film actor during the silent and Nazi periods who was trained by Max Reinhardt (*q.v.*) at the Deutsches Theater. He also played a role as director and scriptwriter in several notable fantasy films, including the original Golem films.
[DIR: *Die Augen des Ole Brandis* (14) (co-dir: Stellan Rye), *Evintrude, die Geschichte eines Abenteurers* (14) (co-

dir: Rye), *Der Golem** (14) (co-dir: Galeen), *Rübezahls Hochzeit* (16), *Der Yoghi* (16), *Der Golem und die Tänzerin** (17), *Hans Trutz im Schlaraffenland* (17), *Der Rattenfänger von Hameln* (18), *Der Fremde Fürst* (18), *Welt ohne Waffen* (18) (documentary), *Der Golem, Wie er in die Welt kam** (20), *Der Verlorene Schatten* (21), *Herzog Ferrantes Ende* (22), *Lebende Buddhas Götter des Tibet* (24), *Ein Mann will nach Deutschland* (34), *Die Freundin eines grossen Mannes* (34), *August der Starke* (36), *Moskau-Shanghai/Der Weg nach Shanghai* (36), *Die Stunde der Versuchung* (36), *Unter Ausschluss der offentlichkeit* (37), *Krach und Glück um Künnemann* (37).

SCEN: for Stellan Ray, *Der Student von Prag* (13); *Peter Schlemihl* (15); for Rochus Gliese, *Der Galeerensträfling* (19), and for most of his own films.]
He acted in dozens of films, including many of his own, ranging from his dual roles in *The Student of Prague* and *The Golem* to the Nazi propaganda film, *Kohlberg* (44).

WEISS, Jiři DIR Czechoslovakia. (Prague March 29, 1913–) The best Czech film maker of his generation, he began his career as a documentarist in Prague (1934–38) and with the Crown Film Unit in Britain during the war (1939–45). His documentary background is evident in his feeling for natural locations but he has also a sense of precise characterization and sometimes of irony.
[DIR (shorts, notably): *People in the Sun* (35), *Give Us Wings* (36), *Song of a Sad Country* (37), *Journey from the Shadows* (38), *The Rape of Czechoslovakia* (Brit39), *Eternal Prague* (Brit 41).]
DIR (features): *John Smith Wakes Up* (Brit41), *Uloupena branice/Stolen Frontier* (47), *Dravci/Wild Beasts* (48), *Pisen o sletu/High Flies the Hawk* (49) (documentary feature in 2 parts), *Posledni vystrel/The Last Shot* (50), *Vstanou novi bojovnici/New Warriors Shall Arise* (50), *Muj pritel Fabian/ My Friend the Gypsy* (53), *Putna a ctyrlistek/Doggie and the Four* (54), *Hra o zivot/Life Was the Stake* (56), *Vlci jama/Wolf Trap* (57), *Takova Laska/Appassionata* (59), *Romeo, Julie a tma/Romeo, Juliet, and Darkness* (60), *Zblabelec/The Coward* (61), *Zlate kapradi/The Golden Fern* (63), *31*

stupnu ve stinu/Ninety in the Shade (Czech/Brit64), *Vrazda po Cesku/Murder — Czech Style* (67).

WELLES, Orson DIR USA/France/Spain. (Kenosha, Wisconsin May 6, 1915–) The cinema would have been the worse for the lack of this disorderly genius, the one-time child prodigy, wise before his time, who loved to make himself up as an old man and yet retained something of his childhood as part of his guiding spirit. Cocteau offered this portrait: "He has the manner of a giant with the look of a child, a lazy activeness, a mad wisdom, a solitude encompassing the world; he is the student who sleeps in class, a strategist who pretends to be drunk when he wants to be left in peace. He seems to have used better than anyone . . . that air of a waif which he sometimes affects, and of a drowsy bear" (1950). At the age of 24 he shot onto the Hollywood scene like a meteorite, having already made himself famous as an actor-director on the stage and radio. In 1931 he joined the Gate Theater in Dublin as an actor and appeared (1933–37) in numerous roles with various companies in New York and also on radio. He directed a *Macbeth* with a black cast in 1936 and Marlowe's *Faust* in 1937. He founded the famous Mercury Theater in 1937 and in 1938 produced his own adaptation of Shakespeare's historical tragedies under the title *Five Kings* for the Theater Guild; he himself played Falstaff. From 1938 to 1940 he wrote, directed, and acted in the weekly radio series *Mercury Theater of the Air.* One of these programs was his famous adaptation of H. G. Wells's *War of the Worlds,* a program that many listeners believed was the broadcast of an actual invasion and that created absolute panic in the New York area. In 1939 he signed a contract with RKO, the terms of which gave him complete freedom to choose his stories and his collaborators. "This is the most beautiful toy train a man could ever dream of," he said after seeing the RKO studios. After working on two projects that he finally abandoned, he created *Citizen Kane,* a prodigious self-portrait of the artist but equally a portrait of the millionaire press magnate, William Randolph Hearst (*q.v.*). Hearst attempted to halt the film's release, but failed; his intervention was then used in the publicity. At its premier it was rightly hailed as a masterpiece and enjoyed considerable success in New York and other large cities before flopping badly in smaller towns. In 1941 Welles began production of three films, *The Magnificent Ambersons, Journey into Fear,* and *It's All True.* But in 1942, after he had already shot many thousands of feet of film in South America for *It's All True,* he was recalled to Hollywood and his contract with RKO was cancelled. *The Magnificent Ambersons* was partially re-edited before its release, while *Journey into Fear* was completed and edited by, and credited to, Norman Foster. Welles abandoned the cinema during the war, working mainly on radio and participating actively in progressive campaigns. On his return to film making, he directed the excellent *The Lady from Shanghai,* but after producing his version of *Macbeth* independently, he settled in Europe, working for stage, radio and TV, acting in several films, and directing an adaptation of *Othello* (51). At this time he seemed to be devoting himself to Shakespearean adaptations, but, as André Bazin wrote: "Even if he has not fulfilled all the promises contained in his first films, those would be sufficient for his glory." He had revolutionized film techniques by picking up already known devices (chiaroscuro and deep-focus photography, one-shot sequences, flashbacks, sets with ceilings, etc.) and uniting and transforming them to give them a whole new power and quality. From radio he developed a new conception of the film sound track so that its rhythm was totally integrated into the construction of the images through the use of the most varied resources. In 1955, however, he returned to contemporary themes with *Mr. Arkadin,* a film whose hero was in some ways similar to that of *Citizen Kane.* After many years' absence, he returned to the USA for a new film, *Touch of Evil,* and transformed a banal thriller into a poignant soliloquy. Then, gradually, he seemed to become trapped by his own myth, entombed even. But suddenly, with *The Trial,* Lazarus rolled back the stone of his tomb. This adaptation of Kafka (but also somewhat autobiographical) was the first film since *Citizen Kane* over which he had had full and personal control and it proved he had not squandered his life and his talent; he had only spent them lavishly for he considered: "I don't think that I will be remembered one day. I find it as vulgar to work for posterity as for money." *Chimes at Midnight* only confirmed his new maturity of vision and style.

DIR: *Too Much Johnson* (38) (16mm insert for a play), *Citizen Kane** (41), *The Magnificent Ambersons** (42), *It's All True* (41–42, abandoned), *Journey into Fear* (42) (replaced by Norman Foster), *The Stranger* (46), *The Lady from Shanghai** (47), *Macbeth** (48), *Othello** (Morocco51), *Confidential Report/Mr. Arkadin* (Sp55), *Around the World with Orson Welles* (Brit55) (TV series), *Touch of Evil** (57), *The Method* (Brit58) (TV documentary), *Voyage to the Country of Don Quixote* (It61) (TV documentary), *Le Procès/The Trial** (Fr62), *Don Quichotte* (57–65, unfinished), *Campanadas a Medianoche/Falstaff/Chimes at Midnight** (Sp/Switz66), *Une Histoire immortelle** (68).

WELLMAN, William A. DIR USA. (Brookline, Massachusetts Feb 29, 1896–) A director since 1923 and a skilled craftsman who is capable of such honest achievements as *Public Enemy** (31), *The President Vanishes/The Strange Conspiracy* (34), *Wild Boys of the Road** (33), *A Star is Born* (37), *Nothing Sacred* (37), and especially the antilynching work, *The Ox-Bow Incident** (43). He has often specialized in war films, e.g., *Wings* (27), *The Story of G.I. Joe* (45), *Battleground* (49), *Lafayette Escadrille* (58), but is also capable of turning out the most extravagant pieces of stupidity, such as *The Next Voice You Hear* (50). He is also responsible for the anticommunist *The Iron Curtain** (48).

WERNER, Gösta DIR Sweden. (Ostra Vemmenhög 1908–) Director of both shorts and features, he established his international reputation with the interesting documentaries *Midwinter Sacrifice* (46) and *The Train* (48) before directing somber melodramas such as *Gatan/The Street* (49). He has not made any features since 1955 but has continued to work in documentaries.

*WHALE, James DIR USA. (Britain July 22, 1889–Hollywood 1957) Apart from

Tod Browning (*q.v.*), he was Hollywood's master of the horror film during the Thirties and responsible for four key films of the genre: *Frankenstein, The Invisible Man, The Old Dark House,* and *The Bride of Frankenstein* — films with a highly sophisticated sense of fantasy and a tone of self-mockery and black humor. Apart from these he made several elegant melodramas, including the excellent *Remember Last Night* (35) and *Showboat* (36). A former cartoonist, actor, producer, and set designer, he originally moved to Hollywood to direct *Journey's End,* a war drama that he had produced and designed in Britain. He retired in 1941 and, after several unsuccessful attempts to revive his career (including an unfinished film in 1952), he was found dead in his swimming pool in 1957 under mysterious circumstances.

DIR: *Journey's End* (30), *Waterloo Bridge* (30), *Frankenstein** (31), *The Imprudent Maiden* (32), *The Old Dark House* (32), *The Kiss before the Mirror* (33), *The Invisible Man** (33), *By Candlelight* (33), *One More River* (34), *The Bride of Frankenstein** (35), *Remember Last Night* (35), *Showboat* (36), *The Road Back* (37), *The Great Garrick* (37), *Sinners in Paradise* (37), *Wives under Suspicion* (38), *Port of Seven Seas** (38) (from Pagnol's *Marius*), *The Man in the Iron Mask* (39), *Green Hell* (40), *They Dare Not Love* (40).

WHEELER, René SCEN France. (Paris Feb 8, 1912–) Author of numerous scripts, including Christian-Jaque's *Fanfan la Tulipe** and Tati's *Jour de fête**. He has also directed an excellent autobiography, *Premières armes* (56).

WICKI, Bernard DIR German Federal Republic/USA. (St. Pölten Oct 28, 1919–) Good German actor, notably for Käutner, he directed his first film in 1958 and then made *The Bridge* (59), one of the best West German films since 1945. [He has also directed an adaptation of Friedrich Dürrenmatt's *The Visit* (64) and has worked in the USA. More recently he has returned to acting.

DIR: *Warum sind sie gegen uns?* (58) (documentary feature), *Die Brücke* (59), *Das Wunder des Malachias* (61), *The Longest Day** (USA61) (German sequences only), *Der Besuch* (It/Fr/GFR 64), *The Saboteur — Code Name Mori-*

turi/Morituri (USA65), *Transit* (Switz 66, unfinished).]

*WIDERBERG, Bo Gunnar DIR Sweden. (Malmö June 8, 1930–) Brilliant new film maker of the "non-Bergman" school, a former novelist and film critic who scathingly attacked the conventions of the Swedish cinema (*Vision in the Swedish Film*, 1962). He is much concerned with the traditions, environment, and social conditions that shape his characters, but, apart from his weakest and most pretentious film, *Love 65,* is not merely concerned with schematically elucidating a thesis. He admires Truffaut (*q.v.*) and, like him, has a feeling for sympathetic characterization and a lyrical vision in which comedy is mixed with intense emotion. His best films are *Raven's End* and *Adalen 31,* both of which brilliantly capture the events and emotions of working-class life in the Thirties and the conventions of the environment which inexorably trap those involved. This same inexorability is present in the intensely poetic and overwhelmingly emotional *Elvira Madigan:* society is betrayed and the lovers must accept the consequences of their escape into idyllic bliss.
DIR: *Pojken och draken/The Boy and the Kite* (61) (TV short, co-dir: Jan Troell), *Barnvagen/The Pram/The Baby Carriage* (62), *Kvarteret Korpen/Raven's End** (63), *Kärlek 65/Love 65* (65), *Heja, roland!/Thirty Times Your Money!* (66), *Elvira Madigan** (67), *The White Game* (68) (documentary, in collaboration), *Adalen 31/The Adalen Riots* (69), *Joe Hill* (USA71).

WIENE, Robert DIR/SCEN Germany. (Sachsen 1881–Paris July 17, 1938) Although he is credited with directing *Das Cabinett des Dr. Caligari** (19), a key film in the history of the cinema, he was only a second-rate director and the success of this masterpiece is more due to an exceptional team of scriptwriters, designers, and actors than to him. His other expressionist films, *Genuine* (20), *Raskolnikov* (23), *I.N.R.I.* (23), and *Orlacs Hände* (24), were still of some interest, but he completely lost his remaining stature in the sound period. Starting in 1914 he also wrote scripts for others, including *Satanas* (19) for Murnau (*q.v.*).

WIENER, Jean MUS France. (Paris March 19, 1896–) An excellent composer, formerly with the musical avant-garde, who has written several notable scores for Bresson, Renoir, Daquin, and Becker (all *q.v.*).
MUS (notably): for Bresson, *Les Affaires publiques* (34), *Au hasard Balthazar* (65), *Une femme douce* (69); for Duvivier, *La Bandera** (35); for Renoir, *Le Crime de Monsieur Lange** (35), *Les Bas-Fonds** (36); for Daquin, *Les Frères Bouquinant** (47), *Le Point du jour** (49), *Maître après Dieu* (51); for Becker, *Touchez pas au grisbi** (54); for Paviot, *Pantalaskas* (60); for Edouard Hofmann and Jean Effel, *La Création du monde* (62).

*WILCOX, Herbert DIR/PROD Britain. (Cork, Ireland Sept 19, 1891–) Doyen of the British cinema who began producing, writing, then directing in 1920. He cofounded Elstree Studios in 1926 and was director of production for British and Dominions from 1928. He has directed several light operettas — from *Chu Chin Chow* (23) and *No, No, Nanette* (USA40) to *The Courtneys of Curzon Street* (47), *Spring in Park Lane* (48), and *Maytime in Mayfair* (49) — and numerous "biographic" films: *The Loves of Robert Burns* (30), *Nell Gwyn* (34), *Victoria the Great* (37), *Nurse Edith Cavell* (USA39), *Odette* (50), *The Lady with a Lamp* (51). Many of these films feature his wife, Anna Neagle, whom he made into an international star.

WILDER, Billy (Billie) DIR/SCEN USA. (Vienna June 22, 1906–) Film maker notable for his cynical, bitter, often misanthropic comedies and dramas characterizing the private and public behavior of Americans. But he often takes two steps forward and one back and, though he has a sense of the absurd, he has not always taken account of his own absurdities, such as *Five Graves to Cairo* and the later sex comedies. [He began as a journalist in Vienna, then became a scriptwriter in Berlin, writing a dozen scripts 1929–33, including *Menschen am Sonntag* and *Emil und die Detektiv*. He left Germany in 1933 and, after a brief period in France, settled in Hollywood, where he was at first a scriptwriter.] His experience in Germany is evident in the somewhat expressionist style of many of his films. He established his reputation after the war with *films noirs,* notably the excellent *Double Indemnity;* a drama about alcoholism, *The Lost Weekend;* a sometimes degrading portrait of old Hollywood, *Sunset Boulevard;* and a satire on the press and its behavior, *Ace in the Hole/The Big Carnival.* Then in the Fifties and Sixties, apart from a few straight dramas, he tended to specialize in bawdy farces in the old central European tradition and had enormous success with *The Seven Year Itch, Some Like It Hot, The Apartment, Kiss Me Stupid,* and *The Fortune Cookie.* [His skillful Victorian period re-creation, *The Private Life of Sherlock Holmes,* is his most accomplished film in recent years and pleasingly broke the circle of sex comedies.]

[CO-SCEN (notably): for Robert Siodmak, *Menschen am Sonntag** (29), *Der Mann, der seinen Mörder sucht* (31); for Ernst Laemmle, *Der Teufelsreporter* (29); for Lamprecht, *Emil und die Detektive** (31); for Paul Martin, *Ein Blonder Traum* (32); for Geza von Bolvary, *Was Frauen träuman* (33); for Dieterle, *Adorable* (Fr34); for Ernst Lubitsch, *Bluebeard's Eighth Wife* (USA38), *Ninotchka** (39); for Mitchell Leisen, *Midnight* (39), *Arise My Love* (40), *Hold Back the Dawn* (41); for Hawks, *Ball of Fire* (41), *A Song is Born* (48); and for all his own films (co-scen, 1942–50: Charles Brackett; co-scen, 1959– : I.A.L. Diamond).]

DIR: *Mauvaise graine* (Fr34) (co-dir: A. Esway), *The Major and the Minor* (42), *Five Graves to Cairo* (43), *Double Indemnity** (44), *The Lost Weekend** (45), *The Emperor Waltz* (47), *A Foreign Affair* (48), *Sunset Boulevard** (50), *Ace in the Hole/The Big Carnival** (51), *Stalag 17* (53), *Sabrina* (54), *The Seven-Year Itch** (55), *The Spirit of St. Louis* (57) (replaced John Sturges), *Love in the Afternoon* (57), *Witness for the Prosecution* (58), *Some Like It Hot** (59), *The Apartment* (60), *One, Two Three* (61), *Irma la Douce* (63), *Kiss Me Stupid* (64), *The Fortune Cookie/Meet Whiplash Willie* (66), *The Private Life of Sherlock Holmes* (Brit 70). AVANTI (1972)

*WILLIAMS, Richard ANIM Britain. (Canada 1933–) Highly talented animator with a remarkable feeling for visual design and a sharp sense of satire who had a signal success with his first complete cartoon, *The Little Island* (58). Like many animators, he also produces commercials and sponsored films in order to finance his own films; notable among these is the famous *Guinness at the Albert Hall.* He has also designed credit titles for *A Funny Thing Happened on the Way to the Forum, What's New Pussycat?, The Liquidator,* and, exceptionally, *The Charge of the Light Brigade.*

ANIM: *The Little Island* (58), *The Story of the Motorcar Engine* (58), *A Lecture on Man* (61), *Love Me, Love Me, Love Me* (62), *Circus Drawings* (64), *Diary of a Madman* (65), *The Dermis Probe* (65), *Pubs and Beaches* (66), *The Sailor and the Devil* (67), *I. Vor Pittfalks* (67), *Nasrudin* (70).

WILLIAMSON, James A. DIR/PROD Britain. (Scotland 1855–19?) With G. A. Smith (*q.v.*) a pioneer British film maker of the Brighton school who was originally a chemist and who entered films in 1898 by filming local events and staging short dramas. He was the first to use parallel action and editing in *Attack on a China Mission* (1900) and *Fire!* (1901), films in which is found the germ of various cinematic techniques, such as parallel editing, whose creation was attributed much later to D. W. Griffith (*q.v.*). [He first used a close-up in *The Big Swallow* (1901), in which the image starts in midshot and ends in a close-up on the actor's tonsils. The comedy, *An Interesting Story* (05), includes many typical Mack Sennett visual gags and tricks. He abandoned production after 1909.]

WILSON, Michael SCEN USA. (McAllister 1914–) One of the best American scriptwriters who demonstrated his sense of realism and his convictions in *A Place in the Sun* and *Salt of the Earth.* Although he was blacklisted during the McCarthy witchhunt years, he continued to collaborate on screenplays without credit until he returned to Hollywood in 1965 and worked on *The Sandpiper* with Dalton Trumbo.

SCEN (notably): several *Hopalong Cassidy* films; for Capra, *It's a Wonderful Life* (46); for George Stevens, *A Place in the Sun** (52); for Mankiewicz, *Five Fingers* (52); for Biberman, *Salt of the Earth** (53); for Wyler, *Friendly Persuasion* (56) (uncredited), *Lawrence of*

Arabia (62) (uncredited); for Minnelli, *The Sandpiper* (65); for Schaffner, *Planet of the Apes* (67); for Richard Fleischer, *Che!* (69).

WISE, Robert DIR USA. (Winchester, Indiana Sept 10, 1914–) A director of integrity, though he has often worked on purely commercial films. Modest, never posing as a genius nor seeking publicity, he directed several excellent films (*Curse of the Cat People, The Set-Up, The Day the Earth Stood Still, Executive Suite, Odds Against Tomorrow*) before directing, with great vigor and intelligence, *West Side Story,* in which Jerome Robbins's choreography contributed to the film's revitalization of the American musical. He originally joined RKO in 1933 as a sound editor, then became chief editor in 1939 before Val Lewton (*q.v.*) gave him his first chance to direct.
ED (notably): H. C. Potter's *The Story of Vernon and Irene Castle* (39), Kanin's *My Favorite Wife* (40), Orson Welles's *Citizen Kane** (41) and *The Magnificent Ambersons** (42), Dieterle's *All That Money Can Buy* (41).
DIR: *The Curse of the Cat People** (44), *Mademoiselle Fifi** (44) (from Maupassant's *Boule de Suif*), *The Body Snatcher* (45), *A Game of Death** (45) (remake of *The Most Dangerous Game**), *Criminal Court* (46), *Born to Kill* (47), *Mystery in Mexico* (48), *Blood on the Moon* (48), *The Set-Up** (49), *Three Secrets* (50), *Two Flags West* (50), *House on Telegraph Hill* (51), *The Day the Earth Stood Still* (51), *Captive City* (52), *Something for the Birds* (52), *Destination Gobi* (52), *The Desert Rats* (53), *So Big* (53), *Executive Suite* (54), *Helen of Troy* (55), *Tribute to a Bad Man* (56), *Somebody Up There Likes Me* (56), *This Could Be the Night* (57), *Until They Sail* (57), *Run Silent, Run Deep* (58), *I Want to Live!* (58), *Odds Against Tomorrow* (59), *West Side Story** (61), *Two for the Seesaw* (62), *The Haunting* (63), *The Sound of Music* (65), *The Sand Pebbles* (66), *Star!* (68), *The Andromeda Strain* (71).

WOLF, Friedrich SCEN USSR/German Democratic Republic. (Berlin Dec 23, 1888 –Berlin Oct 5, 1953) German dramatist, a contemporary and friend of Bertolt Brecht (*q.v.*), he moved to the USSR in 1933 and there adapted his own play into the excellent *Professor Mamlock**

(38), of which he was the principal author. In East Germany after the war he also wrote Kurt Maetzig's *Der Rat der Götter* (50).

*WOLF, Konrad DIR German Democratic Republic. (Hechingen Oct 20, 1925–) Son of the dramatist, Friedrich Wolf, he studied at the Moscow film school, was assistant to Kurt Maetzig (*q.v.*) and Joris Ivens (*q.v.*), and is one of the most skilled East German directors. He is responsible notably for the excellent *Stars,* though his remake of *Professor Mamlock* does not match the original.
DIR: *Einmal ist keinmal* (55), *Genesung* (55), *Lissy* (57), *Sterne/Stars** (GDR/Bulg58), *Die Sonnensucher* (58), *Leute mit Flügeln* (60), *Professor Mamlock** (61), *Der Geteilte Himmel* (64), *Der Kleine Prinz/The Little Prince* (66) (TV), *Ich war neunzehn* (68), *Goya* (GDR/USA70).

WOLFF, David see MADDOW, BEN (*pseud of*)

WOOD, Sam DIR USA. (Philadelphia July 10, 1883–Hollywood Sept 22, 1949) Onetime assistant (from 1915–20) to Cecil B. DeMille (*q.v.*), he directed mediocre films by the dozen and ended by teaching his profession. He was President of the Cinematographic Alliance for the Preservation of American Ideals and his will stipulated that his son would be disinherited if he joined the Communist Party. His best films were: *Goodbye Mr. Chips, For Whom the Bell Tolls,* and the two Marx Brothers films, *A Night at the Opera* and *A Day at the Races,* for which he deserves little credit.
DIR (notably): *The Beloved Villain* (20), *Beyond the Rocks* (22), *Bluebeard's Eighth Wife* (23), *The Barbarian* (33), *A Night at the Opera** (35), *A Day at the Races* (36), *Goodbye Mr. Chips* (39), *Our Town* (40), *Kitty Foyle* (40), *King's Row* (41), *Saratoga Trunk* (43, released 46), *For Whom the Bell Tolls* (43), *Casanova Brown* (44), *Command Decision* (48). He also worked on part of *Gone With the Wind**.

WRIGHT, Basil DIR Britain. (London June 12, 1907–) One of the best English documentary film makers whose most renowned works are *Night Mail* and *Song of Ceylon.* He began his career in 1928 with John Grierson (*q.v.*) at the Empire

Marketing Board Film Unit and during the war was head of the Crown Film Unit. His films reveal his deep sensitivity to rhythm and to the structure and design of images in addition to his humanity.
DIR (notably): *Windmill in Barbados* (30), *O'er Hill and Dale* (31), *The Country Comes to Town* (32), *Cargo from Jamaica* (33), *The Song of Ceylon** (34), *Night Mail** (36) (co-dir: Watt), *Children in School* (37), *The Face of Scotland* (38), *The Battle for Freedom* (42), *This Was Japan* (45), *Southern Rhodesia* (45), *The Story of Omolo* (46), *Waters of Time* (51), *World Without End* (53) (co-dir: Paul Rotha), *Stained Glass at Fairford* (56), *The Immortal Land* (58), *A Place for Gold* (61).

WYLER, William DIR USA. (Mulhouse, France July 1, 1902–) Veteran American director who for some ten years of his career was one of the great film makers to whose style André Bazin devoted several long and penetrating analyses. After studying in Paris he was invited to Hollywood by his uncle, Carl Laemmle (*q.v.*), was an assistant 1920–25 and 1925–28 directed many B-westerns and shorts. His feature debut at the beginning of the sound period was modest, as he diligently and patiently learned his craft on humble B-films and routine commercial films. In his best years, from the mid-Thirties, he was above all an adaptor who owed much to the dramatist Lillian Hellman (*q.v.*) for *These Three* (from *The Children's Hour*), *Dead End*, and *The Little Foxes*. He offered a broad critical fresco of the USA in films like *Come and Get It*, *Dodsworth*, with its clever script, *Jezebel*, *The Westerner*, a vigorous western, and *The Best Years of Our Lives*, which, though not exempt from commercial conventions, gave a very sincere portrait of the return of soldiers from the war, their restlessness, and their difficulties in readapting. Although this film was showered with Oscars, the witchhunt broke out and, as Wyler then said, "From now on, I would

no longer be able to make *The Best Years of Our Lives*." He turned toward academic adaptations like *The Heiress* and *Carrie*, an approach he had already shown a taste for in *Wuthering Heights*. He portrayed an uneasy and isolated America in *Detective Story* and *The Desperate Hours* and, with *Roman Holiday* achieved a lively success in a genre he had never tackled before. America had installed him on the pinnacle and left him there, offering as evidence, "He has never made a bad film." *Ben Hur* and *Friendly Persuasion* proved the contrary despite their international commercial successes. But of his recent films, *The Collector* demonstrated that his former talent had not been entirely lost.
DIR (shorts, notably): *Lazy Lightning* (26), *Hard Fists* (26), *Riders* (27), *Desert Dust* (27), *Border Cavalier* (28), *Stolen Ranch* (28).
DIR (features): *Anybody Here Seen Kelly?* (28), *The Shakedown* (29), *The Love Trap* (29), *Come Across* (29), *Evidence* (29), *Hell's Heroes* (29), *The Storm* (30), *Papa sans le savoir* (Fr31), *A House Divided* (32), *Tom Brown of Culver* (32), *Her First Mate* (33), *Counselor at Law* (33), *Glamour* (34), *The Good Fairy* (35), *The Gay Deception* (35), *Come and Get It** (36) (completed only), *Dodsworth* (36), *These Three* (36), *Dead End** (37), *Jezebel** (38), *Wuthering Heights** (39), *The Westerner* (40), *The Letter* (40), *The Little Foxes** (41), *Mrs. Miniver* (42), *The Memphis Belle* (43), *The Fighting Lady* (44), *Glory for Me* (45), *Thunderbolt* (46) (co-dir: John Sturges) (preceding four films all Army Service features), *The Best Years of Our Lives** (46), *The Heiress* (49), *Detective Story* (51), *Carrie* (52), *Roman Holiday** (53), *The Desperate Hours* (55), *Friendly Persuasion* (56), *Thieve's Market* (57) (abandoned), *The Big Country* (58), *Ben Hur** (59), *The Children's Hour/The Loudest Whisper* (62), *The Collector* (65), *How to Steal a Million* (66), *Funny Girl* (68), *The Liberation of L. B. Jones* (69).

YAMAMOTO, Satsuo DIR Japan. (July 15, 1910–) One of the best of the left-wing independent Japanese film makers, notable for two committed films in a violent and personal style, the antimilitaristic *Vacuum Zone* (52) and *Sunless Street* (53). His costume drama, *Storm Clouds over Hakone* (51), also dealt with a peasant theme that had very modern overtones. He was originally an assistant to Naruse (*q.v.*) and Shibuya and directed his first films for Toho before establishing himself as an independent after the war.
DIR (notably): *Haha no Kyoku* (37), *Denen Kokyogaku/La Symphonie Pastorale* (38) (from Gide), *Neppu/Hot Wind* (43), *Senso to Heiwa/War and Peace* (47) (co-dir: Fumio Kamei), *Boryoku no Machi/Street of Violence* (50), *Hakone Fuunroke/Storm Clouds over Hakone* (51), *Shinku Chitai/Vacuum Zone* (52), *Taiyo no Nai Machi/ the Sunless Street** (53), *Hi no Hate/To the End of the Sun* (54), *Ukigusa Nikki/ Duckweed Story* (55), *Taifu Sodoki/ Typhoon No. 13* (56), *Akai Jinbaori/ His Scarlet Cloak* (58), *Buki Naki Tataki/Battle Without Arms* (60), *Chibusa o Daku Musumetachi* (62), *Shinobi no Mono/A Band of Assassins,* I & II (62 & 63), *Kizu Darake no Sanga/Tycoon/A Public Benefactor* (64), *Shonin no Isu/ The Witness Seat* (64), *Hyoten/Freezing Point* (66), *Zato Ichi Ro-yaburi/The Blind Swordsman's Rescue* (67), *Botan Doru/The Bride from Hades* (68).
NOTE He should not be confused with the slick director Kajiro Yamamoto (Tokyo 1902–), a mentor of Kurosawa (*q.v.*) who specialized in comedies in the Thirties and in war dramas during and after the war, but who was also responsible for the semidocumentary *Uma/ Horse* (41), which greatly influenced the development of Japanese realism.

*YAMAMURA, So DIR Japan. (Naka 1910–) Famous postwar Japanese actor who has also directed several films, most notably his first film, the violent, *The Crab-Canning Ship*.
DIR: *Kanikosen/The Crab-Canning Ship** (53), *Kuroi Ushio/The Black Tide* (54), *Kashimanada no Onna/The Maidens of Kashima Sea* (59), *Haha ko gusa/The Mother and Her Children* (59), *Furyu Fukagawa/The Song of Fukagawa* (60).

YAMANAKA, Sadao DIR Japan. (Tokyo 1907–China 1938) One of the greatest directors of the Thirties, sometimes known as "the Japanese René Clair," responsible for at least one masterpiece, *Humanity and Paper Balloons*. A film maker with great style, sensibility, and a sense of fantasy, he specialized in period dramas and "with Itami he was the first director to escape completely from the conventions of the genre . . . He was rewarded with fame, popularity and, though active only six years, more critical awards than any other costume-drama director in Japanese film history" (Anderson and Richie). He began his career in 1927 as scriptwriter and assistant and died — as young as Vigo — during the war with China.
DIR: *Dakine no Nagadosu/Sleeping with a Long Sword* (32), *Bangoku no Issho/ The Life of Bangoku* (32), *Furyu Katsujinken/The Elegant Swordsman* (34), *Machi no Irezumi Mono/The Village Tattoed Man* (35), *Kunisada Chuji/ Chuji Kunisada* (35), *Mori no Ishimatsu/ Ishimatsu of the Forest* (37), *Ninjo Kami-fusen/Humanity and Paper Balloons** (37).

YEN, Mou-che DIR China. (190?–) Excellent Chinese director of the Thirties who made a pre-neorealist film, *Angels of* *the Street,* in Shanghai in 1936. Other films include: *A Higher Patriotism* (37), *At the Crossroads* (37), *Yenan and the Eighth Army on the Road* (39) (documentary feature). He was later director of the Chinese state cinema.

YERMOLOV, Pyotr PHOTOG USSR. (Moscow 1887–Moscow March 19, 1953) A pioneer of the Soviet cinema, he was a newsreel cameraman during the civil war, then photographed many of Protazanov's films from 1925–35. He also photographed Erwin Piscator's *Vostaniye rybakov/Revolt of the Fisherman* (34) and Donskoy's famous *Gorki** trilogy (38–40).

YORDAN, Philip SCEN/PROD USA. (Chicago c.1912–) Successful American scriptwriter in great demand who has said: "I am against everything that perverts liberty: war, violence, McCarthyism; against all forms of government. But I am not an anarchist. I believe in God and live like a millionaire." However, it is difficult to judge his work because it is claimed that many of his scripts were in fact written by authors on the blacklist — notably Ben Maddow (*q.v.*) — and their work only supervised by Yordan. He has also produced several of the films based on his scripts.
SCEN (notably): for M. Nosseck, *Dillinger* (45); for Mankiewicz, *House of Strangers* (49); for Anthony Mann, *Reign of Terror* (49), *The Man from Laramie* (55), *The Last Frontier* (56), *Men in War* (56) (prod), *God's Little Acre* (57) (prod), *El Cid** (61), *The Fall of the Roman Empire* (63); for Wyler, *Detective Story* (51); for Hugo Fregonese, *Blowing Wild* (53); for Irving Lerner, *Man Crazy* (53) (prod), *Studs Lonigan* (60); for Dmytryk, *Broken Lance* (54); for Nicholas Ray, *Johnny Guitar** (53), *King of Kings* (61), [*55 Days at Peking* (62); for Mark Robson, *The Harder They Fall* (56) (prod); for Ken Hughes, *Joe Macbeth* (56); for Martin Ritt, *No Down Payment* (57); for Henry King, *The Bravados* (58); for Irving Rapper, *Anna Lucasta* (58) (prod); for Andre De Toth, *Day of the Outlaw* (59) (prod); for S. Sekeley, *The Day of the Triffids* (63) (prod); for Andrew Marton, *The Thin Red Line* (64) (prod); for Ken Annakin, *Battle of the Bulge* (67) (prod).]

*YOSHIMURA, Kimisaburo (Kozaburo) DIR Japan. (Hiroshima Sept 9, 1911–) One of the best Japanese directors, though his work is little known in the West. A film maker of studied versatility with an eclectic style, he has made every type of film, from period dramas to those handling contemporary social themes, always with the most appropriate style. He joined Shochiku in 1929 as an assistant and began directing in 1934, but his best period was after the war, particularly after he formed an independent production company in 1950 with Kaneto Shindo (*q.v.*), who has written many of his best films. He is more interested in characterization and dramatic values than expounding theses and has made a considerable number of films about women; he completed *An Osaka Story* after Mizoguchi's (*q.v.*) death and is often considered Mizoguchi's natural successor — though he himself resents this and other classifications of his work.
DIR: *Nukiashi Sashiashi* (34), *Onna Koso Ie o Mamore* (39), *Yoki no Uramachi/Lively Alley* (39), *Ashita no Odoriko/Tomorrow's Dancers* (39), *Gonin no Kyodai/Five Brothers and Sisters* (39), *Danryu/Warm Current* (39), *Nishizumi Senshacho-den* (40), *Hana/Blossom* (41), *Kancho Imada Shisezu/The Spy Isn't Dead Yet* (42), *Minami no Kaze/South Wind* (42), *Kaisen no Zenya/On the Eve of War* (43), *Kessen/Decisive Battle* (44) (co-dir: T. Hagiyama), *Zo o Kutta Renchu/The Fellows Who Ate the Elephant* (47), *Anjo-ke no Butokai/The Ball at the Anjo House* (47), *Yuwaku/Temptation* (48), *Waga Shogai no Kagayakeru Hi/The Day Our Love Shines* (48), *Shitto/Jealousy* (49), *Mori no Ishimatsu/Ishimatsu of the Forest* (49) (remake), *Mahiru no Enbukyoku/Waltz at Noon* (49), *Shunsetsu/Spring Snow* (50), *Senka no Hate/End of War Disasters* (50), *Niju-sai Zengo/About Twenty Years Old* (50), *Itsuwareru Seiso/Under Silk Garments/Clothes of Deception* (51), *Jiyu Gakku/School of Freedom* (51), *Genji Monogatari* (51), *Nishijin no Shimai/The Sisters of Nishijin* (52), *Boryoku/Violence* (52), *Senbazuru/Thousand Cranes* (53), *Yokubo/Desires* (53), *Yoake Me/Before Dawn* (53), *Ashizuri Misaki/Cape Ashizuri* (54), *Wakai Hitotachi/People of Young Character* (54), *Aisurebakoso/Because I Love* (55) (episode), *Ginza no Onna/Women of the Ginza* (55),

*Bijo to Kairu/The Beauty and the Dra-
gon* (55), *Totsugu Hi/Date for Mar-
riage* (56), *Yoru no Kawa/Night River/
Undercurrent* (56), *Yonju Hassai no
Teiko* (56), *Osaka Monogatari/An
Osaka Story* (57) (replaced Mizoguchi),
Yoru no Cho/Night Butterflies (57),
Chijo/On This Earth (57), *Hitotsubu
no Mugi/A Grain of Wheat* (58), *Yoru
no Sugao/The Ladder of Success/The
Naked Face of Night* (58), *Kizoku no
Kaidan* (59), *Jokyo/A Woman's Testa-
ment/Code of Women* (60) (episode),
Onna no Kunsho/A Design for Dying
(60), *Onna no Saka/A Woman of Kyoto*
(60), *Konki/Marriageable Age* (61),
Katei no Jijyo/Their Legacy (62), *Sono
Yo wa Wasurenai/Hiroshima Heartache/
A Night to Remember* (62), *Uso/When
Women Lie* (63) (episode), *Echizen
Takeningyo/The Bamboo Doll* (63),
*Kokoro no Sammyaku/Heart of the
Mountains* (66), *Daraku suru Onna/A
Corrupted Woman* (67), *Nemureri Bijo/
The House of the Sleeping Virgins* (68),
Atsui Yoru/A Hot Night (68).

YUDIN, Konstantin DIR USSR. (Moscow
1896–Moscow March 20, 1957) A talented director of adventure films as
exemplified by *Antosha Rybkin* (43) and
The Bold Ones (50).

YUTKEVICH, Sergei DIR USSR. (St. Petersburg Sept 15, 1904–) One of the best
directors of the first Soviet generation.
He began his career when very young as
a stage artist, designer, and director; in
Petrograd in 1920 he helped organize
FEKS, the Factory of the Eccentric
Actor, with Kozintsev (*q.v.*) and Trauberg (*q.v.*); he worked with other experimental theater groups and designed for
Eisenstein (*q.v.*) in the theater. He directed his first two features only at the
end of the silent period (at the age of
24) and his talents were immediately
apparent on these and his first sound
films. "The majority of my films have
been based on modern themes," he has
said, "beginning with the first, *Lace.
Golden Mountains* showed above all a
psychological development, that of a
peasant, a small landowner, transposed
into a factory. We rightly dreaded the
dangerous mentality of those who arrive
from their village with a *petit bourgeois*
spirit. *Counterplan*, *Miners*, and *The
Man with a Gun* were also contemporary

films. This last was nonconformist in that
it showed Lenin not in an epic manner
but with humor and intimately." Always
in his films of the 1928–41 period one
finds a type of man who, in various
ways, eventually finds his place in society, becoming an innovator and revolutionary, e.g., the foreman in *Counterplan*, the soldier in *The Man with a Gun*,
the men transformed by the influence
and example of *Yakov Sverdlov*. He
attempted to show the interiors of his
characters rather than use monumental
and heroic representations; he reveals his
characters through their behavior in
apparently ordinary events and not
through portentous actions. In fact all
his films carry the mark of his avant-
garde background and his experiments at
FEKS, experiences that led him, for example, to mix comedy and tragedy or to
resort to burlesque, as in *The New Adventures of Schweik*. In 1945, *Liberated
France* was a love poem dedicated to a
country he knew and loved. During the
difficult period of the Soviet cinema,
1946–53, he had to either remain silent
or accept imposed subjects like *The
Great Warrior Skanderbeg*. But later he
was finally able to direct his version of
Othello, a project long dear to him, two
more films on Lenin in the tradition of
The Man with a Gun, and the partly
animated version of Mayakovsky's still
virulent satire, *The Bath House*.
ASSIST: to Room on *Bed and Sofa* (27).
SCEN: Gerasimov's *The Bold Seven* (36)
and many of his own films.
DIR: *Kruzheva/Lace** (28), *Chyorni
parus/The Black Sail* (29), *Zlatye gori/
Golden Mountains** (31), *Vstrechnyi/
Counterplan** (32) (co-dir: Ermler),
Ankara — Heart of Turkey (34) (docu-
mentary; co-dir: Arnstam), *Chakhtiery/
Miners* (36), *Chelovek s ruzhyom/The
Man with a Gun* (38) (see entry *Lenin
films**), *Yakov Sverdlov* (40), *Schweik
in the Concentration Camp* and *The
White Raven* (in *Fighting Film Album*,
No. 7) (41), *Noviye pokhozdeniya
Shveika/The New Adventures of Schweik*
(43), *Liberated France* (45) (documen-
tary feature), *Zdravstai Moskva/Hallo
Moscow!* (45), *Molodost nashei strany/
The Youth of Our Country* (46), *Svet
nad Rossiei/Light over Russia* (47), *Tri
vstrechi/Three Encounters* (48) (co-dir:
Pudovkin, Ptushko), *Przhevalsky* (51),
Veliki voin Albanii Skanderberg/The

Great Warrior Skanderberg (USSR/Albania53), *Otello/Othello** (55), *Yves Montand Sings* (57) (documentary), *Rasskazi o Lenine/Stories about Lenin** (57), *Meeting with France* (60) (documentary), *Banya/The Bath House** (62) (co-dir: Karanovich), *Lenin v Polshe/ Lenin in Poland** (64), *Syuzhet dlya nebolshogo raskaza/Theme for a Short Story* (USSR/Fr69).

ZAMPA, Luigi DIR Italy. (Rome Jan 2, 1905–) Though not a first-rate film maker, he has had his good moments with the neorealistic *Vivere in pace* (46) and *Anni difficili* (48).

*ZANUCK, Darryl Francis (also Mark Canfield) PROD USA. (Wahoo, Nebraska Sept 5, 1902–) One of the most powerful of Hollywood producers during a career that spanned 40 years. He began as a scriptwriter, then became a producer with Warner Brothers. He resigned in 1933 and, with Joseph Schenck (*q.v.*), set up Twentieth Century — which merged with Fox in 1935. He was vice-president in charge of production at 20th Century-Fox until 1956, when he turned independent, producing largely uninteresting films in Europe. He personally directed and supervised *The Longest Day** (62), one of 20th Century-Fox's most successful films whose profits went some way toward counterbalancing the losses on *Cleopatra**. After a power struggle, he took control of 20th Century-Fox from Spyros Skouras (*q.v.*) in mid-1962 and became executive president; but he stayed out of production. His son Richard (Los Angeles 1934–), formerly an independent producer, became head of production. A power struggle between father and son resulted in Darryl resigning as chief executive officer in 1971, though he retained his title of chairman of the board. Few of his productions have stood the test of time, but he did supervise some of John Ford's (*q.v.*) good films and the first films of Elia Kazan (*q.v.*). Under the name of Mark Canfield he wrote the script for Richard Fleischer's *The Crack in the Mirror* (60).
PROD (notably): *Moulin Rouge** (34), *Les Misérables** (35), *Seventh Heaven* (37), *Alexander's Ragtime Band* (38), *Jesse James* (39), *Drums along the Mohawk* (39), *The Grapes of Wrath** (40), *The Mark of Zorro** (40), *Tobacco Road* (41), *Western Union* (41), *How Green Was My Valley** (41), *Wilson* (44), *Anna and the King of Siam* (46), *The Razor's Edge* (46), *Gentleman's Agreement** (47), *Pinky* (48), *All about Eve** (50), *Viva Zapata!** (52), *The Sun Also Rises* (57), *The Roots of Heaven* (58), *The Crack in the Mirror* (60), *Sanctuary* (61), *The Longest Day** (62), *The Chapman Report* (62), *Cleopatra** (63) (replaced Walter Wanger).

ZARKI, Alexander DIR USSR. (St. Petersburg 1908–) Veteran Soviet director with a direct and sensitive style and a feeling for contemporary life and typical detail. He was Heifitz's (*q.v.*) constant collaborator from 1930–1950. For filmography of joint films *see* HEIFITZ, JOSIF.
DIR: *Pavlinka* (52), *Nesterka* (55), *Vysota/The Heights* (57), *Lyudi na mostu/Men on the Bridge* (60), *Moi mladshii brat/My Younger Brother* (62), *Anna Karenina* (67).

ZAVATTINI, Cesare SCEN Italy. (Luzzara July 20, 1902–) The most important scriptwriter and theorist of Italian neorealism, famous, above all, for the series of films he wrote for De Sica (*q.v.*): *Shoeshine, Bicycle Thieves, Umberto D, Miracle in Milan,* etc. He had been a journalist and film critic for some years when he wrote, in 1942, two important examples of neorealism, *Quattro passi fra le nuvole* and *I Bambini ci guardano;* and then, soon after the war, he began his portraits of contemporary Italian life in his scripts for De Sica. In these films he made use of research and investigation that he later set into narrative. He begged for films "useful to man" for "the cinema has used far too few images to open the eyes of our neighbors, to help them understand (and prevent) terrible events." He called for a "deep examination of conscience" (1949). One might have thought he was interested in creating a kind of "neorealistic fantasy" with *Miracle in Milan*, but this film was the fruition of a cherished project. After 1949, he considered that neorealism was only a beginning. He demanded that "as a supreme act of humble confidence in reality, a film should be made of 80 minutes in a man's life." In 1951 he wrote to De Sica of the projected *Italia Mia*: "This will be a film without a script, created directly at the first contact with reality registered by our sight and hearing. That is what neorealism will become I think: the facts are there, it is necessary to capture them and choose them as they appear; sometimes it will be necessary to stage a scene, but always in terms of the theme." But *Italia Mia* was not to be made, neither by De Sica nor by Rossellini. Nonetheless, he was the driving spirit behind *Amore in Città,* a film that not only marked the birth of a new generation of Italian film makers (Fellini, Antonioni, Lizzani, Maselli), but was also, in its detailed re-creation of actual events, an embryonic attempt at *cinéma-vérité* many years ahead of its time. But the Italian cinema fell into a serious financial and artistic crisis and took refuge in old formulas, spectaculars, and sophisticated comedies. For some years, Zavattini was unable to work in the cinema and later had to content himself writing commercial scripts or completing old projects with De Sica. He had to leave to others the realization of the program he described in 1952: "My fixed idea is to deromanticize the cinema; I want to teach people to see daily life with the same passion they experience in reading a book."

SCEN (notably): for De Sica, *Teresa Venerdi* (41), *I Bambini ci Guardano* (42), *La Porta del Cielo* (46), *Sciuscià** (46), *Ladri di Biciclette** (48), *Miracolo a Milano** (50), *Umberto D** (52), *Stazione Termini* (53), *L'Oro di Napoli* (54), *Il Tetto* (56), *La Ciociara* (60), *Il Giudizio Universale* (61), *Boccaccio '70* (61) (episode), *The Condemned of Altona* (62), *Il Boom* (63), *Yesterday, Today, and Tomorrow* (63), *Marriage Italian Style* (64), *Un monde nouveau* (65), *After the Fox* (65), *Le Streghe* (66) (one episode), *I Girasoli* (69); for

Blasetti, *Quattro Passi fra le Nuvole** (42), *Un Giorno nella Vita* (46), *Prima Communione* (50); for Germi *Il Testimone* (46); for De Santis *Caccia Tragica** (47), *Roma, Ore 11** (51); for Emmer, *Domenica d'Agosto* (49); for Clément, *Au-delà des grilles* (49); for Visconti, *Bellissima* (51); for Maselli, *La Donna del Giorno* (56); and the following collaborative films; *Amore in Città** (53), *Siamo Donne* (53), *I Misteri di Roma* (63), *Contresesso* (63).

ZECCA, Ferdinand DIR France. (Paris 1864–Paris 1947) One of the pioneers of the French cinema who contributed much to the fortunes of Pathé with the success of his early *Les Victimes de l'alcoolisme, Histoire d'une crime, La Passion, La Baignade impossible.* Unlike Méliès (*q.v.*) – whom he did not imitate as much as his English rivals – he was less of an artist than a commercial film maker, who was very conscious (1901–08) of the wishes of Pathé's principal clients, the fairground owners. Seen today, this wily fox seems like a primitive and his lively films have a certain charm. He was originally a singer in *caf'conc';* he began his film career with Gaumont and joined Pathé in 1900. During the First World War he was sent by Pathé to the USA as supervisor of Pathé Exchange; on his return he directed Pathé-Baby, Pathé's nontheatrical division, from 1920–27.

DIR (notably): *Les Mésaventures d'une tête de veau* (1898), *Les Dangers de l'alcoolisme* (?) (1898), *Le Muet mélomane* (1900) (with sound), *L'Enfant prodigue, Les Sept châteaux du diable, Histoire d'un crime, Le Coucher de la mariée, La Conquête de l'air, Comment Fabien devint architecte, Par le trou de la serrure, La Loupe de grand-mère, Quo Vadis?** (all 01), *Catastrophe à la Martinique, Les Victimes de l'alcoolisme*, Le Poule merveilleuse, Ali Baba et les 40 voleurs, La Baignade impossible, Une idylle sous un tunnel, Tempête dans un chambre à coucher, La Passion* (co-dir: Nonguet) (all 02), *La Belle au bois dormant, La Chat botté, La Passion* (2nd part) (all 03), *La Grève* (04), *L'Incendiaire, Dix femmes pour un mari, Rêve à la lune, Au pays noir, Les Petits vagabonds, Vendetta, Toto gâte-sauce, Ce qu'on voit de la Bastille* (all 05), *L'Affaire Dreyfus** (08), *Messaline* (10) (co-dir: Andreani), *Scènes de la vie cruelle* (series) (co-dir: Leprince), *La Comtesse noire, Plus fort que la haine, L'Escarpolette tragique, Le Roi de l'air, Le Calvaire, La Lutte pour la vie, Le Calvaire d'une reine, Le Vieux Cabotin, La Fièvre de l'or, La Danse héroïque* (all 12–14).

ZEMAN, Karel ANIM/DIR Czechoslovakia. (Ostromer, Bohemia Nov 3, 1910–) A film maker who has widened the horizons of the eighth art, animation; in his later, and best, films he is justly considered Méliès's (*q.v.*) successor. He undoubtedly brings the old master to mind, not only because he is an artisan impassioned by art, creating his "innocent inventions" with infinite patience rather than with large budgets, but also because of his ingenuous and always ingenious fantasies. Less intellectual than Trnka (*q.v.*), but nonetheless his equal, he has great zest and a marvelous sense of baroque oddities and poetic gags. He was originally a poster designer, window dresser, and director of publicity films for the Bata factory in Zlin (Gottwaldov). Since his first postwar film, *A Christmas Dream*, which combined puppets and live action, he has never stopped experimenting with new techniques and exploring new genres. The didactic film series that he made in the late Forties, which centered on his famous wooden puppet character, *Mr. Prokouk*, was created in a simple functional style, as was his first medium-length feature, *King Lavra*. For *Inspiration* he had accepted a bet: to animate glass figurines. In *The Treasure of Bird's Island* he combined in certain scenes various animation techniques in both two and three dimensions; then, in the didactic *A Journey to Primeval Times,* both puppets and child actors. In *An Invention for Destruction* he broke completely away from didacticism and gave fantasy full rein, combining live action with the animation of old wooden engravings that had illustrated the books of Jules Verne. His marvelously imaginative *Baron Munchhausen* used special effects, tricks, and period illustrations as backdrops for the fantasy world in which his characters moved. It was closer to drama than animation and with his next films, notably *A Jester's Tale*, he moved entirely into live action, though still employing tricks and effects learned from animation.

DIR (shorts, notably): *Vanocni sen/A Christmas Dream* (45), *Podkova pro stesti/A Horseshoe for Luck* (46), *Pan Prokouk jede na brigadu/Mr. Prokouk on a Brigade* (47), *Pan Prokouk uraduje/ Mr. Prokouk and the Red Tape* (47), *Pan Prokouk v pokuseni/The Temptation of Mr. Prokouk* (47), *Pan Prokouk filmuje/Mr. Prokouk Makes a Film* (48), *Pan Prokouk vynalezcem/Mr. Prokouk the Inventor* (49), *Inspirace/Inspiration* (49), *Kral Lavra/King Lavra* (50), *Pan Prokouk, pritel zviratek/Mr. Prokouk the Animal Fancier* (55), *Pan Prokouk akrobatem/Mr. Prokouk the Acrobat* (59) (designed only, dir. Z. Rozkopal).
DIR (features): *Poklad Ptaciho ostrova/ The Treasure of Bird's Island* (52), *Cesta do praveku/A Journey to Primeval Times* (55), *Vynalez zkazy/An Invention for Destruction** (57), *Baron Prasil/Baron Munchhausen** (61), *Blaznova kronica/ A Jester's Tale* (64), *Ukradena vzducholod/The Stolen Airship* (66), *Archa pana Servadaca/Mr. Zervadac's Ark* (69), *Na komete/On a Comet* (70).

ZGURIDI, Alexander Mikhailovich DIR USSR. (Saratov Nov 23, 1904–) The best contemporary specialist in nature films whose work has won many awards; his best film is undoubtedly the dramatic *In the Sands of Central Asia* (43). He began making short nature films in 1932 and tried directing fiction in 1946 with an adaptation of Jack London's *White Fang.* He has headed the Soviet association of documentary film makers for some years and has long been active in the International Scientific Film Association.
DIR (notably): *In the Depths of the Sea* (38) (co-dir: B. Dolin), *The Power of Life* (40), *In the Sands of Central Asia* (43), *White Fang* (46), *Real Life in the Forest* (50), *In the Icy Ocean* (52), *The Story of a Forest Giant* (56), *In the Pacific* (57), *Jungle Track* (59), *In the Steps of our Ancestors* (61), *Magnificent Islands,* (65), *Forest Symphony* (67).

ZHANDOV, Zahari (also, Zachari Shandoff) DIR Bulgaria. (1911–) The best Bulgarian film maker of the postwar years who helped establish the Bulgarian state cinema with several documentaries and features. He has a feeling for narrative and beautiful imagery.
DIR (features): *Tregova/Alarm* (49), *Septemvriisti/Septembrists/The Septem-*

286

ber Heroes (52), *Zemya/The Land/ Earth* (57), *Otvad horizonta/Beyond the Horizon* (60), *Chernata reka/The Black River* (64), *Shibil* (68). Also photographed Bulgarian sequence of Ivens' *The First Years**.

ZINNEMANN, Fred DIR USA. (Vienna April 29, 1907–) An American director of considerable importance in the Forties and Fifties whose work since 1953 has lapsed into conscientious academicism. [He originally trained as a cameraman in Paris and 1927–29 was an assistant cameraman in Paris and Berlin, collaborating notably on *Menschen am Sonntag**. He moved to the USA in 1930 and was an extra in *All Quiet on the Western Front** and an assistant in Hollywood, 1931–32, before joining the New York documentarists and collaborating, notably, with Paul Strand (*q.v.*) on *Redes/The Wave* in Mexico. From 1937 to 1942 he directed 17 shorts for MGM (*Crime Does Not Pay* series, *Passing Parade* series, etc.).] One of his first features, *The Seventh Cross,* was based on an antifascist novel by Anna Seghers. Later, in Europe, he directed the semidocumentary, *The Search,* a harshly realistic portrait of the problem of child refugees. The unexpected commercial success of this film made him welcome in Hollywood, where he made *Act of Violence, The Men* (a film on war paraplegics in which Marlon Brando made his film debut), and *Teresa,* which depicted the poor section of New York seen through the eyes of a young Italian girl. Then, after the Oscar winning short, *Benjy,* came the international success of *High Noon,* a metaphorical western about the mutual defense of liberty that tugged a little too calculatedly at the heart strings. *From Here to Eternity,* a superficially "courageous" film, marked a turning point in his work. From then on he was one of "the lost generation"; his work has been artistically unsatisfying and not always even commercially successful. However, his failings do not justify the indignities heaped on him by certain critics who have lavished praise on Kazan (*q.v.*) and Wilder (*q.v.*).
[ASSIST: to Robert Siodmak *Menschen am Sonntag** (Ger29); to Berthold Viertel, *Man Trouble* (30), *The Spy* (31), *The Wiser Sex* (32), *The Man from Yesterday* (32); to Leo McCarey, *The Kid from Spain* (32).

DIR (shorts): *Friend Indeed* (37), *That Mothers Might Live* (38), *The Story of Dr. Carver* (38), *Trapping the Sleeping Death* (38), *While America Sleeps* (39), *Help Wanted* (39), *The Ash-Can Fleet* (39), *Weather Wizards* (39), *One Against the World* (39), *Forgotten Victory* (39), *The Old South* (40), *The Great Meddler* (40), *Stuffie* (40), *Away in the Wilderness* (40), *Forbidden Passage* (41), *Your Last Act* (41), *The Lady or the Tiger?* (42), *Benjy* (51).]
DIR (features): *Redes/The Wave** (Mex 35), *Kid-Glove Killer* (42), *Eyes in The Night* (42), *The Seventh Cross* (44), *Little Mr. Jim* (46), *My Brother Talks to Horses* (47), *The Search** (Switz/ USA47), *Act of Violence* (48), *The Men** (50), *Teresa** (51), *High Noon** (52), *The Member of the Wedding* (52), *From Here to Eternity** (53), *Oklahoma!* (55), *A Hatful of Rain* (57), *The Old Man and the Sea* (58) (replaced by Henry King, then by John Sturges), *The Nun's Story* (59), *The Sundowners* (60), *Behold a Pale Horse* (63), *Hawaii* (66) (replaced by George Roy Hill), *A Man for All Seasons* (Brit66).

ZUKOR, Adolph PROD USA. (Ricse, Hungary 1873–) Perhaps the most picturesque of the American motion picture pioneers, he was originally a poor immigrant (1889) who became a furrier, bought theaters and, thanks to Sarah Bernhardt (on celluloid), ended up controlling the powerful Famous Players-Paramount.
1903: Entered the penny-arcade business. 1904: Opened a semipalatial film theater in New York. [Merged his interest with Marcus Loew (*q.v.*) in Loew's Consolidated, which eventually controlled a whole chain of theaters. After the success of Zecca's *La Passion* in 1907, became interested in exclusive presentations. 1912: Left Loew to launch the showing of *Queen Elizabeth** (starring Sarah Bernhardt), which he bought for $18,000 and from which he made a fortune. Conceived the idea of "Famous Players in Famous Plays" and in 1913 made films such as *The Count of Monte Cristo* and *The Prisoner of Zenda* starring famous stage stars. Hired Mary Pickford for films in Hollywood. 1916: Merged Famous Players with Jesse L. Lasky's (*q.v.*) Feature Plays, with himself as president. 1917: Also became head of Paramount, Famous Players-

Lasky's distributing company that was earlier founded by W. W. Hodkinson and that later merged with the production company and theater chain. 1919: With the help of a loan of ten million dollars from the Morgan bank he built up a powerful chain of theaters in the USA and abroad. He survived various power struggles in the early Thirties, but in 1935 was replaced as president of Paramount Pictures and became chairman of the board, a position he has retained "emeritus" ever since.]

ZURLINI, Valerio DIR Italy. (Bologna 1926–) One of the best of the younger generation of Italian directors. A film maker of profound sensibility with an excellent visual sense he established his reputation with *L'Estate violenta, La Ragazza con la valigia,* and *Cronaca Familiare.* He has also made many shorts, e.g., *Pugilatori, Il Mercato della Facce, Soldati in Città, Il Blu della Domenica.*
DIR: *Le Ragazze di San Frediano* (54), *L'Estate Violenta* (59), *La Ragazza con la valigia* (60), *Cronaca Familiare* (62), *Le Soldatesse* (64), *Seduto alla sua Destra/Out of Darkness* (67, released 68) (originally planned as part of episode film *Amore e Rabbia/Vangelo '70*).

ZWOBODA, André DIR France. (Paris March 3, 1910–) Formerly an assistant to Jean Renoir (*q.v.*), he has directed in Morocco an excellent film based on Berber folklore, *Noces de sable/Desert Wedding** (48), and many short documentaries.